FROMMER'S
NEW YORK ON $45 A DAY

by Joan Hamburg
and Norma Ketay

1986-87 Edition

Copyright © 1960, 1961, 1962, 1964, 1966, 1968, 1969, 1970, 1972,
1974, 1976, 1978, 1980, 1982, 1984, 1986
by Simon & Schuster, Inc.

All rights reserved
including the right of reproduction
in whole or in part in any form

Published by Frommer/Pasmantier Publishers
A Division of Simon & Schuster, Inc
1230 Avenue of the Americas
New York, New York 10020

ISBN 0-671-55619-3

Manufactured in the United States of America

CONTENTS

Introduction	**NEW YORK ON $45 A DAY**	**1**
Chapter 1	**FINDING A BUDGET HOTEL**	**18**
	1. Rooms for Singles and Students	19
	2. Low-Cost Permanent Residences	25
	3. Rooms for Service Personnel	27
	4. Hotels for General Occupancy	27
	5. Rooms for Families	37
	6. Bed and Breakfast	38
	7. Weekend and Other Packages	39
Chapter II	**EATING CHEAPLY AND WELL**	**42**
	1. Midtown West/Times Square	42
	2. Midtown East	57
	3. Upper East Side and Yorkville	67
	4. Upper West Side	82
	5. Lincoln Center	93
	6. Pennsylvania Station/Chelsea	98
	7. Greenwich Village	103
	8. SoHo	117
	9. Lower Manhattan/Tribeca	122
	10. Chinatown	128
	11. Little Italy	136
	12. Lower East Side/East Village	139
	13. Murray Hill/Gramercy Park	149

	14. Brighton Beach, Brooklyn	165
	15. Especially for Brunch	166
	16. Around the Clock	169
	17. Early-Bird Dinner Specials	170
	18. Big-Splurge Restaurants	171
Chapter III	**THE TOP SIGHTS AND CULTURAL ATTRACTIONS**	**173**
	1. Sights Not To Be Missed	174
	2. Museums	181
	3. Galleries, Theater, Concerts, Opera, and Dance	193
	4. Entertainment	207
	5. Zoos and Botanical Gardens	209
	6. Sports and Recreational Facilities	212
	7. More Sights	217
	8. Churches and Synagogues	221
	9. Historic Houses	225
Chapter IV	**A STROLL OR TWO**	**228**
	1. Greenwich Village	228
	2. The Lower East Side	230
	3. The Garment Center	232
	4. Yorkville	232
	5. SoHo	233
	6. The Upper West Side: Columbus Avenue	233
	7. Chinatown and Little Italy	235
	8. Chelsea	235
	9. Tribeca	236
	10. Central Park	236
	11. Times Square	237

Chapter V	**ONE-DAY EXCURSIONS FROM NEW YORK**	**238**
	1. Up the Hudson Valley	238
	2. Long Island	243
	3. New Jersey	243
Chapter VI	**BARGAIN NIGHTSPOTS**	**245**
	1. Bar Hopping	245
	2. The Music Spots	256
	3. Dance, Dance, Dance	265
	4. Theatrical and Nightclub Entertainment	267
Chapter VII	**THE BEST SHOPPING BUYS IN TOWN**	**272**
	1. Men's and Women's Clothing	272
	2. An Alphabetical Miscellany	286
	3. Food	308
Chapter VIII	**NEW YORK WITH CHILDREN: BUDGET TIPS**	**317**
	1. Cultural and Educational Attractions	317
	2. Recreation	326
	3. Entertainment	329
	4. Shops for Children	332
	5. Services for Children	333
	6. Eating Out With Children	333
	7. Mapping Out Your Days	334
Chapter IX	**HELPFUL NEW YORK CITY LISTINGS AND GENERAL INFORMATION**	**337**

MAPS

The Five Boroughs of New York City	5
Manhattan	6–7
New York City Subways	
IRT-Broadway-Seventh Avenue	13
IRT-Lexington Avenue	14
Independent Subway (IND)	15
BMT Subway	16
Manhattan Areas	21
Midtown Manhattan	43
Greenwich Village	105
Upper Manhattan	188
Central Park	215
Lower Manhattan	231
The SoHo Area	234
Getting Out of New York City	239

INFLATION ALERT: We don't have to tell you that inflation has hit the United States as it has everywhere else. In researching this book we have made every effort to obtain up-to-the-minute prices, but even the most conscientious researcher cannot keep up with the current pace of inflation. As we go to press, we believe we have obtained the most reliable data possible. Nonetheless, in the lifetime of this edition—particularly its second year (1987)—the wise traveler will add 15% to 20% to the prices quoted throughout these pages.

DISCLAIMER: Although every effort was made to ensure the accuracy of the prices and travel information appearing in this book, it should be kept in mind that prices do fluctuate in the course of time, and that information does change under the impact of the varied and volatile factors that affect the travel industry.

Introduction

NEW YORK ON $45 A DAY

The Reason Why

THIS EDITION OF *NEW YORK ON $45 A DAY* marks the 25th anniversary of the first publication of a guidebook that has become a staple in bookstores throughout the English-speaking world.

Twenty-five years ago, when this book appeared with the then-startling title of *New York on $5 a Day,* its authors were two young women fresh out of college. The research for that first edition of what grew to be a travel classic was done after they left their jobs each day. All of their work was done on foot. In a period of nine months they covered practically every street in the city, from the Battery to Harlem, and wore out a total of five pairs of sneakers each.

The experience and subsequent revisions of the book every two years marked the authors for life. They became (and still are) New York chauvinists. A New York chauvinist is someone who thinks that Paris, London, and San Francisco are nice places to visit but he or she wouldn't want to live there. A New York chauvinist is someone who thinks that New Yorkers are the friendliest, most "with-it" individuals in the world. A New York chauvinist thinks he eats the best food, sees the best shows, visits the greatest museums, and lives in the most interesting city in the world. And he loves to show his city off to visitors, even if they only come from a nearby suburban town.

And when they stray too far from their home base, New York chauvinists begin to experience withdrawal symptoms. It's a known fact that New Yorkers transplanted to Los Angeles became major customers several years back of tap water bottled in the Big Apple and airlifted to California. And it's another known fact that New York boasts the tastiest hot dogs in America—they're sold right off the umbrella-topped pushcarts on the streets of the city.

New York is a sensual pleasure, especially at night. Coming across one of the many bridges to the island of Manhattan is a visual happening. The shapes of the buildings silhouetted against the sky, the lights in the windows, the strings of illumination across the bridges—they all add up to the promise of an excitement, mystery, and glamor that is unmistakably New York.

There is no leavening our love for this city. No amount of grafitti on buildings and subways, nor traffic jams, movie lines, irritable salespeople, or slow service in a busy restaurant can dampen our ardor. We've always loved New York, and now as we present the 1986–1987 edition of this book, we love it even more. We've watched the city grow and change in the past 25 years. It gets more beautiful each year. At the same time as we are building

2 NEW YORK ON $45 A DAY

new skyscrapers, we are learning to preserve the lovely old architectural vestiges of the past. New York is coming into its own. Much maligned for years, it is becoming a mecca for savvy travelers who know that it can be easier on the pocketbook than a lot of other American cities, and most European ones.

So here it is. It's our New York. A New York that only New Yorkers know. It's the New York that is affordable to most people—to people who don't want to mistakenly wander into an expensive restaurant and blow their whole week's vacation budget. It's the New York we know and love. It's yours for the reading.

THE TWO NEW YORKS: It's not true that New York is a city only for the rich. There is no other city in the world that offers the diversity in price range for such basic essentials as food and lodging. New York has been called the world's number one performing arts city, and many of the best cultural events in the city are free or available at low cost. The city devotes itself to providing both residents and visitors with a dazzling array of unusual and exciting events. Shakespeare in the Park (Central Park) is presented by the New York Shakespeare Festival. Stars such as Linda Ronstadt, Cleo Laine, Meryl Streep, Kevin Kline, and Dustin Hoffman have played on the open-air stage in Central Park's Delacorte Theatre. Tickets are available on a first-come, first-served basis—absolutely free.

Restaurants to fit any budget can be found with no trouble at all. This book will provide you with enough choices to keep you busy eating out for years. Hotels, on the other hand, are another thing altogether. We have more than our share of good ones with correspondingly high prices—the Helmsley Palace, the Regency, the Waldorf, the Plaza, among others—but finding the smaller, offbeat hotels with satisfactory rooms at lower cost takes a lot of looking. We have nonetheless uncovered several of these hotels with adequate accommodations at budget prices.

If it's nightlife you've come for, there are offerings galore—the widest range of nighttime entertainment possibilities in the world! You can spend evenings on end without exhausting the supply of discos, country-music haunts, belly-dancer palaces, showcase theaters, concert halls, etc.

For food, the selections are even better: hundreds upon hundreds of restaurants where good meals are still in the budget to moderate range. These are in the not-so-easy-to-find category for the inexperienced visitor, but every New Yorker knows that these low-cost finds exist. What we've done is to collect scores of those "little places around the corner" into one volume.

To do that, and to find the rest of the information contained in this book, we devote five to six months yearly to walking, searching, questioning, tasting, and trying. Each edition includes new selections, as well as revisions of acceptable old ones. We've been irritating pests (especially to our friends whom we "shake down" for every restaurant tip they possess), but we've come up with information that we sincerely believe can save you hundreds of dollars over the course of time.

NOTE ON PRICES: The information in this 1986–1987 guide is correct as of the early 1986 publication date. Because prices are changing weekly all over the world, we cannot assume New York will be immune to price revisions. Therefore we cannot be responsible for price changes that occur after publication.

$45 A DAY—WHAT IT MEANS: Our main goal is, of course, to show you how to enjoy New York without spending a fortune. To do that you have to begin with a moderate per-day cost of living. By living costs we refer to basic necessities: your hotel room and three meals. Obviously your transportation, sightseeing, and entertainment costs will all be in addition to this, but we will show you how to enjoy these and other activities with a reasonable expenditure of money.

Inflation, as we all know, has become a way of life across the nation, and New York City is no exception. Prices continue to skyrocket. In updating this book we were truly surprised at some of the gigantic price leaps. Good values in hotels are, alas, becoming almost impossible to find. You can just about squeak by on food for $14 a day and, by traveling with a companion and sharing a double room, spend $30 to $35 a day for your lodgings. For those of you with a little more to spend, we have included more expensive choices; your flexibility will make it a bit easier.

The $45-a-day standard won't bring you a Hilton or a Plaza, but it will usually produce an adequate room, plus very good meals—and this we say without reservations, for our many small foreign restaurants especially offer what we consider gourmet-quality food.

By cataloguing all the choices, *New York on $45 a Day* hopes to service the entire range of budget visitors who come to or live in New York: from the extremely cost-conscious $45-a-dayer to the visitor or resident who has more to spend but wants to get dollar value for every penny he or she puts out.

SOME PRIOR ORIENTATION: New York vies with London and Tokyo for the distinction of being the world's most populous city. Some 7½ million people live within our city limits, and 5½ million more are located in the surrounding suburbs.

New York prides itself on its polyglot mix. It is an ethnic, racial, and religious smörgasbord. Italians, Irish, Jews, Hungarians, Scandinavians, Chinese, Japanese, Hispanic—you name it, New York's got it. The rich blend of cultures is the solid underpinning on which the city is built. Every few decades a new generation of immigrants emerges as the latest entrepreneurial hotshots. Everyone gets a turn and the city respects, even salutes, the hard workers who make it to the top. New York is not the town of the vested interest. It is instead the personification of the American Dream. Just looking at its mayor and its governor is a clear example that the strength of New York is the sons and daughters of its recent immigrants.

New Yorkers have also always prided themselves on being in the vanguard of social and political movements. It is here you can find headquarters for various civil rights organizations; political organizations from far right to far left; sexual rights organizations, both gay and heterosexual; and women's organizations.

New York offers groups for whatever your interest, problem, or cause may be. And the "live and let live" attitude of most residents guarantees you the freedom to pursue your chosen path.

No other American city, with the possible exception of Washington, D.C., has the importance of New York. The city is the center of America's communications industry and the advertising and public relations world. The offices of the major fashion houses and magazines are located here, as is virtually the entire book-publishing industry. New York is the home base of America's commercial theater, the nation's major opera company, and key art galleries. Many of the country's major industrial concerns maintain their headquarters in the skyscrapers of Manhattan. The city is so full of celebrated public figures and important cultural, political, and economic events that most New Yorkers remain blasé and unconcerned about things that would dazzle and excite the residents of almost any other town. We admit, of course, the many flaws and inconveniences of New York, but as you can see, we love our exciting city and grow more aware of its endless opportunities and gifts with every passing day.

Tourists may not be tempted to savor all of the unusual neighborhood areas of New York, but to us there is nothing more interesting than the people who live here. Everyone knows us for our culture, but the huge ethnic population is what makes this city great. We will give you a rundown on these neighborhoods elsewhere in this book. Visit them and meet real New Yorkers. You'll like them. New Yorkers are friendly, open people, and they are proud of their city.

A City of Boroughs

New York is made up of five distinct sections, called "boroughs": **Manhattan, Brooklyn, the Bronx, Queens,** and **Staten Island.**

The island of Manhattan—in the very center of New York—is where the key public buildings are located, and where the most important commercial, industrial, and cultural activities take place. It's here that you'll find virtually all the sights and entertainments you've come to see, all the hotels and restaurants that we'll recommend, and all the other famous places and landmarks that are customarily identified with New York. That's not to say that the other boroughs don't possess some of these attractions, but you'll have more than enough to do if you try to canvass merely the sights of Manhattan. We have, however, included several sights to be seen in other boroughs.

Manhattan is only a small residential section of New York—a fact that ought to clear up the bewilderment you may experience over the predominantly commercial appearance of the island. Most New Yorkers live in the other boroughs of New York and travel back and forth each day to their jobs in Manhattan. If you take a trip into Brooklyn, or the Bronx, Queens, or Staten Island, you'll see the areas in which most New Yorkers live; you'll find streets with trees, private homes, little community centers, schools, fields, and parks similar to those you'd find in the residential districts of any other town. And if you travel into the suburbs of New York—to the villages on Long Island or the county of Westchester, north of Manhattan—then you'll encounter the greener areas in which New Yorkers live, and from which they commute to Manhattan to work.

The Geography of Manhattan

Actually, it's lucky that you'll be staying and sightseeing in Manhattan, because it's the easiest of the boroughs in which to find your way around. Except for the bottom third of Manhattan—that is, the portion below 4th Street on the West Side, 1st Street on the East Side—virtually the entire island is laid out exactly like a grid: the streets and avenues of the town crisscross each other almost at precise right angles.

The **avenues** of New York run directly north and south (uptown and downtown).

The **streets** of New York run directly east and west (crosstown).

With a few exceptions, all of these avenues and streets bear consecutive numbers, enabling you to know at all times where you are.

Thus, starting at 4th Street on the West Side or 1st Street on the East Side, and going north, the streets of New York are numbered 5th, 6th, 7th, 8th, etc., all the way up to around 212th Street at the northern tip of Manhattan. If you're at 42nd Street and want to go to 82nd Street you simply go directly north for 40 blocks.

Similarly, the avenues begin with First Avenue on the East Side of Manhattan, and then proceed across town. Second Avenue, Third Avenue, Fourth Avenue, Fifth Avenue, and so forth until you arrive at Twelfth Avenue on the west

ORIENTATION 5

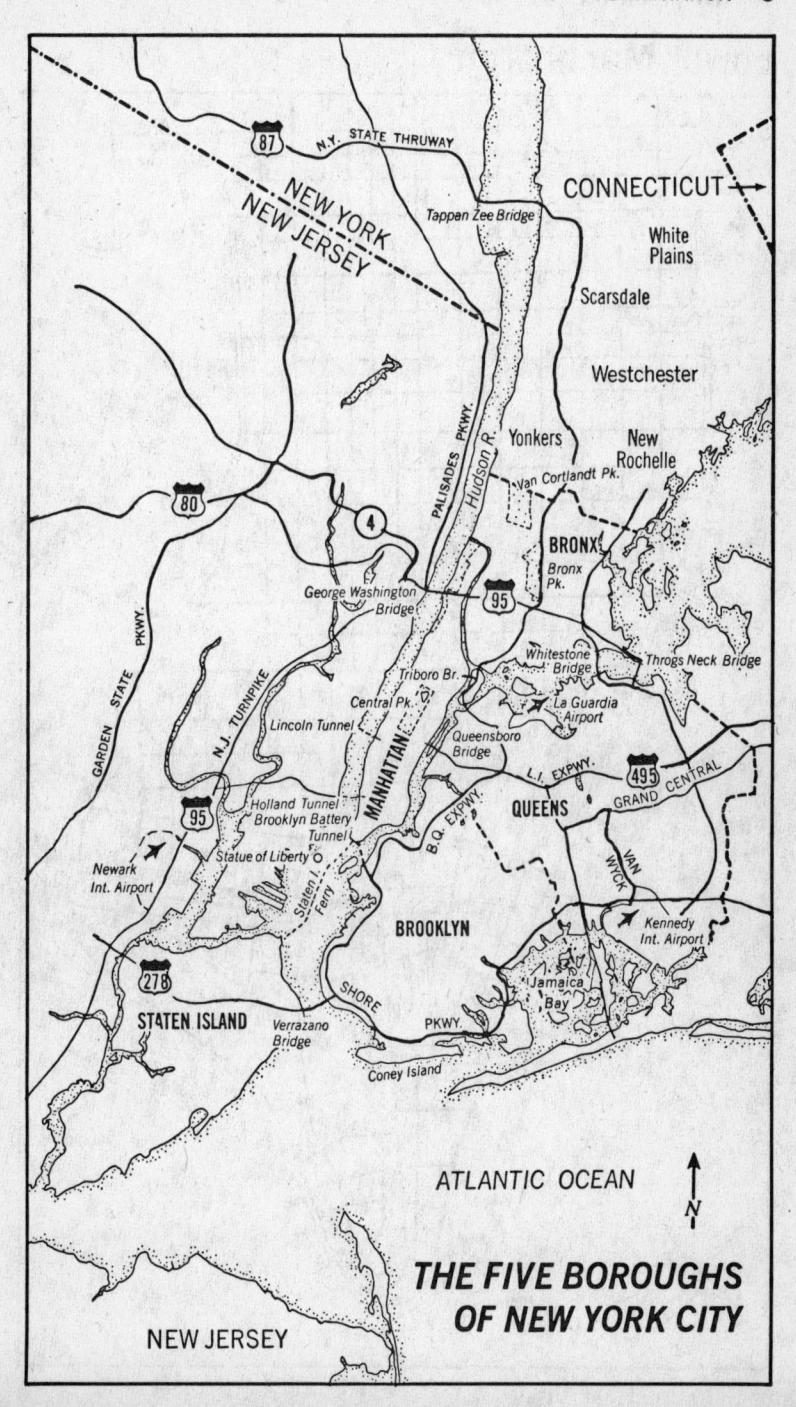

THE FIVE BOROUGHS OF NEW YORK CITY

Lower Manhattan

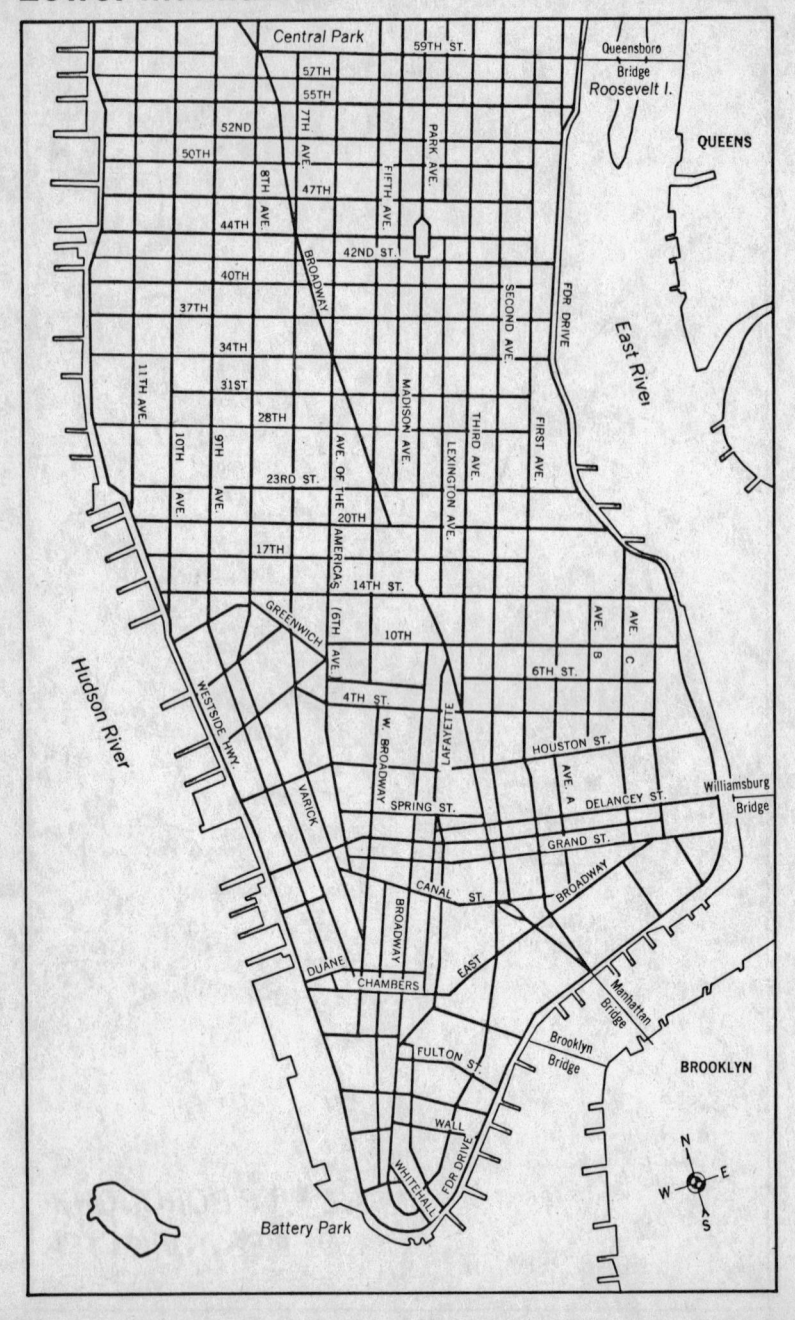

ORIENTATION 7

Upper Manhattan

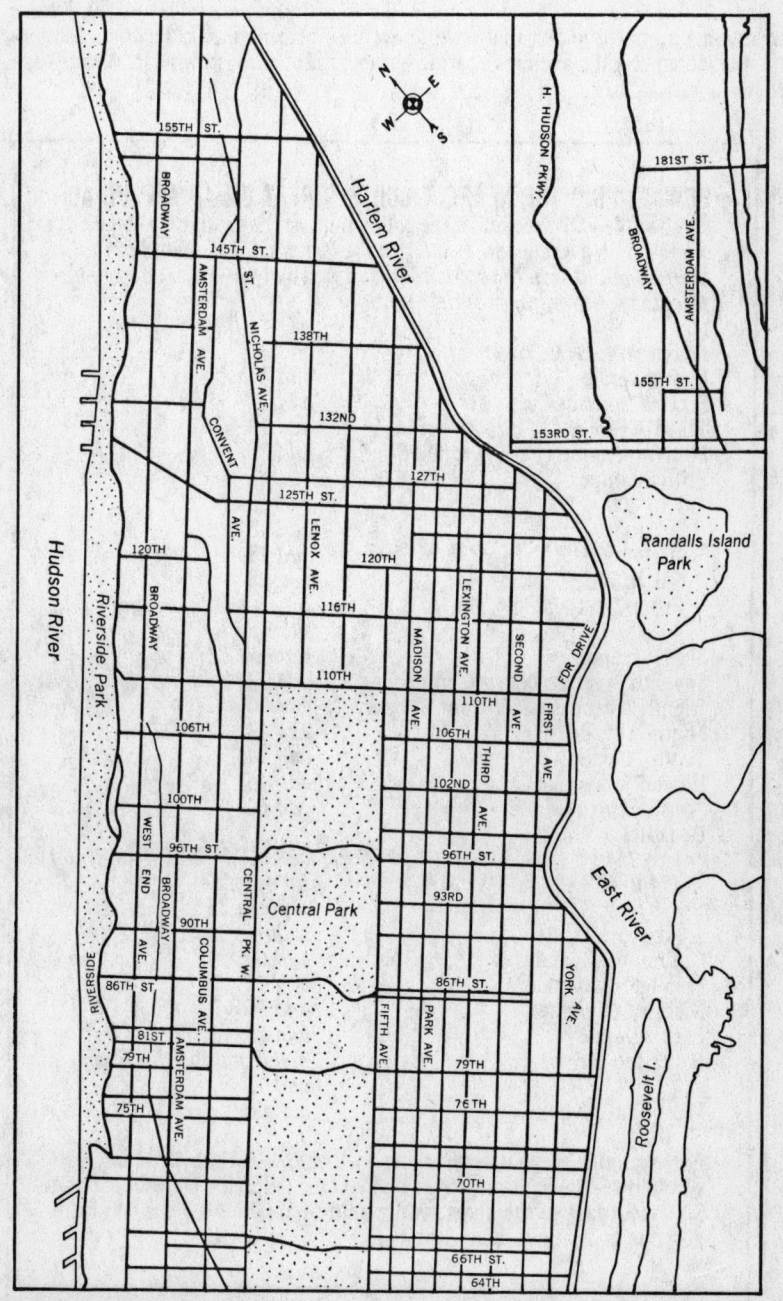

8   NEW YORK ON $45 A DAY

side of Manhattan. Thus if you're on Seventh Avenue and want to go to Ninth Avenue, you simply go west for two blocks.

As we've said, there are some exceptions to this general layout, and these revolve around the fact that several avenues bearing names have been interspersed among the avenues bearing numbers. Thus Broadway (an avenue) ap-

---

HOW TO FIND THE NEAREST CROSS STREET ON AN AVENUE ADDRESS: New Yorkers have the following system for finding the cross street on an avenue address: *Drop the last digit of the number of the address and divide the remaining number by two. Then add or subtract the following appropriate number:*

Avenue A, B, C, or D	add 3
First Avenue	add 3
Second Avenue	add 3
Third Avenue	add 10
Fourth Avenue (Park Avenue South)	add 8
Fifth Avenue	
1 to 200	add 13
201 to 400	add 16
401 to 600	add 18
601 to 775	add 20
From 776 to 1286	*cancel last figure and subtract 18*
Sixth Avenue	*subtract* 12
Seventh Avenue below Central Park	add 12
Eighth Avenue below Central Park	add 10
Ninth Avenue	add 13
Tenth Avenue	add 14
Eleventh Avenue	add 15
Amsterdam Avenue	add 60
Broadway	
1 to 754	*below 8th St.*
754 to 858	*subtract* 29
858 to 958	*subtract* 25
Above 1000	*subtract* 31
Columbus Avenue	add 60
Lexington Avenue	add 22
Madison Avenue	add 26
Park Avenue	add 35
Riverside Drive	*divide number by 10 and add 72*
West End Avenue	add 60

For example, if you were trying to locate 645 Fifth Avenue, you would drop the 5, leaving 64. Then you would divide 64 by 2, leaving 32. According to the chart, you would then add 20. Thus 645 Fifth Avenue is at about 52nd Street.

pears between Seventh and Eighth Avenues on the Upper West Side (and proceeds *diagonally* downtown); Madison, Park, and Lexington Avenues are placed between Fifth and Third Avenues.

And, incidentally, Fourth Avenue is the same as Park Avenue and is called Fourth Avenue only from 8th Street (where it begins) to 14th Street. And Sixth Avenue is officially named "Avenue of the Americas"—but everyone calls it Sixth Avenue, and you'll see both names used in these pages.

The most central avenue in New York, cutting directly through the island lengthwise, is Fifth Avenue.

All east-west street addresses in New York begin at Fifth Avenue and increase in number as they move away from Fifth Avenue. Thus the address 2 West 9th Street would denote a building on 9th Street just a few steps to the west of Fifth Avenue; 56 West 9th Street would indicate a building that is even farther west, and so on. The address 12 East 45th Street would denote a building just a little to the east of Fifth Avenue, while 324 East 45th Street would indicate a building on 45th Street that is way, way east of Fifth Avenue.

A look at the maps printed throughout this book should make it all clear instantly. But as for the bottom portion of Manhattan—that is, the portion below 4th or 1st Streets—there simply is no way that you can easily find your way around. For this is the oldest section of New York (the city grew from south to north), and streets there follow the outlines of old cowpaths and the like. They twist and turn in no defined fashion and bear names instead of numbers: Wall Street, Canal Street, Whitehall Street, etc.

About Times Square

The Times Square area is having a renaissance, although it's only visible to date in a few tall new structures and hotels. Visit Times Square for its theaters, but don't forget our neighborhoods: offbeat Greenwich Village, SoHo and the East Village; dignified Gramercy Square; elegant Park, Madison, and Fifth Avenues (a Fifth Avenue bus ride is an absolute must); and Chinatown and Little Italy, where the flavor is entirely different from the rest of the city. After you've traversed the entire city, you'll realize that life in New York isn't well characterized by the souvenir shops, hot-dog stands, and porno shops of the midtown Broadway area.

A Note on Safety

Perhaps because of exaggerated reports in the media, some first-time visitors to New York approach the city with fears that border on paranoia. While it would be foolish to discount the crime problem, it should not be magnified. New York can be dangerous—like any metropolitan area—but there are ways to keep safe.

Strolling New York streets alone at night isn't usually safe and in some areas should be avoided entirely. These include Harlem, Spanish Harlem, Times Square, and parts of the Upper West Side, Upper East Side, and East Village. This doesn't mean that you must stay away from the city's nightlife. Take cabs to the bars, restaurants, and clubs. Travel in a group, stay on the brightly lit avenues, and avoid the numbered and side streets, which are usually darker and quieter.

During the day or night, walk purposefully. Keep your purse tucked under your arm (or if a shoulderbag, worn *diagonally* over your shoulder) and your wallet in front, not back, pockets. Don't wear expensive jewelry or keep passports and all money in your purse, wallet, or any other single place.

The subways are cheap and fast but also require extra caution. The system is not self-explanatory, so make sure about directions before using it. Don't stand close to the tracks; choose crowded, not empty, cars, and once riding, stay alert. We don't recommend using the subways for late-night travel; the buses are usually safer. But keep in mind that at rush hour, the heavy jostling crowd provides a good camouflage for pickpockets. Neither are hotels and department stores always safe. Don't leave passports and money in hotel rooms, and be aware that some criminals view department-store customers as lucrative and easy targets.

In some parts of the city, people play cards and dice in the streets. Don't join them. First, these games are illegal. But more important, you'll probably lose because the games are rigged—and if you win, you may be relieved of the money. Also, be careful of the traffic. The cars and trucks and especially the cabs move very fast and don't always stop for pedestrians.

A final note: New York is fascinating and exciting but on the flip side are the city's dangers. If you're alert and cautious, you can enjoy the city safely.

MAPS: We've included several maps to make orienting yourself easier. For more detailed color maps, we recommend the *"I Love NYC" Travel Guide*, available free from the New York Convention and Visitors Bureau, Two Columbus Circle, New York, NY 10019; the "Exxon" map to New York City, available at the Exxon Building at Rockefeller Center; and (our favorite) the Flashmaps *Instant Guide to New York* ($4.95), which has maps showing restaurant, theater, hotel, and museum locations, as well as subway and bus routes. For a free full-color subway or bus map of any borough (be sure to specify), send a self-addressed stamped envelope to "Maps," New York City Transit Authority, 370 Jay St., Brooklyn, NY 11202. Subway and bus maps are also available at most subway station token booths.

TRANSPORTATION: New York has few rivals when it comes to fast and inexpensive transportation. Cabs are available 24 hours a day, and except during the rush hours (8 to 9:30 in the morning and 4:30 to 6 in the evening) the subway and bus systems work wonderfully, getting you anywhere in Manhattan and the five boroughs as fast as a private car and with considerably less anxiety.

The charge for all the buses and subways is $1, which must be paid in change or tokens. The bus is the most interesting way to travel and its routes are easiest to understand. The subway system is faster and the graffiti splashed over its walls and trains is as interesting a sight as any in New York. But the crime rate in the subway tunnels is high, and in recent years even New Yorkers have been reluctant to use the system.

North or South in Manhattan by Bus

Virtually every one of the avenues of Manhattan has buses that go either up or down the entire length of that avenue; and since most of the avenues have one-way traffic restrictions, most of the buses go in only one direction.

Along the following avenues, the buses go *north* (uptown) only: First Avenue, Third Avenue, Park Avenue (to 40th Street only), Madison Avenue, Sixth Avenue (Avenue of the Americas), Eighth Avenue, Tenth Avenue.

Along the following avenues, the buses go *south* (downtown) only: Second Avenue, Lexington Avenue, Fifth Avenue, Broadway (below 59th Street), Seventh Avenue (below 59th Street), Ninth Avenue.

Along York Avenue, Riverside Drive, and Broadway above 59th Street, the buses go in *both* directions (uptown and downtown).

East or West in Manhattan by Bus

There are also a number of so-called crosstown buses which go east or west across the entire island, along certain of the important streets of Manhattan.

Along the following streets, the buses go *east* only: 8th Street, 50th Street, and 65th Street. (Important note: This last bus travels along 65th Street on the West Side of Manhattan only; after it crosses Central Park to the East Side, it continues its eastbound route on 68th Street.)

Along the following streets, the buses go *west* only: 9th Street, 49th Street, Central Park South (that's 59th Street between Fifth and Eighth Avenues), and 67th Street. (Another important note: This last bus travels along 67th Street on the East Side of Manhattan only; after it crosses Central Park to the West Side, it continues its westbound route on 66th Street.)

And along the following streets, the buses go in *both* directions (east and west): 14th Street, 23rd Street, 34th Street, 42nd Street, 57th Street, 79th Street, 86th Street, 96th Street, 116th Street, 125th Street, 145th Street, and 155th Street.

If transferring from one bus route to another is necessary, a free "transfer" ticket is available to passengers who have already paid the full fare. The ticket allows you to change from one bus to another, but only where routes intersect. Senior citizens, those 65 and over, who are New York City residents pay half fare (50¢), except during rush hour. For information about the transit system, call 718/330-1234.

Traveling by Subway

Despite the noise and occasional discomfort, especially during the hottest days of summer, the quickest, cheapest, and most efficient way to move around the city is by subway. And from the point of view of pure experience, we recommend that every visitor ride the subway at least once: if you haven't ridden the subway you haven't seen New York—and you certainly haven't seen its graffiti.

Tokens currently cost $1 apiece and are obtained at token booths inside the stations. Purchase tokens with small bills; anything larger than a $20 bill will not be accepted.

To the stranger, the system might appear to operate in an extremely mysterious way, and to unravel its complexities would require a separate tome. Our first and most important piece of advice, therefore, is to obtain a good map. You can pick up a free map at most token booths. This map may confuse first-timers even further, so we recommend you supplement it with a copy of the aforementioned Flashmaps *Instant Guide to New York,* which contains excellent maps not only of the subway system, but of everything in town. Almost every bookstore carries it, as do large newsstands.

Having said all this, here are a few pointers to smooth your subway riding: There are three subway lines running through Manhattan: Interborough Rapid Transit (IRT), Brooklyn–Manhattan Transit (BMT), and the Independent Line (IND). Keep in mind that there are *two* IRT lines: the East Side IRT–Lexington Avenue line, and the West Side IRT–Seventh Avenue line. The East and West branches of the IRT are connected by the Grand Central to Times Square Shuttle and the 14th Street Canarsie (BMT) line. The BMT runs mostly from Brooklyn through lower and midtown Manhattan out to Queens and back. IND trains run along Sixth and Eighth Avenues, with major stops in Greenwich Village at West 4th Street and Sixth Avenue (both lines), at the Port Authority Bus Terminal at 41st Street (Eighth Avenue line), at Rockefeller Center (Sixth Avenue line), and at Columbus Circle (59th Street; Eighth Avenue line). You can switch from line to line—look for the transfer points on your subway map.

Each subway train is clearly numbered or lettered, indicating its specific route. (IND and BMT trains are lettered; IRT trains are numbered). Since differently routed trains will pull into the same station, it is best to know which letter or number you should take. Consult your subway map.

Both express and local trains run on each line. Locals stop at all stations on the route. Express trains do not. For example, if you ride an express (A) train uptown from 42nd Street on the IND Eighth Avenue line, you'll stop first at 59th Street and then zoom right through seven stations to the next stop, 125th Street! So you might be advised to stick to local trains until you know the system. Riding only in Manhattan, you won't lose much time doing this, and it could lessen the strains and frustrations of getting lost, or being whisked 60 blocks north of your destination.

Avoid the rush hours—8 to 9:30 in the morning, 4:30 to 6 in the afternoon. Pushing and shoving is the rule then—as it is most other times—but at rush hour there are at least 100 people per car pushing and shoving (feels more like a thousand).

To avoid waiting in line to buy tokens, carry extras with you—they can also be used on the bus.

It is not a particularly good idea to ride at night. If you do, avoid empty cars. Transit policemen patrol the trains at night, and the conductor rides in either one of the center cars in a tiny compartment at all times.

Do not hesitate to ask questions. Subway personnel (token sellers, conductors, transit policemen) are the best sources of information on exactly which train goes where—and how to negotiate the maze of underground passageways to the entrance to the train you're looking for, or to the exit to the street.

Traveling by Taxi

Obviously the most convenient way to travel around town is by cab, but it's not cheap. At press time, fares start at $1.10 the minute you step into a cab, and thereafter the charge is 10¢ for each ninth of a mile and an additional 10¢ for every 14 seconds of waiting time in traffic. The rider pays bridge, tunnel, and/or highway tolls. Also, as of this writing there is a 50¢ surcharge tacked on each fare after 8 p.m. every day, and all day on Sunday. Of course you are also expected to tip, but don't let any driver intimidate you—give 15% on all fares.

On short rides, if a group of people hop a cab together it can often cost less, or at least the same, as taking a subway. You can often find willing cab sharers at bus stops.

Check the Yellow Pages under the heading "Taxicab Service" for radio-dispatched cabs, which operate on regular meter rates, though sometimes there's an extra charge if you reserve in advance. Although it's usually easy enough to walk out and hail a passing cab, there may be occasions when you'd prefer door-to-door service. We usually call **All City** (tel. 796-1111), **Communicar** (tel. 718/457-7777), or **Ding-A-Ling** (tel. 691-9191).

Cabs are hard to come by during morning and evening rush hours, and furthermore any trip at these times will cost you a fortune in waiting time.

Avoid gypsy cabs. These cabs do not have a medallion on top, many have a somewhat battered appearance, and offer somewhat questionable service—we ourselves have been taken for more than a ride. There are, however, some fine private-car services with radio-dispatched late-model sedans. If you find yourself in an area not serviced by regular yellow cabs, ask a local person for a recommendation or check the Yellow Pages under "Car Service." Ask for the rate when booking service.

TRANSPORTATION 13

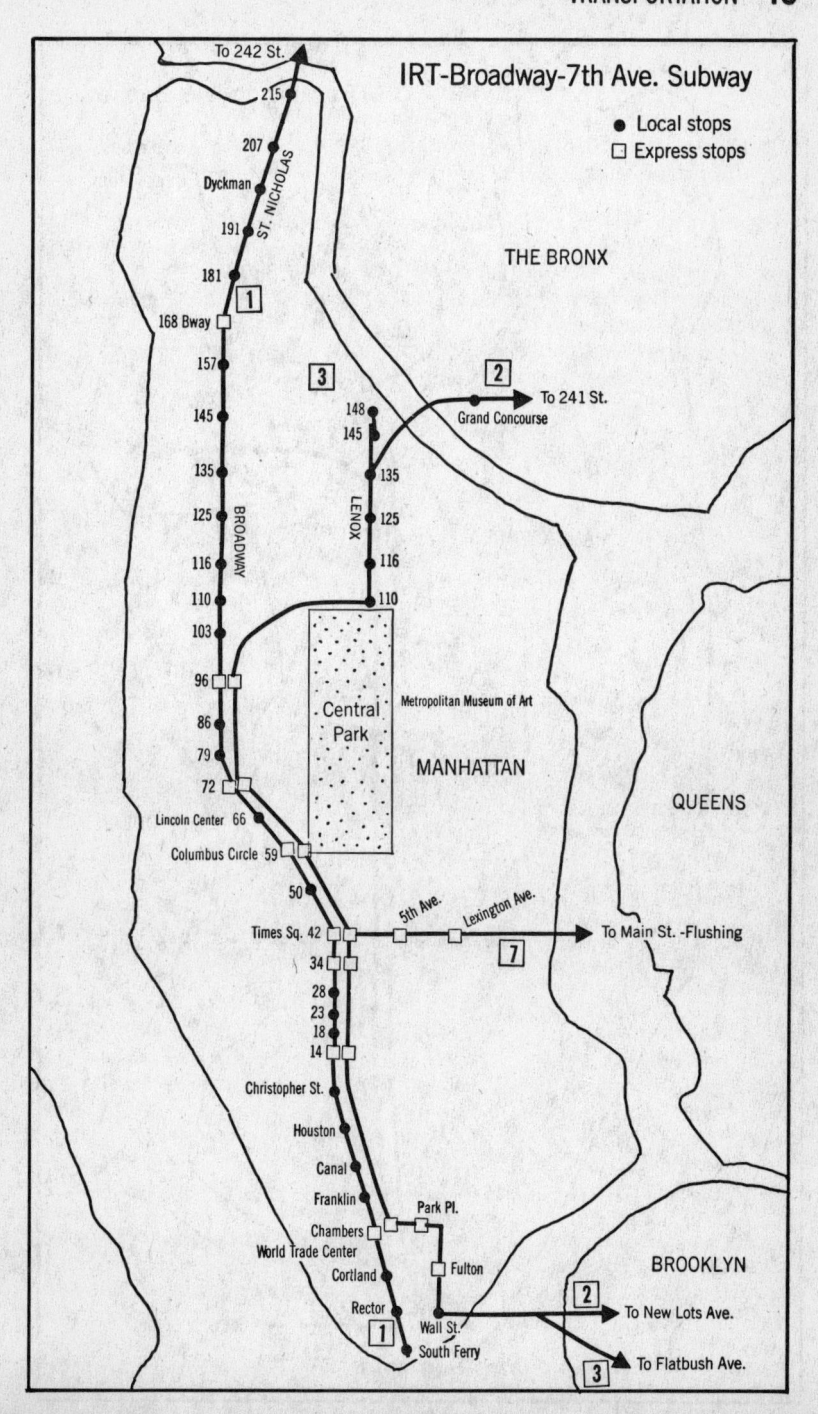

IRT-Broadway-7th Ave. Subway

- ● Local stops
- □ Express stops

To 242 St.
215
207
Dyckman
191
181
ST. NICHOLAS
168 Bway — [1]
157
145
135
125
BROADWAY
116
110
103
96
86
79
72
Lincoln Center 66
Columbus Circle 59
50
Times Sq. 42
34
28
23
18
14
Christopher St.
Houston
Canal
Franklin
Chambers
World Trade Center
Cortland
Rector
[1]
South Ferry

[3]
148
145
135
LENOX
125
116
110

[2] → To 241 St.
Grand Concourse

THE BRONX

Central Park

Metropolitan Museum of Art

MANHATTAN

QUEENS

5th Ave.   Lexington Ave. → To Main St.-Flushing [7]

Park Pl.
Fulton
Wall St.

BROOKLYN

[2] → To New Lots Ave.
[3] ▶ To Flatbush Ave.

14 NEW YORK ON $45 A DAY

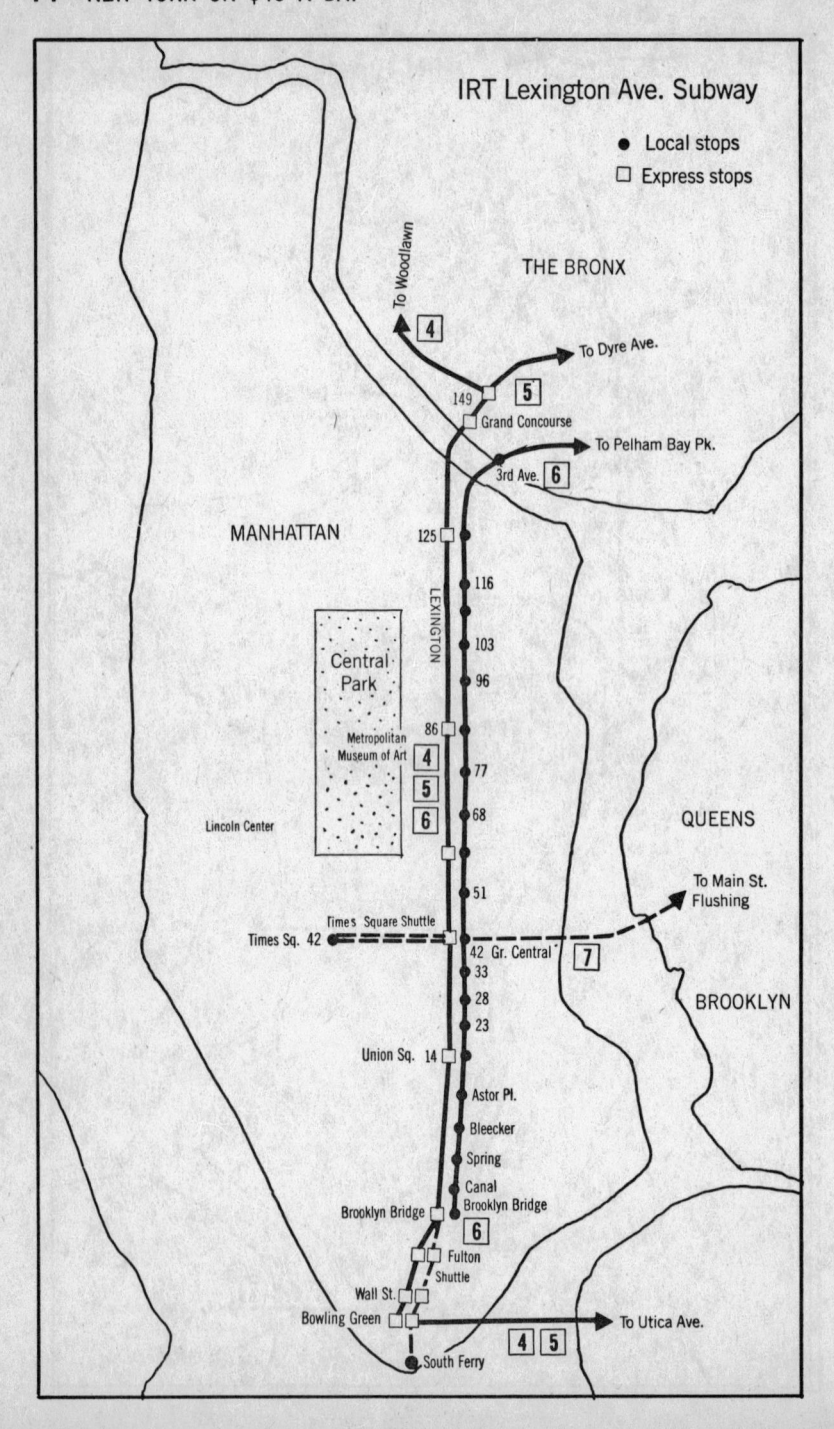

TRANSPORTATION 15

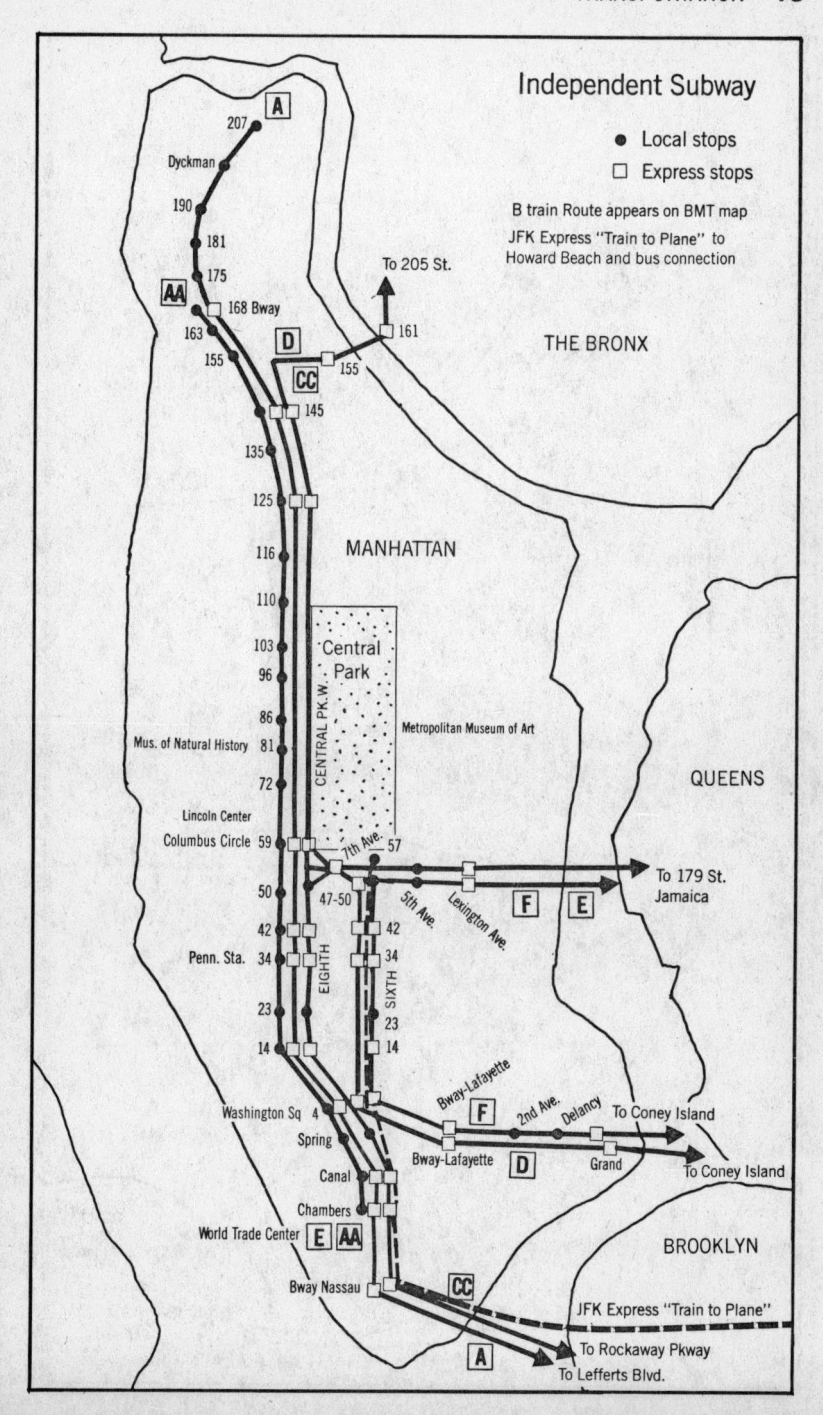

Independent Subway

- ● Local stops
- □ Express stops

B train Route appears on BMT map
JFK Express "Train to Plane" to Howard Beach and bus connection

16 NEW YORK ON $45 A DAY

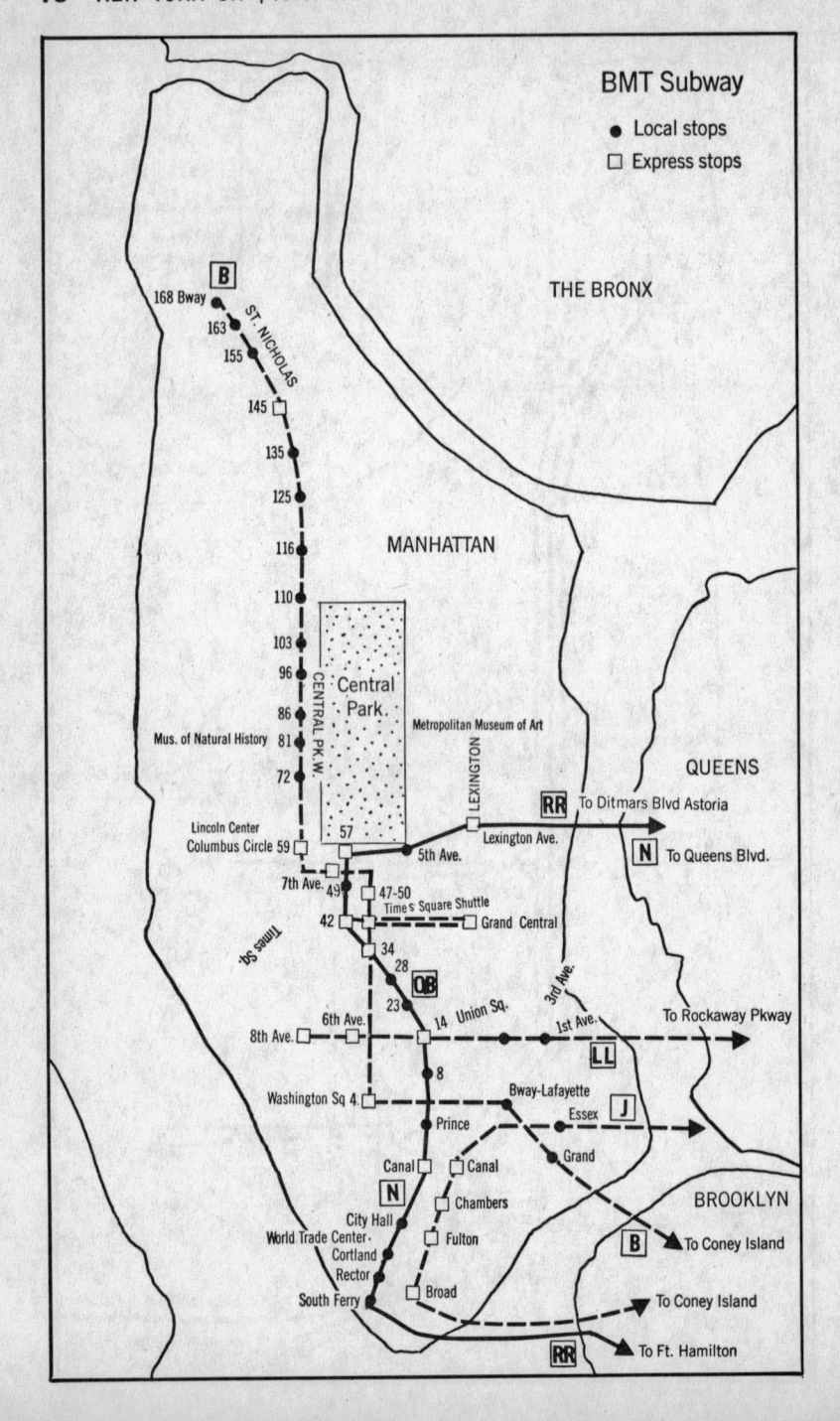

Parking Your Car

People in New York have been known to have fistfights over street-side parking places. Usually the only way to get one is to catch someone leaving a spot, which can take as long as a half hour. Don't wait to see a car pulling out. Watch for telltale signs. A person reaching into a pocket for keys, opening a car door, or even just walking purposefully toward a vehicle often means a space may be free in a few minutes.

Finding inexpensive garage parking is no easy task either. The average price for a space can be $5 or more an hour and more than $20 a day. One way to beat prices is to find a lot with a low maximum—a set charge for minimum parking time. **Square Industries,** 425 W. 52nd St., between Ninth and Tenth Avenues (tel. 664-8476), has ten-hour parking for $6 and is open 24 hours daily. The company has two other low-cost parking locations in Manhattan—at 40 E. 89th St. (tel. 534-9421), and at 309 W. 46th St. (tel. 664-8224).

The **municipal garages** managed by the city are the cheapest in Manhattan. In the **midtown** area, there's one on Eighth Avenue between 53rd and 54th Streets (tel. 997-8901). Parking costs 85¢ an hour; it's open daily 24 hours. The **Wall Street** area has a municipal garage at 103–109 Park Row, underneath the Police Plaza building near the Manhattan side of the Brooklyn Bridge (tel. 962-8524). Parking costs $1 each half hour between 9 a.m. and 4 p.m. Monday through Friday. Other times there's a $2 maximum charge. A third municipal garage is on the **Lower East Side,** at 105–113 Essex St., near Delancey (tel. 475-9814). From Monday through Saturday, parking is 30¢ per half hour with a $2.70 minimum between 7 a.m. and 7 p.m. and $3.90 for 24 hours. On Sunday the charge is 40¢ per half hour. The fourth municipal garage is on **Leonard Street** between Lafayette and Center Streets. Parking is $1 an hour, with a three-hour limit, and the garage is only open between 8 a.m. and 10 p.m. Monday through Saturday.

Low-Cost Car Rentals

Not Nu Car Rental, 415 W. 45th St., between Ninth and Tenth Avenues (tel. 265-3120), rents cars for $19.95 a day weekdays and $24.95 on weekends, with a charge of 12¢ per mile. Open Monday through Friday from 8 a.m. to 6 p.m. and on Saturday from 9 a.m. until noon.

Rent-A-Wreck, State Highway 440, Jersey City, New Jersey (tel. 201/451-9500), does what its name promises. At $21.95 a day, the company rents cars that are three to six years old but mechanically sound and well running. The price includes 50 free miles, with a 15¢ charge for each additional mile. There's a weekend special from Friday to Monday for $65.95, which includes 150 free miles (15¢ for each additional mile), and a full-week special for $119, which includes 500 free miles (15¢ for each additional mile.) Rent-A-Wrecks are individually owned franchises; this is the low cost member—expect to pay more if you rent from the Manhattan branches. Open Monday through Friday from 8 a.m. to 6 p.m. and on Saturday until noon.

U-Drive, 301 Bowery, between Houston and 1st Streets (tel. 982-9680), rents cars for $22.95 a day weekdays and $34.95 weekends, which includes 50 free miles (15¢ for each additional mile). Open Monday through Friday from 7:30 a.m. to 5 p.m., on Saturday until noon.

Chapter I

FINDING A BUDGET HOTEL

1. Rooms for Singles and Students
2. Low-Cost Permanent Residences
3. Rooms for Service Personnel
4. Hotels for General Occupancy
5. Rooms for Families
6. Bed and Breakfast
7. Weekend and Other Packages

YOU'RE PLANNING YOUR FIRST TRIP to New York, or maybe the first one in some years. When it comes to choosing a hotel, confusion reigns. You've heard rumors that Manhattan hotel rooms are vastly overpriced and that some neighborhoods are not safe. Should you choose to stay in midtown near Times Square, in the Lincoln Center area, or over on the East Side? And how much *will* you have to pay for a decent room? Finding a suitable budget hotel is the most difficult task, and the hardest, trickiest, most important job of all. Read and reread this chapter carefully; we have spent months researching the hotel scene, and if you read on, you'll find your choice of clean, comfortable accommodations for a minimum of money.

Like many other major cities of the world, New York has a single section or district noted as a clustering spot for good, inexpensive hotels: Times Square and the midtown theater district. Other budget hotels are widely scattered, and it's necessary to search them out. Nevertheless, they exist. Some, of course, have no fancy doormen or brocaded lobbies, but they do have adequate accommodations whose prices can still be considered reasonable in today's highly inflated hotel market.

And what does a reasonable, budget-minded hotel cost in New York these days? More than it does in most other cities, alas. Plan on spending between $50 and $80 for a double if you wish to stay in one of the regular tourist hotels (see "Hotels for General Occupancy," ahead). High as these rates may seem, they are actually budget by New York standards; in many hotels, rates of $125 and more per night are commonplace. If you stay in a Y, a women's hotel, or are a student or young working person and can qualify at certain places, you will, of course, pay much less. Weekly or longer stays bring down the rates. A bed-and-breakfast arrangement in a private home can save you money. And the best deal of all is to plan your trip for a weekend when first-class and luxury hotels often have special packages—meals, theater tickets, etc.—for not much more than the cost of a budget hotel. We outline all of these options in the pages ahead.

Finding the best bargain rooms is an art, and here are a few tricks that all budget tourists should know. Although there are not many such establishments left, a few hotels still have some of their older rooms without private bath available. Request them when you can; savings are great. This doesn't mean that you have to give up bathing to enjoy these low costs—it means you share a connecting bath with the adjoining room or trek down the hall a few doors to a bath.

Here's another tip: Travel in threes. By forming your own threesome, you will cut costs considerably. A triple is usually a large double room with one double bed and one twin, and—here's the bonus—a private bathroom. It's three for the price of two.

Or as an alternative, if you're a couple you can travel with another couple and share a suite, which usually consists of two well-furnished bedrooms and one bathroom. Some even have kitchen units. By sharing a bathroom here, you'll discover that the cost of a luxury suite doesn't equal the cost of two private rooms with bath.

Write well in advance for reservations. Hotels are busier than ever with many foreign tours and convention groups coming into Manhattan. But to take advantage of the special discount rate that some hotels offer to readers of this book, you *must write* well in advance stating specifically what price room you require. If you don't write ahead you may find that the cheaper bargain rooms have been snapped up, and that only the higher priced variety remains available. You may not get the same discount if you arrive without advance reservations, even if you flash a copy of the book upon registering.

If you haven't written for reservations, then make good use of a phone booth (25¢ per call) before you rush to a particular hotel. In some of the lower-priced establishments, you may want to see your room before paying or registering; quality varies from floor to floor in some budget hotels. It is also possible for hotels to change their rates at will, depending on what the traffic will bear.

OTHER PRELIMINARY POINTS: To clear up a matter that confused some readers of the earlier editions of this book: when we refer to the price of a double room, we are referring to the *total* price for two persons. Thus, for instance, when we say that a double room rents for $60, we mean that the price per person is only $30. Unless otherwise stated, prices are for the cost of the room only, without breakfast.

Also, please note that the prices we quote for rooms do not include the New York City Hotel Occupancy Tax, unless otherwise indicated. In addition to an 8¼% sales tax on your total hotel bill, you will also have to pay the Hotel Occupancy Tax, a rather steep charge of about $2 a day.

Got the general picture? Then let's begin. . . .

1. Rooms for Singles and Students

SINGLE MEN AND WOMEN: For the young and young at heart (men and women, even families), we heartily recommend the **Vanderbilt YMCA,** 224 E. 47th St., NYC 10017, between Second and Third Avenues (tel. 212/755-2410). A 435-room, ten-story structure, it offers some of the finest athletic facilities (including a large pool, gym, and sauna) in town, plus an excellent cafeteria, a self-service laundry, a sundeck with chaise longues, newsstand, and general supply store. The atmosphere of the place reminds us of a European youth hostel—relaxed, young, and friendly—but visitors of any age can stay. It's not a bad idea for families willing to rough it. The cafeteria is a terrific money-saver; it's quite pleasant, offers big, filling meals in the $4 to $5 range, and even serves wine and beer. Guests are given automatic Y membership for the length of their stay and can use all the Vanderbilt Y facilities. The hospitality desk is helpful with sightseeing and other information.

Rooms are small and spartan, but very clean, located off attractive hallways with carpeted walls. All accommodations have single or bunk beds, dresser, and desk. Some have sinks in the room, but baths are down the hall. Phones are also in the hall; the desk will take messages for you.

Rates for single rooms are $24 to $34 per night; doubles (with bunk beds) are $34 to $40. Triples and quads offer savings at rates of $45 to $50 and $56 to $60. Credit cards are now accepted. Considering the superb East Side location and facilities, this Y is quite a bargain. It's also the kind of place parents can feel at ease sending their young sons and daughters. Write or phone for reservations.

SINGLE WOMEN ONLY: Women traveling alone will find the following very comfortable:

Even though there's no name on the door and the lobby looks more like that of an office building than a hotel, **Allerton House**, 130 E. 57th St., NYC 10022, corner of Lexington Avenue (tel. 212/753-8841), continues to hold forth after many years, a dowdy but doughty dowager among the women's hotels. The location is excellent, in a busy midtown business and shopping neighborhood, with Bloomingdale's just two blocks away. The atmosphere is rather sedate (about three-quarters of the rooms are occupied by permanent residents, mostly older women), but there are also enough 20- to 30-year-old guests for younger women to feel at home. Pluses include a terrific wrap-around rooftop terrace ideal for sunbathing, and a laundromat. Tommy Makem's atmospheric Irish Pavilion restaurant, with candlelight, beamed ceilings, a popular bar, and a craft shop to boot, adjoins the hotel. And there's usually a smart crowd lined up at the elevators waiting to gain access to the Living Well Lady Figure Salon on the mezzanine floor (hotel guests are usually entitled to one free visit) or to the Beverly Bridge Club, one of the city's busiest and best (lunch and an afternoon's worth of bridge for $6), on the third.

Above these floors are the hotel rooms, almost all of which, except for those on the 17th floor, could be described as clean and respectable, but without much charm. They are small, with high ceilings, direct-dial phones, sinks, desks, dressers, worn furniture; TV sets can be rented. The units on the 17th floor, however, are another story: attractive new hotel rooms, they have twin beds, private bath, black-and-white TV, air conditioning, nice furnishings, and are an excellent value at $60 double.

A bathless room (facilities down the hall) is $30 per night for one person; a room with connecting bath (you share with an adjoining room), $35; a room with a private bath or shower, $40. The 17th-floor twins are $60. Weekly rates are available for stays of two weeks or longer: $130 for a bathless room, $150 for a room with connecting bath, $160 for rooms with private bath or shower.

Also recommendable is the **Martha Washington Hotel,** 30 E. 30th St. (entrance through 29 E. 29th St.), NYC 10016, between Park and Madison Avenues (tel. 212/689-1900), which accepts women of any age. Built in 1901 "with a view to affording accommodations for self-supporting women in artistic, literary, educational, and kindred pursuits," it is a comfortable and safe middle-class establishment with ordinary furnished rooms. As at most hotels for women, men are not permitted above the lobby floor and are not permitted into the building at all after midnight. About 70% of the 500 rooms are occupied by

ROOMS FOR SINGLES / STUDENTS 21

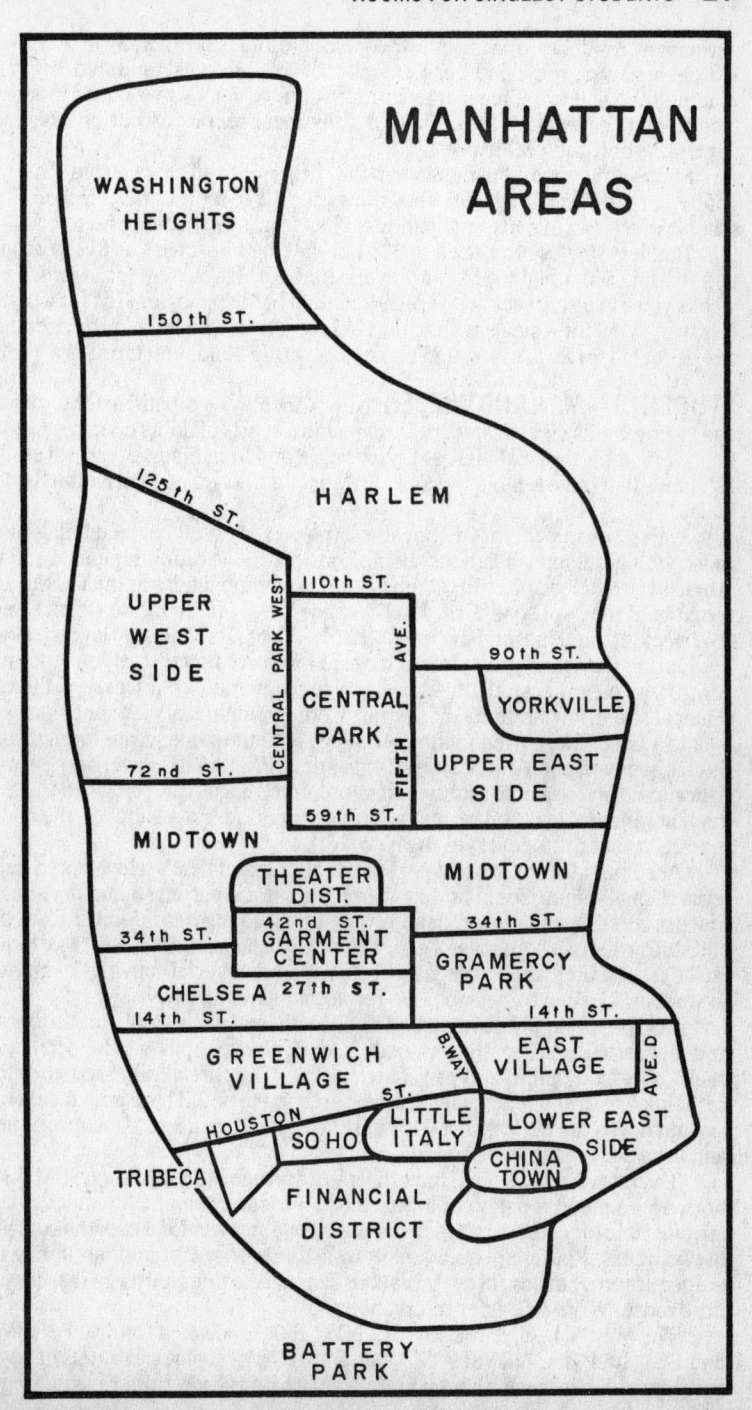

MANHATTAN AREAS

- WASHINGTON HEIGHTS
- 150th ST.
- 125th ST.
- HARLEM
- 110th ST.
- UPPER WEST SIDE
- CENTRAL PARK WEST
- CENTRAL PARK
- FIFTH AVE.
- 90th ST.
- YORKVILLE
- UPPER EAST SIDE
- 72nd ST.
- 59th ST.
- MIDTOWN
- THEATER DIST.
- 42nd ST. GARMENT CENTER
- MIDTOWN
- 34th ST.
- GRAMERCY PARK
- CHELSEA 27th ST.
- 14th ST.
- GREENWICH VILLAGE
- B'WAY
- EAST VILLAGE
- AVE. D
- HOUSTON ST.
- SOHO
- LITTLE ITALY
- LOWER EAST SIDE
- CHINA TOWN
- TRIBECA
- FINANCIAL DISTRICT
- BATTERY PARK

permanent residents, and many, of course, are older women; as in Allerton House, however, you'll find a good number of younger guests and students too. Among the facilities: kitchenettes in rooms rented for two weeks or more, a laundromat, newsstand, sundeck, and daily maid service except on holidays (weekdays only for weekly guests).

Some of the rooms are more worn than others, but all are neat and clean (if you're not satisfied with the one they show you, ask to see another). Decorating schemes vary, but all have sink-vanity cabinets and switchboard phones.

Bathless singles are priced at $28 per day, bathless twins at $42; a single with bath is $40 a night, $55 for a twin with bath. If you stay for at least two weeks you can pay a weekly rate of $94.50 for a bathless single, $154 for a bathless twin, $119 for a single with bath, $182 for a twin with bath. A refrigerator can be rented for an additional $5 a week, and an air conditioner for $14 a week.

STUDENTS—MEN AND WOMEN: New York may be expensive for the average visitor, but flash your student ID card and all sorts of doors open up. We've been very impressed with the quality, warmth, and friendliness of several establishments that put out a big welcome for students and young international travelers.

University students aged 21 or above (possessed of student credentials) and those with academic affiliations should consider the vacation-time (May 15 to August 15 and December 15 to January 15) accommodations at the famous **International House of New York,** 500 Riverside Dr., NYC 10027, at 122nd Street (overlooking the Hudson River; tel. 212/678-5036). Bus and subways are close by. During the school year, International House accommodates, on a permanent basis, over 500 students from all over the world (we discovered there a political scientist from India, a ballerina from Argentina, a Vietnamese lawyer — and a U.N. intern from Idaho). About 65% of the students are foreign, and though many of the American residents attend Columbia University, over 45 educational and training institutes are represented each year. But when the permanent residents leave on vacation (during the periods stated above), the house rents its rooms to students visiting New York.

Accommodations are just part of the offerings. There's a low-priced cafeteria, a small dining room and kitchen for informal parties, a laundry, music practice rooms, general store, and several public lounges including a TV room and study rooms. There's also a gym with volleyball, basketball, and table tennis facilities, and there are dance and aerobics classes. Special activities of interest to students and newcomers to New York occur almost daily.

Rooms are simple but neat and clean, with light walls, linoleum-tile floors, and the necessary furnishings—bed, linens, blanket, pillow, dresser, desk, chair, bookcase, lamp, and private telephone. They are all singles, two-thirds with sinks; bath and toilet facilities are shared in the hall. There is no maid service, but linens can be exchanged for fresh ones for a small fee. Vacuum cleaners and irons are available at no extra cost.

The rates are $22 a night; monthly rates average $12 to $13 a day. (Applications are required for stays of longer than a month.) A limited number of cots are available for guests to stay in your room for $8 a night for a maximum period of two weeks. Rooms are occasionally available to transient students during the academic year, but advance reservations cannot be confirmed more than a week in advance. Write or call for reservations.

The **West Side Y,** 5 W. 63rd St., NYC 10023, between Central Park West and Broadway (tel. 212/787-4400), has one of the best physical setups of any Y in the country. Its location is first rate—just seconds away from Lincoln Center and Central Park—and it abounds with facilities: three gymnasiums (for men and women); sauna; steamroom; two swimming pools; handball, squash, and racquetball courts; indoor track; exercise rooms; etc. Park West Café, the attractive cafeteria on the premises—Spanish in motif with ceramic tile and stucco walls—offers inexpensive meals. There is maid service and an athletic equipment store. The atmosphere is friendly, with many European backpackers and student residents from Julliard and nearby ballet schools.

The 561 single rooms are small and of the no-frills variety, clean and serviceable. Each contains a small bed, desk, dresser, and closet; walls are off-white and unadorned. Communal bath amenities are in the hall, public phones in the lobby; black-and-white TV sets are in all transients' rooms.

Three floors of rooms are set aside just for students, both male and female, but you must have student identification (such as a letter from your school addressed to the Y with starting and finishing dates). A stay of at least one semester is required to qualify for student rates, and you must be 18 or over to stay at any room in the Y. Write for student rates.

Transient rooms are singles and doubles; student rooms are singles only; all share a community bath. Rates start at $25 per night. Air conditioning is available, in both types of rooms, for an additional $2.50 per night. Y membership is included in daily rates; for longer stays there is a nominal membership fee. There are about 20 rooms on the premises with private bath (rather difficult to get) that rent for $34 per night and up. If you'd like to stay at the Y, write well ahead to: Reservations Manager, West Side Y, at the above address.

Despite its name, the **International Student Hospice**, 154 E. 33rd St., NYC 10016, between Lexington and Third Avenues (tel. 212/228-7470 or 228-4689), is not for internationals only: this reconverted Murray Hill town house is the place where Oxford scholars swap stories with Ohio collegians, where students from St. Louis bunk in the opposite room from those from the Sorbonne. Art Stabile, a friendly man who acts like everybody's uncle, has been presiding over this congenial place since 1958, and naturally takes visitors under his wing. Sponsored by a nonprofit foundation, ISH can house 20 guests (students are preferred, but others are sometimes accepted), and charges them $10 per night for groups of eight or more, $15 for one night or in a few tiny private rooms. Bathrooms and showers are down the hall. Rooms are small but clean, and there's a library for studying, even a tiny lounge with color TV. The hospice is within walking distance of Grand Central Terminal, Penn Station, Madison Square Garden, and the United Nations, in a mixed residential-business neighborhood, right in the shadow of the Empire State Building. Write or phone in advance, or call at any hour: the phone is on 24 hours a day.

The artistic talents of a friendly staff have turned the once rather decrepit **Carlton Arms Hotel**, 160 E. 25th St., NYC 10010, corner of Third Avenue (tel. 212/MU4-8337), into a congenial place for young travelers. Especially popular with students from Europe, this four-story hotel has ancient furniture and the halls could use spiffing up, but the beds are all new and good, and the place is kept clean, safe, and comfortable. Vivid color schemes, wall murals, theme rooms (the Frank Sinatra room, for example), posters, and the like create a laissez-faire college dorm atmosphere. Many artworks have been donated by guests or staff: Gil Domingus's outside mural, with mirror insets (you become part of the mural by walking by), is unusual. There is no air conditioning, but they do have fans. Some 40% of the rooms have sinks and baths; other rooms share communal facilities. Rooms with bath are $30 single, $39 double; rooms with sinks only (share the bath down the hall) are $25 single, $33 double. Students and international travelers are offered discounts of approximately 20%.

Not for middle-class comfort, but acceptable for casual types. Two telephone calls are requested to secure a reservation.

FOR A STUDENT QUARTET: If you're a group of four students traveling together, and want to stay near Times Square, you can contact the air-conditioned **Century Paramount Hotel,** 235 W. 46th St., NYC 10036, between Broadway and Eighth Avenue (tel. 212/764-5501). They will rent you a room with private bath and two double beds for $16 to $18 per person—providing you mention this book when requesting reservations in advance. Highly recommended. Details about this hotel are in our upcoming section on "Hotels for General Occupancy."

FOR INTERNATIONAL STUDENTS AND TRAVELERS: The office of the **International Student Center,** 38 W. 88th St., NYC 10024, between Central Park West and Columbus Avenue (tel. 212/787-7706), is jammed with backpacks; you know you're in a student hostel the moment you set foot in the door. Sponsored by the Association for World Travel Exchange, which has a similar house in Holland, ISC has been hosting foreign students and travelers (young people between the ages of 18 and 30) since 1956. They've converted an old brownstone in a pleasant residential neighborhood into seven single-sex dormitory rooms, each with from four to ten beds. Downstairs is an old kitchen which students are free to use, and a ramshackle lounge with TV, the scene for lots of lively socializing. This is a good place to meet someone to travel with. Most summer guests are from Western Europe: in winter, the largest number are from New Zealand, Australia, and Japan. Rates are $8 per night, with a five-day limit from May 1 to the end of October. Guests are also accommodated in midtown, at the Hotel Woodward, Broadway and 55th Street (but there is no kitchen or common lounge area here). Robert Tesdell, the cordial manager, advises that advance reservations are not accepted; the best thing is to phone them as soon as you arrive in town. Passports are required. The residence is open daily from 8 a.m. to 11 p.m.

The newest student hostel in town, the **Chelsea Center,** 511 W. 20th St., NYC 10011, between Tenth and Eleventh Avenues (tel. 212/243-4922), circa 1981, is perhaps the homiest. The teapot is always on and a warm welcome is always available from hostesses Heidi Dubose of Germany and Elli Ali of New York, who have remodeled the first floor of an old loft building and turned it into a real home-away-from-home for wandering students and travelers from abroad. They have a large, sunny, L-shaped room, very clean, with whitewashed walls and six double-decker beds; since there is only one dorm, facilities are completely coed. Rates are $12.85 per night, and that includes breakfast—i.e., three slices of bread and butter and jam, coffee, and milk. The center welcomes backpackers, hikers, and other young travelers as well as students, but always gives first preference to foreigners. Stays are limited to one week during the summer. The location, although it seems a bit out of the way in a mixed residential—light industrial area, is actually excellent: it's a two-minute walk to the 23rd Street crosstown bus which takes you to the heart of Manhattan, and a short walk to Greenwich Village. Guests have the use of the cozy kitchen, and you can usually find them there, having a snack, chatting with Heidi or Elli about goings-on in New York, or perhaps celebrating a birthday. One student from Australia wrote in the guestbook: "Definitely the most friendly place in the USA and a 'secure' place to feel welcome in New York." As in most hostels, there are rules: the house is closed between 10 a.m. and 4 p.m., no visitors or personal phone calls, no drinking, midnight curfew (keys are available for those wishing to stay out later). An excellent choice for a personal welcome in New York.

2. Low-Cost Permanent Residences

For those of our readers who are planning a fairly lengthy stay in New York —say, two months or more— we've scoured the city for good, low-cost, permanent residences. These we'll break down into two categories: permanent residences for students and young working people, and permanent residences for women.

RESIDENCES FOR STUDENTS AND YOUNG WORKING PEOPLE: The **YM-YWHA,** 1395 Lexington Ave., NYC 10128, at 92nd Street (tel. 212/427-6000), is a paradise for those young men and women who plan to stay at least three months. Rates include light housekeeping privileges, and this is one of the city's most exciting institutions. It was here that Dylan Thomas gave his celebrated poetry readings in the 1950s; and the Y continues to present excellent cultural programs ranging from the Juilliard String Quartet (one of countless musical events) to lectures and appearances by writers such as Bernard Malamud, I. B. Singer, Robert Penn Warren, etc. There are also Jewish operas, Israeli and Jewish-themed films (e.g., *Hester Street),* Yiddish theater and theater on Jewish themes (e.g., Paddy Chayefsky's *The Tenth Man)* productions. Residents often get reduced-price or free tickets to these events. Other facilities include, of course, the adjoining gymnasium and pool, with steam and sauna rooms; exercise rooms and equipment; basketball, volleyball, racquetball, handball, and paddleball courts; etc. Other on-premises amenities: laundry facilities, lounges, a library, an art gallery with changing exhibits, and kitchens on every floor.

As for the rooms, they're immaculate and cheerful, painted in pastel colors, with coordinated drapes and curtains and linoleum-tile floors. Furnishings include a single bed or beds, dresser, desk, bookshelves, and lamps. Some are air-conditioned; baths are communal; phones are in the hall (they take messages). If you so desire, you can install a phone in your room at regular New York City rates.

The Y accepts young men and women between the ages of 18 and 26, regardless of race or religious belief, but only if you are a full-time student or employee, or a combination of the two. Every applicant is required to have a personal interview with a member of the Y staff (by appointment) prior to admission. Rates include weekly maid and linen service and begin at $350 per month, depending on the size and location of the room; double rooms are available for women, singles for men or women. In addition to the weekly stipend, residents are required to purchase Y membership ($35 annually), and a $30 fee is payable upon submission of your completed application. During summer months a minimum stay of two weeks is permitted; rates are a little higher than the rest of the year: $124 to $175 per week.

When writing for an application form, specify that you are between the ages of 18 and 26, and employed or in school; otherwise you will first get a letter explaining eligibility requirements. Write as far in advance as possible, and follow up your application with repeated phone calls or further letters. Highly recommended.

RESIDENCES FOR WORKING WOMEN AND STUDENTS: Some of the nicest of the city's permanent residences for women are maintained by the Salvation Army. On the East Side they have the **Parkside Evangeline,** 18 Gramercy Park South, NYC 10003, at Irving Place (tel. 212/677-6200). Located right off lovely Gramercy Park in one of New York's most exclusive neighborhoods (some of the rooms overlook the park, and residents can use this otherwise-locked private facility), the Evangeline has 300 rooms for students and working women ages 18 to 35 of any race or religion. It's the kind of place in which you'd feel good about having your daughter stay. Facilities include a fireplace lounge off the lobby, two outdoor rooftop terraces with chaise longues for sunbathing, a sewing room, a typing room, music practice rooms, washing machines (irons and ironing boards available), exercise machines, hair dryers, library, and a very attractive second-floor lounge where women can entertain visitors. There's also a lovely carpeted dining room with old-fashioned wallpaper and tables covered in white linen cloths.

Rooms (singles and doubles) are small, but clean and rather charming, with curtained windows and maple Ethan Allen furnishings (chairs, dresser, desk, and hutch), switchboard phones, and sinks. Most have bath in the room; some share a connecting bath. No men are allowed in the rooms.

A personal interview or two letters of recommendation are required, and you must show that you work or go to school full time. Rates at this amazing facility are just $111 per week, including breakfast and dinner daily! A visiting friend or sister can get a cot in your room for $7 a night, and occasionally rooms are available on a daily basis for $20 per night, meals extra. A few double rooms are also available. Contact Miss Pierce or Maj. James Miller.

In Greenwich Village, there's the lovely **John and Mary Markle Evangeline Residence,** 123 W. 13th St., NYC 10011, between Sixth and Seventh Avenues (tel. 212/242-2400). Here, on one of the prettiest, tree-lined streets in the Village, the Salvation Army runs another superb facility. Its 300 rooms are divided equally among college students, business women, and senior citizens, which makes for a stimulating mix; you might find students from Parsons School of Design and N.Y.U., nurses from St. Vincent's Hospital, and even an 82-year-old professor from Columbia! A $7-million renovation has made the 57-year-old building better than ever; now all of its rooms have private bath and shower, telephone, and are attractively furnished with Ethan Allen colonial furnishings. Weekly maid service is provided. Everyone has use of an exercise room, typing room, TV room, piano studio, a lounge for entertaining friends, study halls, and a beautiful roof garden. There's also a snackbar and counter on the first floor—and the rates also include two meals a day! Single, double, and triple rooms are available, at rates that begin at $77, $95, and $146 per person a week. Of course there is a waiting list, but rooms are also assigned on the basis of need. Inquiries should be directed to Major Anderson.

During the summer months, when the college students have gone home, rooms are often taken by young ballet students (accompanied by chaperones) who have come to New York on scholarships from some of the leading ballet companies.

Another Salvation Army facility for women is the superbly located **Ten Eyck-Troughton Memorial Residence,** 145 E. 39th St., NYC 10016, between Third and Lexington Avenues (tel. 212/490-5990), which is for women ages 35 to 60 who are employed full time. Rates average over $100 per week, including two meals.

Working Women Only

The **Webster Apartments,** 419 W. 34th St., NYC 10001, between Ninth and Tenth Avenues (tel. 212/594-3950), is an outstanding hostelry with permanent-residence accommodations for 400 women. Heavily endowed by Charles and Josiah Webster, who founded the residence in 1923 and left a vast fortune to the enterprise, it provides the comforts of home (a very stately and elegant home) to young working women at low cost. Facilities of the 13-story brick structure include a gracious lobby, a handsome library with deep leather chairs, an elegant drawing room, television rooms, a charming wicker-furnished garden room, a card-playing room, and even a series of small intime rooms with no doors that serve as "beau parlors" for entertaining "gentleman callers" (the latter are not permitted upstairs). Other amenities are a lovely garden (quite a luxury in Manhattan), sewing machines, typewriters, laundry, and daily maid service.

The rooms themselves, all singles, are pretty and quaint, with freshly painted pastel blue or green walls, blue/green carpeting, and all necessary furnishings, including a sink. Baths are in the hall, as are phones (they can buzz your room if you get a call). Rooms have electric fans; air conditioning is available at extra cost.

Weekly rates are between $85 and $120, depending on your salary, and are subject to change. Although most of the residents are young, women of any age who are employed full time may apply. You can write to the above address, but if you're in the city, come in for an interview any Wednesday evening between 5 and 7:30 p.m. (no appointment necessary).

3. Rooms for Service Personnel

These are the New York tourists who really have it made. For service personnel on active duty, with families, the **USO**, at 1540 Broadway, NYC 10036, at 45th Street (tel. 212/719-2634), is the preeminent place to visit. The staff here will make arrangements in advance (or upon arrival) with approved midtown hotels to house you and your dependents at USO discount rates of about 20% to 40% off. They'll give you the best accommodations they can get in the price range you can afford. Their mission is to refresh visiting servicemen physically, mentally, and emotionally, and help them enjoy the city. In this vein, they not only provide rooms, but also obtain free tickets to movies, Broadway shows, and sports events on a day-to-day basis, and provide information on New York sightseeing and nightlife. Free refreshments—sometimes light, sometimes more substantial—are offered to visitors. You can usually plan on free dinner on Saturday, 4 to 6 p.m., and free breakfast on Sunday, 9 a.m. to noon. Volunteers do the cooking.

For active-duty military personnel, male and female, the **Soldiers', Sailors' and Airmen's Club, Inc.,** 283 Lexington Ave., NYC 10016, between 36th and 37th Streets (tel. 212/683-4353), rents out semiprivate rooms (two to six persons to a room) for just $8 per night (plus $2 key deposit), and there are adequate bath facilities on each floor. Separated personnel (six months or less) pay $10 per night. The rooms are homey, neat, and cheerful, with nice furnishings, cream-colored walls adorned with framed prints, and very high ceilings; many have shuttered windows. Phones are in the hall; they take messages. The building itself is like a gracious old home with elegantly furnished lounges (one houses a jukebox and piano), library/writing room, pool room, and TV room. There's a budget-priced cafeteria on the premises, open Saturday and Sunday only, where you can dine for $1.75 to $3. The club also provides free tickets, when available, to movies, plays, etc., and can arrange hotel accommodations for married personnel or at reduced military rates at other hotels.

4. Hotels for General Occupancy

Now we come to the regular nonspecialized hotels, which accommodate everyone. We list them according to the area of New York in which they are found. Average price of these rooms will be between $40 and $60, some a bit lower, and a few a bit higher for those visitors who don't mind a relative "Big

Splurge." By New York standards, even these are very well priced. Whatever hotel you choose, be sure to write well in advance for a reservation. Advance reservations are your best guarantee for getting the lowest rates possible.

MIDTOWN WEST / TIMES SQUARE TO ROCKEFELLER CENTER: This is by far the most convenient neighborhood to stay in if you wish to take advantage of the Broadway theater. Some of the other aspects of this area—shoddy cinema houses, sleazy bars, and cheap penny arcades—are not so attractive and best avoided. However, the area is being improved constantly, and the streets get better as you go north of 42nd Street and east of Seventh Avenue. And the hotels here are working harder than ever to maintain strict security standards and to make visitors feel comfortable. We were impressed with several hotels and the genuine value they offer.

The 600-room **Century Paramount Hotel,** 235 W. 46th St., NYC 10036, between Broadway and Eighth Avenue (tel. 212/764-5500), offers all the amenities of far higher priced hotels—doormen, a bustling marble-walled lobby, newsstand, coffeeshop, cocktail lounge, airport limousine service, multilingual staff, barbershop, etc. Yet it's an especially good buy for us, because the management, as a special concession to our readers, has agreed to set aside a number of discount rooms during the period from November 1 through March 31 each year.

The Century Paramount prides itself on offering three things: convenience, comfort (they have a better mattress than many more expensive hotels), and cleanliness, and this they do very well. The rooms themselves, although not fancy, are more than adequate, with off-white walls, carpeted floors, European prints on the walls, individually controlled air conditioning, direct-dial phones, cable television, coordinated drapes and bedspreads (most often in an attractive blue print). At least 45% of their rooms have two double beds. All this, plus attentive management, qualifies the Century Paramount as one of the prime tourist-class hotels of the city.

During the period specified above, these rooms are available for rental to our readers for only $40 to $50 per night per room; groups of three can rent the same rooms for an additional $10, bringing the per-person cost way down. Ordinarily, these same rooms rent for $70 to $80 a night, and they will be made available at the $40 to $50 price only if you mention this book when making your reservation by mail (enclose $50 as a deposit), which you should address to Mr. Caplow, manager. And if these special rooms are booked, they'll place you (again from November 1 to March 31 only) in a higher priced room, but still offer a substantial discount. Furthermore, the management has agreed to give readers of this book a discount during other periods of the year (April 1 through October 31), but only if you write or phone ahead mentioning this book, and if the space is available. It's always worth a try. Regular rates here are $65 to $75 single, $70 to $80 double, $74 to $84 twin, $75 to $85 for three persons in two double beds, and $80 to $90 for four persons in two double beds. If you've brought your car, you can garage it across the street for a reasonable fee. Incidentally, this hotel is a favorite of many international airline crews and foreign tourist groups, so don't be surprised to hear more French and Italian spoken in the lobby than English. Highly recommended.

When a hotel has been in business for over 50 years and is still going strong, you know they must be doing something right. Such a one is the **Hotel Edison,** 228 W. 47th St., NYC 10036, just west of Broadway (tel. 212/840-5000), where the owner-management works hard at pleasing its guests. What we like best here is the feeling of spaciousness that the newer hotels, even the more expensive ones, cannot afford to have. You'll sense in the large lobby (plain but comfortable), the wide halls, and the 1000 nicely decorated rooms. The lobby bustles with guests (many of them theater groups from Europe, South America, and Japan), and has a transportation desk and gift and tobacco shop. Right on the premises is the Café Edison, open from 7 a.m. to 11 p.m., which serves homemade cheese blintzes, bread pudding, and cabbage soup, among other offerings; the owner makes fresh corn muffins every morning. Kenny's Steak Pub, on the other side of the lobby (once the Green Room, home to the Big Bands and names like Blue Baron), serves hearty meals, and the Rum House Bar and Lounge is a popular theater-district watering hole.

The rooms themselves are large and comfortable, most with two double beds and two large closets; all are air-conditioned with combination tub and shower, direct-dial telephone, and color TV with cable. The newer rooms (the hotel is constantly being redone) have fashionable laminated "shipboard" furniture. Double-paned windows help control noise. The one-bedroom suites offer particular value: warm and homey, beautifully furnished, and renting for $80, $85, and $90 per night for two persons, they are a far better buy than bedrooms alone in many fancier hotels.

Rates for singles go from $53 to $59 per night; doubles or twin-bedded rooms for two are $63 to $69; family rooms with two double beds and bath, for three or four family members, are $72 to $78. Rollaway beds are available for $7.50 per night. Parking is available, at an additional charge, directly across the street.

We think you'll be as pleased as we were to discover the **Hotel Royalton,** 44 W. 44th St., NYC 10036, between Fifth and Sixth Avenues (tel. 212/730-1344). A few doors from the Princeton Club on its 43rd Street side, across the street from the Algonquin on its 44th Street side, the Royalton still has the aura of refinement of the private men's club it once was. The building was designed by Stanford White in the early 1900s, which accounts for the lovely lobby with its marble archways, fountains, and plants, Oriental scatter rugs, and the unusually gracious feeling of many of the guest rooms. Although the clientele now is perhaps more Garment Center than theatrical and literary as in the past, there are still many people in the arts who stay here, following in the tradition of such famed Royalton guests as Robert Benchley, George Jean Nathan, Tennessee Williams, William Inge, and Yul Brynner.

The Royalton is a small hotel, with only 142 rooms, no two of which are the same—they are all individually decorated. What they do have in common is thick carpeting, good-sized bathrooms, air conditioning, large closets, color TV (the higher priced rooms also have radios), and—a rarity in many hotels—a desk to work on (which must account for its popularity with so many writers). Refrigerators are available on request. The most inexpensive rooms, which go for $75 single, $85 double, are small but perfectly adequate. If you go a little higher—$85, $95, and $105 single, $10 more for doubles, still very low for New York—you can command a large, lovely room, handsomely furnished and decorated, with such amenities as easy chairs and perhaps even a fireplace. One-bedroom suites, also handsome, run from $85 to $105 for three—great buys at the price. The coffeeshop on the premises will provide room service. Highly recommended: reserve at least two weeks in advance.

Just a few steps from Fifth Avenue, the 200-room **Mansfield Hotel,** 12 W. 44th St., NYC 10036 (tel. 212/944-6050), is a modest but perfectly acceptable budget choice, very popular with European, South American, and Japanese guests. What it has going for it is a good location, on the same block as the Harvard Club and the New York Bar Association, a warm and friendly staff, and a cute little lobby that adjoins O'Lunney's, a delightful Irish pub that offers country music and folk singing four nights a week. Limited room service is available via the Sandwich Shop. What it lacks—aside from the splendid staircase intact in this Stanford White 1907 building—is charm. Rooms are clean, and all have either tub or shower, air conditioning, direct-dial phones, private safes, and cable color TV, but they are small and rather minimally decorated. The cozy suites are perhaps the best buy here, and refrigerators can be furnished on request.

Single rooms go from $40 to $44; doubles or twins, from $42 to $48. Suites for three are $55 to $65; suites for four to six, $70 to $85. Rooms with adjacent bath are $28 to $36, single or double. A discount is offered on parking at a nearby garage.

It's hard to find a more convenient location to the Broadway theater than the **Hotel Consulate,** 224 W. 49th St., NYC 10019, west of Broadway (tel. 212/246-5252): the Eugene O'Neill Theater is a few doors away, the Ambassador is across the street, and so is the Actor's Church. This newly remodeled oldtimer (once the Forrester Hotel, home to the likes of Walter Winchell and José Greco), has about 225 rooms, and they have been tastefully—if rather sedately—decorated and furnished with brown-and-white spreads and drapes, brown carpeting. All have color TV with AM-FM radio, direct-dial phone, air conditioning, and private bath. There are reproductions of old prints on the walls and safety locks on every door. Hunan Eaters Restaurant is on the premises, and a moderately priced coffeeshop, open from 7 a.m. to 8 p.m., will provide room service. Popular with European and South American businessmen, the Consulate is also a good bet for individuals and tourist groups (special rates on request).

The management has agreed to offer those readers who contact them directly and mention this book a discount of 10% on their rates: singles, from $45 to $60; doubles, from $65 to $80; suites, which can sleep up to four, from $90 to $100. Children under 14 can stay free with their parents, according to room availability.

Most of the guests at the **Hotel Remington,** 129 W. 46th St., NYC 10036, between Sixth and Seventh Avenues (tel. 212/221-2600), seem to be from Brazil, Venezuela, or other South American countries. They—and the large numbers of Europeans who frequent the hotel in summer—know the value of the dollar, and the very good value that can be had at this small, 80-room hotel that was totally renovated a few years ago. The tiny lobby has crystal chandeliers, red-flecked wallpaper, and one small elevator to navigate the nine floors of the hotel. Rooms are not bad: they are nicely furnished, with white furniture, floral wallpaper and bedspreads, and all have air conditioning, cable color TVs, new bathrooms, and direct-dial telephones. Rooms with private bath are $45 single, $50 double, $55 triple, and $60 quad. Some rooms do not have private bathrooms, but they do have a sink, and a very clean bathroom is shared by three rooms. These are an excellent buy at $30 single, $32 to $35 double. With its central location, modest but cheerful and very clean accommodations, the Remington offers good value for the dollar.

If you can't get into the Remington, consider a larger, sister establishment run by the same management, where the rates are a bit higher but also reasonable by New York standards. This is the **Hotel Wentworth,** 59 West 46th St., NY 10036 (tel. 212/719-2300), between Fifth and Sixth Avenues. Renovated from top to bottom about five years ago, the Wentworth now offers some 250 pleasant rooms, cheerfully decorated with flowered wallpaper and spreads; all rooms have air conditioning, cable color TVs, private bathrooms, direct-dial phones. Singles are $60; twins and doubles, $70; double-doubles, $85; triples, $80; and suites, $90. An additional person is charged $10. The Wentworth is well located, close to Fifth Avenue and the new People Plaza, a mini-park between 45th and

46th Streets, laced with interlocking gardens. In spring and fall, midtown workers pause here for lunch and free noontime entertainment. The hotel's winding, crystal-chandeliered lobby boasts its own 60-booth Jewelry Exchange, to give guests a head start on New York shopping. The staff is multilingual, the better to serve, again, a preponderance of South American and European guests.

Big Splurges

The new star of New York theater hotels is Best Western's **Milford Plaza,** 270 W. 45th St., NYC 10036, at Eighth Avenue (tel. 212/869-3600). There's an air of excitement about this place, which has become the preeminent spot in town for theatrical events: in one recent six-month period, at least 17 Broadway opening-night parties were held here. All of which means that you could easily bump into Lauren Bacall or Elizabeth Taylor or Robert Redford in the graceful three-story marble lobby, so pretty with its red carpets and black chairs.

The excitement extends right up the 28 floors to the 1300 rooms, all of which have a star on the door and are decorated with red carpets no less, and attractive spreads and wallpaper—even in the bathrooms. The view from your window is of Broadway's theater marquees. Rooms are compact rather than large, but they have everything you need, including color TV, AM-FM radio, direct-dial phone, self-controlled air conditioning and heat; there is free ice on every floor. Security is excellent, since everyone coming up to the rooms must show a key.

Milford guests can take all their meals right at home if they wish. A lavish breakfast buffet, featuring something like 27 items (with eggs cooked to order), costs under $10 and is on from 7 to 11 a.m. The Stage Door Canteen specializes in barbecued food and nostalgia: its walls are decorated with photos of the original Stage Door Canteen. Kippy's 44 is one of the city's most popular continental restaurants. And the Celebrity Deli is popular with just about everybody, especially with traveling Texans, who fall in love with the corned-beef sandwiches. The lobby also offers a travel and theater-ticket desk, a sundry shop, and a unisex hair salon.

Unfortunately, the Milford Plaza rates have recently zoomed out of our budget category, up to $75 to $100 for a single, $90 to $125 for a double. But wait! They've also kept us budget folks in mind with their "Lullaby of Broadway" deal, functional any day of the week (unlike most packages). Subject to availability, they offer a room plus continental breakfast, a meal at Kippy's 44, and a welcoming cocktail for the rate of $43 per person in a double, or $63 single. And on regular rates, the management will extend a 10% discount if you book directly and identify yourself as a reader of this book. Do so by dialing toll-free 800/221-2690 in the continental United States; in New York state, the toll-free number is 800/522-6449.

The **Gorham Hotel,** 136 W. 55th St., NYC 10019, between Sixth and Seventh Avenues (tel. 212/245-1800), is especially nice for families who appreciate its spacious bedroom suites and cooking facilities. But it's also very popular with theater people, buyers, independent business people, many Europeans. Close to the theater district, but away from the hustle-bustle of Times Square, it couldn't be more conveniently located. The mirrored, all-oak lobby, with its crystal chandelier is small and charming, indicative of the friendly service offered at the Gorham. A concierge is always on hand to provide help with sightseeing or theater tickets. Adjoining the lobby, but out of our price range, alas, is one of New York's most rarified restaurants, Castellano, a northern Italian establishment, which has the food crowd agog.

Rooms at the Gorham are immaculate and attractive, some with wood-paneled walls. All are equipped with air conditioning, modern bath, cable color

TV, Touch Tone phones, in-room safes, many closets, comfortable furnishings, and wall-to-wall carpeting. But the most important offerings are the kitchenettes in each room which consist of a two-burner hotplate, sink, refrigerator, and necessary light housekeeping utensils. Many of the larger suites at the Gorham have been redone to consist of one large bedroom with two double beds, table, and chair, plus a smaller bedroom with one double bed; there are 40 such rooms, and they're a big hit with families.

As for the rates, singles run from $70 to $80; doubles, from $75 to $95. Suites are $95 for two, $10 for each extra person (up to six). It's a bit pricey for us, but the kitchenettes, concerned management, spacious rooms, and good upkeep make it well worth the price. Since the Gorham does most of its business from repeat customers, it's advisable to write or call collect well in advance for reservations, especially if you want the lower priced rooms.

Among our splurgy selections there's no better value for your money than the utterly delightful **Wyndham Hotel,** 42 W. 58th St., NYC 10019, between Fifth and Sixth Avenues (tel. 212/753-3500). From the moment you enter the charming lobby—furnished with plush velvet chairs and couches—you know you've arrived at someplace special. It's no surprise that many celebs choose this sedate hostelry; among them Ben Gazzara, Jack Klugman, and Dick Van Patten. It has a Palm Springs–like air of luxury; its rooms are actually nicer than those costing much more at the nearby Plaza, and the service is superb.

All of the 212 rooms are large and exquisitely furnished in a cheerful and charming motif with superior decorator pieces and well-chosen paintings adorning the walls, and each has been individually decorated. They're equipped with air conditioning, tub and shower bath, switchboard phones, and cable color TV. Even the hallways are elegantly papered in flocked wallpaper.

The price for all this luxury: $85 to $95 single, $95 to $105 double. Suites, with living room, bedroom, and pantry, go for $140 to $170. The Wyndham is a gem, unparalleled in its price category. Reserve as far in advance as possible.

Two Motor Hotels in the Heart of Town

The **Travel Inn Motor Hotel,** 515 W. 42nd St., NYC 10036, between Tenth and Eleventh Avenues (tel. 212/695-7171), has always been popular with visitors who want the convenience of a central location, free parking, and a refreshing swim when they come home from a hard day's sightseeing or business. But now that a total renovation of the 250-room property—all-new rooms, hallways, public areas—has been completed, Travel Inn is better than ever, truly one of the most extraordinary values in the city. For rates of $50 to $70 single, $60 to $80 double ($10 for an extra person or rollaway bed), you stay in surroundings that could easily cost twice as much elsewhere. Even standard rooms are enormous, most furnished with two double beds, imported white furniture from France, matching draperies and spreads done in seashell motifs on blue-and-pink or wine backgrounds. A few rooms have chintz spreads and Japanese lamps; all have a desk and chair, air conditioning, direct-dial phone, cable color TV with remote control, and digital clock. Wallpapers usually have a Japanese floral motif. The halls are handsome, with marble and glass panels on the walls. The lobby is small, but the gathering places here are an Olympic-size outdoor swimming pool (reserved strictly for guests of the hotel), several pretty courtyards, and sunbathing areas decked out with garden furniture. All of this makes the hotel an excellent choice for families with children. There may be an outdoor café in the pool area by the time you read this.

The location is excellent, one block from the off-off-Broadway 42nd Street Theater Row, and just a few blocks from Times Square (easily accessible by crosstown bus). There is free self-parking in an indoor garage with no in-and-out charges. With all this going for it, Travel Inn is highly popular, so try to reserve at least two weeks in advance if possible, especially in the summer.

Right on the premises is the Stage One Restaurant, serving three meals a day. Walk one block to the corner of Ninth Avenue and 42nd Street, and you're at Ninth and Natural, a natural-foods restaurant for gourmets with very low prices and a wonderfully congenial atmosphere. A delicious find.

Although the rooms are more expensive than at Travel Inn, the values are still quite good (for New York) at **Best Western's Skyline Motor Inn,** 49th to 50th Streets on Tenth Avenue, NYC 10019 (tel. 212/586-3400). This is a large hotel, with some 230 rooms in two buildings, a free garage (although there's a $2 in-and-out charge), and best of all, a beautiful glass-enclosed rooftop swimming pool, complete with sundeck and sauna, heated and open all year. The rooms are very large, done in attractive color schemes; each has color TV, direct-dial telephone, individually controlled air conditioning and heat, and modern tile bath with tub-shower combinations. These run from $62 to $76 single, $69 to $83 double, $76 to $90 double-double or twin. Comfortable suites, with a sofa bed in the living room, run $125 and up. There is no charge for cribs; each additional person over age 2 is charged $10; rollaways are $10. You can get three meals a day in the coffeeshop, or have gourmet meals and drinks in the restaurant and cocktail lounge. For reservations, call Best Western toll free: 800/528-1234.

LOWER WEST SIDE—CHELSEA: In a city where the old is often torn down to make way for the new and modern, the **Chelsea Hotel,** 222 W. 23rd St., NYC 10011, between Seventh and Eighth Avenues (tel. 212/243-3700), has stood since 1882, catering to the bohemian, the creative, the offbeat, and those who thrive among them. It was the first hotel in the U.S. to be proclaimed a national landmark. This is the place where Andy Warhol made the movie *Chelsea Girls;* where Dylan Thomas, Brendan Behan, Lenny Bruce, Jane Fonda, and Elliot Gould all came to rest, retreat, and get inspiration. Among the works that have been written at the Chelsea are Arthur Clarke's *2001,* Thomas Wolfe's *You Can't Go Home Again,* Arthur Miller's *After the Fall,* and William Burrough's *Naked Lunch.* Manager Stanley Bard reigns over the scene, and his art collection (including many works from grateful tenants) turns the lobby here into a veritable art gallery. Note especially the sculpture called *Chelsea People*—you'll recognize many of the celebrities who have called the Chelsea home. A good Spanish restaurant, El Quijote, adjoins.

Many of the guests stay here for a long time—or forever—attracted by the soundproof walls (three feet thick!), the friendly family feeling, and the enormous rooms, each with unique features (perhaps working fireplaces or kitchens). Transient rooms are available as well, and even the smallest is large by New York hotel standards. The furnishings are adequate (there are, for example, no pictures on the walls, since most tenants want to hang their own), and the furniture is not brand new, but the rooms are nice enough, and usually kept up. About half the rooms have air conditioning, all have direct-dial phones, and color TV can be rented for $15 per week.

Singles run from $30 with semi-private bath, from $50 with bath, from $60 with bath and kitchenette. Doubles with semi-private bath are from $40; with private bath and shower, from $60; with private bath and kitchenette, from $70. Family rooms with kitchen, for four people, go for $75 to $85. The management advises that readers of this book will be given the seventh night of a week's stay free if the week is prepaid.

LINCOLN CENTER AND COLISEUM AREA: Just opposite the Coliseum and

Central Park, around the corner from Carnegie Hall and a short walk from Lincoln Center, is a little jewel of a hotel in a stellar location: **Westpark Hotel,** 308 W. 58th St., NYC 10019 (tel. 212/246-6440). This 100-room, nine-story hotel has plenty going for it: it's an old, well-insulated building, which makes it very quiet; and it's been totally remodeled and decorator-designed with a graceful and elegant touch, which makes it luxurious. Yet this peace and luxury comes with one of the most moderate pricetags in town: singles run $45 to $55, doubles go for $55 to $70 for a room with one bed, and double-doubles for two to four persons are $65 to $80. One-bedroom suites, for two to four persons, are $80 to $125. Prices for rooms of comparable quality could easily be twice as much at some of New York's "name" hotels. And as if this weren't enough, the management has agreed to provide readers of this book, who write to them directly, a 10% discount on rates.

Just a few years old, the Westpark has become a hit with businessmen, tourists, and small groups. The modernistic lobby, quite lovely with glass doors, mirrored columns, a fireplace, and soft-green velvet chairs to sink into, adjoins the Café Comedy next door. And the rooms are lovely, many decorated with deep-maroon quilted bedspreads, ginger-jar lamps, and other nice touches: of course, all have direct-dial phone, air conditioning, color TV with AM-FM radio, and private bath. The higher priced rooms have views of Central Park. Especially handsome are the one-bedroom suites: one of our favorites has pink drapes, a four-poster bed, two television sets, velvet sofas, a desk, lovely lamps and prints. Considering that the price is $80 to $125 for two to four, these have to be among the best bargains in town. Discount parking is available at a nearby garage. Many languages are spoken at the Westpark, and service is helpful and friendly. A real discovery.

Many of the guests who stay at the **Hotel Olcott,** 27 W. 72nd St., NYC 10023, between Columbus Avenue and Central Park West (tel. 212/877-4200), are performers at nearby Lincoln Center, diplomats, and U.N. personnel. The Royal Ballet of London calls it their New York home, so do half a dozen singers from the Metropolitan Opera Company and a few movie and sports celebrities, as well as lots of business people and visitors from overseas. Happily for us, this largely residential hotel still has plenty of space for transients. It offers a terrific location, close not only to Lincoln Center, but also across the street from Central Park and in the very heart of the exciting Columbus Avenue scene; a subway station is on the corner. Its Dallas Jones Bar-B-Q Restaurant is one of New York's best inexpensive restaurants, serving meals averaging $5 or $6 in the plushest of settings (more details in Chapter II).

As for the studios and suites, they're spacious, clean, and comfortable, with attractive furnishings, big closets, nice prints adorning the white walls, and carpeted floors. Homey—very comfortably homey—would be the best way to describe them. All have direct-dial phones, air conditioning, tub and shower baths, and fully equipped kitchenettes with hotplates and refrigerators. The suites, which are very spacious, also have living rooms, and two-bedroom suites have two baths. Color TV can be rented for $3 a night, $15 a week.

Here's how the rates go: studios are $60 single, $65 double, $325 weekly for a single, $350 for a double. One-bedroom suites are $80 for one or two persons, $465 per week; an extra person is charged $7 daily or $35 weekly (up to four can be accommodated). Long-term rates are lower. The management advises that you reserve four weeks in advance for an extended stay of a week or more; for three or four days, a week in advance; and for one night only, call during that week.

Another of our special finds is here on the West Side, this one north of the Lincoln Center area. Across the street from the American Museum of Natural History, in a residential block, is the 300-room **Excelsior Hotel,** 45 W. 81st St., NYC 10024 (tel. 212/362-9200), a charmer in the European manner. In fact, many European visitors—including consular people and titled types—are frequent guests. Curators and couriers from the Metropolitan Museum of Art and the Museum of Modern Art stay here (and so do neighbors from nearby apartment buildings like Liv Ullman who might move in when their own apartments are being redecorated or painted). Three marble steps lead down to a graceful, high-ceilinged lobby, with an accommodating coffeeshop off to one side to provide room service at breakfast. Rooms, constantly being updated and renovated, are done in pale tones, nicely if not lavishly decorated with furnishings of light woods, blue quilted bedspreads and matching draperies, plus color TV, individual air conditioning, direct-dial telephones, and large closets. Upper-floor rooms at the front of the house offer views of the museum's park and the midtown skyline; those in the rear, of the gardens of houses on 82nd Street. The management prides itself on running "a respectable hotel, one where you can bring your children and not have to worry." They will not book conventions, carefully screen wedding parties, and quickly dispense with noisy or obstreperous guests. It's easy for families to save money and cook in here, as the suites have fully equipped kitchens, and there's a supermarket just around the corner on Columbus Avenue. You could comfortably stay here for quite a while.

Single rooms go for $56 to $61; doubles, from $66 to $71. Very comfortable kitchenette suites that can sleep four (sofabed in the living room, twin beds in the bedroom) are $94 to $101 for four people. The Excelsior is at the top of the Columbus Avenue shopping-and-restaurant neighborhood, 16 blocks from Lincoln Center, and a short bus ride to midtown shops and theaters. The management is helpful, and security here is excellent. A find.

MIDTOWN EAST / UPPER EAST SIDE: You simply can't beat the location of the **Pickwick Arms Hotel,** at 230 E. 51st St., NYC 10022, between Second and Third Avenues (tel. 212/355-0300), in a lovely East Side residential neighborhood, a few blocks from all major shopping, cinemas, restaurants. It's a surprise to find a budget hotel here. This half-century-old hotel, which is being spruced up all the time, is quite pleasant, offering an attractive lobby with Tudor-style fireplace, a rooftop sun deck, airport limousine service, and some 370 economy-minded rooms.

The Pickwick Arms is one of the few hotels left in New York where you can realize major economy by sharing the bath down the hall. Some of the older singles, small but quite cozy, have washbasins only, and share a bath/shower with five or six other rooms; these rent for $26. Two such rooms sharing one shower are $35 each. Many of the smaller, older rooms, however, have been converted into large double- and twin-bedded rooms, which are color coordinated, have individual direct-dial phones, attractive bamboo-like white furniture, air conditioning, and private showers. These rent for $56. Every room has cable color TV and an AM-FM radio. The management prides itself on excellent mattresses and careful housekeeping.

Families who don't mind all living in one room can take advantage of the eight efficiency apartments. They're furnished with one or two doubles or twins and a sofa bed, have a sidewall kitchen with under-the-counter refrigerator, and their own bathrooms. These rent for $65 for two, $5 for each additional guest (up to five). We especially liked the ones in the rear, overlooking the garden.

Although the neighborhood abounds with restaurants, the Pickwick Arms has a few of its own. On one side of the building is the Beekman Deli, open from 7 a.m. to midnight, with all kinds of takeout food that can be delivered to the rooms. On the other is the world-famous (and expensive) Spanish restaurant, Torremolinos.

Many of your fellow guests at the Pickwick Arms will be South Americans or Europeans here on tours. Reserve several weeks in advance during the summer months.

If you'd like to have the feeling of being in your own unique apartment or spacious room on the Upper East Side, the **Hotel Wales,** 1295 Madison Ave., NYC 10028, between 92nd and 93rd Streets (tel. 212/876-6000), would be perfect. Uptown's answer to the Chelsea (although much more sedate, and in a gracious residential-art gallery area), the Wales is that kind of European-type hotel with space, peace, quiet, and a certain ambience that nurses artistic and literary spirits: famous guests who have lived here have included writers Norman Mailer and George Axelrod, British artist Anthony Caro, even the director of London's Tate Gallery, Sir John Rothenstein. Built in 1900 and still going strong (the Silverman family management takes great pride in maintaining the hotel in excellent shape and constantly improving it), the Wales has one of the highest occupancy rates in the city, and it is a rather remarkable bargain for New York. Of the 77 rooms available to transient guests, 45 of them are suites. Priced at $60 to $100 per night (similar accommodations would go for three times as much downtown—if they existed), they are all very large, with long entrance halls, big closets, full kitchens, dining room tables—a feeling of being in a private home. Regular rooms are $45 to $65 single, $45 to $75 double, $65 to $100 triple. Each suite or room is one of a kind, with traditional, sometimes slightly eccentric furnishings, and charming antique reproductions. Most contain some surprise element—perhaps a fireplace, a compass mirror, other interesting bric-a-brac. All are tasteful and personal, worlds away from the standard hotel-motel room. About 90% are air-conditioned, all have direct-dial phone, TV, and tile or marble baths with tub and/or shower. Since the building is brick, with thick walls, you can count on rooms being much quieter than those in newer hotels around town.

The lobby of the Wales is old-fashioned and homey, with a deep-blue carpet and easy chairs, a vaulted ceiling and a colonnaded winding marble staircase leading off it to the first floor. Adjoining is Sarabeth's Kitchen, a New York gourmet favorite for quiches, omelets, and other light food; they serve three meals a day, beginning with a luscious breakfast. Room service is available from Sarabeth's for hotel guests. Reserve in advance, as the Wales is deservedly very popular. Guests who write directly, mentioning this book, will be granted a 10% discount from June 20 to September 5, 1986.

The newly redecorated lobby of the **Hotel Tudor,** 304 E. 42nd St., NYC 10017, off Second Avenue (tel. 212/986-8800), seems to be always alive with the animated conversation of the many U.N. delegates who make this hotel their home away from home. Lobby decor ranges from the art deco look of the Café Tudor (for leisurely dining) to the Tudor-style main entrance and registration desk. Adjoining the Café Tudor is the Dreamstreet Café, an elegant restaurant specializing in regional American fare.

The 525 rooms, located off cheerful, carpeted hallways, are small but quite attractive. They're neat and clean, with color-coordinated drapes and curtains, framed prints adorning the walls, and wall-to-wall carpeting. All are equipped with air conditioning, color TV, private bath with tub and/or shower, and direct-dial phone.

Rates for singles begin at $75, $85 for doubles, $95 for twins, $115 for triples. Junior suites (some of which offer two baths) go for $130 to $165. Group rates are available upon request.

5. Rooms for Families

Many of our hotels possess unusually large rooms in which additional cots can be placed, or cater specifically to families traveling with children. Here is a recap of those previously mentioned hotels that have family rooms or large suites.

In the Times Square area, check out the family rooms at the **Century Paramount,** 235 W. 46th St., NYC 10036, between Broadway and Eighth Avenue (tel. 212/246-5500), where rooms with two double beds are $60 per night if you mention this book.

Hotel Consulate, 224 W. 49th St., NYC 10019, west of Broadway (tel. 212/246-5252), has suites that can sleep up to four persons for $90 to $110.

Very large double-doubles can easily house you and the kids, and there's a swimming pool too, at **Travel Inn Motor Hotel,** 515 W. 42nd St., NYC 10036, between Tenth and Eleventh Avenues (tel. 212/695-7171). Doubles are $64 to $80, $10 for extra persons.

The kids will enjoy the pool and all of you can bunk in double-doubles ($76 to $90) at **Best Western's Skyline Motor Inn,** 49th to 50th Streets on Tenth Avenue, NYC 10019 (tel. 212/586-3400). There is no charge for cribs, but those over 2 must pay $10, and it's $10 for rollaway beds. Toll-free reservations: 800/528-1234.

Family rooms with two double beds, sleeping three or four, run from $76 to $86 at the **Hotel Edison,** 228 W. 47th St., NYC 10036, just west of Broadway (tel. 212/840-5000).

One-bedroom suites at the **Hotel Royalton,** 44 W. 44th St., NYC 10036, between Fifth and Sixth Avenues (tel. 212/730-1234), go from $85 to $105 and can sleep three in style.

Cozy suites sleep four to six at the **Hotel Mansfield,** 12 W. 44th St., NYC 10036 (tel. 212/944-6050), and cost $70 to $85.

Up to six family members can share a spacious two-room unit (two doubles in one room, one double in the other) at the very fine **Hotel Gorham,** 136 W. 55th St., NYC 10019, between Sixth and Seventh Avenues (tel. 212/245-1800). Triples start at $95.

A pretty room with two double beds is just $60 at the **Hotel Remington,** 129 W. 46th St., NYC 10036, between Sixth and Seventh Avenues (tel. 212/221-2600). Double-doubles begin at $85, suites at $90 at a sister establishment, **Hotel Wentworth,** 59 W. 56th St., NYC 10036, between Fifth and Sixth Avenues (tel. 212/719-2300).

In **Chelsea,** the renowned but offbeat **Chelsea Hotel,** 222 W. 23rd St., NYC 10011, between Seventh and Eighth Avenues (tel. 212/243-3700), has family apartments for four—two rooms with kitchen—from $70 a night, less for weekly and longer stays.

At Columbus Circle, and not far from Lincoln Center, decorator-designed, luxuriously appointed one-bedroom suites which can sleep four can be found for $80 to $125 at the **Westpark Hotel,** 308 W. 58th St., NYC 10019, between Eighth and Ninth Avenue (tel. 212/246-6440). Even more reasonable are the lovely double-doubles for two to four persons at $65 to $80.

And a very good bet is the **Hotel Olcott,** 27 W. 72nd St., NYC 10023, between Columbus Avenue and Central Park West (tel. 212/877-4200). Two to four people in a spacious one-bedroom suite with fully equipped kitchenette and living room pay $80 to $90 a night. Larger suites are sometimes available in summer. Weekly rates are especially good here. Inquire of the management.

Another Upper West Side favorite is the sedate **Excelsior Hotel,** 45 W. 81st

St., NYC 10024, off Central Park West (tel. 212/362-9200), across from the American Museum of Natural History, which offers beautiful suites with full kitchens, housing two to five people, for $87, $94, and $101.

On Manhattan's East Side, families who don't mind sharing the bath can stay at the **Vanderbilt YMCA,** 224 E. 47th St., NYC 10017, between Second and Third Avenues (tel. 212/755-2410). Triples and quads (bunk beds) rent from $45 to $50 and $56 to $60, and full use of all health club facilities—including a terrific pool—is included.

The **Pickwick Arms Hotel,** 230 E. 51st St., NYC 10022, between Second and Third Avenues (tel. 212/355-0300), is a budget hotel in a fashionable location. One-room efficiency apartments with full kitchens are $65 per night, plus $5 for each additional person (up to five).

And farther uptown, try the **Hotel Wales,** 1295 Madison Ave., NYC 10028, between 92nd and 93rd Streets (tel. 212/876-6000), where large and gracious suites—some with kitchenettes—accommodating six people are $65 to $120 per night; weekly rates are lower.

On weekends only, four luxurious residential hotels of the **Manhattan East** Hotel Group (see below) offer studio apartments and suites at reduced rates: $60 for studios, $85 for a one-bedroom suite (up to five guests), $160 for a two-bedroom suite that can sleep up to six. The hotels are the **Shelburne Murray Hill,** 303 Lexington Ave. at 37th Street; the **Beekman Tower,** 49th Street and First Avenue, opposite the United Nations Plaza; the **Eastgate Tower,** 222 E. 39th St., between Second and Third Avenues; and the **Southgate Tower,** 371 Seventh Ave., at 31st Street, opposite Madison Square Garden. Phone, toll free, 800/223-6663 outside of New York state; in New York state, 800/522-5680. Or write to Mr. Arden, 303 Lexington Ave., NYC 10036.

6. Bed and Breakfast

What with the unusually high cost of New York hotel rooms, the bed-and-breakfast concept of staying in a private residence and receiving breakfast as part of your rent is growing more popular than ever. New York has at least three major B & B organizations at this writing. The oldest and largest is **Urban Ventures,** which offers comfortable, carefully chosen rooms in private apartments —mostly on Manhattan's Upper West Side, Upper East Side, and Greenwich Village, and also in close-to-Manhattan areas of Brooklyn and Queens—at rates that are often less than those at budget hotels. Singles go for $23 to $36, doubles run from $34 to $50 or $60, and entire apartments can be rented from $55 to $100 or more daily. Stays usually average several nights to two weeks (there is a two-night minimum). This is a good bet if you'd like not only to save money, but to establish some personal contact with New Yorkers, since Urban Ventures' hosts are usually outgoing types who genuinely like people. Write to the people at Urban Ventures, Mary McCauley and Fran Tesser, at P.O. Box 426, NYC 10024, or phone them at 212/594-5650.

The **B & B Group (New Yorkers at Home),** headed by Farla Zammit, is another active bed-and-breakfast organization. Ms. Zammit handles space in Manhattan and also in the lovely beach vacation area of the Hamptons during the summer. Write to 301 E. 60th St., NYC 10022, or phone 212/838-7015 Monday to Friday from 9 a.m. to 4 p.m. only.

Roy Schiff and Janice Ikola are in charge of a third popular outfit, **New World Bed and Breakfast,** Suite 711, 150 Fifth Ave., NYC 10011 (tel. 212/676-5000). Their rooms are in Manhattan only.

All three of these agencies require no membership fee. They do, however, request that you make reservations in advance (the farther in advance the better), and there will be a charge should you cancel out. All accommodations and hosts are inspected and screened. And the letters of appreciation all of these groups have received from satisfied guests are truly impressive.

7. Weekend and Other Packages

Many New York hotels and travel companies offer weekend package deals that prove to be relatively inexpensive. Here's how it works. During the week, most of the city's top hotels are occupied by out-of-town business executives. When the weekend comes, off they go, back home. This leaves many rooms empty. To fill the gap, the hotels can offer couples excellent rates for a two- or three-day period, throw in a few breakfasts and dinners in the package, and sometimes a few theater tickets as well. Some packages are also available during the week.

For a complete rundown on hotel packages, pick up or write for a free pamphlet called *New York City Vacation Packages Directory*. It's available from the New York Convention and Visitors Bureau, 2 Columbus Circle, NYC 10019. Your travel agent will also know of many packages.

Keeping in mind that all rates are subject to change, and that bookings are based on availability, here are some examples. The hotels, of course, can be approached directly.

If you'd much rather live in a suite with your own kitchen than in a hotel bedroom, you can't do better than to book one of the extraordinary weekend packages offered by the **Manhattan East Hotel Group.** This company manages (among many others) four of the city's most prestigious luxury residential hotels: the **Shelburne Murray Hill,** 303 Lexington Ave., at 37th Street; the **Beekman Tower,** 49th Street and First Avenue, opposite the United Nations Plaza; the **Eastgate Tower,** 222 E. 39th St., between Second and Third Avenues; and the **Southgate Tower,** 371 Seventh Ave., at 31st Street, opposite Madison Square Garden. When corporate guests go home for the weekends, their exquisite apartments become available at ridiculous prices: a studio for one or two persons, normally renting for $85 to $105, is $60; a one-bedroom suite that can sleep four to five, normally renting for $95 to $140, is $85; a two-bedroom-two-bathroom suite that can sleep up to six, normally renting for $180 to $250, is $160. A little quick arithmetic will show you that since these apartments rent by the room and not the number of occupants, they have to be the best deals in town; a large family or two couples traveling together can realize enormous savings. And the apartments are simply beautiful: large, gracious, decorator-designed, exquisitely furnished, all with large and fully equipped kitchens, down to the dishwasher, silverware, and glassware. Of course all the usual hotel services and amenities are available.

Which of these hotels to choose is your only problem. Since all are lovely, base your decision on what part of town you wish to be closest to. The Eastgate Tower and the Southgate have on-premises garages. Southgate has no two-bedroom suites. Rooms will be assigned on the basis of availability (you may get your second choice, but that will be no hardship). Reservations can be made up to six months in advance. The company asks that you do not contact the individual hotels, but either write to Mr. Arden, 303 Lexington Ave., New York, NY 10036, or phone the following toll-free numbers: outside of New York state, 800/223-6663; in New York state 800/522-5680. The local phone is 212/689-5227.

Note: Rates are good on Friday, Saturday, or Sunday night, but you must arrive on Friday or Saturday to qualify for the Sunday rate.

A small jewel of a hotel, the **Westpark,** 308 W. 58th St., across the street from the Coliseum and Central Park (tel. 212/246-6440), has one of the most reasonable weekend package deals of all: $25 per person (based on double occupancy) for accommodations for two nights.

Both **Howard Johnson's Motor Lodge,** at Eighth Avenue and 51st Street, NYC 10019 (tel. 212/581-4100), and the **Ramada Inn,** Eighth Avenue at 48th Street, NYC 10019 (tel. 212/581-7000), offer an attractive three-days/two-nights package for theater lovers called "On The Town Plus Broadway." It is not limited to the weekend, but can begin any day. It includes a large, comfortable room; an hour-long backstage tour of Radio City Music Hall; one theater ticket to a hit musical or comedy; free parking, taxes, and tips on package items. The package includes a large, comfortable room, one complete dinner at the Sizzler Steak House in the Ramada Inn, one theater ticket to a hit musical or comedy, free parking, and taxes and tips on package items. Rates are $159.25 per person, double occupancy.

If you're the kind of person who hates to break your exercise routine when you're on vacation, take advantage of the "Summit Weekender" plan offered by **Loew's Summit,** Lexington Avenue at 51st Street, NYC 10022 (tel. 212/752-7000). It's for two days and one night, with arrival on Friday or Saturday only. In addition to a deluxe room at this lovely hotel, you receive a two-for-the-price-of-one dinner at Maude's Restaurant, breakfast in your room or Sunday brunch at Maude's, plus unlimited use of the Summit Health Club, which contains Nautilus equipment, exercise bicycles, a ballet bar, and a sauna and whirlpool. Storage of your car and some gratuities are included. The per-person double-occupancy charge is $59.50.

Sheraton Hotels in New York have a "Time of Your Life Big Apple" discounted program you should know about. It includes, for example, a one-night weekend stay at the Sheraton Centre Hotel for approximately $50 per person, double occupancy. For this you receive a complimentary cocktail in any bar or lounge in the hotel, plus wine and cheese and fruit in your room on arrival. The program varies throughout the year to include special seasonal features for the holidays; for example, between Thanksgiving and New Year's you'll receive champagne and caviar on arrival. Sheraton Hotels in New York also has an extended-stay discount program known as "Celebrate New York." Your stay of six days and five nights includes one orchestra seat to a Broadway show, a Grey Line sightseeing tour, five continental breakfasts, plus a welcome cocktail. Prices range from approximately $350 to $450 per person, double occupancy, at such hotels as the Sheraton Russell, Sheraton City Squire (which has an indoor pool), Sheraton Centre and Towers, and the St. Regis. For exact rates and reservations, phone Sheraton's toll-free reservations number: 800/325-3535.

The luxurious **New York Hilton,** 1335 Avenue of the Americas, NYC 10019, between 53rd and 54th Streets (tel. 212/586-7000), has a three-day/two-night "Rainbow Weekend." Rooms must be booked for Friday or Saturday arrival. It's priced at $109 per person, that rate including two nights' accommodation (based on double occupancy), a welcome cocktail, Sunday buffet brunch at Hurlingham's, discounts on sightseeing, shopping, and entertainment, all taxes and gratuities.

The chic **Marriott's Essex House,** 160 Central Park South, NYC 10019, between Sixth and Seventh Avenues (tel. 212/247-0300; or toll free 800/228-9290), offers an "Escape to Luxury" for one to three nights that can be booked on Friday, Saturday, or Sunday. A couple pays $249 for a luxury accommodation for the first night, that price including dinner at the hotel's Devereux restaurant and breakfast the following morning; subsequent nights are priced at $135 per couple without meals. Pretty splurgy for us, but a good price for these very posh digs.

"Le Weekend Français" offers luxury with a French touch at the lovely **Parker Meridien,** 118 W. 57th St., NYC 10019, between Sixth and Seventh Avenues (tel. 212/245-5000; or toll free 800/223-9918 outside of New York state, 800/

442-5917 in New York state). Two nights' (Friday arrival) accommodations, room service or breakfast in Le Patio, chilled champagne waiting in the room, and even membership in the hotel's health club (year round pool, Nautilus equipment, sauna, etc.) are included for the price of $130 per person (based on double occupancy).

Remember the famed Barbizon Hotel for Women? It's undergone a complete metamorphosis and has emerged as the lovely **Golden Tulip Barbizon Hotel,** 140 E. 63rd St., NYC 10021, between Lexington and Third Avenues (tel. 212/838-5700). Its weekend package, priced at $49.50 per person (based on double occupancy) includes a welcome bottle of champagne, continental breakfast in bed, and copies of Saturday's and Sunday's *New York Times*. A two-night stay is required, which means a Friday arrival and a Sunday departure. On the premises of the hotel is the exclusive La Marée Restaurant.

Chapter II

EATING CHEAPLY AND WELL

1–14. Restaurants by Neighborhoods
15. Especially for Brunch
16. Around the Clock
17. Early-Bird Dinner Specials
18. Big-Splurge Restaurants

NEW YORK'S MELTING POT is home to the world's largest array of cuisine. Here you can sample everything from hearty peasant fare to refined French cooking, take in the friendly atmosphere of a family-run trattoria or sip wine in chic art deco surroundings. The biggest problem you'll have is deciding where you want to go—the possibilities are endless.

We've arranged the restaurants in this chapter by geographic location. At the end we have included a list of good brunch spots and restaurants with early-bird specials. We've also listed the restaurants open 24 hours a day and the ones worth a once-in-a-blue-moon splurge.

1. Midtown West/Times Square

Here, in an area encompassing the Broadway theater district and the diamond district, there is an abundance of restaurant discoveries for the budget traveler. Midtown West is bounded roughly by 40th Street on the south, 57th Street on the north, Fifth Avenue on the east, and Ninth Avenue on the west.

AMERICAN/CONTINENTAL: If you want to eat at reasonable prices in unpretentious surroundings and still find yourself in the company of stars, try **Joe Allen's,** 326 W. 46th St., between Eighth and Ninth Avenues (tel. 581-6464). We've seen Al Pacino, Roy Scheider, and Angela Lansbury here on separate occasions. The atmosphere is warm, if too noisy to be intimate. Exposed brick walls bear framed theatrical posters which are an inside joke—the shows are either flops or little known. Tables are covered with red-checkered tablecloths and plants hang in brick archways that separate the busy bar from the larger dining area. Out in back there's dining beneath a skylight.

Prices on the blackboard are usually low. There are generally three or four dinners in the $8 to $10 range. Recommended are liver and onions or chopped steak ($9.50) or fried chicken ($10.50). Huge salads, priced from $6 to $9.50, are meals in themselves. Try the chicken salad, said to be the "only chicken salad in

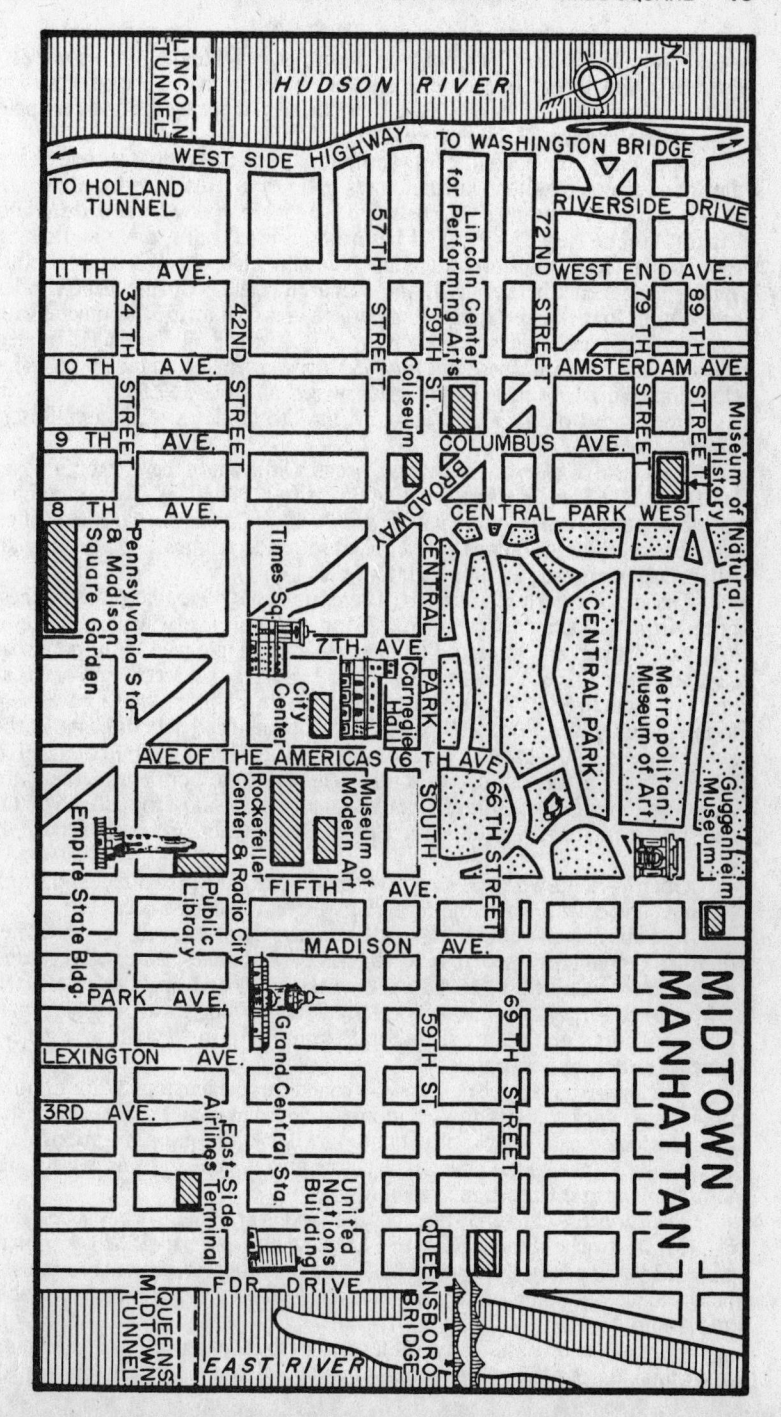

RESTAURANTS: MIDTOWN WEST / TIMES SQUARE 43

Manhattan made without mayonnaise" ($8.50). Brunch—served seven days a week until 2:45 p.m. (3:45 p.m. on Saturday and Sunday)—has omelets, creamed chipped beef, or Monte Cristo sandwiches (ham and cheese dipped in batter and grilled) for about $6.50 each. For dessert, there are the favorite apple crisp and pecan pies ($3.25) or cheesecake ($3.50).

Open daily from noon to 2 a.m. (from 11:30 a.m. on Wednesday and Saturday for matinee-goers); the kitchen closes at 1:30 a.m. Reservations advised.

A similar restaurant is **Charlie's,** 263 W. 45th St., between Broadway and Eighth Avenue (tel. 354-2911). It has exposed brick walls, a bar and dining room separated by brick archways, and blue-and-white checkered tablecloths. While the ambience here is just as warm, Charlie's blackboard menu has a wider selection of lower-priced items: hamburgers and chili are $3.75, quiche with salad is $6.75, and daily specials run from $6.95 to $8.50. Try half a broiled chicken for $7.50 or Chinese ribs for $8.95. Desserts made on the premises include lime pie, carrot cake, and fudge brownies, all around $2.50.

Open daily from 11:30 a.m. to 4 a.m.; the kitchen closes at 1:30 a.m. Reservations suggested.

For a taste of "Anywhere U.S.A.," head a little out of the way to the **Market Diner,** 572 Eleventh Ave., at 43rd Street (tel. 244-6033). There's nothing special about the diner, but that's what makes it so familiar: a sweeping coffee counter, large orange booths, a foyer filled with video games, and a parking lot where customers can park one hour for free.

The menu is virtually endless. There are some 40 kinds of sandwiches, priced from $1.30 for a fried egg to $5.75 for a toasted bagel with cream cheese, lox, sliced onion, and tomato. Full dinners—including a meat dish, potato or rice, and vegetable or salad—run from $4.50 for baked breast of lamb or chicken chow mein to $7.95 for veal parmigiana. There are more than a dozen seafood dinners priced from $5.95 to $8.95, including fried sole or clams at the lower end, up to the garlicky shrimp scampi. And with any entree of $5.50 or more, you get a "bonus" cup of soup or glass of juice. For dessert, there are baked-on-the-premises fruit pies, muffins, and cakes—most for under $1.50—and ice-cream treats made with Breyer's ice cream. A super-sundae is $1.95.

Open 24 hours a day, as are its two other locations: 33rd Street and Ninth Avenue, and downtown on the corner of West and Laight Streets.

Rise above it all—18 stories—and encounter the classiest university cafeteria you'll probably ever see. It's **City University's Graduate Center Dining Commons,** 33 W. 42nd St. (18th floor), between Fifth and Sixth Avenues (tel. 790-4433). It's not just a university cafeteria, either. There's a lounge and bar, where hot hors d'oeuvres are served gratis from 5:30 p.m. "until they're gone," which is usually by 6:30 p.m.

The lounge has a large oak bar with caned chrome barstools. Along one of the exposed brick walls is a row of chrome-and-canvas lounge chairs, where studious customers can sit back with a book and a drink. The more gregarious gather around the low, round tables. The dining area has cream-colored walls and ferns hanging in shutter-framed windows.

The service is cafeteria style, but the food is first rate. It consists of soup ($1.15), sandwiches (about $2.30 to $4.50), and a salad bar ($2.95 for a small plate, $3.95 for a large). For about $5.50 you can order hot entrees like braised beefsteak with scallions or the fish of the day, served with a gourmet vegetable and potato.

Continental breakfast is available from 10 to 11:30 a.m., lunch and dinner from noon to 8 p.m. The Commons is a good place to stop by for a cheap cup of coffee (40¢) and dessert (pies and cakes run $1.25 to $1.75), or for an afternoon drink (house drinks are $2.50; call drinks, $2.50; draft beer, $1.25).

Beggar's Banquet, 125 W. 43rd St., between Sixth Avenue and Broadway (tel. 997-0959), is a not-so-typical midtown bar/restaurant in the heart of the theater district. It's a warm retreat from the flashy midtown lights, with an almost woodsy, mountain feel that derives from rich wood paneling, wooden booths, brick-tile floors, and exposed brick walls. Up front there are a few tables in a plant-filled window area.

For lunch, there are hearty homemade soups and stews—types change daily—served with freshly baked bread for under $5. Or try one of six kinds of quiche, most priced under $6. There are large, meal-size salads of beans and greens, or fruit, nuts, and cottage cheese, each for $5.95. The dinner menu offers the same soups, salads, and quiches, but for about $1 more. There are also a dozen dinner entrees, including eggplant parmigiana or spaghetti carbonara ($8.95) and New York sirloin ($13.95). All are served with salad and homemade bread. Desserts—also homemade—change daily and may include a chocolate silk pie or champion peach pie ($1.95).

Lunch is served Monday to Saturday from 11:30 a.m. to 5 p.m., dinner from 5 to 11 p.m. (except on Monday, when the kitchen closes at 8 p.m.). Closed Sunday.

A favorite weekday lunch spot is the **Embassy Gourmet,** 1431 Broadway, at 40th Street (tel. 354-0550). As you enter, you can view sweets and deli salad treats in glass cases to the left and right. The eating area has potted trees in the windows, wine bottles on the shelves, and plants hanging from latticework overhead.

Embassy Gourmet's specialties are the salads: chunky chicken or tuna, served with cole slaw and German potato salad, is $4.95. Another special dish is the quiche with salad, or escargots and croissant ($5.25). Two can happily split a cheese and sausage board, priced $6.95 to $7.95, and save room for a dreamy gourmet dessert. After walking midtown all day, you might treat yourself to chocolate mousse or praline cake ($2.65), or a rich and fattening Black Forest cake ($2.75).

Between 7:30 and 11 a.m. you can get a continental breakfast which includes fresh-squeezed orange juice, croissant or brioche, cream cheese wedge, and coffee (all orders à la carte) for less than $3.50.

Open Monday to Friday from 7:30 a.m. to 6 p.m.

A similar set-up in an altogether different part of midtown is **Juliana** gourmet shop and café, 891 Eighth Ave., at 53rd Street (tel. 582-4503). Here you can sample vegetable and pasta salads, such as tortellini al pesto or fusili primavera ($3.75), or "heroic sandwiches" of meatballs, ham, roast beef, or mortadella ($5), at outdoor sidewalk tables. For snackers there are croissants, scones, and cheesecake (all $1.75), and espresso and cappuccino.

Open Monday through Saturday from 9 a.m. to 8 p.m., on Sunday from 10 a.m. to 6 p.m.

One of New York's oldest favorite fast-food spots is **Nathan's Famous,** 1482 Broadway, at 43rd Street (tel. 382-0620). It's got a happy, Coney Island feel to it (the first Nathan's started in Coney Island). The split-level restaurant, which seats 500, has yellow Formica tables, orange vinyl chairs, and paintings of Coney Island scenes on its walls.

The food is fast and good: the best New York hot dogs you'll try ($1.25), and great french fries (99¢). The superburger with cheese is $1.99, and a bacon cheeseburger, $2.09. For the non-burger, non-hot dog crowd there's other fare: chili con carne ($1.40), fish and chips ($1.75), shrimp and chips ($3.75), knishes

(99¢), corn on the cob ($1.07), an individual pan pizza ($1.89), and even frog legs ($3.69).

Open Sunday through Thursday from 7 a.m. to 2 a.m., on Friday and Saturday to 4 a.m.

Robert's Restaurant, 736 Tenth Ave., tucked between 50th and 51st Streets (tel. 581-4244), is the kind of place you'd want in any neighborhood—inviting, friendly, clean, a place to drink and chat. Not surprising, then, that it's a neighborhood hangout. The brick walls, black piano, and long mirror-backed mahogany bar give the interior a homey feeling, and in the summer there's a patio open in the rear. On evenings and weekend afternoons a piano player undercuts the chatter with soothing melodies. The menu is limited but generally good; the salmon tortellini ($8.75) is excellent. For the rich-at-stomach there's an inviting dessert menu, featuring the aptly titled "chocolate orgasm," a big, nutty brownie smothered with chocolate sauce.

Open seven days a week from noon till whenever the bar closes, which can go into the wee hours of the morning if the mood is festive.

With a bright, airy interior, **Miss Brooks,** 1379 Sixth Avenue, at 56th Street (tel. 581-1931), is the right place to visit. The decor is attractive and modern, with baskets hanging on the walls and candles on the tables. Service is cafeteria style, and meals are a health-food gourmet's delight. A plate of crisp stir-fried vegetables costs $3.75, and a vegetable casserole, $3.85. Spinach, Niçoise and Oriental salads sell for $4.35, and garden salads with lettuce, cucumbers, and peas are $2.25 each. Desserts are special, fresh-baked treats. The banana-walnut cake ($1.60) is a moist delight.

Open daily from 7 a.m. to 11 p.m. There is another Miss Brooks at 926 Third Ave., at 56th Street (tel. 581-1931).

ARGENTINIAN: To see where the New York Argentinian community socializes, go to **La Milonga,** 742 Ninth Avenue, corner of 50th Street (tel. 541-8382). It has a Latin club atmosphere that is festive and convivial. A busy bar greets the visitor, and the dining areas bear travel posters of Argentina and a huge oil painting of Argentinian tango singer Carlos Cardel.

The lunch specials on weekdays are the best buy ($4.95), and there are nine to choose from. Try La Milonga's empañadas (called "gaucho pies" here); you get two, with salad and rice, at the lunch special price. Or order chili con carne, with rice, bread, and butter. For something truly Latin American, try the black beans.

At dinner there's a $4.95 minimum, and for that you can get Italian spaghetti with meat sauce. Or try a dinner platter that reflects the Argentinian predilection for meat: it has sweetbreads, kidney, steak, sausage, short ribs, and salad, for $9.95. Seafood specials such as lobster gumbo or marinera are more, but not overpriced at $14.95.

Lunch is served from noon to 3 p.m. weekdays only, dinner from 3 p.m. to 2 a.m. daily, with a limited late-supper menu available until 3 or 4 a.m. On Friday, Saturday, and Sunday nights there's live Argentinian folkloric or tango music from 9 p.m. with a moderate cover charge, and dinner prices are a couple of dollars higher. Reservations are suggested for weekend nights.

BRAZILIAN: Climbing the stairwell up to **Cabana Carioca,** 123 West 45th St., between Sixth Avenue and Broadway (tel. 581-8088), is like coming upon the gay and gaudy minstrel caravan in the movie *'Bye 'Bye Brazil.* Cabana Carioca is one of the least expensive, and certainly the most colorful of midtown's Brazilian restaurants. The second-floor restaurant is almost as colorful as the folkloric scenes painted on the stairway walls. A large window overlooking 45th Street is filled with plants, the walls are hung with oil paintings by a South American artist, and the tables are gaily covered with green linen cloths and yellow napkins.

Three specials are offered daily, priced from $8.25 to $11.95. Portions are generous enough to share between two. Try the broiled chicken gaucho style ($8.95) or fish stew Brazilian style ($11.95). These come with rice, more black beans than you can eat, and a basket of fresh bread. The Brazilian national dish, feijoada completa, is a stew of black beans and three kinds of meat—pork, beef, and sausage ($8.95). At the lower priced end of the menu there's a Portuguese omelet, made with sausage ($4.95). Consider sampling the desserts ($1.50); select from guava with cheese, coconut custard with cheese, or Portuguese pastry. Highest recommendation.

Open daily from 11 a.m. to 11 p.m., on Sunday to 10 p.m. Reservations suggested.

More in the style of modern Rio is a lovely, sophisticated little bar and restaurant called **Via Brazil,** 34 W. 46th St., between Fifth and Sixth Avenues (tel. 997-1158). The decor is very '80s, with mahogany-stained wainscotting trimmed in rich turquoise and watercolors of Brazilian scenes hung above on white walls. There is seating to the side in semiprivate cubicles, or at the front in a glassed-in patio. Samba music plays in the background.

The menu offers an extensive selection of entrees with a Brazilian accent for under $10. There's fried sea trout served with fried bananas, a shrimp omelet, broiled lamb, veal, and pork, all served with rice and salad, and priced from $9.95 to $11.95. Via Brazil serves several versions of muquecas—an herby fish stew made with tomatoes and coconut milk—priced from $10.75 for trout stew to $13.95 for a stew with fish, shrimp, and lobster tail. All come with rice, beans, and salad. If you decide to share an entree, expect to be charged $2 for an extra plate.

Open from noon to 10 p.m. Monday to Saturday. Closed Sunday.

CAJUN/CRÉOLE: You can take a train uptown to Harlem or a plane down south to Dixie for down-home southern cooking, or you can stay in midtown and head for **The Barking Fish,** 705 Eighth Ave., between 44th and 45th Streets (tel. 757-0186).

The tall, distinguished-looking chef, Arthur DeCuir, offers traditional Créole and Cajun delights such as seafood jambalaya ($14.95), shrimp créole ($14.95), and seafood gumbo ($12.95), which comes with yellow rice and cornbread. Or go for the blueplate special, which includes catfish ($10.95) or whiting ($9.95), cornbread, rice, and your choice of collard greens, black-eyed peas, or red beans. But the Barking Fish's real specialties are offered during holiday festivals such as Mardi Gras (February), when New Orleans dishes are featured, or the Summer Softshell Crab Festival (May through August), when eight different varieties of softshell crabs are served.

Open Monday through Friday from 11:30 a.m. to 11:30 p.m., on Saturday from 4:30 to 11:30 p.m., and on Sunday from 5 to 10 p.m. There's also a brunch featuring Dixieland music on Sunday from noon to 5 p.m.

CHINESE: For Chinese food lovers who can't make it down to Chinatown, there is the exceptional new **Kofu Spring,** 257 W. 55th St., between Broadway and Eighth Avenue (tel. 315-3556). At first glance the interior appears cramped as one steps down from the street level through the entrance, but in back there's a comfortable, brick-walled seating area with "mood lighting" for evening and a skylight for illumination during the day. The cooking is Szechuan style, with fine appetizers of spring rolls and hot-and-sour soup (each $1), and more than 60 different entrees, ranging from chicken with orange flavor ($6.50) to ten-ingredient lo mein noodles ($4.25) to sliced prawns, snow peas, carrots, straw mushrooms, and baby corn in white egg sauce ($8.95).

Open seven days a week from 11:30 a.m. to 11 p.m.

For a more stylish setting, **Lai Lai West,** 859 Ninth Ave., corner of 56th Street (tel. 586-5083), offers a neon-lit exterior with a slick black decor—black tiled floors, black tables with wood siding, and black booths, all lit in a soft, indirect way. The food, like most Chinese restaurants, is reasonably priced. Appetizers begin at $1 for spring rolls, and go up to $6.95 for the Lai Lai special hors d'oeuvres for two—shrimp toast, fried wonton, pillow chicken, spring rolls, and honey spare ribs. Entrees vary from $6.55 for moo shu pork and pancakes, to $8.75 for General Ching's chicken with assorted vegetables in hot sauce, to $10.95 for shelled lobster in chili sauce.

Open Sunday through Thursday from 11:30 a.m. to 10:30 p.m., on Friday and Saturday to 11:30 p.m.

CUBAN/CHINESE: Thanks to a sizable Chinese immigrant population in Latin America, Chinese food is as popular south of the border as it is in the U.S. With the post-revolutionary exodus from Cuba, many Chinese restaurateurs settled in New York and established a number of binational eateries that are a budget-minded, ethnic-food-lover's paradise. One of Manhattan's best is **Asia Numero Uno,** 920 Eighth Ave., between 54th and 55th Streets (tel. 541-4137). Its interior is uncharacteristically—for Chinese/Latino restaurants—attractive, with butcher-block tables and caned chrome chairs, lots of greenery, a mirrored wall, and a modest number of red-tassled Chinese lanterns.

The food is cheap and served in ample portions. You can go either Latin or Chinese—the cuisines are kept distinct—or combine the two. Though China and Cuba are several oceans apart, their cuisines are remarkably compatible. Where else might you eat egg foo yung alongside fried plantains? Our favorite Cuban entree is ropa vieja (Spanish for old clothes), shredded beef with a spicy Cuban sauce, served with black beans, rice, and fried plantains ($4.15). Daily Cuban specials include beef stew Cuban style, codfish, and oxtails, all served with rice and beans or plantains ($5.45). On the Asian side of the menu are such traditional Cantonese favorites as tomato or pepper beef ($4.45), and shrimp with lobster sauce or sweet-and-sour pork ($6.35). For dessert, try coconut, guava, or papaya served with cream cheese ($1.85).

Open daily from 11:30 a.m. to 11 p.m.

There is also an Asia Numero Uno crosstown at 788 Lexington Ave., between 61st and 62nd Streets (tel. 951-3140).

ENGLISH/IRISH: A little out of the way, but one of New York's most charming dining places is the **Landmark Tavern,** 626 Eleventh Ave., at 46th Street (tel. 757-8595). An inn-like, Irish tavern that dates back to 1868, the Landmark has an antique feel to it that few New York restaurants can match. There is dining on the second floor, in what served for a century as home to the Carly family, the Landmark's first owners. It is still the restaurant's homiest part; eating there is much like having Thanksgiving dinner at grandmother's. There are old floor rugs, antique furniture, brick fireplaces, and even a functioning grandfather clock.

Downstairs in the main dining area is a gorgeous old Victorian bar with huge, beveled mirrors. Tables are covered with white linen and adorned with candles and fresh flowers.

For lunch, there's shepherd's pie ($7.25) or fish and chips ($6.25). There are also sandwiches ($4.75 to $5.75) and Irish potato soup ($2.75). Dinner equivalents run about $1 higher. For dessert, there's hot apple pie ($1.95) or pecan pie or carrot cake ($2.50). Sunday brunch at Landmark is a newer tradition. The above-mentioned entrees are served for lunch prices. There are seven types of omelets ($6.95) and plain, corn, or strawberry griddle cakes with ham, bacon, or sausage ($5.50). Have a bullshot, Bloody Mary, screwdriver, or fruit juice on the house with brunch.

Open daily for lunch from noon to 4 p.m. and for dinner from 5 p.m. to midnight (on Saturday and Sunday to 1 a.m.).

The English Pub, 900 Seventh Ave. between 56th and 57th Streets (tel. 265-4360), is felicitously located between Carnegie Hall and City Center and is a popular stop for a quick, filling meal. The low ceilings with exposed beams, the abundance of wood, and the soft green lamps give this New York eatery a truly British feel. London street signs decorate the walls and British flags embellish the menus—you may be tempted to settle in for a convivial pub evening.

Daily blackboard specials like fish 'n' chips ($7.25), shepherd's pie ($6.50), and bangers 'n' mash ($7.25) should warm the heart of anyone homesick for the empire. The lunch menu offers big salads, hamburgers, and sandwiches ($4.25 to $6.95), as well as more substantial entrees like London broil and pork chops ($7.95 and up). At dinner the English fare is the most reasonably priced and the best bet, like the steak-and-kidney pie ($7.50).

Weekend brunch, from noon to 4 p.m., includes your choice of egg dishes, toast, coffee and *two* drinks, for $6.95.

Open daily from 11:30 to 4 a.m.

There's always a boisterous Irish-pub crowd gathered around the bar at the **Shandon Star,** 938 Eighth Ave., near 55th Street (tel. 664-8181). At lunchtime the locals are joined by broadcast and business types who come from nearby for the restaurant's famous meat sandwiches, filled with generous portions of corned beef, pastrami, ham, or roast beef ($3.25), and for sandwich platters, which come with two vegetables ($4.95). Drinks at the bar are unusually cheap. A large shot of Gordon's gin or Bacardi rum is $1.35, a shot of vodka costs $1, and J&B scotch is $1.50.

Open daily from 8 a.m. to 4 a.m.

FRENCH: In fair weather, dine on a terrace overlooking 55th Street on the second floor of **La Bonne Soupe,** 48 W. 55th St., between Fifth and Sixth Avenues (tel. 586-7650). In winter there's warmth and intimacy inside on the street level. Low ceilings, subdued lighting, walls covered with red-and-white checked gingham, and tables covered with red-and-white checked tablecloths give La Bonne Soupe a close, cozy ambience. So does the small bar in back, which you'll pass if you go upstairs to sit on the outdoor terrace, or to view the restaurant's private collection of Haitian primitive paintings which adorn the upstairs walls.

Lunch and dinner at La Bonne Soupe are from the same menu, at the same low prices. Omelets, filled with ratatouille or gruyère cheese, are $5.95, and a meal of soup, bread, salad, dessert, and coffee or wine is only $5.95. Soups are mushroom-barley with lamb, sweet-and-sour cabbage, and French onion. There are also salads—Niçoise, chef's, or "Popeye" (spinach)—for $6.95, and fondues of cheese ($5.95) or chocolate ($3.95).

Open daily from 11:30 a.m. to midnight (on Sunday to 11 p.m.).

Not far away is another low-priced French restaurant, part of a nationwide chain but without a hint of franchise uniformity. **La Crêpe,** 57 W. 56th St., between Fifth and Sixth Avenues (tel. 247-1136), has French provincial decor with Tudor-beamed stucco walls adorned with ceramic decorative plates and copper cooking utensils. There is a lovely ceramic water fountain near the entryway, and the waitresses are dressed in milkmaid costumes. If you sit near the center of the restaurant, you can watch your crêpes being created at the open crêperie.

There are 15 crêpe entrees, filled with cheese, vegetables, and sausages, singly or in combinations. The latter are nice if you can't decide. We tried a crêpe filled with both ratatouille and sweet Italian sausages ($5.75 at lunch). Served with salad, bread, and butter, the crêpes cost between $5 and $8.50 (about $1 higher at dinner). There are omelets too, served with french fries and salad (about $6 to $7). They are good choices if you want to follow your meal with one of the 14 dessert crêpes, filled with imported French chestnut spread ($4), bananas and ice cream ($5.70), or simple traditional jam ($2).

Open daily from 11:30 a.m. to 12:30 a.m. On Saturday and Sunday, brunch is $7.95 and includes crêpes, omelets, quiche, or eggs Benedict, plus french fries, salad, and coffee, as well as a cocktail or wine.

The entrees are expensive at **Café Un, Deux, Trois,** 123 W. 44th St., between Sixth and Seventh Avenues (tel. 354-4148). But this restaurant's distinctive ambience may be worth the price. Boisterous, bustling, brightly lit, and airy like a loft, it's the kind of restaurant to go to when you don't want intimacy. In the heart of the theater district, the café is packed both before and after shows.

Butcher paper instead of linen serves as tablecloths, and with crayons supplied by the café, your table becomes an adult playground. Waiters will demonstrate their remarkable memories by reproducing the evening's menu on your tablecloth—that is, if your own graffiti doesn't take up all the space before your waiter arrives. If it's your birthday, by all means request a serenade. The waiters' chorus sounds professional.

Though entrees run upward from $10.95 for brochette de poulet to $16.95 for roast duck or mixed grill, there are omelets ($6.95), quiche ($4.95), and appetizers for under $5. Try pâté de canard ($3.95) as a before- or after-theater snack. Or for a big-splurge sweet, consider ordering profiteroles—three cream-puff pastries filled with vanilla ice cream and topped with bittersweet fudge sauce ($4.95).

Open daily from noon to 12:30 a.m. Prices are somewhat lower before 5 p.m.

GREEK: For the best in Greek cuisine and a possible peek at a celebrity patron, go to **Molfeta's,** 307 W. 47th St., between Eighth and Ninth Avenues (tel. 840-9537). This popular Greek coffeeshop is a longtime family operation, run by Nick and Bill Fillos, and a longtime source of low-priced, reliably good Greek food. It has pleased the likes of Liza Minnelli, Chita Rivera, and Telly Savalas. Molfeta's coffee counter, chrome-and-vinyl barstools, and rusty orange vinyl booths are reminiscent of New York in the '40s, when the restaurant was founded.

Prices and selections are the same at lunch and dinner. Many of the lamb entrees—Molfeta's specialties—cost about $5 and include two vegetables. Begin a full meal by sharing a Greek antipasto—caviar salad, stuffed grape leaves, feta cheese, eggs, and finger vegetables ($2)—or have it for a simple lunch. Don't forget baklava for dessert or the similar but less-known galaktoboureko, filled with eggs and farina and drizzled with honey ($1).

Open daily from noon to midnight.

The food is similar but the dining more elegant at the nearby **New Acropolis,** 767 Eighth Avenue, at 47th Street (tel. 581-2733). Lamb entrees here start at $7.25, except for a recommended combination plate of baked lamb, eggplant moussaka, baked macaroni, stuffed grape leaves, spinach, and cheese ($8.75). There are dozens of other entrees, from fried or broiled shrimp ($10.75) to roast baby veal ($9.75) or chicken ($5.95). Acropolis serves its own version of Greek antipasto, with caviar and eggplant salads, stuffed grape leaves, feta cheese, and tzatziki—yogurt seasoned with garlic, oil, salt, and cucumber at ($3.25). This dish includes a huge hunk of fresh bread and butter.

Open daily from 11 a.m. to 11 p.m.

INTERNATIONAL: The newest addition to the diversity of choices on 46th Street between Eighth and Ninth Avenues, known to theater locals as Restaurant Row, is **Lido,** 345 W. 46th St., between Eighth and Ninth Avenues (tel. 582-4801). The restaurant, with its pink painted walls, light-grained wood bar, and oil paintings of tropical flowers, has a pleasant, cheerful look that is southern in essence.

At the piano, drinks are about $3, and you are welcome to tickle the ivories yourself if the piano is free. We liked the pink bird ashtrays decorating the bar, and continue to debate whether they are storks or pelicans. Go and decide for yourself.

In the main dining room, music from the '30s and '40s plays over a superior sound system while diners peruse a menu of international pastas. You can choose among various tempting dishes, including ravioli Mexicali (cheese ravioli made with hot sauce and avocado) for $8, penne à la Grêque (spaghetti with feta cheese, olives, and olive oil) for $8, or the more extravagant angel's hair à la Russe (pasta with caviar, vodka, and cream sauce) for $11. An equally rich array of desserts changes daily and costs $4.

Open from noon to 1 a.m. seven days a week. Reservations suggested.

Want a chance to meet New Yorkers, have a good dinner or brunch, and get to practice a foreign language too, for all of $10? An evening at **The Language Club** has to be one of the best values in New York. Started in April of 1984 by the popular broadcast talk-show host Barry Farber, the club has caught on so quickly that any given week should see at least five or six meetings in the metropolitan area. Farber, a student of 14 languages, thought he was the only language freak around; when he mentioned the fact on a radio show, hundreds of others came forward, and now the meetings are extremely popular, especially with older singles who would like to meet people in a congenial and cultural environment. For $10, the visitor receives a drink, a buffet meal that runs from "generous to limitless," depending on the restaurant, and a chance to converse in small groups in any number of tongues, everything from Albanian to Zulu, though the most popular languages are, of course, French, Spanish, Italian, and German. There's no guarantee that you'll find somebody with whom to discuss world affairs in Mandarin Chinese or Serbo-Croatian or Turkish, but the chances are good. A joint program on teachings and tactics (i.e., learning to memorize words once and for all) is presented to the entire group. And students are also offered discounts on classes at language schools, cassette courses, books, dictionaries, and more. The purpose of the club is to bring together those who wish to begin, refresh, improve, or practice a language, so you are welcome at whatever your level of skill. Internationals are especially welcome: they quickly become "superstars, celebrities," says Farber, and get a chance to make American friends and practice their English in a pleasant, nonthreatening environment."

As for the restaurants, they are always of excellent quality, from dinners at La Maganette or Dallas Jones Bar-B-Q, to Sunday brunches at Charlie O's in the Citicorp Center. Says Farber: "The bargain is so good it pays to come to the Language Club even if you keep your mouth shut!"

For information on all Language Club activities, phone their 24-hour hotline at 877-1413.

ITALIAN: No, that's not an Italian villa you see in the heart of Manhattan, it's **Mama Leone's,** 239 W. 48th St., between Broadway and Eighth Avenue (tel. 586-5151). The yellow stucco exterior barely hints at the crazy interior design—a labyrinth of stairways and arches, complete with a fountain and dotted with marble sculptures. The eclectic design is all part of the fun here, where friendly waiters and Italian hospitality make for enjoyable dining. The dinner menu runs high ($15.50 to $27), but lunches are reasonable and filling. Pasta entrees are your best bet, running from $5.95 to $11.95. If you plan to make lunch the main meal of the day, we strongly suggest the all-you-can-eat buffet. For $8.95 you get a beautiful selection of cold salads and an assortment of pastas, as well as chicken cacciatore. Be sure to try the shrimp salad, the marinated calamari, and the marinated mushrooms. Fresh tortellini salad, hot ravioli, and tangy meatballs are also a must. Coffee or tea is included in the buffet price. If you have room for dessert, we suggest the homemade pastry assortment ($1.95).

Lunch is served from 11:30 a.m. to 2:30 p.m. Monday through Friday, from noon to 2 p.m. on Saturday. Dinner is 3:30 to 11:30 p.m. Monday through Friday, 2:30 to 11:30 p.m. on Saturday, and 2 to 10 p.m. on Sunday. Free parking for dinner customers only.

JAPANESE: Carefully prepared and presented Japanese food can often run up a hefty bill, but **Yakitori,** 210 W. 49th St., at Seventh Avenue (tel. 586-2272), serves first-rate Japanese food at bargain-basement prices. Right off Times Square, this bustling little diner-style restaurant delivers more than its cheap prices and modest interior would imply.

The young clientele likes to choose among the 20 different kinds of sushi available, from shrimp and crab sushi ($2.50) to the ever-popular California sushi with rice rolled on the outside ($2). Six pieces are in one order and come accompanied with extremely fresh slices of ginger and a mound of pungent horseradish.

If you're not a sushi fan, there are eight entrees that come with salad and rice, including kiji-don (broiled chicken and vegetables), negimaki (beef rolled around scallions), and shumai (steamed Japanese dumplings), ranging from $3.50 to $6.50. Our favorite is the yakisoba, a plate of spicy sauteed noodles topped with chicken and vegetables that have been lightly grilled ($3.50).

While you wait for your meal, you can watch the three young male chefs working busily at the grill behind the counter, or you can read one of the English-language or Japanese newspapers stacked near the door.

Open Monday to Friday from noon to 10 p.m., on Saturday and Sunday from 3 to 10 p.m.

Tucked away up a dingy apartment-house stairway is an excellent little restaurant called **Hide** (pronounced "hee-day"), 304 W. 56th St., between Eighth and Ninth Avenues (tel. 582-0030). Almost totally lacking in ambience, Hide nevertheless draws a loyal crowd for its hospitality and delicious, low-priced Japanese dishes. Favorites are chicken and beef teriyaki ($10.25), and shrimp and vegetable tempura ($10.50). Complete dinners, including entree, soup, pickled vegetable, rice, and dessert, run up to $11.75 for sukiyaki. There are assorted sushi platters for $9 and $11.

Lunch is served weekdays from noon to 2:30 p.m.; dinner, Monday to Saturday from 5:30 to 10:30 p.m.

For more atmosphere and food at somewhat higher prices, try **Sushiko Restaurant,** 251 W. 55th St., between Eighth Avenue and Broadway (tel. 974-9721). Its distinguished clientele has included celebrities like Anthony Quinn, Eli Wallach, and Mitch Miller, all of whose autographs and best wishes are displayed prominently by the management. The interior is modest, with Formica "wood-look" tables and lighting from rice-paper fixtures. There is a sushi bar and a bar for liquor.

An entree with soup, appetizer, and pickled vegetables ranges from $8.50 à la carte and $9.50 (with soup, salad, and dessert) for chicken yakitori to $8 and $10 for shrimp and vegetable tempura, sashimi, and sukiyaki. A veritable feast of soup, appetizer, salad, rice, pickled vegetables, green tea, sashimi, tempura, and chicken teriyaki or broiled fish is available for about $15. At the lower-priced end of the menu are noodle-based dishes for $3.95 and $4.50.

Open weekends from noon to 3 p.m. for lunch, from 5:30 p.m. to midnight for dinner.

Step inside **Iroha,** 142 W. 49th St., between Sixth and Seventh Avenues (tel. 398-9049), and you'll swear you've been transported to the Orient. With its sushi bar, kimono-clad waitresses, tatami-matted floors, and Japanese-businessmen clientele, Iroha's atmosphere is as authentic as its food. The sushi is not only fresh and delicious, but artfully prepared (individual pieces cost from $1.75 to $3.25; a regular full plate of about 20 assorted pieces is $12.50). Those who don't like raw fish, however, need not feel like a fish out of water; try the deep-batter-fried shrimp and vegetable tempura ($9.95) or teriyaki beef, the thin-sliced meat grilled in soy sauce. For a uniquely Japanese dining experience, order shabu shabu, which is a sort of ritual in sharing. You order for two ($16.95 per person) and cook enoki mushrooms, cabbage, clear noodles, and paper-thin raw beef in boiling water at the table, then dip the cooked food into sesame or soy sauce. If you're the daring sort, go with a Japanese friend or ask the waiter to translate the Japanese menu for you; it offers buckwheat noodles in soy sauce ($4.50) and midten items not offered on the English version.

Open daily for lunch from noon to 3 p.m. and for dinner from 5 to 11:30 p.m.

For a more expansive sushi setting, there is **Iroha Sushi,** 1634 Broadway, on the corner of 50th Street (tel. 315-3808). The sushi bar twists around a whole side of the room, manned by traditionally garbed Japanese sushi chefs, who yell orders in their native tongue to waiters dashing to and fro. As with most places in New York, the sushi is not cheap—prices can run up to $16.50 for the deluxe sushi platter—but the presentation of the food is sheer beauty, a masterful demonstration of raw-fish-as-art-form. Individual pieces, ordered one by one at the sushi bar between sips of hot sake rice wine, range from $1.75 to $3.25. There is good food other than sushi as well. In particular, the chicken cutlet, breaded and deep-fried with a thin layer of cheese and served with soy bean soup, steamed rice, and a Japanese salad, is exquisite at $8.95.

Open for lunch Monday through Friday from 11:30 a.m. to 3 p.m. and 5 to 11:30 p.m. for dinner, on Saturday and Sunday from 5 to 11:30 p.m. only.

JEWISH DAIRY: Diamond Dairy, 4 W. 47th St., just west of Fifth Avenue (tel. 719-2694), is a tiny, coffee-counter luncheonette that serves kosher cuisine to Orthodox Jews working in Manhattan's diamond district. Sit near the mezzanine window and watch the trade in precious gems below.

The food here is tasty, healthful, and inexpensive. Traditional dishes like cheese blintzes, potato pirogie, and cheese kreplach are $4, as are the salads of vegetables, chopped egg, and pickled herring. Gefilte fish, salmon cutlet, and fish balls with spaghetti cost $4.95 or less. Sandwiches are generally around $3, and desserts—freshly baked—are $1.50 or less. No eggs are served between noon and 3 p.m.

Open Monday to Thursday from 7:30 a.m. to 5:30 p.m., on Friday to 3 p.m.

KOREAN: Ho Shim, 120 W. 44th St., between Sixth Avenue and Broadway (tel. 575-9774), is an attractive little restaurant serving Japanese and Korean cuisines. Tables have royal-blue linen tablecloths and wooden planters with thriving greenery. On the walls are poetic Oriental watercolors. At the entry there's a bar for drinks, and in the back, a bar for sushi and sashimi.

The best buy at Ho Shim is the Korean lunch special. For $6.50 you get an entree such as barbecued chicken or batter-fried sole, plus sauteed vegetables, steamed rice, soup, tea, and ice cream. For a lighter and more adventurous meal, step back to the sushi bar and sample rice specialties with raw tuna, abalone, and shellfish, priced from $1 to $2.80 a dish.

At dinner there are several à la carte entrees for under $10, including tasty fried chicken strips and vegetables in a spicy sauce for $7.95. The full Korean dinner costs $15, which shows what a bargain the lunch special is.

Lunch is served Monday through Saturday from noon to 3 p.m., and dinner every night from 3 p.m. to midnight.

MEXICAN: Texans and others "in the know" will complain that there is no real Mexican food in New York (Mexicans will agree). But among the best the city has to offer is the Mexican cooking at **Caramba!,** 918 Eighth Ave., at 55th Street (tel. 245-7900). Relax, enjoy the festive but tasteful decor—white walls adorned with colorful folk art, woven wall hangings, and Indian masks. Tables are covered with pink linen tablecloths and glass. The floors are rustic cement, and there's a patio-garden in the back beneath a sunny skylight and nearby a running fountain with live goldfish.

Forget about authenticity and fill up on truly tasty food. Start with nachos, covered with melted cheese and jalapeño peppers ($2.75); then go for one of the combination plates ($7.95). The pork burrito, with green chiles and salsa verde, approaches the authentic. And you should consider a chile relleno, stuffed with chicken or cheese, dipped in egg batter, and fried. If you have trouble choosing only two dishes, pay another $2 and get a third choice. But arrive hungry; with beans and rice on the side, you'll be leaving stuffed. If you're restrained, save room for the delicious Mexican doughnuts, buñuelos, served with New York's favorite Häagen-Dazs ice cream ($2.95).

Lunch is served from noon to 4 p.m. (prices are slightly lower), dinner from 5 p.m. to midnight. There's a brunch served on Saturday and Sunday from noon to 4 p.m. featuring various Mexican versions of eggs and a cocktail or wine ($6.95).

If the wait at Caramba! is too long, which it often is, try the Mexican restaurant just across the street, **Cancún,** 937 Eighth Ave., near 55th Street (tel. 307-7307). Its owners are also its chefs, and though not Mexican, they come with experience from other New York Mexican restaurants. The food here—if not authentically Tex-Mex, much less Mex-Mex—is tasty and priced right.

Cancún has combo plates, with a choice of either enchiladas or tacos priced at $7.25 (for three items, $8.95). Cancún also serves Mexican-flavored casseroles of eggplant or beef for $7.95 and $8.95, and seafood entrees for $10 and $11. For "gringos" who don't like chili and cumin, there are hamburgers and cheeseburgers (around $4) and California chicken, sauteed in wine ($8).

Cancún is open daily from 11 a.m. to midnight, on Saturday and Sunday to 1 a.m., with weekend brunch ($6) served until 4 p.m.

In competition with Caramba! for the well-heeled crowd is **Arriba Arriba,**

762 Ninth Ave., between 51st and 52nd Streets (tel. 489-0810). Since opening last year, the restaurant has fed a steady clientele of young professionals and theater types—both goers and doers—who enjoy the socializing as much as the margueritas (from the $2.95 "bebe-size" to $5.95 "mama-size") and the nachos, layered with beans, cheddar cheese, and jalapeño (single portion $2.95).

While dining at pink-linen-covered tables surrounded by colorful Mexican murals on the stucco walls, enjoy a combination platter, choosing from tacos, tostadas, burritos, enchiladas, or tamales, all with refried beans and rice on the side. (Combination of two, $6.45; three, $7.45). If after that you still have room, finish with homemade flan, an authentic Mexican recipe of rich custard covered with brandy-caramel sauce ($2.50) or a buñuelito, a deep-fried flour tortilla dusted in cinnamon and sugar, topped with chocolate or vanilla ice cream ($2.25).

Open daily from noon to midnight. Brunch, featuring five different selections with a cocktail and coffee, is served Saturday and Sunday from noon to 4 p.m. for only $5.95.

What **Viva Mexico,** 801 Ninth Ave., between 53rd and 54th Streets (tel. 315-4470), lacks in decor, it makes up in authenticity. Though the narrow, dimly lit space pales next to the skylit garden room of Caramba's, the food is more traditional—as are the waiters, who are mostly Mexican. The combination platters offer more than the usual taco and burrito fare; try combo Guadalajara, a cheese-stuffed pepper, chicken burrito, and beef burrito for $7.50, or sample the Mexican fondue ($4.25). Wash everything down with a pitcher of fruity sangría (small pitcher, $4.50; large, $8.50). The fast and friendly service has the extra touch of a guitar-strumming balladeer who serenades each table in Spanish.

Open from noon to midnight Monday through Friday, from 5 p.m. to midnight on Saturday, and 5 to 11 p.m. on Sunday.

SEAFOOD: King Crab, 871 Eighth Ave., corner of 52nd Street (tel. 765-4393), is a thoroughly classy restaurant with superb seafood at remarkable prices. The interior is exceptionally pretty, with a black marble bar, gilt-framed mirrors, oak floors, ample greenery, and Tiffany-style lamps.

Lunch entrees are the best bet here, priced significantly lower than the dinner meals. Fish of the day costs less than $5; shrimp scampi, less than $8; and a seafood combination or seafood brochette, just under $7. At dinner the menu is more varied, and there are several entrees for under $10, like sea bass, cod, or brook trout ($8.50), flounder or bluefish ($6.95), and salmon steak ($8.95). Among the shellfish entrees, shrimp scampi and scallops are within budget, just under $10. Lunch and dinner come with vegetable, potato or rice, bread, and butter; dinner adds a salad. Favorite desserts at King Crab are the chocolate cheesecake and pecan pie ($2).

Open weekdays from noon to midnight (lunch specials served until 3:30 p.m.), on Saturday and Sunday from 5 to 11:30 p.m. No reservations.

If waiting at King Crab doesn't suit you, there's a newer, very similar operation called **K.C. Place,** 807 Ninth Ave., between 53rd and 54th Streets (tel. 246-4258). The decor and menu are equally appealing. Lunch is served from noon to 4 p.m., dinner from 4 to 11:30 p.m., brunch from noon to 4 p.m. on Sunday—and here you *can* get reservations.

THAI: Slightly more exotic than either Szechuan Chinese or Korean, but similar to both, is the cuisine of Thailand. **Bangkok Cuisine,** 885 Eighth Ave., between 52nd and 53rd Streets (tel. 664-8488), is one of New York's most popular Thai restaurants. The decor is somewhat chaotic. Metallic Thai paintings are hung on black walls; Thai figurines keep vigil from strategic vantage points; black tablecloths with jungle-animal prints cover tables, and plastic Tiffany lamps are hung overhead. Cozy or crowded, depending on your mood, the restaurant's center tables are close enough for eavesdropping.

If you go in for spicy, by all means go for it here: try any of the dishes so designated by a little star. For a dish like few you've tried before, have minced pork with lime juice and peanuts, served on a bed of iceberg lettuce—$7.75, a generous serving. Less spicy dishes are still perfectly tasty. There's double delight—with chicken and shrimp in sauce—for $9.25, and egg noodle topped with chicken curry and Chinese vegetables for under $8.25. Slightly higher, but a real treat, is roast duck with the chef's special sauce for $10.95.

For vegetarians or just stricter budgetarians, meatless dishes include sauteed mixed vegetables with hot curry and sauteed bean curd with oyster sauce, both for $5.75.

Open daily from 11:30 a.m. to 11:30 p.m., on Sunday from 5 to 10 p.m.

Seeda Thai, 204 W. 50th St., between Seventh Avenue and Broadway (tel. 586-4513), offers similar fare in a less exotic, but more tasteful setting. Tables are covered with bright print cloths and glass tops; a mirrored wall makes the darkened room seem roomier, Thai paintings and ornamental plates adorn the other wall, and the exposed-beam ceiling adds a rustic quality.

At lunch, Seeda Thai serves fried-rice dishes with shrimp, beef, pork, or chicken, noodle dishes with chicken and bamboo or beef and broccoli—all under $5. Many of the dinner entrees are in the $8 and $9 range, including such exotic meals as sauteed beef with coconut milk and hot sauce; Chinese sausage salad with onion, cucumber, chili, and lettuce; and the intriguing Thai crispy noodle dish, mee krob, with pork, shrimp, and beansprouts. For dessert, try Thai coconut cake or pumpkin custard, both under $2.

Lunch is served at Seeda Thai Monday through Friday from 11:30 a.m. to 3 p.m., dinner from 5 to 11 p.m. Dinner starts on Saturday at 4 p.m., and on Sunday at 5 p.m. No weekend lunch.

Siam Grill, 585 Ninth Ave., between 42nd and 43rd Streets (tel. 307-1363), is one of the few Thai places in the city that offers take-out and delivery service. Not that its interior is anything to scoff at. A large aquarium, in which colorful and exotic fish swim lazily back and forth, graces the entry way, and the take-out area does not intrude on the dining area. House specialties include a seafood combination of crab legs, shrimp, scallops, and squid served in a coconut sauce ($8.50), and pla mug pad bai gra prou, a sauteed squid with basil leaves and chili ($6.95). In addition, there are fine soups and appetizers ranging from $1.50 to $3.95.

Open Monday through Friday from 11:30 a.m. to 11:30 p.m., and on Saturday and Sunday from 5 to 11:30 p.m. Delivery is free with a $10 minimum order.

One of the newest Thai restaurants in town is **Thai Orchid**, 769 Ninth Ave., between 51st and 52nd Streets (tel. 397-8997). Intimately set, with lacquered wood walls, frosted mirrors, and stylish pastel-violet tablecloths, the restaurant's native Thai owners eagerly set about pleasing patrons by personally visiting tables to check on the course of your dinner. The pad ped nor-mai ($6.95), a sauteed chicken, pork, or beef dish with bamboo shoots and chili paste, is particularly good, as is the pla tod grob, a deep-fried crispy fish ($7.95). Appetizers such as sate, a thin-sliced beef or pork grilled in coconut milk and curry, delightfully whet the appetite.

Open Monday through Saturday from noon to 11:30 p.m., and on Sunday from 5 to 11:30 p.m.

Perhaps the best Thai cuisine in all of Manhattan is at **Siam Inn,** 916 Eighth Ave., between 54th and 55th Streets (tel. 489-5237). The cozy restaurant space is not too cramped, not too spacious—perfect for parties of three or four—and the food is exquisite. There is a five-stool bar near the entrance at which to wait for a table, but rarely is a wait necessary. Up and down the menu one can't go wrong, be it the cold spring rolls with a sweet peanut sauce ($3.25 for one, $5.95 for two), the sauteed chicken with mushrooms and baby corn ($7.95), or the sauteed squid with basil leaves and chili ($8.95). Save room for dessert: the house-made ice cream—in banana, mango, and green-tea flavors— is a treat at $1.75.

Open Monday through Friday from noon to 5 p.m. for lunch and 5 to 11:30 p.m. for dinner, on Saturday from 4 to 11:30 p.m., and on Sunday from 5 to 11 p.m.

2. Midtown East

With the chic lunchtime hustle of suited-up business crowds, U.N. diplomats, and elegant shoppers, the Midtown East section of town, located between 42nd and 60th Streets east of Fifth Avenue, seems like a formidable challenge to budget-conscious diners. But there are a surprising number of restaurants in this area that are reasonably priced.

AMERICAN/CONTINENTAL: With a dark wood interior and regular patrons from the neighborhood, the **Mayfair Restaurant,** 964 First Ave., at 53rd Street (tel. 421-6216), has a familiar old-fashioned feel. There's a large bar at the front, decorated with a huge set of antlers. Leather-covered wooden booths are in the back of the restaurant for diners. Green checkered tablecloths, green curtains hung on thick brass rods, and softly lit green lamps add the proper accent to the mahogany-colored wood paneling.

Special entrees change on a rotating basis throughout the week, but all are hearty and filling. Prices for entrees range from $8.50 to $14.25, but there is usually at least one item on the low end of the scale for each day. Chopped steak ($8.50) and broiled chicken ($9) are items that are offered at all times. Try the beef stew ($8.25), offered Monday, or the beef goulash with noodles ($8.50) on Wednesday. We suggest pie at $2.45 or the peach Melba for $3.25 for dessert.

Open daily from noon to midnight. No reservations.

A beautiful varnished blond-wood exterior is the first clue that the **Electra Restaurant,** 949 Second Ave., at 53rd Street (tel. 421-8425), is no ordinary Greek coffeeshop. While the interior reverts to familiar bright Formica tables and brown booths, the wide variety of dishes is anything but "run of the mill."

Everything from breakfast dishes to hamburgers is served throughout the day. Try the special feta cheese with tomato omelet for $4.65. For a full meal, order the breaded veal cutlet ($6.65) or the Yankee pot roast ($3.95). Roast sirloin costs $6.95, and is served with potato, vegetable, and a salad. There are also Greek specialties like shrimp à la Santorini ($9.95). Hamburger specials cost between $2.05 and $4.55. Try the homemade baklava or galaktoboureko for dessert ($1.25).

The Electra is open from 6 a.m. to 1 a.m. weekdays, until 2 a.m. on weekends.

For 1920s-style decor, visit **Knickers,** 928 Second Ave., between 49th and 50th Streets (tel. 223-8821). Once a speakeasy, the restaurant is now run by the Halberian family, who have owned it for over 20 years. The dining room, located behind a mahogany bar room, has an authentic old-world feel, complete with an art deco chandelier, wall sconces, and antique Chinese porcelains.

Members of the Halberian family can be seen chatting with regular customers at the bar, and they are ready to furnish newcomers with information about the restaurant's history. They'll even take you to see the hidden escape door where Prohibition customers made speedy exits.

Prices are fairly high, but the chef's salad ($6.95) and the marinated chicken salad ($6.95) make full meals. Sandwich platters range in price from $4.95 to $7.95, and desserts are about $2.75. Brunch, served on Sunday, is a terrific bargain. For as little as $5.75 you can have eggs Benedict smothered in creamy hollandaise sauce and served with home-fried potatoes. Coffee and a choice of a Bloody Mary or two glasses of champagne are included with all seven brunch entrees.

Open from noon to 4 a.m. daily. Reservations suggested.

For a quick sandwich in art deco surroundings, try the **Horn and Hardart Automat,** 200 E. 42nd St., at Third Avenue (tel. 599-1665). Food at the Automat is dispensed from glass boxes decorated with art deco mirrors. Coffee pours with a turn of a crank and comes out of ornate dolphin-shaped spouts.

To "order," you must go to a central booth and buy silver and brass tokens to use in the machines, although some dispensers accept quarters. Hot sandwiches cost $3.80 and up; cold sandwiches, between $2 and $3; bread and butter, 35¢; and pie, 90¢. There's a stand for **David's Cookies** where fresh-baked cookies with mouthwatering names are sold for $1.65 per quarter pound.

Open daily from 6 a.m. to 10 p.m.

Despite its name, the **Alpine Tavern,** 131 E. 45th St., between Lexington and Third Avenues (tel. 986-9725), does not serve Swiss food. But the fare here is simple, inexpensive, and well suited to this New York pub-restaurant. The pub section is large and often filled with boisterous sports fans who gather on weeknights to watch the large TV screen. Look for daily specials like the chicken-and-ribs platter for $6.80. Quiche is served with salad for $4.95, and the slices look like they equal a quarter of the pie. A wide assortment of hamburgers —some with bleu, swiss, and cheddar cheeses—range in price from $3.25 to $3.75. Onion rings ($1.25 for a basket side order) are juicy and come in generous portions. Dessert is not served. If your initials match those displayed at the bar, you get a free lunch.

Open from 9 a.m. to 4 a.m. Monday through Friday, from noon to 4 a.m. on Saturday and Sunday.

Decorated with green plants and simple blond-wood furniture, the **Something Else Eatery,** 1 East 43rd St., off Fifth Avenue (tel. 661-3420), is the place to go for a relaxed atmosphere and fresh, satisfying food. Try one of the many crêpes as an entree or dessert. The broccoli Italiano crêpe ($4.25) and the asparagus Italiano crêpe ($4.80) are filled with ricotta and mozzarella cheese and topped with tomato sauce. The curry chicken crêpe ($3.95) combines chicken, potato, and onion in a mild curry sauce. There is even a moussaka crêpe, which is a deliciously unorthodox mixture of the classic Greek dish and the traditional French pancake ($4.15). For those with a bigger appetite, we suggest the chopped steak, served with vegetable of the day and a baked potato. Something Else features numerous breakfast items, ranging in price from $1.50 to $2.40.

Open from 7 a.m. to 7 p.m. weekdays, to 3 p.m. on Saturday. Closed Sunday.

With a name like **Joe Burns' Restaurant and Art Gallery,** 903 First Ave., at 51st Street (tel. 759-6696), you might expect to find this eatery hidden away in Greenwich Village somewhere. True to its name, the restaurant displays Joe Burns's works on the walls. They are brightly colored paintings of houses done with childlike simplicity. Diners are encouraged to try their hand at drawing. Bright-yellow tablecloths are covered with white paper, and every table is set with a glass of Crayola crayons so you can design your own placemat.

Owner Joe Burns has created a menu that caters to the budget-conscious with delicious but simple fare in generous portions. To start, try the artichoke vinaigrette ($2.95). Then move to the all-you-can-eat tortellini or ravioli ($6.95), or the all-you-can-eat fettuccine or linguine ($4.95). Homemade chicken pot pie is $6.75 and cold smoked trout runs $6.95. For a lighter meal, try the avocado and chicken platter, with fresh chunks of white meat under a creamy house dressing ($6.95). For dessert, we suggest the apple-walnut pie ($2.50). Coffee here is $1 per cup.

Lunch is served from noon to 2:30 p.m. on weekdays and dinner is from 4 p.m. to 1 a.m. With some exceptions, the menu and prices remain the same for both meals. Brunch is served on Saturday from noon to 4:30 p.m. and on Sunday from 10 a.m. to 4 p.m.

Jr. Dallas' 8 Oz. Burgers, 250 E. 58th Street, between Third and Second Avenues (tel. 980-1421), is a great burger house, which also serves hearty breakfast and dinner basics. The restaurant is nicely attired (for a burger house) in oak tables, an oak counter, and tiled floors. The burger patties, which weigh no less than eight ounces, are made from huge mounds of lean red meat, slowly grilled with whatever extras you can think of ordering. The house specialty is the East Side burger, with bacon, cheese, ham, mushrooms, and fried onions for $5.30. Burger items come as a platter with french fries, lettuce, and tomatoes for about $1 extra. For breakfast, french toast with ham and two eggs is $4.05.

Breakfast hours are 6 to 11 a.m. The restaurant closes at 10 p.m. daily.

On the rise in New York are charcoal grill houses like **Checkers Char-Grilled Chicken & Ribs,** 1047 Second Ave., between 55th and 56th Streets (tel. 355-0994). The black-and-white tiled restaurant holds a number of small tables, from which you can watch the grill man work in his tall white chef's hat. Special combination plates (served with salad, bread, sauce, and tea) include a half chicken ($4.95) and a half portion of baby back ribs ($6.25).

Open weekdays from 11:30 a.m. to 11 p.m., and on Saturday and Sunday from 3:30 p.m. to 1 a.m.

When the urge for steak and potatoes strikes, try **Kenny's Steak Pub,** 565 Lexington Ave., between 50th and 51st Streets (tel. 355-0666). The old wooden bar in the front of the restaurant is a good place to watch sporting events; when the bar opened in the 1950s, it was a favorite watering hole for pro baseball players. Red-and-white checkered tablecloths and brass fixtures add to the sense that this is a classic steakhouse. Filet mignon at lunch is only $9.95, with dinner prices higher. In addition, you can also get such delicacies as clams on the half-shell or cherrystone clams ($8.50).

Kenny's is open from 7 a.m. to 11 p.m. daily.

If midnight munchies are a problem, try **Jumbo Bagels & Bialys,** 1070 Second Ave., between 54th and 55th Streets (tel. 355-6185). Along with some of the best bagels in the city, the shop in front of the bakery serves bialys, muffins, and croissants, and offers accompanying salads and juices. Any of the dozen types of bagels are 35¢ each, and fruit muffins are 85¢. Whitefish or baked salmon salads are $3.50. For only $3 you can get a lox, bagel, and cream cheese sandwich—the bagel combination New Yorkers adore. No tables, but late-night munchers often sit in the large bay window facing the street.

Open 24 hours daily.

CHINESE: Just around the corner from the U.N. is the **Wan Fu** restaurant, 801 Second Ave., between 42nd and 43rd Streets (tel. 599-1231). It offers reasonable prices and a pleasant, relaxing decor. There are two dining rooms, one at ground level and one up on an interior balcony. The wall-to-wall carpeting is red, but Chinese paintings and murals are of subdued tones. Every table is set with silk flowers.

Lunch platters, served from noon to 3 p.m. on weekdays, range in price from $3 to $4. There's a wide variety of dishes, including spicy diced chicken with broccoli and eggplant with garlic sauce. The house specialties are more expensive ($6.50 to $9). Try the fresh meat and noodle soup ($4.25), or one of the combination platters ($5 to $6.25). The chef will make the dishes only as spicy, as you want and will leave out salt or MSG at your request. There is a small, full bar in the front of the restaurant. The minimum charge is $3.75 to $5 with credit cards.

Open noon to 10:30 p.m. Monday through Thursday, till 11:30 p.m. on Friday, and till 10:30 p.m. on weekends. Reservations are suggested at lunch.

We are told that for Hunan cuisine, U.N. diplomats often frequent **Peng Teng**, 219 E. 44th St., between Second and Third Avenues (tel. 682-8050). The spacious restaurant has served Henry Kissinger, and the restaurant's owner, Peng, used to cook for Chiang Kai-shek. The Peng Teng features large dining rooms and china place settings, with plants and carved-wood dividers. The atmosphere is dignified but unpretentious.

Food prices run on the high side of our budget, but are worth the splurge. The chef's specialties tend to be expensive while à la carte dishes are cheaper. Try shredded chicken with garlic sauce for $8.95. Vegetable dishes, like braised vegetable hearts and mushrooms with oyster sauce, range in price from $7.50 to $15. The most inexpensive dishes are the rice and noodle dishes, which are priced from $6.50 to $11.50.

Hours are noon to 10:30 p.m. daily. There's free parking across the street after 5:30 p.m. We suggest reservations, particularly for lunch on weekdays when the restaurant gets crowded.

True to its name, the **Beijing Duck House,** 144 E. 52nd St., between Lexington and Third Avenues (tel. 759-8260), serves Peking duck throughout the day. There is no need for advance notice, but the limited supply goes on a first-come, first-served basis. The cost is $27 for two people. The restaurant is small, with white tablecloths and fresh red carnations on every table.

The specialty here is the crisp-skinned duck, prepared through a sophisticated process that includes pumping air into the skin before roasting; it's served with thin pancakes. But there are other, less expensive dishes for those who do not want to splurge. Entrees range in price from $6.75 for vegetable dishes to $11.95 for seafood. Poultry dishes average about $8.25. Try the sliced duck meat with green scallions and hoisin sauce ($8.95), a kind of Peking duck without the skin.

Open from noon to 10:30 p.m. Monday to Thursday, to 11:30 p.m. on Friday.

GREEK: One of the best things about **Seven Steps Down**, 231 E. 53rd St., between Second and Third Avenues (tel. 759-3256), is the family feel of the restaurant. We once went there and found a birth announcement for the proprietor's new baby proudly posted outside. The restaurant is cozily tucked away in a cellar, and there is a hint of the Mediterranean in the white stucco walls and the royal-blue tablecloths. Greek decorator items are hung around the dining room.

The menu, which changes daily, is posted outside. Entrees range from $6 to $10 for lunch, and are about $1 more at dinnertime. Try the bluefish or the sea bass ($7.50). Moussaka is $7, and leg of lamb runs $8. Greek pastries are served for dessert.

Open from noon to 2 p.m. for lunch, 6 to 9 p.m. for dinner. Dinner only on Saturday; closed Sunday.

INDIAN: A man in a turban will usher you through a beautiful wood-and-brass door to the **Tandoor Restaurant,** 40 E. 49th St., between Park and Madison Avenues (tel. 752-3334). Tandoor is elegantly decorated with red plush seats and sculptured wooden beams. The restaurant is owned by two Indian families, the Khibunis and the Aduanis, who live in India but stop in to visit every month or so. The waiters, dressed in suits and ties, are very attentive and willing to explain what the dishes are and which are extra-spicy. The best deal is a lunch buffet, served daily for $9.95. This buffet includes a variety of curry dishes, as well as a cold salad buffet and raita and chutney sauces. The majority of à la carte entree items cost $6.95 to $9.95. Try the lamb kebab for this price, or the chicken curry. The navrattan curry—nine vegetables cooked with nuts and cream—is very good for $6.95. For dessert, we suggest Indian ice cream flavored with saffron and nuts, priced at $2.

Open seven days from noon to 3:30 p.m. for lunch, and every night from 5:30 to 11 p.m. for dinner. We suggest making reservations, especially for large parties.

IRISH: For a taste of Ireland, stroll into **Tommy Makem's Irish Pavilion,** 130 E. 57th Street, between Park and Lexington Avenues (tel. 759-9040). The long dark wooden bar up front leads into a dining area with wooden beams and dark-green decor, which give the area a cozy and earthy feel. The Irish smoked salmon is prepared in the old Gaelic manner with capers and lemon for $6.95. Mixed-grill specialties, including pork or lamb chops, sausage, bacon, black pudding, and kidney and tomatoes, cost $11.75, but they're enough for two persons. Although most of the kitchen help is Chinese, most of the waitresses and barmen speak Irish with a brogue. And folk musicians of international renown, including owner Tommy Makem, play here on a regular basis.

Open from noon to 4 a.m. Monday to Saturday; closed Sunday.

ITALIAN: Jazz up a pasta meal by going to **Mimi's,** 984 Second Ave., at 52nd Street (tel. 688-4692). This Italian piano bar has a glassed-in terrace that looks out onto Second Avenue. Three stained-glass windows from an old temple serve as dividers between the terrace and main dining room. Tables are set with flowers in Perrier bottles. Mimi's has many loyal local patrons, who can often be found singing around the piano. Thursday and Friday are particularly crowded evenings.

Though many of the entrees may strain your budget, pasta dishes range from only $6.50 for spaghetti to $7.75 for fettuccine Alfredo. Chicken parmigiana and cacciatore are both $7.95. For dessert, try spumoni or tortoni, both $3.

Open from noon to 4 a.m. on weekdays, and from 5 p.m. to 1 a.m. on Sunday.

An autographed picture of Frank Sinatra is proudly displayed over the bar at **Eduardo's,** 1140 Second Ave., at 60th Street (tel. 688-7390). The restaurant is located right next to the Roosevelt Island tramway, which may pass by several times during the course of your meal. The restaurant is evenly divided between a large cocktail lounge, complete with rotating fans from the ceiling à la *Casa-*

blanca, and a simply furnished dining room. Tables are covered in bright-red tablecloths with white paper placemats.

Pasta dishes are your best buys here, ranging in price from $4.75 to $6.75. You might want to begin your meal with minestrone soup ($1.75). Pizza is also served, with small-size pizzas from $6 to $6.75 and large pizzas from $8 to $9. Seafood and chicken dishes cost between $6 and $9.25, and there are a wide number of veal dishes starting at $7. For dessert, we suggest the cheesecake ($1.50) or the tortoni ($1.25).

Eduardo's serves the same menu at lunch and dinner. Open Monday through Saturday from noon to 2 a.m., and on Sunday from 2 p.m. to 2 a.m.

Ray's Original Pizza, 961 Second Ave., at 51st Street (tel. 752-2143), serves thick Sicilian and thin Neapolitan pizzas that will make you forget Mama Leone. Ray's is frequented by customers wearing everything from Gucci's to rollerskates as the night wears on; rock music plays at a reasonable decibel, and the tables are simple. Pizzas start at $8.50; sausage, ricotta and mozzarella cheese, green peppers, eggplant, and spinach are among the toppings and fillings you can order. You can also get calzones—a small "pizza-hero" sandwich—for $3 and up.

Ray's is open daily from 10 a.m. to about 2 a.m.

Café Fonduta, 120 E. 57th St., near Lexington Avenue (tel. 935-5699), offers light northern Italian fare and a pleasant atmosphere for conversation before or after the theater. Owner Luis Levero will usher you into the restaurant past a glass cabinet stocked with an excellent section of Californian, French, and Italian wines. Be sure to taste the pasta dishes. Among them: rigatti a quattro formaggio, with cheddar, swiss, fontina da osta, and parmesan cheeses, mushrooms, and zucchini ($8.50); tagliarini and chopped spinach in a light cream sauce ($8.50); fettuccine Alfredo with vegetables and a cream sauce ($8.80); and angel-hair fonduta, a mixture of pasta, tomatoes, and basil ($8.50).

Open weekdays from 11 a.m. to 10 p.m., and on Saturday from 11:30 a.m. to 4 p.m. Closed Sunday.

JAPANESE: A small stone fountain is the first thing you'll see in the front window of **Yodo of Japan,** 13 E. 47th St., between Madison and Fifth Avenues (tel. 751-8775). Inside, you'll find a full bar and a sushi bar, decorated with autographed pictures of famous Japanese stars who frequent the restaurant when they're in town. The dining room at the back of the restaurant has separate booths with soft lighting that enhances the cozy atmosphere.

For lunch, try the hot-pot dishes, which offer a variety of items at low prices. The salmon and vegetable stew flavored with sake is $5.75. Sliced beef, vegetables, and noodles with sukiyaki sauce is $6. Broiled mackerel is $5.75, and broiled salmon with butter costs $6.25. Dinners are more expensive, but come with soup, tempura, pickles, rice, and dessert. Try the shrimp and vegetables for $6 or the chilled bean cake (which can also be ordered cooked in seaweed soup) for $7.50.

Open weekdays from noon to 2:30 p.m. for lunch, from 5 to 10:30 p.m. for dinner, and on Sunday from 5 to 10 p.m. Closed Saturday.

The **Larmen Dosanko Noodle Shop,** 423 Madison Ave., between 48th and 49th Streets (tel. 688-8575), features huge steaming bowls of noodles mixed with a variety of meats and vegetables. The decor is informal, with seats at the counter up front or in orange booths toward the back. While the Dosanko chain may strike you as the Japanese equivalent of "fast food," the noodles are good, inexpensive, and filling.

There are four larmen noodle dishes to choose from, and you can order any of them with beef or pork for between $4.10 and $4.30. The chef's special, which changes daily, is $5.40. You can also order combination platters for between $4.95 and $5.40. Ice cream is served for dessert for $1.40. Alcoholic beverages are also served ($1.45 to $2).

Open 11:30 a.m. to 10 p.m. Monday through Friday, and from noon to 8 p.m. on weekends. There are several Larmen Dosankos located elsewhere in the city.

Modern and stylish, **Hatsuhana,** 17 E. 48th St., between Fifth and Madison Avenues (tel. 355-2967), offers exciting Japanese cuisine that is beautifully served. If you eat at the sushi bar, your orders will be served on ti leaves from Hawaii. The decor includes individual booths with blond-wood dividers and round portholes.

Prices are a little high, but the food is worth the splurge. At $9, luncheon specials are your best deal. A tempura luncheon special with fried shrimp, seafood, and vegetables is $12 to $16. Salmon teriyaki is the same price. Dinners are more expensive, with specials ranging from $14.50 to $18. There are sushi items on the dinner menu for $11; sushi à la carte is $1.50 to $2 per piece.

Open Monday through Friday from 11:45 a.m. to 2:30 p.m. for lunch, and from 5:30 to 9:30 p.m. for dinner. Weekend hours are 5 to 9:30 p.m. Reservations suggested.

Shima of Japan, 213 E. 45th St., between Second and Third Avenues (687-0127), serves a full menu of Japanese cuisine at reasonable prices, not always the case for sushi houses outside the Village. The decoration includes a number of objects that owner-chef Y. Endo brought from Japan, including wooden masks, fine basketry, and prints. The restaurant is fairly dark, but a large fish tank with vivid goldfish lights up the center of the table area in front of the sushi bar. Popular for his lunchtime specials, Endo even serves vegetable sushi, a concoction he claims to have originated in New York to keep up with health and diet crowds. Avocado, squash, and tofu are among the many veggies with which Endo lovingly crowns his sushi. Sashimi and teriyaki are $4.25 and $8 during lunch; a sukiyaki dinner is $8.75. Appetizers like fried softshell crab at $4.75 are plentiful.

Hours are noon to 3 p.m. for lunch and 5 to 10:30 p.m. for dinner Monday through Saturday. Closed Sunday.

MEXICAN: Good Mexican restaurants are scarce in New York, so the wide range of dishes offered at **Bonampak,** 235 E. 53rd St., between Second and Third Avenues (tel. 838-1433), makes it a special find indeed. The small basement restaurant, run by Francisco Reynos and his family, is simply decorated with lush plants in the window, and Mexican pottery and other curios displayed in nooks and crannies along the stucco walls. Pretty colored blown-glass lamps give off a warm glow to the relaxed, unpretentious atmosphere.

Bonampak offers entrees with exotic sauces. Try the chicken in unsweetened chocolate sauce for $7.35 or the beef with lime and garlic juice for $7.35. Combination platters with tacos, tostadas, burritos, and tamales are reasonably priced at $6.95 at lunchtime. For dessert, we suggest the mangos flambés for $2.50. The lunch and dinner menus are virtually the same, with dinner prices 25¢ to 40¢ higher than lunch prices. The menu is written in both Spanish and English, and the staff is quite willing to answer any questions.

Open from noon to 10 p.m. Monday through Friday, on Saturday from 5 to 10 p.m. Closed Sunday.

MIXED BAG: For relief from the hustle of midtown, the **Citicorp Center,** which covers the block from 53rd to 54th Streets, bordered by Lexington and Third Avenues, is a greenery-filled escape. The three-story skylit atrium below the shimmering steel office tower with a dramatically angled roofline, is a bustling, but not hectic, arcade of shops and restaurants. Citicorp sponsors frequent concerts and exhibits in the central public space, and tables and chairs are scattered about, suited to brown-bagging and people-watching.

If you bring your own lunch, you can top it off with a freshly baked chocolate-chip cookie from the **Famous Chocolate Chip Cookie** on the third level. Variations on the chip theme are 40¢ apiece and $5 a pound. Cookies and pastries are also sold at **Café Buon Giorno** on the main level. Soups, sandwiches, and quiche are also served for take-out only. The scents of freshly baked bread wafting across the main floor from **Au Bon Pain** (tel. 838-6996) are enough to send you heading for their take-out croissant sandwiches made with ham, turkey, salami, tuna, and French cheese ($2.75 up). Breads, from rye to challah, are made fresh daily. No seating, only take-out.

If the weather is cooperative, take a stroll to the Citicorp plaza below Lexington Avenue, and stop at the **Bear Café,** famous in midtown for its cinnamon coffee at 50¢ a cup ($4.50 by the pound). The Bear also features stuffed potatoes, filled with your choice of nacho cheese, chili jalapeños, or sour cream ($2.50). You can load the same toppings on a foot-long hot dog ($2). Homemade soups include chicken vegetable and gazpacho. And to go with the fragrant coffee, homemade muffins ($1) in every conceivable flavor, from banana to cranberry, are made fresh daily.

Open daily from 5:30 a.m. until 7 p.m. (closes earlier on rainy days, and from December until April). Chairs and tables fill the plaza in warm weather, so you can have your lunch al fresco.

For less casual fare, there are seven other restaurants to choose from inside the Citicorp Center. Some can be expensive, but most offer weekly specials well worth the visit.

Auberge Suisse (tel. 421-1420) is an elegant restaurant, specializing in Swiss and French dishes. Prices are high for entrees, but dishes include a salad. A unique specialty here is fondue for two, for $22, which includes a salad and fresh, crusty bread for dipping into the bubbling cheese concoction. Other specialties include suprême de volaille en croûte, a breast of chicken in pastry with tomatoes and gruyère cheese, for $12.50; and veal sausage, St. Gallen style, with potatoes and onions, for $10. Dessert here is truly a treat, thanks to the chocolate fondue, to be shared by two with fresh dippable fruit like strawberries for $9.50. Appetizers are also unusual and reasonably priced, and two are ample for a meal. A beignet de fromage, a pastry filled with gruyère cheese and homemade tomato sauce, is $4. Duck mousse à l'orange is $4.50. There is a minimum of $10 per person.

Open Monday through Saturday from noon to 2:30 p.m. and 5 to 10:30 p.m.

Avergino's (tel. 688-8828), with white stucco walls and colorful hangings, and a kitchen open to full view, serves authentic Greek food like taramosalata, fish roe dip, at $3.95 for an appetizer (but ample) portion, stuffed grape leaves at $3.95 as an appetizer, and moussaka at $8.95. Lunch and dinner menus vary by a few dollars, with most entrees in the $8.95 to $10.95 range. Lunchtime here is sometimes frenetic, but always fun, with Greek music and waiters at your service. There is a $5.75 minimum per person from 11:30 a.m. until 2 p.m.

Open daily from 11:30 a.m. until 10:30 p.m.

Charley O's Bar and Grill (tel. 752-2102) has the feeling of an old pub: dark-green walls, copper lamps, brass-framed mirrors, and a large round clock.

Tables in the dining room sport crisp white tablecloths and individual booths are separated by etched-glass dividers. Checkered-glass skylights in the back take in lots of natural light in the daytime.

Main courses at lunchtime are priced between $6.75 and $14.25. Meat sandwiches and hamburgers run between $5.95 and $11.50. You can also get large salads for $6.50 to $9.15, and omelets for $7.95. Desserts run between $2.50 and $2.95. Dinner entrees are slightly higher than at lunch; between $8.25 and $15.95. There's a free hot and cold buffet (appetizers and hors d'oeuvres) during Happy Hour after 6 p.m. in the bar.

Open from 11:30 a.m. to 3 p.m. for lunch, from 5 to 9 p.m. for dinner on weekdays, from noon to 4 p.m. for brunch and 4 to 8 p.m. for dinner on the weekends.

The Market (tel. 935-1744) has a stand-up counter with tables, where you can get coffee and pastry as well as a limited number of sandwiches. Sandwiches run between $3.95 and $4.25. Pita specials (tuna melt, etc.) run between $4.25 and $5. Pastries range from 90¢ to $1.50. There's a $1 minimum to sit at the large red booths.

Hours are 8 a.m. to 9 p.m. on weekdays, and 10 a.m. to 6 p.m. on weekends.

Healthworks (tel. 838-6221) is a busy health-food restaurant, brightly decorated with red chairs and green trim. There are daily specials like vegetarian lasagne ($5.50), as well as numerous salads and pita platters for $4.50 to $4.95. Fresh baked goods can be purchased for dessert, along with frozen yogurt. You can order items for take-out, but some take-out prices are more expensive.

Open from 7 a.m. to 9 p.m. weekdays, from 11 a.m. to 9 p.m. on Saturday, and from 11 a.m. to 6 p.m. on Sunday.

Alfredo's (tel. 371-3367), whose founder in Rome lays claim to the original recipe for fettuccine Alfredo, specializes—naturally—in pasta. Best bets here are the special Sunday brunch offerings, served from noon until 4 p.m., and the all-inclusive pasta dinner ($8.95), served on Monday between 3 and 6 p.m. Brunch ($9.50) is a choice of soup, tomato juice or melon, along with either an Italian omelet, lasagna bolognese, or eggplant parmigiana. A Bloody Mary or mimosa is $1. Dessert and coffee are also included. The pasta dinner gives the choice of minestrone or melon, followed by either broccoli with spaghetti, rigatoni al Alfredo, or linguine with mussels. On the regular menu, veal and chicken dishes start around $8.75. Daily specials are $8.95 for dinner and $5.95 for lunch. Lunch is always a good buy, with fettuccine Alfredo at $8.95 and an ample medium-sized portion at $5.95. Salads are included with specials.

Open from 11:30 a.m. until 11:30 p.m. weekdays and Saturday, on Sunday, from noon until 11:30 p.m.

Les Tournebroches (tel. 758-3265) is a quiet French enclave in the midst of the hustle of the Citicorp Center. Prices here can be high, but an evening special dinner for $8.75 is a bargain. It includes soup du jour, choice of roasted half chicken, fish of the day, or mixed-grille brochette, salad, and coffee. Hors d'oeuvres here are also delicious, with pâté and la truite fumée for $5.50. Clam chowder is $3.25; French onion soup, $3.50. Grilled swordfish is $15.50. The prices are all in the $13.95 to $14.95 range. Wine is $10 a carafe and is also sold by the glass. Lunch has a minimum of $10.50 per person.

Open from 10 a.m. to 5:45 p.m. Monday through Saturday. Closed Sunday.

Oscar's Salt of the Sea II (tel. 371-2201) is a cousin of Oscar's at 1153 Third Ave., and has the same fresh seafood. Appetizers—like clams, served steamed or on the half shell—range from $3.75 to $4.25, and a crabmeat cocktail is $8.95.

Oysters are also served in season. Salads, shrimp, crabmeat, and lobster range in price from $13.95 to $18.95. Sirloin steak for those planted firmly on the ground is $15.95, and chicken is $10.95. Fried or broiled fish, such as scrod, sole, or snapper, is about $8.95. A combo fish plate is $10.95. Swordfish steak "Oscar" is $14.95. Lobster here is $18.75.

Open daily from noon to 10 p.m.

NATURAL FOODS: The **Salad Bowl,** 717 Lexington Ave., between 57th and 58th Streets (tel. 752-0777), is a natural vegetarian restaurant run by four brothers from Turkey. A number of tables are available at the back of the narrow but bright and cheery restaurant, which caters to a large breakfast and lunch crowd. Combination platters—a sandwich or hot dish, with a salad—are $4; and you can get soups, quiches, and hot-dish specialties like curried chickpeas and eggplant casserole, also in the $4 range. Frozen yogurt and a variety of fresh juices including carrot, celery, and cucumber are available for $1 to $2.

Open Monday to Friday from 8 a.m. to 8 p.m., on Saturday from 10 a.m. to 7 p.m. Closed Sunday.

Naturally beautiful people flock to the **Au Natural** at the corner of Second Avenue and 55th Street (tel. 832-2922), where butcher-block tables, tiles, mirrors, and fresh flowers give the place the feel of a designer's kitchen nook. Among the many entrees are soybean steak and vegetables for $7.25, boiled Boston scrod for $8.50, and vegetable fettuccine for $8. Salads, omelets, yogurt, and juices round out the menu. Sunday brunch features cottage cheese blintzes for $6.50, and eggs Benedict au naturel with a country chicken sausage patty for $8.

Hours are 8 a.m. to midnight daily, with brunch served on Sunday from 10 a.m. to 3 p.m.

SEAFOOD: Boasting fresh fish that's caught right off Montauk Point, **Hobeau's,** 988 Second Ave., between 52nd and 53rd Streets (tel. 421-2888), is a midtown seafood find, if you don't mind a packed house. With a typically nautical interior, Hobeau's is best for lunch, as dinner prices generally run $1 or $1.50 more for most dishes, and the service is fast and no-nonsense. (You're even entitled to a free cocktail if your waiter doesn't tell your his name or forgets to take your drink order—it doesn't happen often.) Fish is it at Hobeau's, and from fried shrimp stuffed with crabmeat ($5.95) to a mixed seafood platter ($7.95), the fish is the main attraction. There are also poultry and beef entrees—from $3.75 for a hamburger platter to steak teriyaki for $6.95, duck with orange sauce for $7.95, and steak and crab legs for $9.95. Appetizers include oysters Rockefeller (75¢ each) and baked mushrooms stuffed with shrimp and crabmeat ($2.75). Lobsters range from $9.45 for a 1¼-pound crustacean to $13.95 for a two-pounder. Twin pound-and-a-quarters are $14.95 ($5 charge for sharing twin lobsters). Brunch, which comes with a half carafe of Bloody Marys, screwdrivers, wine, or beer, is $4.25 on Saturday, Sunday, and holidays. Midnight brunch is $5.25.

Hobeau's is open for lunch from 11:30 a.m. until 4 p.m. Monday through Sunday and holidays; brunch, 11:30 a.m. until 4 p.m. on Saturday, Sunday, and holidays; dinner, 4 p.m. until 3 a.m. daily; and midnight brunch from midnight until 3 a.m. Monday through Sunday.

The graceful arches of Grand Central Station are echoed in the **Oyster Bar and Restaurant** in the station's lower concourse (tel. 490-6650). Here the tiled arches are festooned with white lights, giving them an added elegance. The large restaurant has a main dining room, counter service for quick meals, a cocktail lounge, and a redwood-paneled saloon. Opened in the 1930s when trains were widely used, the restaurant serves up seafood with style. There is a take-out booth modeled after a ship's deck for commuters on the go.

The seafood is all fresh, and the menu changes daily to accommodate the current catch. Prices are high, but you can get oyster stew for $8.45 and pan-roasted oysters for $8.95. Broiled fish runs between $10.95 and $18.95, and main dishes like bouillabaisse and coquille St. Jacques are $15.95. If you want to go all out, try the full shore dinner with clam chowder, steamers, and a whole lobster for $18.95 (available after 5 p.m.). Lobster is $16.95 a pound.

Open Monday through Friday from 11:30 a.m. to 10:30 p.m. The last seating is at 9:30 p.m., and reservations should be made for both lunch and dinner.

3. Upper East Side and Yorkville

East of Central Park at Fifth Avenue, between 61st and 90th Streets, is what New Yorkers call the Upper East Side. Once pooh-poohed by Village and SoHo types who found it too plastic and scorned by Upper West Siders proud to be "roughing it," the Upper East Side has a chic all its own. It is home to young professionals and established executives. On Madison Avenue in the 60s you'll find some of the world's most exclusive shops, and on Park Avenue you'll see the brass shingles of Park Avenue doctors, renowned for their skill—and fees! And you'll also find traces of old German New York, in the 80s along First and Second Avenues in the area still known as Yorkville. Along the East River there is everything from modest apartments of five-story walkups to the beautiful homes of Sutton Place—some of the most expensive real estate in the country. The East Side is also home to the mayor. Gracie Mansion, his manor house at 89th Street and East End Avenue, is the last remaining 19th-century country seat on the East River. It's no longer country up here, but there's lots of good walking—and eating—to be done!

AMERICAN/CONTINENTAL: Exclusive Park Avenue has a neighborhood secret in the Armory at 643 Park Ave. at 66th Street—a restaurant with good food at reasonable prices. It's the **Seventh Regiment Mess** (tel. 744-4107), run by the U.S. Army! In spite of all the combat fatigues you'll see in the Armory, the public is welcome and the mood at ease. We think you'll agree that the Mess is a unique find!

You can't miss the Armory—this 19th-century red-brick building occupies the whole block. You enter through massive wooden doors studded with iron. Tell one of the soldiers inside the door that you'd like to go to the Mess—he'll show you to the elevator to the left side of the Great Hall. Take time to look around. The Grand Staircase is grand indeed, and the Great Hall is full of antique cannons, military portraits, and flags that are black with age and so thin you can see through them. The Mess is on the fourth floor.

You can take a drink first in the long lounge, where there are comfortable green tweed sofas, red leather chairs, and small metal plaques on the walls honoring members of the Seventh. The dining room, like the lounge, has a beamed ceiling, half-timbered walls, and mounted heads of long-dead moose and rams. The dining room also has a beautiful wood floor, tables covered with red and white linen, and pleasant waitresses. Entrees come with tomato juice, consommé, or the day's soup, as well as a vegetable, potato, and coffee. Most prices are under $9. Choices include scrod or fried butterfly shrimp ($9 each), baked manicotti ($5.50), chicken à la Seventh au gratin ($7), and chef's salad ($5.25). Desserts are $1.75.

The Mess is open weekdays only, from 5 to 9 p.m. *(Note:* The restaurant closes for the summer, late June until Labor Day.)

The original **Mumbles,** 1622 Third Ave., at 91st Street (tel. 427-4355), has been home-away-from-home for legions of East Side singles, many of whom live just down the block in the massive Ruppert Towers. Mumbles even looks homey, with wooden shingles inside and out, multipaned windows with lots of plants in them, a timbered ceiling, a well-trod wood floor, and small tables covered with yellow-and-white checkered cloths. Most of Mumbles' menu and all the specials are written on blackboards—the fare runs from hamburgers to veal marsala. Most items cost less than $7.95. (See the Murray Hill/Gramercy Park section for more details on the extensive menu.)

Mumbles keeps longer hours than most of us did at home, however. It's open daily from noon to 4 a.m. Food is available at all hours, but for the day's specials, come before 11 p.m. After that you can still have sandwiches, salads, and steaks. No reservations.

The newest **Mumbles,** 1491 Second Ave., at 78th Street (tel. 772-8817), is all white and airy. You can dine inside near the bar or in a glass-enclosed terrace decorated with lush green plants. When the weather's warm, the sidewalk surrounding the restaurant becomes a lively outdoor café—an excellent spot to relax and people-watch. Open daily from 11:30 p.m. till 4 a.m.

The Green Kitchen, 1477 First Ave., at 77th Street (tel. 988-4163), is a fancy coffeeshop with something for everyone. There's an oval-shaped area with your basic booth set-up; but there's also a small bar, and an attractive restaurant-style porch with tablecloths, fresh flowers, and glass walls.

The extensive menu also has a little of everything. There are "Famous Salads," priced from $4.05 to $9.25, and sandwiches for $1.50 and up. Most popular here are the daily chef's specials. For $5.95 you can have your choice of entree—veal, beef, pasta, chicken, or fish—served with potato or vegetable. The dessert choices are vast, with prices starting at 95¢. All desserts are baked on the premises. Chocolate cheesecake, assorted pastries, fruit pies, layer cakes, and cookies are under glass and temptingly on display.

The Green Kitchen is open 24 hours daily. And there's brunch too, from noon to 4 p.m. on weekends, for $3.50 and up.

Bagels Plus, 1367 Third Ave., at 78th Street (tel. 744-6114), combines the unlikely duo of deli foods and natural foods—and makes it work. It's a kind of fast-food cafeteria, with lots of butcher-block tables and pine captain's chairs to sit at. Mirrors, a ceramic tile floor, and pine paneling give it a modern appearance. Bagels Plus sandwiches come, of course, on bagels (plain, sesame, poppy, onion, pumpernickel, and cinnamon-raisin), or on rye or whole-wheat bread. Many sandwiches are priced under $2. There's also shrimp salad, chopped liver, and hot pastrami, all under $3. You can have a knish for 85¢, a buttered bagel for 55¢. Quiche is $1.75, and an omelet of ham, salami, swiss, or muenster cheese with a buttered bagel is $2.35. Olive salad is 95¢; three-bean salad, 75¢; and a salad platter, $3.25. You can also have fresh-squeezed orange or carrot juice, and cheesecake or apple pie for dessert. The morning special, available until 11 a.m., includes eggs, bagel, coffee and juice for $1.85.

Bagels Plus is open daily from 7 a.m. to 6 p.m.

The **Bantry Bar and Restaurant,** 161 E. 86th St., between Lexington and Third Avenues (tel. 722-3771), has a devoted neighborhood following and is a bargain to boot. The Bantry has a sense for the bright side, literally—an outside chalkboard posts the day's weather report for all who pass by. There's also a mounted clipping that honors a mysterious hero of the 1982 plane crash at National Airport. There is no menu at the Bantry—you read it on chalkboards and order by sight from the fresh-looking choices at the steam counter by the door.

Waitress service is available in the dining area to the rear. Regulars at the long bar to the left chat or watch the several TVs, usually tuned to the news or to sports. There's even a giant color screen on the back wall. Decor at the Bantry is simple—a beamed ceiling, leaded colored windows at the entrance, a few objects on the white walls, a linoleum floor.

Prices are low but the quality is high—a sandwich of roast sirloin or Virginia ham with a choice of the day's soup or potato salad or cole slaw is $3.99. Roast chicken with rice and Mexican beans is $5; a roast sirloin dinner is $5.50. All entrees come with a choice of two vegetables and bread and butter. The waitress will tell you the day's desserts, all at very low prices. Draft beer goes for 85¢ to $1.65.

Open Monday through Saturday from 8 a.m. to 3 a.m., and on Sunday from noon to 3 a.m. There is waitress service until 11 p.m. daily. For chops, roasts, pastrami, meatballs—and a helping of Irish accents on the side—the Bantry is hard to beat.

It may have something to do with the way New Yorkers look at the rest of the world. There's only one real Jackson Hole, but there are **Jackson Hole Hamburger Restaurants** all over the Upper East Side. They're everything from the very small original restaurant to the glass-walled spaciousness of the one at 91st Street and Madison Avenue. They all have attractive if simple decor, ski posters of a Wyoming ski resort, and good, inexpensive hamburgers. Prices range from $3 to $8.50 (the highest the menu goes), but most are $5 or less. There's lots more: eggs and omelets for $1.80 to $5.25, sandwiches for $1.20 to $3.60, honey-dipped fried chicken with salad and french fries for $5.50, and salads, desserts, and beer and wine.

There are Jackson Holes at 232 E. 64th St., between Second and Third Avenues (tel. 371-7187), and at 1633 Second Ave., at 85th Street (tel. 737-8788). Open daily from 10:30 a.m. to 1 a.m., till midnight on Sunday. The Jackson Hole at the corner of Madison Avenue and 91st Street (tel. 427-2820) is open daily from 7 a.m. to 11 p.m. There is another restaurant in Murray Hill and one on the West Side at 86th Street and Columbus Avenue. Reservations not needed.

J. G. Melon, 1291 Third Ave., at 74th Street (tel. 650-1310), is made irresistibly charming by its profusion of—what else?—melons, in painting, in neon, even in the real thing. A few retired squash racquets and other objects also hang on the brown walls, but the decor is really given over to the kith and kin of watermelons, etc. J. G. simply stands for the owners, Jack and George. We think the restaurant (really more of a pub) is delightful. It's especially nice to get one of the four tables up front in the bar room, tucked on a platform under mullioned windows. Tables are covered with green-and-white checkered cloths, and the high ceiling is reddish tin—perhaps in keeping with the melon motif.

The tiny kitchen is smack in the middle, across from the bar. From it comes simple fare. There's no menu—you make your choices from the blackboard listings. A hamburger is $4.10; a bacon burger, $4.75. A roast beef sandwich is $4.75. A chef's or Niçoise salad is $7.25; a chicken salad, $6.75. Chili is $3.10 by the cup, $3.50 by the bowl. There are also entrees like a cornish hen with potato and salad for $8.75. For dessert, there are pies ($3.25) and cheesecake ($3.75).

J. G. Melon is open Monday through Saturday from 11:30 a.m. to 2:30 a.m. The West Side J. G. Melon (at Amsterdam and 76th Street) kitchen is open till 1:30 a.m. Both restaurants open at noon on Sunday.

We are curious about only one thing at J. G. Melon—why no melon liqueur at the bar? The bartender didn't know.

T.G.I. Friday's, 1152 First Ave., at 63rd Street (tel. 832-8512), was New York's first singles bar. It's still a show-stopping landmark, in an outrageously blue corner building with red-and-white candy-striped awnings at every window. Friday's has mellowed with the years and the proliferation of other singles bars, but the small tables are still great for an intimate rendezvous and the waiters (decked out almost as outrageously as the building) are still flirty. Friday's decor is a fun hodgepodge of Victoriana.

The menu is printed in a spiral notebook full of suggestions for solid American fare. Prices are reasonable. There are 14 ways to order a hamburger, including the "name your own"; a platter with french fries and onion rings is $6.50. Burgers come on an English muffin or on hamburger buns. Salads are $6.75 and up. The steak salad ($8.25) might even change the minds of those who think that salads are wimpy rabbit food. Four-egg omelets with fries, rolls and butter, and a salad start at $6.50.

Entrees include London broil for $8.75, the catch of the day with spinach and mushrooms for $9.25 (we've seen lots higher), and a light fruit-and-cottage-cheese salad for $7.50. The "Outrageous Dessert" is just that—chocolate pudding spooned with chocolate chunks, marshmallows, and whipped cream ($2.75). Or turn to the back page to take your chocolate in liquid form—the Chocolate Monkey's ice cream/banana/chocolate liqueur concoction ($4.75) is worth hanging around for.

If that's not enough there is also brunch—juice; french toast; three eggs; ham, bacon, or sausage; English muffin; coffee or tea; and a Bloody Mary or all the champagne you can drink—for $8.75.

Open daily from 11:30 a.m. to 1 a.m. On Saturday and Sunday brunch is available from 11:30 a.m. to 4 p.m. The bar is open till 1:30 or 3:30 a.m., depending on the crowd.

Martell's, 1469 Third Ave., at 83rd Street (tel. 861-6110), isn't all blue, but it does have a blue-painted sidewalk that becomes an outdoor café in warm weather. Inside, this former speakeasy is a clutter of Victorian memorabilia and charm. The front room has the usually crowded bar and several tables behind a wood partition. Next is a dining room with walls entirely covered by old posters and signs. Beyond, there are three more rooms, all loosely referred to as the Fireplace Room, and all delightful. One area is rustic, with a pot-bellied stove and a ceiling hung with salamis and dried herbs, followed by a brick-walled room with alcoves and a working fireplace. Last is a more elegant area with stained-glass windows, Victorian chandeliers, and wall sconces.

Dinner entrees, served with a salad, start at about $8.95, but there are many hearty lower-priced sandwiches and omelets. A sour cream and caviar omelet is $6.95; a grilled croissant with Black Forest ham, mozzarella, and swiss is $4.95. A hamburger on pita bread is $4.75, and an order of flat fries, $1.75. Martell's is also popular just for drinks and dessert, especially in the wintertime when people come by for coffee next to the fire. Homemade peanut butter pie, warm apple pie, and the "Total Abandon" chocolate mousse cake are all $3.50 a slice.

On Saturday and Sunday brunch at the "oldest bar in Yorkville" is $8.95, including a drink, an entree, coffee, and dessert.

Martell's is open from 4 p.m. till 4 a.m. Monday through Friday (food served till about midnight). Saturday and Sunday hours are noon to 4 a.m. (food till about 1:30 a.m.). Reservations are not necessary, except for large parties or the Fireplace Room.

Ruppert's, 1662 Third Ave., at 93rd Street (tel. 831-1900), takes its name from the former Jacob Ruppert Brewery, once across the street. Its fame comes from its elegant decor, good food, and refreshing prices. Ruperts is serenely modern, with grays, maroons, and touches of brass at the bar rail and at the stairs to the split-level dining room in back. The two-story ceiling is black and has overhead fans turning lazily. Rupperts' 54-foot bar is stunning—a gleaming mahogany structure that spent its first 50 years in a newspaperman's bar downtown.

Lunch prices are under $7. Quiche with salad is $5.75; an omelet with a wide choice of stuffings is $4.50; an open-face Reuben sandwich is $4.95. There are reasonably priced entrees, such as curried chicken salad with apples and chutney for $6.95 and fettuccine with artichoke hearts for $5.75. The waiter will tell you the day's desserts. At dinner there are entrees like chicken au poivre ($7.75), grilled leg of lamb with mint mustard ($10.50), and chicken pot pie ($8.75). Dinner entrees range from $5.50 to $14.95; appetizers, from $3.25 for strips of chicken breast with honey-mustard sauce to $4.75 for baked whole Little Neck clams.

We think Rupperts is at its most lovely at brunch. There's usually a musician playing—a classical pianist, or a guitarist playing mellow '60s music. There are a variety of omelets ($5.95); other choices include eggs Benedict ($6.95) and smoked salmon, tomato, onion, and cream cheese on a bagel ($7.95). Or you might go light and choose an appetizer of fresh melon ($2.50) and a croissant with fruit preserves ($1.95). Brunch entrees come with a complimentary drink, glass of wine or juice, and coffee or tea.

Rupperts is open daily from 10:30 a.m. to 4 a.m. Lunch is served until 4 p.m., dinner from 5 p.m. to 12:30 a.m. Brunch is Saturday and Sunday from 11 a.m. to 4 p.m. There's also live music Thursday through Saturday nights. Reservations recommended.

Michael's Restaurant-Café, 1412 First Ave., between 74th and 75th Streets (tel. 772-2430), is a pleasant and economical establishment, best for its cold salads (15 varieties) and seafood dishes.

Daily dinner specials range between $7.25 and $9.95; there is a hearty lunch special for $6.25, including soup and salad. Between 6 and 10 p.m. there are early-bird specials for $6.25. Triple-decker sandwiches cost between $4.75 and $5.25. An enormous Greek salad à la Athenian (with feta cheese, anchovies, grape leaves, black olives, and more) costs $5.75. Other Greek specialties include moussaka ($6.95) and spinach pie ($6.45). An excellent English grill (spring lamb chop, liver, sausage, grilled tomato and bacon strips) comes complete with salad and vegetable for $8.95. The seafood menu includes stuffed filet of sole with crabmeat ($8.95), stuffed filet of flounder Florentine ($8.95), and a delicious broiled brook trout ($7.25). Prices for these dinners include salad and vegetables.

Michael's is also a great place to pause for a quick afternoon snack, sitting at sidewalk tables and enjoying delicious homemade pastries (carrot cake is $1.75; mouthwatering blueberry cheesecake is $1.95; baklava is $1.75).

Michael's is open 24 hours, seven days a week.

Rascal's, 1286 First Ave., at the corner of 69th Street (tel. 734-2862), is a large, friendly bar-restaurant that attracts an upscale crowd. It offers a standard continental menu, including pasta, seafood, and chops. Dinner specials, served every night between 5 p.m. and midnight, range from $8.95 to $13.95. On weekends brunch is served from 11:30 a.m. to 5 p.m., offering an entree, rolls and fruit, coffee or tea, and all the Bloody Marys or mimosas you can drink, for $9.95. Sunday brunch is the best bet, because there is live music (jazz).

Rascal's is open from 11:30 a.m. to 4 a.m. seven days a week. Although no reservations are necessary, Rascal's does have a dress code (no sneakers, no faded jeans).

Mr. Babbington's Larder, 1454 First Ave., between 75th and 76th Streets (tel. 737-5110), boasts one of New York City's tiniest dining rooms, with only five tables and 18 seats. The reason is that Mr. Babbington's originally began as a caterer, and still does most of its business with take-out orders. The tables command a full view of the immaculate kitchen facilities, so you can watch your dinner take shape. But the real attraction here is the high quality and low prices of the food. The menu is simple, and each dish is prepared with care. A half chicken grilled with plum sauce is $4.99, and comes with noodles mixed with fresh vegetables or french-fried zucchini or french-fried eggplant, as well as a salad and biscuits or cornbread. Fresh, pit-grilled country rib dinners cost $5.99, complete with the fixings as served with the chicken. Beef dinners cost $4.99, as do fresh fish dinners. Desserts (including carrot cake with currants and nuts, or spicy apple pie with raisins) are only 99¢ each. Soups (including chicken chowder with giblets) are 99¢ a bowl.

Mr. Babbington's is open from 4 to 9:30 p.m. Monday through Saturday.

Jim McMullen's, 1341 Third Ave., near 76th Street (tel. 861-4700), is where many of New York's "beautiful people" go to unwind. This successful restaurant is always crowded with well-dressed people, a sprinkling of celebrities among them. It's an attractive place, with huge vases of flowers, random-width planked floorboards, and exposed brick walls with decorated wood panels. The dining room is more spacious than the elbow-to-elbow bar. Tables are covered with maroon cloths, with white linen set over that. A lavish flower arrangement dresses up each table. Waiters are dressed preppy in blue oxford shirts and khaki pants and skirts. There is also an atrium where you can dine overlooking a garden.

The menu is not inexpensive, so stick to the low side. You might start with clams on the half shell ($3.25 at lunch; $3.75 at dinner), or beef-barley soup or tomato and onion salad ($2.95 at lunch, $3.25 at dinner). Lunch prices start at $4.75 for a club sandwich and go upward of $12. On the low side of the menu—omelets, salads (hot chicken salad with pine nuts gets our attention any day), pastas, and chicken pot pie. Dinner choices range from broiled chicken ($8.25) to shell steak ($16.75). Most prices are in the $10 range. Served with your meal is a bread basket filled with hot buttermilk biscuits and cornbread. Specials change daily, including the wine specials.

This is not the place to skip dessert, thanks to the resident pastry chef. Try the profiteroles ($3.25), chocolate brownie pie ($2.95), or cheesecake ($2.95).

Open daily from 11:30 a.m. till the wee hour of 3 a.m. (food served until 1:45 a.m.). No reservations.

Camelback & Central, 1403 Second Ave., corner of 73rd Street (tel. 249-8380), has a minimalist decor that is somehow perfect for fine dining. The floor is bare wood, but the center banquette is carpeted. Windows are great expanses of glass, and the brick walls are painted a flat gray. A few cactus plants and white candles at the tables are the only decoration, and the art deco bar is the oldest thing to be found. The staff is friendly—chef Allan Katz may even take your reservation on the phone—and the food excellent.

Chef Katz trained at the famed Culinary Institute of America, and spent several years cooking in Key West. He brings a nouvelle-continental touch to the menu that is inspired. There's no need here to go to the high end of the menu to find a superlative dinner (although entrees do go as high as tournedos béarnaise for $17.50). Pasta Camelback is a primavera vegetable combination with snow peas, broccoli, carrots, and pine nuts—healthy and pleasing at $10.95. Vegetable tempura and a roasted herbed chicken with pâté as entrees are also under $10.50. Roast duck with prune stuffing and a port wine-currant sauce is superb ($14.95). Fresh swordfish with herb or anchovy butter ($15.50) is an equal delight; you may also find swordfish as a special with the likes of a caper-and-mushroom sauce—making choices difficult. All entrees come with potato or rice and a vegetable. Desserts here are rich and chocolate-laced—fruit and ice cream parfait with chocolate sauce, apple fritters with chocolate brandy sauce, chocolate sin, and chocolate silk pie (priced $2.75 to $3). Certainly one of the city's best culinary buys is the pre-theater dinner offered from 5 to 6:30 p.m. For $11.95 you have your choice of soups, a salad, a choice of five tempting entrees with potato and vegetable, dessert, and coffee or tea.

Expect the same inspiration in the weekend brunch. For $8.95 you can savor a drink, an appetizer (mostly fruits or fruit-based), and an entree such as sauteed whitefish in strawberry sauce, vegetable tempura, or eggs Benedict. The maître d' will tell you with unabashed pride that it's the best brunch on the East Side. Lunch is simpler than dinner and brunch, and comparably lower in price. The soup of the day is a good opener ($2.25), and there's a seafood antipasto with squid, shrimp, and scallops ($4.25). Lunch entrees are as American as a hamburger with cottage fries ($4.25), and as European as a pâté salad plate ($5.95), the highest priced entree on the luncheon menu.

In the summer, on clear days and mellow Manhattan evenings, the outdoor café is open for lunch, brunch, and drinks.

Lunch is served weekdays from 11:30 a.m. to 3 p.m., and dinner is served daily from 5 p.m. to midnight. Camelback & Central is open for brunch Saturday and Sunday from 11:30 a.m. to 4 p.m.

Reservations are usually required. The name, by the way, comes from a crossroads in Phoenix, Arizona—we're glad it migrated this way.

Agora, 1530 Third Ave., at 87th Street (tel. 860-3425), is not to be missed. "Agora" means marketplace, and that's exactly what owners George and Paul Gorra have created. The turn-of-the-century ice-cream parlor, which you enter through a velvet-curtained archway, is not a replica, but a faithful reassembling of an 1896 parlor that was transported, piece by piece, from Haverstraw, N.Y., to its present Manhattan location. Most impressive is the 20-foot onyx soda fountain on which sits an enormous brass cash register. The dark mahogany cabinetry is supported by onyx columns with gold-leaf trim, and stained-glass windows abound. Tiffany-style lamps, ceiling fans, and elegant beaded chandeliers hang from the high tin ceiling. Adjoining the ice-cream parlor is a smaller, second dining room—a two-tiered windowed café. The restaurant has its share of celebrity customers, and has itself starred in three major motion pictures and over 70 television commercials.

Dinner entrees are mostly under $13. Appetizers, such as the pâté du maison, quiche, or soup du jour, are all $3.95. Hamburger platters and salads range from $6.95 to an avocado shrimp salad at $9.95. Dinner choices also include a filet of sole meunière ($10.95) and chicken sauteed in lemon and chablis ($11.95). A waiter will tell you about the evening's specials. Lunch prices are lower, mostly under $9. A hamburger on pita bread is $4.95; a sliced turkey sandwich with cranberries is $5.50; and quiche with a salad is $7.50. On weekends there's a complete brunch for $9.95, including juice, a drink, choice of entrees (eggs Benedict, omelets, fish of the day), and coffee.

Last, but not least, is the old-fashioned "confectionary menu," a dessert lover's dream. Always available from the ice-cream parlor, there are ice-cream sodas ($3.25) and sundaes ($4.25) and nostalgic favorites—sarsaparilla, egg creams, and birch beer, each $1.

A piano plays a soothing blend of popular contemporary tunes and old standards during weekend brunch, lunch (daily from noon to 3 p.m.), and during dinner on Thursday through Saturday night.

Open Monday through Friday for lunch from 11:30 a.m. till 4 p.m. Dinner is served from 5 till 10:45 p.m. Sunday through Thursday; on Friday and Saturday night the restaurant stays open until 11:45 p.m. Ice cream is served on Saturday until 1 a.m. Brunch hours on Saturday are 11:30 a.m. till 3:45 p.m., and from noon to 3:45 p.m. on Sunday. Dinner reservations suggested.

Note: Before or after your meal, be sure to wander into the charming Agora boutiques. The fine women's and men's apparel is expensive, but there are good sales, and even an occasional bargain. Anyway, it's an ideal place for browsing.

LIGHT AND GRACIOUS:

The Summerhouse, 1269 Madison Ave., at 91st Street (tel. 289-8062), is an airy café with a pleasing simplicity. Ficus trees and ivy, and a stunning carousel horse from bygone days, are in the windows. Tables are set with white linens, fresh flowers, and tiny oil lamps; chairs are turn-of-the-century oak with high backs. A bare terracotta floor and open kitchen keep things informal. Outside, there are two real park benches for conversation.

The menu is appropriately light and summery. The same menu is used for both lunch and dinner. An avocado and bay shrimp sandwich and a curried chicken salad are each priced at $8.50. An omelet filled with spinach and sour cream is $7. A large bowl of soup (spring vegetable or chicken velvet) with a salad is $7.50. Entree prices (chicken, fish, pasta) are about $12.50. For Saturday and Sunday brunch, in addition to the luncheon entrees, there are sweet cream waffles at $5.50, and eggs Benedict at $7.50. A particularly nice touch with every meal is the strawberry butter served with a basket of warm biscuits.

The Summerhouse is open from 11:30 a.m. to 10 p.m., except on Saturday and Sunday when it's open from noon to 10 p.m. Closed Monday. Reservations suggested.

Sarabeth's, 1295 Madison Ave., near 92nd Street (tel. 410-7335), is a pastry-lover's dream. Sarabeth's serves more than mouthwatering, melt-away pastries, however, because it's also a lovely place for a meal—morning, noon, or night. The restaurant is French provincial, with wallpaper flocked with tiny flowers, white table linens, ivory Wedgwood china, and crown moldings with rosettes at the ceiling. There are sprays of fresh flowers in the two bay windows, and the floor is black-and-white marble. If you're lucky the gracious Sarabeth (yes, there *really* is a Sarabeth) will be on hand to advise you about the daily specials.

At Sarabeth's you can have omelets any time of the day, apple butter and cheddar cheese among them, for $3.95 to $6.25. Brunch—including porridge with honey, wheatberries, brown sugar and raisins, and/or bananas—is served until 3 p.m. daily. And for dinner there are daily specials like poached chicken breast in mustard sauce ($10.25) and lemon chicken salad ($8.95).

The pastries can't be missed—even if you have to take your sticky buns, elephant ears, and fabulous double-chocolate-chip cookies home with you! You may also be tempted to buy one of the delicious homemade preserves (even at $8 a jar). Every diner at Sarabeth's is brought a croissant or roll with a generous serving of Sarabeth's award-winning orange-apricot preserves, so you'll get to savor some with your meal.

Sarabeth's is open daily from 9 a.m. to 10:30 p.m. Brunch is served until 3 p.m.; dinner begins at 5:45 p.m. Reservations suggested.

Across the park, the West Side Sarabeth's, 423 Amsterdam Ave. at 80th Street, is a spacious, dressier restaurant with a slightly more extensive menu. The delectable pastries and breads are the same though, and there's a bakery in which to indulge the whims of every sweet-tooth.

Hanratty's, 1410 Madison Ave., near 97th Street (tel. 369-3420), is a congenial neighborhood spot, decorated with tasteful simplicity. The attractive, long wooden bar runs almost the length of the restaurant, and a large blackboard announces the daily specials. You can sit at a table by the window or in the more private dining area beyond the bar. There are candles on the table at dinner, and flowers in Perrier bottles. Waiters and waitresses wear maroon aprons, and if you'd like an apron as a souvenir, see the bartender (they're on sale, along with tote bags, polo shirts, and ski caps, all bearing the Hanratty's logo).

Most of the dinner entrees are available for under $10 and are served with a choice of two side orders—salads, vegetable, potato or rice. The daily pasta and beef specials are about $8; seafood specials are priced at $9 and $10. Always on the menu are sandwiches and salads, from a hamburger on English muffin ($4) to a curried chicken salad ($6.25). You can find out about desserts from the blackboard. Lunch is reasonable with a large selection of hot and cold sandwiches from $3.20 for a hamburger, to $5.50 for the elaborate Hanratty's sandwich (turkey, avocado, bacon, and beansprouts). For a lighter lunch, there's a bowl of chili ($3.50) or homemade soup ($2.25). For weekend brunch, entrees and salads ($6.75 and under) are served with your choice of two drinks.

Open 11 a.m. to 4 p.m. Monday through Friday for lunch, from 11:30 a.m. to 4 p.m. for brunch on weekends. Dinner is served from 5 till 11:30 p.m. daily. The bar closes between 2:30 and 4 a.m., according to the whims and energy levels of the customers.

Head east, and there's another **Hanratty's** at 1754 Second Ave., at 91st Street (tel. 289-3200). The lunch and dinner menus are similar to the other restaurant and only slightly more expensive. A dinnertime hamburger here is $4.95; lemon chicken is $8.95; salad entrees are $6.25 and up. At lunch, potato pancakes or omelets are $4.95; hamburgers are $3.75. What makes this restaurant unique is clearly visible as you walk past the red gingham-covered tables, the long bar, and into the softly lit main dining area where a grand piano reigns. Nightly, Hanratty's is the place to come to hear solo jazz piano. On Friday and Saturday there's music at 9 and 11 p.m. On Sunday through Thursday the music starts at 8:30 p.m. The cover charge is $5. If you're not having dinner, there's a two-drink minimum.

Open from noon till 11:30 p.m. on weekdays, to 12:30 p.m. on weekends, the bar takes its cues for closing time from the crowd.

Another Hanratty's is located on the West Side at 732 Amsterdam Ave., near 96th Street (tel. 864-4224).

CHINESE: Szechuan Kitchen, 1460 First Ave., at 76th Street (tel. 249-4615), is one of those small, favorite eating places that New Yorkers try to keep to themselves. This simple, cozy restaurant is always packed, but everyone's friendly and the wait is worthwhile. If it's a very busy night you'll be issued a number, but there's a bench to sit on which gives you time to decide what to choose as you watch the waiters bustle by with tempting platters of food. The glass-topped tables are close together so it's not unusual here to get to know your neighbors. When we were there, enthusiastic devoted customers were describing entrees to newcomers at adjoining tables.

For starters, try the hot sesame noodles ($3) or the spring roll ($1.20). All the main dishes are reasonably priced; most expensive is the widely praised hot spiced lobster meat at $9.60. Try the chef's special chicken (diced chicken with vegetables and pine nuts) at $6.95, beef with broccoli at $5.90, string beans with garlic sauce at $5.20, or the hot spiced ginger shrimp at $7.20. Fried-rice dishes are $5 and under.

Open daily for dinner only from 5 till 10:30 p.m. No reservations.

High Noon Express, 1291 Lexington Ave., between 86th and 87th Streets (tel. 876-5160), has fast-food service with eat-in comfort. This little shop, across the street from Gimbel's is simple, but someone has also made a real effort to keep it attractive. There are yellow Formica tables, wood captain's chairs, and linoleum-tile floors. You order at the red-and-yellow counter, backed by the three-wok open kitchen. Powerful exhaust fans keep the air clean. The cashier brings your order to you at your seat; some foods on Styrofoam, some on real china (take-out containers are a few cents extra). Soups are 75¢ to 90¢; an egg-roll, 75¢. Side orders (basically entrees) are all under $4. There are 22 combination plates, most in the $4 or under range. Sweet-and-sour pork with fried rice or lo mein is $3.20. Mongolian beef (with shrimp, chicken, and vegetables) and white rice is the most expensive item on the menu ($4.95). There are also daily specials like chicken with broccoli ($3.70), chicken or beef with asparagus ($3.75), and fried chicken with rice or lo mein ($2.65). For something refreshingly different, try the cold sesame noodles in a peanut sauce ($2.50)—big enough to share. At High Noon Express you'll see everyone from older ladies taking a shopper's lunch to junior-executive types having dinner after an evening jog.

High Noon Express is open Monday to Saturday from 11 a.m. to 10 p.m. Closed Sunday.

CZECHOSLOVAKIAN: Ruc, 312 E. 72nd St., between First and Second Avenues (tel. 650-1611), is a jewel of a restaurant with European style. You enter through a brick walkway three steps down from the street. There is a small lounge with a copper-topped bar with red glazed tiles. The dining room, through an arched brick entry, positively glows with soft color and light. Tables are set with peach tablecloths, candles, and sparkling glassware. The walls are peach with white panels. Pastel crayon art completes this elegant European setting. There's also an outdoor dining terrace for warm-weather nights.

Ruc has a full dinner with soup, consommé, or juice, an entree, dessert, and coffee, priced from $11 to $15. The chef's special is the boiled beef with dill sauce, dumplings, and cucumber salad. Other entrees include beef goulash or Stroganoff with dumplings and salad, chicken paprika with rice and salad, breaded calf brain with home fries and salad, and wienerschnitzel with home fries or salad. Desserts include apricot dumplings and tempting pastries. You can also order omelets, cold plates, and salads for $7.50.

Ruc is open for dinner only, Monday through Friday from 5 to 11 p.m., and on Saturday and Sunday from noon till 11 p.m. Reservations strongly suggested.

ENGLISH: We love **Drake's Drum,** an English pub at 1629 Second Ave., between 84th and 85th Streets (tel. 988-2826). It's favored by rugby players (which one owner used to be and one still is), homesick Brits and other Europeans, and neighborhood fans. Drake's Drum is appropriately dim, with lanterns, dark wood, red-and-white checkered tablecloths, sawdust on the floor, and huge, wonderful oil paintings, including one of the restaurant's interior. Regulars crowd the copper-topped bar to watch the latest world sports competition. The pillars, wound with thick rope from floor to ceiling, are good to lean against if you can't get a bar seat. In warm weather you can dine outdoors under the sidewalk awning. Prices for food are very, very low.

There's an unbeatable lunch special—with a $2 beer or drink, you get a free quarter-pound hamburger on a roll, weekdays from 11:30 a.m. to 4 p.m. Other lunch prices are (almost) as good. You can try a chef's salad for $3.75, a ham-and-cheese omelet with french fries for $3.95, or a steak sandwich with salad and potato for $4.95. Dinner prices are slightly higher; the same items will cost you $5.50 to $6.95. The dinner menu also features entrees like eggplant parmigiana, Polynesian pepper steak, southern fried chicken, broiled scrod, and yes, even quiche, all with varying combinations of salad, french fries or baked potato, rice, and vegetable. The "Draught and Steak" is a good deal with a 12-ounce sirloin, salad, and baked potato, and choice of 32-ounce pitcher of beer or 16-ounce carafe of wine for $8.95. Also, check the menu for nightly low-priced specials; and on British holidays like St. George's Day (April 23), look for extra-specials like "toad in the hole," "bangers and mash," and roast beef with Yorkshire pudding.

Drake's Drum has two weekend brunch selections—the "Rugby," with a charcoal-broiled steak, two eggs, bacon, french fries, English muffin, and a 16-ounce pitcher of sangría or Bloody Mary for $5.95; or the "Bicycle," with french toast, bacon, and sangría or a Bloody Mary for $3.50.

Lunch is served daily from noon to 4 p.m., dinner from 5 p.m. to 1 a.m. Brunch is from noon to 4:30 p.m. on Saturday and Sunday. Drake's Drum is open for drinks nightly until the early hour of 4 a.m. No reservations needed.

GERMAN: Years ago thousands of German families called the Upper East 80s home. Today, even though many have moved away, you'll see that their German influence still makes this an interesting neighborhood. Stroll down East 86th Street between Second and Third Avenues, where even the newsstands carry German papers. You might want to stop at the **Bremen House,** 220 E. 86th St. (tel. 288-5500; open between 9 a.m. and 8 p.m. Monday through Saturday, 10 a.m. to 6 p.m. on Sunday), for a look at everything from imported Belgian pâté to German crystal lamps. And there are plenty of restaurants here, from plain to fancy, many of them German.

Ideal, 238 E. 86th St., between Second and Third Avenues (tel. 650-1632), is a straightforward luncheonette that's been serving hearty food since 1932. There are a few tables, a long lunch counter stacked with reserves of beer, and fluorescent lighting overhead. Ideal has a character all its own, and it's a good place to eat for $7 or less. A meal of Yankee pot roast with potatoes and red cabbage is $5.25, as is schweinebraten (fresh ham with sauerkraut and potatoes). Lamb stew is $5.75; potato pancakes with applesauce costs $3.95. For the more adventurous, there are pig's knuckles with sauerkraut and potatoes, or liver dumplings, both priced at $4.95. In addition, most meat sandwiches are about $4. Desserts are 95¢; a draft American beer, only 60¢.

Open daily from 7 a.m. to 11:30 p.m., as it has been, the counter clerks will tell you, for the past 50 years.

After you leave Ideal, stroll two doors down the street to your left and take a peek at **Elk's Candy.** You'll probably be too full to eat, but the marzipan (almond paste) fruits and pebbles are worth seeing.

Kleine Konditorei, 234 E. 86th St., between Second and Third Avenues (tel. 737-7130), is another of the block's oldtime German restaurants. It has been around since 1923. In the front windows are exquisite pastries and whipped-cream cakes, and a counter at the front offers pastries and European chocolate. It's all much more elegant than it sounds: the dining rooms up the stairs have flowers, white linen, and burnished brass. The carpet and wallpaper are red, and there's cherry paneling. The shaded sconces and chandeliers are reminiscent of old Vienna.

Complete meals are featured at lunch and dinner. At lunch you might start with a homemade herring salad or fresh melon, with an entree of wiener würstchen (German frankfurter) with potato, salad or vegetable, and a dessert of vanilla pudding ($10.75). Lunch prices range from $7 to $13; à la carte, the wiener würstchen is $7.75. Choices for the full dinner are similar, with an appetizer or soup, salad and vegetable, potatoes, dessert, and coffee, tea, or milk. A complete dinner with an entree of rainbow trout amandine is $11.75, $12.25

with Hungarian goulash, and $12.75 with fresh sole. À la carte, a chef's salad or herring salad is $9.25.

Kleine Konditorei is open daily from 10 a.m. until midnight Sunday through Thursday, until 1 a.m. on Friday and Saturday. Reservations recommended.

Café Geiger, 206 E. 86th St., between Second and Third Avenues (tel. 734-4428), will catch your eye with its two front windows: one full of pastries as fanciful as chocolate ETs and edible elephants, the other with an exquisite tableau of a Bavarian village, complete with cog trains, waterfalls, and a castle atop. Inside there's a spacious, cheerful dining room with elegant touches like wood paneling and oil paintings. The staff is polite, and the Café Geiger has a loyal following.

There are many reasonably priced items on the menu, although entree prices can go as high as $14. Potato pancakes with applesauce is $6.75, wiener würstchen (the Vienna-style frankfurter) with sauerkraut and potato is $6.50. Hard-boiled eggs Russian style come with caviar, vegetable salad, mayonnaise, and fresh greens for $6.50. Daily specials are priced similarly. The menu lists 40 mouthwatering desserts, including fresh-baked tortes, strudels, waffles, cakes, and pies, most for $2 to $2.50 each. All bar drinks are available.

Open daily from 9 p.m. to midnight, on Friday and Saturday to 1 a.m. Reservations suggested.

GREEK: The **Argonaut,** 1020 Third Ave., between 60th and 61st Streets (tel. 838-6554), is a Greek coffeeshop as we think one should be. It has paneled walls (some with rich wood, others with imitation), the requisite calendars and pictures of Greece, and a bustling, happy atmosphere. An open kitchen in the middle divides the counter area from the dining room. It's not fancy up front, but there are cheerful Tiffany-style lamps in the front window, a curving orange counter with matching stools, and a floor worn by lots of traffic—but clean, like everything else. The dining room in back has wood tables and chairs, and a chandelier. We recommend an order of dolmades, delicious rice-stuffed grape leaves ($3.75), big enough for two to share as an appetizer. The menu is large: sandwiches range from simple cheese to triple-deckers with french fries and cole slaw ($5.45). Entrees run as high as a steak for $12.95. Look for specials like cheesy spinach pie served with vegetables ($4.25) or a hearty souvlaki sandwich of lamb ($3.35). And try a dessert, a slab of cheesecake ($1.60), apple pie à la mode ($2.25), or a large sundae smothered in whipped cream ($2.10). All bar drinks are available.

The Argonaut is open daily from 6 a.m. to midnight, which makes it a great place for a late-night breakfast.

HUNGARIAN: The **Mocca Hungarian Restaurant,** 1588 Second Ave., between 82nd and 83rd Streets (tel. 734-6470), is clean and inviting. It's cozy too, even with its turn-of-the-century mosaic floor and marble. Brass wall lamps, mirrored panels, and front windows (one with a dessert case, the other with curtains) add to the charm.

The Mocca's portions are usually generous, and the food generally good. A three-course lunch here will cost you between $7.75 and $8.75, depending on your entree choice. Dinner prices are similar. All entrees come with potato, vegetable, and salad. You might start with a warming bowl of homemade noodle soup—good broth, fine noodles, and sliced carrots ($2.25). Calf liver with green peppers and paprika or a crisp breaded wienerschnitzel is $8.25 each. An entree of stuffed cabbage is $7.25, and there's also a good duck entree on the menu ($8.25). For dessert, definitely give the chocolate orange torte ($2.50) or rich somloi galuska ($3.50) a try. That is, if a cake soaked in rum, with nuts and chocolate sauce, and a smothering of whipped cream doesn't intimidate you!

The Mocca is open daily, for lunch from 11:30 a.m. to 4 p.m., and for dinner from 4:30 to 11 p.m. Reservations suggested.

INDIAN: The **Agra,** 807 Lexington Ave., between 62nd and 63rd Streets (tel. 308-8281), is a charming retreat tucked away on the second floor of an otherwise nondescript building (go up the stairs and turn right). The Agra has Indian-print cloth on the walls, a brown ceiling with yellow beams, and tables set with white linen and flowers. Ask for a seat by the windows, which are cut to look like Indian arches. The Agra is sunny and bright by day, dark and mysterious by night. Many regular patrons are Indian or have traveled in India—a good indication of its authenticity.

Come between noon and 3 p.m. weekdays for a bargain lunch—$3.95 buys a good beef, lamb, chicken, or keema (chopped lamb) curry, served with fiery red onion relish, mild dhal (a soup-like blend of lentils and onions), a vegetable dish such as cooked cabbage, white or saffron rice, and coffee or a pot of bracing Indian tea with cream.

Dinner prices are also reasonable. For openers, try the coconut soup ($1). The duck curry is a good choice ($7.75). Most prices range from $4.75 for vegetarian dishes to combination dinners like the tandoori dinner with shami kebab (chopped meat), bread, choice of soup and dessert, mango chutney, tandoori chicken, rice pilaf, dhal, and tea or coffee ($9.95 for one person, $20.95 for two). And don't pass any meal without one of the excellent Indian breads, such as the poori—puffy, slightly sweet, and large enough for two ($1.50).

The Agra serves wine for $1.50 a glass, $3.75 to $7.50 a carafe. Eagle, an Indian beer, is $1.95; other brands are $1.95.

Open from noon to midnight Monday through Saturday, and from 4 p.m. to midnight on Sunday. Reservations are suggested for one of the window tables, otherwise not necessary.

Tanjore, 1229 First Ave., between 66th and 67th Streets (tel. 535-8718), is a pleasant Indian restaurant that looks much bigger than it is because of its mirrored walls. There's also lots of brick and many plants, with ceiling fans overhead. Napkins are tucked into stemmed glasses on the bare wood tables. Tanjore first caught our eye with its lunch special, served Monday through Friday from noon to 3 p.m. The lunch includes rice and soup, and prices vary with the entree. A chicken curry lunch here is only $4.95. A mango chicken or lamb entree is $5.95. Most entrees on the regular dinner menu are priced under $9.95, and there are complete dinners for $11.95 to $15.95. À la carte, you might ask for an appetizer of chicken chat ($3.95), crisp-fried pieces of chicken in a spicy lemon marinade. For dessert, there's mango sliced over ice cream, or fresh strawberries ($2.25).

Tanjore is open for lunch from 11:30 a.m. to 3 p.m., and for dinner between 5:30 and 11 p.m. Reservations not needed.

ITALIAN: No need to go all the way downtown to Little Italy with the reasonably priced **Café and Restaurant Divino,** at 1544 Second Ave., between 80th and 81st Streets (tel. 861-1096). Café Divino is *molto buono,* with intimate charm. The small restaurant is decorated in bright greens and crisp white: green-and-white tablecloths, a green awning over the bar, green curtains, with posters of

Italy on the white walls. At night it glows with candlelight and conversation. The menu is the same at lunch and dinner. There are 12 different types of pasta, such as tortellini alla Panna and conchiglie ortolana, priced between $7.75 and $8.50. The six or so specials of the day include chicken sorrentina ($8.75) and filet of sole in wine sauce ($9.75). Cold platters like pasta fredda ($4.75) and Caesar salad ($4.75) are available. A chef's salad is $4.75. For dessert there are delights like zuppa inglese and torta Divino ($2.75 each), cannoli ($2), and six Italian ice creams ($2 to $3). Plus there's a selection of Italy's wonderful mineral waters and fruit drinks, and of course espresso ($1) and cappuccino ($1.50).

Open daily from noon to midnight weekdays (lunch till 3 p.m., dinner from 5 to 11:45 p.m.). Friday and Saturday hours are noon until 1 a.m. (kitchen open until 12:45 a.m.). On Sunday it's open from 2 until 11 p.m.

MEXICAN: Mañana, 1136 First Ave., between 62nd and 63rd Streets (tel. 223-9623), is elegant, with soft lights, white stucco walls, dark heavy woods, tapestry chairs, touches of red in escutcheons, and candles. In spite of its subdued, graceful atmosphere, though, meals are substantial and attractively priced. Lunch appetizers cost between $3.25 and $3.95; an appetizer of chalupas (chili- and pork-filled mini-tortillas) or nachos are $3.25 each at dinner. Hearty combination platters of Mexican favorites with rice and beans are $5.25 at lunch, $7.95 at dinner. There are daily specials, usually about $6.95. Chili con carne is $4.50; three beef tacos rancheros are $6.95 at lunch, $8.95 at dinner. For dessert there's crème caramel for $1.50 at lunch, $2.25 at dinner; or ice cream for $1.50 at lunch, $2.25 at dinner. Or you might want to try something different in the ice cream with fruit and sweet Malago wine sauce ($2.50 and $3.25, depending on the meal). Sangrita, a hot and spicy Bloody Mary, is also served ($2.50).

Mañana is open weekdays for lunch from noon to 3 p.m., and for dinner on Saturday and Sunday from 1 to 11:30 p.m. No reservations accepted.

Bright reds make **Tijuana,** 217 E. 86th St., between Second and Third Avenues (tel. 289-9627), a cheery place. The door and beams on the ceiling are red, and the walls stucco white with red panels where coats-of-arms are hung. Amber wall lights add to the coziness.

Tijuana offers an inexpensive luncheon special, including soup and coffee. Choices include enchiladas ($2.75 for one, $3.50 for two) and chile rellenos ($2.85 for one, $3.65 for two). The vegetarian combination—one bean burrito, one cheese taco, and one enchilada guacamole—is $3.50, and Mexican shrimp and avocado salad is $3.75; chalupa is $3.50. Dinner prices go up about $3: combination platters (for instance, one taco, one enchilada, and one tostada) are priced from $6.25 to $7.85. Entrees like two chile rellenos are $6.25. The menu also has Spanish and Swiss (chicken-liver enchiladas Swiss, for example!) entrees. Generally, only the shrimp and some chicken entrees are priced higher than we want to spend ($11 and $12). Special south-of-the-border cocktails are $2.50; sangría is expensive ($9.75 for a full pitcher, $7.25 for a half). For dessert there is flan ($1.75).

Tijuana is open for lunch daily from 11:30 a.m. or noon to 3:30 p.m., and for dinner from 4 p.m. until midnight (kitchen closes at 11:30 p.m.). On Friday and Saturday nights Tijuana stays open until 2:30 a.m. Reservations accepted.

Acapulco, 1586 Second Ave., between 82nd and 83rd Streets (tel. 650-9097), is owned by the same people who own Tijuana, but it's a bit more casual in atmosphere. In warm weather there are outdoor tables for sidewalk dining. Inside there is as much cheerfulness as at its sister restaurant, with a long padded bar with tall captain's chairs up front, lots of wrought-iron, Spanish-influenced chandeliers, and red candles set at each table. The restaurant is narrow, with dividing arches—we like the back with its stained-glass windows.

The menu is identical to Tijuana's—in fact, it even has the same name. Acapulco does not serve lunch, however. It's open for dinner from 5 p.m. to midnight Tuesday through Thursday, until 1 a.m. on Friday and Saturday. Reservations suggested.

MIDDLE EASTERN: Falafel 'n' Stuff, 1586 First Ave., between 82nd and 83rd Streets (tel. 879-7023), has lots more imagination than its name. This Egyptian restaurant has the narrowest of dining rooms, with white brick walls and yellow wall lamps. There is also some Egyptian art. On the tables are flower-print oilskin tablecloths and fresh carnations with babies' breath.

On the menu are 14 vegetarian platters, priced from $5.50 to $6.50. Each comes with salad and pita bread, making a filling and inexpensive meal. We think these maza dishes—falafel (crisp-fried chickpea balls), tabouli (crushed wheat salad), hummus (chickpeas and tahini)—are the best on the menu. The Pharaoh chicken (barbecued and served with a vegetable, rice, salad, and pita) is also a good deal at $7.90. Other meat dishes are in the $9 range, and go as high as $12.50 for baby lamb rib chops.

Jumbo sandwiches with maza fillings are another low-priced consideration. They start at $2.95 and none is higher than $4.50. An appetizer of zucchini pie or spinach and feta cheese ($1.50 to $5.50) is recommended. For dessert, try the magnificent bird's nest, a homemade concoction of phyllo and nuts ($1.50), baklava ($1.50), or a not-too-sweet custard ($1.50).

Open daily from noon till midnight (till 1 a.m. on Friday and Saturday). Reservations suggested for parties of more than two.

SEAFOOD: Barbra Streisand used to live upstairs of **Oscar's Salt of the Sea,** 1155 Third Ave., between 67th and 68th Streets (tel. 879-1199), a huge bustling seafood house. Just about the entire restaurant is paneled in wood, and there are planked wood floors, heavy wood tables, and wood captain's chairs. It all has a glowing patina from much use.

Oscar's has a daily luncheon special for all seafood lovers. For $9.25 you get the special entree of the day, soup, cole slaw, french fries, and coffee or tea. The soup may be a hearty chowder, the entree a sea trout—you check the blackboard for the day's offering. Oscar's serves the luncheon special until 4 p.m., and also offers a full dinner menu all day long. The complete dinner includes an appetizer (Little Neck clams, cherrystone clams, herring slices, and others), a choice of chowders, potatoes, cole slaw or salad, and coffee or tea. Dinner prices are $11.95 to $19.95 (à la carte is $1 less), and include choices like scrod, halibut, salmon steak, sole stuffed with crabmeat, and fried oysters. The same complete meal at lunch is $9.25 or $11.25.

Oscar's is open from noon to 11 p.m. weekdays, from noon to midnight on Saturday and Sunday.

There's also a **Captain's Nemo's** in this area (see the Lincoln Center section for details), at 1131 Lexington Ave., between 78th and 79th Streets (tel. 988-6756). Lunch is served from noon to 5 p.m., dinner until midnight, seven days a week. Brunch on Sunday. Reservations suggested.

Other inexpensive seafood restaurants include **Nodeldini's,** 1399 Madison Ave., at 97th Street (tel. 369-5677); **Cockeyed Clams,** 1673 Third Ave., at 94th Street (tel. 831-4121); and **Squid Roe,** 1468 Second Ave., at 77th Street (tel. 249-4666).

TEA: For tea before or after seeing the Metropolitan Museum, nothing could be nicer—or more convenient—than the **American Stanhope Hotel,** 81st Street and

Fifth Avenue (tel. 288-5800). The Stanhope is literally just across the street from the Met, and a treasure in its own right. It's packed with American antiques, and has as gracious 19th-century elegance to it that isn't overwhelming.

Tea is held in the **Furnished Room,** to the back of the small black-and-white marble-floored lobby with its wonderful grandfather clock. The Furnished Room is just that—a cozy room with small but overstuffed chairs set at marble tables. The wainscotted walls are a dusky blue, and are hung with 19th-century still-lifes (Currier and Ives among them). The drapes (not curtains here) are blue, the carpet blue flocked. The chair fabrics, like the teapots and china upon which tea is served, are Laura Ashley florals. Civilized types like the Prince and Princess of Kent have taken tea here.

At afternoon tea, a fresh-brewed pot of Earl Grey, Ceylon, and Red Zinger, among others, costs $2.25. To go with it, there are tea sandwiches ($4.50); fresh currant scones served with raspberry jam, marmalade, and honey ($3.50); hot blueberry cobbler ($3.50); a selection of pastries ($3.75) or toast with butter and preserves ($2.75). Most people spend $10 or less. There is also a sandwich and salad menu offered, with prices from $4.50 to $10.

JUST DESSERTS: While you're on 86th Street window-shopping or walking off a hearty German meal, consider the **Treat Boutique,** 200 E. 86th St., near Third Avenue (tel. 737-6619), for an ice-cream cone. The scoop is Alpen-Zauber ice cream; like many fancy-sounding confections, it's local, not imported (it's from Brooklyn), but still highly recommended. A large cone is $1.10; a double dip, $1.95. There are 15 toppings (crushed M&Ms, trail mix, walnuts, etc.) for 35¢ each, if your sweet tooth is truly insatiable.

Open from 11 a.m. to 11 p.m. daily, on Sunday and Monday from noon to 10 p.m.

Peppermint Park, 1225 First Ave., at the corner of 66th Street (tel. 879-9484), is a favorite for young and old. Everything is fresh (no preservatives), and there's a long list of 40 delicious flavors of ice creams, sherbets, and frozen yogurts. Take-out cones here are $1 for a single scoop, and there are also sodas, egg creams, sundaes, and floats. In another case there are mouthwatering Italian pastries. There's also a small dining area behind a green glass partition, where you can order fountain specialties (a banana split for $4.50, the white crêpe Gatsby for $3.25, or a Belgian waffle with ice cream and fudge sauce for $4.25). You can also have a full meal here—quiches for $3.75, salads for up to $5.25, entree crêpes in creamy sauces for $4.25, and a cream cheese and salmon sandwich for $5.95.

Peppermint Park is open from 10 a.m. to midnight Monday through Thursday, till 1 a.m. on Friday, till 2 a.m. on Saturday, and from 11 a.m. to midnight on Sunday.

4. Upper West Side

This neighborhood offers a wide variety of international foods and has a lively spirit due to its large student population. Columbia University, at 116th Street between Broadway and Amsterdam Avenue, is the city's only Ivy League institution and wields considerable influence despite its distance from downtown Manhattan. Barnard College is just a block north from Columbia on Broadway; and there are many other schools and seminaries in the area. The Upper West Side is also permanent home to many different groups, and you can see how ethnic flavors change almost block by block. It also is a neighborhood in transition, not from the students who come and go with each academic year, but from the influx of trendy, artsy stores and restaurants moving in next to the older mom-and-pop shops. Some welcome the change; others deplore it. Whatever the outcome, you'll find an exciting and energized neighborhood, where something's always going on.

AMERICAN/CONTINENTAL: According to its management, "every doggone thing" gets ordered at the **American Restaurant,** 2020 Broadway at 69th Street (tel. 724-4000). This family-style diner—with comfortable booths, wooden arches, and red swivel stools at the lunch counter—offers plenty of cheap, tasty food. A grilled cheese sandwich costs $2.15. A beefburger on a toasted bun with cole slaw and a pickle is $2. A hot roast beef sandwich with potato and vegetable is $5.05. The American also offers a variety of diet delights if you're watching calories. A chicken salad platter on a bed of lettuce with tomato, scallions, cucumber, cole slaw, and sliced egg is $4.30.

Open 24 hours.

Celebrate a victory at **Pershings,** 232 Columbus Ave., between 70th and 71st Streets (tel. 595-5420). This pleasant restaurant features World War I and World War II enlistment and victory posters, wainscot paneling, and a high pressed-tin ceiling. Pershings is a winner with the theater crowd, who come here after hours. Among the favorites here are Pancho Villa's chili, served with your choice of a combination of sour cream, grated cheddar cheese, and chopped onions ($6.25). The Big Bertha burger, made of lean, chopped beef, served on an English muffin with steak fries, lettuce, and tomato, is $4.50. Try one of the Stout-hearted sandwiches, such as the Allies' roast beef, served with Florence Nightingale's cole slaw and steak fries for $5.25.

Open from noon to 4 a.m. daily. Kitchen closes at 3 a.m.

Amsterdam's Bar & Rotisserie, 428 Amsterdam Ave., between 80th and 81st Streets (tel. 874-1377), is a French bistro-style restaurant and bar that is standing-room-only until it closes. Gay red homespun tablecloths, shiny black wood chairs, and freshly painted white brick walls create a cheery atmosphere. The chef guards no secrets from diners as the kitchen is visible in the center of the restaurant. Whole chickens and cuts of beef roast dramatically on a spit while french fries sizzle in a fryer underneath.

Some prices are high, but the roast half chicken, with a fresh green herb sauce and a pile of crispy thin fries with their skins, is a good and savory buy at $6.95. By all means try the spicy homemade catsup that sits on every table. The gravlax, thinly sliced marinated salmon with dill mustard sauce ($4.50 for a small serving, $9.95 for a large), is refreshing and delicious when served with a cold Norwegian beer or a shot of frosty aquavit, "the water of life," a vodka-like Scandinavian liquor.

Small salads (which come with the entrees) are made with arugula, radicchio, and other flavorful greens, flavored with a balsamic vinegar dressing that would send Peter Rabbit into raptures.

The restaurant is open noon until 1 a.m. on Sunday and Monday; till 2 a.m. on Tuesday, Wednesday, and Thursday; and till 2:30 a.m. on Friday and Saturday. The bar stays open until 2:30 a.m. on weekdays and until 3:30 a.m. on weekends.

West Side Story, 700 Columbus Ave., at 95th Street (tel. 749-1900), is about ten blocks north of the chic Columbus Avenue strip. But if you're willing to take a stroll, a delightful meal is in store for you. This restaurant is a little hidden at the corner, but customers seek it out, and often are found waiting for the doors to open in the morning.

Breakfast dishes feature a special french toast—challah bread dipped in cream and served with real Vermont maple syrup ($3.95). Three-egg omelets are also a treat, with fillings such as country cream cheese and watercress ($3.95) or chorizo, a spicy Spanish sausage ($4.95).

Lunch brings in another big crowd. The sandwich selection includes Emmenthaler swiss with ham for $4.25, served on your choice of bread, or fresh roast turkey for $4.25. A dish of Moroccan chili with sour cream and a small salad is $4.75, and a grilled hamburger on a seeded roll with fries is $3.95. Dinners are quiet, but there is still a good selection that includes chicken gai yang with Thai hot sauce for $7.95, and chicken livers sauteed in sherry with mushrooms for $7.95. All entrees are served with two choices of salad, potato, rice, french fries, or the daily vegetable. Meals may also be prepared for low-salt or low-calorie diets.

Hours are 7 a.m. to 11 p.m. daily, with deli take-outs too.

The owner of both **Teacher's** and **Teacher's Too**, sister restaurants at 2249 and 2271 Broadway, near 81st Street (tel. 787-3500 and 362-4900), likes to be known as "Murray the Cap." He prides himself on the fact that much of his business comes from the repeat visits of satisfied customers. But both his restaurants also have an appealing and congenial atmosphere, with a schoolhouse theme carried out in the red walls, red lamps over the tables, and blackboards for the day's specials. There are also large, realistic paintings of the city in a style that recalls the paintings of Edward Hopper.

You might try the chicken gai yang, a half chicken that's marinated and then broiled in a hot spiced sauce—a favorite here ($5.95 at lunch, $7.25 at dinner), and a Thai beef salad (sauteed beef with onion, hot crushed pepper, lime, and fresh coriander) for $5.25. There's an obvious Thai influence on the menu —the chefs at both restaurants (Teacher's Two was opened to take up the overflow) are Thai. But there's also lots of continental flair, and you might want to begin your meal with an appetizer of smoked filet of trout ($3.75), homemade country pâté ($2.95), escargots, and oysters ($3.75 per half dozen). There's also a big trade in basic American hamburgers, all under $5 at lunch and dinner.

For dessert there are cakes, cheesecakes, and daily specials, arranged beautifully on a front table where you can't miss them.

Both restaurants are open from 11 a.m. to 1 a.m. Sunday through Thursday, and until 2 a.m. on Friday and Saturday. "Murray the Cap" says his brunch —served between 11 a.m. and 4:30 p.m. on weekends—is the "best on the West Side." It features poached eggs with lean pastrami hash, eggs Benedict, pastrami Benedict, an eggplant and tomato omelet, and a sour cream and caviar omelet. Brunch prices range from $3.95 to $6.95 (a sirloin steak with eggs is tops in price), and all include a cocktail.

If you can get past the waitress dancing by the jukebox as she totals a check, you'll enjoy lunch or dinner at **Hanratty's**, 732 Amsterdam Ave., between 95th and 96th Streets (tel. 864-4224). The restaurant has a comfortable atmosphere with lots of oak tables and an old mahogany bar that dates from the early 1900s. This former speakeasy is now a charming restaurant, one which does some great things with food. There is a fresh broiled salmon with hollandaise sauce ($8.75), sole meunière ($7.50), the pasta of the day (ranging between $6.95 and $8.25), and honey-dipped fried chicken ($6.25). Sauteed liver is $7.25. All entrees are served with a choice of two side dishes, from a list including cole slaw, rice, baked potato, marinated zucchini, or the vegetable of the day. You could also have quiche or a bowl of chili, or just enjoy some talk and TV at the bar.

Open daily from noon to 1 a.m. (dinner served till about midnight). On weekends brunch is featured with some unusual omelets and fish and chips. Reservations are taken, and by 8 p.m. there may be a wait if you want a booth.

The Burger Joint, 2175 Broadway (tel. 362-9238), and **The Pizza Joint**, 2165 Broadway (tel. 724-2010), have been Upper West Side institutions for over 20 years. Located a couple of doors away from each other between 76th and

RESTAURANTS: UPPER WEST SIDE 85

77th Streets, they are unpretentious eateries that offer a staggering array of wholesome, reasonably priced food. Since they are run under the same ownership, you can order from both menus at either "Joint."

The house specialties are, logically enough, burgers and pizzas—topped with everything from the conventional cheese to hearty chili con carne. A 100% beef char-broiled burger served with french fries, lettuce, and tomato costs $1.85; the Big Nick hamburger, named for the Joint's owner, has a half pound of beef and should satisfy even the most ravenous traveler ($2.75). The pizzas range in price from $3.25 for an individual cheese pizza to $10.85 for a large one with everything on it. Other fare includes heros and submarine sandwiches ($2.50 to $3.85), spinach, meat, or cheese pie ($2.85), minestrone soup ($1.45), spaghetti and meat sauce served with fresh bread ($4.05). The Joints also serve breakfast, with a cheese omelet, fries, and toast ($2.55), and pancakes (about $2.10).

The Burger Joint is open daily from 6:30 a.m. to 1:30 a.m.; the Pizza Joint, from 11 a.m. to 1 a.m. Monday through Saturday and from noon to 1 a.m. on Sunday.

A great place for brunch or any other meal is **Shelter,** 2180 Broadway, on the corner of 77th Street (tel. 362-4360). Ask for a window table at this attractive restaurant—you'll have a great view of the street outside. This pleasant restaurant is filled with leafy green plants, streamlined tables, and neon signs. The back room is wood paneled, with European art posters on the walls. The oak bar is framed with hanging ferns and neon art deco designs. Fresh flowers and a basket of unusual breads (salty twists, pumpernickel, french rolls) are on every table. Even the menu at Shelter is elegant.

For brunch you can order grilled Italian sweet sausages and eggs ($6.50), curried chicken salad with apples and chutney ($6.50), or scrambled eggs, smoked salmon and onions, served with a croissant ($6.95). All are delicious and come with a drink such as a mimosa or champagne with cassis. For dinner at Shelter, several attractive plates are offered: mussels marinara ($6.25) is quite reasonable, as is the tortellini ($6.25). Tempting dishes from the newly installed grill include southern glazed duck with chili pepper jelly ($8.95), and grilled, boned fresh rainbow trout ($7.25).

Open Sunday through Thursday from 11:30 to 1:45 a.m., on Friday and Saturday till 2:45 a.m. A weekend brunch is served from 11:30 a.m. to 4:30 p.m.

One of the classier restaurants on the Upper West Side's "restaurant row," near the Museum of Natural History, is **Dobson's,** 341 Columbus Ave., at 76th Street (tel. 362-0100). Inside this large, showy establishment, brick archways and brass coatracks set off the antique mahogany bar and cabinets, and bentwood chairs and blue-and-white checked tablecloths give a classy but festive air. Palmy plants, recessed lighting, and lacy white curtains round out the quaint but chic charm.

For a special dinner, try an appetizer such as Nova Scotia salmon garni ($4.95), two generous salmon-wrapped blocks of cream cheese on dark bread with lots of onions and tomatoes, attractively presented. And don't miss the dinner specials, such as broiled baby flounder ($8.50) or broiled ginger chicken ($8.50). You could opt for a spinach salad with bacon, shrimp, tomato, and egg ($6.50), or pick out two unusual cheeses for a cheese-and-fruit board ($6.25). Combination platters of fried shrimp and ginger chicken or sliced steak are generous and delicious ($9.25). Desserts are tempting: chocolate-chip cake to a hula pie or chocolate marnier mousse.

Dobson's is open every day from noon to 12:30 a.m. Make reservations to avoid a wait.

Marvin Gardens, 2274 Broadway, between 81st and 82nd Streets (tel. 799-0578), is instantly appealing, with lots of plants and brick, natural wood, and intimate booths. Dinners, which are in the $7.50 to $14.95 range, include the fish of the day, chicken stuffed with bacon and cheese, spare ribs, and a fancy shell steak with peppercorns. You could also order from the pasta section. A full order of fettuccine white (egg noodles, heavy cream, and aged parmesan cheese, priced at $7.25) will satisfy big appetites. Lighter eaters should ask for the small order, available at $5.50. There are also sandwiches and salads to choose from at lunch and dinner, as well as a vegetable plate, and you could have a side order of ratatouille or beansprouts with sesame dressing.

Marvin Gardens opens Monday through Friday at 7:30 a.m., on Saturday and Sunday at 10 a.m. Sunday through Wednesday it closes at 2 a.m., Thursday through Saturday at 3 a.m. Weekend brunch is served with a full array of omelets, crêpes, and daily specials. Reservations are recommended for this popular spot.

Light and airy is the look of **The Front Porch** restaurant, 2272 Broadway at 82nd Street (tel. 877-5220). Plants in the windows and casual tables set inside make it a comfortable place to enjoy lunch or dinner. The fare is definitely on the natural and healthy side, with homemade soups (hearty, vegetarian, or chilled, $1.95 to $3.50), championship chili ($2.50 to $3.75 for meat or vegetarian), pita-pizza sandwiches ($3.25), and many other interesting and creative dishes. There is an assortment of salads—fruit, cabbage, pasta, or mixed beans—in the $5 range, all served with bread and butter. For dinner only, try spinach bountiful, a vegetarian dish with fresh spinach and a variety of cheese in flaky pastry ($5.95, with salad), and chicken Morocco, a chunky chicken dish with raisins, onions, and coriander in puff pastry. The Front Porch also offers unique salad spreads, served open-face with vegetables. They include tuna Olivia, and chicken and egg spreads. The restaurant takes pride in its own home-baked pies and cakes, and also has puddings and yogurt for dessert. Special coffees with whipped cream make a nice ending to a relaxed meal in these pleasant surroundings.

Hours are 11:45 a.m. to 1:30 a.m. Sunday through Thursday, to midnight on Friday and Saturday.

If you want to mix and mingle with Columbia students at a famous old hangout, visit the **West End,** 2911 Broadway between 113th and 114th Streets (tel. 666-8750). The whole neighborhood is familiar with this dark, woodsy inn with a steam table and busy oval bar. The rundown look is part of its charm. Some come for quiet conversations, others after sports events, still others to finish schoolwork. There are 70 varieties of beer at the bar as well as 14 beers on tap. You can take a bowl of popcorn back with a pitcher and listen to the jukebox, or get dinner or lunch from the steam table. Pizza is $1 per slice, and there are hot sandwiches, such as an open-faced steak, with french fries and cole slaw ($6.50). Barbecued ribs are $5.95 and a fried clam platter is $4.25. Burgers, topped with bleu cheese or pizza sauce, range from $2.45 to $5.25.

Hours are 9:30 a.m. to 3 a.m. or later daily. There is also the Jazz Room, where older types eschew the collegiate crowd for live music.

Diane's Uptown, 249–251 Columbus Ave. between 76th and 77th Streets (tel. 799-6750), is a great find. A stained-glass entry sets the mood. Inside, high-backed wooden booths, mahogany tables, lush green plants, and dark-green walls with art deco flower motifs complete a feeling of luxury and relaxation. The menu is an even greater find, with bargains galore. A plain seven-ounce hamburger is $2.60. But you can create your own combinations with toppings ranging from mushroom and bacon to bleu cheese and onions. Each topping is

85¢. If you'd rather try something different, select a Virginia ham and cheese sandwich for $3.65, or a bacon and egg sandwich for $2.60.

Devotees of Diane's heartily recommend rounding your meal off with an old-fashioned egg cream, a steal at $1.35. Many customers make the trip to Diane's simply for the delicious desserts. These include caramel apple cake for $2.95 or key lime pie for $2.50. There is also a large selection of milkshakes, malts, and double dips.

Open from 11 a.m. to 2 a.m. daily.

With a huge flag of Texas hanging over it, the **Yellow Rose Café,** 450 Amsterdam Ave., between 81st and 82nd Streets (tel. 595-8760), is hard to miss. Cactus plants add more of the Texas flavor to this small restaurant. Waiters in cowboy outfits complete the scene. Start your meal with a "Texas Teaser," such as "Might Fine Mushrooms" ($3.50). The favorites among the "Main Spread" dishes are "Cattle Annie's Chicken Fried Steak" and "Barbara Ann's Southern Fried Chicken"—each for $9.25 with choice of potato and vegetable. Finish off your dinner with a selection from "The Last Round-up," such as sweet potato pie ($3).

Open Monday through Thursday from 11 a.m. to 11 p.m., to midnight on Friday and Saturday. On Sunday, brunch is served from 10 a.m. to 3 p.m. and the café closes at 11 p.m.

The Four Brothers, 2381 Broadway at 87th Street (tel. 874-7532), run by four Greek brothers named Lolos, is half coffeeshop, half fancier dining room. There is a homey bar where locals sit and watch TV for hours. Behind the bar is a lamp made from a whiskey bottle with a sombrero perched on top, twinkly Christmas lights, numerous bar mugs and accessories, and a balalaika next to a rope of seed beads hanging on the wall.

The diner offers one of the most reasonable breakfasts in town: $1.35 for two eggs, home-fries, toast, coffee or tea, or a breakfast of juice, wheat cakes or french toast, and beverage. Lunches and dinners at this local hangout are very good and also quite reasonable. The Greek salad is $4.50, omelets run from $2.75 to $4.50, and several roasts and fish and chicken dishes are between $4.75 and $11. There is a daily special list every weekday and a wide variety of sandwiches. Drinks from the bar are quite inexpensive ($1.50 for a wine spritzer). Not surprisingly, there are a lot of regulars!

Open from 6 a.m. to 11 p.m. daily.

College Inn, 2896 Broadway, between 112th and 113th Streets (tel. 663-0257), is a long-standing tradition in the Columbia University neighborhood. The menu, which is almost too extensive to absorb, features American and Greek food. Each wooden table is set with a large, bright-colored plastic water jug, or you can sit at the lunch counter on one of the red swivel stools. There are mirrors on three walls; above Mediterranean street scenes are depicted on the wallpaper. You are likely to find this diner as crowded with students studying at 3 a.m. as it is during the evening dinner rush.

The daily specials have plenty of family-dinner appeal. You might be tempted by the Irish lamb stew, with a cup of soup, a green salad, bread and butter ($4.35), or the baked meatloaf, with potato and vegetable ($3.80). Chopped steak with potato and vegetable is $3.80. The shish kebab ($6.50) is always a favorite. Soup here is 75¢ for a cup, and 85¢ for a bowl. And if you have any room left over, splurge with an old-fashioned banana split ($2.25).

Open 24 hours daily.

Columbia University's gracious **Faculty House,** tucked away behind a dormitory at 400 W. 117th St., close to Amsterdam Avenue (tel. 856-4700), is a little-known secret even among neighborhood residents. Delicious buffet lunches and dinners are open to nonmembers. Visitors can eat in the cafeteria or on the fourth floor, in a lovely large room with a great view of the city. Buffet lunches are $9.85 for nonmembers, and include two hot entrees, cold selections, vegetables, a full salad bar, and a sumptuous dessert table. The soups are homemade and delicious, including delicate bisques, cream soups, and fresh vegetable creations. Baking is done mainly in-house. Waiters will bring coffee and tea to your table, and you may eat all you want from the buffet tables. The dinner buffet has a set price of $12.45, plus a $1.50 service charge. Dinner often features delectable fish dishes with smooth sauces, coq au vin, and veal and lamb.

Hours are noon to 2 p.m. for lunch, 6 to 8 p.m. for dinner, Monday through Friday. Closed for the summer.

ARGENTINIAN/LATIN: **La Tablita,** 65 W. 73rd St., just off Columbus Avenue (tel. 724-9595), is a half-Italian, half-Argentinian restaurant with a lot of charm. Small, romantic tables are set creatively with candles and fresh flowers. Animal skins are draped on the brick and stucco walls, and there are lots of travel posters.

The dinner menu is on the high-priced side, so order carefully. There are several fish dishes, including a fresh catch of the day, priced around $13. Italian dishes—such as clams and mussels marinara ($10.95), or veal scaloppine marsala ($14.95)—are excellent. Fettuccine Alfredo ($10.95) is rich with butter and cream sauce, just the right consistency and delicately spiced. From the Argentine side of the menu, you can choose paradilla, a mixed grill with skirt steak, short ribs, sweetbreads, Argentine sausage, and black sausage, for $15. And save room for dessert. A peach Melba dessert ($3.95), loaded with raspberry sauce, ice cream, and whipped cream, is out of this world; and chocolate-covered frozen ice-cream balls ($3.95) are a wonderful complement to a cup of coffee or cappuccino. There are also Argentinian crêpes at $4.95, and sweet milk paste (dulce de leche) at $2.75 for those who want something unusual.

The brand-new bar here is an elegant, comfortable place to try La Tablita's deliciously potent frozen margaritas ($5) and sample the spicy empañadas ($4.25 for two).

Open from noon to midnight during the week, from noon until 1 a.m. on Friday and Saturday.

CHINESE: If you're looking for a nice restaurant for a group, or just a fancier-than-average Chinese place, the **Hunan Balcony,** 2596 Broadway at 98th Street (tel. 865-0400), is a perfect choice. The comfortable two-story restaurant has a window view and some nice touches: for instance, fruit drinks served with colorful parasols. Service is fast, and the food is delicious and reasonable.

Try the fried dumplings ($3.25) and cold noodles with sesame sauce ($2.50) for appetizers, and favorite entrees such as beef with four flavors ($7.50), shredded beef and red pepper, garlic, green scallions, ginger, and watercress, or moo shu pork ($5.75) served with pancakes to make what has been called a "Chinese burrito." Shredded pork with garlic sauce ($5.95) is also delicious.

Open from noon to midnight on Monday, Tuesday, and Sunday; Wednesday through Saturday until 2 a.m. Reservations are suggested for parties over five people.

The **Moon Palace Restaurant,** 2879 Broadway, between 111th and 112th Streets (tel. 666-7517), isn't one of the area's cozier spots, but its generous portions of good food at low prices have made it a favorite with local students, Columbia faculty, shopkeepers, and secretaries. The weekday lunch special is an especially good deal: an entree with soup, rice, dessert, and a pot of tea costs from $3.50 for vegetable chow mein to $9.75 for lobster Cantonese. The sweet-and-pungent (also called sweet-and-sour) shrimp for $6.50 is quite tasty and loaded with shrimp.

In addition to the specials, there are six pages of Peking- and Shanghai-style dishes to choose from. The velvet chicken ($6.75) practically melts in your mouth, and if you're feeling adventuresome, you can try sauteed shrimp with pork kidney ($6.50). Of course, there are customary family dinners, with a five-course meal for two starting at $14. Service is efficient, and low-priced cocktails, wine, and beer are available.

The airy **Empire Szechuan**, 2574 Broadway, at the corner of 97th Street (tel. 663-6004), is very popular. Although it's often crowded, the large dining area is divided into more intimate sections by rows of hanging pots and by planters with miniature palms.

Its weekday luncheon special offers soup, an eggroll, and fried rice with an entree for $3.55 to $3.95. The regular menu offers a variety of hot and spicy dishes, which can be toned down—or up!—to suit your taste, plus such exotic dishes as sliced chicken with fermented rice sauce ($7.25) and aromatic Chinese eggplant ($6.25).

Open from 11:30 a.m. to 1:30 a.m. Wednesday through Sunday, to 11:30 p.m. on Monday and Tuesday. Reservations suggested for dinner.

CUBAN: The **Ideal Restaurant**, 2825 Broadway, at 109th Street (tel. 866-3224), has the warm, friendly atmosphere of a Spanish *tasca*. The walls have exposed brick and wood paneling, and the tables are covered with bright red-checked oilcloth. Straw-covered wine jugs hang from the walls. Much of the Ideal's clientele comes from the local Latin community, and the restaurant is also popular with the student crowd. During dinner the tables are reserved for those ordering full-course meals, and smaller orders can be eaten at the luncheon counter.

The Ideal offers a variety of meat, seafood, and rice dishes, all prepared in the hearty Cuban style. Pot roast in gravy or beef stew with potatoes—both served with rice and beans or fried plantains and french fries or fried yucca—costs $7.25; sliced fish is $6.75; a thick soup of chicken and rice is $7.50. For a real treat, try the paella valenciana ($22.50 for two), a zesty dish of saffron rice, chicken, seafood, onions, garlic, and vegetables. Dessert selections include such tropical treats as guava shells, papaya chunks, or grated coconut with cream cheese ($1.75). You can top it all off with one of the Upper West Side's most reasonably priced cups of espresso (75¢). An extensive wine list is available.

Open weekdays from 11:30 a.m. to 11 p.m., weekends from 4 to 11:30 p.m.

CUBAN/CHINESE: Cuba and China merge at **La Victoria-China,** 2532 Broadway, between 94th and 95th Streets (tel. 865-1810). This restaurant offers an adventure in mix-and-match eating. It's a neighborhood eatery full of New York craziness. It's noisy, bustling, and full of people. It is full of Formica and vinyl booths, with wall hangings and bustling Chinese waiters making it bright and busy. For a Cuban experience, try one of the generous combination plates such as chopped beef, with moros y cristianos (rice and beans) and salad ($4.65). The savory sauce on the beef and the rice studded with black beans is delicious and hearty. Green or ripe plantains make an interesting and tasty dish ($1.15). When you mix a meal with Chinese favorites like moo goo gai pan (chicken with mushrooms, bamboo shoots, and vegetables, at $6.55), a crazy but satisfying blend can be yours.

A perfect and appropriately wacky finish to your meal is a dish of Carvel ice cream sent over through an actual hole in the wall from the Carvel store next door.

Open from 11 a.m. to 10:30 p.m. daily. No reservations.

GREEK: As you go downstairs on a quiet side street near Columbia University, **The Symposium** Greek restaurant, 544 W. 113th St., between Broadway and Amsterdam Avenue (tel. 865-1011), is a pleasant surprise. There are folk-art paintings on the ceiling, painted lightbulbs, Greek art on the walls, and drawings on the tables. The friendly, festive atmosphere will add to a very good meal.

This is the only restaurant we know of where the prices have gone down! Under new management this year, the food is the same, but the prices are significantly lower. Moussaka (eggplant and meat pie) and pastitsio (stuffed macaroni) are $4.95. "Feta"ccini (Greek spinach noodles with feta cheese) is also $4.95. A carafe of wine is $5. For dessert, flogera (the shepherd's flute) is a custardy roll of dough with a sweet sauce ($1.35). If the weather permits, dine in the lovely rear garden decorated with strings of lights, hanging plants, and more paintings.

Open daily from noon until 11 p.m.

FRENCH BISTRO: Amsterdam Avenue is the latest address in New York's restaurant renaissance. All along the avenue in what used to be junk shops, package stores, hardware and fabric emporiums are chic new restaurants, open late and packed with young professionals as well as celebrities.

HUNGARIAN: A lot of restaurants say that they have home-style cooking, but the **Green Tree**, 1034 Amsterdam Ave., at 111th Street (tel. 864-9106), really does. Even if your mother never cooked a Hungarian meal in her life, the food will make you think you're eating in somebody's home. The decor is well worn and homey: the wood-paneled walls are decorated with bright plates, and plants are scattered throughout the dining room.

The food is hearty and plentiful. Daily specials include stuffed chicken ($5.35), veal shank ($5.95), and chicken liver à la Budapest ($5.75)—all served with rice, potatoes, and string beans. On Thursday, Friday, and Saturday, roast loin of pork ($5.75) and stuffed veal ($5.95) are added to the specials; on Friday, roast duck ($7.95) is also featured, and on Saturday all these specials, plus sauerbraten ($5.75), are offered.

Try a cup of cold borscht ($1.35) for an appetizer, and perhaps an entree of plum dumplings ($5.95), potato pancakes ($4.45), Hungarian goulash ($5.55), or chicken paprikash ($5.25). Add $2.50 to the price of any entree and you'll get an appetizer, coffee or tea, and a dessert. The fresh apple strudel ($1.45) and palacsinta ($1.65), a Hungarian crêpes suzette, are the most popular sweets.

Owners Ali and Clara Kende have been giving students a break here for 28 years. The student lunch, served from 11:30 a.m. to 3 p.m., features 11 dishes such as fried filet of sole ($3.45), chopped steak à la Budapest ($3.45), and stuffed pepper ($3.95). Every day after 3 p.m. all students ordering a full dinner get a free beer.

During the busiest hours, service can be slow—don't come here if you'll be in a rush.

The Green Tree is open from noon to 9 p.m. Monday through Saturday; closed Sunday. Reservations accepted only for groups of seven or more.

INDIAN: "Though curry is Indian food, not all Indian food is curry," reads the slogan at the **Indian Kitchen**, 2200 Broadway at 78th Street (tel. 362-8760). This interesting restaurant has a lot more than its storefront looks suggest. Luciano Pavarotti and Zubin Mehta are reputed to be regulars here, where creative Indian dinners as well as vegetarian Indian specialties are served. Chicken tika tandoori, chunks of white meat barbecued and served with vegetables and a sauce ($7.95), and shrimp tika, jumbo shrimps sauteed in a green masala and steamed with vegetables ($9.95), are perennial favorites. Four kinds of homemade chutney (tomato, tamarind, mango, and ginger) are available to take home as well.

There are eight different curry dinners on the menu—egg, meatball, chicken, and more—and also special pulav dinners made with choice meats cooked in rice with vegetables, herbs, and spices. All are in the $4.95 to $8.95 range.

Don't leave without trying tofutti, a nondairy ice cream made from tofu, soy milk, fresh fruits, and honey. It's kosher and has only 26 calories per ounce ($2).

Open daily from 1 p.m. to midnight. No reservations. You may bring wine or beer.

JAPANESE: The **Aki Dining Room**, 420 W. 119th St., between Amsterdam Avenue and Morningside Drive (tel. 864-5970), is a serene retreat. Located in a side street in the bottom floor of an apartment building, it evokes the tranquility of a Japanese tea room. The walls are lined with rice-paper panels and bamboo-patterned wallpaper, and paper lanterns hang all around. Though not elegant, it is charming and comfortable.

On the lunch special you can get shrimp or vegetable tempura, beef or chicken teriyaki, or shoga yaki (pork cooked in ginger sauce)—all served with white rice, soup, and tea—for $4.25. Combination plates are also available for $5.25. Seventeen dinners are offered, ranging from nabeyaki, a chicken, shrimp, and fish-cake casserole ($6.95), to teishoku, a combination plate of tempura, sashimi, and teriyaki ($9.25). All the entrees come with rice, soup, salad, and tea, and many are served in a hot iron dish atop a wooden platter.

Open Monday through Saturday from noon to 3 p.m. and from 5 to 11 p.m. Reservations accepted.

Suki's, 433 Amsterdam Ave., between 80th and 81st Streets (tel. 496-8940), is one of the newest Japanese sushi restaurants on the Upper West Side. The atmosphere is chic and intimate. Rock and roll plays softly in the background. There is a small sleek black-lacquered wood bar and a vase of elegant fresh flowers at the entrance. Potted plants sitting by the big front window and a wall covered with brightly colored paintings add to Suki's charm.

The food here is excellent and affordable. For the intrepid, sitting at the sushi bar and watching the masterful sushi chefs slice and sculpt colorful mouthfuls of raw fish and seaweed is as much fun as going to the theater. The mackerel handroll, raw mackerel with minced scallops and ginger and rice, wrapped in a cone of toasted seaweed ($3.50), is fresh and delicious. Grilled eel sushi ($2.20) is an unusually sweet treat. And if you're really brave, try the creamy raw sea urchin ($2.20)—you'll feel positively affectionate for the spiny species.

The Japanese chef salad (baby shrimp, squid, and marinated beansprouts with tofu and the chef's dressing at $6) is also good. Kiki yaku, broiled sea scallops with the house sauce ($5.50), and tatsutage, Japanese fried chicken ($4.50), are more conventional fare but with a unique flair.

Open from 5 p.m. to 1 a.m. Monday through Saturday, from 3 to 11 p.m. on Sunday.

MACROBIOTIC: With a basis in Eastern philosophy, the macrobiotic diet is intended to balance the two universal principles, yin and yang, within the individual and thus lead to a more harmonious, healthy life. Macrobiotic food is made from whole grains, beans, fresh fruits and vegetables, seafood, and seaweed. Forbidden "fruits" include meat and eggs (too yang), sugar, honey, alcohol, and even seemingly innocuous foods such as dairy products (too yin).

But even if you can't tell your yin from your yang, you'll find enjoyable macrobiotic fare at **Souen,** 2444 Broadway, between 90th and 91st Streets (tel. 787-1110). Most of the dishes are based on Japanese cuisine, and as long as you don't have your heart set on meat and potatoes, you'll appreciate the freshness of the food.

Souen is small and spotless, with 16 little tables in two neat rows and a few counter seats as well. The decor is simple without being stark: oak parquet floors and exposed brick lend warmth, while wood-slatted lanterns keep the place softly lit. You can try some agetofu ($3), deep-fried tofu in ginger burdock sauce, along with some brown rice ($1.50 for a small bowl, $2.50 for a large), which comes with a sesame-oat sauce. A bowl of tabouli salad costs $2.75; vegetable soba (noodles and vegetables in broth) is $4.50.

House specials include karaage (a trout filet deep fried with ginger burdock sauce) at $7, and seitan (whole-wheat protein cutlets deep fried, with the same sauce), at $5.95. If you're not feeling adventurous, you can get broiled sole, shrimp, sea trout, or brook trout for $7. Try some bancha tea (25¢) or mu tea (75¢) with your meal. Sugar-free desserts, such as the tofu pie ($2.50) or apple crunch ($1.75), are a boon for the less-than-iron-willed dieter, though perhaps not as satisfying as a gooey hot-fudge sundae.

Souen is open Sunday through Thursday from noon to 10 p.m., on Friday and Saturday to 11 p.m.

MIDDLE EASTERN: The **Sultan's Table,** 2337 Broadway, between 84th and 85th Streets (tel. 787-5811), may not be as plush as the name implies, but you can get a good variety of Middle Eastern food here at reasonable prices. The walls are decorated with a hodgepodge of red-flocked saloon-style wallpaper, artificial wood paneling, mirrors, and wallpaper murals depicting country scenes. The place is tiny, and the service is pleasant.

Many patrons order the Aleppo special salad ($4.25), named for owner Nader Shayet's hometown in Syria. It has a combination of hummus (ground chickpeas with sesame oil and lemon), baba ghanouj (mashed eggplant salad), and falafel (deep-fried balls of ground, spiced chickpeas). Appetizers, enough for a meal, include foolmoudamas, fava beans with parsley, for $3; tabouli salad ($2.50); and a mixed salad with feta cheese ($3.25). Stuffed chicken, lamb, grape leaves, or squash cost $6.25. Mideastern desserts such as halvah, baklava, and sahlab (a milk pudding) are $1.25.

Open from 12:30 to 10:30 p.m. daily.

NATURAL FOODS: Peter's Pumpkin Eater, 2452 Broadway, near 91st Street (tel. 877-0132), features "natural cuisine," an eclectic menu of macrobiotic, Middle Eastern, and Mexican fare. Recently expanded, this is a quiet, peaceful restaurant, even at its busiest. Classical music plays in the background. The small wooden tables are set with fresh flowers and candles. Abundant green plants hang near the front windows. Diners here all look healthy, which is the best advertisement for this cuisine.

While there's no red meat on the menu, there's a varied selection of boiled fresh fish ($8.50 to $10.95). Guacamole ($3.25) and hummus ($2.95) are popular appetizers. If you've ever had Indonesian "rice table," you won't recognize this Indonesian curry ($7.95), but it's delicious nonetheless. A hearty helping of coarsely cut vegetables—carrots, zucchini, broccoli, cabbage, and chickpeas on a bed of brown rice, smothered in an unusually sweet and spicy cashew sauce—is delicious. A diner at a nearby table was overheard saying, upon tasting this dish, that "it's like coming home." Mango lemonade ($1.50 for a small glass, $2.75 for a large) is a refreshing beverage, or try a cool papaya smoothie ($2.25) that is both thirst-quenching and a reputed digestive aid.

Peter's Pumpkin Eater is open for breakfast. You can start your day with homemade scones or carrot raisin muffins, fresh-squeezed orange juice, and coffee or tea for $2.95. Or if you like a heavier breakfast, the "Primrose Patty" (tofu and chopped scallions scrambled together, with paprikash potatoes, toast, apple juice, coffee or tea, at $3.95) will wake you up as well as fill you up.

Open from 8 a.m. until 10:45 p.m. Monday through Friday, from 11 a.m. to 10:45 p.m. on Saturday and Sunday.

5. Lincoln Center

The Lincoln Center neighborhood has changed radically since it inspired the Broadway musical *West Side Story*. Although you can still find some oldtime "bodegas" (Spanish neighborhood markets), the area has filled up with slick, expensive restaurants that can gobble up your budget in no time. When you've got tickets to a Lincoln Center concert and want to go someplace nearby for dinner or dessert, we suggest one of the reasonably priced restaurants and cafés listed here. All are within walking distance of Lincoln Center, which is bounded by Broadway and Amsterdam Avenue, between 62nd and 66th Streets.

AMERICAN/CONTINENTAL: The **Opera Espresso,** 1928 Broadway at 65th Street (tel. 799-3050), is sort of an elegant coffeeshop—a perfect place to have something simple before or after the show without having it cost more than the Lincoln Center tickets. The walls are covered with burgundy paper and adorned with framed copies of old Metropolitan Opera programs, a Gregorian chant on parchment, and pictures of performers from Pavlova to Nureyev. Graceful brass chandeliers cast a soft glow. You can sit either at the counter or in one of the comfortable wood booths.

Entrees run from $7.50 to $8.75, including baked eggplant stuffed with ricotta and mozzarella, served with a salad, and fresh-baked fish du jour with potato and salad. You can also get sandwiches ($3.25 to $4.95), burgers ($3.75 to $4.95), omelets with potato or salad ($4.75), and a fresh cup of espresso ($1) with dessert ($2.50 or $3.75).

Open from 7:30 a.m. to midnight Monday through Saturday, from 8 a.m. to midnight on Sunday. Reservations accepted for large groups only.

The **Lincoln Square Coffee Shop,** 2 Lincoln Square, between 65th and 66th Streets, "where Broadway meets Columbus" (tel. 799-4000), is much more than a coffeeshop. It had all the requisites, like coffee (Viennese coffee, with lots of whipped cream, is $2.50) and hamburgers (from $4.25), soups ($1.95), sandwiches (from $3.45 to $4.95), homemade pies and ice-cream sundaes or "brownies all-the-way" ($2.75 to $3.75), but it also has one of the most unusual salad bars found under a sneeze guard. Served with fresh rolls and butter, the salad bar is billed as a meal in itself, and it is—with the expected vegetables and lettuce, but also special seafood salads, nuts, fruits, and marinated mushrooms —an ever-changing supply of ingredients. It's $6.95 alone, $7.95 with soup (homemade chicken noodle, cold borscht, matzoh ball, boiled potato, or chicken rice). French onion soup in a crock is $2.35. There are other special entrees like eggplant milanese ($5.95, $8.95 with salad bar) or Indian curried chicken ($6.75, $9.25 with salad bar).

Hours are 7 a.m. to 11:30 p.m. seven days a week.

The Saloon, Broadway at 64th Street, across from Lincoln Center (tel. 874-1500), is an outdoor café with roller-skating waiters in the summer and a high-ceilinged, exposed-brick gathering spot for West Siders in chillier months. Colorful banners float over tables where a varied selection of Mexican, all-American, and continental dishes are served. The menu is huge, in size and assortment, but appetizers and salads are exotic and affordable, as are sandwiches and other specialties. Blue corn nachos chivera, with goat cheese, jalapeños, and guacamole ($4.95); Cajun popcorn (deep-fried crawfish tails, $5.95) and homemade goose liver pâté ($4.95) are almost enough for a full meal. Hot and cold salads are featured, including duckling and macadamia nuts ($10.95), hot gulf shrimp salad ($10.95), ratatouille Niçoise ($7.95), and a chef's salad for $7.50. Sandwiches (from $6.95 to $7.95) are inventive—as are the omelet and egg dishes ($5.50 to $7.95). Pizzelles, wafer-thin pizzas, are $4.95 to $6.95 for a lighter meal. There is a huge list of daily specials, which include fresh seafood (steamers are $7.95).

Open daily from 11:30 a.m. to 2 a.m. for food, till 4 a.m. for drinks.

CHINESE: The **Hunan Café,** 214 Columbus Ave., between 69th and 70th Streets, is refreshingly simple in appearance. It has white walls, white tablecloths, and white dishes, with plants and a single flower on each table to soften the effect.

Every day there are seven chef's specials (about $7.50 to $9). On a given day these might include duck, chicken, or beef with asparagus, or crispy whole sea bass. The regular menu is extensive, offering a variety of Hunan, Szechuan, and Peking dishes. The chef's specialties include hot-and-spicy orange beef ($8.50), lemon chicken ($6.95), and jumbo shrimp Hunan style ($8.50). Specials are shrimp with asparagus and softshell crab (both $8.50).

Open Sunday through Thursday from 11:30 a.m. to midnight, on Friday and Saturday to 1:30 a.m.

CRÊPES: **Crêpe Inn Plus,** 332 W. 58th St., between Eighth and Ninth Avenues (tel. 757-7241), offers crêpes and other good food at low prices in a clean, cheery, fast-food eatery. Little orange Formica tables are lined up along the wall and in a small dining area in the rear. The floors are terracotta tile; two walls are decorated with murals of autumn forests and the others are faced with imitation brick. Greek music crackles from the radio behind the counter.

Crêpes filled with cheese, spinach, moussaka, and even chicken curry are priced from $1.90 to $2.60; sandwiches range from cream cheese and jelly ($1.70) to ham and swiss ($2.80). A cottage cheese and fresh fruit salad costs $2.30; a hamburger is $1.95. You may want to splurge a bit and have a dessert crêpe stuffed with rice pudding ($1), fruit salad ($1.50), or fresh strawberries ($2.05)—all topped with a dab of whipped cream.

From 6 to 11 a.m. there's a breakfast special of two eggs with potatoes, toast, and coffee ($1.50).

Open Monday through Saturday from 6 a.m. to 6 p.m.

ITALIAN: **Al Buon Gusto,** 143 W. 72nd St. (tel. 874-9560), is a home-style Italian restaurant owned by Pietro Secci, a native Genoan. The Genoa lighthouse is a symbol for this friendly eatery, which has a red-and-white checked floor, ceiling fans, paintings on the walls, and a large inlaid wood map of New York (the only one in the world).

Entrees include veal done several ways—veal parmigiana and spaghetti ($8.50), veal goulash ($6.50), or veal piccante or scaloppine with peppers and spaghetti ($8.50)—and steak pizzaiola and spaghetti ($9.50). There are several seafood selections in the $7.50 to $10 range.

If you want good Italian food on a lower budget, there are 13 kinds of spaghetti to choose from, including dishes with butter sauce, garlic, and anchovies or clams, all in the $4 to $7 range. Manicotti and cannelloni are each $5.50, and Italian-style sandwiches are also on the menu.

If you're in a pizza mood, you can get regular or Sicilian (thick) pizza by the pie or the slice. Small pizzas start at $6.75, with toppings $1.25 extra. Large pizzas start at $8, with $1.50 extra for topping.

Several imported Italian wines are on the menu, served European style in glass tumblers. Beer is also available.

Open noon to midnight daily.

Genoa Ristorante, 271 Amsterdam Ave., between 72nd and 73rd Streets (tel. 787-1094), is one of a new breed of family restaurants. Owners Pamela and Bob Arena, a young couple who used to work on Wall Street, decided to go into the restaurant business five years ago, and the result has been a charming little trattoria offering fresh northern Italian cooking at prices that cause double-takes from passersby who see the menu in the window. The Arenas do the cooking, and judging from the crowds that line up for tables, they do it the way the people like it. The tables are elegantly set with pink linen cloths and white napkins, and the service is friendly.

Pasta entrees, with salad, are mostly in the $6.50 range; chicken genovese, marsala, or francese costs $7.75, veal scaloppine costs $8.75, and shrimp marinara, served with three cherrystone clams and spaghetti, is $7.95. By adding $1.25 to any of these entree prices, you can get minestrone soup or a stuffed pepper, and coffee or tea. If you like to try a little of a lot of things, you might want to make a meal of some minestrone ($1.25 a cup, $1.50 a bowl) or a half order of pasta ($3.50) with the hearty hot antipasto ($8.50 for two), which includes broiled clams, shrimp, stuffed mushrooms and peppers, and eggplant rollatine.

Open Tuesday through Sunday from 5:30 to 10:30 p.m. No reservations.

Once you've discovered **Noodles,** 40 W. 72nd St. (tel. 873-3550), you'll keep trying to find excuses to go back. You'll dine amid old copper pots and red-checkered tablecloths in this pleasant restaurant, which is full of friendly waiters. A special dinner offer—two full dinners for $10.95 between 4 and 6 p.m. on Sunday—makes for economical indulgence.

Regular prices are reasonable and range from $3.95 to $7.95, with a daily special at $7.95. You can get noodles from the East or West at this establishment. Italian-style dishes include a wonderful tortellini Alfredo with rich cream sauce ($6.95) and spaghetti with a variety of fresh sauces, with meat and tomatoes and plenty of robust flavor. If you try Eastern noodles, we recommend the Korean cellophane-noodle dish with stir-fried veggies arranged in a sherry-and-soy sauce atop threads of noodles ($6.95). One-pot meals come in generous individual cauldrons, such as soba ($5.95), which has mixed vegetables and buckwheat noodles simmered in a savory sauce. One person can hardly finish this delectable meal.

A new Noodles is open at 115 E. 57th St., in the Galleria. Hours are Monday through Thursday from 5 p.m. to midnight, on Friday and Saturday till 1 a.m., and on Sunday from 4 to 6 p.m. Plan to arrive early for the dinner special.

ITALIAN PASTRIES: Café La Fortuna, 69 W. 71st St., between Columbus Avenue and Central Park West (tel. 724-5846), is one of those delightful places where you should forget that calories exist. It's the perfect place to linger over a cappuccino ($1.50) or espresso ($1.20) and pastry ($1.75 to $2) after the show. The walls are laden with old opera records and pictures of singing stars from Caruso to Pavarotti. The owner's favorite photo is the one of John Lennon, Yoko Ono, and their son, Sean—former regulars at the café—mugging it up in oldtime costumes. During the summer you can enjoy the evening on the café's fenced-in patio.

Most of the pastries, including the sinfully rich cannoli, are Italian, although there are also some German delights. A variety of cookies, cakes, homemade Italian ices, and gelati ($2.50) are also available.

Open Tuesday through Thursday from 1 p.m. to 1 a.m., on Friday to 2 a.m., on Saturday from noon to 2 a.m., and on Sunday from noon to 1 a.m. Closed Monday.

JEWISH DELI: New York's Jewish delis are legendary, and **Fine and Schapiro**, 138 W. 72nd St., between Broadway and Columbus Avenue (tel. 877-2721), is one of the nicest around. Started in 1927, this family-run place has a charmingly simple, old-fashioned decor. The walls are of cedar—something you'd be hard pressed to find in a newer place—with brown-painted wainscotting. Dinner is a fancy production, complete with double linen tablecloths on the blond wood-grained Formica tables. Many regular customers have been coming here for decades.

Lunch is the best deal here. For about $5.25 to $6 you can get one of a variety of sandwiches, such as pastrami, chicken salad, or chopped liver, with soup, cookies, and tea or black coffee (no butter or milk is served). You can also choose from a changing list of luncheon specials, such as stuffed cabbage ($6.05), gefilte fish ($5.70), or potted meatballs ($6.10), served with potatoes or vegetables, soup, tea, and dessert. Of course you can also order items à la carte. Potato pancakes cost $1.35; potato salad or cole slaw costs $1.25. A club sandwich is $7.20, a bottle of beer costs $1.55 to $1.95, and 95¢ buys a glass of Dr. Brown's Celery Tonic or a traditional cream soda. Homemade soups such as pea, lentil, and cabbage are $1.60 for a cup and $2.20 for a bowl. Omelets range from $4.65 for onion to $8.50 for chicken liver, all served with relish and french fries.

Dinners are huge—served with appetizer, soup, vegetable, potato, dessert, and beverage—and offering everything from corned beef and eggs ($10.20) to stuffed homemade kishke ($11) and broiled baby lamb chops ($16.30). If you'd like to turn any of these generous meals into a dinner for two, add a $2 charge for the extra plate. For those on low-sodium diets, Fine and Schapiro offers several salt-free dishes.

Open 8:30 a.m. for the take-out counter and from 11:30 a.m. to 10:30 p.m. daily.

MEXICAN: If you're in the mood for some south-of-the-border cuisine, try **Los Panchos**, 71 W. 71st St., between Columbus Avenue and Central Park West (tel. 874-7336). From the street, you step down into a pleasant bar/lounge (known for its Cuervo margaritas at $2.75) into a dining room with white cloths and candles on the tables. The stucco walls are brightened, though not to garish excess, with sombreros, serapes, and Mexican paintings. When the weather is nice, you can also eat in the quiet back patio or at one of a few tables on the sidewalk.

Lunch here is the best deal; most entree prices rise by $1.50 to $2 for dinner. Weekdays from 11:30 a.m. to 4 p.m. lunch specials offer such plates as a beef-stuffed tomato and a chile relleno or a shrimp enchilada and guacamole tostada for $5.50. The regular menu includes typical taco, tostada, enchilada, and burrito combination plates ranging from $5.75 to $8.50 with rice and beans. Other dishes include flautas—corn and flour tortillas stuffed with muenster cheese, deep-fried and covered with guacamole—served with tomato sauce, rice, and beans for $8.50, and a bowl of hot and spicy chili, served with rice on the side for $5.95 ($7.50 at dinner). Guacamole dip ($3.25 at lunch, $4.25 at dinner) is a popular appetizer, and flan ($2.50) is the perfect dessert after a hot, spicy meal. At lunch, selected wines are available for $1 a glass.

Open Sunday through Thursday from 11:30 a.m. to midnight, on Friday and Saturday to 1 a.m. Brunch is served on Saturday and Sunday from 11:30 a.m. to 4 p.m. Reservations for large parties only.

SEAFOOD: Dining at **Capt. Nemo's,** 137 W. 72nd St., between Columbus and Amsterdam Avenues (tel. 595-5600), is fun. You enter through the pleasant front bar area, which has a pretty leaded-glass window that looks onto the street, and walk past a tankful of ill-fated lobsters into a dining room fitted out in copper and brass to resemble a submarine. For dinner, white linen cloths cover the tables, and candles add a touch of romance.

At lunch you can start with a cup of New England or Manhattan clam chowder for $1.25, then have a filet of sole, scrod, or bluefish, prepared just about every way possible for $4.45. Scampi broiled in herbal garlic butter is $6.25, as is the broiled scallops. Entrees are served with salad or cole slaw and french fries or rice. If you don't want fish, you can have chopped sirloin, or marinated chicken for $5.95. You'll have to order carefully at dinner to avoid breaking your budget: most entrees cost $8.95 to $12.95. If you really feel like going all-out, there's a lobster dinner with appetizer, potato or saffron rice, salad, and wine for $16.95.

Open Sunday through Thursday from 1 p.m. to midnight, on Friday and Saturday from noon to 1 a.m. Reservations accepted.

VIENNESE: Eclair, 141 W. 72nd St., between Columbus and Amsterdam Avenues (tel. 873-7700), is a charming old neighborhood institution with a suitable old-fashioned decor. The dining room is nicely lit and airy; the marble floors and white linen tablecloths speak of the proud Viennese heritage of owner Alexander Selinger.

As you might guess from the name, Eclair's specialty for 42 years has been pastries and cakes. You'll have a hard time choosing from over 200 varieties of scrumptious strudels, tortes, eclairs, fruit tarts, danish, croissants—you name it. Prices range from $1.50 to $2.25. For an extra 50¢ you can have your delicacy à la mode or with a mound of whipped cream. The perfect complement for one of these pastries is a cup of rich, smooth Viennese coffee with whipped cream ($1).

But don't write Eclair off as just a coffee and pastry shop. It's a pleasant place for dinner before or after a concert, with such continental treats as Hungarian goulash ($7.25), Viennese fried chicken ($7.25), and sauerbraten with potato pancakes ($7.95)—all served with creamed spinach or the vegetable du jour, potato, and your choice of cucumber, tossed salad, or applesauce. Add $3 to any of these dinners and you can get a soup (perhaps chilled borscht) or appetizer, dessert, and coffee or tea. Check the daily specials, which include paprika chicken with a vegetable and tossed salad ($7.25) or a breaded liver steak with potato salad ($6.25). A glass of wine with a dinner is only 95¢.

If you're looking for lighter fare, try the quiche, served with a tossed salad for $3.95, or one of a variety of sandwiches and burgers most priced from $2.75 to $4.25. With a full soda fountain, wine, beer, and apéritifs, Eclair offers such a variety of choices that it's ideal for groups of people with different tastes or appetites.

An excellent breakfast is also served. Open from 8 a.m. to midnight daily. Reservations accepted.

6. Pennsylvania Station/Chelsea

The area that includes Pennsylvania Station and Chelsea, from 15th Street to 40th Street west of Fifth Avenue, is characterized by two distinct neighborhoods. Located in the heart of the garment district, Penn Station is surrounded by a nine-to-five stream of commuters and delivery trucks. The emphasis here is on fast food—but don't be led astray by the familiar chains. There are plenty of unique eateries here, offering low-priced meals. Farther down, the residential area known as Chelsea is a neighborhood in transition. Developers are moving in quickly, and may soon change the face of this area entirely. Carpenters are already busy building new, slick facades on old structures, but there are still a lot of small, unpretentious restaurants here.

AMERICAN/CONTINENTAL: There's an "olde" English feel to the **Old Garden,** 15 W. 29th St., between Fifth Avenue and Broadway (tel. 532-8323). It has a Tudor exterior of red brick and black-wood framing. The front arched wooden doorway leads to a cozy dining room and a large bar called the Winery, which is lit by electric gas lamps. Tables are set with patchwork cotton tablecloths, and archways toward the back are hung with curtains of the same material. The exposed brick walls have still-life pictures of fruits and flowers.

Lunch is your best bet here, with entrees ranging from $5.95 to $9.50, and luncheon salads ranging from $4.95 to $8.50. To begin, you might try the chopped liver ($1.50) or split-pea soup (95¢). Entrees are served with potatoes and vegetables. Fried Louisiana shrimp with sauce for dipping costs $7.75, and veal marsala with wild mushrooms runs $7.95. For dessert, try the strawberry shortcake for 95¢.

Open from 11:30 a.m. to 9 p.m. Monday through Friday, from 4:30 to 9 p.m. on Saturday. Reservations suggested.

The food is cooked long and slow at **Smokey's Real Pit Bar-B-Q,** 230 Ninth Ave., at 24th Street (tel. 924-8181). It can take up to 12 hours to cook a 12-pound brisket of beef in their charcoal brick oven. Josh and Elisa Lewin, the young couple who own the restaurant, decorated Smokey's with weathered gray wood walls and wood-grained Formica tables. Over in one corner there's an old-fashioned water pump with a wood barrel drain for washing barbecue sauce off sticky hands.

Try the rib snack here for $5.35, or half a barbecued chicken for $5.99, served with cole slaw and fried potatoes. A bowl of Smokey's award-winning chili is $3.90, and a sliced beef sandwich is $3. For dessert there's key lime pie for $1.25, or pecan pie for $1.50.

Open Monday through Friday from 11 a.m. to 11 p.m., from noon to 11 p.m. on weekends.

The menu changes every two weeks at **Miss Ruby's Café,** 135 Eighth Avenue, between 16th and 17th Streets (tel. 620-4055), a self-styled haven of "American Eclectic" cooking that features different regional cuisines fortnightly. Inside, beyond the long bar in front, there's a light and airy room, whose bare-brick walls are done in pastels. Hanging plants, track lighting, and three skylights add to the effect, and the open kitchen at the rear affords a view of your own meal being prepared.

Cooking styles you might encounter here range from New England to Deep South to California; we recently sampled Tex-Mex, feasting on carne adobada ($8.50), shredded pork that's marinated and broiled and served with a verde sauce on a soft corn tortilla, along with rice and beans. Six other entrees, from cheese and onion enchiladas ($7.95) to baked pickled kingfish ($9.95), rounded out the offerings. Beer and wine are available, as are specialty drinks and wines that change with each menu.

Desserts are sinfully rich, with the likes of fudge pie ($4.50) and sopaipillas ($4), fried biscotto dough drizzled with honey. Coffee, espresso, and cappuccino are always available.

Much the same fare is offered at lunch, and there is an "interim" menu—soup and salad—in effect between 4 and 6 p.m. Sunday brunch ($3 to $7) features blackboards of changing specials.

Open from noon to midnight Monday through Saturday, to 10 p.m. on Sunday. Sunday brunch is from noon to 4 p.m.

Chelsea's neighborhood spirit is still thriving at **Dunleavy's,** 236 Eighth Ave., at 22nd Street (tel. 242-8255). This relaxed, unpretentious restaurant is housed in one room, with a full bar. The local crowd is low-key, and although the bar takes up a good portion of the restaurant, it isn't a pickup joint. The decor is simple, with a long wooden bench lining one wall, and green brocade patterned wallpaper. Fresh flowers are set on every table and the yellow pressed-tin ceiling has a hanging fan. The staff—one waitress and a bartender—is friendly and helpful. Dinner items are reasonably priced between $6.50 and $7.95, and include homemade soup and a salad. Try the chicken parmigiana ($7.95) or the sauteed bay scallops (market price). Specials are posted daily on the blackboard. For dessert there are assorted home-baked specials like chocolate rum cake and pecan pie for $3, or fresh strawberries in heavy cream (in season) at $2.25.

Open from 11 a.m. to 1 a.m. Sunday through Thursday, to 2 a.m. on Friday and Saturday. Brunch ($5.95) is served from 11 a.m. to 4 p.m. on weekends and holidays.

As the name implies, **West Boondock,** 114 Tenth Ave., at 17th Street (tel. 929-9645), is about as far from the madding crowd as you can get, situated as it is in the middle of an area devoted to warehouses, trucking firms, and light industry. But make the effort to find this unpretentious spot with its brick and wood-paneled walls, long bar up front, photos and posters of jazz greats, and fresh flowers on every table, and you'll discover some of the best soul food in town.

Start with an appetizer like breaded and fried okra ($1.50) or fried chicken wings ($2.50), then choose one of 13 entrees, including chitterlings, barbecued pork ribs, or deep-fried catfish (each is $7.95). Entrees come with warm corn-bread and two vegetables (try the collard greens and blackeyed peas). Sandwiches and sandwich platters run from $2.95 to $4.95, and for dessert there's delightful sweet potato pie ($1.50), peanut fudge pie ($1.75), and five other choices. The lunch menu (served from noon to 3 p.m.) features most of the same dishes for $1 less, plus daily specials (like roast pork loin or chicken curry) for only $3.95.

In addition to a first-rate selection of older jazz recordings on the jukebox, there is live jazz piano nightly.

Open from noon to 1 a.m. Monday through Thursday, to 3 a.m. on Friday, from 5 p.m. to 3 a.m. on Saturday, and from 5 p.m. to 1 a.m. on Sunday.

CHINESE: Chinatown Express, 425 Seventh Ave., between 33rd and 34th Streets (tel. 563-3559), is attractively designed with green-and-white tiles at the front counter and behind the stove. Entrees are temptingly displayed in a curved alcove covered by glass slats. Downstairs there are two dining rooms, decorated with plastic shields painted with Chinese characters. An upstairs dining room, with a view of the avenue below, is furnished with orange chairs and live plants. The restaurant is kept bright and clean by a hardworking staff.

The menu features combination platters served in large portions. Wonton soup is $1.07 and eggrolls cost $.88. The four platter combinations are all about $4, with a peppersteak, eggroll, and fried-rice platter for $4.17; a platter of spare ribs, fried wonton, chicken wings, fried rice, and shrimp toast is $3.66. Roast pork egg foo yung costs $2.22 and a large order of chicken wings is $3.38.

Open 11 a.m. to 9 p.m. daily, and from 9:30 a.m. to 10 p.m. on nights when there's a big show at Madison Square Garden across the street.

The food at **Sung Ho Lo,** 211 Seventh Ave., between 22nd and 23rd Streets (tel. 924-8580), is undeniably fresh; we once watched as the staff sat stemming mountains of green beans at a back table. The informal, quiet restaurant is decorated with framed black calligraphy letters painted on rice paper, and Chinese watercolor prints. Tables are set with pretty green Chinese-design placemats. Plants adorn the front window and a tall bamboo tree stands by the counter.

Luncheon specials, ranging in price from $3.95 to $4.95, are the best deals of the day. Try the chicken with broccoli, the sweet-and-sour pork, or the peppersteak, each $3.95. Shrimp with cashew nuts is $4.95. The à la carte menu, for lunch and dinner, includes hot-and-spicy orange beef ($5.95), and lemon chicken that's batter-fried and dipped in lemon and honey sauce ($5.95). For dessert, try the chilled lichee nuts (75¢). Main dishes can be served with brown rice, if you prefer it to the white rice.

Open Monday through Friday from 11:30 a.m. to 11 p.m., on Saturday from 5 to 11 p.m., and on Sunday from 5 to 10:30 p.m.

CUBAN/CHINESE: Housed in an old shiny aluminum diner, **Mi Chinita** is at 176 Eighth Ave., at the corner of 19th Street (tel. 741-0240). Here the character is set by the diner decor—a long Formica counter and blue Formica tables matched with aqua-colored linen curtains. Two Chinese hanging lamps and a few other Chinese decorator items reflect the Asian half of the menu.

The menu offers a wide selection of both Chinese and Cuban food. Eggdrop soup is $1.25 and two eggrolls cost $2. The Chinese menu includes roast pork and mushrooms ($4.95), vegetable egg foo yung ($4.35), and chicken with broccoli ($5.15). From the Cuban menu you can choose peppersteak with rice and beans ($4.55), tongue with rice and beans ($4.35), or paella ($12). This is only a small view of the wide number of dishes offered. For dessert, try the flan or bread pudding (75¢).

Open from 11:30 a.m. to 9:40 p.m. Monday through Saturday.

GREEK: Hidden away behind a freight entrance on 39th Street is **Nick's Place,** 550 Seventh Ave., between 39th and 40th Streets (tel. 221-3294). This restaurant is a real find, with delicious homemade Greek specialties. There are only seven tables in the dining area, but the small room is cozily decorated, with blue-and-orange patterned cloth covering walls that are simply adorned with large straw baskets and an old-fashioned French poster.

Traditional Greek offerings include moussaka with vegetable or salad ($4.25), spinach pie with salad ($4.05), and stuffed grape leaves ($1.40). There is also a wide variety of salads, including avocado salad vinaigrette ($4.35), and a spinach salad ($3.75). For dessert, try the fresh carrot cake ($1.60) or the baklava ($1.10).

Hours here are limited to 11 a.m. to 3 p.m., weekdays only.

For more elegant dining, there's the **Atlas Greek Restaurant,** 171 W. 29th St., around the corner from Seventh Avenue (tel. 695-6998). Don't be discouraged by the gray stairway leading up to the restaurant. You'll find that the Atlas has a spacious, airy dining room with a good view of Seventh Avenue from the window tables up front. The decor here is simple, with mirrors and warm wood paneling that takes on a golden glow when the sun streams in. Tables are covered in white linen draped over red cloths. Many patrons are Greek businessmen, who stop in at lunchtime to sample the authentic food and drink retsina or ouzo.

The menu here changes daily, with most entrees around $6. Omelets cost $4.50 and lamb pilaf or shish kebab is $6.25. A small Greek salad is $1 and wine or beer is $1. For dessert, try the baklava ($1.25).

Open from 11:30 a.m. to 3 p.m. Monday through Saturday.

ITALIAN: A colorful, working-class deli, **Manganaro's Grosseria,** at 488 Ninth Ave., between 37th and 38th Streets (tel. 563-5331), consists of a large store that sells imported specialty items, with a small luncheonette in the back. The store is decorated with hanging baskets and a red, green, and white canopy at one counter. It's now run by five of the seven Manganaro sisters, who see to it that the biscotti and the delicious cheeses are all beautifully displayed. The sit-down deli is simply decorated, with a green floor and brown-wood Formica tables.

Sandwiches here are a real treat, served in long, fresh hero rolls. A meatball hero is only $2.50, and an eggplant parmigiana sandwich is $3.50. Baked ziti and eggplant, served only on Friday, costs $4.95. A cappicola sandwich is only $2.50, and the Manganaro special, with mixed meats, cheese, and peppers, is $3.75. For dessert, try the extraordinary ricotta cheesecake ($4 per pound).

Open from 8 a.m. to 7 p.m. Monday through Saturday.

It means meatball, but **La Polpetta,** at 257 W. 34th St., between Seventh and Eighth Avenues (tel. 244-2876), offers more than that. The atmosphere here is jovial, with a full bar and two window tables up front, and booths toward the back. The walls are white stucco, with wood-framed mirrors at every booth. The rose-colored ceiling is decorated with a white fan. There is a small dining room toward the back, with tables for parties bigger than four. This is decorated with a stained-glass picture of rose orchids and orange tulips. The staff here is friendly, and your check comes with a piece of candy, even though you won't need it to sweeten the restaurant's reasonable prices.

Lunch specials at the bar are under $6 and include a free beer or glass of wine. Lasagne is $4.67, sausages with spaghetti are $4.95, and spaghetti with meatballs runs $4.62. Dinner specials change daily. Pasta dishes, like meatballs with spaghetti or ziti ($4.45), or breaded veal cutlet with spaghetti ($4.85), are always available. Small pizzas range between $3.95 and $5.95. For dessert, try the cheesecake ($2.05).

Open from 11 a.m. to midnight Monday through Saturday, from 2 to 10 p.m. on Sunday.

JEWISH DAIRY: Kosher businessmen can be found eating at **Gefen's Kosher**

Dairy, 297 Seventh Ave., between 26th and 27th Streets (tel. 929-6476). The restaurant is clean and unpretentious, with white Formica tables set with blue paper placemats and blue chairs to match. On the walls are original drawings of the Wailing Wall, the Burning Bush, and Jewish rabbis. There's a sit-down counter in the back, as well as a take-out stand. Waiters, dressed in black outfits with white shirts and black bowties, add a touch of old-world elegance. The atmosphere here is boisterous, with plenty of lively chatter.

Your waiter will immediately set a metal dish filled with pumpernickel bread and fresh rolls at your table, but save some room for other items. To start, try the borscht with cream ($2.25) or the homemade soup of the day ($1.95). Entrees include baked gefilte fish ($7.95) and broiled salmon ($9.50), served with a choice of two vegetables and mashed or boiled potatoes. The dairy dishes include potato pirogen ($5.25), cheese blintzes ($5.50), and potato pancakes ($4.95). There are daily specials, including Hungarian vegetarian goulash on Tuesday and stuffed cabbage on Wednesday (each $5.95). For dessert, try the homemade danish ($1.10) or the homemade cheesecake ($1.65).

Open from 6 a.m. to 7:30 p.m. Monday through Thursday, on Friday to 2:30 p.m., and on Sunday from 11 a.m. to 6 p.m. Closed Saturday.

To dine in more elegant surroundings, try **Hershey's,** 167 W. 29th St., between Sixth and Seventh Avenues (tel. 868-6988), smack in the center of the furrier district. The interior has wood paneling, with a large modern chandelier in the middle of the room. Tables here are dark imitation wood, and the walls are decorated with family crests (nobody in the restaurant seems to know why they're there).

The menu offers traditional Jewish cooking, with cheese blintzes for $5.50 and kreplach for the same price. Sandwiches are priced between $2.25 and $7.25, and include a belly lox sandwich ($6.25) and a Norwegian sardine sandwich ($5.75). Matzoh brei with applesauce is $6.95 and a kasha varnishke casserole is $5.75. For dessert, try a homemade fruit pie ($1.50) or the homemade coffee cake (also $1.50).

Open from 6 a.m. to 8 p.m. Monday through Thursday, on Friday to 2:30 p.m.

JEWISH DELI: Smart and sassy, **J. J. Applebaum's Deli Co.** points out on its three-foot menu that it is "sandwiched" between 33rd and 34th Streets at 431 Seventh Ave. (tel. 563-6200). Puns like this abound on their long list of offerings, including the "son of a botch" and the "U.R.A. turkey" sandwiches. The decor here is modern and airy, with exposed brick walls and black-and-white checkered tile floors. Maroon booths are separated by wood siding, lit by large white half-glove lights suspended from lattices on the ceiling.

To start, try the borscht served with sour cream and a boiled potato ($2.75). Sandwiches served with homemade cold slaw, potato salad, and a pickle are huge. The grilled Reuben, a mountain of hot pastrami covered with cole slaw, russian dressing, and gobs of melting cheese, is $6.75. You can also get zucchini latkes, with sour cream or applesauce ($3.85), and a steak sandwich, with charcoal-broiled steak is only $5.75. For dessert, try the fresh pound cake ($1.35) or the carrot cake ($1.95).

Open from 8 a.m. to 9 p.m. weekdays, and until 8 p.m. on weekends.

MEXICAN: One of the newest additions to Chelsea's burgeoning "Restaurant Row" on Eighth Avenue, **Mary Ann's,** 116 Eighth Ave., at 16th Street (tel. 242-9455), offers a nice variety of well-executed Mexican and Tex-Mex dishes at very affordable prices. Stucco and brick walls, ceiling fans, south-of-the-border decorative crafts, and a tiny candle on each table are the simple but effective design touches that, along with the menu, attract a young neighborhood crowd.

After working your way through a bowl of tortilla chips and pungent dipping salsa, try an entree like the chile relleno plate ($5.95), two Monterey peppers stuffed with cheese and covered in a delightful sauce, served with rice and beans. Mole poblano ($7.95), breast of chicken with a red-chili-and-chocolate sauce, comes with hot flour tortillas and is quite good. Such daily specials as roast duck in a mole of green tomatoes and pumpkin seeds, served with rice and zucchini ($7.95), generally run $8 to $9. From a limited but respectable wine list you can choose a bottle of a good French table white for only $6 (beer is also available). A cup of flan ($1.95) tops off the meal.

Open from noon to 10 p.m. Monday through Thursday, to 11 p.m. Friday through Sunday.

SEAFOOD: For years a fixture at its old 34th Street address, **Paddy's Clam House,** 367 Seventh Ave., between 30th and 31st Streets (tel. 244-1040), recently moved its act downtown a few blocks. The feel of the new place, though, is much the same as the old, with nautical-motif decorations, waiters in red jackets and black bowties, and a congenial, informal atmosphere.

The dinner special is $9.95 and includes choice of juice or chowders, fresh fish of the day, potato, cole slaw or salad, dessert, and coffee. (A slightly abbreviated version of the dinner special is offered at lunch at $7.95.) À la carte entrees start at $5.95. To begin, sample either the Manhattan clam chowder ($1.65) or Boston fish chowder ($1.75). Fresh bluefish is $5.95 and salmon is $8.45. For those who don't love seafood, half a chicken with potatoes and salad ($5.95) is a good bet. Featured desserts include fruit pies and chocolate mousse (each $1.10) and cheesecake ($1.75). The à la carte menu is the same at lunch and dinner.

Open from 11 a.m. to 10 p.m. Monday through Saturday.

SPANISH: From its blue-tiled exterior to its stucco walls, the **Centro Vasco,** 208 W. 23rd St., between Seventh and Eighth Avenues (tel. 741-1408), has an authentic Spanish feel. Inside, the restaurant is decorated with original abstract art pieces painted by a Peruvian artist, in addition to more standard paintings of flamenco dancers. The setting here is elegant, with candle-shaped wall sconces and chocolate-colored tablecloths draped over beige linen. Arched doorways and wooden beams complete the Mediterranean setting.

This restaurant is expensive, with entrees between $6.25 and $23.95. But dinners, served in large portions, can be split by two people, with a $2.50 charge for an extra plate. To start, we suggest the black-bean soup or gazpacho ($1.75). The seafood paella, big enough for two, is $11.95. The lower priced entrees— veal parmigiana ($8.50) and shrimp in wine sauce ($9.75)—are also good. If you really want to go all-out, try the stuffed lobster dinner ($17.95). For dessert, try the flan ($2) or cheesecake ($2.50).

Open for dinner only, from 4 p.m. to midnight during the week, to 1 a.m. on Saturday.

7. Greenwich Village

Greenwich Village, perhaps like no other place in all the city, encompasses the special diversity that is New York. Centered around Washington Square Park and including New York University, it is both frenetic and serene, commercial and residential. It offers the intimacy of quiet, crooked streets, and is one of the few places where one can wander quite accidentally onto an absolutely still street filled with rows of trees and town houses that evoke the feel of a European city. Yet within another few blocks one returns to Sheridan Square, the honky-tonk of 8th Street, and the whirl of Washington Square Park.

That park, once a potter's field, then a parade ground, is the hub of the Village—especially on a sunny weekend or a warm summer night, when it's peopled by magicians, musicians, street artists, mothers and their toddlers, men bent intently over chess boards, young people on skateboards and roller skates, hustlers hawking the latest fad to anyone who will buy, and hundreds of spectators soaking up the scene. The entire area is filled with antique stores, unusual boutiques, small restaurants and bars in all price brackets. The area covered in this section is bounded north and south by 14th and Houston Streets, and on the east and west by Broadway and the West Side Highway.

AMERICAN/CONTINENTAL: The thoroughly quaint little **Ye Waverly Inn** tavern and restaurant, 16 Bank St., at Waverly Place (tel. 929-4377), has been making customers happy since the 1920s, and the building that houses them dates to over a century ago. You can almost smell the age in the yellowing, cracking wallpaper, dark-wood wainscotting, oaken booths, and pendulum clocks. There's even an 1868 engraving of Manhattan to really take you back in time.

In spring and summer there's patio dining in the back (though the patio isn't nearly as charming as the inn-side). In winter, two of the four dining rooms are heated by working fireplaces. At all times, in all seasons, the ambience is friendly and intimate, and the food good enough to draw the likes of Al Pacino, Robert DeNiro, and Richard Gere.

Dinner prices at Ye Waverly Inn have begun to climb over budget, but an early-dinner special, served Monday through Thursday from 5 to 6:30 p.m., is worth scheduling your evening around. For $7.95 you get soup, an entree of southern fried chicken, meatloaf, calf liver, or quiche and Waldorf salad, plus a vegetable, dessert, and coffee. Lunch is also a good deal. You can get soup, fresh muffins, salad, coffee and dessert for only $5.25. There are sandwiches—like a hearty grilled cheddar or swiss with ham or bacon—for around $5. And the inn makes its own desserts—pecan pie, Wellesley fudge cake, and carrot cake cost around $2.50.

Perhaps the best time to head for Ye Waverly Inn is on Sunday, when a classical guitarist serenades partakers of a champagne/cocktail brunch. Choose from eggs Benedict, fluffy omelets, quiche, french toast, or apple fritters with bacon and maple syrup. Complete with drink or juice, homemade rolls or muffins, and coffee or tea, the brunch is $7.75.

Ye Waverly Inn serves lunch Monday through Friday from 11:45 a.m. to 2 p.m. and Sunday brunch from noon to 3:30 p.m. Dinner is served Monday through Thursday from 5 to 10 p.m., on Friday and Saturday to 11:15 p.m., on Sunday from 4:30 to 9:30 p.m. Reservations are advised at all meals.

The Lion's Head, 59 Christopher St., just off Seventh Avenue South (tel. 929-0670), is known as a popular writers' hangout, the sort of place where at the bar you might meet the body behind a famous byline or the author of one of the books whose jacket covers line one wall. A hand-carved lion's head of oak, dating from the turn of the century, looms above the bar, which adjoins the dining room. With its low ceilings, dark-wood paneling, exposed brick walls, and amber lighting, the place is dark, den-like, and cozy.

Dinners here can easily break a budget. For a low-priced alternative, order the chili con carne ($5.75), a quiche with salad ($5.25), or a hamburger platter ($5.25). Or check the blackboard for daily specials, like potato leek or scotch egg soup ($3 and $4). Other, more expensive specials typically include such offerings as cold pasta with smoked chicken ($7.50) and baked bluefish ($8.50).

RESTAURANTS: GREENWICH VILLAGE 105

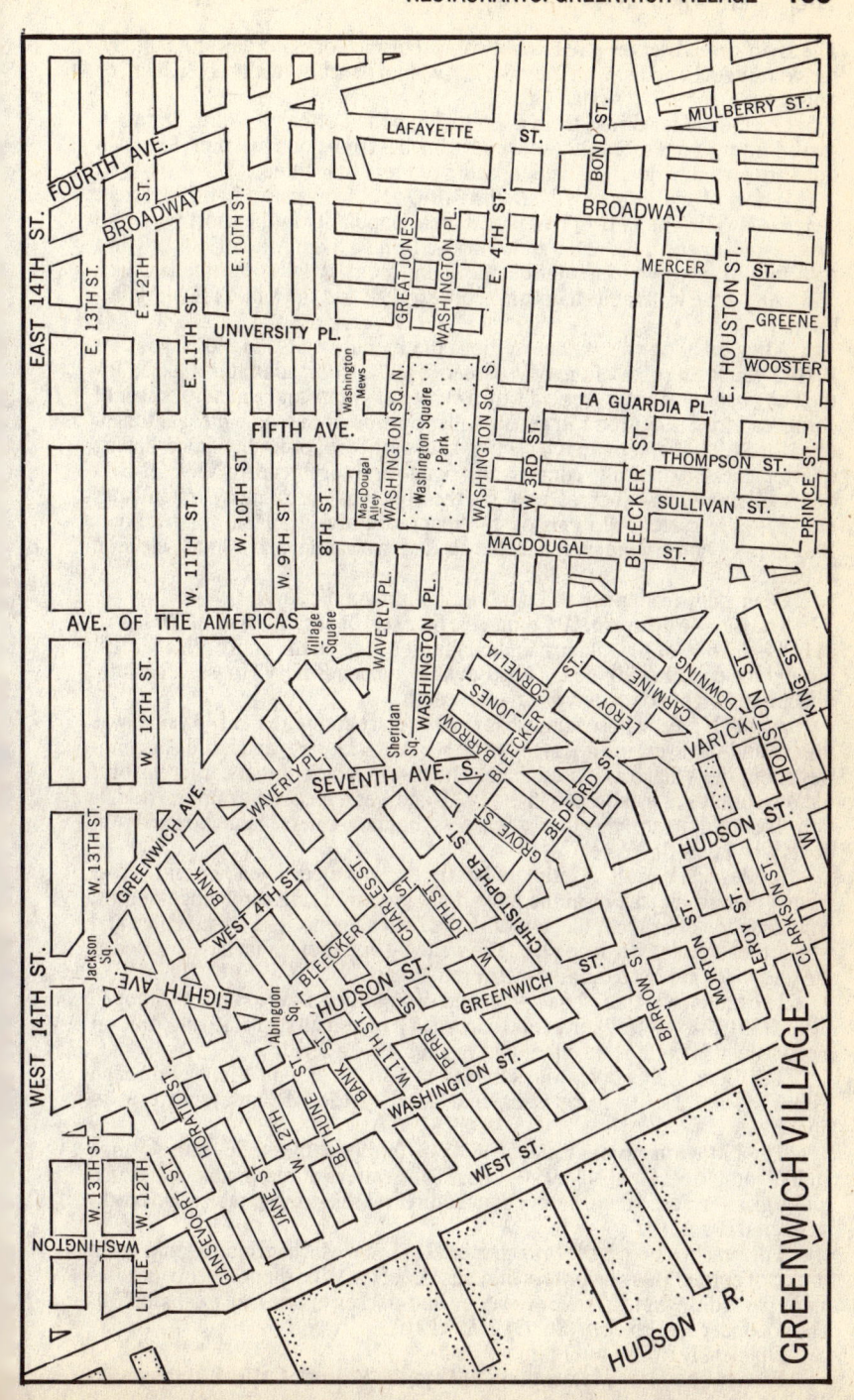

The Lion's Head serves a reasonably priced brunch on Saturday and Sunday, including eggs Benedict with fries ($4.75), walnut pancakes with bacon, ham, or sausage ($5), or a chef's salad ($6.95).

Open daily for drinks from noon to 2 a.m. and often till 4 a.m. Dinner is served from 5 p.m. to 2 a.m., weekend brunches from noon to 4 p.m. Reservations are recommended for dinner parties of more than three.

A new village hot spot is the **Dallas B-B-Q** at 21 University Pl., off 8th Street (tel. 674-4450). The B-B-Q has gained great popularity in the short period of time since it opened. From the glass-enclosed dining room you can look out on a colorful Village street scene. Inside, the dining room is wildly decorated in black and white—the walls and chairs are zebra-striped, and the tables are black lacquered.

After entering this unique setting, the menu won't disappoint you. At B-B-Q you'll get some of the best barbecue and cornbread in the Village. Try the baby back spare ribs, served with a choice of potato and a generous slab of cornbread for $8.95. You can get a smaller portion of the same meal at lunchtime for $4.95. If you prefer chicken to beef barbecue, order the finger-licking quarter chicken which also comes with a potato and cornbread for $2.95. B-B-Q offers other tidbits—such as corn on the cob (95¢) or crunchy onion rings ($2.95)—à la carte. All items on the menu are also available for take-out. B-B-Q has a house wine served by the glass or in a carafe, and a small selection of beer.

Open daily from noon to 1 a.m., until 2 a.m. on Friday.

The Blue Mill Tavern, 50 Commerce St., west of Seventh Avenue (tel. 243-7114), is on one of the quietest and quaintest streets in the entire Village. Just around the corner from the famous Edna St. Vincent Millay House, it's a little difficult to find but definitely worth the search.

Alcino Neves, whose family has run the place for more than 40 years, was raised (and still lives) in an apartment above the restaurant, and is full of memories about the Village as it used to be. The tavern is part of that earlier history; the restaurant was established in the 1920s and was a speakeasy during Prohibition. It once did a thriving tourist business, but now caters mainly to local residents who know the place.

Inside, one can sit at intimate booths, upholstered in leather and across from a mahogany bar, or in the main dining room, where three huge murals, painted to look like Delft tile, establish the Dutch theme. The china is blue and white, the tablecloths a deep blue. The waiters—many of whom have worked at the tavern for at least a decade—wear red jackets.

The food too is traditional—the kind that mothers used to make. Chopped sirloin ($5), fish stew ($9), liver and bacon ($7), or a small steak ($9) all come on a platter with a potato and either two vegetables or a salad.

The Blue Mill is open for dinner from 5 to 10:30 p.m. Monday through Thursday, until 11:30 p.m. on Friday and Saturday. Closed Sunday. No reservations.

The Little Mushroom Café, at 183 W. 10th St. between Seventh Avenue and W. 4th Street (tel. 242-1058), offers light entrees at reasonable prices in a sunny glass-enclosed dining room that features marble-topped tables and black-lacquered chairs.

The best buy here is the brunch special ($5.95), which includes drinks and a choice of entree. (Our favorite is the eggs Benedict.) The dinner menu includes many pasta dishes and a range of seafood and chicken entrees, all for under $10. The coconut curry chicken ($6.95) is delicious.

Open daily from 4 to 11 p.m.

Bring a good book and a thin wallet to the **Peacock Caffè,** 24 Greenwich

Ave., off West 10th Street (tel. 242-9395). It's a quiet, romantic place, with classical music playing in the background, baroque columns, busts, a life-size statue of Pan playing his flute, and a carved-wood peacock perched over what was once a fireplace.

During the day the Peacock serves a variety of sandwiches on Italian bread, such as prosciutto and provolone ($4.95) and salami and provolone ($5.50). It also offers plates of fruit and cheese ($4.50 to $5.95), an array of salads served with Italian bread and butter ($3.75 to $5), and soups (less than $3).

At night you can order any of the above, or choose a pasta dish like gnocchi with butter sauce, or tortellini or fettuccine with meat sauce (less than $4). For dessert, try the homemade Florentine apple torte served with whipped cream ($2.85), or the Milanese coffeecake served with butter ($1.60). And of course there's cappuccino, espresso, and special concoctions of coffee, chocolate, cinnamon, and whipped cream.

Open Tuesday through Thursday and on Sunday from 1 p.m. to 1 a.m., on Friday and Saturday till 2 a.m. Closed Monday.

Weary of the New York scene? The **Cottonwood Café**, 415 Bleecker St., between West 11th and Bank Streets (tel. 924-6271), may offer the perfect respite from urban overload. As one of its owners likes to say, the Cottonwood is "a T-shirt and blue jeans sort of place."

A bank of windows facing Bleecker Street lends a bright and breezy air to the front dining room, where the walls are decorated with huge framed photographs of Texas ranching scenes and a state map. The back dining room, just as large but darker, is where the music begins at about 10:30 p.m. on weekdays and 11:30 p.m. on Saturday. Most of the performers are original songwriters, often playing folk or country and western music on acoustic guitar. Performances continue until the bar closes, between 12:30 and 2 a.m. depending on the size of the crowd.

The menu is limited and excellent, offering such Tex-Mex culinary delights as chicken and cheese enchiladas with refried beans and rice ($6.50). Other main entrees—chicken fried steak ($6.25), pork chops ($6.75), or smoked barbecued ribs ($8.50)—all come with a choice of two vegetables (also available à la carte). We recommend the mashed potatoes—cooked with their skins and slathered with creamy gravy—and fried okra or blackeyed peas. Come hungry; the portions are Texas size.

At brunch, served from 10 a.m. to 3 p.m. on Sunday, try the huevos rancheros (hot Mexican eggs) or fresh fruit pancakes (both $4), and perhaps a bowl of grits ($1).

Dinner is served daily from 5 to 11:30 p.m.

One of the Village's most popular hangouts is **Sandolino's**, 9 Jones St., off West 4th Street (tel. 255-6669). It's a relaxed and casual place, where at almost any hour of the day or night people lounge around wooden tables, sipping coffee, talking, and greeting friends. A long corkboard wall is covered with posters, announcements, and notices of local and citywide events. A wall of windows up front lets in lots of sunlight for an outdoor feel during the day.

The entire menu is available at all times. It offers over 35 regular sandwiches, such as sliced egg and anchovy ($2.75) and turkey salad with bacon ($3.35), 12 gigantic club sandwiches ($4.50 to $5.35), and hot sandwiches such as roast beef with french fries or baked potato or salad ($5.25). Omelets, served with a choice of breads or bagel, are $3.60 to $4.50; cheese blintzes with sour cream are $3.35; and waffles with blueberries, whipped cream, and Häagen-Dazs ice cream, $5.75. A glass of wine with your meal is $1.75, and Sandolino's has an international selection of beers.

Open Sunday through Thursday from 9 a.m. to 1 a.m., on Friday and Saturday to 3 a.m.

For another great view of the Village spectacle, try **Montana Eve**, on Seventh Avenue South between 10th and Charles Streets (tel. 242-1200). Seated in either the glass-enclosed front porch or the sidewalk café, you can watch the parade of pedestrians passing by. Inside there's an elaborate 150-year-old hand-carved mahogany bar from Bavaria and a pleasant lounge area with a view of the street. The bar is always casual and on weekends it's rowdy and noisy. The main dining area is dark and den-like, with earth-toned walls adorned with photographs of people from the neighborhood. It's furnished with oak booths and pedestal tables; in the winter two fireplaces burn brightly, lending a cozy atmosphere.

A limited menu includes burgers and sandwiches, such as roast beef with Russian dressing ($4.75) or herbed cream cheese and cucumber ($3.25), and a variety of omelets ($4) at lunch. For dinner, served daily from 6 p.m. to 2 a.m., you might try steamed mussels simmered in a sauce of tomatoes and white wine ($5.50), or the three-fish and sausage stew ($7.50). The chili, a house specialty and made with top round, is always a good bet ($5.25, depending on the topping). Or check the blackboard for specials at both lunch and dinner.

Sunday brunch, served from 11 a.m. to 5 p.m., ranges from $5.75 to $8, including a drink, muffin or bagel, and coffee or tea. Bloody Marys are $1.50 all day on Sunday.

Montana Eve is open daily from noon to 2 a.m.; dinner is served from 6 p.m. onward. The bar stays open until 4 a.m. No reservations except for parties of more than eight.

The perfect place to sit and linger alone with a book or dine on a light meal with friends is **Blazing Salads,** 228 W. 4th St., just west of Seventh Avenue South in the heart of the Village (tel. 929-3432). The staff is congenial, the decor (with baskets of plants suspended from an emerald-green ceiling) is cheery, and the homemade desserts (many of them pies with whole-wheat crusts and sweetened with honey, for $2) are delectable.

As the name suggests, Blazing Salads specializes in salads—scrumptious, huge, and nutritious ($4.25 for a garden salad to $5.50 for a shrimp salad), topped with a choice of dressings that includes tofu or tahini. Also on the menu are omelets ($3.25 to $3.95 at lunch, up to $4.95 at dinner), sandwiches (about $4), and burgers (also about $4), including a vegetarian burger on whole-wheat pita bread. Lunch and dinner specials—which come with a salad, brown rice, bread, and butter—might be a vegetable cheese casserole or vegetable lasagne ($4.25 at lunch, $6.50 at dinner) or flounder stuffed with spinach, onions, mushrooms, and walnuts ($5.25 at lunch, $7.25 at dinner). Most items can be ordered to take out.

Brunch, served on Saturday and Sunday from noon to 4 p.m., includes fresh-fruit whole-wheat pancakes ($3.75) and a variety of egg dishes (mostly at $3.75).

Blazing Salads is open from noon to midnight Monday through Thursday, until 1 a.m. Friday through Sunday. The small eatery seats only 34, so there's often a wait during the lunch and dinner hours. No reservations except for parties of more than four.

David's Pot Belly, 98 Christopher St., between Bleecker and Bedford Streets (tel. 243-9614), is another tiny eatery (45 people is a squeeze) that's popular with the Village crowd and tourists. It has wood-paneled walls, small wooden tables and booths, mirrored walls, and at night, soft candlelight.

The menu consists primarily of omelets, egg casseroles, burgers, and salads. Omelets—priced from $4.25 to $4.95—come with every imaginable filling;

corn, jelly, peanut butter, sardines, chutney, olives and pimiento cheese, walnuts, peach, pineapple, eggplant, artichokes, and more. Those and a variety of egg casserole dishes ($6.25) are served with potato pancakes, applesauce, and an English muffin. Half-pound burgers (in the $4 range) come with an array of toppings—from chili to cream cheese, anchovies to egg. Crêpes, topped with mornay sauce ($4.95), may be filled with anything from asparagus and mushrooms, tuna and corn, to chopped beef and onions or hot mixed fruit. The menu also offers a variety of salads ($5.25 to $6.50). Desserts consume an entire page of the menu, and include floats ($2.75) and sundaes ($3.75) made with Häagen-Dazs ice cream.

Open Sunday to Thursday from 11 a.m. to 5:30 a.m., on Friday and Saturday to 6 a.m. No reservations.

The **Cedar Tavern,** 82 University Pl., between 11th and 12th Streets (tel. 929-9089), is a comfortable joint, as the manager likes to say. Downstairs it's dark and woody. In the back there are cozy booths lit by lantern-like lamps; up front there's an elaborate maple bar, over 100 years old, with panes of stained glass; and on the second floor there's a garden under a peaked glass roof. In the late 1950s and early '60s the tavern was a hangout of abstract expressionist artists like Mark Rothko, Franz Kline, and Jackson Pollock. Now the clientele is more likely to be the neighborhood crowd—antique dealers, professionals, and students.

Meals here are tasty, simple, and cheap. Sandwiches and burgers are $4.50 to $5.50. You can order a cheese, mushroom, or ham omelet, served with a vegetable, potato, and salad, for $5. Softshell crabs ($7) and lamb or beef stew ($5.50) are two of the more popular items, and both are served with a salad and potato. At the weekend brunch, served from 11:30 a.m. to 4:30 p.m., you can get a cocktail, coffee, home-fries, and a choice of eggs Benedict, french toast, or eggs with ham, bacon, or sausage, for $7.25.

Open from 8 a.m. to 4 a.m. daily; the kitchen is on duty from 11:30 a.m. to 1 a.m. Reservations accepted.

Covent Garden, 133 W. 13th St., between Sixth and Seventh Avenues (tel. 675-0020), is New York posh: elegant, lavish, lovely to look at, and formal. The room is graced by Tiffany-like lamps, velvet couches, and a grand piano that sits near the entrance and is reflected in a huge mirror. There is music nightly, with a pianist whose repertoire runs from show tunes to classical to jazz. Out back is an appealing garden terrace under a skylight roof, with abundant hanging plants and an ivy-covered wall.

Lunch in this setting is surprisingly affordable. The menu is large and varied. Entrees range from a chef's salad ($5.25) to roast chicken ($6.95). Or you can order a French-dip roast beef sandwich for $5.75 or a hamburger for $4.25. Most dinner entrees are well above budget, but you can order a Caesar salad for two for $7.95, or roast duckling flambé or brook trout stuffed with vegetables for $13.95.

Sunday brunch is a fair bet. For $8.95 you can have cocktails or unlimited champagne with an entree of cold chicken breast, quiche, and spinach salad, or a small prime sirloin with eggs.

Covent Garden is open for lunch Tuesday through Friday from noon to 3:30 p.m. Dinner is served from 5 to 11 p.m. Sunday through Thursday, till midnight on Friday and Saturday. Sunday brunch is served from noon till 3:30 p.m. Reservations advised.

You'll be lured inside by the café-curtained windows of **The Big Dish,** 283 W. 12th St., corner of West 4th Street (tel. 243-9898). In one window an employee operates a pasta machine on a marble counter, and the sight of the fresh noodles folding out is a real treat (although eating them is better!).

The Big Dish is a pleasantly informal restaurant. An old oak bar stands under antique amber lamps, and a slow-moving ceiling fan hangs from the black pressed-tin ceiling. Unlike most such places, the Big Dish bears the personal stamp of its owner. Joseph Coppolo is a fan of Sophia Loren, and the walls of the restaurant are covered with photos from her many motion pictures.

Dinner prices run up to $12.95, but daily specials are usually under $10, and include a salad, vegetable, and baked potato or rice. Also recommended are the homemade fettuccine with meat sauce or heavy cream and cheese sauce. ($7.95). Or try the homemade ravioli with or without meatballs ($9.95). All come with salad.

Sunday brunch, served from noon till 4:30 p.m., offers eggs Benedict or Florentine, fresh-fruit pancakes or french toast (the latter two with bacon or sausage), and a drink and coffee, for $6.50.

Open daily except Monday for dinner from 5:30 to 11:30 p.m., until 12:30 a.m. on Friday and Saturday. Reservations advised for parties of more than four.

CHINESE: Szechuan Taste Restaurant, 189 Bleecker St., on the corner of Mac-Dougal Street (tel. 260-2333), sits in the very heart of the West Village. From its glass-enclosed wrap-around patio you can watch the passing parade of foot traffic while dining on reasonably priced traditional Szechuan fare. The decor is modern, with an exposed brick wall, new brick floors, and a dark-brown ceiling. Sunlight streams in through the glass porch.

The cold noodles in sesame sauce paste ($2.10 for a small serving) are a spicy and delicious way to begin a meal, and the portion is large enough for two. The menu includes entrees of vegetable, pork, beef, lamb, seafood, poultry, and fried-rice dishes (most priced from about $5 to $8), as well as excellent specialties, such as chicken with a spicy orange-flavored sauce ($5.75), hot-and-spicy shrimp cooked in a tomato and ginger-flavored sauce ($7.50), and combination dishes (about $7 and up). Szechuan Taste also serves American fare—fried chicken, scallops, and shrimp. Lunches run $1 to $1.50 less than dinner. Beer is available ($1.35 and $1.75) or you may bring your own wine.

Open Monday through Thursday from noon to midnight, on Friday to 1 a.m., on Saturday from 1 p.m. to 1 a.m., and on Sunday from 1 to 11:30 p.m. Reservations recommended for parties of more than five.

CRÉOLE: A new, glassed-in sidewalk café hides the fact that **Sazerac House**, 533 Hudson St., corner of Charles Street (tel. 989-0313), is the oldest structure on Charles Street. The 1926 landmark building was once part of a farm.

Sazerac's interior is old-style Village, with an old mahogany bar, rough hardwood floors, oak booths and tables, antique lighting fixtures, and a working fireplace. Menus from New Orleans restaurants and pictures of Dixieland and jazz musicians grace the walls. The atmosphere is casual and attracts primarily a neighborhood crowd, plus a few celebrities now and then.

The menu offers New Orleans favorites like jambalaya—a Créole stew—served with garlic bread ($7.95), and deep-fried oysters ($9.25). Lower-priced items include more traditional New York fare: hamburgers and cheeseburgers for around $5, chef's and spinach salad for $5.95. Sazerac is a favorite Village spot for brunch, serving à la carte pain perdu (Louisiana-style french toast), a variety of gourmet egg dishes, hash and eggs, and quiche—all $4.95 to $5.95. There are also burgers for the hungrier.

Sazerac serves lunch daily from 11:30 a.m. to 4 p.m., dinner from 4 p.m. to 1 a.m., and brunch on Saturday and Sunday from 11:30 a.m. to 3:45 p.m. Reservations recommended.

CUBAN: Bayamo, at 704 Broadway, between 9th and 10th Streets (tel. 475-5151), is a splashy new addition to the Village restaurant scene. The owners call it a Cuban restaurant with Chinese overtones, but the decor is pure New Wave. If you can, sit at a table in the balcony. From there you can get a great view of the comings and goings of a whole variety of chic-looking Village folk.

When you cast your eyes over the extensive menu, you'll see that you can get almost anything at Bayamo. In the mood for a salad? Try ensalada de pollo escabechado ($6.95), which is spiced chicken mixed with cold vegetables. Maybe you want eggs. Order the huevos revueltos con palmito y pimiento ($6.95), scrambled eggs with pimiento and hearts of palm. For a taste of the East, sample any of this restaurant's Oriental spring rolls, made to order with your choice of filling, and filling enough to be a whole meal ($6.95).

There's also a large dessert menu. The homemade almond-coconut macaroons covered with milk chocolate come highly recommended ($3). For something lighter, try the mandarin orange sorbet ($3.50).

Open daily from 11 a.m. until 3 a.m.

FRENCH: Chez Brigitte, 77 Greenwich Ave., between Bank and 11th Streets (tel. 243-9542), is an easy place to overlook: six paces and you've passed it. It has two counters, 12 seats, minimal decor, and a sense of humor: a sign in the window declares, "Chez Brigitte will seat 250 persons at one time." If you don't mind the luncheonette ambience, you'll be pleased with the Provence-style fare at reasonable prices.

You can begin with pea, onion, or soup du jour for 90¢ or $1.40, and then choose either a daily special ($6, and served with a vegetable and potato, rice, or macaroni) or entrees like beef bourguignon, filet of sole meunière, veal cutlet, or chicken fricassee for $5.50 or $6. Omelets are $3.30; sandwiches, $1.85 and $2.80. A fresh homemade dessert—such as chocolate chiffon or banana pie—is $1.50.

Open from 11 a.m. to 9 p.m. Closed on Sunday.

Unlike most eating spots in the Village, **14 Christopher Street,** right off Gay Street (tel. 620-9594) begins to fill by 6 p.m. That's because of its popular "early-bird special"—a complete dinner, with salad or soup, entree, dessert, and beverage, all for $6.95. The cuisine is "French country," the chef/owner British, and the decor American 1980s sophisticate.

Early-bird specials change from time to time, but are generally simple, sauce-less entrees. The regular menu is more adventurous but also more expensive. Filet of flounder with scallop stuffing, or chicken Cordon Bleu, is $10.95. A tasty cottage pie is $9.95. Daily specials always include entrees for under $12. Wine dresses it all up, at $6.50 for a half carafe of "house."

Early-bird dinner is served Tuesday through Saturday from 5 to 7:30 p.m. and on Sunday from 4 p.m. Regular dinner goes until 9 p.m. Lunch on weekdays is from noon to 5 p.m., on Sunday to 4 p.m. Closed Monday.

ITALIAN: You don't necessarily have to head for Little Italy to find a good Italian restaurant in the city, or even to find a cluster of them. Along Thompson Street in the Village, between West 3rd and Bleecker Streets, there are three moderately priced Italian eateries.

The **Grand Ticino,** 228 Thompson St. (tel. 777-5922), is a gracious restaurant with a restful air and friendly service. Established in 1919, it's the oldest Italian restaurant in the Village. It is a few steps below street level, and entered via a small alcove of plant-filled windows. The deep-green walls are background for black-and-white framed photographs. The tables are covered with white linen, softly lit with individual lamps, and surrounded by simple black chairs. A few pieces of pottery line a shelf that runs across the room and a huge vase of flowers sits beside the bar. The effect is one of understated elegance.

The dinner and lunch menus are essentially the same, with prices running about $1 less at lunch. Most of the soups are priced at about $3 for dinner; pasta dishes run from $7.50 to $8.50. Main entrees come with a vegetable of the day or spaghetti. Desserts are $3 to $4; half a carafe of house wine, $5.50.

Open Monday through Friday from noon to 3 p.m. for lunch, from 5 to 11 p.m. for dinner. On Saturday, open continuously from noon to 11 p.m. Closed Sunday. Reservations recommended.

A few doors away is **Livorno,** 216 Thompson St. (tel. 260-1972), which has a charming, festive air. In the front room there's a bar under a shingled eave, and the walls are decorated with prints, paintings, and maps of Italy. Pass through a latticework plastic grape arbor to enter the main dining room in the back, where trompe l'oeil windows are framed by wood shutters and boxes of plastic geraniums. Tables are covered with white linen over deep-green cloths.

Begin with a soup, such as spinach or escarola in broth ($2), or a hot antipasto ($3.25). Homemade pasta dishes are priced between $5.50 and $6.50. Veal scaloppine entrees cost $8.50; veal cutlet or chicken cacciatora, $7.95. All include a side order of vegetables or pasta.

Livorno is open daily from noon to 11:30 p.m. Reservations recommended.

Ponte Vecchio, 206 Thompson St. (tel. 228-7701), is less elegant than the Grand Ticino, but casually tasteful. The dining area is graced with prints of Leonardo da Vinci sketches, a few large impressionist oil paintings, and posters of Florence.

Pastas are priced $6.95 to $7.95. You might try the linguini with clam sauce or spaghettini with shrimp ($7.75). Main dishes are served with salad or vegetable.

Open Monday through Saturday from 5 to 10:45 p.m., on Sunday from 2 to 9 p.m. Reservations recommended.

Another Italian restaurant, this one sleek and smooth, is **Trattoria Villaggio,** 192 Bleecker St., between Avenue of the Americas and MacDougal Street (tel. 533-5414). The 14-table café is painted silver-gray, with rose-pink curtains on the large front window, rose-pink linens on the tables, ceiling fans, and large framed florals on the walls.

The menu includes many old favorites and a few surprises. You may want to start your meal with a bowl of zucchini fritti (fried strips of zucchini) for $3.50. If you want pasta, there's lots of choices. The house special is pasta Raphael, a spaghetti with tomato and Italian sausage sauce ($6.50), and regulars recommend the spaghetti with white clam sauce ($9.50). Entrees include veal scaloppine for $10.25, and calamari Lucino for $10.

Trattoria Villagio is open from 5 to 11 p.m. Tuesday through Thursday, from 5 to 11:30 p.m. on Friday and Saturday, and on Sunday from 4 to 10 p.m. Closed Monday.

There are dozens of Italian pastry shops in Manhattan, and again they're not all in Little Italy. **Caffè Cefalu,** 259 W. 4th St., between Charles and Perry Streets (no telephone), offers what's been described as "a relaxed atmosphere in a sophisticated neighborhood."

Cefalu is the name of a village in Sicily that was settled in different centuries by both Arabs and Normans. It boasts a Mediterranean melting-pot culture and its own very special sweets. Cannoli is the house specialty, but equally appealing are baba al rum, sfogliatelle, napoleons, and eclairs—all priced at $1.35. Espresso runs 90¢; cappuccino, $1.50; a pot of tea, $1.35; and Italian soft drinks,

$1.25. Not very Italian, but memorably rich, is the chocolate mousse cake, priced at $2.35.

Open Tuesday through Friday from 6 p.m. until midnight, on weekends from noon until midnight or later.

JAPANESE: A huge vase of calla lilies framed by a small front window beckons the passerby to **Taste of Tokyo**, 54 W. 13th St., between Fifth Avenue and Avenue of the Americas (tel. 691-8666). Appealingly simple, the restaurant has small, black-topped tables set with white napkins, ceiling lamps covered with rice paper, framed Oriental prints on the walls, and bamboo caning separating the kitchen from the small dining room.

Dinners—served with soup, salad, and rice—are in the $7 to $9 range. There's a chicken broiled with teriyaki sauce or shrimp and vegetables tempura (each $7.35); and deep-fried breaded oysters, served with a special sauce, or salmon steak (each $8.75). Sushi (raw fish) is also available, as are a number of seafood, meat, and vegetable appetizers ($2.50 to $3.50).

Taste of Tokyo is open for dinner Monday through Thursday from 6 to 11:30 p.m., on Friday and Saturday till 12:30 a.m., on Sunday from 5:30 to 11 p.m. No reservations.

Shima, 12 Waverly Pl., between Greene and Mercer Streets (tel. 674-1553), serves excellent food at reasonable prices. The decor here is also simple, with wood-paneled walls tastefully decorated with Japanese block prints. A small separate room has knee-level tables and cushions for seating on the floor. Overhead in the main dining area, paper lanterns hang from an Oriental-style peaked ceiling.

For lunch you can order à la carte: vegetable tempura is $4.50; chicken teriyaki, $5.45; sukiyaki, $5.25. At night, full dinners come with soup, salad, rice, and an appetizer. A chicken teriyaki dinner is $7.75; beef teriyaki, $9.50. A bottle of sake, served slightly warm as the Japanese drink it, is $2.10.

Shima is open weekdays for lunch from noon to 2:30 p.m. and for dinner from 5:30 to 11 p.m. On Saturday and Sunday only dinner is served, from 5:30 to 11 p.m. Reservations accepted.

MEXICAN: People who hail from places where Mexican fare is usually the best buy in town often greet the prices for New York City's south-of-the-border food with some dismay. The dinners at **El Coyote**, 774 Broadway, between 9th and 10th Streets (tel. 677-4291), are no exception to the higher price tabs in the city. But you might try this popular and classy restaurant for lunch, when the selections run about $2.50 less than in the evening.

It's festively decorated with cut-tin lanterns, wainscotting, wooden booths in front, and tables in the large back dining room. The white stucco walls are adorned with Mexican rugs, bullfight paintings, and a huge mural of a Mexican market scene.

Popular choices are the two- or three-item combination plates served with rice and beans ($4.95 and $5.95), the enchiladas with green sauce and sour cream, or the Mexican casseroles (all $6.50). Burritos filled with chicken, cheese, beans, and onions are priced at $7.50. Vegetarians can opt for vegetable enchiladas ($6.50). Mexican hot chocolate, highly recommended, is $2.95.

Open daily, serving lunch from 11:30 a.m. to 4 p.m., dinner from 4 till 11:30 p.m. No reservations.

Panchitos, 105 MacDougal St., between Bleecker and West 3rd Streets (tel. 473-8963), is a more casual, more crowded, noisier place, and so popular at peak hours that the lines of hungry customers snake back through the long grotto-like hallway. The wait can be as much as 30 minutes.

The restaurant is rustic, dark, and spacious. It runs the width of a block; in the back, plant-filled windows look out onto a quiet street. The floors are concrete set with marble, and the main dining room is lined with black-walnut booths and Mexican folk art. Overhead, large ceiling fans whir gently. Cut-tin lamps and candles on every table are the only lighting. Many evenings a local musician plays Spanish classical guitar.

Panchito's may be as popular for its drinks as for the food it serves. The bar boasts 101 different double-rum piña coladas and frozen daiquiris, 25 types of rum, and 30 cognacs; the drink list consumes almost three pages of the menu. But the food is good and affordable, and the portions are generous. In fact unless you're simply ravenous, an order of Panchito's popular nachos ($5.45) and one entree may be quite enough for two.

Combination plates with two or three entrees are $6.45 and $7.95, respectively. Chiles rellenos with rice, beans, and salad are $6.95; three turkey enchiladas are $7.95.

Open daily from 11 a.m. to 4 a.m. No reservations; be prepared to wait.

The hi-tech dining room at **Caramba!**, on the corner of Broadway and East 3rd Street (tel. 245-7910), may not seem particularly south-of-the-border, but after you've tasted the food you'll know why this is considered one of the best Mexican restaurants in the Village.

Caramba! is a favorite hangout for the young, professional crowd, who come on weekend nights to enjoy the giant slush margaritas ($4). If you don't want to wait for a table, come to this restaurant at lunchtime; it'll be far less crowded.

There's a wide selection of appetizers, and many of them are filling enough to be a whole meal if you aren't very hungry. Try the chicken quesadilla, a soft flour tortilla filled with cheese, shredded chicken, salsa verde, and served with guacamole and jalapeños ($5.25). For an entree, have a Caramba! combination plate, a choice of two items from a long list of Mexican specialties ($6.95), or the beef chimichangas, crisp-fried burritos topped with enchilada sauce and served with rice and beans ($7.50).

Caramba! is open daily from noon to midnight.

Manhattan Chili Company, 302 Bleecker St., right off Seventh Avenue (tel. 206-7163), offers a mouthwatering selection of different kinds of chili. What they call the "Real McCoy" is the standard mixture of chili beans, beef, onion, and hot pepper. For variety, you may want to try the seafood chili, or if you like hot food choose the "Texas Chain Gang" chili. All the chilis cost between $4.50 and $8, depending on the size of the bowl you order.

Besides chili, the menu includes a few other Tex-Mex favorites. A bowl of chunky gazpacho costs $5. For dessert, sample the Mississippi mud pie ($2.75). The restaurant also has a wine list and offers a large selection of beers.

The Manhattan Chili Company is open Sunday through Thursday from 2 p.m. until midnight, and on Friday and Saturday from noon until 2 a.m.

MIDDLE EASTERN: Amy's, 108 University Pl., between 12th and 13th Streets (tel. 741-2170), is a cafeteria-style eatery, with a bit of a fast-food atmosphere, specializing in Middle Eastern food. The tables are long, laminated affairs, the walls are simply decorated with posters from Israel, and the food is served on plastic dishes. It does a big take-out business. But what it lacks in ambience, it makes up for in wholesomeness and tasty fare at prices that can't be beat.

One of the most popular items is a hamburger on pita bread, served with fresh salad and tahini dressing ($2.75), or with a combination platter that includes falafel, baba ganoush, stuffed grape leaves, feta cheese, and a salad ($5.30). The platter alone is $3.45, or $4.45 for a larger portion. The meatless sandwiches are top-notch; you might try the baba ganoush (mashed eggplant, vegetables, and spices) or the hummus (mashed chickpeas, vegetables, and spices). Both are served with salad for $2.85. For dessert there's baklava (nuts and honey), halvah (sesame and nuts), or carrot cake (each 99¢), among other choices.

Amy's is open from 11 a.m. to 10 p.m. on weekdays, from noon to 9 p.m. on Saturday and Sunday.

As travelers often do, you may tire of rich sauces, vegetable-less entrees, and spicy ethnic foods. If so, take a trip to **Boostan,** 85 MacDougal St., between Bleecker and Houston Streets (tel. 533-9561). It's a popular, totally unpretentious restaurant that prides itself on large helpings of extremely healthy foods based on Middle Eastern recipes. You can dine at lacquered tree-trunk tables adorned with flower-filled vases, amid guitars and wooden flutes and weavings hung on the walls. Or if weather permits, you can sit outside at small Formica tables.

Boostan's under-$6 vegetarian dinners are widely appreciated for their freshness and ample servings. A favorite among regulars is couscous (a Middle Eastern grain dish) topped with stewed vegetables ($6.75), but other dishes are more imaginative and tastier. Try the falafel plate, with four deep-fried chickpea patties, a heaping salad, and tahini dressing ($3.75), or eggplant or spinach parmigiana ($5.75). There are any number of dishes for around $6; choose by your favorite vegetable (broccoli, eggplant, spinach) or your favorite Middle Eastern bean dish (falafel, hummus).

Desserts at Boostan should not be ignored. Baloza, made of fresh orange or apricot, low-fat milk, and whipped cream, is particularly popular, as is Boostan's carrot cake (each $2). Try a Turkish coffee to top it all off ($1).

Open from noon to 1 a.m. weekdays, to 2 a.m. on Friday and Saturday.

PIZZA: There must be at least a dozen pizzerias in the city which all claim to be the "original" **Ray's** pizza house. But most in-the-know New Yorkers seem to agree that this one, on the corner of 11th Street and Avenue of the Americas (tel. 243-2253), is the authentic one and worthy of its fame. The pizza here has a nearly perfect crust and gobs of mozzarella. On any given day—and seemingly at any hour—the line of people waiting for a slice snakes out the door and more are jammed around the stand-up counters and the restaurant's few tables.

The pizza is $1.05 for a slice, $1.50 for Sicilian. Optional extras are 50¢ each. An entire large pie is $6.75; with one topping, $10.75.

Ray's is open every day from 11 a.m. to 2 a.m., until 3 a.m. on Friday and Saturday.

Pizza Piazza, at Broadway and 10th Street (tel. 505-0977), is the place to go if you like deep-dish Sicilian-style pizza. The pizzas come in three sizes: small is recommended for one person, medium for two, and large for three or four. The menu features a list of 11 types of pizza ranging from the "Basic," with tomato sauce and three kinds of cheeses ($3.95, $7.95, $14.95), to the "Californian," with tomato sauce and seasonal vegetables ($5.50, $10.50, $16.50), to the "Shrimp Créole," with baby shrimp and green peppers marinated in a spicy créole sauce ($5.95, $11.50, $17.95).

Cooking the pizzas takes 20 minutes, so you may want to while away the waiting time by trying an appetizer. Guacamole ($2.95) and broccoli and shrimp vinaigrette ($3.95) are both tasty.

Open from noon until midnight Sunday through Thursday, until 2 a.m. on Friday and Saturday.

PUERTO RICAN: La Taza de Oro, right outside the Village at 96 Eighth Ave., between 14th and 15th Streets (tel. 243-9946), is a great place for anyone interested in eating some of the best Latin food around at bargain-basement prices. La Taza de Oro is a simple luncheonette with Formica counters and Formica tables, where the music from the jukebox is Latin and almost everyone speaks Spanish. It's nothing if not a neighborhood joint, a fact that's evident from the way everyone seems to know each other. But the secret about the food here has been leaked to a few outsiders: maybe it's for them that the menu, posted on two blackboards, is in English as well as Spanish.

Many people come for the pork chops ($5) or the roast chicken ($4.50), both served with rice and salad. But the specialties are more exotic: tripe soup ($3.50), mofongu (crushed green banana covered with a meat sauce, $3.75), and octopus salad ($6.25) are a few among many. Recommended, too, are the drinks—mavi (an apple-cider drink) and tamarindo (a tropical fruit juice), each 95¢.

Open daily from 7 a.m. to 11:30 p.m. Sometimes the owners close on Sunday, so you might call first if you're planning on dropping by that day.

SOUL FOOD: The **Pink Teacup,** 42 Grove St., near Bleecker Street (tel. 807-6755), is one of the few eateries in the Village where a yearning for true southern cooking can be satisfied. Nearly everything in this luncheonette is pink, including the walls, curtains, menu, and shirts worn by the waitresses and waiters. The entrees include pigs feet, giblet stew, grits, and freshly baked southern biscuits.

The place is small with ten counter stools and seven oilcloth-covered tables. The walls are adorned with an assortment of photographs of Stevie Wonder, Martin Luther King, John F. Kennedy, and the Supremes. But the menu is remarkable for bounteous fare at budget prices. A breakfast of eggs, grits, and bacon will cost you $3.95, or you can dine in true southern style on pecan or blueberry pancakes and a grilled pork chop or fried chicken with a biscuit for $7.25. Dinner offerings are equally generous: all come with hot bread, soup, salad, two vegetables—such as blackeyed peas, yellow turnips, or okra—and dessert. With a main entree of Virginia ham, the cost is $8.50; with pigs feet, $7.25; with barbecued pork, $8.75. All homemade, all hearty, all deliciously authentic.

Open from 7 a.m. to midnight on weekdays and around the clock from Friday morning until Sunday midnight. No reservations.

SPANISH: There's something appealingly unpretentious about a restaurant simply called **Spain,** 113 W. 13th St., west of Sixth Avenue (tel. 929-9580). The friendly service and apparent lack of attention to decor further emphasizes the casual atmosphere of the restaurant, which has been run by the same family for two generations. You enter from the street under a long red awning. Up front there's a bar and a few tables. The main dining room is in back, through a hallway and past one small alcove with a few more tables and booth seating. Paintings with a Spanish flavor line the walls.

The fare is northern Spanish, and seafood is its specialty. Here too the portions are large, and you might want to split one portion between two people. (Extra-plate charge is $1.50.) The menu at lunch and dinner is the same, with prices running about $1.50 to $2 more for dinner. Shrimp with wine or green sauce is $6.25 at lunch, $8.50 at dinner; paella marinera with seafood and paella Valenciana with chicken, sausages, and seafood are $7.95 and $9.50, respectively. All the entrees are served with Spanish rice and tossed salad. A half bottle of sangría is $4.75; a dessert of caramel custard costs $1.60.

Spain is open daily from noon to 3 p.m. for lunch, and from 3 p.m. to 1 a.m. for dinner; open Sunday for dinner only. Reservations recommended, especially on weekends.

Tío Pepe, 168 W. 4th St., between Sixth and Seventh Avenues (tel. 242-9338), is one of the most dramatic-looking restaurants in Greenwich Village. A leopard skin covers the bar wall, crystal chandeliers hang from the ceiling, gilt-framed mirrors adorn the four corners, and candles grace the tables. Overlooking West 4th Street out back is a lovely glass-enclosed garden and Spanish-style patio. A flamenco guitarist adds to the atmosphere.

The best buy at Tío Pepe is the Mexican "all-you-can-eat" combo platters —tacos, enchiladas, tamales, burritos—served with soup, salad, rice and beans ($7.25 at lunch, $9.95 at dinner). Most dinner entrees are in the $11.50 to $12.50 range. At lunch, however, most of the same entrees—chicken paella, shrimp in green sauce, rainbow trout with almonds, and others—are $6.50 to $8. They are all delightful departures from regular Mexican restaurant fare.

Open Sunday to Thursday from noon to midnight, on Friday and Saturday till 1 a.m. No reservations.

THAI: If you've never eaten Thai food, **A Pinch of Love,** 210 Thompson St., between Bleecker and West 3rd Streets (tel. 477-2558), is a great place to make the introduction; some people swear it's the best in town. The restaurant is a small (only nine tables), unassuming place, and simply decorated. Travel posters of Thailand cover the walls, fish mobiles swing gently from the ceiling, silk flowers top the cloth-covered tables, and Thai music sets the mood. The location couldn't be better (Thompson Street is a delightful Village stretch and the restaurant's big front window provides a fine view of the street), nor could the food. We recommend it highly.

Many of the dishes are hot and spicy; if you can't distinguish from the menu descriptions, don't hesitate to ask. Those that come with Thai sauce are especially hot, but milder dishes include pork, shrimp, beef, or chicken with eight kinds of vegetables. We tried one of each—beef with eight vegetables ($6.45) and chicken with spicy Thai sauce ($6.25)—and both were excellent. Most pork, chicken, and beef dishes are between $6.25 to $6.75; most seafood dishes are $7.75. A bowl of all the rice you can eat is $1. It's a bargain of a meal. A glass of house wine ($1.85) complements the meal nicely.

Open from 5:30 to 11:30 p.m. daily. Reservations accepted.

VEGETARIAN: For a light lunch or dinner, **Michael's,** at 4 Waverly Pl., just off of Broadway (tel. 475-1722), is a good bet. The restaurant offers salads and hot vegetarian entrees at reasonable prices. The dining room is high and airy, and its walls are decorated with paintings by local artists. As you eat, you can people-watch through the huge windows.

Start a meal at Michael's with a cup or bowl of soup ($1.25 and $2). There's always a special soup du jour, and lentil bean and cream of vegetable to choose from. Salad platters cost between $3 and $4. Cold pasta salad, tuna fish, or curried chicken salad are the house specialties. Hot entrees include spinach pie for $2.95 and sauteed vegetables for $2.75.

Michael's is open weekdays from 8 a.m. until 8 p.m., on weekends from 10 a.m. until 8 p.m.

8. SoHo

This former industrial area, whose buildings date from the early 1840s, derives its name from its location south of Houston Street (thus SoHo). It encompasses the area from Houston to Canal Streets, between Lafayette and West

Broadway. When Manhattan's industrial center began to shift from Manhattan, many of SoHo's cast-iron warehouses were left empty. They didn't stay that way for long; over the past decade hundreds of artists and other loft dwellers have moved in, and today SoHo is a lively, colorful, and urbane neighborhood. On the weekend, hundreds of New Yorkers crowd the narrow streets taking in an incredible variety of art galleries, boutiques, gourmet food shops, nightclubs, and theaters. And as could be expected, dozens of restaurants have sprung up to feed the crowds. Below are some of the most reasonably priced.

AMERICAN CONTINENTAL: From noon until early in the morning, the publike **Broome Street Bar,** corner of Broome Street and West Broadway (tel. 925-2086), is filled with a typically eclectic SoHo crowd of artists, writers, and musicians, all of whom are noisily—and sometimes vehemently—discussing the latest trends in art or literature or exchanging the news and gossip of the neighborhood. Broome Street is especially attractive in the late afternoon when jazz plays on the sound system, and you can sit over a beer or coffee and study the passing SoHo scene through the plant-filled front windows. There's a venerable old mahogany bar, small tables with comfortable bentwood chairs, and old-fashioned "Sydney Greenstreet" fans overhead.

The menu is posted: salads, quiches, burgers, sandwiches, and omelets are $5 or less. There's a wide assortment of desserts at around $2.50, and the ice cream is a New Yorker's favorite: Häagen-Dazs. Be sure to try the pineapple fizz.

Open daily from 11 a.m. to 2:30 a.m. The kitchen closes at 1:30 a.m.

Our favorite place for lunch in SoHo is **Food,** 127 Prince St., at the corner of Wooster Street (tel. 473-8790). It's big, bright, airy, and tastefully adorned with modern art and photographs, many by local artists. People sit at simple butcher-block tables, under high ceilings and surrounded by a forest of greenery.

Meals are served cafeteria style, and the ample portions are absolutely delicious. The homemade soups served with big slabs of whole-wheat bread and butter are meals in themselves and, at $2.95, a bargain. Huge sandwiches are priced $3.95 to $5.75, and large, fresh salads run from $4.75 to $6.50. But for a real treat, try one of the daily specials. We recently enjoyed Cajun chicken with a mushroom garnish, baked pumpkin, corn on the cob, bread and butter ($6.95). Desserts are homemade and include poppyseed cake and rhubarb-strawberry pie ($2.95). Sunday brunch specials are served with fresh-baked croissants ($4.95 to $6.95).

Food is open Monday to Wednesday from noon to 10 p.m., Thursday through Saturday until 11 p.m., on Sunday from 11:30 a.m. to 4:30 p.m. for brunch. No reservations, but sometimes there's a short wait for tables during the crowded lunch hour.

Housed in a 150-year-old landmark wood-frame house, **Tennessee Mountain,** 143 Spring St., at Wooster Street (tel. 431-3993), is a welcome addition to the SoHo culinary scene, offering southern-style chicken, ribs, steak, and fish. The downstairs part houses a big, open kitchen at one end and a fully stocked bar at the other. Diners sit at polished, light-wood booths and tables. Upstairs there's a more tranquil dining room with exposed brick walls, a beamed ceiling, and lots of light shining through the skylight.

The menu is the same, lunch or dinner, although prices are slightly higher and portions slightly larger at the latter meal. All entrees come with steak-fries and homemade cole slaw. A heaping platter of barbecued baby back ribs is $11.95. Chicken and ribs, and barbecued beef ribs are $9.95; ale-batter shrimp with orange mustard sauce is $9.95. Tennessee Mountain also offers a selection of char-broiled burgers and chilis ($4.95 to $5.95). For an excellent weekend brunch, served on Saturday and Sunday from noon to 10:30 p.m., we recommend barbecued baby back ribs served with eggs Benedict and a glass of champagne ($8.95 per person).

Open Monday to Thursday from 11:30 a.m. to 10:30 p.m.

The **Cupping Room Café,** 359 West Broadway, between Broome and Grand Streets (tel. 925-2898), is simply one of the most comfortable places in town for a leisurely breakfast or brunch. With exposed brick walls, captain's chairs, blackboard menus, and a working pot-bellied stove, it's suggestive of a charming rural restaurant. A huge vase of colorful flowers sits on an oak counter and more flowers adorn marble-topped tables. The skylight-lit back room is a perfect place to enjoy excellent croissants and delicious freshly brewed coffee, while jazz or classical music plays in the background.

A croissant is $1.50; a cup of coffee is 90¢. A cheese-and-fruit plate with fresh-baked rolls and butter is $4.25; chicken tarragon salad, $6.50; a hot waffle topped with raisins, nuts, fresh fruit, and homemade whipped cream, $5.75. For dessert, try the delicious Austrian plum cake or perhaps the fruit torte, each $3. Breakfast specials are offered every morning.

The Cupping Room Café is open from 8 a.m. to 6 p.m. Monday to Thursday, to midnight on Friday and Saturday, to 10:30 p.m. on Sunday.

Early risers who want to breakfast in SoHo before taking on the galleries should head to **Elephant and Castle,** 183 Prince St., between Sullivan and Thompson Streets (tel. 260-3600). Here you'll find 22 different kinds of omelets to choose from, including a delicate fines-herbes omelet ($3.25), smoked salmon with dill ($6.75), and scrambled eggs with sour cream and curry ($2.95). The warm croissant with sliced apple ($1.75) makes a nice accompaniment, as does the fresh-squeezed orange juice ($1.25). Cheerful jam jars decorate the shelves mounted on mirrored walls and give the place a cozy, early morning feel.

Hamburger lovers may want to lunch at Elephant and Castle. There are 12 different toppings for the juicy thick burgers, including guacamole and horseradish ($4.50 to $6.95). For the famished, there's even the Elephant burger—a colossal creation of chopped beef served with curried sour cream, bacon, scallions, cheddar, and tomato ($6.95). Indulge, but bring a toothbrush for afterward. There's also a variety of sandwiches for $4 to $6.

Open Monday through Thursday from 8 a.m. to midnight, on Friday until 1 a.m., on Saturday and Sunday from 10 a.m. to midnight.

The **Prince Street Bar and Restaurant,** 125 Prince St., corner of Wooster Street (tel. 228-8130), is a comfortable bar-restaurant and hangout, offering reasonably priced food and drink. The crowd here is constantly changing, with an interesting cross section of the SoHo populace. The back of the dining room is dimly lit by pink overhead bulbs and houses a bar covered with framed mirrors; up front, natural light streams in through high, plant-filled windows. The menu offers almost everything under the sun: we counted over 95 separate dishes, including many Indonesian specialties. A small sampling: guacamole dip ($4.50); tofu parmigiana with salad, french fries, and bread ($7.25); mixed vegetables with lemon butter ($5.50); fresh-fruit salad marinated in orange juice and Galliano ($4.95); and a roast beef and creamed horseradish sandwich in toasted pita ($4.95).

Then there are the hot toddies for the winter months ($3.50), refreshing piña coladas for the summer ($3.50), and a slew of fresh-baked desserts—try the "tunnel of fudge" cake ($2.75). Sunday brunch, served from noon to 4 p.m., includes specials such as a choice of a screwdriver, Bloody Mary, or wine, plus juice and coffee, with any egg, omelet, or french toast entree for $1.50 plus the price of the entree.

The kitchen is open Sunday through Thursday from noon to 1 a.m., on Friday and Saturday until 2 a.m. The restaurant closes an hour later.

CHINESE: Operating on two levels in a small building that used to be an art gallery, the **Bamboo Corner,** 331 West Broadway, corner of Grand Street (tel. 966-3355), features excellent Szechuan and Mandarin food at bargain prices. It's a simple and comfortable place to eat, with wood floors, exposed brick walls, high ceilings, and neat tables adorned with white tablecloths.

There are 15 different luncheon specials, including beef with Chinese cabbage, double-spicy chicken, green and red pepper steak, and sweet-and-sour pork—all served with hot-and-sour or egg-drop soup ($3.55 to $4.95). The regular menu is also always available: pan-fried dumplings are $3.50; lemon chicken, $5.75; sliced chicken in Chinese wine sauce with bamboo shoots, snowpeas, and carrots, $6.25; beef with broccoli, $5.75.

Open Monday to Thursday, and Sunday, from 11:30 a.m. to 11:30 p.m., on Friday to 12:30 a.m., on Saturday from 12:30 p.m. to 12:30 a.m. Reservations suggested at dinner.

ETHIOPIAN: Abyssinia, 35 Grand St., between Thompson Street and West Broadway (tel. 226-5959), offers excellent Ethiopian cuisine in an intriguing ethnic setting. Diners are seated on tiny three-legged stools around a short round table decorated with a dome of straw. When the meal is served, the dome is removed and hung on the wall.

The exotic variety of vegetarian, beef, and fish dishes cost an average of $7 and are all accompanied by an ample serving of "injera," the porous Ethiopian pancake that takes the place of knife and fork and can be used to soak up every last bit of the spicy red-pepper sauce known as "berbere." Doro wot, a popular Ethiopian dish of chicken marinated in berbere, is served exceedingly tender and spicy ($8.50). Also excellent, and a bargain at $9.75, is kitfo, a national dish of steak tartare seasoned with spiced butter and hot chili powder.

Desserts are equally unusual, from a simple plate of papaya with lime ($3.25) to a rich dark African chocolate-chip cake ($3.75). For those who can never get enough chocolate there's even a trio of handmade chocolate truffles ($3.75). Cocoa beans never tasted so good.

Currently open for dinner only, from 6 to 11 p.m. nightly.

INTERNATIONAL FARE: At **Central Falls,** 478 West Broadway, near West Houston Street (tel. 475-3333), patrons get a generous helping of SoHo culture along with their meals: monthly art exhibitions give a gallery-like feel to this airy space, classical musicians perform chamber music during weekend brunches, and the seats by the window offer some of the best sidewalk watching in all of SoHo.

At the bar, oysters on the half shell ($1) wash well with the icy draft beers ($2). The menu is an eclectic international mix, including rumaki, grilled chicken livers wrapped in bacon and served with tamari and watercress ($5.25), broiled hamburgers with french fries ($6.25), and an open-faced chicken salad sandwich with almonds ($7). For a great late-afternoon snack, try the small loaves of french bread stuffed with mozzarella cheese and laced with garlic ($4.75) or the deep-fried zucchini ($3.50). Portions are generous and well prepared, and if you're lucky, you just might catch Richard Gere or Susan Sarandon sitting by one of the spectacular neoclassical columns that decorate the place.

Open Monday to Saturday from noon to 2 a.m., on Sunday from 11:30 a.m. to 2 a.m. Reservations suggested for dinner and brunch.

Although slightly west of SoHo proper, the **Ear Inn,** 326 Spring St., between Washington and Greenwich Streets (tel. 226-9060), is well worth the few extra blocks of walking. This small, casual restaurant is a deservedly beloved neighborhood hangout whose outstanding feature is its clientele of writers, musicians, and artists. The Ear Inn offers its discerning patrons live music, poetry readings, and tables covered with butcher paper and crayons, should the creative urge strike while dining. The restaurant is housed in an ancient landmark structure dating from 1817 and the decor is minimal—a collection of old glass bottles on the bar, a few fish on the walls, a wood floor. There are tables with blue-and-white checkered tablecloths in the front and in a small back room. The jukebox, which plays the latest in New Wave, reggae, and jazz, is very, very good.

The Ear Inn's specialty is "homemade international cuisine" and the food is inexpensive and imaginatively prepared. You might sample the cowboy chili ($3.50 a bowl), an excellent hot-and-spicy offering, along with a mixed green or Niçoise salad ($5.50). Or there are sirloin burgers, pasta of the day, Bhutan vegetables with curry sauce, and daily specials such as sausage ragoût stew ($5.50 to $8). The desserts are all homemade and very large. There's a full bar too.

The kitchen is open from noon to 1 a.m., and there are poetry readings every Saturday at 3 p.m. Sunday brunch is served from noon to 4 p.m. Reservations are accepted.

Standing in marked contrast to the rest of the SoHo scene is **Fanelli's,** 94 Prince St., corner of Mercer Street (tel. 226-9412). The last of the neighborhood taverns, it's been around for over a century, and owner Mike Fanelli has been there almost that long—he's somewhere in his 80s, we're told. It's a small place with a handful of tables and an eclectic clientele of SoHo-ites, truckers, and students. Mike Fanelli was a boxer in his youth and he's lined the walls with photographs of old fights and famous boxers. The food is simple, but filling. For $5 to $7 you can have linguine with marinara sauce, eggplant parmigiana, or shepherd's pie with salad. Escarole rice soup is $2.50. Thick sandwiches are $4.25 to $4.95.

The bar is open from 10 a.m. to 2 a.m. Monday through Saturday, from noon to 2 a.m. on Sunday; food is served from 11 a.m. to 1 a.m.

ITALIAN: A young sophisticated crowd is already flocking to **I Tre Merli,** 436 West Broadway, between West Houston and Prince Streets (tel. 254-8699), the new SoHo sister of a wine bar and restaurant in Genoa, Italy. Indeed, the Genovese owners have taken pains to give their New York hangout a sleek Italian look. The trendy interior, including floors and furniture, is a highly glossed black, and the clever modular bar with movable sections encourages an Italian attitude toward meeting strangers.

Wine and champagne come by the glass or bottle ($3 to $4) and are imported exclusively from the I Tre Merli vineyards in northern Italy. If you need to prolong your wine sampling, there's a snack menu for late afternoon and evening that includes plates of assorted salamis, cheeses, and pastas ($4.25 to $6.75).

The cuisine, like the wine, is Genovese, and the fragrant and spicy dishes served at brunch may bring back memories of lazy afternoons in Italy. An aromatic plate of fusilli with basil is $6.50, breast of chicken with herbs and pine nuts is $7.50, and eggs with sweet Italian sausage are $6. Dinner is more expensive, but the view from the mezzanine of the late-night action at the crowded ground-floor bar may make the splurge worthwhile.

Open daily from noon until 2 a.m., and until 4 a.m. in the summer on Saturday and Sunday.

9. Lower Manhattan/Tribeca

Financiers and tourists alike who find themselves in lower Manhattan at lunch or dinnertime would do well to resist the urge to grab a bite around the corner. A much better idea is to stroll a little to the east, toward the waterfront, or to the west and a bit uptown, to Tribeca (Triangle below Canal Street). Both these areas—the former steeped in history, the latter the site of an old produce market that's redefining itself into a loft-and-office district—offer a number of restaurants with good food at reasonable prices, served in interesting environs.

AMERICAN/CONTINENTAL: The **Bridge Café**, 279 Water St., at Dover Street (tel. 227-3344), two blocks from the South Street Seaport, has a 19th-century Cape Cod charm other landmark restaurants in the area have lost. From the outside, the red wood-frame building looks as if it's bowing before the towering Brooklyn Bridge above it. Inside, there are photos of the bridge on the café's cream-colored slat-board walls. There are potted flowers in the entry and front windows and red-checked cloths on the tables.

The menu changes daily, but generally offers sandwiches, soup ($2.95 for a bowl of clam chowder, $6.95 for a soup-and-sandwich combination), a hot and a cold pasta dish, and fish, chicken, and meat entrees, usually braised with a subtle sauce. Most are priced under $9. Dinner entrees run higher, but there's usually an under-$10 choice, such as tagliatelle with a smooth mushroom, prosciutto, and cream sauce ($9.95).

Lunch is served daily from 11:45 a.m. to 3 p.m., dinner from 6 p.m. to midnight. Brunches featuring omelets (try the one with tangy goat cheese, $6.75), apple pancakes ($6.50), and pastas such as fettuccine primavera ($6.95) are served from noon to 3:30 p.m. on weekends.

Reservations are not accepted—unless you are Mayor Ed Koch, who pops in here for lunch at least once a week. Hizzoner is such a regular here that the restaurant frees up the table it sets aside for him only after his secretary calls to say he *won't* be coming.

It's a friendly Tribeca crowd that frequents the bar and restaurant at **Smoke Stacks Lightnin'**, 380 Canal St., at West Broadway (tel. 226-0485). If you can get yourself past the video games at the entry, you can make yourself at home at the large, roomy, wooden tables. The green-and-brown motif and lofty, green pressed-tin ceiling give Smoke Stacks a woodsy atmosphere, and lighting from theatrical fixtures lends added drama to the decor.

Smoke Stacks is particularly nice at sundown for a drink and an appetizer, perhaps country pâté ($3.25) or liver mousse ($3.75). Bistro fare is served at lunch and dinner, with most entrees under $10. At the lower-priced end of the menu are hearty sandwiches under $5, served at lunchtime, and a meal-size Caesar ($3.50) or seafood salad ($6.95). On Sunday, Smoke Stacks serves a champagne brunch for $7.50—a good deal, even for brunch-crazy Manhattan.

Smoke Stacks is open from noon to 2:30 a.m. weekdays, till 4 a.m. on Friday and Saturday. The kitchen closes at midnight on Sunday and Monday, at 1 a.m. on Tuesday, Wednesday, and Thursday, and at 2 a.m. on Friday and Saturday. Brunch on Sunday is served from 11:30 a.m. till 4 p.m.

Less out-of-the-way than most of Tribeca's warehouse restaurants is **211 West Broadway**, at Franklin Street (tel. 925-7202). This one is cool gray and typically lofty, with a gray pressed-tin ceiling held high by Grecian-style columns, floor-to-ceiling windows screened with venetian blinds, and a large acrylic canvas of a southwestern *Last Picture Show* scene. Tables are marble tops on wrought-iron pedestals, graced by bud vases filled with fresh flowers.

The lunch menu offers a number of items for the budget-conscious. Try the grilled breast of chicken with a tarragon cream sauce ($7.50), angel hair pasta primavera ($7.95), or a fluffy omelet ($5.95) or the "Two-Eleven burger" ($4.50), both with shoestring potatoes. The price goes up at dinnertime, but the juicy house burger is still affordable at $6.50, fettuccine with spinach, mushrooms, and marsala wine costs $10.25, and chicken cooked with three fruits and mandarin Napoléon liqueur costs less than $11.

The restaurant serves cocktail brunches on Saturday and Sunday. Once again, the house burger with shoestring potatoes costs least ($6.50). Among the other choices: eggs with smoked salmon and salmon caviar ($9.50), seafood crêpes bathed in a creamy saffron sauce ($8.95), and a French peasant omelet ($7.50). All brunch entrees are served with a mimosa, a Bloody Mary, or a screwdriver.

Lunch is served daily from 11:30 a.m. to 4:30 p.m., dinner from 5 p.m. to 1 a.m., and weekend brunch from 11:30 a.m. to 4:30 p.m. Live music on an occasional Sunday.

A favorite of Tribeca's "locals"—the loft dwellers who call the district home—is **riverrun**, 176 Franklin St., between Greenwich and Hudson Streets (tel. 966-3894). Healthful food, manageable prices, and rotating displays of the work of neighborhood photographers are three good reasons for this cozy restaurant's popularity. At lunch, if you're in the mood for a meal-size salad, you can choose among several, including a mixed seafood salad ($5.95), a hearty Niçoise ($5.95), and a bracing mixture of lettuce, chicken, apples, walnuts, swiss cheese, and onion ($5.95). Perhaps you'd prefer the full smoked trout with bean salad ($7.95), chicken and vegetables in spicy garlic sauce with rice ($6.95), or a mound of steamed mussels floating in a zesty sauce of garlic, white wine, and tomatoes ($6.95). Omelets with french fries are cheaper still ($4.95 for one stuffed with smoked trout, sour cream, and scallions), as are sandwiches such as the avocado on whole wheat ($4.75) and the cheeseburger with french fries ($5.75).

Many of the items on the luncheon menu reappear on the dinner menu at the same bargain prices. Among the additional entrees: steak teriyaki, with rice and a vegetable ($8.95); fried chicken with cornbread and homemade potato salad ($7.50); and linguine in a cream sauce with mixed seafood ($7.50). If you've a yen for carrot cake, riverrun's, with cream-cheese icing, is one of the best ($2.75). The friendly waitresses will bring you extra forks if you want to share.

Their unlimited-champagne brunch, on weekends, features eggs Florentine or Benedict ($5.50), french toast with bacon or ham ($5.25), and a selection of omelets from $4.95. Also available are items from the regular lunch menu: salads ($5.95), burgers ($5.25), and quiche with french fries ($5.25).

The restaurant is open for lunch from 11:30 a.m. to 5 p.m. weekdays and from 11:30 a.m. to 2 p.m. on Saturday. Dinner runs from 5 p.m. to 1 a.m. Sunday through Thursday, to 2 a.m. Friday and Saturday. Brunch is served on Saturday from 11:30 a.m. to 5 p.m. and on Sunday from 11 a.m. to 5 p.m.

One block west and one block south from riverrun is another neighborhood hangout, a festive Cajun place, **how's bayou**, 355 Greenwich St., at Harrison Street (tel. 925-5405). By design, there's nothing fancy here. The restaurant is housed in a former meat market whose many doors stay open on summer nights to give diners the feeling they're eating al fresco. Fans hang from the pressed-tin ceiling, as does a large neon sign that spells out the restaurant's name. Paper bags of tortilla chips adorn every butcher-block table—a clue that the kitchen produces Mexican as well as Cajun specialties. The staff makes you feel like an instant regular by snapping Mardi Gras beads around your neck.

How's bayou's food won't win accolades from restaurant critics, who don't hand out stars for good home-cooking. But the food here is hearty and served in generous portions. For lunch you can have chunky chili ($3.50), Créole meatloaf ($4.95), or a "Bayou raft" of fried catfish filet on fresh hero bread ($5.95). Specialties from the dinner menu are also served at lunch, including a chicken, sausage, shrimp, and crayfish jambalaya ($5.95), enchiladas ($6.95), and southern fried chicken ($6.95). (These items are about $1 more at dinnertime.) Evenings, you can choose from the New Orleans (or N'awlins) gumbo ($5.95) and mesquite chicken ($8.95) among the Cajun offerings, fajitas ($9.95) and spaghetti Tex-Mex ($6.95) from the Mexican list, and chicken fried steak ($6.95) and barbecued pork ribs ($8.95) from the section of the menu labeled "Southern Hospitality." Round out the meal, if you're still hungry, with homemade apple pie or Créole bread pudding with whiskey sauce ($2.50). Ya hear? Weekend brunch ($7.95 and up) offers items from lunch and dinner plus huevos rancheros, corned-beef hash and eggs, omelets, and side orders of grits, biscuits, and gravy.

Food is served from 11:30 a.m. to midnight Sunday through Thursday, to 1 a.m. on Friday and Saturday. The bar stays open till 2 or 3 a.m.

For some of the city's most acclaimed hamburgers, drop into **Hamburger Harry's,** 157 Chambers St., near Greenwich Street (tel. 267-4446). "Ha-Ha's" decor is a functional mix of butcher block and art deco—just the right setting for charcoaled burgers with a gourmet touch. If you want to watch the red-capped chefs in action, ask to be seated at the counter. Plush seats there are spaced for the maximum in comfort and elbow room. Ha-Ha's hefty but lean hamburgers are broiled over live charcoal and mesquite—the wood that gives these burgers their distinctive taste. You'll have 17 varieties of hamburgers to choose from, ranging from a "naked burger" (plain without the roll, $2.95) to burgers topped with béarnaise sauce ($4.25), gorgonzola cheese ($3.95), guacamole and pico de gallo (spicy, $4.95), or the works (chili, cheddar cheese, chopped onion, guacamole, and pico de gallo, $5.95). Don't pass up Ha-Ha's fresh french fries ($1.50), which, like the burgers, have received top marks from New York's discriminating restaurant reviewers.

Instead of hamburgers, you might try the fajitas—a house specialty that combines char-broiled beefsteak or chicken with pico de gallo, refried beans, guacamole, and steaming flour tortillas ($6.95 for the chicken, a dollar more for the beef). Other items on this surprisingly eclectic menu: chili ($3.50), Ha-Ha tostadas ($4.95), specials such as lobster salad platter ($5.95), corn chowder ($1.60), desserts such as chocolate-raspberry ice cream ($2.25), and in season, strawberries and whipped cream ($2.85). Ha-Ha's serves wine and beer.

Open seven days a week from 11:30 a.m. to 11:30 p.m.

What Ha-Ha's is to the hamburger, **Ham Heaven,** 49 Warren St., between West Broadway and Greenwich Street (tel. 513-7224), is to ham. Come here if you want to taste succulent, sweet Virginia ham at its best. Owned by Paul and Kathy Domitrovich and named after Kathy's family's place in Detroit, Ham Heaven is, well, "hamazing," as the proud Domitroviches will be the first to tell you. On the street level, where sun slants in from a skylight, green tablecloths and counter service give this former hardware warehouse a homey warmth. Downstairs, theater seats salvaged from an uptown disco and walls decorated with porcine art put you in the mood for . . . well, ham and dinner theater—a dream of the owners which may be a reality when you read this book. They "import" their hams from Michigan—meat from other sources proved too salty —and bake about 20 a day in brown sugar and ginger ale. You can savor the finished product in an overstuffed sandwich ($3), in homemade navy-bean or split-pea soup loaded with ham ($1.25); as healthy slices served with macaroni salad, potato salad, or baked beans ($4.25); in quiche ($4.50) and omelets

($3.50); creamed on toast ($3.50), or chopped and sauteed with fresh vegetables and stuffed into pita bread. Breakfast features "Detroit Heavenly Hash" ($3.50 for a hearty mix of hash browns, chopped ham, green peppers, and onions, fried together with an egg added on top). The menu provides options for diners who don't feel like ham—but ham's the thing, and it draws ham lovers from all over town.

The restaurant serves breakfast and lunch all day, opening at 6:30 a.m. weekdays and 8 a.m. weekends. Closing hours in this business district one block below Tribeca are 4 p.m. weekends and 6 p.m. weekdays, except for jazz nights (Wednesday and Thursday during the summer, Thursday and Friday at other times), when the restaurant stays open until 11 p.m.

Sports fans lonely for the home team might find it in action at a unique Tribeca restaurant, **The Sporting Club,** 99 Hudson St., between Harrison and Franklin Streets (tel. 219-0900). The main draw is a ten-foot video screen and its companion, a computerized scoreboard, which tower above the oval bar and can be seen from every table in this mahogany-paneled, multilevel restaurant. TV monitors spotted around the restaurant enable Bill Rose, the owner, to show anywhere from three to six events simultaneously. (Call ahead and he'll tell you if he'll be able to pull your favorite team off a satellite or cable link. The scoreboard keeps almost instantaneous track of every game being played in the nation.) Sports lovers flock to this restaurant as much for the camaraderie as the food and drink. The clientele, about two-thirds male, often includes well-known sports figures, sometimes working behind the bar. The menu is eclectic and moderately priced, running from "O.J.'s Buffalo Wings" ($3.75) and "Super Bowl" chili ($5.50) to the "Rose Bowl" chef's salad ($6.50), barbecued chicken ($8.75), and a steamed vegetable platter ($8.95). On Saturday and Sunday from noon to 5 p.m., brunch ($6.95 and up) is popular—only partly because every home run will earn you a free drink during baseball season.

The restaurant opens every day at 11:45 a.m. and closes anywhere from 2 to 4 a.m. The kitchen stays open till midnight.

FRENCH: By far the prettiest of Tribeca's warehouse restaurants is **Capsouto Frères,** 451 Washington St., at Watts Street (tel. 966-4900). The neo-Romanesque warehouse is housed in a landmark building dating to 1891, and the restaurant's owners have done wonders with its interior. From the high, exposed-beam ceiling hang gently turning antique ceiling fans and chandeliers of brass with fogged-glass tulip shades. Stately cast-iron columns appear to support the lofty ceiling. The floors are brightly polished hardwood, the walls exposed brick with large, floor-to-ceiling windows framed by maroon velvet drapes. White linen cloths cover the tables, with fresh flowers on each.

Main entrees run upward of $10.50, but there's a varied selection of seven "petits plats" with delicious portions of coquille Saint-Jacques, crêpes farcies, and a vegetarian plate with wild rice—all for $6.75 to $11.50. The dishes are à la carte, but servings are generous. Desserts are laid out on a table in the restaurant's center, to be assembled by waiters. They feature pastries and fruits and are irresistibly pretty. They cost about $3.50.

Capsouto Frères is open daily from noon till 2 a.m., except Monday when it opens at 5 p.m. Lunch is served before 4 p.m., with prices somewhat lower.

GREEK/MEDITERRANEAN: Tribeca has a bustling Greek restaurant, **Delphi,** 109 West Broadway at Reade Street (tel. 227-6322), which is well worth a visit. Delphi has an enclosed terrace and a small room on the ground floor with a room full of hanging plants above. Travel posters advertise Greece from nearly every wall—as if the food weren't advertisement enough. As an appetizer, try the stuffed grape leaves ($1.80) or the Delphi specialty, spinach cheese pie ($3.15); then move on to a hearty Greek salad ($5.95) or tomatoes stuffed with pignola nuts, raisins, rice, and cooked with herbs and spices ($5.15). For filling meat dishes, you might turn to the souvlaki platter (roasted marinated beef and lamb), the mixed grill of souvlaki, shish kebab, sausage, and stuffed grape leaves, or the golden-baked pastitsio (macaroni layered with ground beef, cheese, and tomato sauce). The meat dishes all cost $5.95 and include a small Greek salad, rice or baked potato, and fresh broccoli. Definitely a good deal.

Open seven days a week from 11 a.m. to midnight.

Chrisa's Café, 127 West Broadway at Chambers Street (tel. 267-5115), has food similar to Delphi's but a less ebullient atmosphere. If you're ravenously hungry and truly curious about Greek food you might stop here just for the "Pikilia for Two" ($13.95)—a combination of the most popular Greek specialties: souvlaki, kebab, moussaka, spinach pie, and pastitsio served with rice, vegetables, and a bowl of salad.

Across town, a few blocks from the South Street Seaport, you'll find **Chrisa II,** 76 Fulton St., near Gold Street (tel. 964-4136). Greek specialties here are served in a coffeeshop atmosphere, brightened by Greek island scenes painted on the walls and Greek music playing in the background. The prices are definitely right for the budget traveler. You might lunch on pita-bread sandwiches filled with souvlaki, shish kebab, or sausage ($2.55), or Greek antipasto for $4.55. There's also cheese or spinach pie for $2.55 and a Greek salad for $3.25.

Open every day of the week at 10:30 a.m., Chrisa II closes Monday through Friday at 9:45 p.m., on Saturday at 8:30 p.m., and on Sunday at 7:30 p.m.

MEXICAN: For a true south-of-the-border taste, Tribecans go to the **Beach House,** 399 Greenwich St., at Beach Street (tel. 226-7800). The interior of this Civil War–era building is dark and warm. Large fans spin lazily from the high ceiling, painted mirrors adorn the walls, and you're as likely to sit at a large booth as at a candlelit table near the bar. You can buy burritos, enchiladas, tacos, and tostadas, served with refried beans and rice, either separately or in combinations of two ($6.75) or three ($8.25). For something unusual, try the flautas (deep-fried corn tortillas filled with chicken and topped with guacamole and sour cream, $7.75), or the pollo mole poblano (half a chicken sauteed in mole sauce, $8.75). Fire-eaters will delight in the puntas Albanil (corn tortillas filled with strips of shell steak, fresh tomatoes, scallions, jalapeño pepper, and garlic, $8.50). Prices are as much as $2.50 per item cheaper at lunch.

Open for lunch weekdays only, from noon to 4 p.m. Dinner is served Sunday through Thursday from 4 p.m. to midnight, on Friday and Saturday to 1 a.m.

MIXED BAG: Take a ride into the sky, climb 107 stories in less than a minute, walk through a simulated crystal cave, and arrive at the **Hors D'Oeuvrerie,** One World Trade Center (tel. 938-1111). After 3 p.m. the cocktail lounge is open to the public, and after 4 p.m. you can enjoy spicy ethnic hors d'oeuvres with afternoon or evening drinks.

The corridor leading from the super-smooth, super-fast elevator to the lounge looks like the inside of a precious gem, with glass, mirrors, and enlarged travel photos arranged into a three-dimensional collage. Mounted on pedestals fixed to the floor are giant semiprecious stones: African rose quartz, Eurasian pegmatite, and amethyst geode.

Inside, seating is on multiple terraces, with a 180-degree view. Pick your table to afford a view of the Statue of Liberty, Staten Island, or the Brooklyn Bridge and Queens.

Though the view is clearly the real treat, the hot and cold hors d'oeuvres run a close second. For under $8 you can choose from sushi and sashimi (raw fish), sliced roast pork, Indonesian lamb, Korean barbecued short ribs of beef, grilled marinated chicken, and much more. There are even "main course" entrees: sliced breast of chicken in a tangy lemon sauce ($6.50), for example, and Thai beef salad (spicy ground beef stir-fried with coriander and mint, $7.50). Espresso is $1.35; drinks, upward of $3.50.

The Hors d'Oeuvrerie is open to the public daily from 3 p.m. to midnight for food, till 1 a.m. for drinks. A scrumptious Sunday brunch ($8.95 and up) runs from noon to 3 p.m. Piano music begins at 4 p.m. daily (a trio at 7:30), except Sunday, when the trio begins at 7:30. Men must wear jackets (a very few house jackets can be borrowed); blue jeans of any sort are not allowed.

SEAFOOD: The **Front Street Restaurant,** 228 Front St., between Beekman Street and Peck Slip (tel. 406-1560), is a madhouse on weekdays from noon to 2:30 p.m., when it serves some 400 to 500 self-service lunches, all priced between $1.95 and $5. Housed in an 1831 landmark seaport building, the restaurant has a New World, marine ambience. The main dining area has a jukebox, Formica tables, exposed brick walls, and concrete floors; out back there's outdoor dining at tables on a slat-board patio where empty beer kegs have been tossed out. Fried shrimp, clams, and scallops are the favorites, along with juicy bratwurst, bauernwurst, and knockwurst. There are also quiches, cheesemelts, and seafood salads—none priced above $3.60 at lunch. A dinner menu offers similar fare, plus barbecued chicken ($5.25) or lamb ribs ($6.45), and broiled fish specials ($6.95), served with salad, garlic bread, and a choice of rice pilaf or french fries. Beer on tap is 75¢; a glass of house wine, $1.25.

Open weekdays from 10 a.m. to 10 p.m., on Saturday from 11 a.m. to 9 p.m., on Sunday from noon to 9 p.m. The dinner menu begins at 5 p.m. everyday. A musical brunch ($7.95) runs from noon to 4 p.m. weekends and features folk music and a choice of fresh broiled or fried fish, quiche, a burger platter, or three-egg omelets, all served with french fries, salad, garlic bread, and a half liter of beer, wine, or sangria.

A classier, but higher-priced seafood place, also in a landmark building, is **Fulton's Steamer,** 144 Beekman St., corner of Front Street (tel. 267-9490). The tavern/restaurant has wood floors and walnut-stained wainscotting beneath mauve-colored walls adorned with chrome-framed photos. The split-level room is cooled in spring and summer by large ceiling fans. There's a lovely mahogany bar that came from the old fish market.

There's a $6 minimum weekends only. All entrees served at lunch and dinner are fresh seafood, priced under $11. Choose from smoked brook trout with potato and salad ($7.25), fried clams ($8.75) or oysters ($8.25), served with potato, vegetable, and salad, or sauteed shrimps and bay scallops ($9.95). For dessert there's a sumptuous chocolate whiskey cake ($2.25).

Open for lunch Monday through Friday from noon to 3 p.m., for dinner Tuesday through Friday from 5 to 9 p.m. On weekends the restaurant is open on Saturday from 2 to 9 p.m. and on Sunday from 2 to 7 p.m.

SOUTH STREET SEAPORT: Dining options at this inviting four-block complex that so remarkably evokes the atmosphere of 19th-century New York include a fantastic variety of fine restaurants (most regrettably too pricey for more than a brief mention here), cafés, and foodstalls (see the "Gourmet's walk at the South Street Seaport" in Chapter VII). For gourmets and gourmands on a budget, the **second floor of the Fulton Market building** offers the next best thing to an around-the-world food cruise. You can munch on dim sum (Chinese dumplings), empañadas (Argentine meat turnovers), cheese steak sandwiches, burgers, chili, raw-fish bar goodies, Indian tandoori cooking, Greek barbecue, Japanese soup and noodle dishes, chicken and ribs, pizza, sushi, frozen yogurt sundaes, fresh fruit, salads, sausages, New York delicatessen, and enough cake, candy, and ice-cream specialties to satisfy the most demanding sweet tooth.

Gianni's, 15 Fulton St. (tel. 608-7300), an art deco study in black and white, is one of the Seaport's most attractive restaurants, and the one that offers diners the best view of the bustling world outside. Avoid its pricey upstairs menu and opt for the first-floor café, where you can get sausage sandwiches and giant burgers for less than $7. Or, weather permitting, sit at the outdoor café, where Caesar salads are $5, seafood or cold pasta salads run $8.50, and Virginia baked ham sandwiches, $6.50.

The popular **North Star Pub,** 93 South St., at Fulton Street (tel. 509-6757), is decorated like a British ale house, so it's no wonder the menu has a British flavor. Among the choices: bangers and mash (English sausages and mashed potatoes, $4.50), Cornish pasties (meat, potato, and vegetable turnovers, $4.75), and a fishmonger's basket (shrimps, scallops, and fish filet, coated in beer batter and deep-fried, $7.75). The pub's light menu offers samplings from the regular menu at reduced prices. You can get one Cornish pasty, for example, for $2.75, and English cheese and apple slices for $2.50.

The turn-of-the-century atmosphere in **Roeblings Bar and Grill** (tel. 608-3980), on the mezzanine of the Market building, provides the perfect setting for the hearty (and rather expensive) American fare: steaks, ribs, Cajun fried chicken, broiled lemon sole (at $8.95, the cheapest dinner entree), oysters (raw or fried in beer), and smoked trout. No dinner served on Friday evenings, when the place is crammed with Wall Streeters celebrating the week's end and taking advantage of a *free buffet*. You might want to join them.

Resist the urge to visit the rooftop Coho, where the cheapest dinner entree, broiled salmon steak, will set you back $15.95. Prices are more down-to-earth at the ground-floor **The Grille,** across from the Trans-Lux Seaport Theatre on Beekman and Front Streets (tel. 227-9328). During warm months the Grille moves outdoors and serves lunch and dinner on pink tablecloths. Dinner entrees begin at $8.75, for sesame chicken, and run to $11.95 for batter-fried shrimp. Weekend brunch offers a variety of choices, from an apple, brie, and walnut omelet ($6.95) to filet of sole meunière ($9.95).

We would be remiss not to mention two of New York's landmark restaurants still very much in business in the busy Seaport. **Sloppy Louie's** (tel. 952-9657) and **Sweet's** (tel. 344-9189) are both in Schermerhorn Row on Fulton Street. At either place you'll find fresh seafood at moderate prices, with a full dinner ranging from about $10 to $17.

10. Chinatown

For street shopping and divine dining, there's no place like Chinatown. The neighborhood located south of Canal Street and loosely bounded by the Bowery, Park Row, and Centre Street is a bustling hodgepodge of fascinating shops and restaurants. The streets are crammed with crowds buying low-priced fish, fruit, and vegetables from a lively market of sidewalk vendors. The biggest crowds come to Chinatown during January or February to celebrate the Chinese New Year with a steady stream of firecrackers and firewater.

During the rest of the year Chinatown's main attraction is its restaurants, where you'll probably find the greatest concentration of Chinese cuisine in America. Cantonese, Szechuan, Hunan, Mandarin, Shanghai, and Fukien—all varieties of Chinese fare from the country's different provinces are represented in force.

Many of these restaurants offer a unique treat called dim sum, the traditional Chinese tea lunch, which is an economical way to sample some of Chinatown's most interesting dishes.

What you'll find lacking in most Chinese restaurants is elegant ambience. The Chinatown standard of interior design is hard Formica furnishings placed under harder fluorescent lighting. Plastic tablecloths and simple spindleback chairs complete the spartan style of decor. But don't be put off by conventionally banal settings, for it's also a Chinatown truism that some of the plainest places serve some of the most memorable meals.

CANTONESE: This is the food served by a majority of Chinese restaurants and characterized by specialties that include fried wontons or wonton soup, sweet-and-sour pork, and shrimp with lobster sauce. Unfortunately, Cantonese fare has been given a bad name by restaurants that serve cliché wonton dishes full of cornstarch and sauces laden with fruit out of a can. In Chinatown, less Westernized versions of Cantonese favorites prove that at its best, Cantonese food can meet the standards of the most sophisticated and demanding gourmet. A word of caution: Some restaurants will doctor dishes served to Westerners, so if you want to sample something Chinese style, make that clear to your waiter.

The Chinatown institution for superior Cantonese fare is the **Yun Luck Rice Shoppe,** 17 Doyers St., near Pell Street (tel. 571-1375). Located on a charming curved side street, Yun Luck was for years an out-of-the-way favorite among Chinatown residents and in-the-know tourists. Then Mimi Sheraton, the tough food critic for the *New York Times,* gave the 150-seat restaurant her seal of approval with a rare three-star (excellent) rating. Now it's hard to find a seat for lunch. If you're lucky or patient enough to get a table, stay away from the tried-and-true chow mein and wonton dishes and try some truly inventive Cantonese cooking. Among the house specialties are crabs Cantonese style ($6.75), stir-fried with a sauce of pork, ginger, black beans, and scallions; and treasurer duck ($9.75), garnished with jumbo shrimp, roast pork, chicken, mushrooms, and snowpeas. The much-raved-about steamed flounder and steamed bass are not on the menu, so ask your waiter.

Our favorite nonseafood dishes are steak with jade tree, meat that melts in your mouth served on a bed of broccoli ($9.75), beef with mixed vegetables ($7.75), and watercress soup ($4.25 for a large tureen serving two to four). The thick, chewy noodle dishes are quite good, with roast duck lo mein ($3.75) near nirvana for noodle nuts.

While the food is guaranteed to please the palate, the decor is less successful at pleasing the eye. Waiters cover the tables in white Hefty Bag–style plastic, removing the top layer every time the table is used. The tacky tablecloths and the dismal lighting give Yun Luck all the ambience of a greasy-spoon diner, but patrons say the magnificent meals make it easier to ignore the mundane surroundings.

The price on the à la carte dinners ranges from $3.75 to $9.75, and $15.95 for a few seafood and lobster dishes. Most dishes cost between $5 and $8. No dessert is on the menu. Bring your own wine or beer, since the house serves no liquor. Reservations, especially for large crowds, are a must.

Open from noon to 11 p.m. Sunday through Friday, from noon to midnight on Saturday.

Also top-notch is **Wong Kee Restaurant,** 113 Mott St. (tel. 966-1160), a small establishment which provides very good inexpensive noodle and soup dishes without the frenetic fast-food atmosphere found in other Chinatown noodle houses. A couple of years ago the management moved from the old restaurant into a newly renovated place down the street. The new Wong Kee looks very different from the Wong Kee Chinatown residents grew to know and love. Gone are the red-and-gold flocked wallpaper and the red Formica tables. The new place is cheerily decorated in shades of steely gray, lemon yellow, and dark turquoise, and the overall effect is soothing and attractive.

It's hard to believe that the Wong Kee restaurants can stay in business, since their prices are just about the cheapest in Chinatown. Hearty dishes over rice, such as beef with green peas, cost as little as $2. Nearly half of Wong Kee's 47 other rice dishes cost less than $3; the other half run from about $4.90 to $5.75. There are other more expensive house specialties, like pineapple roast duck ($7.50), Wong Kee spiced pork ($6.35), and crab Cantonese ($5.75). A Chinese friend told us about this place and we can understand why it's his favorite.

Open daily from 11 a.m. to 10 p.m. No bar. Reservations accepted for large groups.

The menu of **Hong Ying,** 11 Mott St., between Worth Street and Park Place (tel. 962-9821), boasts that "all our Chinese food is delicious, the price reasonable." Critics and customers agree. Renowned food critic Craig Claiborne called the food "uncommonly good." Here you can find offbeat Cantonese seafood delicacies like mussel casserole with black beans and garlic, and eggplant with garlic. These dishes are not on the menu, so ask your waiter for suggestions. Ask him for prices too.

Our favorite meal is wor shu opp—fried duck with a thin coating of finely chopped almonds under skin as crisp as parchment and topped with a delicate sauce. Also on our interesting yet inexpensive meal list is lor hon jai, mixed vegetables in bean-curd sauce topped with sesame seeds ($3.95); Canton-style crabs or snails ($4.95); steamed fish ($7.35); and a unique dish called fun gone har kew, fried chicken livers and jumbo shrimps with water chestnuts, bamboo shoots, snowpea pods, and other vegetables ($5.95).

Hong Ying offers four basic Chinese noodle dishes at prices ranging from $2.15 for fried rice to $3.45 for noodles with shrimp in black-bean sauce. The à la carte dinners cost between $3.25 for a vegetable dish of steamed mustard greens and $8.95 for steak and lobster. Most dishes are priced between $5.95 and $7.95.

Open Sunday through Thursday from 11 a.m. to 2 a.m., on Friday and Saturday to 4 a.m. No reservations. No bar.

Bo Bo's or **Toong Lai Shoon Restaurant,** 204½ Pell St., is between Mott Street and the Bowery (tel. 267-8373). The neon sign in the window still reads "Bo Bo's," but the larger sign hanging above the small establishment reads "Toong Lai Shoon" restaurant. Customers are likely to be confused until they find out that the ownership of Bo Bo's has changed and the new management has been reluctant to part with the legendary star appeal of Bo Bo's name. The former owners, the Tams, had been Hong Kong stage actors and the place attracted many Far Eastern entertainers and a roster of New York celebrities; Marlon Brando and Dick Cavett were en route to Bo Bo's the night they had their famous run-in with paparazzi photographer Ron Galella. The new staff admits that there are few chauffeured limousines parked outside the door these days. The Bo Bo's mystique may have faded with the change in menu as well as the different name above the door.

The old Bo Bo's specialized in Cantonese specialties like butterfly shrimp; the new Bo Bo's cooks some Cantonese dishes, but prefers to serve spicier Mandarin and Szechuan fare. The new management has also introduced special full dinners, including soup, appetizers, an entree, fried rice, and dessert, for $7.50 per person. Touted by the chef are dishes like lake tung ting ($9.50), scallops with dry orange peel in Hunan hot-pepper sauce; and Hunan beef ($7.65) with scallops and snowpeas. The price for à la carte dinner dishes ranges from $4.95 for moo shu pork to $6.75 for crispy fried duck. Specialties of the house cost between $9.50 for changsha fish and $7.65 for Confucius prawns.

Open Sunday through Thursday from noon to 11 p.m., on Friday and Saturday to midnight. No bar. Reservations accepted.

Another place to go for quality Cantonese food is the **Kam Bo Rice Shoppe,** 51 Bayard St. (tel. 233-5440). In addition to inexpensive yet filling noodle dishes ($2.50 to $4.85), you can get stir-fried vegetable and beef dishes with rice here for as little as $2.50. For seafood lovers there's mussels in a black-bean sauce served in a hot clay pot ($5.75), or the "Three Stars Sea Food Pot," with lobster, crabmeat, jumbo shrimp, and mixed Chinese vegetables ($9.95). For more daring palates, we recommend the peanut dice-cut chicken with hot-pepper sauce ($6.25).

Open daily from 11 a.m. to 3 a.m.

SZECHUAN: The hot-pepper province in southwestern China is a center for savory, spicy cooking where dishes are seasoned with generous portions of garlic and scallions. Some of the better-known Szechuan dishes are twice-cooked pork, shredded beef with garlic sauce, chicken with hot peppers, and hot-and-sour soup.

A hard-to-find little restaurant, but well worth the search, is the **Little Szechuan,** 31 Oliver St., off Chatham Square (tel. 349-2360). The name is appropriate: the tiny place has only eight tables. A golden dragon covers most of the one wall, tables are clothed in red and covered with glass, and a single tassled lantern sports flashing Christmas-tree-style lights.

The service is extremely hospitable, the food is superlative, and the prices are unbeatable. We recently had a veritable feast of ginger shrimp ($5.25), fried flounder ($7.50), orange beef—the best we've tried—($5.25), chicken with asparagus ($4.95), hot-and-spicy vegetables ($4.25), and a cold noodle appetizer with sesame sauce ($2.50). You'll be hard pressed to find either better or cheaper fare.

Open daily from 11:30 a.m. to 10 p.m.

The **Szechuan State,** 22 Chatham Square (tel. 619-1435), serves excellent yet inexpensive food in a comfortable environment. Golden Tiffany-style lamps cast a warm glow on the wood- and mirror-paneled room and its rust-colored vinyl booths.

We recently took the waiter's advice and tried the sliced prawns and scallops in a garlic sauce ($8.95). The dish was neither too garlicky nor too leaden, and the sauce was robust but not overwhelming. Also highly praised are the imperial shrimp with peanuts ($7.95), ta chien chicken ($5.95), double-sauteed pork ($5.25), and sliced beef with broccoli ($5.75).

Most dishes are reasonably priced, with lamb, poultry, and beef à la carte dinners costing between $5.25 and $6.50. Fish dishes are, on the average, the most expensive meals on the menu, priced at $6.75. Pork, vegetable, bean, and noodle dishes are least expensive, with prices ranging from $4.25 to $5.50.

Open from 11 a.m. to midnight Sunday through Thursday, to 1 a.m. on Friday and Saturday. Reservations accepted.

SHANGHAI: Chefs from every part of China were drawn to this sophisticated city in days of yore and combined their regional culinary skills to create what we know as Shanghai cuisine.

One of the best places in Chinatown to sample Shanghai delicacies is **Say Eng Look,** 1 East Broadway, off Chatham Square (tel. 732-0796). Say eng look means "four, five, six" in Shanghai dialect—an unbeatable combination in Chinese games of chance. Indeed, owner/chef A. K. Chang leaves nothing to fate as he fixes such sure-fire winners as finely sliced deep-fried pork cutlets ($6.25), fish roll wrapped in sheets of bean curd ($5.25), shrimp with sizzling rice ($7.50), sweet-and-sour sliced fish ($6.95), and shrimp with kidney ($6.75). You might also try the casseroles—another Shanghai specialty—particularly the fish-head casserole ($7.50) and chicken with cashew nuts ($7.25). Most à la carte dinner dishes cost between $6.25 and $7.50, with double-digit prices for some seafood and duck meals.

Say Eng Look's interior is spotless and attractive. Subdued lighting tones down the flamboyant red walls and the beamed ceiling gives the restaurant a homey charm.

Open from 11 a.m. to 10:30 p.m. Sunday through Thursday, to 11 p.m. on Friday and Saturday. Reservations are necessary for large groups.

Under the same ownership and bearing the same name in English, **Four Five Six,** 2 Bowery, corner of Doyers Street (tel. 964-5853), offers a similar menu in slightly less appealing surroundings. It's also more touristy, offering Westernized versions of Shanghai specialties; so if you want the real thing, talk to your waiter or go to Say Eng Look.

Open from 11:30 a.m. to 11 p.m. Sunday through Thursday, to midnight on Friday and Saturday. Reservations suggested for large groups.

FUKIEN: The province of Fukien on the southeast coast of China is famous for spicy but not super-hot seafood and clear soup. Chefs in this province also created the eggroll, suckling pig, pork liver, and noodle soup.

Chinatown boasts the only known Fukien restaurant in the city. It's **Confucius Restaurant,** 13 Division St., off the Bowery (tel. 431-4931), and it's worth bragging about. Recommended are the strongly seasoned fried fish rolls ($3) served with spicy cabbage salad. Don't miss the seafood entrees like hon shu ya pai, fresh fish filets with Chinese mushrooms ($8.50). Delicious pork dishes include pork chops with scallion sauce ($7.75) and sweet-and-pungent lichee pork ($6.50). Also on our delectably edible list are the spiced beef ($6.50) and lemon chicken ($6.95).

Open daily from 11:30 a.m. to 11:30 p.m. No reservations. No bar.

MIXED BAGS: There are some restaurants in Chinatown offering the culinary specialties of several provinces, the variety of which allows you to put together an interesting meal and to sample a few types of cooking at one sitting.

One of the best of the genre is the **Mandarin Inn Pell,** 34 Pell St., corner of Mott Street (tel. 267-2092). If you like the melange of Mandarin, Cantonese, Szechuan, and Hunan dishes coming out of the kitchen, chef and restaurant raconteur Peter Wong will show you how to make them at the inn's free monthly Chinese cooking classes. Wong's recipes must be good because the Mandarin Inn Pell is an offshoot of his highly successful Mandarin Inn on Mott Street. It's also the second-largest restaurant in Chinatown (the Silver Palace is the first), with seating on two floors for 300 people. The main floor is dominated by two huge electrically lit photomurals of wild horses, and another of a coastal setting. Upstairs the decor is even wilder, with walls bizarrely paneled in aqua and red tiles depicting leaves and berries. There is wine-red carpeting, scarlet drapes, and crystal chandeliers.

Among the chef's prize recipes are those for lobster and black-bean sauce ($7.95) and Mandarin spare ribs ($5.95). The house offers a complete family dinner for $8.95, or a gourmet dinner for $12.95 which includes soup, appetizer, entree, and dessert.

When ordering an à la carte dinner, we like to begin by sharing an order of sizzling rice soup, almost a meal in itself, containing shrimp, chicken, pork, and snowpeas ($3.50), or perhaps an order of scallion pancakes ($1.75). Exciting entrees include lemon chicken ($5.95), Mongolian lamb ($7.50), spicy Kung Pao shrimps ($7.50), and spicy sauteed string beans or eggplant ($4.95). Most à la carte dinner dishes fall in the $6.25 to $7 range, a bit higher than other restaurants of comparable quality. For dessert there's no other choice but the Peking honey crisp banana, deep-fried in batter and then dipped in honey, sugar, and sesame seeds ($3.25 for two).

For large groups, the restaurant will also arrange a tour of Chinatown—the fee is 75¢ for children and $1.50 for adults.

Open Sunday through Thursday from 11:30 a.m. to 11:30 p.m., on Friday and Saturday from noon to 1 a.m., and on Sunday from noon to 10:30 p.m.

Under the same ownership and offering identical fare is the **Mandarin Inn**, 14 Mott St., between Worth Street and Park Place (tel. 962-5830). Soft lighting, comfortable leather booths, and cheery orange-flowered tablecloths give this restaurant a relaxing ambience. A mural of the Great Wall of China is tasteful and pretty, and mirrors on the opposite wall make the quaint establishment seem even more spacious.

Open from 11:30 a.m. to midnight Sunday through Thursday, to 1 a.m. on Friday and Saturday. Reservations accepted for large groups. No bar.

The **Peking Duck House**, 22 Mott St. (tel. 962-8208 or 227-1810), is on Mayor Koch's list of his ten favorite restaurants. It's easy to see why. The restaurant is famous for its way of cooking Peking duck. When the chef carves the roasted duck ($24 for a whole duck) with surgeon-like skill at your table, the skin has been browned to a golden lacquer. The meat is moistly tender and folds neatly into the paper-thin crêpes served with the meal. A velvety hoisin sauce and cool cucumbers and scallions make the roasted duck sandwich a succulent taste sensation.

The Peking Duck House offers an extensive variety of Mandarin, Szechuan, and Hunan dishes, but the most popular order, as you would guess, is the duck. If duck isn't for you, sample the sliced pork double sauteed with chili sauce ($6), the spiced cold beef ($6.50), or the sliced beef with watercress in hot garlic sauce ($7.25). Although the duck is expensive, other à la carte dinners are priced more moderately, with most dishes costing between $6 and $8.95. Noodle and vegetable dishes are less expensive, costing an average of $4.50.

Open Sunday through Thursday from 11:30 a.m. to 10:30 p.m., on Friday and Saturday from 3 to 11:30 p.m., on Sunday from 11:30 a.m. to 3 p.m. (just dim sum). No bar, but Chinese beer is served.

Chi Mer, 11 Chatham Square, near Doyers Street (tel. 267-4565), offers a tasteful ambience and gourmet Chinese food at affordable prices. Tables are covered with simple white linen over a gold cloth; the lighting is recessed and the atmosphere is elegant. With walls of exposed brick, mirrors, and pale paisley wallpaper, the restaurant is a pleasing change from the fire-engine red that covers the walls of many other Chinatown restaurants.

The rave-winning menu of Hunan, Mandarin, and Cantonese fare offers patrons over 150 choices of critically acclaimed Chinese food. Diners recommend the Szechuan orange-flavored beef, the eggplant with garlic sauce, and the beef with watercress. Also recommended are Chi Mer's fried dumplings and Oriental fondue of shrimp balls, pork balls, and lobster liver dipped into a simmering broth.

The beef, chicken, and pork à la carte dinner dishes range from $4.75 to $7, with the average $5.50. Seafood and fish dishes are a little more expensive, ranging from $6.75 to $8.75. The egg and bean-curd dinners are the least expensive, costing (with the exception of dishes with crabmeat) $4.50 and $4.75, respectively. Dinners of vegetables and noodles generally run from $3.75 to $5.25.

Open Sunday to Thursday from 11:30 a.m. to 11:30 p.m., on Friday and Saturday till 1:30 a.m. Reservations advised on weekend nights. There is a small bar.

DIM SUM: Many Cantonese and larger mixed-bag restaurants offer a dim sum brunch, usually served from 10 a.m. to 3 p.m. Waiters bring trays of Chinese delicacies and other food in bite-size portions; you choose what you like and are charged by the number of plates on your table at the brunch's end. A satisfying dim sum brunch generally costs between $3 and $5.

Our favorite place for dim sum is the **Nom Wah Tea Parlor,** 13 Doyers St., near Pell Street (tel. 962-6047). The decor hasn't changed much since the Choy family opened for business over 40 years ago, so walking in is like stepping back in time: the parlor with its red-vinyl booths, white pressed-tin ceiling, and old-fashioned paintings has all the flavor of a 1940s-style luncheonette. There's no menu: the food comes to you from scurrying waitresses bearing delicacies like their delicious cha shao pao (fluffy steamed buns filled with pork and sweetened red beans), ha gow (chopped shrimp with Chinese vegetables wrapped in rice flour dough), woo gork (Chinese potato grilled with meat and vegetables), py gwut (sauteed spare ribs marinated in red bean sauce), or authentic dim sum (minced pork with vegetables in a wonton covering). They cost between $1 and $2 a plate. Then there are dessert dim sum—doughnuts, almond cookies, custard pies, and sponge cake to sweetly end the meal—priced at 50¢ to $1. A variety of choice teas is always available. Dim sum is always a great crowd pleaser, so don't pass up the opportunity to share Chinese tea with large groups of friends.

Open daily from 10 a.m. to 6 p.m. Reservations suggested on weekend mornings.

Dim sum literally means "to take one's heart's delight," and at **China Royal,** 17 Division St., off the Bowery (tel. 226-0788), you have over 50 chances to sample some delightful dumpling, rice, and noodle creations, plus a sugary assortment of dessert dim sum. Dim sum is served every day from 8 a.m. to 3 p.m., and prices per plate range from $1.30 to $2.25. China Royal also offers a full Cantonese menu, with some challenging entrees that just demand to be eaten, like bird's nest with shredded chicken ($12), braised duck with mushroom ($9), and preserved bean-curd sauce with watercress ($3.75).

China Royal's atmosphere is befittingly more regal and formal than Nom Wah's. The two-story restaurant seats over 200 and is open from 8 a.m. to 10:30 p.m. daily.

Hee Seung Fung, 46 Bowery, between Canal Street and Chatham Square (tel. 374-1319), prides itself on offering the largest choice of dim sum in the city. Plates of dim sum are continuously wheeled around the restaurant from 7:30 a.m. to 5 p.m., with each plate costing $1.30 to $1.75 per person.

The à la carte menu of Cantonese fare offered by the restaurant after noon presents some interesting possibilities for the demanding palate. To snap your taste buds to attention, try the snail with black-bean sauce ($5.25) or the shark fin with shredded chicken soup ($6.25 per person).

Hee Seung Fung is decorated in the modest style of most other Chinatown restaurants with one enlivening exception—a large magenta screen covering a back wall is festooned with a dragon, a phoenix, and a scalloped arch framing three statues of Buddhist deities, the symbol for double happiness.

Open from 7:30 a.m. to 11 p.m. daily. Reservations accepted.

Where do the Chinese go for dim sum? They go to **Hop Kwan,** 20 Catherine St. (tel. 285-9183), a tired-looking restaurant located at the bottom of a flight of stairs. The restaurant only has about 25 varieties of dim sum, but they're excellent and inexpensive, with many dumplings and dessert dim sum priced at $1.10 or less. The clientele is largely Chinese and they have two different menus, one in Chinese and one in English, the latter geared to tourists. If you want authentic fare, put away the menu and point to the brightly colored pieces of paper hanging on the walls announcing the day's specials in Chinese and tell the waiter you want a meal like that.

Open from 8 a.m. to 10:30 p.m. daily. No reservations.

NOODLE HOUSES: Throughout Chinatown are many small places specializing in Chinese noodle dishes served in bowls with pork, shrimp, chicken, duck, fish, vegetables, and beef. These noodle meals are filling, delicious, and very low in price.

Hong Fat, 63 Mott St., between Bayard and Canal Streets (tel. 962-9588), is the premier noodle emporium, but it resonates with the noisy atmosphere of a fast-food burger chain. It's a good eatery for a quick lunch, not a restaurant for a relaxing dinner.

China's four basic noodles are served: lo mein (soft noodles) for $2.25 to $2.70; show fon (broad noodles), also $2.25 to $2.70; chow mai fon (fine rice noodles) for $2.35 to $2.80; and special noodles with gravy for $2.50 to $3.90. You can also order your noodle dish fixed "your way," with any combination of roast pork, beef, shrimp, fish, chicken, or duck.

The restaurant also serves several non-noodle Szechuan specialties, including beef with Szechuan preserved vegetables ($5.75) and dried sauteed string beans with minced pork ($4.50).

Open from 9 a.m. to 5 a.m. daily.

Chinatown's most popular lo mein eatery has found its formula for success in inexpensively priced food served in heaping helpings so huge that a meal can often feed two people. **Lin's Garden Restaurant,** 53 Bayard St., at the corner of Elizabeth Street (tel. 962-9085), is decorated in the same no-frills style as other Chinatown restaurants, yet Lin's is the place to go for over 40 varieties of noodle dishes priced between $2.50 and $4.50.

In addition to four basic types of noodle dishes, Lin's serves over 100 Cantonese specialties, including clams Chinese style ($5.75), served hot in the shell in an oyster sauce; iron steak with broccoli ($7); roast duck ($5.50); and sweet-and-sour pork ($5). Parties of two to five can eat special dinners, including soup, entree, and dessert, for $7.25 per person.

Open from 9 a.m. to 6 a.m. seven days a week.

Wo Hop is actually two restaurants, at 15 and 17 Mott St. (tel. 766-9160 or 962-8617, respectively). The two establishments are different in decor but similar in menu. Devotees of both restaurants recommend the chunky, meat- and seafood-filled soups and noodle dishes. The Wo Hops offer over 50 noodle dishes priced under $4. Many of the steamy plates of silky noodles, such as roast pork chow fon and beef chow fon, cost $2 or less. Other low-priced Cantonese fare: roast pork with green peppers and onions ($3.45), beef with beansprouts ($3.45), and sweet-and-pungent pork ($3.85).

Number 15 is the more attractive place to eat. Decorated with bright-red tiles and electrically lit photomurals of the Chinese countryside, the 50-seat restaurant is cheerful and pleasant. Number 17, located at the bottom of a flight of stairs, has been in that location for over 40 years.

The restaurant at 15 Mott St. is open daily from 11 a.m. to 4 a.m.; the one at 17 Mott is open 24 hours a day. Only 15 Mott will accept reservations.

Wo On, 16 Mott St. (tel. 962-6475), is one of the few restaurants in the district that stays open late. It attracts crowds until 4 a.m. in the morning. Manager

Wesley Lee, who speaks Oxford English, offers a number of seafood specials like the "House Sea Food in a Basket," a combination of shrimp, scallops, conch, fishcake, and lobster, sauteed with Chinese vegetables and served in a fried taro root basket, at $7.25. The chef's specials, apart from the normal noodle fare, range in price from $5 to $8. There is also an upstairs dining room for groups of six or more people.

Open daily from 11 a.m. to 4 a.m.

A good place to try the famous whole braised carp in brown sauce is **Wu Fan,** 36 East Broadway (tel. 925-7498). The dish is prepared with black mushrooms, brown-bean sauce, bamboo shoots, and other Chinese vegetables for $6.95, enough for two or three people. The restaurant is run by a single family, country style, and the service is performed courteously by a number of the owner's daughters. Among appetizers try the jellyfish with sesame oil and scallions for $2.95, the in-house smoked fish for $2.75, or the boiled dumplings with minced pork and leeks for $2.50.

Open from 11 a.m. to 11 p.m. daily.

For some of the best soup in Chinatown, try the **Shanghai Snack Bar,** 14 Elizabeth St. (tel. 964-5640), at the end of the covered Elizabeth Street mall walkway. Offering more than 20 varieties of soup and noodle dishes, this is the perfect place for a quick yet filling meal. Try the Shanghai noodles in a bowl of hearty broth, with diced chicken and pork, shrimp, bamboo shoots, green peas, and Chinese mushrooms ($2.75), or the several appetizing dumpling dishes that range in price from $2 to $3.

Open daily from 10:30 a.m. to 9:30 p.m. (approximately).

For refined dining, try **Siu Lam Kung,** 9 Elizabeth St. (tel. 219-3590). Here, crisply uniformed waiters serve seafood that's undeniably fresh; in fact, the tank in the window of the restaurant is home to such future dinner fare as frogs, served with black-bean sauce, and eels, served sliced and sauteed in a mild sauce (prices vary seasonally). You can also get a delicious sizzling dish of Sang Kang scallops in a spicy brown sauce ($8.25), or lobster prepared in either black-bean sauce or with ginger and scallions (around $10, depending on the season).

Open daily from 9 a.m. to midnight.

ICE CREAM: Don't fill up on fortune cookies when you dine in Chinatown; some of the most flavorful Chinese desserts can be tasted at the **Chinatown Ice Cream Factory,** 65 Bayard St., between Mott and Elizabeth Streets (tel. 608-4170).

This is Chinatown's answer to Baskin-Robbins. Here you can try 36 homemade flavors as Chinese as chow mein or as exotic as the Orient, including almond cookie (our favorite), lichee, ginger, red bean, green tea, papaya, and mango. For the less adventurous, Occidental favorites from vanilla to Rocky Road are on the menu. A cone is 90¢, a pint is $2.10, and a quart is $3.45.

The five Seid Brothers—William, Henry, Eugene, Philip, and Otis—make all the flavors from all-natural ingredients in a huge freezer on the premises. Try the milkshakes, ice-cream sundaes, banana splits, and ice-cream cakes for a tasty alternative to the double-dip cone.

11. Little Italy

Little Italy is the ultimate ethnic neighborhood for the New Yorker and tourist alike. Its lively street life serves as a magnet to people from all over the city. The area's Italian character is reflected in its plethora of bakeries, coffeehouses, restaurants, and food shops. In the summer and fall, street festivals spring up almost every week. Best known is the feast of San Gennaro, held in

September. Cars are exiled from Mulberry Street, fried pastries and sausage steam the air, and you can become part of the gregarious scene. Later, the tired street reveler can rest in a café and indulge in fresh pastries. Some of the best are listed in this section.

No one should miss the experience of eating at **Puglia,** 189 Hester St., near Mulberry Street (tel. 966-6066). Although the food is excellent, the main attraction is the atmosphere: Puglia is crowded, noisy, rowdy (in a friendly way), and on weekends the house singer often leads the customers in a sing-along. Accordion and mandolin players are also known to put in an appearance; the entertainment is all free. The Puglia is a venerable New York institution in which patrons have been partying since 1915. The restaurant has marbled floors and walls decorated with friezes of Little Italy scenes. The festive diners sit at long tables out front, and there's an adjoining garden-like backroom with a bar. In the summer a few tables grace a small garden outside.

The portions of food are inexpensive and hefty, and there are some unusual dishes—try the grilled sheep's head, a house special ($3). On the more traditional side is spaghetti with meatballs, mussels, or sausage ($6), a wide selection of veal dishes ($8 to $9.50), and lasagne, ziti, or manicotti ($5 to $6). An order of garlic bread is 50¢; a glass of wine with your meal is $1.50. Good food, great fun.

Open Tuesday through Sunday from noon to 1 a.m.

The only Little Italy restaurant that has been around longer than Puglia is **Vincent's Clam Bar,** 119 Mott St., corner of Hester Street (tel. 226-8133). Giuseppe and Carmelo Siano established the place in 1904 and the Siano family has been running it ever since. The front room houses a bar and a long counter, behind which Vincent's chefs cook up steaming pots of their famous hot sauce. The main dining room in the back is informal but pleasant, with beamed walls, two big arched windows, and tables and booths covered with red-and-white checked tablecloths. On the wall, watching over it all, is a large oil painting of the Siano brothers.

Fresh fish, seafood, and pasta are the specialties here: for only $5 you can get an order of linguine with medium or hot sauce, $5.50 for backed mussels, $6.95 for a dozen Little Neck clams; an Italian seafood combination platter, such as calamari and oysters is $10.20; a glass of burgundy or chablis, $1.50.

Open Sunday through Thursday from 11:30 a.m. to 2 a.m., on Friday and Saturday until 5 a.m. No reservations.

One of Little Italy's more reasonably priced restaurants is **Luna,** 112 Mulberry St., between Canal and Hester Streets (tel. 226-8657). Like many of the area's kitchens, it's family owned and family run. Luna has a justifiably loyal clientele and at dinnertime the booths (there are only 12) fill quickly, so be prepared to wait.

The antipasto ($4.50) is very good, and comes with stuffed pepper, mushrooms, scallops, and clams. Pasta dishes—spaghetti, lasagne, ravioli, and linguine—are all $5 to $6.50, and veal cacciatore with mushrooms and peppers costs $4.50. In general the seafood dishes are outstanding; we favor calamari arregante, a tender, sliced squid baked with a topping of breadcrumbs, garlic, oregano, and olive oil ($8). There are also healthy platters of steamed mussels and clams ($7), wine by the glass ($2), and a full complement of bar drinks.

Open daily from noon till 1 a.m.

For first-rate, southern-style Sicilian cuisine, **Benito's II,** 163 Mulberry St., between Broome and Grand Streets (tel. 226-9012), is the place. It's a rustic restaurant, with a dark wood-paneled ceiling and exposed brick walls punctuated by floor-to-ceiling wood beams. Neat tables are covered with white linen tablecloths.

The veal, seafood, and pasta are excellent, as are the antipasta. The entrees are all between $8 and $11, but you can get a much better deal if you order in courses, Italian style, and share. Two people might begin with the pepper stuffed with vegetables in marinara sauce ($4.75) or the mozzarella in carrozza (fried cheese sandwiches, $5.25); or go on to share one of the pastas, such as linguine marinara style ($6.75) or homemade manicotti ($6); then perhaps a main dish, octopus Sicilian style ($10.50), veal scaloppine ($10.50), or the delicious striped bass, broiled and served in a light tomato sauce with capers and anchovies ($12.75). You might also order a small carafe of wine with your meal ($5), and if you decide to splurge on dessert, try the zabaglione ($5.25).

Benito's II is open Monday through Saturday from noon to 11 p.m. And, yes, there is a Benito's I, just down the street at 174 Mulberry St. (tel. 226-9012); same hours, same menu. No reservations at either restaurant.

Umberto's Clam House, 129 Mulberry St., corner of Hester Street (tel. 431-7545), is perhaps the best known of Little Italy's restaurants. During the wee hours (the real crowds don't start arriving until 3 a.m.) the place is filled with actors, actresses, and other restaurateurs. One whole wall is devoted to autographed pictures of the celebrity clientele—among them Frank Sinatra, Johnny Carson, Cher, Jackie Gleason, and Fellini. Nevertheless, Umberto's is an attractive and unpretentious place with butcher-block tables, large windows, blue-tiled floors, and fishnet and ship models on the walls. In good weather a row of umbrella tables is placed outdoors on a small patio.

Umberto's is most renowned for its clams ($6.50 for a dozen cherrystone or Little Necks) and its linguine in hot sauce ($6). Seafood, such as calamari (squid), scungilli (conch), and mussels are served with a choice of hot, medium, or sweet sauces and biscuits ($6 and $6.50). A fish salad combination—shrimp, calamari, mussels, and scungilli with lemon, oil, garlic, and parsley—is $8, also served with biscuits. Fish and chips or a plate of smelts with french fries, lemon, and tartar sauce is $6.50. Most of the traditional Italian pastries are $1.50 and homemade Italian cheesecake is $2.50.

Right down the street is **Teresa's of Mulberry Street,** 117 Mulberry St. (tel. 226-6950), a pretty and intimate little place with barely enough room for its 11 tables. It has plant-filled windows, beautiful latticework over room-length mirrors, a gold floor, and tables covered with green oilcloth and graced with fresh flowers. The entire effect is rather charming and very Italian. The menu is the same at lunch and dinner, and the prices are extremely reasonable: most of the pastas are under $5.75, fettuccine Alfredo is $5.50, linguine and spaghetti are $4.75, and a delicious vegetarian pasta plate is $5.50. A glass of wine is $1.50.

Open daily from noon to 11:30 p.m. Reservations are recommended at dinner.

Housed in a Federal two-story domed brick house that dates from the early 1800s, **Paolucci's,** 149 Mulberry St., between Grand and Hester Streets (tel. 925-2288), is one of Little Italy's top-rated restaurants, family owned and family run. The decor is very ornate, with black-and-gold wallpaper, black-and-gold vinyl chairs, a pressed-tin roof from which hang huge chandeliers, and white-linen-covered tables. Next to the bar is a large, working brick fireplace.

All of the food is homemade and first rate. Most entrees cost less than $10.50: huge servings of manicotti and lasagne are $8.25; veal cacciatore with mushrooms and peppers is $10; a cold antipasto is $4.75; a hot antipasto for two, $8.50. We like to finish up a meal with a dessert of homemade Italian cheesecake ($3.25) and a cup of espresso with anisette ($1.75). Wine and liquor are also available.

Paolucci's is open Monday through Thursday from noon to 10:30 p.m., on Friday and Saturday until 11:30 p.m. Reservations are suggested on weekends.

What would a visit to Little Italy be without a thick slice of pizza or a hefty cheese calzone? For both, go to **Florio's,** 192 Grand St., between Mott and Mulberry Streets (tel. 226-7610). Entered via an alcove with large plant-filled windows, the interior has exposed brick and stucco walls decorated with oil paintings, a beamed ceiling, and tables covered with red tablecloths under glass. There's a very comfortable backroom with a skylight and thriving potted trees and plants.

A thick-crusted regular pizza here is $7, $8 for a large pie. A piece of cheese calzone (sort of like a fried, rolled slice of pizza with filling) is $2.50; you can also get cheese and sausage and cheese and prosciutto varieties for $3. Florio's also offers huge hero sandwiches—meatball, sausage and peppers, veal cutlet, and more—for between $2.50 and $3.75. There are also homemade pasta dishes; fish, chicken, and veal entrees (most between $9.50 and $10.95); and Italian ice creams and pastries ($2).

Open daily from 11 a.m. to midnight. No reservations.

PASTRY SHOPS AND CAFÉS: Since 1892, **Ferrara's,** 195 Grand St., between Mott and Mulberry Streets (tel. 226-6150), has been tempting New Yorkers with an outrageous variety of cake and pastry. Just a peek at the long pastry counter laden with every imaginable confection and cake will have your mouth watering. The demand for Ferrara's goodies has made the café a nationally known business; Ferrara's ships its own brand of coffees, candies, and hundreds of other Italian delicacies all over the world.

The traditional Italian pastries—cannoli, eclairs, babas au rum, babas au ricotta, napoleons, cream puffs, and many others—are $1.75. Specialties of the house include Italian rum cake, filled with layers of vanilla, chocolate custard, and topped with whipped cream; almond and cheese cakes; and a rustic peasant pie, filled with salami, fresh eggs, and smoked cheese ($3.50 each). An espresso is $1.40; a cappuccino, $2.40.

Once you've made your choice, and if the weather is good, walk outside and sit under the white-and-red awning, while the rest of Little Italy strolls by.

Ferrara's is open daily from 7:30 a.m. to midnight.

Caffè Roma, 385 Broome St., at Mulberry Street (tel. 226-8413), is a traditionally charming Italian café. The decor is lovely and authentic: high ceilings, white tiled floors, marble tables and counters, with numerous paintings on the wall by Frank Mason, an internationally renowned artist. The long gold pastry case is filled with some of the most delicious pastries in all of New York.

Caffè Roma is known for its milk Sicilian cassatina, a special cake filled with ricotta, vanilla, and pieces of chocolate ($1.75). Other assorted pastries are $1.25; an espresso is 90¢; a cappuccino, $1.35.

Open daily from 8 a.m. to midnight.

The **Primavera Caffè,** 51 Spring St., at Mulberry Street (tel. 226-8421), is the area's newest pasticceria and it has attracted a devoted and chic clientele. It's sparkling clean, with wrap-around, plant-laden windows facing onto both Spring and Mulberry Streets. The walls are a pale yellow with fluted columns, and there are tables both inside and out.

Most of the traditional pastries are $1.25; Amaretto cheesecake is $2.50; chocolate fudge cake is $2.50. In addition to espresso ($1) and cappuccino ($2), Caffè Primavera also serves cool Italian ices and beverages.

Open Sunday to Thursday from 11 a.m. to 1 a.m., on Friday and Saturday till 3 a.m.

12. Lower East Side / East Village

A stroll through the East Village is like entering a time machine that spans six decades of American history. Here you'll find restaurants and coffeeshops that grew up in the '20s, '30s, and '40s, as waves of immigrants, making their way past Ellis Island, landed in Manhattan and made their first homes in places called Hester and Grand Streets. Today the Orthodox Jewish population still thrives below Houston Street, but it shares this area with new immigrant groups from Latin America and Southeast Asia.

St. Mark's Place was traditionally the home of Ukrainian immigrants, and the Ukrainian community is still very much in evidence. Every year a Ukrainian festival livens up East 7th Street between Second and Third Avenues. But in the 1960s St. Mark's became the center for New York's counterculture movement—the East Coast's Haight Ashbury. Now you're more likely to see young people sporting New Wave outfits and punk hairdos than hippie get-ups here. The area is also home to artists and actors, and most recently to the New York Public Theater and other off-Broadway companies.

Restaurants here are a bargain hunter's dream. The food here is some of the best you'll find in the city.

A word to the wise: While the East Village is filled with streets that bustle with activity into the wee hours of the morning, there are some side streets that are deserted and unsafe. Don't miss the excitement here, but exercise a little extra caution, especially at night.

AMERICAN/CONTINENTAL: Around the Clock Café, 8 Stuyvesant Pl. (tel. 598-0402), a new addition to the neighborhood, is already drawing a loyal following. Passersby who stop to admire the café's large, centerpiece clock stay for the delicious food. The menu includes a wide range of Benedicts and crêpes. Sample the tender sliced beef teriyaki crêpe with mushrooms and scallions, served with a salad and home-fries ($4.95), or try the bananas, walnuts, and strawberries crêpe, served with a fruit salad and a choice of a chocolate or fruit sauce ($3.75). The New England seafood Benedict is another favorite, two baked puff-pastry shells with poached eggs and hollandaise sauce, served with steamed vegetables and home-fries ($5.50). If you're feeling exotic, you might try the tender, crunchy calamari (deep-fried squid) at $5.75.

The café's riverboat-era antique bar, imported from Missouri, adds to the timeless atmosphere.

Open 24 hours on Thursday, Friday and Saturday. Sunday through Wednesday, open from 9 p.m. to 2 a.m.

If you think **Eat,** 11 St. Mark's Pl. (tel. 477-5155), sounds like the name of a rough, no-frills hash house, you're in for a pleasant surprise. This long, low-ceilinged restaurant offers a touch of class with its eye-catching art, wood trim, and fresh flowers on the tables. The menu is a mix of vegetarian dishes and pita (Middle Eastern pocket bread) sandwiches. A few fish and chicken dishes are offered too. Try the cheese and chili-melt pita stuffer or the stir-fried vegetable pita stuffer—both at $2.95. A small dinner salad, overflowing with lettuce, cheese, carrots, mushrooms, tomatoes, and scallions, is only $1 when ordered with a sandwich or soup. Pasta dishes are a bargain. We suggest the broccoli fettuccine topped with mushroom sauce for $4.50. Or ask about the fish selection of the day ($4.50).

Eat has an extensive imported beer and wine list. Open from 10 a.m. to midnight Sunday through Thursday, on Friday and Saturday to 1 a.m.

For a break from the whirl of sightseeing, try the relaxed atmosphere of the **Cloister Café,** 238 E. 9th St. (tel. 777-9128). An outdoor garden patio offers its own small fountain and goldfish pond. Ivy-covered brick walls and festive night lighting also add to the patio's charm. If it's raining or cold outside, move indoors to admire the Cloister Café's antique religious stained-glass windows. The Strauss salad, with chicken, crabmeat, spinach, garnishes, and fruit ($5.25), is a meal in itself. Tortellini al pesto is another favorite here ($6.75). You are invited to bring your own wine or beer. Or linger over a café-au-lait, served French style in large bowls ($1.50).

Don't come here if you're in a hurry, though. The help is as relaxed as the atmosphere. They don't like to rush. Open from noon to 12:30 a.m. Sunday through Thursday, to 1:30 a.m. on Friday and Saturday.

If you sit long enough at **Phebe's**, 361 Bowery at East 4th Street (tel. 473-9008), you're bound to run into a few young, struggling actors—and maybe a few established ones as well. Theater posters decorate the walls, and the bar, a renowned actors' hangout, is crowded after a show. There is a glassed-in terrace at the outer perimeter of the restaurant, covered by a faded yellow awning. Tables here are light butcher block. Inside there's a spacious bar with a jukebox, and another cozy dining room. The food here is simple and satisfying.

Entrees range from $6.25 for barbecued half a spring chicken to $14.95 for a ten-ounce filet mignon. Hamburgers and meat sandwiches run between $2.75 and $3.95. Omelets are good buys at $2.95, and come with french fries and toast or an English muffin. For dessert, try the chocolate decadence for $2.50, or the homemade apple pie for the same price.

Hours are 11:30 a.m. to 4 a.m. daily.

It's easy to see that a lot of thought went into making **Hiro Gallery-Café**, 112 First Ave., near 7th Street (tel. 777-1250), a place you will want to come back to. This combination art gallery and café features lively art displays that change every four weeks. The food is arranged artistically too. For a light meal, try the fresh-fruit salad: strawberries, melons, apples, bananas, and grapes, with honey lemon mint dressing ($3.59). A sandwich favorite here is the avocado, tomato, and turkey, served on your choice of bread ($2.99). For dinner, try a daily special such as the broiled monkfish with ginger sauce, served with brown rice and a salad ($5.95), or the vegetarian lasagne with a salad ($4.95).

When the weather is warm, the Hiro Café opens its outdoor garden, one of the most attractive and spacious in the East Village. Relax here and listen to water spilling into a small pool. Butcher-block tables with folding chairs of mixed colors are placed among distinctive sculptures, small fruit trees, and potted plants. One of the garden's centerpieces is a large hanging metal sculpture painted with camouflage colors of green, black, and yellow.

Open daily from 10 a.m. until 4 a.m.

7A, 109 Avenue A., at 7th Street (tel. 475-9001), is a bright, airy café with pink-and-white walls, lots of wood and plants, and outdoor sidewalk seating. For entrees, try the bay scallops sauteed with herbs and wine over linguine, served with a vegetable and your choice of rice or potato ($5.95). Or stay with simpler fare, such as the hearty half-pound burger on pita bread or an English muffin, served with a garden salad or home-fries ($3.50).

If you're getting a late start in the morning, try 7A's weekday breakfast special, served until 1 p.m. For $2.45, order your choice of three eggs any style, with home-fries, toast or an English muffin, and coffee. For the same price you can also get blueberry pancakes with coffee.

Desserts here are a local treasure. Treat yourself to the wickedly rich chocolate diablo ($2.50), or the cool, irresistible strawberry-kiwi pie ($2.25).

Open from 10 a.m. to 2 a.m. Sunday through Thursday, to 6 a.m. on Friday and Saturday.

The Pharmacy, 141 Avenue A, at 9th Street (tel. 260-4798), is a pioneer in the Tompkins Square area of the East Village. This bar and restaurant opened when these streets were still the domain of drug addicts and Bowery bums. Today this pleasant restaurant with weathered-brick walls and glassed-in corner walls draws a mixed crowd ranging from yuppies and older, established regulars, to visitors from uptown. Comfortable booths, wood floors, and a bar dating from the 1800s complete the atmosphere.

Once you're settled into an inviting booth or at your table, begin your meal with the popular and tasty rumaki, an appetizer consisting of chicken livers and water chestnuts wrapped in bacon ($2.75). Then move on to another favorite—the chicken and vegetable tempura with a house salad ($6.95). The steak sandwich served on garlic bread with a salad or fries is unbeatable ($5.25). Or check one of the five specials offered daily. If you come to the Pharmacy for lunch, you might order a fresh roast turkey, bacon, and tomato sandwich for $3.75. Brunch is also offered here on Saturday and Sunday from noon until 4:30 p.m. You have your choice of a drink, breakfast entree, home-fries, and coffee or tea for $6.50.

Open Sunday through Thursday from noon until 2 a.m., on Friday and Saturday until 4 a.m.

CHINESE: Some local Chinese-food lovers won't eat anywhere besides the **Bamboo House,** 104 Second Ave., at East 6th Street (tel. 254-3502). This small, unassuming restaurant is well known for its heaping portions and tasty dishes. The vegetables here are crisp and the meats are carefully prepared. Try a mixed dish of chicken, shrimp, and scallops in garlic sauce for $6.55. Or we recommend the sauteed tender chicken with broccoli for $5.15. Another chicken favorite is the moo goo gai pan, also $5.15. If you want spicy seafood, try the prawns sauteed with hot spicy paste for $6.25. Most of the cooking is traditional Szechuan, but brown rice is also available.

The medium-sized square dining room features a modest decor, with Chinese prints and calendars and festive red Chinese trim. The food here is the main attraction.

Open from 1 to 11:15 p.m. daily.

CRÉOLE/SOUTHERN: Hungry and in high spirits? Go to the **Pig,** 12 First Ave., near Houston Street (tel. 982-1089). A huge pig mural outside the building will guide you to the door. Inside is a 1980s version of streamlined 1950s style, including stylized light fixtures and a beautiful mahogany bar. The food is a spicy mix of Tex-Mex and Cajun cooking. Start off with a serving of red and green spicy slaw ($1.50), then move on to the grilled breast of chicken with mustard sauce, served with baked cheese grits ($7.25). Or try the spinach quesadilla, made with fresh spinach, piquant sauce, green chiles, sour cream, and cheddar cheese wrapped inside a flour tortilla ($6.25). For dessert, indulge in Pig's specialty, Death by Chocolate cake ($2.75). Open from 5 p.m. to about 2 a.m. daily.

Brunch, served Saturday and Sunday from 11:30 a.m. to 4:30 p.m., is a great way to round out your weekend. For $4.75 you may choose among specialties such as Grillades and Grits, pan-fried steak with Cajun-style tomato sauce, served with grits and biscuits; or Eggs Basin Street, fresh poached eggs and smoked ham served with a tangy Créole and choron sauce. While away the morning by watching passersby through either of the large glassed-in windowfronts.

When the **Great Jones Café,** 54 Great Jones St., just off the Bowery (tel. 674-9304), opened two years ago, the owners planned a little neighborhood bar with food as a side attraction. But the word got out about some of New York's finest Cajun cooking. Now the crowds that usually fill up the bar are waiting for a table. Begin your meal with an order of honey-sweetened, fresh-baked jalapeño cornbread ($2). Then for a real treat try the blackened redfish, charred and crunchy outside, succulent and juicy inside, served with a salad and vegetable ($7.95). Another big favorite here is the rich, thick, Louisiana gumbo, cooked old style, and served with a salad and vegetable ($6.95). Don't forget to check the daily specials, posted on the blackboard. If you're caught waiting for a table, join the bar drinkers for a Cajun martini, a shot of straight vodka or gin flavored with jalapeño pepper ($1.50). You might need a beer chaser. If so, order a Rolling Rock, the café's unofficial beer.

The kitchen is open from 5 p.m. to 1 a.m. Monday through Friday, and until 2 a.m. on Saturday and Sunday. Note: Tables are placed side by side, so privacy is at a minimum.

INDIAN/BANGLADESHI: The Ahmed brothers were the first to open their small basement restaurant on East 6th Street between First and Second Avenues, and soon others followed suit, turning the block into an Indian-food lover's haven.

Boasting that it was "the first on the block," **Shah Bagh,** 320 E. 6th St., between First and Second Avenues (tel. 677-8876), is a most unpretentious restaurant in decor, with interior wood paneling and barely a hint of Indian decorator items. There are two dining rooms, filled with small wood tables that are set with flowers and white cloth napkins. Tea is on the house.

To start your meal, you might want to try the coconut soup for 60¢, or the banana fritter for 95¢. The à la carte menu features vegetable, chicken, beef, lamb, and crabmeat curries for between $2.75 and $4.50. There are also several kinds of biryani, dishes cooked with saffron rice, coconut, and spices, for between $3.50 and $4.50. All entree dishes are made mild, so ask for hot orders if it suits you. For dessert, try the honey cake or the gulab jaman, a sweet fried cheese ball, each for 75¢.

Hours are noon to midnight daily.

The Ahmed brothers' second enterprise, **Anar Bagh,** at 338 E. 6th St. (tel. 533-2177), features a similar menu with fancier decor. A bright green, yellow, and red canopy hangs from the ceiling in the interior dining room, and there is an open garden for dining in back.

The menu here is translated into English, with explanations of traditional dishes. Try the poori (puffed Indian bread) as an appetizer for 70¢, or the mulligatawny tomato soup (65¢). Kurma dishes, cooked in a creamy sauce with mild spices, cost between $3.95 and $4.50. Curries here run $2.50 to $4.75. There's a wide selection of seafood dishes, including lobster, for $3.75 to $7.25. For dessert, try a rosh-golla cheese ball (95¢) or firni custard sprinkled with rose water (75¢).

JAPANESE: Only in New York would you find a restaurant like the heady, trendy, New Wave sushi restaurant called **Avenue A,** 105 Avenue A between 7th Street and St. Mark's Place (tel. 982-8109). Immerse yourself in A's black-and-purple interior (the owner's favorite colors) with highlights of blue lighting, irreverent art displays, and two black-lacquered bars, one for sushi and one for drinks. In the back is more intimate seating with fresh flowers on the tables.

You might make a meal by sampling the appetizers and the sushi à la carte. If so, try the Masa specialties, prepared by Masa, a 15-year veteran sushi chef. These include the yado-kari—mushrooms, carrots, and bamboo shoots sauteed with crabmeat and baked in a clam shell with a white sauce ($4.95). Or try the "Dynamite"—scallops, mushrooms, and smelt roe baked in white sauce with sesame seeds ($5). Another favorite is the "Tiger's Eye"—salmon, spinach, and seaweed surrounded with squid to look like a tiger's eye ($5). For bargain entrees, try the katsu tama, a deep-fried pork cutlet and vegetables cooked with egg in a sukiyaki sauce ($5.50), or the rolled beef, stuffed with scallions, with teriyaki sauce ($7.95).

Open Sunday through Wednesday from 6 p.m. to 1 a.m., Thursday through Saturday to 4 a.m.

In the East Village, **Tanaka,** 58 St. Mark's Pl. (tel. 677-8663), is a Japanese restaurant that New York's Japanese come to. Nothing is mass-produced here! This is a very small restaurant, seating about 25. And the intimacy means that the owner, the waiter, and the chef are very happy to answer your questions and prepare special orders. Tanaka is one of the few restaurants in the area that prepares traditional Japanese dishes, as well as creative chef's specialties. Try the tempura noodles ($8.25), the yosenabe ($9.25), or the eel teriyaki ($8.50)—all served with a house appetizer, soup, and salad. For sushi, try the combination roll ($6.25), or the California roll ($6.75).

Open Sunday and Tuesday through Thursday from 5 p.m. to midnight, on Friday and Saturday to 1 a.m. Closed Monday.

Hisae's Place, 35 Cooper Square, between 5th and 6th Streets (tel. 228-6886), brings a bit of uptown style to the East Village. Rich purple velvet-covered couches and chairs, frosted lighting, black wooden leaf mirrors, and a cozy fireplace add up to an intimate formality. Hisae's best deal is a complete dinner for two including soup, entree, and coffee or tea for only $10.95, available between 4:30 and 6:30 p.m. Entrees include the niunabe, thinly sliced beef with Oriental vegetables in soy sauce ($5.95), and the steamed mussels cooked in a wine, garlic, and tomato broth ($6.95). For a sure-fire hit, rely on one of Hisae's old favorites, such as the filet of flounder with mushrooms ($7.95). For sushi, Hisae's offers one of New York's best bargains. Try the California maki with avocado and crab for $2, or the salmon roe or the shrimp sushi for $1. On Monday many sushi dishes are half price. Salt-free or fat-free dishes are prepared upon request.

Open at 11 a.m. for lunch on weekdays. Dinner begins at 4:30 p.m. daily. Hisae's closes at 11:30 p.m. Monday through Thursday, on Friday and Saturday at 12:30 a.m., and on Sunday at 10:30 p.m.

Dojo, 24 St. Mark's Pl., between Second and Third Avenues (tel. 674-9821), offers a great mix of Japanese dishes, natural foods, and good old-fashioned American meals. Here you will find one of the widest selections and some of the best prices in the East Village. The highest-priced meal on the menu is the steamed seafood plate, with mussels, scallops, shrimp, and fish, served with salad and rice for only $6.50. Other bargains include the hamburger dinner, served with salad and home-fries for $3.50, and any of the salad plates ($3.25 to $4.95), each a meal in itself. For dessert we suggest the chocolate mud cake ($2.50).

Situated in the heart of the East Village, Dojo's offers a great view of the East Village scene from its canopied sidewalk seating. Otherwise, enjoy yourself in any of the three inside rooms.

Open Sunday through Thursday from 11 a.m. to midnight, on Friday and Saturday to 2 a.m.

JEWISH DAIRY: The huge, open dining room at **Ratner's,** 138 Delancey St., between Norfolk and Suffolk Streets (tel. 677-5588), is reminiscent of a ballroom from the 1940s, with a pink scalloped ceiling and mirrored walls. There are a lot of oldtimers on the staff, dressed in mustard-colored uniforms, who can tell you about the early days when the Harmatz and Zankel families first opened the restaurant. The bakery counter up front offers tempting treats, and the restaurant menu is world famous for its wide selection of Jewish specialties, like matzoh brei and kreplach.

To start, we suggest the cold borscht, with a generous helping of sour cream ($2.50). Try the potato pancakes with applesauce ($6.25), or the cheese, potato, or sour-cream blintzes for the same price. Splurge on the baked gelfilte fish with créole sauce, vegetable, and potato ($9). The matzoh brei with applesauce is $6.25. For dessert, if you have room, try the strawberry cheesecake for $2.25.

Hours are 6 a.m. to 11 p.m. Monday through Saturday, till 1 a.m. on Sunday.

On a smaller scale there's **Yonah Schimmel**, at 137 Houston St., between Eldridge and Forsyth Streets (tel. 477-2858). The knishes here are famous citywide, and on Sunday mornings it's not unusual to see limousines lined up outside this unpretentious eatery, buying knishes for fancy East Side brunches. Inside, a dumbwaiter on rope pulleys still delivers hot knishes and strudels from the kitchen. Lillian Berger, the present owner, is a descendant of Yonah Schimmel, who opened the restaurant in 1910.

While potato and kasha knishes are the star attractions at $1.10, you can also get a homemade borscht with sour cream for 85¢. Cheese bagels and apple strudel are $1. Open daily 8 a.m. to 6 p.m.

These days, students from the local Seward Park High School are as likely to be found at the **Grand Dairy Restaurant,** 341 Grand St., at the corner of Ludlow Street (tel. 673-1904), as are Jewish matrons stopping for coffee and blintzes after shopping. The dining area is separated from the counter by a long divider, with a battered metal coatrack above it. While Formica tables and orange chairs make for simple decor, with orange curtains in the window and granite-speckled floors. The strictly kosher restaurant has a menu filled with hundreds of dairy items.

Try the cabbage soup (Sunday) for $2 or the borscht with sour cream for $2.15. Dairy items include matzoh brei and kasha blintzes, $4.25 each. Omelets here ($2 to $7) are delicious. Fish dishes cost between $4 and $7.25. For dessert there's a wide variety of pastries, including homemade coffee cake (90¢) and hamantaschen cakes ($1).

Hours are 6 a.m. to 4 p.m. Sunday through Friday; closed on Saturday and Jewish holidays.

JEWISH DELI: Although Abe Lebewohl established his delicatessen late by Lower East Side standards (1954), meals at the **Second Avenue Deli,** 156 Second Ave., at the corner of East 10th Street (tel. 677-0606), have become a thriving tradition. With its flashy green stained-glass windows, the restaurant is easily spotted from a distance. The late Sam Levenson, a great Second Avenue Deli fan, wrote that the "vital ingredient" found here is "common sense based on years of scenting." In addition to common sense, Lebewohl has a good deal of promotional skill, and he has managed to turn Second Avenue Deli events into major New York happenings. For the 20th anniversary of the restaurant, he set prices at their 1954 level for a day, and deliveries were made by horse and buggy during the energy crisis.

The interior decor is bright, with glass lamps hanging from the ceiling and a large take-home counter. Pickles are set at every table. There's a small café in back as well, decorated with posters and plants.

The mushroom-barley soup ($1.95) is a good bet to start your meal. Matzoh-ball soup is another specialty here (same price). The deli is famous for its pastrami, and a heaping hot pastrami sandwich is $4.70. There are traditional knishes and kugels for $1.75. Hungarian goulash with noodles is $8.75 and chicken with matzoh balls is $9.25. For dessert, try the warm apple strudel or marble cake ($1.50).

Hours are 7 a.m. to 11 p.m. daily. No reservations.

MACROBIOTIC—KOSHER STYLE: Only the crazy melting pot of cultures, old and new, that is found in the East Village could have created the **Caldron,** 308 E. 6th St., between First and Second Avenues (tel. 473-9543). While it originally opened as a macrobiotic restaurant in the '60s, it's now strictly kosher, attracting both leftover hippie types and Orthodox Jews from the community. The outside of the restaurant is distinguished by a crazy brown-wood front, with odd-shaped windows. Inside, the dining furniture is made of heavy light-colored wood.

The combination of macrobiotic and kosher diet restrictions makes for a limited menu. Gone are the dairy delights we've seen in other Jewish restaurants because they're too yin; banned are the unkosher fruits of the sea like shrimp.

To start, try the miso soup for $1.35. Then move to one of the dinner combinations, served with brown rice or whole-wheat noodles. The simple rice and vegetable dinner costs $4.35, and sole Provençal with mushroom sauce and salad is $6. A whole-wheat noodle Alfredo dish, made with tofu and soymilk, comes with a salad for $4.95. Brown rice or noodles is available with tahini and tamari sauces for $1.25. For dessert, try one of the fresh-baked cakes or the tofu yam pie for $1.50.

Hours are 12:30 to 11 p.m. Sunday through Thursday; closed Friday and Saturday. The same menu is served at all hours.

MEXICAN: The **Life Café,** 343 E. 10th St., at Avenue B (tel. 477-8791), in the East Village, attracts a fringe crowd of punk types, yet-to-be-discovered artists, and 1960s holdovers. The café gets its name from the montage of pictures from old *Life* magazines pasted on its walls.

The food here is mostly Mexican, with assorted burgers and vegetarian dishes. If you've got an appetite, order the "mega burrito," two flour tortillas stuffed with rice, beans, lettuce, tomato, onions, and salsa, topped with more salsa and sour cream ($4.25). Or order the deep-fried chimichangas, topped with salsa, guacamole, and sour cream, and served with rice, beans, and salad ($6.95). Burgers range from a "regular deluxe," served with Life fries (sweet baby red potatoes with the skins left on) for $3.50 to the "Ultra Burger" for $6.75.

Open daily from 11 a.m. to 1 a.m.

MIDDLE EASTERN: For spicy Middle Eastern food, step into **Caffè Kabul,** 32 St. Mark's Pl., between Second and Third Avenues (tel. 677-1490). There's an outdoor café that attracts the trendy New Wave crowd and an interior dining area is filled with the aromatic smell of herbal teas. It can get a bit hot inside despite the air conditioning, so you might want to try getting an outdoor table in warm weather. The interior is decorated with traditional Afghani dress and headwear. There's a low-lying booth at the front of the restaurant, where you can recline on plump cushions or sit cross-legged during your meal. The other tables are set with fresh flowers, and traditional Middle Eastern music plays in the background.

The appetizers here are a special treat. Try the bulanee kadu, a fried turnover filled with pumpkin or scallions and herbs, with cool mint yogurt, for $1.75.

The tabouli salad, made with kasha, vegetables, and mint, is $2.50. For a main course, try the Cornish game hen kebab ($6.95), or the eggplant Afghan style, with mint yogurt ($5.50). Daily specials can include Afghan meatballs with rice ($5.75), or pilaf rice with raisins, almonds, and lamb ($6.50). For dessert, we suggest the custard, sprinkled with rosewater, at $1.75; or pomme beignets, deep-fried apple slices with powdered sugar, a splurge at $4.

Hours are 11 a.m. to 1 a.m. daily.

POLISH: Some customers eat three meals a day at **Teresa's**, 103 First Ave., between 6th and 7th Streets (tel. 228-0604). This family-run coffeeshop and restaurant offers some of the lowest-priced food in the city, and Teresa and her family are quite rightly proud of their delicious home-cooking and special recipes. Breakfasts here range from blueberry pancakes to western omelets, all under $3. Sandwiches such as grilled cheese with bacon, sausage, or ham are a treat at $1.85. A wide variety of soups are offered too. A bowl of the potato soup is $1.20. So is a bowl of the red Ukrainian borscht. Lunch and dinner entrees are a steal. And here is where Teresa's family recipes really shine. Try one of Poland's national dishes, such as the boiled beef cooked with horseradish sauce, served with a vegetable and potato ($4.50); or the breaded pork chops, served with vegetable and potato ($4.50). The inside of Teresa's is simple and appealing, with wooden tables, fresh flowers, and an orange lunch counter in the back.

Open daily from 6 a.m. to midnight.

UKRAINIAN: When a fire destroyed the **Ukrainian Restaurant**'s original home, its many regulars could hardly wait until their favorite restaurant reopened at 132 Second Ave., between St. Mark's Place and East 9th Street (tel. 533-6765). Entering the newly decorated restaurant is like stepping into a Ukrainian chalet. Ukrainian prints, traditional plates, and musical instruments called banduras decorate the stone walls. Ukrainian music is played, and the waiters and waitresses even wear traditional dress.

One thing that hasn't changed is the delicious food. For a traditional meal, order the bigos: a mixture of sliced kielbasa, beef, and sauerkraut served with potato for $3.95. Another wonderful meal is the steak tartare, prepared to order with a basket of homemade challah bread, black or rye ($6.25). If you can't decide among all of the tempting dishes, then choose the combination plate. It includes one stuffed cabbage, four varieties of pirogis, bigos, slices of kielbasa, tossed salad, and a basket of bread for $6.95.

Open daily from 11 a.m. until 11 p.m.

Owner Michael Hrynenko's success with the Ukrainian Restaurant inspired him to set up **Kiev International Coffee House and Restaurant**, 117 Second Ave., at East 7th Street (tel. 674-4040). Open 24 hours a day, seven days a week, this coffeeshop is the late-night hangout for local residents. The decor is diner style, with a take-out counter in front and Formica tables in the glassed-in dining room toward the back. The challah here is just as delicious as it is at the Ukrainian Restaurant, and the menu includes breakfast items as well as Ukrainian specialties.

Kielbasa and eggs served with bread and home-fries is $3.25, and potato pancakes are $3.50. Meat entrees range in price from $4.50 to $6.95. Pirogen are $3.95 and blintzes are $4.25. Pita sandwiches are also served, filled with falafel or liver for $2.50. A homemade babka costs 95¢ for dessert, and apple cake costs the same.

The informal decor at the **Odessa**, 117 Avenue A, between East 7th Street and Saint Mark's Place (tel. 473-8916), runs toward cheery red booths and bright white Formica tables. There's a sit-down counter in the center of this restaurant, and the menu boasts of fine home-cooking. The Odessa has become a regular hangout for punk crowds, who seem to feel quite at home in the traditional old-fashioned diner.

The large menu offers everything from Ukrainian specialties to American hamburgers. Potato pancakes are $2.50 and a variety of pirogen cost between $2 and $2.75. Homemade blintzes are $2.50. Italian specialties, like veal parmigiana, cost between $3 and $4.95. A broiled salmon steak is $4.35, and there are daily seafood specials. For dessert, try the homemade cheesecake, a bargain at $1.

Hours are 7 a.m. to 11 p.m. Tuesday through Sunday. Closed Monday.

A block away from the Odessa is **Leshko's Coffee Shop and Restaurant**, 111 Avenue A, at East 7th Street (tel. 473-9208). Like the Odessa, this is another diner-style restaurant, serving homemade dishes. Green plants brighten the front window and stained-glass Tiffany-style lamps hang over the booths. Portions are generous.

Homemade soups, such as cabbage soup (75¢) and hot or cold borscht (80¢), make good openers. Meat entrees, served with a choice of potato and vegetable, cost between $2.30 and $4.30. Pirogi here are $1.90 to $2.45, and blintzes are about $1.55 each. Meat sandwiches cost between $1.90 and $2.15. For dessert try the apple noodle pudding (75¢) or the bread pudding (50¢).

Hours are 6 a.m. to 10 p.m. Monday through Saturday. Closed Sunday.

LUNCH ONLY: Every inch of **McSorley's Old Ale House**, 15 E. 7th St., between Second and Third Avenues (tel. 473-8800), is covered with historical memorabilia. This bar dates from 1854, when members of General Custer's 69th Army Regiment convinced old McSorley, a blacksmith, to turn his blacksmith forge into an alehouse. The rest is history.

Only McSorley's special recipe ale is served here. Order the light or dark ale, two steins for $1.50. Many regulars swear by McSorley's corned-beef sandwiches ($3.50). Others champion the daily special. Once you're settled with your beer and food, look around at the treasures covering the walls, including a pair of old shoes that the owner, Irishman Matt Maher, swears were worn by Joe Kennedy, father of President John F. Kennedy, when he immigrated to the U.S. Also hanging from the bar is the chair that President Abraham Lincoln reputedly sat in while he made his famous Emancipation Proclamation speech, freeing U.S. slaves. Both students and oldtimers fill McSorley's to the packing point, often smoking up a storm with McSorley's special-order cigars (25¢ each). But bear with the crowds, because you'll never forget your visit here.

Open from 11 a.m. to 1 a.m. daily.

OPEN 24 HOURS: At **103 Second Restaurant**, 103 Second Ave., at East 6th Street (tel. 533-0769), you'll find the atmosphere of a comfortable diner, but with a twist, such as tables that angle out from the wall. The front window and ceiling with wooden rafters also emphasize slanted angles. Here you'll find an older artsy crowd, many of them longtime New Yorkers who have fled the expense of SoHo's restaurants.

103 offers a wide range of dishes. For a hearty meal, try the slow-stewed beef with onions, carrots, and potatoes, with a dinner salad and rolls and butter ($5.75). For a lighter meal, try the delicious Niçoise salad ($5.75). Omelets range from $3.75 for an omelet with swiss cheese and ratatouille (a spicy eggplant/tomato filling), to $5.75 for an omelet with Nova Scotia salmon and

fresh dill. Order beer or wine from the bar to complete your meal, or splurge on a French coffee, with Grand Marnier and whipped cream, for $3.50.

13. Murray Hill/Gramercy Park

These two East Side neighborhoods stretch from 15th Street up to 42nd Street, from the quaint Village to bustling Grand Central Station. You'll find towering apartment complexes near the East River, and bucolic surprises like the Third Avenue Organic Garden, a community effort between 31st and 32nd Streets complete with summertime scarecrows and zinnias. There are traces of very old New York—the Federal house at 122 E. 17th St. and Irving Place, where Washington Irving used to meet with a literary salon; a white clapboard house at 203½ E. 29th St., still with a wooden fence and carriage house (now a home). The Players Club, founded by Edwin Booth, stands in all its Gothic splendor at 16 Gramercy Park South; the National Arts Club is right next door at 15 Gramercy Park South. A statue of Booth portraying Hamlet is located in the center of the park. There is an order of Carmelite Fathers in a Romanesque church at 26th Street and First Avenue, just behind Phipps Plaza, and the famed Little Church Around the Corner at 1 E. 29th St., scene of many a wedding. There are contrasts—exclusive Gramercy Park, and grimy commercial areas in the 20s between Madison and Third Avenues, also home to many Indian and Pakistani restaurants. Which brings us back to the business of eating, of course!

AMERICAN/CONTINENTAL: The **Orchid**, 81 Lexington Ave., at 26th Street (tel. 889-0960), won itself a name with its nouvelle American menu, based on reasonable prices and fresh ingredients. You'll recognize it by its art deco facade. Inside, the Orchid's decor combines old and new New York—it has a dark and massive wood bar dating back to when it served as a pub in an Irish neighborhood, and it has the sophisticated veneer of its current owners, Judy Schiff and Howard Wexler. There are sleek banquettes, pictures of flowers and champagne glasses, and fresh flowers in arrangements. The bar is frequented by a suited after-work crowd. Farther back is the dining room with its black-and-white color scheme.

Lunch prices range from $4.50 for a cheese omelet (cheddar, swiss, parmesan, or bleu) with fries, to $8.95 for a seafood salad with shrimp, mussels, scallops, lobster, avocado, mushrooms, and alfalfa. A strudel of spinach, mushrooms, and cheese, served with a salad ($6.95), is a nice change from lunchtime quiche. There is always bisque ($3.50) and homemade soups ($2.95). Sandwiches and burgers are priced from $5.50 to $6.95, and come with cottage fries. Desserts are rich and tempting—walnut pie with whipped cream or chocolate mousse pie, each $2.75.

The dinner menu is similar and—for a pleasant change—very few of the prices go up. The strudel, in fact, passes as an appetizer at dinner and costs less ($4.95). We recommend the lemon chicken, or the popular spare ribs barbecued in a tangy honey sauce (both entrees are $10.95). Dinner entrees come with a salad. There is a daily diet special for weight watchers, such as grilled salmon steak with basil and shallots ($13.95).

The Orchid's weekend brunch includes eggs Benedict with cottage fries; smoked whiting with scrambled eggs, and a bagel with scallion cream cheese; a caviar and sour cream omelet with fries; steak and eggs with fries; and french toast with fruit salad and bacon. Your choice is $9.95 with unlimited mimosas, screwdrivers, Bloody Marys, and coffee or tea, or $7.95 without drinks.

Lunch is served from noon to 4 p.m. weekdays, and dinner from 5 to 11:30

p.m. Sunday through Friday. Saturday dinner is on from 6 p.m. to 12:30 a.m. Brunch is noon to 4 p.m. on Saturday and Sunday. Closed most holidays. Reservations suggested for large groups (five or more), especially at lunch and brunch. Not necessary at dinner, but calling ahead helps.

Shelter, 540 Second Ave., at 30th Street (tel. 684-4207), draws a young, lively crowd. It's an airy, attractive place, with its mirrored, columned mahogany bar (15 types of beer available) and slate-gray/blue color scheme. Tables are set with blue-and-white checkered tablecloths and white carnations, and the booths up front have white globe lights. The varied menu is reasonably priced. At lunch there are appetizers such as avocado or artichokes vinaigrette ($2.50 each), and entrees like sliced steak with bordelaise sauce, salad, and steak fries ($5.95), or tortellini and salad ($4.95). Or you might try one of the many salads —chef's, seafood, curried chicken—priced from $5.25 to $6.95. Dinner prices are about a dollar or two more. Mussels marinara with a salad is $5.95, chicken Florentine is $6.95, and a roast Cornish hen with vegetable is $7.25. The waitress will tell you the day's desserts.

Shelter's weekend brunch includes a Bloody Mary, mimosa, screwdriver, Kir royale, or juice, and an appetizer such as soup, cold mussels vinaigrette, a salad, or fruit. Brunch prices depend on the entree you choose. The brunch omelet is $5.50; steak and eggs or seafood in pastry is $8.25; french toast with ham, Canadian bacon, or Italian sweet sausages and pure maple syrup is $5.50. Coffee or tea is included.

Shelter is open daily; for lunch from 11:30 a.m. to 4:30 p.m., for dinner from 5 p.m. to 1:45 a.m., and for brunch on Saturday and Sunday from 11:30 a.m. to 4:30 p.m. The bar stays open until 4 a.m. Reservations advised.

Mumbles, downtown at 603 Second Ave., at 33rd Street (tel. 889-0750), is a lot like its older uptown sister. The exterior is shingled, and there's a white door and window boxes with real flowers. The floor is covered with sawdust. A low wooden bar takes up half the restaurant, but there are more tables in the window porches. The menu is printed on paper placemats set over the yellow-and-white checkered tablecloths, and is also written on chalkboards. The blackboard specials change daily, with the likes of zucchini-walnut quiche with salad ($5.25), roast duckling ($7.95), coquilles St. Jacques ($5.95), and calf liver with bacon and onions ($7.75). Entrees come with the vegetable of the day. The menu has even lower prices—fettuccine Alfredo ($5.95), spinach salad ($4.25), a Mumbleburger platter ($4.75), and a tuna melt sandwich ($5.25)—a meal in itself. End your meal with a rich slice of chocolate chocolate-chip cake ($2.25).

Mumbles' weekend brunch includes a Bloody Mary or mimosa, and coffee or tea. For $6.50 you get three eggs with steak, bacon, ham, or sausage, fries, and an English muffin or bagel. French toast with bacon or sausage is $5.95; eggs Benedict or Florentine is $6.50.

Mumbles is open from 11:30 a.m. to 4 a.m. or later daily, and for brunch on Saturday and Sunday till 4 p.m. Reservations not necessary.

Kitty Hawk, 565 Third Ave., between 36th and 37th Streets (tel. 661-7406), is a popular Third Avenue restaurant. It can be noisy and the service slow, but also fun. Kitty Hawk is an airplane buff's delight, for the walls are crammed with memorabilia from the early days of aviation—pictures, models, propellers. Tables and walls are dark wood, with colored lights about. On each table there is a seltzer bottle. The mood is informal and cozy.

Two light eaters can share the Frammis Feast, with spare ribs, fried chicken, a few shrimp, a salad, and fries ($9.95). A big chef's or spinach salad is $6.75; a mushroom-and-onion omelet, $5.75. A French-dip sandwich is $6.25, and a half-pound sirloin burger with fries is $5.75, $6.25 with cheese or mushrooms. Kitty Hawk serves an Amaretto, Kahlúa, and ice-cream drink that makes a delicious dessert splurge, but at $4.50 they run up a bill faster than even regular bar drinks.

Kitty Hawk has a "Say When" brunch on weekends. For $7.95 you get a choice of three eggs with ham, bacon, or sausage and an English muffin, stuffed french toast, and home-fries; spinach or chef's salad; a burger platter; eggs Benedict; or a club sandwich. It includes all the champagne, Bloody Marys, or screwdrivers you can drink.

Kitty Hawk is open daily, for lunch from noon to 4 p.m. and for dinner from 5 p.m. to midnight. Brunch is noon to 3:45 p.m. on Saturday, 11:30 a.m. to 3:45 p.m. on Sunday. The bar stays open till 2 a.m. or later. Reservations are not necessary, except for large parties. There is often a wait for brunch.

Earth Angel Natural Café, 611 Second Ave., between 33rd and 34th Streets (tel. 684-9637), is a refreshing throwback to the early '70s and the heyday of Alice's Restaurant. Small but not cramped—with butcher-block tables and plants aplenty—the atmosphere here is mellow and friendly. The food here is eye-pleasing and filling—Earth Angel believes in serving gargantuan portions of everything.

For our money the most rewarding menu selection is the Earth Angel burger deluxe—your choice of a bulghur soy-bean patty or nutburger on a whole-wheat sesame bun with onions, pickles, sprouts, shredded carrots, tahini-based sauce, tomato, and cheddar cheese, served with homemade french fries (with skins intact), bread, and a picture-perfect house salad ($5.95; a burger à la carte is $3.25). The sun salad—cheese, lettuce, red cabbage, carrots, sunflower seeds, raisins, and cashews—is too large for one person ($6.50); try ordering the half portion of it instead ($4.25). Cold sandwiches range in price from $2.95 for a cheese, sprouts, and tomato combo, to $3.95 for chunky white tuna on whole-wheat bread. A pita pizza is $3.95 and a grilled eggplant sandwich is $4.50. Omelets, served with fries or brown rice, start at $3.95. Minestrone, baked in a crock and topped with a thick layer of cheese, is $2.50. Entrees, served with bread and a house salad, include vegetarian lasagne ($7.25) and vegetable fontana—steamed vegetables in a Spanish tomato sauce on a bed of brown rice covered with cheese and baked in a casserole ($6.75). Daily fish and chicken specials are offered—most are in the $6.95 to $8.95 price range.

Desserts include a homemade brown rice pudding with almonds and whipped cream ($1.95), maple pecan pie ($1.95), chocolate cake or cheesecake ($2.50), and carrot cake ($2.25). Tofutti ($2.25) and Bassett's ice cream ($2.25) are served. Strawberry or banana smoothies—fresh fruit blended with juice, honey, and ice—are $1.35 and $1.95 (depending on size). Protein shakes—made with ice cream, milk, and protein powder—are $2.25. A glass of red or white house wine is $1.75.

Saturday and Sunday brunch includes unlimited champagne and a main entree (we recommend the banana-walnut pancakes) for $5.95.

Open daily from noon to midnight. Saturday and Sunday brunch from noon to 4 p.m.

Pete's Tavern, 66 Irving Pl., on the northeast corner of 18th Street (tel. 473-7676), opened in 1864 and is the oldest established bar in New York City. Originally known as Healy's Bar, Pete's (bought in 1935 by Pete De Bella) was a Tammany Hall meeting place. During Prohibition it was one of New York's most notorious speakeasies, operating from behind a storefront florist's shop. Pete's also has a notable literary history—O. Henry penned "Gift of the Magi" while sitting in the very first booth after you enter the main doorway. Butch Cassidy and the Sundance Kid were said to have eaten at Pete's; President Kennedy dined here when he was staying in the Gramercy Park Hotel.

Although the original eating area has been expanded (the two backrooms used to be stables), Pete's has retained the feel of a real neighborhood tavern. Its authentic pub appearance—the original tin ceiling, tile floor, antique mirrors, rosewood bar, and walls cluttered with photographs taken over the past 60 years—has made it a prime set location for TV commercials and films: the Miller Lite ads are filmed here; a scene from *Ragtime* (with James Cagney) was shot here. "Pete's has always played down its image," according to its personable night manager, and today it's a melting pot for everyone—politicians, policemen, tourists, actors, sports figures . . . the list goes on and on.

Menu prices can go as high as $18 for a 16-ounce sirloin steak, so you will do best to stick with the more reasonably priced burgers and pasta dishes. Pete's is famous for its eight-ounce burgers, served with fries, cole slaw, lettuce, and tomato ($5.50 at lunch, $5.75 at dinner). Main entrees, served with a mixed green salad (ask for the house dressing, a creamy herb blend) or a side of spaghetti, include eggplant parmagiana ($5.75 at lunch, $7.25 at dinner), filet of sole, broiled or fried ($7 at lunch, $9.25 at dinner), and London broil with mushroom sauce ($7.50 at lunch, $9 at dinner). Spaghetti with tomato, meat, or marinara sauce is $5.25 at lunch, $6.50 at dinner. Linguine with clam sauce is $6 at lunch, $7.50 at dinner. The best lunch bargain is the $3 daily special—the day we were there it was tortellini.

The most popular dessert is the hot pecan pie ($2.75 at both meals). There is also chocolate cheesecake ($3), rum cake ($3), and zabaglione, a mixture of eggs, sugar, and wine served chilled ($3.25).

A weekend brunch menu includes a Bloody Mary or mimosa, main entree (an omelet with fries and french toast with bacon are among the choices) and coffee or tea for $7.50.

Pete's is open seven days a week. The bar is open daily at 8 a.m. Lunch is served from 11:30 a.m. to 3 p.m. Dinner is served from 3 to 11:45 p.m. (until 12:45 a.m. on Friday and Saturday). Brunch is Saturday and Sunday from noon to 4 p.m.

Pie in the Sky, 194 Third Ave., between 17th and 18th Streets (tel. 505-5454), is an inviting restaurant with an artistic ambience and a touch of class. The likes of Andy Warhol and Paloma Picasso can often be found dining within its walls (which, incidentally, are adorned with rotating art shows—you may find yourself surrounded by patchwork quilts or oil portraits). Most entrees fall into the $6.95 to $7.95 price range. The emphasis is on regional American cooking, and the hands-down favorite entree is the chicken pot pie, served with a tossed salad ($5.95 at lunch, $6.95 at dinner). Southern fried or barbecued chicken, served with a tossed salad or potatoes dijonnaise, is another house specialty ($6.95 at both lunch and dinner). Sandwiches range in price from $3.95 for a three-cheese and tomato melt to $4.95 for smoked chicken with horseradish. Salads range in price from $2.25 for a vegetable side salad (such as pasta pesto or dilled carrots) to $6.25 ($7.50 at dinner) for a zippy curried chicken salad, served on mixed greens with fresh fruit salad. An entree-size portion of hot ratatouille with grated parmesan cheese is $5.25 at lunch, $6.95 at dinner. Desserts are numerous and unbelievably delectable. The apple pie is oh-so-tart and jampacked with apples. Chocolate truffle cake, made with bittersweet chocolate, is indescribably decadent ($2.50). Ben & Jerry's ice cream is served ($1.95). The bakery in front of the restaurant is open for breakfast, and European visitors swear by the coffee (75¢ for regular or brewed decaffeinated). Cappuccino is $1.50; espresso is $1. A glass of wine ranges from $2.25 for house red or white to $3.75 for Kir royale.

Weekend brunch entrees range from $5.95 for french toast made with brioche bread and served with bacon and real maple syrup and homemade preserves, to $7.95 for a caviar and sour cream omelet. Breakfast goodies—served at the small tables located in the bakery at the front of the store—include croissants and scones ($1.25), pain au chocolat ($1.50), and sour cream coffeecake ($2.50).

Pie in the Sky is open Monday to Thursday from 8 a.m. to 11 p.m., on Friday and Saturday to midnight, and on Sunday from 9 a.m. to 10 p.m. The brunch items are served Saturday and Sunday from 10 a.m. to 3 p.m.

Caffè Bonnelle, 208 E. 34th St., between Second and Third Avenues (tel. 684-8662), is a European-style café cheerfully presided over by its owner, Arthur Bonnelle. The brickface walls are host to revolving art shows, and classical music is played in the background—but never too loudly to drown out intimate conversations. No alcohol is served, and patrons are sophisticated yet low-keyed. There are butcher-block tables and comfortable chairs. In short, this is the sort of haven where you want to hang out—quite possibly alone—with the "Arts and Leisure" section of the *Times*.

A variety of sandwiches, quiches, and casseroles are served, and all are good. Ratatouille ($5.25), meat lasagne ($7.95), vegetarian lasagne ($7.25), and a broccoli and cheddar cheese quiche ($4.25, $5 with a salad) are among your choices. Our favorite is Susan's spinach magnifique, spinach baked with mozzarella, parmesan, and provolone cheese, wrapped in a light pastry shell and served with ratatouille ($7.25). Sandwiches include tuna salad ($3.25), ham ($3.75), and turkey ($4.25), or you might want to try the delightful date-nut bread and cream cheese finger sandwiches served with fresh fruit ($5.25).

Go sparingly on the main course, however, for you will surely want to partake of one of Bonnelle's 55 different desserts, such as banana cheesecake ($3.25), fudgy chip pie ($3.50), raspberry mousse cake ($3.75), mocha torte ($3.75), apple pie ($3), strawberry rhubarb pie ($3.50), Kahlúa chocolate mousse pie ($3.25), or a vanilla napoleon ($2.25). We especially recommend any of the 18 chocolate-based desserts. Dessert crêpes range from $4.75 to $5.25. Häagen-Dazs ice cream is served ($2.25 for a dish, $4.50 for one of several luscious sundae concoctions). The iced cappuccino, thick and creamy, is served in a huge goblet and is thick enough to eat with a spoon—they include one, just in case ($3.25)! Hot beverages include several varieties of regular and decaffeinated coffee ($1 to $2.50) and hot chocolate ($2), as well as several varieties of tea ($1.25).

Caffè Bonnelle is open Sunday to Thursday from 11 a.m. to 1 a.m., on Friday and Saturday to 2 a.m.

The **Brickwork Café,** 497 Third Ave., at 34th Street (tel. 686-8422), is a delightful café. Colorful crayoned drawings dot the walls, and you can add to the art by decorating your paper tablecloth with the crayons supplied at each table. For lunch, try salads ($2.75 to $6.75) or Brickwork burgers ($5.25 to $5.75). Also tasty is the cheese steak sandwich, roast beef and melted cheese on an onion roll, with french fries on the side ($5.95). Wash it down with a Watney's Ale ($1.50). For dinner, try the mussels marinara ($8.75), which comes with salad and potato or vegetable. Desserts include an assortment of cakes ($2.75) or apple pie ($2.50).

Open for lunch from noon to 4 p.m. Monday to Friday with a $3-per-person minimum. Dinner is served from 5 p.m. to 2 a.m. Monday through Saturday, until 1 a.m. on Sunday.

Down the block is **The Back Porch,** 488 Third Ave., at 33rd Street (tel. 685-3828), a pleasant eatery that's arranged in three ascending tiers, from a lower bar level inside the door, to a mid-level dining room, to a raised terrace in the rear. Chandeliers hang over each table adding an intimate air to the dining area. The à la carte menu offers basic American cuisine. Entrees start at $7.50 and range from sandwiches to egg dishes and mixed salads.

Dinner is served from 5 to 11 p.m. Monday through Thursday, on Friday till midnight, and on Saturday from 6 p.m. to midnight. Sunday brunch ($4.95 to $9.95) is from noon until 5 p.m.

BARBECUE, BURGERS, AND RIBS: **R.J.'s Saloon,** 220 Madison Ave., at 37th Street (tel. 889-5553), brings a slice of the West to Murray Hill. You bring your biggest appetite, because R.J.'s serves a lot of food. R.J.'s, with a saddle slung at the front door, a huge barrel of unshelled peanuts to snack from, its cactus and miscellaneous old tools, is a rarity in Manhattan. It has some winning civilities more common in costly restaurants. Like the hot towels that come after you've finished feasting, or the free hot-meat appetizers at Happy Hour (5 to 8 p.m. every weekday) that alone will fill you up.

Just about anything you order here is sure to be giant-size—even a half order of crispy onion loaf ($1.95) is still more than two people can eat. A half order of vegetable tempura ($3.50 for a half, $4.50 full-size) is a meal in itself. The barbecued beef is succulent—ribs with choice of potato, cornbread, and extra sauce is $8.95 (baby ribs are $11.95 at dinner, $6.95 at lunch). We like the tangy barbecue sauce best, even more than the Oriental sauce. The half chicken, charcoal roasted and served with potato, corn muffin, and sauce, is also good ($5.95). The menu has lots of other choices, including chicken salad or two types of spinach salad at $6.50 each (and served in chilled bowls). Wines are $1.75 a glass; draft beers, $1.75 to $2.25 (there's a long list). And the desserts, should you be able to manage one, are knockouts. There are treats like Yankee apple crumb cake ($2.50) and Arkansas pecan pie ($2.50). And the chocolate climax is a boggling concoction of chocolate cake, chocolate chips, vanilla ice cream, fudge, nuts, and whipped cream, served in a huge goblet ($3).

R.J.'s also has a Sunday brunch—$7.95 for ribs, grits, eggs, hot biscuits, and champagne, mimosas, or Bloody Marys. There are free square-dancing lessons during brunch for those who can still move.

R.J.'s has other entertainment too—western performers (no designer jeans here) on Wednesday and Thursday nights from 7 to 9 p.m. or later (overlaps with Happy Hour and those free goodies), and on Friday and Saturday from 9 p.m. to 1 a.m.

R.J.'s is open daily for lunch from 11:30 a.m. till 4 p.m. and for dinner from 4 till 11:30 p.m. (till 1 a.m. on Friday and Saturday night). R.J.'s opens at noon on Saturday and Sunday. Reservations are not needed except for large parties.

Checkers, 201 E. 34th St., just off Third Avenue (tel. 684-7803), is a fast-food barbecue place with eat-in room and lots of Manhattan pizzazz. Checkers promises healthy food at reasonable prices. The focus of the shop is the huge grill, with its lines of chicken and ribs in various stages of cooking. The aroma is wonderful. But Checkers is also decorated with imagination, so you won't feel that you're just chowing down in a take-out kitchen (even though you are!). The floor is black-and-white tile, very clean in spite of the traffic. There are black tables set with red ashtrays, and modern art on the white walls and salsa music overhead.

You can order à la carte—a quarter of a three-pound chicken is $3.25 (also available in half- or whole-bird sizes). A half portion of Canadian baby back ribs is $6.25. There are three sauces: the traditional red barbecue sauce with a kick (some may find it too salty), a sweet-and-sour, and a mustard. A small portion of salad costs $1.75 and is enough to feed two—choose from potato salad with natural mayonnaise, potato salad, pasta salad, and our favorite, red cabbage cole slaw with white raisins and a sweet-sour dressing. You can also order meat-salad combinations, like a quarter of a three-pound chicken with a choice of salad, extra barbecue sauce, and fresh whole-wheat, rye, or pita bread, for $3 ($4.95 for a half of that chicken). A chicken and ribs combination with the same accompaniments is $8.45. Checkers has canned sodas, and apple-walnut pie, carrot cake, and brownies for dessert ($1.50 to $2.45 each).

Open daily from 11:30 a.m. to 2:30 p.m., and again from 4:30 to about 10:30 p.m.

Jackson Hole came east (to the Upper East Side of New York, that is), and now it's come south, to Murray Hill. The hamburger cookery chain has a restaurant at Third Avenue and 35th Street (tel. 679-3264). It's a good local place to satisfy a craving for a big, round, seven-ounce hamburger at low prices in a restaurant setting. This one is quite attractive (if a little smokey), with an original mosaic floor, wood tables, and the requisite ski posters of the real West. A hamburger here is $2.80; a baconburger, $4.05; and a cheeseburger, $3.40. There are all sorts of toppings and platters, plus omelets priced from $1.75 to a loaded combo for $6.30. Nothing on the menu is more than $7, and most items are a lot less. From salads to sandwiches to burgers and beer, there's something for everyone. The older Jackson Holes (except the resort!) are all uptown, but the menus are the same.

Open Monday to Saturday from 10:30 a.m. to 11 p.m., on Sunday from noon to midnight.

Also, see "Steakhouses," at the end of this section.

COFFEESHOPS AND SPECIALTY SHOPS: **East Bay,** 491 First Ave., at 29th Street (tel. 683-7770), is our idea of a good coffeeshop. It's clean and spiffy with no worn corners. The spacious interior is Early American, with Delft-look tiles behind the counter, comfortable booths with blue seats, a brick floor, paneling, and a beamed ceiling with chandeliers.

East Bay's menu is almost as big as the dining room—over 200 items. There are 49 sandwiches alone, as varied as salami and egg ($2.35), and jumbo daily specials include a chopped sirloin steak with onion rings, potato, vegetable, and salad ($5.15); meatloaf with potato, vegetable, and salad ($4.25); baked shrimp with mushrooms, rice, and salad ($4.50); and quiche with soup or salad ($2.75). The owners are Greek, and pastitsio—a baked, layered macaroni dish—is served intermittently throughout the week ($2.40). Cakes and pies are baked on the premises—try the strawberry cheesecake ($2), chocolate-chip cake ($1.60), or the dreamy lemon meringue pie ($1.50). The rice pudding ($1.10) is not to be overlooked. There is a full bar. The staff is polite, and the dining room is often full of doctors and nurses from Bellevue Hospital across the street.

East Bay is open 24 hours a day every day.

The **Tivoli,** 515 Third Ave., between 34th and 35th Streets (tel. 689-6856), is another first-rate coffeeshop. In the heart of Murray Hill, it's worth a short walk from 34th Street stores (Macy's, Ohrbach's, B. Altman and Co., etc.) or anywhere. The Tivoli has what we call class—it's spotless and modern, with a long wooden counter up front and tile floors. The dining room in back seems almost private and is quite attractive—blond-wood tables, fresh flowers, brass, a mirrored back wall, and Ultrasuede-like seats. The food is excellent, and the Tivoli has nice touches, like leaving baskets of pickles at each table.

Sandwiches are priced from $3.35 for tuna salad or chicken salad to $5.95 for a turkey club. A hamburger with fries is $3.95. Entrees—seafood, steaks, Italian pastas, chicken, and chops—are priced from $5.95 to $12.50, with most around $8.95. Daily specials include the likes of moussaka with a vegetable and salad ($6.95), or chicken à la king ($5.95). Our favorite seafood dish is stuffed filet of sole with crabmeat ($12.95).

The Tivoli is also open 24 hours daily.

Sarge's, 546 and 548 Third Ave., between 36th and 37th Streets (tel. 679-1177), is worth a visit, even just to look. It's freshly decorated with a light-toned tile floor and sparkling glass. There are imported delicacies and a case of fresh candies and cannolis. But the deli counter is the real treat. There are trays of unusual salads within, good bagels atop, and a veritable gourmet feast of take-home foods—heaping platters of roasts, tortellini, etc., even brunch in chafing dishes on weekends. You see how New Yorkers survive with their tiny kitchens—no one uses them!

Next door at 548 Third Ave. is the restaurant itself (tel. 679-0442), with a counter full of roast meats and pies up front and the dining room with wood walls and wood captain's chairs beyond. The food is delicious, the portions large, and the prices reasonable. Sandwiches are priced from $1.95 for cream cheese and jelly to $5.25 for roast beef or fresh turkey. A burger with lettuce, tomato, and onion is $3.25. A bacon cheeseburger with fries is $5.25. Entrees include corned-beef hash with poached egg and potato at $5.95, and go as high as $12.95 for a one-pound boneless sirloin with salad and baked potato. Desserts are 95¢ to $2.50. Sarge's serves a $7.95 weekend brunch between 11 a.m. and 3 p.m. that includes a drink or fresh-squeezed orange juice, and coffee. Entrees include eggs Benedict; french toast stuffed with meat and cheese; and a lox, eggs, and onion omelet with a bagel and cream cheese.

Sarge's is open 24 hours daily, of course. The Gourmet Shop is open daily from 7 a.m. to midnight, till 1 a.m. on Friday and Saturday night.

CHINESE: Our selections in this section of town are listed in order of expense and elegance.

The delights of a dim sum lunch or brunch at **Hee Seung Fung,** or **HSF,** 578 Second Ave., near 32nd Street (tel. 689-6969), will teach you that it's not rude to point. Dim sum is the venerable Hong Kong tradition of dining on many tidbits, and it literally means to point to what your heart wants most. At HSF, the sister of a famed Chinatown restaurant, it is civilized indeed. You pick from a cart, or order from the special menu (ask). HSF is very elegant, very hi-tech, with subdued browns and whites, thick linens, and columned walls. Set way back from the hurly-burly street (HSF is one of the few suburban-looking shopping arcades in Manhattan), lunching here is a real respite. Dim sum morsels are not inexpensive—at $1.50 and $2.75, they can add up quickly—but keep in mind that three or four will satisfy most people. Among the delectables: beef shiu mi, stuffed crab claws, shredded chicken roll, crispy spring roll, and pork dumplings.

On the regular lunch menu, chicken dishes are $6.95; pork, $6.50; beef, $7.25; and seafood, $7.95. The dinner menu is past our budget, alas.

HSF is open from 11:30 a.m. to 11:30 p.m. Sunday to Thursday, to 12:30 a.m. on Friday and Saturday. Reservations suggested.

Dragon Szechuan, 338 Lexington Ave., between 39th and 40th Streets (tel. 370-9648), is done in bright Oriental reds and greens, with linen and flowers on the tables and traditional tasseled lamps hanging from the ceiling of the narrow room. Its decor is that of the old-fashioned Chinese restaurant—very dragon-y, with dressed-up glitz. On the back wall, a lit-from-within cartoon salutes your good dining. The food is good, and priced comparably to other restaurants. We recommend going at lunchtime, when entrees are 50¢ to $1 less. For an appetizer, try sharing a dish of cold noodles with nutty-tasting sesame sauce ($3.35). The menu also has two "king-size" entrees that are easily shared: the Buddhist delight, a medley of sauteed vegetables ($6.35 at lunch), or the sweet-and-sour combination of pork, shrimp, and chicken ($7.95 at lunch). Other entrees are $5.50 to $7.95 at lunch, about $6.20 to $8.55 at dinner. Expect to spend $5 or more a person at lunch, $6 at dinner.

Open daily for lunch from 11:30 a.m. to 3 p.m., and for dinner from 5 to 10 p.m. Reservations suggested.

Hunan K's, 455 Second Ave., between 25th and 26th Streets (tel. 689-3857), is a good place for lunch, when the weekday special is only $3.95. You get a choice of 12 entrees, including pork and broccoli with garlic sauce, spicy beef and Buddhist delight, a choice of white or fried rice, a choice of soup or an eggroll, and a pot of tea. Shrimp dishes are $4.25. A fortune cookie and a dish of delicious caramelized walnuts follow your meal, a treat not on the menu. Another charming gesture also not on the menu—with new customers, owner Kent Huang brings over a complimentary cordial of plum wine, one for you and one for him, and he toasts you! You probably won't even have to say you're a newcomer; he'll know.

Hunan K's also serves dinner, with many entrees under $6. But you can't beat the luncheon special. The service here is fast, attentive, and friendly. The restaurant itself is pleasantly dressed up, with cane chairs, brown tablecloths, and fabric roses in bud vases on each table. There are two rooms and a full bar.

Hunan K's is open daily Monday to Thursday from 11:30 a.m. to 11 p.m., on Friday and Saturday to 11:30 p.m., and on Sunday from 1 to 11 p.m. The luncheon special is served Monday to Friday only, from 11:30 a.m. to 3 p.m. Reservations not necessary.

CHINESE/JAPANESE: Extraordinary is the only word for **Genroku Sushi,** 366 Fifth Ave., between 34th and 35th Streets (tel. 947-7940), a completely automated Chinese/Japanese restaurant. There are over 125 in Japan alone, and you'll find that the restaurant here is almost always crowded. The chain is the brainstorm of Taiwanese fast-food magnate Kin Syo Chin, who brings a *Modern Times* efficiency to the old Hong Kong dim sum. We'd love to see Charlie Chaplin have a go at the morsels here. How? You sit on backless stools at a Formica counter, as food travels by, believe it or not, on an oval conveyor belt from the kitchen. What you like, you take, and at the end the waitress counts up your plates and gives you the tab. All dishes are a standard $1.71 each, except sashimi ($4.25) and a beef or curry bowl ($3.33).

Among the many choices are Japanese miso soup (clear broth) and tempura, Chinese chop suey, fried rice, fried chicken, and lots of sushi—tuna, shrimp, salmon, octopus, egg, mackerel, squid, etc. It's clanky and clattery, but great fun.

Open Monday to Friday from 11 a.m. to 7:30 p.m. (to 8:30 p.m. on Thursday), on Saturday to 7 p.m., and on Sunday from noon to 6 p.m.

ENGLISH: We love **David Copperfield,** 322 Lexington Ave., between 38th and 39th Streets (tel. 684-8227), a neighborly place in the middle of expensive Murray Hill. It's all quite upbeat, from the young but capable waitresses who seem like family, to pianist Lenny Metcalfe who plays nightly Monday to Saturday. A Britisher like the owner, Metcalfe tinkles out tunes from "I'm a Londoner" to the theme from the movie *Chariots of Fire*—and well too. Diners often sing along. The restaurant is as dark as a Dickensian garret, but cozy. Wood tables are set with small white candles and heavy pewter service plates. Brass bedwarmers, scuttles, and hunting horns hang everywhere on the dark paneling, and brass letters spell out the names of well-loved Dickens characters.

Lunch and dinner are similar except for a slight increase in price. A huge chef's salad is $6.25 at each meal. Good and hearty fish and chips is $6.25 at lunch, $6.85 at dinner. Chicken McCawber is rich and lemony at dinner ($7.75). Entrees come with salad and potato. There are also British staples like steak-and-kidney pie ($7 at dinner), but the waitresses will kindly make sure you don't mind kidneys before placing your order. The house special is sliced steak on garlic bread topped with onions and melted cheese ($6.50 at dinner). On Saturday, Sunday, and Monday nights there's a special dinner of thick prime rib, baked potato, and salad for $7.95, but supplies run out before the evening does because of the demand, so come early. For dessert, trifle (whipped cream, fruit, and pound cake, with a nip of sherry—$1.50 at lunch, $1.75 at dinner) hits the spot.

Sunday brunch includes a Bloody Mary, entree or eggs, and trifle and coffee ($4.75).

David Copperfield serves lunch from 11:30 a.m. to about 4 p.m., then dinner until about 1 a.m. daily. Sunday brunch is from noon to 4 p.m. Reservations are not necessary, except for Lenny Metcalfe's *British Music Hall* show on the first Saturday of each month. He brings in other performers and there's a $3 cover charge.

GREEK: Z, 117 E. 15th St., between Irving Place and Park Avenue South, a block from Union Square (tel. 254-0960), is one of the nicest restaurants anywhere. Its red awning, spotless white paint, and tiled entry brighten an otherwise drab street; three steps down is the beautiful taverna. Owner Jerry Vontas is usually at the door—for 14 years he's been getting rave reviews for excellent food, service, and atmosphere. You walk past the spotless open kitchen, where waiters heap generous portions of delicious-looking food. The narrow front room positively glows: gleaming wood tables set with red napkins and red candles, a wine bar with red-and-white checkered cloths and more candles, a fireplace. Beyond, there are two more rooms and a fenced summer garden with benches and ten tables. Throughout, there are white stucco walls, cozy low ceilings, and wall hangings of colorful woven fabrics.

Lunch and dinner menus are similar, except that at lunch there are sandwiches, like souvlaki for $3.25. The antipasto is big enough to share: $3.25 at lunch, $3.95 for dinner. Or you might try a taramosalata appetizer of caviar and raw onion ($2.10 at lunch, $2.95 at dinner). Entrees come with a Greek salad, rice, vegetable, and bread and butter. Moussaka is $5.50 at lunch, $6.75 at dinner; and there is lamb and seafood. Customer favorites include yavetsi—shank of lamb baked with seasoned Greek pasta ($6 and $7.50, depending on the meal)—and the broiled scampi ($7.90 and $8.50). There are Greek wines and rich desserts—try the baklava ($1.40 and $1.45).

Z is open daily: Monday to Friday from 11:30 a.m. to 3 p.m. for lunch, 4:30 to 11 p.m. for dinner (to 11:30 p.m. on Friday). On Saturday dinner is from 1 to 11:30 p.m., on Sunday to 11 p.m. (no lunch). Reservations suggested for parties of five or more.

Deno's Place, 155 E. 26th St., at the corner of Third Avenue (tel. 725-9386), is actually two restaurants and an ice-cream café sprawling over half a block. Nary a name is in sight, but you'll recognize their brick and ironwork, very Victorian and lovely. The glass-enclosed **Corner Café** (tel. 725-9386) is white and summery inside, with yellow-and-green cushions on white bentwood chairs, lots of flowers, a few small antique carousel horses in the window, white wrought iron, a terracotta tile floor, and white latticework and a stained-glass effect at the ceiling. The café is as expensive as it looks, however. Dinner is past our budget. For lunch, you might want to share an appetizer of mussels marinara ($4.95) or saganaki—a Greek cheese fondue ($5.50). Linguine is $6.95 with meat sauce, $7.95 with red or white clam sauce. Frutta di mare—translated as "fruits of the sea," which includes shrimp, clams, mussels, calamari, scallops and octopus, served over a bed of lettuce—is slightly high for those on a strict budget, but well worth the splurge ($11.50). More reasonable choices are ravioli ($5.95) and stuffed eggplant parmigiana ($6.95). Wine and sangría are $2.25 a glass.

The other two restaurants are on 26th Street, past a video store. Out front there's a fanciful wrought-iron fence, painted white. Upstairs is the **Greek Taverna** (tel. 684-9339), a charmer with its white stucco walls, bare polished tables, sawdust on the floor, and open kitchen with red heat lamps. There's a big picture window, and vines grow on the ceiling. An appetizer of grape leaves is $4.50; a salad big enough for two, $5.50. Spanakopita—spinach pie—is $4.50. Chicken parmigiana is $8.50; moussaka, $7.95. Pastitsio, a Greek pasta dish, is $6.95. Veal, most lamb dishes, and shrimp are in the $9.95 to $10.95 price range. A side order of garlic bread is 75¢. For dessert, try a crème caramel ($2.50) and a cup of Greek coffee ($1.25).

You might prefer to end your visit to Deno's with a trip to the **Ice Cream Café** (tel. 684-8679), located beneath the Greek Taverna. Wrought-iron tables are covered with crisp white cloths, and the atmosphere here is cozy and friendly, the sort of place you'd like to have your child's next birthday party at. Sundaes are $3.95; Belgian waffles, $4.95; and baklava, $2.50.

Lunch at the Corner Café is Monday to Friday from noon to 3 p.m. The Taverna serves dinner only, from 5:30 p.m. to midnight every night but Tuesday, when it's closed. The Ice Cream Café is open from 6 p.m. to midnight every night but Tuesday, when it's closed.

INDIAN / PAKISTANI / BANGLADESHI: Curry in a Hurry, 130 E. 29th St., between Lexington and Third Avenues (tel. 889-1159), is a no-frills, fast-food place for Indian, Pakistani, and Bangladeshi meals. Decor consists of an orange zigzag stripe painted around the walls. Seating is on orange dinette chairs at orange Formica tables. The linoleum floor is well worn, but everything is clean. You'll often see Indian families eating here. There's a small steam table, which fills the room with the smell of cumin. You order from the overhead menu. À la carte items are priced at $1.50 to $2.75. A platter of beef or chicken curry, with one vegetable curry, pilaf rice with vegetables, bread, and salad, is $4.50, or $4.25 with just vegetable curries. The special of beef or chicken curry, pakora (a savory fritter) or a kebab, a vegetable curry, pilaf rice, bread, and salad is $5.45. Milk or tea is 50¢; soda, 70¢; and sweets, $1.50 to $2.

Open Monday to Saturday from 11:30 a.m. to 9 p.m., on Sunday and holidays till 7 p.m.

Shaheen, 99 Lexington Ave., at the corner of 27th Street (tel. 683-2139), is a little Pakistani cafeteria—clean, bright, and new. There's Indian music overhead but no decoration. The menu is on the wall. A half plate of lamb or chicken curry, rice, a piece of bread, and raita (yogurt) or dhal (lentil sauce) is $4, or 4.50 with a vegetarian curry. Niharee, a beef curry, with two pieces of nan (or naan) bread and dhal is $3.50. Lentil curry and tandoori chicken are $2.25 each. Snacks and sweets are the real treats here, priced $1.50 to $2, or $6 per pound. There are Pakistani doughnuts, jalaby (a sweet pretzel of sugar and flour), kheer mohan (deep-fried cottage cheese with cream on top), coconut and cheese balls, and several kinds of halvah including pistachio, milk fudge, pink and almond fudge, and many more.

Shaheen is open daily from 11 a.m. to 10:30 p.m. Monday through Saturday, till 9:30 p.m. on Sunday.

Jay Hind, 31 E. 30th St., between Park and Madison Avenues (tel. 684-6226), is small and as mysterious as a casbah: you'll find couples dallying in a romantic corner as well as Indian businessmen. The maroon interior includes a tented ceiling with gold braid. Tables are set with white linen, Indian tapestries are on the wall, and Indian music plays in the background. There are Pakistani camel-skin lamps, painted like stained glass, but the light is dim.

Lunch is a bargain: between noon and 3 p.m. weekdays (not holidays) you choose any one of seven curries that come with saffron rice, dhal (mild lentil sauce), onion chutney, and tea or coffee, all for between $4.45 and $4.95. Be sure to order one of the delicious Indian breads, large enough to share, like poori or chapati ($1 to $1.50). À la carte prices are higher, ranging from $5.95 to $11.95. A curry dinner is $7.95 for lamb, $7.50 for beef, and $7.25 for chicken, and comes with pilaf rice, dhal, and onion chutney. Indian tea, served with cream, is much like British tea except for a trace of cloves. It's worth trying for a few cents more.

Jay Hind is open Monday to Friday from 11 a.m. to 11 p.m. (the kitchen closes about 10:30 p.m.), and on Saturday from 5 to 11 p.m. Closed Sunday.

Shalimar, 39 E. 29th St., between Park Avenue South and Madison Avenue (tel. 684-8327), has offered good northern Indian food in a charming setting since 1977. From a nondescript commercial street, you step into an attractive bar/lounge area and then into the dining room. All is kept very simple—white walls with Indian-motif mosaics imbedded in the stucco, plants and fresh flowers, white tablecloths draped over red, and a tin ceiling.

The lunch special is a good deal. For $4.50 you choose from fish, lamb, chicken, pork vindaloo, and vegetable curries. Lunch comes with rice, dhal (lentil sauce), onion chutney, and coffee or tea. The shrimp curry is $5.95. Definitely do not miss those marvelous breads—the huge, unleavened naan, or deep-fried poori, puffed and light.

Dinner à la carte is not out of reach. You might try an appetizer of bhujia, fried vegetable and chickpea balls ($1.50), or a samosa turnover (85¢). Entrees are served with rice, dhal, and onion relish. Chicken curry or spicy vindaloo is $7.25; a keema muttar (minced beef with peas) is $7.25. Lamb entrees are $7.50 to $7.25. Fish masala (curry) is $7.50, and other seafood is more expensive. For dessert, gulab jaman, a deep-fried pastry in syrup, is good ($1.50). Or for more money ($10.95 to $16.95), you can feast on a complete dinner with appetizer, soup, entree, dessert, and beverage.

Open daily from noon to midnight. The luncheon special is also served daily, from noon to 3 p.m. Reservations for large parties only.

IRISH: The first thing you'll notice walking into **Molly Malone's Pub,** 287 Third Ave., at 23rd Street (tel. 725-8375), is the sawdust on the floor, and the second, the friendly banter of the bartender who greets the regulars and nonregulars alike with the same Irish charm. Molly's is the place to go in the winter, when the fireplace is kept crackling throughout those long nights. The bar runs almost the entire length of one wall, and is backed by wood beams crisscrossed on an off-white stucco wall giving the room a down-to-earth, relaxed feeling. Against the other wall, and flanking the fireplace, are sets of wood booths just perfect for quaffing a stein of Irish beer or sipping a cup of good Irish coffee.

For traditional Irish fare try the Cork Dublin Irish lamb stew, a combination of fresh vegetables and lamb in a thick sauce for $8.25. The roast leg of lamb with mint jelly is $8.75. For $8.50 you can try fish and chips Dublin style—filets of gray sole dipped in ale batter. All dinners come with salad and french fries. For the hearty appetite, try Molly Malone's shepherd's pie, at $8.25, which consists of ground beef sirloin with sauteed fresh vegetables, topped with mashed potatoes and baked. Of course dinner wouldn't be complete without Irish coffee, which Molly's serves for $3. And for dessert, try cheesecake, $2.75; or apple pie, with or without melted cheese, $2.75.

Lunch is served from 11:30 a.m. to 5 p.m. weekdays, and dinner from 5 p.m. until 2 a.m. On Saturday and Sunday, brunch is from noon until 5 p.m.

JAPANESE: Akasaka, 715 Second Ave., between 38th and 39th Streets (tel. 867-6410), is popular with locals and writers from nearby *New York* magazine. Akasaka is simplicity itself, with a red-and-white tiled floor, and a red-and-white sushi counter up front with red enamel lights above. Here you can watch sushi platters being made while you eat. In back there's a dining room with large rice-paper lanterns, tables covered with blue-and-white checkered tablecloths, and blue triangular graphics painted on the walls. Yakitori, three skewers of grilled chicken, is a good appetizer ($3.95). You can order sushi à la carte after 4:30 p.m., at $1 (for mackerel) to $2 (for tuna) apiece. Entrees include fish and shrimp tempura ($6.75), pork shu mai dumplings ($6.25), and katsudon deep-fried pork cutlets ($5.75). A Kirin or Asahi beer is $1.80, and there's a full bar.

Lunch is noon to 2:30 p.m. Monday to Friday, and dinner from 5 to 10 p.m. Open Saturday for dinner only. Closed Sunday. No reservations, but sometimes there is a wait.

There's a branch of **Larmen Dosanko**, a chain of Japanese noodle shops, at 329 Fifth Ave., between 32nd and 33rd Streets (tel. 686-9259). It's all day-glo orange, from the tiled floor to the Formica tables, but also spacious and modern. The noodles—fried, in soup, in soy sauce, or chilled—are tasty and different. And cheap! Nothing on Dosanko's menu costs more than the chef's daily special, which is $4.85. A bowl of larmen (noodles) in soup is $3.85; stir-fried with beef and vegetables, and with a salad, is about $4. Six pork dumplings with sauce (gyoza) are $2.85, or $4.45 with a salad. Or you can really stuff yourself: Japanese-style fried chicken, with salad, vegetable, and rice or noodles for $4.85. To drink, there are Japanese and American beers and wines for $1.10 to $1.75. Find out why there are over 12,000 Larmen Dosankos in Japan. They're fun, fast food!

The Fifth Avenue Larmen Dosanko is open from 11 a.m. to 10 p.m. Monday to Friday, and from noon to 8 p.m. on Saturday and Sunday.

JAPANESE/FRENCH: La Maison Japonaise, 334 Lexington Ave., at 39th Street (tel. 682-7375), is one of the most beautiful restaurants we've seen. On the street you'll see passersby looking in, entranced. The front window always has a huge, striking floral arrangement in it, the carpet and back wall are black, the table linens are plum, and the two rows of track lighting pull it all together with soft elegance. Oriental simplicity pervades, but the collection of French brass pots hung at the back are a clue to the restaurant's dual French-Japanese nature (only in New York!). Tastes like cinnamon and ginger in cream sauce are surprising, but worthwhile for the adventurous.

Lunch includes omelets such as spinach and cheddar cheese, eggplant, watercress, and sour cream with green chilis or caviar ($6.95 to $11.95), a cold ginger chicken salad ($8.50), curried pork à la Japonaise ($8.50), and quiches, chicken teryaki, and shu mai noodle dumplings, all priced at $7.95. The most expensive lunch is the hot seafood salad (shrimp, scallions, and vegetables, sauteed and tossed with soy sauce and sake) at $10.50. Most lunch entrees are priced from $7 to $12.

Dinner prices are slightly higher, and there are more entrees: chicken flambé with cinnamon, brandy, and madeira ($9.95), a lightly battered kakiage tempura ($9.25); and steak béarnaise, the most expensive dinner item at $12.95. Dinner appetizers like heart-of-palm salad ($3.95) and clear, spicy miso soup ($1.95) are good choices. Entrees come with a choice of tossed salad or a bean-sprout salad, both with a delicious vinaigrette and soy sauce dressing.

Desserts are Western concoctions—brandy Alexander pie ($2.50), glacé Dame Blanche (ice cream, fudge, and crème de cacão for $3.25), chocolate mousse ($1.95 and $3.25), crème caramel with strawberries and whipped cream ($2.50), raspberry sherbet ($1.50), and the Mount Fuji sundae with fudge sauce, crème de menthe, and coconut ($3.25).

La Maison Japonaise is open weekdays for lunch from noon to 2:30 p.m., and for dinner from 6 to 10:30 p.m. On Saturday dinner is from 6 to 10:30 p.m., and on Sunday from 5 to 9:30 p.m. Reservations suggested.

MEXICAN: White candles, red table linen, blue tiles, and a beamed ceiling make **Mexico Lindo,** 459 Second Ave., at 26th Street (tel. 679-3665), a convivial place. Amber lamps, a terracotta tiled floor, and attractive oil paintings add to the south-of-the-border atmosphere. And a strolling guitarist, Wednesday through Sunday nights (6:30 to 11 p.m.), will win your heart.

Menus are similar at lunch and dinner, except for price. There are 17 combination platters with favorites like tacos, chicken enchiladas with green sauce and sour cream, and tamales, priced from $3.95 to $4.50 at lunch and $5.75 to $6.95 at dinner. There's seafood too, including four spicy shrimp entrees for $5.75 at lunch and $7.25 at dinner. A half pitcher of sangría is $4.25 or $4.95 (depending on the meal), and $6.95 or $7.25 for a full pitcher. Flan for dessert is $1.25 at lunch and $1.75 at dinner.

Mexico Lindo serves lunch Monday from noon to 3 p.m., and then closes until dinner, served from 5 to 11 p.m. Tuesday through Thursday it's open from noon to 11 p.m., and on Friday to midnight (lunch prices are in effect until 3 p.m.). On Saturday dinner is 3 p.m. to midnight, and on Sunday to 11 p.m. Reservations not required.

Grab your topsiders, khaki slacks, and a striped shirt and join the rest of New York's yuppies at the **Lorango** Mexican restaurant and bar on Third Avenue at 24th Street (tel. 679-1122). The long, rectangular room offers plenty of opportunity for those up and coming to size up the competition. Large windows flank the street and provide ample lighting for those milling around the bar. Seating is minimal and the service can be brusque, but the restaurant serves up authentic Mexican food. Portions can be on the small size—so heartier appetites may want an appetizer plus main course.

For starters try the quesadillas at $3.75 and you get three soft flour tortillas filled with cheese. Single-entree dinners range from about $6.50 and up. The typical double-entree combination dinner—from a choice of tacos, enchiladas, tostadas, or burritos, with rice and beans on the side—is $7.75. Wash it down with Dos Equis beer for $2.50.

Lunch is served from 11:30 a.m. until 5 p.m., dinner from 5 p.m. until midnight, seven days a week.

MIDDLE EASTERN: Cedars of Lebanon, 39 E. 30th St., between Park and Madison Avenues (tel. 725-9251), takes its name from the national symbol of Lebanon. Under the green awning, you enter the first of its two rooms, the bar/lounge. The bar is black and padded, and the walls are covered with textured wallpaper. The dining room has a simple, spacious elegance. Chairs are cushioned in red, tables are covered in white linens, and the wallpaper has a gold-toned tree motif. Oil paintings hang on the walls.

A weekday lunch special includes soup, a choice of entree (the likes of shish kebab, lamb chops, and keftah kebab), baklava for dessert, and American coffee, for $6. There is also a dinner special for $12.50, with soup, appetizer, a choice of most of the entrees on the menu, any dessert, and American or Turkish coffee. Or you might try the mezza, or appetizers, instead of an entree. With pita bread, the mezza can be a full meal. Among them are hummus (mashed chickpeas with sesame), falafel (deep-fried vegetable burgers), and tabouli (chopped parsley, mint, and scallions), priced from $1.75 each. Prices for dinner à la carte range from $5 for grape leaves stuffed with minted lamb to $10 for a club steak (but who's eating American?).

Cedars of Lebanon is open daily from 11:45 a.m. to 11 p.m., till 3 a.m. on Friday and Saturday. The luncheon special is served Monday through Friday from 11:50 a.m. to 3 p.m. Reservations are suggested, especially for Friday and Saturday, when entertainment (dancers and musicians) starts at 10 p.m.

NATURAL FOOD: Near newly refurbished Union Square is **Dennis'**, 91 Fifth Ave., between 16th and 17th Streets (tel. 741-0770). Dennis' serves meat, like the natural hot dog (no nitrites or nitrates), with sauerkraut, mustard, a wholewheat bun, and mini-salad for $2.15. The food is imaginative and good. There are baked potatoes stuffed with tuna and mozzarella, taco, or pizza potato, at $3.60 each. Meatless veal parmigiana is $3.25; pastas like high-protein spaghetti and Chinese noodles are $3.10 each. All are served as "mini-meals" with soup or salad. There are sandwiches and salads for under $2.50, and daily homemade soups for $1.85. There's even organic popcorn (75¢ buttered), and delicious frozen yogurt ($1.05 and $1.45). Everything comes take-out style in Styrofoam, but the atmosphere is pleasant. There are lots of white patio chairs and tables, with large round rice-paper lanterns overhead. The ceiling is hung with green canvas stretched over white frames, so it almost looks like the deck of a ship.

Dennis' is open Monday to Friday from 10:30 a.m. to 7 p.m., and on Saturday from 11:30 a.m. to 6:30 p.m.

SPANISH: It may not be sunny Spain, but the authentic atmosphere at the **Olé** restaurant at 434 Second Ave., between 24th and 25th Streets (tel. 725-1953), will take you there for the space of one meal. Run and owned by the Lugares brothers, the restaurant features live entertainment every night except Monday. Patrons sometimes sing along to familiar tunes, and Pepe Lugares sometimes gets up on a table to display his talent for downing an entire decanter of wine in one long gulp.

The food here is simple, peasant-style cooking, served in generous portions. For lunch, try the Spanish red sausages with rice ($4.95) or the veal in wine sauce ($6.95). Shrimp in garlic sauce and a beautiful paella with chicken, sausages, clams, mussels, shrimp, and rice cost $6.50. For dinner, we suggest splitting one order of paella, served in a huge pot for $10.50, which is more than enough for two people. Dinner prices are slightly higher than lunch prices in general. Try the gazpacho soup (a cold vegetable soup) or the caldo gallego (a traditional peasant soup made with beans or other vegetables). Scallops in garlic sauce costs $10.75, and veal in wine sauce goes for the same price. For dessert, we recommend the pine nut cake, which is a moist, light delicacy for $2.50. Open 4 p.m. to 11 p.m., on Friday and Saturday till midnight.

STEAKHOUSES: Farnies Second Avenue Steak Parlor, 311 Second Ave., at 18th Street (tel. 228-9280), is well on its way to being a New York institution. For a thick juicy steak or barbecued ribs at reasonable prices, it's hard to beat. In the window is a beef chart—a sure sign of serious eating. Inside it's decorated for fun: the walls are carpeted, mirrored, and cluttered with memorabilia, including huge likenesses of Laurel and Hardy, Charlie Chaplin, and W. C. Fields, oversize coins, and authentic advertisements from the turn of the century. The bar has turned spools and the whole atmosphere is old New York—bustling and a little offbeat. Tables are covered with newsprint tablecloths, and red globe lights shed just enough light for you to see. Dinner entrees include chopped sirloin steak ($6.95), barbecued spare ribs or Dublin broiled steak ($7.95 each), and char-broiled chicken ($6.95). A large sirloin, filet mignon, lobster tail, or shrimp scampi entree, plus a choice of chicken, ribs, or sole (you figure out a combination) is $10.55. Dinner entrees come with a bottomless bowl of salad, garlic bread, and a choice of french fries, onion rings, baked potato, vegetable, or spaghetti. Lunch entrees come with a smaller salad and garlic bread, and are priced from $3.75 to $4.75 for hamburgers, omelets, ribs, steaks, sole, etc.

Farnies is open Monday to Thursday from 11:30 a.m. till midnight, on Friday till 1 a.m. On Saturday and Sunday it opens at 3 p.m. for dinner and closes at 1 a.m. on Saturday, at midnight on Sunday. There is free two-hour parking at dinner. Reservations suggested for parties of three or more only.

TEX/MEX: One of the hottest spots in town, **America,** 9–13 E. 18th St., between Fifth Avenue and Broadway (tel. 505-2110), is one of those places where people from all walks of life will find their niche, and have fun and a good meal at low prices. You'll find no sign outside so look instead for the raised star standard out front. The dining area is lit by track lights that accentuate the high ceilings and the art deco murals on the walls. Strips of red and white neon tubes stream along the center walkway that separates the dining room into two halves. Seating capacity is 400, and unlike many New York establishments, gives the diner ample elbow room. The atmosphere here is just plain fun. Dress is anywhere from New York sloppy to evening wear. Late nighters lounge around the raised bar in the back that stretches nearly the width of the room. Gaze around. On one wall the Statue of Liberty gazes down on New York. On the other you get a bird's-eye view of a farm.

The menu conjures up a taste of Americana, with a variety of dishes from all four corners of the country. Try the Tex-Mex fare with a generous portion of marinated beef grilled on charcoal, served with sour cream, salsa sauce, and tortillas for wrapping it all up. Or try the Cajun oyster po' boy sandwich, served with cole slaw and spuds for $6.95. Move over a few states and partake of fresh Tupelo catfish filet, fried in cornmeal for $9.95. A meal from a little farther north might be the Tuscaloosa BBQ pig-pull platter of boneless ribs for $8.95. The good old all-American hamburger is also available, and with a choice of toppings ($8.95).

Open daily from 11 a.m. to 3 a.m.

TIBETAN: The **Tibetan Kitchen,** 444 Third Ave., at 31st Street (tel. 679-6286), offers a varied menu of Tibetan food. There are only a few seats, but servings are generous and prices reasonable. Beef, lamb, and chicken entrees run from $5 to $7. Try the Himalayan khatsa—spicy hot cauliflower, fresh leeks, and bean curd, served cold on green leaf and hot bread—for $5.50. Or warm yourself up on a cold day with a cup of thang soup, a sort of spinach and egg-drop concoction that's delicious ($1.50). Another traditional Tibetan beverage is bocha, a buttered and salted tea ($2 a pot), which is a perfect dessert complement to deysee—a steamed sweet rice with raisins, served with cold yogurt ($1.75).

Open Monday to Friday from noon to 3 a.m., and on Saturday from 5:30 to 11:30 p.m. Closed Sunday.

JUST DESSERTS: **Café Caruso,** in the mall at the northeast corner of 33rd Street and Second Avenue (tel. 689-0067), is an attractive place for dessert—cakes as well as Gaslight ice cream—and coffee and cappuccino. The café is airy, modern, and clean—with blond slatted wood, bentwood chairs, mirrored walls, and track lighting. Single-scoop cones or cups are $1; a double-scoop, $1.75. A small sundae is $1.50; large, $2.25; and a banana split, $3.50. Toppings are 35¢. Cappuccino with whipped cream and Swiss chocolate, served in a china cup, is $2.50. A delicious moist lemon pound cake is $1 if you can get it—regulars skulk the shop waiting for it and buy the entire cake on the spot. Other delectable treats include double chocolate-chip layer cake ($2.75), and harvest pie with plums and peanuts ($2.25).

Open daily from about 1 to 10 p.m. or later.

AFTER-HOURS ENTERTAINMENT: Even the master of ceremonies may sound surprised to see people having dinner at **Good Times,** 449 Third Ave., at 31st Street (tel. 725-8130). People come to Good Times mostly for the floor shows. The attraction for us is the Tuesday audition night, when aspiring singers and comedians try out for the regular shows this small establishment puts on. Audition night is free (there isn't even much pressure to order lots of drinks), and there is some real talent. You might see a college kid honing a comedy routine, or a great torch singer singing her own songs. Restaurant people say that rock singer Pat Benatar got her start here.

Decoration is minimal: some framed posters and framed record jackets on the wall, including one by actress Cheryl Ladd. There are window seats tucked under brick arches with nice views of 31st Street, but for watching performers, sit at one of the platform tables covered with oilskin cloth. If you come around 8 p.m., you can meet the night's aspirants—they are invited at that time for a hamburger (you have to pay). The burger platter, a passable combination of lettuce, tomato, onion, fries, and pickle, is $5.50. Other entrees are $7.50 to $11.50, and a chef's salad is $5.95. A beer is $2.50; a small soda, $1.

Audition night on Tuesday starts at about 9:30 p.m. On other weeknights there's a $4 cover charge, but now you know better. Reservations are not necessary.

14. Brighton Beach, Brooklyn

If you're heading to Coney Island for a day at the beach or to visit the New York Aquarium, or if you simply have the time: find your way to Brooklyn's Brighton Beach, where fantastic food, drink, and a full evening's worth of entertainment can be had for less than $10. The thousands of Russian Jews who have settled here in recent years call it "Little Odessa by the Sea." On the weekends they go all-out, partying and eating at dozens of local, authentic Russian restaurants. For the price of a subway token, and with the patience for the ride, you can join them. Take the IND D train all the way to the end of the line, Brighton Beach. Stop in at any one of the following restaurants for some of the best food in the area.

The **Kavkas Restaurant,** 405 Brighton Beach Ave. (tel. 718/891-5400), serves authentic Georgian food, considered the finest cuisine in the Soviet Union. The clientele is a mix of Russian immigrants and other New Yorkers, and it's the kind of place where friends and relatives wander in, pull up a chair, and reach without asking for one of the dishes of exotic food piled on the tables. Start with the red caviar, served with pita bread ($3.30), or with Ukrainian borscht, served hot and full of beef, cabbage, potatoes, and sour cream ($2.80), one of the ten different soups. Then try the specialty of the house, shaslik: grilled chunks of lamb that arrive on a skewer the size of a small sword, accompanied by a mountain of fried potatoes and raw onion. The price is only $4.95. Other specialties, none of them over $5, include chicken Kiev, stuffed Ukrainian meat dumplings, and eggplant in walnut sauce. Things really heat up around 9 p.m., when a Russian band begins playing and the dance floor fills.

Open daily from 11 a.m. to 2 a.m. Entertainment nightly; reservations a must on Saturday.

More of the same can be found at **Primorski,** 282B Brighton Beach Ave. (tel. 718/891-3111). This is a somewhat fancy place: dark-blue walls adorned with triangular mirrors, and tables covered in white linen. Try some of the cold appetizers, such as cabbage with spring onions and apples ($1.50) or herring with onions, boiled potatoes, and vinaigrette ($1.85). House specialties include loolya kebab, ground meat with spices, grilled on skewers ($4.25); roast lamb with plums ($4.25); chicken shaslik ($4.25); and fish in walnut sauce ($4.25).

Owner Buba Khotovli has also instituted a "party" menu ($22 a head for groups of four or more on Saturday, slightly less on other nights) that features a bottle of domestic vodka or Lambrusco, every hors d'oeuvre on the menu, three or four main courses, and a basket of fruit. A daily lunch special offers soup, salad, one of the sixteen entrees, and coffee or tea for only $3.99.

Open daily from 11 a.m. to 2 a.m. Russian, Georgian, and Israeli music played nightly around 9 p.m.

Just up the street at the **Café Tashkent,** 306 Brighton Beach Ave. (tel. 718/934-8398), Uzbekian cooking is the specialty. There are six hearty soups to choose from daily, including lagman à la Uzbek, a huge bowl of vegetables, beef or lamb, homemade noodles, and broth topped with chopped scallions and parsley ($3.20) that's a meal in itself. A selection of 25 entrees includes everything from the meat-filled dumplings called chuchvara ($3.20) to roast pheasant ($10.90). At the conclusion of your meal, send your compliments to chef/owner Azad, who toils away by himself in the restaurant's tiny kitchen.

Open daily from 11 a.m. to 2 a.m. Music nightly starting around 9 p.m. Reservations strongly recommended on weekends.

Other spots to try in the neighborhood are the **Zodiac Restaurant,** 309 Brighton Beach Ave. (tel. 718/891-2000); **Sadko,** 129 Brighton Beach Ave. (tel. 718/372-3088); and the **National Restaurant,** 273 Brighton Beach Ave. (tel. 718/646-1225). Each is a delight.

15. Especially for Brunch

Sunday, after an evening out on the town, treat yourself to a late morning in bed and then join native New Yorkers in their favorite weekend pastime: brunch. Even at expensive restaurants, brunch can be a real bargain. In the restaurant section we included many places that offer special deals for this in-between meal, and we've listed them here for easy reference.

MIDTOWN WEST/TIMES SQUARE: **Landmark Tavern,** 626 Eleventh Ave., at 46th Street (tel. 757-8595).
    La Crêpe, 57 W. 56th St., between Fifth and Sixth Avenues (tel. 247-1136).
    Caramba!, 918 Eighth Ave., at 55th Street (tel. 245-7910).
    Cancún, 937 Eighth Ave., near 55th Street (tel. 307-7303).
    K.C. Place, 807 Ninth Ave., between 53rd and 54th Streets (tel. 246-4258).
    The **English Pub,** 900 Seventh Ave., between 56th and 57th Streets (tel. 265-4360).
    Arriba Arriba, 762 Ninth Ave., between 51st and 52nd Streets (tel. 489-0810).

MIDTOWN EAST: **Hobeau's,** 963 First Ave., corner of 53rd Street (tel. 421-2888).
    Knickers, 982 Second Ave., between 49th and 50th Streets (tel. 223-8821).
    Joe Burns's Restaurant and Art Gallery, 903 First Ave., at 51st Street (tel. 759-6696).
    Charley O's Bar and Grill, Citicorp Center (tel. 752-2102).
    Au Natural, 1043 Second Ave. at 55th Street (tel. 832-2922).

UPPER EAST SIDE AND YORKVILLE: **Mumbles,** 1622 Third Ave., at 91st Street (tel. 427-4355).
    The Green Kitchen, 1477 First Ave., corner of 77th Street (tel. 988-4163).
    T.G.I. Friday's, 1152 First Ave., at 93rd Street (tel. 832-8512).
    Martell's, 1469 Third Ave., at 83rd Street (tel. 861-6110).
    Ruppert's, 1662 Second Ave., between 84th and 85th Streets (tel. 831-1900).
    Camelback and Central, 1403 Second Ave., corner of 73rd Street (tel. 249-8380).
    Sarabeth's, 1295 Madison Ave., at 92nd Street (tel. 410-7335).
    Drake's Drum, 1629 Second Ave., between 84th and 85th Streets (tel. 988-2826).
    Nodeldini's, 1399 Madison Ave., at 97th Street (tel. 369-5677).
    Cockeyed Clams, 1673 Third Ave., at 94th Street (tel. 831-4121).
    Squid Roe, 1468 Second Ave., at 77th Street (tel. 249-4666).
    Rascal's, 1286 First Ave., at 69th Street (tel. 734-2862).
    Agora, 1530 Third Ave., at 87th Street (tel. 860-3425).

UPPER WEST SIDE: **Teacher's,** 2249 Broadway, between 80th and 81st Streets (tel. 787-3500).
    Hanratty's, 732 Amsterdam Ave., between 95th and 96th Streets (tel. 864-4224).
    Shelter, 2180 Broadway, corner of 77th Street (tel. 362-4360).
    Dobson's, 341 Columbus Ave., at 76th Street (tel. 362-0100).
    Marvin Gardens, 2274 Broadway, between 81st and 82nd Streets (tel. 799-0578).

LINCOLN CENTER: **Opera Espresso,** 1928 Broadway at 65th Street (tel. 799-3050).
    Crêpe Inn Plus, 332 W. 58th St., between Eighth and Ninth Avenues (tel. 757-7241) (Saturday only).

168 NEW YORK ON $45 A DAY

Los Panchos, 71 W. 71st St., between Columbus Avenue and Central Park West (tel. 864-7336).
Captain Nemo's, 137 W. 72nd St., between Columbus and Amsterdam Avenues (tel. 595-5600).
Eclair, 141 W. 72nd St., between Columbus and Amsterdam Avenues (tel. 873-7700).
Lincoln Square Coffee Shop, 2 Lincoln Square, between 65th and 66th Streets (tel. 799-4000).

PENNSYLVANIA STATION/CHELSEA: Miss Ruby's Café, 135 Eighth Ave., between 16th and 17th Streets (tel. 620-4055).
Dunleavy's, 236 Eighth Ave., at 22nd Street (tel. 242-8255).
Gefen's Kosher Dairy, 297 Seventh Ave., between 26th and 27th Streets (tel. 929-6476) (Sunday only).

GREENWICH VILLAGE: Ye Waverly Inn, 16 Bank St., at Waverly Place (tel. 243-9396).
The Lion's Head, 59 Christopher St., just off Seventh Avenue South (tel. 929-0670).
The Cottonwood Café, 415 Bleecker St., between West 11th and Bank Streets (tel. 924-6271).
Montana Eve, 140 Seventh Ave. South, between 10th and Charles Streets (tel. 242-1200).
Blazing Salads, 228 W. 4th St., just west of Seventh Avenue South (tel. 929-3432).
David's Pot Belly, 98 Christopher St., between Bleecker and Bedford Streets (tel. 243-9614).
The Cedar Tavern, 82 University Pl., between 11th and 12th Streets (tel. 929-9089).
Covent Garden, 133 W. 13th St., between Sixth and Seventh Avenues (tel. 675-0020).
The Big Dish, 283 W. 12th St., corner of West 4th Street (tel. 243-9898).
Sazerac House, 533 Hudson St., corner of Charles Street (tel. 989-0313).
Sandolino's, 9 Jones St., off West 4th Street (tel. 255-6669).
The Pink Teacup, 42 Grove St., near Bleecker Street (tel. 807-6755).

SOHO: Food, 127 Prince St., corner of Wooster Street (tel. 473-8790).
Tennessee Mountain, 143 Spring St., at Wooster Street (tel. 431-3993).
Cupping Room Café, 359 West Broadway, between Broome and Grand Streets (tel. 925-2898).
Spring Street Natural Restaurant and Bar, 149 Spring St., between West Broadway and Wooster Street (tel. 966-0290).
Prince Street Bar and Restaurant, 125 Prince St., corner of Wooster Street (tel. 228-8130).
The Ear Inn, 326 Spring St., between Washington and Greenwich Streets (tel. 226-9060).
Elephant and Castle, 183 Prince St., between Sullivan and Thompson Streets (tel. 260-3600).
Central Falls, 478 West Broadway, near West Houston (tel. 475-3333).

LOWER MANHATTAN/TRIBECA: Bridge Café, 279 Water St., at Dover Street (tel. 227-3344).
Smoke Stacks Lightnin', 380 Canal Street, at West Broadway (tel. 226-0485).

211 West Broadway, at Franklin Street (tel. 925-7202).
riverrun, 176 Franklin St., between Greenwich and Hudson Streets (tel. 966-3894).
how's bayou, 355 Greenwich St., at Harrison Street (tel. 925-5404).
Ham Heaven, 49 Warren St., between West Broadway and Greenwich Street (tel. 513-7224).
Hors d'Oeuvrerie, One World Trade Center (tel. 938-1111).
Front Street Restaurant, 228 Front St., between Beekman Street and Peck Slip (tel. 406-1560).

CHINATOWN: **Nom Wah Tea Parlor,** 13 Doyers St., near Pell Street (tel. 962-6047).
China Royal, 17 Division St., off the Bowery (tel. 226-0788).
Hee Seung Fung, 46 Bowery, between Canal Street and Chatham Square (tel. 374-1319).
Hop Kwan, 20 Catherine St. (tel. 285-9183).

LITTLE ITALY: **Ferrara's,** 195 Grand St., between Mott and Mulberry Streets (tel. 226-6150).
Caffè Roma, 385 Broome St., at Mulberry Street (tel. 226-8413).
Primavera Caffè, 51 Spring St., at Mulberry Street (tel. 226-8421).

LOWER EAST SIDE / EAST VILLAGE: **Ratner's,** 138 Delancey St., between Norfolk and Suffolk Streets (tel. 677-5588).
Yonah Schimmel, 137 E. Houston St., between Eldridge and Forsyth Streets (tel. 477-2858).
The Pharmacy, 141 Avenue of the Americas, at 9th Street (tel. 260-4798).
Pig, 12 First Ave., near Houston Street (tel. 982-1089).
103 Second Avenue, at 6th Street (tel. 533-0769).

MURRAY HILL / GRAMERCY PARK: **Orchid,** 81 Lexington Ave., at 26th Street (tel. 889-0960).
Shelter, 540 Second Ave., at 30th Street (tel. 684-4207).
Mumbles, 603 Second Ave., at 33rd Street (tel. 889-0750).
Sarge's, 548 Third Ave., between 36th and 37th Streets (tel. 679-0442).
R.J.'s Saloon, 220 Madison Ave., at 37th Street (tel. 889-5553).
David Copperfield, 322 Lexington Ave., between 38th and 39th Streets (tel. 684-8227).
Hee Seung Fung (HSF), 578 Second Ave., near 32nd Street (tel. 689-6969).
Kitty Hawk, 565 Third Ave., between 36th and 37th Streets (tel. 661-7406).
Earth Angel Natural Café, 611 Second Ave., between 33rd and 34th Streets (tel. 684-9637).
Pete's Tavern, 66 Irving Pl., at 18th Street (tel. 473-7676).
Pie in the Sky, 194 Third Ave., between 17th and 18th Streets (tel. 505-5454).
Molly Malone's Pub, 287 Third Ave., at 23rd Street (tel. 725-8375).

16. Around the Clock

New York City is the place that never stops. When a craving for pastrami on rye, bagels and lox, a hamburger, or an honest-to-goodness breakfast strikes at 5 a.m., chances are that a place is right around the corner to satiate your munchies. And for the ultimate in convenience, many of them deliver for free, so ask. Listed here are 24-hour (or close) eateries; for full details, see their write-ups in the restaurant sections.

MIDTOWN WEST/TIMES SQUARE: Market Diner, 572 Eleventh Ave., at 43rd Street (tel. 244-6033). Open 24 hours daily.

MIDTOWN EAST: Jumbo Bagels & Bialys, 1070 Second Ave., between 54th and 55th Streets (tel. 355-6185).

UPPER EAST SIDE/YORKVILLE: The Green Kitchen, 1477 First Ave., at 77th Street (tel. 988-4163). Open 24 hours daily.

Michael's Restaurant-Café, 1412 First Ave., between 74th and 75th Streets (tel. 772-2430).

UPPER WEST SIDE: College Inn, 2896 Broadway, between 112th and 113th Streets (tel. 663-0257).

GREENWICH VILLAGE: David's Pot Belly, 98 Christopher St., between Bleecker and Bedford Streets (tel. 243-9614). Open Sunday to Thursday from 11 a.m. to 5:30 a.m., on Friday and Saturday till 6 a.m.

The Pink Teacup, 42 Grove St., near Bleecker Street (tel. 807-6755). On Friday and Saturday only, open 24 hours (till midnight on Sunday).

CHINATOWN: Wo Hop, 17 Mott St., between Worth Street and Park Place (tel. 766-9160). Open 24 hours daily.

Lin's Garden, 53 Bayard St., corner of Elizabeth Street (tel. 962-9085). Open till 6 a.m. daily.

Wo On, 16 Mott St. (tel. 962-6475). Open until 4 a.m.

LOWER EAST SIDE/EAST VILLAGE: Kiev International Restaurant, 117 Second Ave., at 7th Street (tel. 674-4040). Open 24 hours daily.

Around the Clock Café, 8 Stuyvesant Pl. (tel. 598-0402).

Hiro Gallery-Café, 112 First Ave., near 7th Street (tel. 777-1250). Open until 4 a.m.

103 Second Avenue, at 6th Street (tel. 533-0769). Open 24 hours.

MURRAY HILL/GRAMERCY PARK: East Bay, 491 First Ave., at 29th Street (tel. 683-7770). Open 24 hours daily.

Tivoli, 515 Third Ave., between 34th and 35th Streets (tel. 689-6856). Open 24 hours daily.

Sarge's, 548 Third Ave., between 36th and 37th Streets (tel. 679-0442). Open 24 hours daily.

17. Early-Bird Dinner Specials

Some restaurants offer dinner at lower prices during certain hours—hard-to-find specials dear to the hearts of budget-wise travelers. Listed here are a few good bets.

UPPER EAST SIDE: The Green Kitchen, 1477 First Ave., at 77th Street (tel. 988-4163).

GREENWICH VILLAGE: 14 Christopher Street, at 14 Christopher St., between Sixth and Seventh Avenues off Gay Street (tel. 620-9594).

18. Big-Splurge Restaurants
Here are some special choices to consider for a big night on the town.

MIDTOWN WEST / TIMES SQUARE: Café Un, Deux, Trois, 123 W. 44th St., between Sixth and Seventh Avenues (tel. 354-4148).
   Mama Leone's, 239 W. 48th St., between Broadway and Eighth Avenue (tel. 586-5151).

MIDTOWN EAST: Mimi's, 984 Second Ave., at 52nd Street (tel. 688-4692).
   Oyster Bar, in Grand Central Station (lower concourse level), 42nd Street, between Vanderbilt and Lexington Avenues (tel. 490-6650).
   Hatsuhana, 17 E. 48th St., between Fifth and Madison Avenues (tel. 355-2967).
   Kenny's Steak Pub, 565 Lexington Ave., between 50th and 51st Streets (tel. 355-0666).
   Auberge Suisse, Citicorp Center (tel. 421-1420).
   Les Tournebroches, Citicorp Center (tel. 758-3265).
   Oscar's Salt of the Sea II, Citicorp Center (tel. 371-2201).
   Peng Teng, 219 E. 44th St., between Second and Third Avenues (tel. 682-8050).
   Beijing Duck House, 144 E. 52nd St., between Lexington and Third Avenues (tel. 759-8260).

UPPER EAST SIDE/YORKVILLE: Camelback and Central, 1403 Second Ave., at 73rd Street (tel. 249-8380).
   Agora, 1530 Third Ave., at 87th Street (tel. 860-3425).
   Ruc, 312 E. 72nd St., between First and Second Avenues (tel. 650-1611).
   Kleine Konditorei, 234 E. 86th St., between Second and Third Avenues (tel. 737-7130).

UPPER WEST SIDE: Dobson's, 341 Columbus Ave., at 76th Street (tel. 362-0100).
   Marvin Gardens, 2274 Broadway, between 81st and 82nd Streets (tel. 799-0578).
   Faculty House, Columbia University, 400 W. 117th St., near Amsterdam Avenue (tel. 865-4700).
   La Tablita, 65 W. 73rd St., just off Columbus Avenue (tel. 724-9595).

LINCOLN CENTER: Captain Nemo's, 137 W. 72nd St., between Columbus and Amsterdam Avenues (tel. 595-5600).

PENNSYLVANIA STATION/CHELSEA: Centro Vasco, 208 W. 23rd St., between Eighth and Ninth Avenues (tel. 741-1408).

GREENWICH VILLAGE: Covent Garden, 133 W. 13th St., between Sixth and Seventh Avenues (tel. 675-0020).
   The Big Dish, 283 W. 12th St., at West 4th Street (tel. 243-9898).

Trattoria Villaggio, 192 Bleecker St., between Avenue of the Americas and MacDougal Street (tel. 533-5414).

LOWER MANHATTAN/TRIBECA: Capsouto Frères, 451 Washington St., at Watts Street (tel. 966-4900).

Chapter III

THE TOP SIGHTS AND CULTURAL ATTRACTIONS

1. Sights Not To Be Missed
2. Museums
3. Galleries, Theater, Concerts, Opera, and Dance
4. Entertainment
5. Zoos and Botanical Gardens
6. Sports and Recreational Facilities
7. More Sights
8. Churches and Synagogues
9. Historic Houses

NEW YORK ALMOST BECAME the permanent capital of the United States after the American Revolution, although that honor went farther south for political reasons. Today New York is viewed by many as the artistic and cultural capital of the country, if not the world. We think New York's art and entertainment are simply the best anywhere! You could take years and not exhaust the city's diverse treasures, but since you're here for only a short time, we've planned this chapter as your key to unlocking as much as you can. Don't be surprised if you're tired—but happy—at the end of a sightseeing day, because just walking around this on-the-go city is a wonderful adventure. If we sound biased, we are, and avidly so. Do as much exploring as you can, and you'll see why!

Don't let stories about how expensive New York is intimidate you. Yes, it can be costly here, but the city is a never-ending show packed with loads of freebies from street musicians (the good and the outlandish) to the U.N. General Assembly. In fact your biggest expense might be for a sturdy pair of walking shoes, for this chapter will take you on those freebies, from a tour of the venerable New York Stock Exchange on Wall Street, to swank midtown art galleries, to upper Central Park.

We've put almost 300 places on your list to visit. To help you choose among them, here's a quick outline of how we've arranged everything.

Sights Not To Be Missed: These are what we consider New York's best: things not be missed by anyone lucky enough to visit the city.

Museums/Galleries, Theater, Concerts, Opera, and Dance: New York City is recognized throughout the world as a leader in cultural happenings. Not only are some of the most prestigious museums in the nation and the world located here, but Manhattan art galleries are known for setting trends in the art world.

Entertainment: We have tips for beating the skyrocketing costs of movies, as well as for seeing a taping of a favorite TV show or a pilot series.

Zoos and Botanical Gardens: The Bronx Zoo is superb; the Central Park Children's Zoo endearing. The New York Botanical Garden is astonishingly beautiful.

Sports and Recreational Facilities: If you haven't joined the national fitness craze, we'll show you how it's done in New York. Look at all the business suits with sneakers—walking (like you'll be doing) is a popular exercise here. And we'll tell you how to see your favorite sports star or team.

More Sights: For those with more time, or a penchant for the different.

Churches and Synagogues: New York's melting pot has filled the city with buildings sacred to countless sects and faiths. Many of these buildings are noteworthy for their history and architecture.

Historic Houses: Beneath that famed Manhattan skyline you can still find Old New York, in buildings and homes preserved by concerned citizens and the city government.

Have fun!

1. Sights Not To Be Missed

WORLD TRADE CENTER: They have none of the romance inherent in the Empire State Building, but the twin towers of the World Trade Center—each 110 stories and 1350 feet tall—are imposing and impressive. On any given day nearly 130,000 people pass through the center's revolving doors—50,000 to work, another 80,000 as tourists. Many of the latter come to marvel at the breathtaking panorama from the observation deck on the 107th floor in the No. 2 World Trade Center building—a quarter of a mile in the air—and from the rooftop platform just above it (open only when the weather permits; tel. 466-7377). The vista can't be beat: on a crystal-clear day you can see 60 miles in every direction. Diagrams on the floor-to-ceiling windows identify buildings and other points of interest. The ride up is swift (at 20 miles per hour, it takes just under a minute) and silent. In addition to the view there's a display on the history of trade, a souvenir shop, and a classy fast-food snackbar with a stupendous view.

The observation deck is open daily from 9:30 a.m. to 9:30 p.m., except on Thanksgiving and Christmas Eve (9:30 a.m. to 5 p.m.) and Christmas and New Year's Day (11 a.m. to 7 p.m.). Admission is $2.95 for adults, $1.50 for children ages 6 to 12 and individuals over 62, and free to children under 6.

Down below the concourse, underneath the buildings, there's a complete city in itself, with restaurants and shops. There's also a pleasant, if windy, outdoor plaza with benches and plants centered around a large fountain and a huge bronze sculpted globe. It's a pleasant place to picnic.

To get there, take the IRT–Seventh Avenue subway or the BMT subway to Cortlandt Street; or the IND–Eighth Avenue subway to the Chambers Street–World Trade Center Station. Located at Liberty, Church, Chambers, and Vesey Streets.

EMPIRE STATE BUILDING: When it opened its doors in 1931, the 102-story Empire State Building, on Fifth Avenue between 33rd and 34th Streets, was the tallest building in the world and was often called "The Eighth Wonder of the

World," "The Everest on Fifth Avenue," or "The Miracle on 34th Street." Depression-struck New Yorkers scrimped for weeks to save the then-$1 admission fee.

It no longer is the tallest building in the world, of course (it was eclipsed by two Chicago skyscrapers and the twin-towered World Trade Center downtown), but it remains one of the most beloved of the city's buildings, and a symbol of romantic skylines everywhere.

It's difficult to imagine a picture of New York's skyline without the profile of the 1250-foot tower and familiar silver spire. Each year more than 1.75 million tourists flock to the building's observation decks on the 86th and 102nd floors, where on a clear day the view is a spectacular one of 60 miles or more. The building provides an entirely different vista of the city from the view at the World Trade Center tower; from here, you're right in the middle of a concrete forest of skyscrapers, looking down on them. The viewing area on the 86th floor has been opened up with a raised walkway platform backed by mirrors, and you can venture outside to the promenade if you wish. On the 102nd floor, viewing is from the inside only, through round porthole windows.

Take one of the building's elevators to the observation deck any day of the year, from 9:30 a.m. to midnight (last admissions before 11:25 p.m.). Cost is $3 for adults, $2.60 for students with identification, $1.75 for children under 12 and senior citizens. Summer days and weekends all year long are especially crowded, so you might want to try a weekday, or better still, a star-studded evening. If you've got children along, you might also want to stop in at the **Guinness World Record Exhibit Hall,** on the concourse level (open from 9:30 a.m. to 6 p.m. daily; $3 for adults, $2 for children). See Chapter VIII for details.

STATUE OF LIBERTY: Liberty Island is temporarily closed to the public until July 4, 1986, while major restoration work on the statue, which began in 1984, is under way. This is the statue's first major overhaul since 1938.

The statue, a gift from France, welcomes to America the world's "homeless, tempest-tossed . . . huddled masses yearning to breathe free." She's 152 feet tall, weighs 18,000 pounds, has a 35-foot waist and a 4½-foot nose. Since she was shipped to the United States in 214 crates and erected in 1886, she has stood in New York's lower harbor as a symbol of freedom and a lady of hope for the country's immigrants.

When the island reopens, be sure to visit the **American Museum of Immigration,** located inside the statue's base. The museum offers a picture of America's immigrants, complete with artifacts, slides, and evocative black-and-white photographs of the country's famous and obscure immigrants. There are also films shown daily, although schedules are not available in advance.

To get to Liberty Island, take a Circle Line boat leaving from Battery Park (at the bottom tip of Manhattan; take the IRT–Seventh Avenue local subway to South Ferry station, the IRT–Lexington Avenue express subway to Bowling Green, or the BMT local to the Whitehall Street–South Ferry Station). At this writing, the boat will leave every hour (every half-hour in July and August) from 10 a.m. to 4 p.m., and the round-trip fare is $2 for adults, $1 for children under 12. The trip takes 45 minutes if you stay on the boat, or if you wander around the small park, allow at least one hour and 45 minutes. The island will be open every day, but call 269-5755 for exact times and more information.

UNITED NATIONS: Like a sea-green monolith, the Secretariat building at the United Nations, on First Avenue between 42nd and 49th Streets (tel. 754-7713), towers over a white marble plaza with the grandeur befitting its international status. Built on land that is internationally owned, it's the meeting place for delegates from over 150 nations, who discuss everything from disarmament to fishing rights.

General Assembly meetings are sometimes open to the public, and admission is free. Check the *New York Times* or call for information about meetings. Tickets are issued on a first-come, first-served basis, and meetings are sometimes cancelled on short notice.

The U.N. also offers a guided tour of its huge assembly halls, decorated with donations from Scandinavian countries. Your tour guide will probably speak more than one language, and will describe the U.N.'s history from its inception. Tours are given every 15 minutes from 9 a.m. to 4:45 p.m. daily. Admission is $3 for adults, $1.75 for college and high school students, and $1.25 for children in the ninth grade and below. Children under 5 are not admitted.

The U.N. also shows free films about its history and about different U.N. projects. Call for a schedule.

LINCOLN CENTER FOR THE PERFORMING ARTS: New York City has nothing more impressive than Lincoln Center. It's home to the city's premier performing artists—the Metropolitan Opera, the New York City Opera, the New York Philharmonic, the New York City Ballet, and the Juilliard School of Music. It's a complex of eight tremendous theaters separated artfully by fountains, cafés, and tree-filled parks which stretches in length from 62nd to 66th Streets and in width from Amsterdam to Columbus Avenues. When you walk up the steps to the central plaza, the noise of the traffic fades and there is a sense that this is an island untouched by the city's commotion. It's worth a visit just to sit on the fountain's edge and watch the sleek and glittery theater-goers gather outside during the intermission, or to see the two immense and colorful Chagalls behind the glass facade of the Metropolitan Opera House.

The construction of Lincoln Center in the 1960s—at a cost of about $165 million—was surrounded by controversy. It transformed what was once a sprawling ghetto into a prime real estate area, but also increased traffic. Architects and architectural critics alike debated endlessly and angrily over whether to build it in the classical or modern style. What finally emerged was a blend of both.

The 2800-seat **New York State Theater** (at the left side of the plaza), designed for ballet and musical theater, is the most clearly classical building. It has a lobby decorated lavishly in the baroque style, and above that there's a grand foyer with decorative metal balcony railings, colored chain drapery, and a gold velvet ceiling.

The **Metropolitan Opera House**, also built in classical style, has a sensuous auditorium of red and gold, but most noteworthy here are the Chagalls in the front lobby facing the central plaza.

Avery Fisher Hall (on the right side of the plaza), built for musical performances, was the most architecturally controversial because of its widely publicized acoustical problems. Rebuilt several times, the building finally emerged as a mix of modern and classical styles. Its auditorium is a classic European rectangle, but its simple flat planes derive from modern architectural notions. These three buildings, separated by an open plaza with a fountain, are banked by five other theaters, including **Alice Tully Hall** and the **Vivian Beaumont Theater.**

This cultural playground should not be missed by anyone visiting the city. Performances are expensive, but anyone can wander in and out of the buildings, or for the price of a drink, sit in one of the outdoor cafés or indoor restaurants. There are also one-hour tours every day for $5.25 for adults, $4.75 for students, and $3 for children 14 and under. The schedule changes daily, so call 877-1800, ext. 512, before 10 a.m. the day you plan to visit. A special program, Meet-the-Artists, offers visitors a chance to talk with some of the performers. For information, call 877-1800, ext. 547.

Nestled behind the Metropolitan Opera House is the **New York Public Library at Lincoln Center** (the Library and Museum of the Performing Arts), 111 Amsterdam Ave., near 65th Street (tel. 870-1630). On the first floor are four exhibition galleries and an auditorium which often offers free performances. The second floor has a projection room for films, and the third, a gallery collection of old clippings, photos, playbills, and costumes. There are research libraries with large and varied collections of material on dance, music, and theater. It also has records, earphones, and turntables available for public use. Open Tuesday through Saturday from 10 a.m. to 6 p.m., on Monday and Thursday until 9 p.m., and on Friday from noon to 6 p.m. Closed Sunday.

ROCKEFELLER CENTER: To see Rockefeller Center is to see a microcosm of New York. Skyscrapers, plazas, stores, and theaters all come together between 47th and 50th Streets from Fifth to Sixth Avenues in this magnificent complex—America's first and foremost urban mall. Unlike Lincoln Center, which serves only the arts, Rockefeller Center is multidimensional. A promenade lined with stores and offices leads to Rockefeller Center's famous sunken ice-skating rink, marked by an immense gold-colored statue of *Prometheus*. This winter playground becomes a festive outdoor café in the summer. At the center of the mall is a cluster of skyscrapers capped with rooftop cafés and gardens that offer spectacular views of Manhattan. One of the most noteworthy structures is the **RCA Building,** which has a magnificent black granite lobby lined with murals by José Maria Sert. But most impressive is the celebrated **Radio City Music Hall.** It has a 6000-seat theater and 60-foot-high lobby. On one wall is Ezra Winter's richly gold-and-bronze painting *Fountain of Youth,* and on the staircase is a perfectly patterned art deco rug. Taken as a whole, the building is empowered with all the grandeur of the decade in which it was built—the 1930s.

The theater's productions are as grandiose as its architecture. There are concerts, ice extravaganzas, the traditional Rockettes shows, and at Christmas and Easter special 90-minute spectaculars.

No view of New York is complete without seeing this mall. And unlike many of the city's attractions, Rockefeller Center can be enjoyed inexpensively. Tickets for performances at Radio City start at $18, but for only $3.95 there's a guided tour of the theater that might prove just as entertaining. For information, call 246-4600, ext. 263. There's also an observation roof on the 70th floor of the RCA Building at 30 Rockefeller Plaza (tel. 489-2947). At 850 feet (260 meters) above street level, it offers a spectacular, 360-degree view of the city and surrounding areas. Tickets are available at the 65th-floor sales desk of the RCA Building—a 37-second elevator ride—every day, April through September from 10 a.m. to 9 p.m., October through March to 7 p.m. Admission to the rooftop is $3.25 for adults and $1.75 for children under 12; but a rate increase is expected.

TRUMP TOWER: One of the newest buildings in the city, and certainly one of the most spectacular, glamorous, and exciting to visit, is the Trump Tower on Fifth Avenue between 56th and 57th Streets. The tall glass-sided building is primarily a residence for tenants capable of shelling out upward of three-quarters of million for an apartment. But the best part is a gorgeous pink-marble lobby and atrium where browsers can stop in at expensive shops and just look around. There is something so New York about the Trump Tower that we definitely recommend a visit.

NEW YORK STOCK EXCHANGE: At the heart of Wall Street—so named because in 1653 the Dutch governor, Peter Stuyvesant, ordered that a wall of thick planks be constructed to protect the city from marauding Indians from the north—lies the New York Stock Exchange. The forerunner of the present day Exchange was founded in 1792 by 24 brokers who sealed the bargains with a mere handshake. Times have indeed changed, as any visitor to the Exchange will see firsthand. From the gallery overlooking the floor of the Exchange you can watch the frenetic and seemingly chaotic trading from 10 a.m. to 4 p.m. Monday through Friday. There is a taped explanation of the floor activities, and audio-visual exhibits and a short film presentation of the Exchange's history and present-day operations.

The Exchange is located at 20 Broad St., off Wall Street, on the third floor. For groups of more than ten, reservations are recommended: phone 623-5168. You can get there on either the IRT–Seventh Avenue or the IRT–Lexington Avenue trains; get off at the Wall Street station.

COOPER UNION FOUNDATION BUILDING: The brownstone building at 41 Cooper Square (tel. 254-6374), at Third Avenue and East 7th Street, is today a tuition-free school of art, architecture, and engineering. It was founded by Peter Cooper, an industrialist and philanthropist whose early poverty prevented him from gaining an education, and spurred him in later years to begin the first privately endowed, tuition-free college in the country. The building, which opened in 1859, is technologically interesting—it was among the first anywhere to use rolled-iron beams in construction, which earned it the designation as a forerunner to the modern skyscraper. It is also of political and historical interest. It provided New York City with its first free reading room, and the building's "Great Hall" (which seats about 950), was once the largest public auditorium in the city. That hall was the site of the first free public lecture series in the nation, and it has been a mecca for debate. It drew Abraham Lincoln arguing against the extension of slavery, Susan B. Anthony calling for women's suffrage, Mark Twain, Ulysses S. Grant, Theodore Roosevelt, and Margaret Mead, among many others. It was here that the campaign to overthrow the New York Tweed Ring was launched and here that a meeting leading to the establishment of the National Association for the Advancement of Colored People was held. The three-nights-a-week music, poetry, and lecture series—and the roster of notable speakers—continues today. Closed Friday, Saturday, and Sunday in the summer. Call for scheduled events.

SOUTH STREET SEAPORT: In these days of telecommunication and air travel, it's easy to forget that New York rose to its present greatness from its original role as the nation's greatest seaport. At the newly restored South Street Seaport, located way downtown along Fulton and Water Streets and on Piers 15, 16, and 17 on the East River, that heritage is preserved in a revitalized area that contains one of the city's most exciting educational and recreational attractions. As you explore the Seaport's all-pedestrian cobblestone streets, restaurants, specialty stores, public terraces with waterfront views, and restored 19th-century rowhouses, you'll be caught up in the whole new spirit of enterprise and imagination that has magically brought the old port back to life.

Your tour should begin at the Pilot House on Pier 16, where you can purchase an admission ticket to the South Street Seaport Museum that includes a guided walking tour of the historic district and antique ships, and admission to the Seaport Gallery ($4 for adults, $3 for senior citizens, and $2 for children under 12). You might also want to take in *The Seaport Experience*, a multi-screen, multimedia entertainment at 210 Front St. in the Trans-Lux Seaport

THE TOP SIGHTS 179

Theater. Complete with seaspray and fog, the presentation ($3.75 for adults, $2.50 for children under 12) provides a fine introduction to the Seaport's past and present and the ships that have docked at its piers. Call 608-6696 for show times.

On the same museum block of new and renovated buildings as the theater, visit the **Seaport Gallery,** 215 Water St., for a schematic indoor tour of the area's historic buildings. See Chapter VII for a full description of the shops in the Museum Block, along **Cannon's Walk,** a charming interior courtyard tucked away in the center of the block, and along **Fulton Street,** named for Robert Fulton, inventor of the steamboat who inaugurated the Fulton Ferry to Brooklyn at the foot of the street. Also on Fulton Street is **Schermerhorn Row,** an architectural treasure of a red brick blockfront dating back to 1811.

The festive-looking three-story brick-and-granite building occupying the block bordered by Fulton, Front, Beekman, and South Streets is the fourth **Fulton Market Building** on this site since 1822. Colored with the vitality and rich confusion of traditional market activity, the new Fulton Market incorporates the stalls of honest-to-goodness fresh fish and seafood merchants (along South Street) as well as an extraordinary variety of restaurants, outdoor cafés, and food shops. Just like the good old days, only better.

The tang of salty air will lead you across South Street to the **piers** where the old ships are moored: the four-masted steel bark **Peking** and the U.S. Coast Guard lightship **Ambrose.** You can also take a 90-minute excursion on the **Andrew Fletcher,** a new sidewheel paddle ship modeled after 19th-century excursion boats. (Andrew Fletcher was the name of a father and son who were leading builders of sidewheel engines in the latter half of the 19th century.) The cost of the four-times-daily excursion is $5 for adults, $3 for children. Call 964-9082 for information.

Finally, you might cap off your trip to the Seaport with a visit to the brand-new **Pier 17 Pavilion,** a three-story glass-and-steel structure on the water's edge. Inside are more than 100 shops and restaurants; each floor has an outdoor promenade, and the top floor offers spectacular views of the Statue of Liberty, Brooklyn Bridge, and waterborne traffic on the East River.

Most Seaport attractions are open from 10 a.m. to 5 p.m. daily, except Thanksgiving, Christmas, and New Year's Days, with ship hours shorter during the winter. Call S-E-A-P-O-R-T for more information. To get there, take the IRT–Lexington Avenue express no. 4 or no. 5 train, or the IRT–Seventh Avenue express no. 2 or no. 3 train, to Fulton Street and walk east toward the waterfront.

STATEN ISLAND FERRY: The ferry is probably the best deal in town, and certainly one of the most restful things any tour-weary visitor can do. For a mere 25¢ you can take a five-mile, 25-minute voyage and watch tugs nosing tankers and sun sparkling off the water, gaze on the shadowy silhouette of the Verrazano Narrows Bridge, glide past the Statue of Liberty and Governor's Island, and listen to the cry of gulls. Day or night, the view of the Manhattan skyline from the ferry is superb.

The ferry runs every half hour from 9:30 a.m. to 9:30 p.m., then every hour until the next morning. With a car, the trip costs $2 from the Manhattan side and $1.75 from the Staten Island side, plus 25¢ per person.

To get to the ferry, take the IRT–Seventh Avenue local subway to South Ferry, the IRT–Lexington Avenue express to Bowling Green, or the BMT local to the Whitehall Street–South Ferry station.

CHINATOWN: Tucked below Greenwich Village and Little Italy is Chinatown

—smaller than its San Francisco counterpart but no less charming. Many of its residents are recent immigrants, and there's a sense in this area that English is a second language. Bordered by Canal Street to the north and Worth Street to the south, stretching west from the Bowery, its narrow, winding streets are packed with shops selling Oriental clothing, jewelry, and art, and with food stores selling herbs, teas, and fresh fish—even live chickens and ducks. There are just as many restaurants, and while some are lavishly decorated, others are no more than storefronts with a few wooden tables. During the Chinese New Year (held in February) the streets explode with fireworks, and are animated with masked dancers and paper lions and dragons.

GRAND CENTRAL TERMINAL: This is no mere train station: it has been New York City's great hall for almost 70 years, a place consummately public yet able to provide a private nook. It is a distillate of the city itself, a collision of the rich with the destitute, an intermingling of a glamorous past with a less romantic and more commercial present.

The Beaux Arts building at Park Avenue and 42nd Street, completed in 1913, has often been called "a city within the city," and aptly so. It houses more than 60 stores and banks; within its corridors you can buy French pastries or potted plants, books, bric-a-brac, booze, or a basketball. You can place a bet, fill a prescription, have a pair of shoes or a watch repaired, dine on a fine meal or a variety of fast food.

It throbs at rush hour. On a normal weekday one million people stride through its corridors, concourse, and waiting room, plunging into or out of the tubes and tunnels. In their wake they leave six or seven tons of litter daily—enough to require a 55-man cleanup crew. Yet for all its swirling hubbub, there are quiet eddies too. The lower level is nearly always tranquil, and one can sit peacefully on the long wooden benches of the waiting room, underneath the ornate brass chandeliers and carved ceiling beams. At 1:30 a.m. when the station is vacant but for those few huddled to catch the last train, to Stamford, Connecticut, the building is magnificent and still, and not unlike a cathedral. A quiet time like this is a good time to note the ceiling mural of the Mediterranean winter sky, with 2500 stars painted in gold, vaulting over the concourse. The subdued marble and stone elegance of both that room and the waiting room evoke an earlier era, when your train might be the *Twentieth Century* to Chicago, instead of a commuter to Connecticut. A sign of modern times is provided, however, by the presence of the world's largest color slide, courtesy of Kodak, and the world's largest clock and running news-strip, courtesy of *Newsweek* magazine, both in the main concourse.

THE BROOKLYN BRIDGE: "All modern New York, heroic New York, started with the Brooklyn Bridge," said the British art historian Kenneth Clark. The bridge, which celebrated its centennial on May 24, 1983, was the first link over the East River between what were then the separate cities of New York and Brooklyn. But it was—and is—much more than that. It was the first great bridge, the longest suspension bridge in the world at the time, a brilliant feat of engineering. It took 16 years to build, piece by piece, by hand. In its time it was as daring an event as a space shot. And it is an architectural triumph: its roadway and great stone gateways on either end make the cables look more like delicate cobwebs than the heavy steel strands they are. And the bridge provided New York City, which then had buildings of only five and six stories, with its first skyscrapers: the two huge granite towers, each 276 feet above high water, were the tallest and grandest man-made thing in the city. The roadway itself provided a spectacular panorama of Manhattan.

Today the panorama is far different, but no less stunning. Daily, some 5000 pedestrians and bicyclists walk or wheel across the bridge's mile-long wooden promenade; and if you have time, you should consider becoming one of them. For a walk across the bridge is an experience unlike anything else New York offers: the view of the Manhattan skyline is spectacular, and strolling underneath the crisscross of cables, with the tumult of the traffic below, all makes the crossing a kind of ceremony.

You can reach the bridge by taking the IRT–Lexington Avenue subway to the Brooklyn Bridge–Worth Street station. (If you feel like continuing your jaunt after crossing the bridge, you can journey a short distance to the East River promenade in Brooklyn Heights, where benches provide a perfect place to rest.) Or take the Eighth Avenue subway to High Street–Brooklyn Bridge in Brooklyn and return on foot to Manhattan over the bridge.

ELLIS ISLAND: The drafty old brick buildings on Ellis Island are empty now, and restoration work is under way, and the island is expected to reopen by "Liberty Weekend" (July 4–6, 1986).

Between 1892, when the federal government opened the buildings as an immigration center, and 1924, when the massive influx of immigrants tapered off, these buildings and its island were the first point of entry for more than 17 million hopeful, weary, anxious people seeking a new beginning. But the buildings have been long neglected since the island closed in 1954 and have deteriorated badly. In 1965 it was proclaimed a national monument, and now there are plans afoot to remake the entire island, which may take until 1998. The Great Hall and other key buildings are currently being restored.

To get to the island, take a Circle Line boat, leaving from Battery Park (at the lower tip of Manhattan). At this writing, sailing times and prices were unavailable. For more information on the boats and the proposed opening of the island, call the Circle Line ticket office at 269-5755.

To get to Battery Park, take either the IRT–Seventh Avenue local (no. 6) train to South Ferry station, the IRT–Lexington Avenue express train to Bowling Green, or the BMT subway to the Whitehall Street–South Ferry station.

2. Museums

New York City is one of the world's great art centers, a mecca for artists, art dealers, and collectors. But it is the city's museums that draw the public to the world of art. There are more than 100 museums, and many contain some of the greatest examples ever made of man's creativity: Picassos, Rembrandts, Renoirs, and Manets, among others. Along with fine art museums, there are also museums devoted to other fields, such as natural history, crafts, history, and ethnic cultures. Chances are good that if you have a specialized interest, New York has a museum that caters to it. But in this section we have chosen to concentrate on those museums that every tourist should try to see.

Points to remember: Some museums have fixed fees; others ask for contributions. Senior citizens and students should carry some form of identification to qualify for special rates. Few museums open before 10 a.m., and most are closed one day during the week, so a call beforehand is often wise.

METROPOLITAN MUSEUM OF ART: The grande dame of American museums, the Metropolitan Museum of Art, located at Fifth Avenue and 82nd Street (tel. 535-7710), has something to interest almost everyone. Its collection, the largest in the Western Hemisphere, comprises everything from ancient Greek vases and Renaissance paintings to Native American masks and a room designed by Frank Lloyd Wright. In addition to its permanent collection, the Met offers several special exhibitions of works on loan from around the world each year. The museum's Costume Institute, which preserves clothing from as far back as the 1600s, organizes some gorgeous exhibitions of period or regional clothing, and rooms exquisitely furnished in period styles offer a glimpse of life in ages past. The American Wing gives a comprehensive picture of three centuries of American life and art, and its glassed-in sculpture garden is a lovely place to pause and relax a bit. At one side of the garden you'll find some breathtaking stained-glass windows created in the much-acclaimed Tiffany Studios. There is also a Junior Museum for the kids (see Chapter VIII) with its own galleries, snackbar, and gift shop.

Something's always new at the Met. In June 1983 the final 13 galleries of its Egyptian collection opened, marking the end of a 25-year project and the first time that the entire collection has been on public view. With an estimated 40,000 objects spanning over 300,000 years of Egyptian history, it is breathtaking—the largest such collection outside Cairo. Also new is the Michael C. Rockefeller Wing, which exhibits a fascinating array of native art from Africa, the Americas, and the Pacific Islands. Slated to open in 1986 are the Far Eastern and the Greek and Roman Treasury Wings. If you're interested in seeing the Met's newest additions to its collections, go to the Gallery for Recent Acquisitions.

Gorgeous as it is, the Met's size can be taxing for even the hardiest of museum-goers, so even if you've budgeted a whole day to see it, you should take a few minutes with a copy of the floor plan (available free at any of the information booths at the entrances) to plot out which exhibits you want to see. You also might want to take a guided tour (free), which takes place daily in English and weekly in Spanish and French. (Inquire at the Visitors' Center for details.)

If you'd like to take a breather, you can get a cup of coffee or a bite to eat at the museum restaurant, which is quite nice compared to most other museum eateries. Weather permitting, you can also sit on the steps outside the front entrance and join other museum-goers munching hot dogs and watching the antics of street performers. A bit more tranquil are the tree-shaded park benches off to the side, where the splashing of the fountains drowns out the noise of the traffic.

The Met sponsors a variety of special activities (many during weekends) such as gallery talks, lectures, and concerts; call for details. The Met is open on Tuesday from 9:30 a.m. to 8:45 p.m. and Wednesday through Sunday from 9:30 a.m. to 5:15 p.m. Closed Monday. A contribution of $4 is suggested for nonmembers; students and senior citizens, $2. Children under 12 are free with an adult.

MUSEUM OF MODERN ART: Recently expanded and refurbished, the Museum of Modern Art (MOMA), on West 53rd Street between Fifth Avenue and Avenue of the Americas (tel. 708-9500), is one of the world's great museums. Founded in 1929, the museum offers an unrivaled survey of the modern arts from 1880 to the present. Its collection includes over 100,000 paintings, sculptures, drawings, prints, photographs, architectural models and plans, and superbly designed objects, as well as 8000 films, 3 million film stills, and a library containing some 80,000 books and periodicals. The museum's changing exhibitions focus on specific artists' works, styles, and modern art movements. In more than 20 galleries, you can explore the development of modern art—from the masterpieces of post-impressionists like van Gogh and Cezanne to works by modern masters Rauschenberg and Stella. And—against a soothing backdrop of weeping birch and beech trees, reflecting pools, and fountains—you can enjoy the sculpture of Picasso, Rodin, and many others in MOMA's Abby Aldrich Rockefeller Sculpture Garden.

Films—mainly by international and American independent filmmakers; and free with admission—are shown daily in the museum's two theaters, and video exhibitions are screened in the Video Gallery. For information on film showings, call 708-9400; for information on current exhibitions, phone 708-9480.

MOMA is open daily from 11 a.m. to 6 p.m., to 9 p.m. on Thursday; closed Wednesday and Christmas Day. Admission is $4.50 for adults, $3 for students, $2 for senior citizens, and free for children under 16 accompanied by an adult. Thursday, from 5 to 9 p.m., pay as you wish.

GUGGENHEIM MUSEUM: Called a "giant snail" by some and "the most beautiful building in New York" by architect Philip Johnson, the Solomon R. Guggenheim Museum, 1071 Fifth Ave., at 89th Street (tel. 360-3500), is justly famous for its striking design by Frank Lloyd Wright and for its collection of more than 3000 works from every major period in 20th-century painting and sculpture. The museum is shaped like a chambered nautilus, and in order to view most of the paintings, you must walk along the gently curving ramp that coils for seven stories down to the large circular ground floor. Displayed on the ramp are works by new artists, as well as rotating exhibits of art by modern masters. On permanent display are such modern masterpieces as Picasso's *Mandolin and Guitar,* Braque's *The Buffet,* and Chagall's *The Green Violinist.* The museum also has 20 other Picassos and one of the largest collections of works by Vasily Kandinsky in the world. In the permanently installed Justin K. Thannhauser Collection, off the main building, hang paintings by such luminaries as Manet, Renoir, Cézanne, Gauguin, and van Gogh.

The Guggenheim is open Wednesday through Sunday from 11 a.m. to 5 p.m., on Thursday until 8 p.m. To get to the museum, take the no. 2, 3, or 4 Madison Avenue bus to 88th Street and walk a block to Fifth Avenue; or take the IRT–Lexington Avenue subway to 86th Street and walk over to Fifth Avenue. Admission is $3 for adults, $1.75 for students and senior citizens; children under 7 are free. On Tuesday evening from 5 to 8 p.m. no admission is charged.

WHITNEY MUSEUM OF AMERICAN ART: In the heart of the gallery district, the Whitney Museum, 945 Madison Ave., at 75th Street (tel. 570-3611), is devoted exclusively to 20th-century American art. Even the building is a piece of modern art. Designed by Marcel Breuer (the creator of the tubular-steel chair that bears his name), the Whitney is made out of rich gray granite and looks like an inverted pyramid. Here you'll see paintings that reflect all the historical trends in American art from John Sloan to Julian Schnabel: naturalism, impressionism, pop art, throwaways, abstractionism, up to the stylistic pluralism of the present. Don't miss the whimsical *Circus* stabile by Alexander Calder on the first floor. Made out of steel, metal, felt, and fiber, this circus is a delightful creation of cavorting animals and swinging acrobats. On the upper floors, the Whitney displays pieces from its renowned permanent collection and highlights changing exhibits. Every two years the Whitney presents a show that features the work of both new and accomplished artists, and provides a revealing look at new trends in American art. There is also a pleasant, plant-filled restaurant where you can have a light meal and a cup of coffee. The Whitney operates the **New American Filmmakers' Series,** which provides a showcase for the work of independent film producers. (Admission to the films is included in the general admission fee.)

Open Wednesday through Saturday from 11 a.m. to 5 p.m., on Sunday from noon to 6 p.m., and on Tuesday 1 to 8 p.m. Closed Monday. Admission is $3 for adults, $1.50 for senior citizens, and free for students and children. On Tuesday nights no admission is charged.

FRICK MUSEUM: The Frick, 1 E. 70th St., at Fifth Avenue (tel. 288-0700), is a jewel. Its collection belonged to Pittsburgh coal-and-steel magnate Henry Clay Frick, and the museum was once his home. Although the Frick is not as large or as well known as some of her New York sisters, it is priceless in presentation. It's much like visiting the home of a very rich—and hospitable—friend who just happens to have Gainsboroughs in the dining room, a drawing room full of Fragonards, Titians in the living room, and an El Greco over the fireplace. The Fricks collected art for 40 years, lived with it, and arranged to turn it over to the public upon their deaths. The museum trustees have abided by their wishes; and even though the magnificent house has been expanded to almost double its original size, it still looks like a home complete with books and easy chairs among the grander antiques. Two of the more notable additions made since the Frick opened in 1935 are the serene garden court with splashing fountain, and a lovely garden designed by British landscape artist Russell Paige.

The Frick is open Tuesday through Saturday from 10 a.m. to 6 p.m., on Sunday and holidays from 1 to 6 p.m. Closed Monday. Admission is $1 for adults, 50¢ for students and senior citizens. Sunday admission is $2. No children under 10 are allowed in, and those under 16 must be with an adult. Call or write for information on lectures and weekly concerts (tickets must be arranged in advance).

THE CLOISTERS: Isolated on a Manhattan hilltop in Fort Tryon Park (tel. 923-3700), this uptown branch of the Metropolitan Museum of Art resembles a medieval monastery in location and appearance. Built in the 1930s by Charles Collens, the architect of Riverside Church, this stone complex combines parts of five medieval monasteries, a 12th-century chapter house, a Romanesque chapel, and a 12th-century Spanish apse into one. The Cloisters contains the Met's vast collection of medieval art, including the famous *Unicorn Tapestries* (seven 16th-century tapestries that depict the hunt of the mythical one-horned creature). Among other spectacular pieces on view is the famous *Altarpiece of the Annunciation,* as well as important illuminated manuscripts and striking stained-glass windows. You may want to take a free guided tour, which is given at 3 p.m. Tuesday through Thursday (on Wednesday only in January and February). After looking at the collection, sit in the herb garden and soak in the tranquility of this serene oasis far removed from the noise and hustle of midtown.

This unusual museum is well worth the half-hour trip from downtown. To get there by subway, take the IND–Eighth Avenue A train to 190th Street–Overlook Terrace. Then take the no. 4 bus or walk to Fort Tryon Park to the museum. By bus, take the Madison Avenue no. 4 to the Fort Tryon Park–The Cloisters stop. Open Tuesday through Sunday from 9:30 a.m. to 5 p.m. Suggested admission is $4 for adults, $2 for students and senior citizens.

THE BROOKLYN MUSEUM: At Eastern Parkway and Washington Avenue (tel. 718/638-5000), the Brooklyn Museum contains perhaps the finest collection of Egyptian art in the country. The museum also owns a large selection of Oriental art, as well as an excellent group of American paintings from colonial times to the present. There are 28 American period rooms, the best assortment of Russian costumes and textiles outside the Soviet Union, and an outdoor sculpture garden consisting of architectural sections from demolished New York buildings. In the gift shop you can purchase original folk art from around the world, including Peruvian textiles, Thai parasols, and Polish boxes. The museum has an art reference library with more than 100,000 volumes and the Wilbur Library of Egyptology that has more than 25,000 books on the subject.

To get to the museum, take the IRT–Seventh Avenue subway line to the Eastern Parkway stop. Open Wednesday through Saturday from 10 a.m. to 5 p.m., on Sunday from noon to 5 p.m., on holidays from 1 to 5 p.m. Suggested contribution is $2 for adults, $1 for students; free to senior citizens and children.

AMERICAN MUSEUM OF NATURAL HISTORY: Animal and human life in all its forms is the theme of this vast museum located at Central Park West and 79th Street (tel. 873-4225). With more than 34 million artifacts and specimens, the museum offers the visitor an incredible range of objects to view, from a miniscule chromosome to a 94-foot replica of the blue whale, the largest mammal that ever lived. But don't try to see all the exhibits or else you'll quickly become overwhelmed. Among the many excellent exhibits are the new Gardner D. Stout Hall of Asian Peoples, which features over 3000 artifacts and artworks; the Hall of Mexico and Central America, which has an impressive collection of pre-Columbian jade and carved stone pieces; and the Hall of Man in Africa. Also on display are dioramas of many preserved animals shown in every type of habitat from the savannah to the tundra. The museum also has a pleasant shop, a reference library, a cafeteria, a restaurant, and a theater where the popular films *To Fly, Living Planet,* and *Man Belongs to Earth* are shown daily (call 496-0900 for show times and admission prices).

Open every day from 10 a.m. to 5:45 p.m., until 9 p.m. on Wednesday, Friday, and Saturday. Suggested admission is $3 for adults, $1.50 for students and children. On Friday and Saturday evenings admission is free.

THE HAYDEN PLANETARIUM: The closest thing to stargazing you're likely to get in Manhattan is a Sky Show at the Hayden Planetarium, at Central Park West and 81st Street (tel. 873-8828). When the lights go out and the quarter-million-dollar Zeiss VI projector splashes a star-studded sky on the 75-foot dome ceiling, you'd almost believe you were sitting on a mountaintop. That is, until the prerecorded show begins. The shows, which vary from season to season, trace man's fascination with the stars and the planets, the mythical and scientific explanations for cosmic phenomena, and the possibilities for future exploration. Shows take place weekdays at 1:30 and 3:30 p.m., on Saturday and Sunday at 1, 2, 3, and 4 p.m. (Saturday shows at 11 a.m. and 5 p.m. are added October through June).

The planetarium also contains exhibits explaining such things as orbital patterns, gamma rays, rainbows, and why the sky is blue. Its Hall of the Sun is the largest exhibit in the world devoted entirely to our nearest star. And if you're curious to know what you'd weigh on Mars, Jupiter, Venus, the sun, or the moon, jump onto a scale in "Your Weight on Other Worlds."

Most popular with the young crowd is the **Laser Show,** a dazzling show that combines laser images with rock music to create a vibrant kaleidoscopic effect. Shows are Friday and Saturday at 7:30, 9, and 10:30 p.m. Tickets cost $5 and at times sell out, so you should plan to arrive early or to buy tickets in advance at Ticketron. For Laser Show information, call 724-8700.

The planetarium is open from noon to 4:45 p.m. every day. Admission is $3.25 for adults, $2.25 for students with ID and for senior citizens, and $1.50 for children 12 and under.

To get to the planetarium, take the IND–Eighth Avenue subway (AA line) to 81st Street, or the IRT–Seventh Avenue local (no. 1) to 79th Street and walk east from Broadway.

NEW-YORK HISTORICAL SOCIETY: This museum's old punctuation of "New-York" shows how determined it is to preserve the past. At 170 Central Park West and 77th Street (tel. 873-3400), this library and museum of American history (with a special emphasis on New York) was founded in 1804 and is the oldest in the city. But along with age came an impression of stuffiness, and in the past few years the society has been rejuvenating its image with educational and entertaining exhibits of Americana, such as pot-bellied stoves and summer brass bands. The museum has an excellent collection of colonial silver, plus period rooms from the 17th and early 18th centuries, fire engines, Early American toys and carriages. The museum can also boast of 422 *Birds of America* watercolors by John Jay Audubon, a print and photographic department, and an excellent research library (for which a small user's fee is charged).

Open Tuesday through Saturday from 11 a.m. to 5 p.m. (opens at 10 a.m. on Saturday), and on Sunday from 1 to 5 p.m. Suggested donation is $2 for adults, $1.50 for senior citizens, 75¢ for children. Tuesday, pay as you wish.

FRAUNCES TAVERN MUSEUM: This fascinating museum of early American history and culture is housed in the site of Fraunces Tavern, a landmark 18th-century building at the corner of Broad and Pearl Streets in lower Manhattan (tel. 425-1778). The museum's permanent collections include Early Americana, Revolutionary War memorabilia, and portraits of President George Washington, the tavern's most famous guest. The museum also boasts two fully furnished period rooms: the Long Room, site of Washington's emotional farewell to his officers in 1783, and the 19th-century Clinton Dining Room. The museum hosts lectures, workshops, concerts, and theatrical performances, as well as special exhibitions on such topics as "The History of Health Care in Early America" (on view from mid-October 1985 until mid-June 1986) and "The Legacy of Lafayette."

Open Monday through Friday from 10 a.m. to 4 p.m. Admission is free, and group tours are available by appointment.

MUSEUM OF THE CITY OF NEW YORK: In a beautiful old Georgian building at Fifth Avenue and 104th Street (tel. 534-1672), this museum contains a collection of New York City memorabilia presented in an entertaining and informative way. Even if you yawn at the thought of history, this museum will spark your interest. Through slide shows, colorful dioramas, and detailed exhibits, the museum will glide you through the "Big Apple's" history from the time when the city was the Dutch colony of New Amsterdam to the present. Permanent exhibits capture the mood of Wall Street and the activity of New York Harbor with slide shows, taped sounds, and enlarged photographs. The museum has an excellent collection of American silver and some fine portraits of early American patriots and statesmen. Rooms filled with models, photographs, old fire engines, maps, toys—plus period recreations of furniture and dress—provide a sense of the city's rich social and cultural past.

Open Tuesday through Saturday from 10 a.m. to 4:45 p.m., on Sunday from 1 to 4:45 p.m. Suggested donation is $1.

THE COOPER-HEWITT MUSEUM: The Smithsonian Institution established its **National Museum of Design** in the elegant former Andrew Carnegie mansion at 2 E. 91st St., at Fifth Avenue (tel. 860-6868). The museum's name honors its founders: Peter Cooper, a 19th-century philanthropist and his three granddaughters; and the Hewitts, who envisioned a museum for the designer, the artisan, and the student. Since the Hewitt sisters started the museum in 1897, the collection has grown into one of the foremost collections of decorative arts and design in the world, including objects from every historical period over a span of 3000 years: drawings, prints, wallpapers, textiles, porcelain, glass, furniture, woodwork, metalwork, jewelry, and woven and printed fabrics. The museum's collection of original architecture and design drawings is the largest in the United States.

The permanent collections are not on view, but the regularly changing exhibitions always relate to some aspect of design—from the dash and style of engraved and sculpted cane handles to the skyscrapers built in Manhattan in the 1920s and 1930s. Watch for coming exhibitions on a variety of themes: crafts of India, Bronislava Najinska's ballet sets and costumes, Hollywood and its influence on American life. Don't miss the peaceful garden on the southern side of the museum, which is lined with shaded benches; it's a very pleasant place for a moment's rest.

Open Wednesday through Saturday from noon until 5 p.m., on Sunday to 5 p.m., on Tuesdays from 10 a.m. to 9 p.m. (free after 5 p.m.). Admission other times is $2 for adults, $1.50 for students and senior citizens. Closed Monday and major holidays.

THE JEWISH MUSEUM: This museum, housed in the former Warburg mansion at 1109 Fifth Ave., at 92nd Street (tel. 860-1888), contains the largest and most important collection of Jewish ceremonial objects in the United States. On view are spice boxes, Torah headpieces, menorahs, and rings. Featured permanent displays include one devoted to Jewish life in colonial America and another containing religious and social artifacts dating from antiquity—the days of the Roman conquest. Though once known as a forum for any type of avant-garde art, the museum now displays only modern art with a Jewish content. Films, lectures, and children's programs are scheduled regularly, along with art courses and music programs.

Open Monday, Wednesday, and Thursday from noon to 5 p.m., on Tuesday to 8 p.m., on Sunday from 11 a.m. to 6 p.m., and on Friday from 11 a.m. to 3 p.m.; closed Saturday and major Jewish holidays. Admission is $2.50 for adults, $1.50 for children, $1 for students and senior citizens.

MUSEUM OF THE AMERICAN INDIAN—HEYE FOUNDATION: Located on the Upper West Side at Broadway and 155th Street (tel. 283-2420), this museum contains the world's largest and finest collection of artifacts made by the Indians of the Western Hemisphere. Attractively arranged in three floors of exhibits, these artifacts vividly catalogue the ceremonies and daily activities of Indian culture. The first and second floors focus on the different North American Indian societies. Here you can see everyday tools, such as the tomahawk, along with dramatic false-face masks worn by the Iroquois and personal possessions of Chiefs Red Cloud, Sitting Bull, Crazy Horse, and Arapoosh. On the upper floor are exhibits describing Indian life in South and Central America, plus collections of wampum, games, pipes, weaving, and other Indian crafts. The museum currently occupies one of the imposing and elegant buildings that make up the Audubon Terrace complex; but there's been talk of moving the museum either out of state or downtown into the Museum of Natural History complex—so be sure to call the museum before making a special visit to see it.

Open Tuesday through Saturday from 10 a.m. to 5 p.m., on Sunday from 1

188 NEW YORK ON $45 A DAY

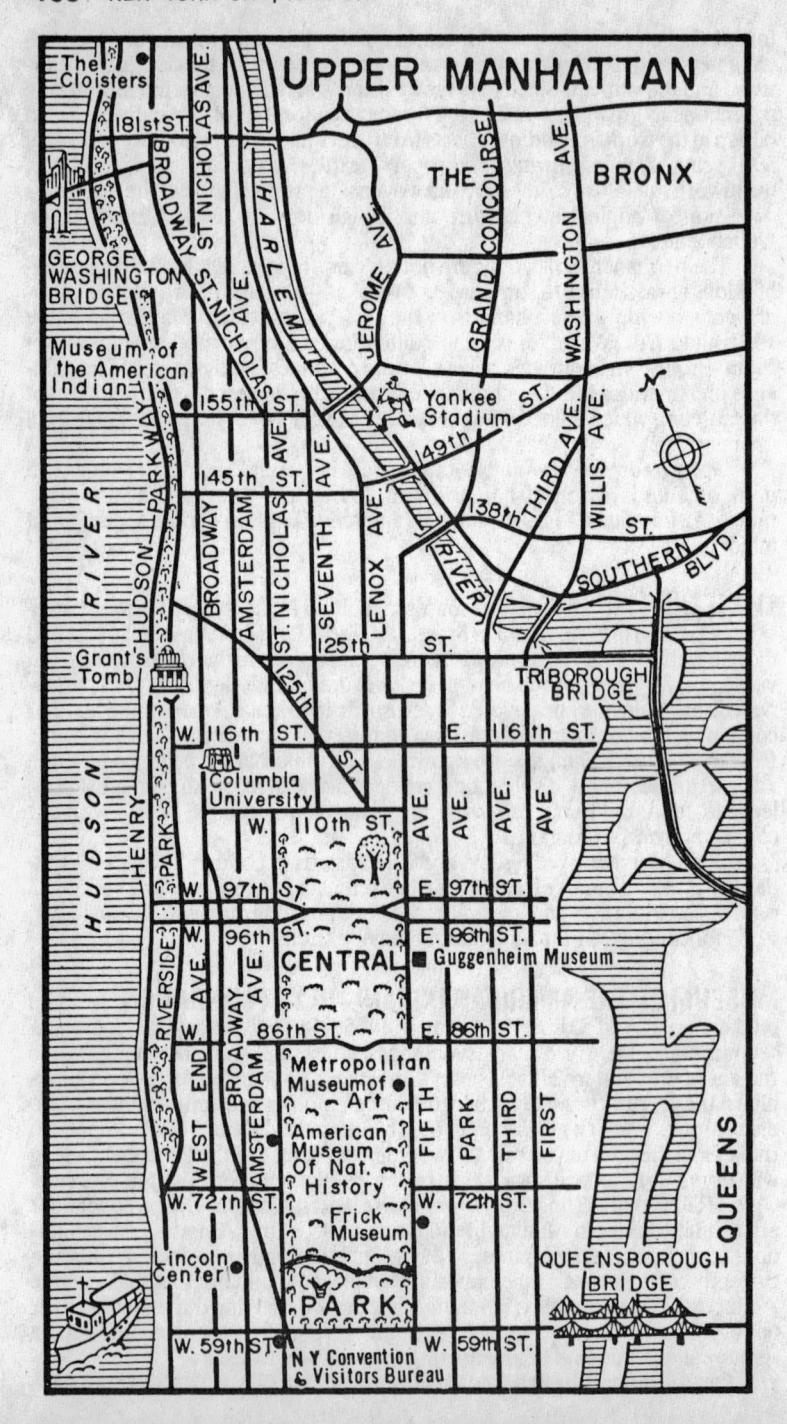

UPPER MANHATTAN

THE BRONX

- The Cloisters
- 181st ST.
- BROADWAY
- ST. NICHOLAS AVE.
- HARLEM
- JEROME AVE.
- GRAND CONCOURSE
- WASHINGTON AVE.
- GEORGE WASHINGTON BRIDGE
- Museum of the American Indian
- 155th ST.
- Yankee Stadium
- 149th ST.
- 145th ST.
- THIRD AVE.
- WILLIS AVE.
- 138th ST.
- SOUTHERN BLVD.
- AMSTERDAM AVE.
- ST. NICHOLAS AVE.
- SEVENTH AVE.
- LENOX AVE.
- HARLEM RIVER
- 125th ST.
- HUDSON RIVER
- HUDSON PARKWAY
- Grant's Tomb
- TRIBOROUGH BRIDGE
- W. 116th ST.
- E. 116th ST.
- Columbia University
- W. 110th ST.
- W. 97th ST.
- E. 97th ST.
- RIVERSIDE
- HENRY PARK
- WEST END AVE.
- BROADWAY
- AMSTERDAM AVE.
- W. 96th ST.
- E. 96th ST.
- CENTRAL
- Guggenheim Museum
- W. 86th ST.
- E. 86th ST.
- Metropolitan Museum of Art
- American Museum Of Nat. History
- FIFTH AVE.
- PARK AVE.
- THIRD AVE.
- FIRST AVE.
- W. 72nd ST.
- W. 72nd ST.
- Frick Museum
- Lincoln Center
- PARK
- QUEENSBOROUGH BRIDGE
- QUEENS
- W. 59th ST.
- W. 59th ST.
- NY Convention & Visitors Bureau

to 5 p.m. Closed Monday and holidays. Admission is $2 for adults, $1 for students and senior citizens. To get there, take the Madison Avenue no. 3 or no. 4 bus, or the Avenue of Americas (Sixth Avenue) no. 5 bus to 155th Street and Broadway. By subway, take the IRT–Seventh Avenue local (no. 1) uptown to 157th Street.

THE HISPANIC SOCIETY OF AMERICA: Part of the Audubon Terrace complex at Broadway and 155th Street (tel. 690-0743), the society owns an impressive collection of paintings, sculpture, and decorative arts representative of Hispanic culture from prehistoric days to the present century. Though the society specializes in the art of Spain and Portugal, it also features a good selection of Latin American pieces. Included in the collection are paintings by El Greco, Velázquez, and Goya, plus such objects as Mexican ceramics and Spanish earthenware.

With its rich terracotta floors, Valencia tapestries, and high ceiling, the museum's interior resembles a grand and majestic cathedral in tone. The air of solemnity is accented by the sculptured effigies of Spanish nobility lined up against one wall. The society's library, filled with books about Hispanic culture, conveys a similar air of hushed grandeur.

Open Tuesday through Saturday from 10 a.m. to 4:30 p.m., on Sunday from 1 to 4 p.m. Admission is free. See the listing for the (next-door) Museum of the American Indian (above) for transportation directions.

PIERPONT MORGAN LIBRARY: Designed by Charles McKim, the Pierpont Morgan Library, 29 E. 36th St., at Madison Avenue (tel. 685-0008), is a Renaissance palazzo befitting its collection of 15th-century and earlier books, illuminated manuscripts, and drawings. The library often has collections on loan—for instance, in early 1987 you'll be able to see the first major loan exhibition of 16th-century Dutch drawings by Bruegel and his contemporaries ever shown in the U.S. Almost always on exhibit are selections from Morgan's collection, including Erasmus's *Defense of Folly* and one of the Gutenberg Bibles—both on display with other rare books in the ornate East Room library.

Open Tuesday through Saturday from 10:30 a.m. to 5 p.m., on Sunday from 1 to 5 p.m. Closed Monday, holidays, Sunday and Monday in July, and all of August. Suggested admission is $2.50 for adults. Senior citizens, students, and children are asked to donate as they can. Be forewarned: this is not a place for young children; they will get restless.

AMERICAN CRAFT MUSEUM: If your impression of crafts is limited to coil pots and potholders, then let the American Craft Museum introduce you to the latest trends in clay, wood, fiber, glass, and metal crafts. Currently located at 29 W. 53rd St., between Fifth and Sixth Avenues (tel. 869-9422), the museum soon will be moving a few steps away into its new facility (with a new phone number) at 40 W. 53rd St., with an inaugural exhibition planned in the fall of 1986. Sponsored by the American Craft Council, the museum mounts thematic and group exhibitions and single-artist shows; it also houses a permanent collection whose objects represent high points in the 20th-century American craft movement. Call for hours and admission fees.

MUSEUM OF AMERICAN FOLK ART: Located at 125 W. 55th St., between Sixth and Seventh Avenues (tel. 581-2474), this museum boasts a wonderful collection of 18th- and 19th-century artisanry that includes quilts, handmade dolls, decoys, weathervanes, and carousel horses. Open Tuesday from 10:30 a.m. to 8 p.m., Wednesday to Sunday to 5:30 p.m. Admission is $2 for adults, $1 for students and senior citizens, and free for children under 12. On Tuesday admission is free for everyone.

INTERNATIONAL CENTER OF PHOTOGRAPHY: One of the museums on Fifth Avenue's "Museum Mile," the ICP is in an elegant landmark building at 1130 Fifth Ave., at 94th Street (tel. 860-1777). Its exhibitions, under the stewardship of Cornell Capa, show the sophistication and diversity of contemporary photography and the techniques and styles of the past. Changing exhibits sometimes focus on one photographer or on one genre, such as still-lifes, photo essays, or portraits. In the permanent collection are works by such famous photographers as Henri Cartier-Bresson, W. Eugene Smith, and Andreas Feininger. For those striving to become famous, the museum offers photography classes throughout the year for every level of experience. A large selection of photography books, postcards, and posters are sold in the first-floor shop.

Open Tuesday from noon until 8 p.m. (free after 5 p.m.), Wednesday through Friday from noon until 5 p.m., and on Sunday from 11 a.m. to 6 p.m. Admission is $2.50 for adults, $1 for students and senior citizens, and 50¢ for children under 12.

THE NEW YORK PUBLIC LIBRARY: On the steps of the enormous New York Public Library, on Fifth Avenue between 40th and 42nd Streets (tel. 340-0849), street musicians, vendors, and undiscovered comedians vie for the attention of the bustling crowds. Inside the library, the horns and noise of the street are forgotten. At table after table, in room after room, people pore intently over books. But there is more to do here than read. The library also has exhibition rooms, art galleries, and permanent displays of 19th-century American paintings. To find out about special events, check the library's publication titled *Events*, available at all branches. All exhibits and programs are free.

The main branch is open on Monday, Tuesday, and Wednesday from 10 a.m. to 9 p.m., on Thursday, Friday, and Saturday to 6 p.m. Closed Sunday. (Other branches have different hours.)

ASIA SOCIETY GALLERIES: Located in the society's earth-toned new headquarters at 725 Park Ave., at 70th Street (tel. 288-6400), the galleries provide a permanent home for the Mr. and Mrs. John D. Rockefeller III Collection of Asian Art. Included in this prodigious collection of art from China, Japan, India, and Southeast Asia are dancing Krishna statues, Ming porcelain, and delicate Japanese folding screens. On the second floor, small colored-porcelain lions scowl from within their elegant display cases where a ritual vessel with dragon handles and a small statue of a Chinese court lady playing cymbals are also displayed, among many other objects. The first-floor exhibit space is devoted to changing exhibits on specific themes in Asian art such as "Photography in China, 1850–1912" or early Indian dyed textiles.

Open Tuesday through Saturday from 10 a.m. to 6 p.m., on Sunday from noon until 5 p.m., on Thursday until 8:30 p.m. Admission is $2 for adults, $1 for students and senior citizens.

YESHIVA UNIVERSITY MUSEUM: Featured in this university collection at 2520 Amsterdam Ave., at 185th Street (tel. 960-5390), are paintings, photographs, and ceremonial objects that record the Jewish historical experience. Of special interest is the museum's exhibit of detailed architectural models of ten famous synagogues.

Open Tuesday through Thursday from 10:30 a.m. to 5 p.m., on Sunday from noon to 5 p.m. Admission is $2 for adults, $1 for students and senior citizens.

CHINA HOUSE GALLERY: Fascinating exhibits of classical Chinese art are presented semiannually at the China House Gallery at 125 E. 65th St., between Lexington and Park Avenues (tel. 744-8181). A past show featured "The Sumptuous Basket," an exquisite collection of Chinese lacquer, with basketry panels.

Open Monday through Friday from 10 a.m. to 5 p.m., on Saturday from 11 a.m. to 5 p.m., on Sunday from 2 to 5 p.m. Admission is free.

MUSEUM OF BROADCASTING: With more than 10,000 videotaped television shows and 7000 radio shows, this comfortable place at 1 E. 53rd St., just off Fifth Avenue (tel. 752-7684), is a mecca for fans of popular culture, entertainment, and American history. Founded in 1975, this museum collects, preserves, and interprets radio and TV programs. All tapes can be screened by the public. At 23 broadcasting consoles, you can listen to Edward R. Murrow's London broadcasts or FDR's fireside chats. You can also view TV programs of all kinds, from Sid Caesar's comic routines to shots of the moon or serious documentaries.

Open on Tuesday from noon to 8 p.m., Wednesday through Saturday from noon to 5 p.m. Suggested admission is $3 for adults, $2 for students, $1.50 for senior citizens and children.

MUSEUM OF HOLOGRAPHY: At 11 Mercer St., in SoHo, half a block north of Canal Street and one block west of Broadway (tel. 925-0581), this museum is devoted to the display of a new art form made with laser light. The museum has four galleries of holograms, three-dimensional images made by exposing photographic film to laser beams. The result is images that never stop moving and often trick the eye. For example, a wine-glass appears whole though it is constructed half out of glass and half out of light. In one display, miniature holographic images of famous celebrities, such as the artist Andy Warhol and the opera singer Beverly Sills, seem to move and vibrate as though alive. This is a fascinating museum for anyone curious about light, science, or new directions in art made possible by technology. The museum store has books, jewelry, pendants, and fine art by holographic artists for sale. For example, you can buy a holographic recording of a human eye, or the inside of a clock.

Open Wednesday through Sunday from noon to 6 p.m. Admission is $3 for adults, $1.75 for children and senior citizens. To get there, take the bus or subway to any Canal Street stop.

THE NEW MUSEUM: At 583 Broadway in SoHo, between Houston and Prince Streets (tel. 219-1222), this museum is devoted to contemporary art. What makes it different from more traditional institutions is its support for new and unrecognized art. The museum has no permanent collection, but shows all kinds of artworks, from painting to sculpture to conceptual art, in temporary exhibits. The works, never more than ten years old, are often experimental, innovative, and radically different. But social acceptance is not a prerequisite for art displayed by this museum, which rather than recording the past serves as a link between the public and the contemporary artist.

Open from noon to 6 p.m. Thursday through Sunday, till 8 p.m. on Wednesday. Suggested admission is $2.50 for adults, $1.50 for students, artists, and senior citizens.

UKRAINIAN MUSEUM: Tucked away in a small building at 203 Second Ave., at 13th Street (tel. 228-0110), this museum features Ukrainian folk art from the 19th and 20th centuries: textiles, ceramics, metalwork, and woodwork. Because of the museum's limited space, only a few of its 2000 craft items can be displayed at any one time. Highlights of the collection include 14 colorful peasant costumes on permanent display and the museum's annual Easter exhibition of pysanky (colored Easter Eggs). Pieces from the permanent collection are shown throughout the year in rotating exhibits.

Open Wednesday through Sunday from 1 to 5 p.m. Admission is $1 for adults, 50¢ for students and senior citizens. Children are admitted for free.

STUDIO MUSEUM IN HARLEM: By focusing on the work of one painter or presenting a group show, this museum at 144 W. 125th St., near Lenox Avenue (tel. 864-4500), features the work of prominent and emerging black artists. The permanent collection contains works by Afro-American, African, and Caribbean artists. Changing exhibits present the work of such artists as Romare Bearden, James Van Der Zee, and Beauford Delaney. Also included in the permanent collection are paintings, prints, sculpture, and photographs. The gift shop has arts and crafts from all over the world.

Open Wednesday through Friday from 10 a.m. to 5 p.m., on Saturday and Sunday from 1 to 6 p.m. Closed Monday and Tuesday. Suggested donation: $1.50. To get there, take the IRT–Seventh Ave. line (no. 2 or 3 train) to Lenox Avenue, then the BX 29 bus to 125th Street.

EL MUSEO DEL BARRIO: Located at 1230 Fifth Ave., at 104th Street (tel. 831-7272), this museum records the vivid culture of Puerto Rico and Latin America through sculpture, paintings, graphics, and photography. On permanent view are pre-Columbian artifacts, supplemented by changing exhibits that focus on Puerto Rican culture on the island, in New York City, and in the Americas.

Open Tuesday through Friday from 10:30 a.m. to 4:30 p.m., on Saturday and Sunday from 11 a.m. to 4 p.m. Voluntary contributions.

THE NATIONAL ACADEMY OF DESIGN: Founded in 1825 as an art school and exhibition space, the National Academy of Design, 1083 Fifth Ave., at 89th Street (tel. 369-4880), is still a school of fine arts and honorary artists' organization of elected members. It has a permanent collection of 19th- and 20th-century fine arts, and organizes exhibitions whose eclectic range aims to introduce new subjects to an American audience. Recent exhibits have introduced little-known European masters or neglected American 19th-century talents.

The museum is open from noon to 8 p.m. on Tuesday, and from noon to 5 p.m. Wednesday through Sunday. Admission is $2.50 for adults, $2 for students and seniors, and free for friends of the Academy and for all on Tuesday from 5 to 8 p.m.

THE GROLIER CLUB: This private club for bibliophiles and book collectors, which recently celebrated its centennial, runs changing exhibits on anything to do with books, from the 19th-century British Gothic Revival, to the art of stencil, to Ezra Pound. The museum, at 47 E. 60th St., between Park and Madison Avenues (tel. 838-6690), is open to the public free of charge Monday through Saturday (Friday in the summer) from 10 a.m. to 5 p.m. The library at the club is open to scholars and members only.

3. Galleries, Theater, Concerts, Opera, and Dance

ART GALLERIES: For artists, dealers, collectors, and art lovers around the world, New York is an irresistible magnet, the center of the newest, the finest, the most prestigious in the visual arts. Dozens of art galleries are continually redefining the meaning of art and making new reputations. Whatever you may want to see or buy, it's here—from the paintings of old-world masters to graffiti-inspired visual mayhem. Each gallery is an adventure, and after a quick tour of a few you'll feel like a knowledgeable insider to a chic and beautiful world.

Most galleries don't charge admission (they've got work to sell!), and they're open Monday or Tuesday through Saturday, from about 10 a.m. to 6 p.m. Some are closed on Saturday, and may have special summer hours.

Here's a listing of the galleries the art world takes seriously, as well as the type of work and artist you're likely to encounter. For those who want the most current and up-to-date listings, the gallery-goers' bible is *Gallery Guide,* a glossy paperback published monthly that lists virtually every gallery's shows, plus maps. It's available free in most galleries.

57th Street

The **Sidney Janis Gallery,** 110 W. 57th St., between Sixth and Seventh Avenues (tel. 586-0110), is famous for showing a wide range of modern and contemporary art—from cubism to graffiti art. See the works here by well-known artists like Mondrian, Léger, Segal, and Marisol, and lesser-known new artists like Crash, Daze, Noc, and Toxic.

Visit the **Frumkin Gallery,** 50 W. 57th St., between Fifth and Sixth Avenues (tel. 757-6655), to see the ceramic sculptures of Robert Arneson, the rigorous realism of Jack Beal, the witty drawings of Californian William T. Wiley, the wood sculptures of Texan James Surles, and other well-known contemporary artists. Also featured in a special drawing gallery are 20th-century master drawings by artists like Matisse, Giacometti, and German expressionist Max Beckmann.

If you are a modern art aficionado, the **Marlborough Gallery** is not to be missed. Located in a skyscraper office building at 40 W. 57th St., between Fifth and Sixth Avenues (tel. 541-4900), this prestigious gallery has exhibited the gurus and greats of modern art, masters like Moore, Picasso, Calder, Sutherland, Botero, Feininger, and Arp. The list goes on, so if you only have time to visit a few galleries, put Marlborough on the list.

While you're in the building, stop in at the **Kennedy Gallery** (tel. 541-9600), where the walls are lined with collector-quality 18th-, 19th-, and 20th-century American paintings, drawings, and prints. Savor especially the works of Charles Burchfield, John Copley, and Charles Prendergast.

Another famous and important gallery not to pass by is the bustling **Pace Gallery,** 32 E. 57th St., between Fifth and Madison Avenues (tel. 421-3292), which shows an impressive array of modern and contemporary artists from Picasso and Calder to photorealist Chuck Close and the maverick Julian Schnabel. Other modern greats on the gallery roster are Nevelson, Dubuffet, Noguchi, and Dine. In the same building, **Pace Editions** (tel. 421-3237) shows contemporary and master prints, and **Pace Primitive and Ancient Art** (tel. 421-3688) features African sculpture.

Traveling to the **André Emmerich Gallery,** 41 E. 57th St., at the corner of Madison Avenue (tel. 752-0124), is almost as much fun as browsing through this contemporary art establishment. The gallery is located in the beautiful Fuller building, an architectural knockout that's considered one of the best city examples of art deco design. Look at the bronze doors, wall decorations, marble fixtures, and mosaic walls and you'll understand why. The art inside Emmerich is as good as the art outside the building, with major work by Hockney, Rothko, and Picasso.

Marion Goodman, 24 W. 57th St., between Fifth and Sixth Avenues (tel. 977-7160), shows contemporary art in all media—from pop art prints to conceptual art, with an emphasis on European artists.

In the same building, stop into the **Arnold Herstand & Co. Gallery** (tel. 664-1379) and you may be surprised to see either ancient African art or its other specialty, modern and contemporary painting and sculpture.

At **Blue Helman,** 20 W. 57th St. (tel. 245-2888), the focus is on American and European postwar and contemporary painting and sculpture, with work by heavyweights like Rauschenberg and Baziotes, as well as by younger artists who make hanging cubistic sculptures that are spotlit, or found sculptures.

The work at the **Holly Solomon Gallery,** 724 Fifth Ave., off 57th Street (tel. 757-7777), defies easy classification but should not be missed. Solomon is something of a legend in the art world for showing provocative work by younger artists. And you never know what you may see here—conceptual art done mostly with a typewriter, wildly colorful room installations, humorous photographs, or romantic oil paintings of animals.

In the same building are two other galleries you should visit. The **Edward Merrin Gallery** (tel. 757-2884) shows only ancient art—classical Greek and Roman, Etruscan, pre-Columbian, and Egyptian—from finely woven textiles to polished stone sculptures from the past. And at **Grace Borgenicht** (tel. 247-2111), which shows an eclectic mix of old masters, established modern artists, and emerging younger artists, you are likely to see anything from small landscape paintings in oil to large, abstract bronze sculptures.

The **Daniel Wolf Gallery,** 30 W. 57th St., between Fifth and Sixth Avenues (tel. 586-8432), is the place to go to see fine-art photography—of every era—at its finest. See the very earliest examples of European photography, photos of the American West, including Yosemite and Yellowstone, the current photography scene, and much, much more.

Madison Avenue

Prestigious Madison Avenue is lined with art galleries and expensive shopping, and each block abounds with architectural and historic landmarks. It is among the most pleasing areas in Manhattan for strolling, so take your time. Window-shop, browse, and join the well-heeled residents of the brownstones, town houses, mansions, and apartment houses that line the side streets off Madison Avenue.

At the **Wildenstein Gallery,** 19 E. 64th St., between Fifth and Madison Avenues (tel. 744-2925), you can lose yourself in the dreamy colors of master French impressionists Monet, Manet, and Renoir, and see more recent examples of French art too.

The **Richard York Gallery,** 21 E. 65th St., between Fifth and Madison Avenues (tel. 772-9155), is the place to see important American art dating from 1800 to 1950. Featured are works by Kensett and others of the Hudson River School, American impressionists like William Merritt Chase, early works by Georgia O'Keefe, western art by Remington, and still-life and marine paintings.

The **Knoedler Gallery,** 19 E. 70th St., near the Frick Museum (tel. 794-0550), has an old masters department, but much of its focus is on modern masters like Robert Motherwell, Frank Stella, Richard Diebenkorn, David Smith, and Adolph Gottlieb.

Up the stairs at 851 Madison Ave., between 70th and 71st Streets, are two top-notch galleries. **Barbara Mathis** (tel. 249-3600) shows Americans of the early 20th century such as Calder and Arthur Dove, works on paper by such Europeans as Matisse and Picasso, as well as contemporary artists. And the **Hirschl / Adler Modern** (tel. 744-6700) features mostly well-known living artists, including painter Philip Pearlstein and sculptor Isaac Witkin.

If you're looking for abstract art, the place to find it is the **Willard Gallery**, 29 E. 72nd St., corner of Madison Avenue (tel. 744-2925). Here you may see comical environmental installations, small gem-like clay sculptures, large colorful paintings, or enormous sculptures of aluminum pieces hammered around trees and rocks.

An intimate and handsome gallery housed in a brownstone, **Xavier Fourcade Gallery**, 36 E. 75th St., near the Whitney Museum (tel. 535-3980), boasts an impressive roster of modern and contemporary artists, like deKooning, Gorky, LeCorbusier, Westermann, and Eva Hesse. Don't miss the pleasant courtyard, where the exhibits include banged-up and colorful car parts made into sculpture by John Chamberlain.

The focus at the **David Findlay Gallery**, 984 Madison Ave., at 77th Street (tel. 249-2909), is 19th- and 20th-century French art. The ambience is appropriately intimate and chic, and you can view old French favorites like Dufy and Vuillard.

Nothing is too bizarre for **Castelli Graphics**, 4 E. 77th St., between Fifth and Madison Avenues (280-0673), to exhibit. The specialty of the house is graphic pop and minimal art by luminaries such as Andy Warhol (whose Campbell Soup cans and Marilyn Monroe pieces are sold here), Jasper Johns, Robert Rauschenberg, and Roy Lichtenstein. In the photography section you'll find photographs by Sandy Skögland, Eve Sonneman, and Eve Arnold.

Three floors of art at the **Graham Gallery**, 1040 Madison Ave., at 78th Street (tel. 535-5767), are enough to give any art lover an eyeful. The first two floors show 19th- and 20th-century American paintings and sculpture, plus British pottery. The third floor shows contemporary paintings and sculpture.

Two galleries at 1020 Madison Ave., between 78th and 79th Streets, are recommended visits. **Jeffrey Hoffeld & Co.** (tel. 734-5505) is a new gallery that's becoming well known in the art world for interesting showings of contemporary and modern art. And at the **James Goodman Gallery** (tel. 772-2288), see modern favorites like Botero, Calder, Giacometti, Lichtenstein, and Klee, as well as contemporary artists like Twombly and Steinberg.

At the **Forum Gallery**, 1018 Madison Ave., between 79th and 80th Streets (tel. 772-7666), you can enjoy your art al fresco, because the gallery exhibits its contemporary sculpture in a charming penthouse roof garden. Inside, admire the works of American figurative painters and sculptors.

The **Rachel Adler** gallery, 58 E. 79th St., between Madison and Park Avenues (tel. 831-3824), specializes in early 20th-century Russian art. It also shows works by the Dadaists and Italian Futurists.

SoHo

Saturday afternoon is *the* time to visit SoHo, when the art scene is moving at full speed. This charming neighborhood of art galleries, restaurants, antique shops, bookstores, and boutiques is a flourishing artist's colony. When rents in nearby Chelsea and Greenwich Village became prohibitive in the early 1960s, artists moved to SoHo (which stands for south of Houston Street), attracted to airy lofts in the commercial buildings. Now it seems that every other storefront is an art gallery.

Art is found everywhere south of Houston Street: in the historic facades of

19th-century cast-iron buildings, on the streets, even in the urban chic dress of many of SoHo's strollers. Artists-in-residence never let an opportunity escape to express themselves; even some building walls have been transformed into street art. Notice the trompe l'oeil mural painted on the building at the southwest corner of Prince and Greene Streets. Visually SoHo is one of the most stimulating neighborhoods in the city, with art affixed to fire hydrants and street lights, and displayed in bars and boutiques.

The uncontested leader of the gallery scene in SoHo is **Leo Castelli,** the wise old impressario of modern art whose unerring knack of spotting groundbreaking artists has made him a New York legend since the early 1950s. Begin your tour at 142 Greene St., between Houston and Prince Streets (tel. 431-5160), one of Castelli's three galleries in the city. There you'll see work by the stars of modern art—Lichtenstein, Rauschenberg, Stella, Warhol, and Johns, to name a few. Also expect eye-opening canvases by rising stars like the Italian Sandro Chia and the much talked-about David Salle.

In the same building are two other galleries on the forefront of the art scene. The **John Weber Gallery** (tel. 966-6115) is associated with conceptual, minimal, and architecturally oriented art. In plain words, that means you may see anything from a row of elegant white grid-like cubes stacked on the floor in the shape of a cross, to a photograph of an Indian woman weaving on a hand loom (titled *St. Laurent Demands a Whole New Lifestyle*). **Sperone Westwater Gallery** (tel. 431-3685) shows contemporary painting, sculpture, and conceptual work in traditional and alternative materials such as the neo-expressionist paintings of the Italians Cucchi, Clement, and Chia, the scribble drawings of Cy Twombly, and the landscape-inspired sculptures of Richard Long.

Up the street at the **Barbara Toll Gallery,** 146 Greene St. (tel. 431-1788), you may find anything from a group of figures falling about the canvas in unexpected ways, to a large black painting with an oval antique mirror in the middle of it.

The **Paula Cooper Gallery,** 155 Wooster St., just south of Houston Street (tel. 674-0766), shows a mixed bag of known contemporary artists. They include painters Jennifer Bartlett and Elizabeth Murray, and sculptors Linda Benglis and Donald Judd.

At the **Barbara Gladstone Gallery,** 99 Greene St. (tel. 431-3334), the work is hard to classify but worth a peek. You may find a moving electric sign or a painting of large greenish figures lying next to a pool.

The checkerboard floor at the **Tony Shafrazi Gallery,** 163 Mercer St., between Houston and Prince Streets (tel. 925-8732), is a fitting setting for the bold, rebellious, and sometimes playful works of younger artists. Best known is the graffiti artist Keith Haring, whose works you may also see in the subway stations. Also crowd-pleasers are Ronnie Cutrone's paintings of Casper the Friendly Ghost and other comic heroes.

The top-notch **Diane Brown Gallery,** 100 Greene St., between Prince and Spring Streets (tel. 219-1060), shows mainly sculpture by emerging artists. Brown is known for her interesting theme shows. For example, one show exhibited pieces that artists considered their failures—and discussions of how such failures often spurred the artists' development into new directions.

The **Mary Boone Gallery,** 417 West Broadway, between Prince and Spring Streets (tel. 431-1818), has quickly become one of SoHo's institutions, with an impressive roster of artists like the minimalist Brice Marden, the German painter Georg Baselitz, and others well known in contemporary art. *New York* magazine called Boone "the New Queen of the Art Scene" and her handsome gallery is a must to see.

Stop into the **Sonnabend Gallery,** 420 West Broadway (tel. 966-6160), to see the works of the famous British team Gilbert and George, the photographs of John Baldessari, and other important contemporary European and American artists. In the same building, see the other **Leo Castelli Gallery** (tel. 431-5160), his second in SoHo, with more works by his stable of illustrious artists.

Tribeca

Just a few blocks south of SoHo is an old loft district on the fast track to trendiness—Tribeca. Here again, nomenclature describes geography: the triangle below Canal Street. For several years the area has been touted as "the next SoHo," and indeed Tribeca resembles its high-rent neighbor of, say, ten years ago. Young galleries and glossy restaurants dot blocks still dominated by rumbling trucks, warehouses, and greasy spoons. Among the key attractions. . . .

The **Bette-Stoler Gallery,** 13 White St., between West Broadway and Church Street (tel. 966-5090), shows contemporary painting and sculpture by younger American and European artists. Fashion-conscious visitors may recognize the gallery's large, elegantly unfinished space, which the French and Italian *Vogue* magazines have adopted as a favorite setting for photo-spreads.

Just around the corner is the always-interesting and often-fascinating **Artist's Space,** 223 West Broadway, between White and Franklin Streets (tel. 226-3970). One of New York City's most active "alternative spaces," it has nurtured many young artists now emerging as trailblazers. Here the work ranges from the recognizable to the outlandish—such as moosehead trophies covered with colored foil and sequins. The gallery also stages performances and avant-garde video showings.

Another "alternative space" is—yes, the name says so—the **Alternative Museum,** 17 White St. (tel. 966-4444). In addition to its regular—and often bizarre—exhibitions, the museum is known for its music series. One series features music from far-flung places like Zimbabwe, Poland, and India; another series focuses on what's been dubbed "new music"—challenging work by young composers. Call ahead for program information. Admission generally runs from $7 to $12.

Seven blocks south is the **Hal Bromm Gallery,** on the second floor at 90 West Broadway, at Chambers Street (tel. 732-6196). This gallery's well-lit ambience makes it a pleasant place to see interesting work in a variety of media. One recent exhibition, for instance, featured "Chain-Saw People"—human figures hacked with a chain-saw out of tree trunks and painted in the brightest of colors.

The East Village

The East Village is the art world's newest—and strangest—frontier. Not long ago this area—between Second Avenue and Avenue B, from East 2nd to East 13th Streets—wasn't even a blip on the cultural map. Today it's making headlines, drawing packs of younger collectors, and sparking a boom of real-estate gentrification. Rents for fixed-up tenement apartments are skyrocketing as well-scrubbed yuppies clamor for quarters alongside green-haired punks, and the neighborhood's long-ignored poor worry about being squeezed out. If you're looking for a sense of adventure and artistic risk, the still-scruffy streets of the East Village are a fresh place to explore.

Among the area's two score galleries, **Gracie Mansion,** 167 Avenue A, between 10th and 11th Streets (tel. 477-7331), clearly has grabbed the spotlight. The owner, Gracie Mansion, named herself and her gallery after the New York City mayor's official residence. But the gallery, a storefront, is a far cry from its namesake. And the work shown—how new is it? "They call it post-contemporary," said one young gallery worker, "because they hang it before the paint's dried."

Another acknowledged East Village trendsetter is **P.P.O.W.,** 216 E. 10th St., between First and Second Avenues (tel. 477-4084). Here the overtones are often political. One recent group show, for instance, featured carved wooden fish in various states of pollutant-caused decay, and violent, angry paintings that protest such things as South African apartheid and the effects of U.S. policy in Central America.

Other Galleries

The **Center for Inter-American Relations,** 680 Park Ave., at 68th Street (tel. 249-8950), has changing exhibits of ancient and contemporary fine art and crafts from Latin America and Canada. Recent shows have included 19th-century Latin American photographs and the work of a Canadian architect. The gallery is open Tuesday to Sunday from noon to 6 p.m. free of charge.

The **Institute for Urban Resources** has two exhibition spaces: **The Clocktower,** at 108 Leonard St. (tel. 233-1096), and **P.S. 1,** at 46–01 21st St., in Long Island City, Queens (tel. 718/784-2084). Both show provocative contemporary art in group or one-person shows of painting and sculpture, run concert programs, and have studios available to artists from home and abroad at low rents.

The Clocktower has extraordinary gallery space inside one of Manhattan's few existing clocktowers. It is open Thursday through Sunday from noon until 6 p.m. free of charge, though donations are welcomed.

P.S. 1 is housed in the city's first public school, a Romanesque Revival building of the 1890s. As well as changing exhibits, it curates site-specific installations, and has a fashion wing. It is open Thursday through Sunday from noon to 6 p.m. Admission is $1. Take the E or F train to 23rd Street and Ely Avenue, or the no. 7 train to Courthouse Square.

The **African-American Institute,** located at 833 United Nations Plaza, between 46th and 47th Streets (tel. 949-5666), has two nice-size galleries, and runs three exhibitions a year of African art. Most exhibitions are of traditional art, but a recent show was of a contemporary South African artist.

The gallery is open Monday through Friday from 9 a.m. to 5 p.m. and on Saturday from 11 a.m. to 5 p.m. free of charge.

AUCTION HOUSES: The quality of a new piece of work can often be measured by the amount one is willing to bid for it. Artistic movements are made or forgotten at the city's great auction houses. Although you may have to pay a "bidding paddle" fee in order to buy something—one doesn't bid here by raising a hand—there are pre-auction exhibits open for public inspection at no charge.

Mention art auction and you must mention **Sotheby Parke Bernet,** the premier auction house, at 1334 York Ave., between 71st and 72nd Streets (tel. 472-3400). The million-dollar art sales will have you holding your breath, but don't forget to check out the less pricey, more down-to-earth auctions of quilts, furniture, antique clothes, and autographs.

Christie's Galleries, 502 Park Ave., at the corner of 59th Street (tel. 546-1000), auctions paintings and sculpture fit for a millionaire or a museum. At **Christie's East,** 219 E. 67th St., between Second and Third Avenues (tel. 570-4141), you can pick up an entire collection of mounted hunting trophies, or if you have no room in your home for those, settle for perhaps a few prints, some antique clothing, dolls, or Victoriana.

THEATER: Many visitors shun the New York theatrical scene because they consider it too expensive for all but the most avid and wealthy fans. But with a little imagination and persistence, almost anyone can see even the glossiest productions at reasonable prices.

THEATER

For those with hearts set on the expensive, glittery **Broadway** shows, there are services that can help you beat the price. We have listed several of them below. For those willing to venture beyond mainstream theater, there's a vast array of small theaters and companies that produce highly competent, motivated work at lower cost. These are the **off- and off-off-Broadway theaters.** They produce more experimental and original shows, and because of that, have gained a luster of their own in recent years. Many theater-goers prefer off- and off-off-Broadway to their more conventional Broadway counterparts. With the increased patronage, off- and off-off-Broadway shows have also become more expensive, though they still undercut Broadway prices. Off-Broadway tickets cost between $15 and $20. Seats for off-off-Broadway performances, which are even more experimental and unusual, usually cost between $7.50 and $15.

Obtaining Tickets

Without careful financial planning, the lights may be the only thing you'll see on Broadway. Tickets for most orchestra seats run between $35 and $50, and even the less expensive second-balcony tickets seldom start at less than $20. Inexpensive seats are more accessible during the slower, summer months. But even then, finding good, low-priced seats is difficult on short notice.

One solution is to attend previews, the New York name for out-of-town tryouts. You get to see the show before opening night at prices reduced by as much as a third. You also risk spending money on an unsuccessful performance. However, most New York theater-goers consider previews a good bet. They're listed in the *New York Times,* the *Village Voice,* and other local publications. Using **twofers** is another way to beat the system. These are coupons that buy two tickets for the price of one. When a production is nearing the end of its run or when the audience is sparse, producers distribute twofers to fill up empty seats. Less popular Broadway shows distribute the coupons prodigiously to hotels, drugstores, and barbershops. More successful productions keep circulation low key to protect sales of full-price tickets at the box office. Producers send the coupons out through mailing lists and to clubs, organizations, labor unions, and doctors' offices, which makes obtaining them without an insider's knowledge difficult.

One reliable source of twofers is **Hit Shows.** Send a self-addressed, stamped envelope to their office at 303 W. 42nd St., Room 303, New York, NY 10036, and ask to be placed on their mailing list. You can also call them at 212/581-4211, and after requesting their schedule, pick up the coupons at their office. The service is open Monday through Friday between 9:30 a.m. and 5 p.m. Another good source for twofers is the **New York Convention and Visitor's Bureau** at 2 Columbus Circle.

TKTS, the Times Square Theater Center, at Broadway and 47th Street (tel. 354-5800), is a third way to enjoy theater without blowing your budget. The nonprofit service sells half-price tickets to Broadway and off-Broadway shows on the day of the performance (with a $1.25-per-ticket service charge). It's open Monday through Saturday from 3 to 8 p.m., and on Sunday from noon to 8 p.m. Tkts has a second office at 2 World Trade Center in the financial district, which is open Monday through Saturday from 11:30 a.m. to 5:30 p.m. Tickets may be paid for with cash or travelers checks only. The group that sponsors Tkts, the Theater Development Fund, also offers $6.50 Broadway and off-Broadway tickets to teachers, students, performers, and members of unions.

Some Special Theaters

The number and variety of theatrical productions in New York is unsurpassed in the world, and deciphering the scene to pick between Broadway, off-

and off-off-Broadway can be a tricky business. One solution is to peruse the ads and reviews in the *New York Times,* the *New Yorker,* the *Village Voice,* and *New York* magazine. We have highlighted some of the most interesting, unusual, and inexpensive shows in town.

One of the best deals is the summertime **New York Shakespeare Festival.** Tuesday through Sunday from late June to early September, some 2000 people fill the outdoor Delacorte Theater in Central Park (tel. 598-7100). Against a backdrop of thick, green summertime trees, the audience watches classic and modern plays such as *Measure for Measure* and the *Mystery of Edwin Drood.* The theater is one of the best in town, and it's free. No surprises, then, at the long lines in front of the Delacorte, which distributes tickets, two per person, at 6 p.m. each night before the 8 p.m. show. The theater is accessible by the 79th Street entrance on the East Side and 81st Street entrance on the West. Try to get there before 5:30 p.m. because the tickets run out fast.

When the summer months are over, the Shakespeare Festival returns to its permanent home at the **Public Theater,** 425 Lafayette St., south of 8th Street and just east of Greenwich Village (tel. 598-7100). The theater's seven playhouses offer high-caliber shows year round by a variety of companies. Among the Shakespeare Festival's most notable productions here were *A Chorus Line* and *The Pirates of Penzance,* which became hits on Broadway. Public Theater tickets cost between $18 and $20 apiece. But one-quarter of the seats are held to be sold at half price the day of the performance. These discount seats, known as Quiktix, are available at 6 p.m. before evening shows and at 1 p.m. on matinee days.

The **Library and Museum of the Performing Arts,** 111 Amsterdam Ave., at 65th Street (tel. 870-1600), is another source of good, free theater. This Lincoln Center branch of the New York Public offers plays, solo and chamber concerts, dance programs, musicals, and films between June and September with no admission fees. Monday through Friday performances begin at 4 p.m. On Saturday the show is at 2:30 p.m. Information about current schedules is available at 870-1630 or at any public library branch.

The Performing Arts theater has a rival in the **Manhattan Theater Club,** 321 E. 73rd St., between First and York Avenues (tel. 288-2500). The club, which now produces its shows at The Space at the City Center, 155 W. 55th St., between Sixth and Seventh Avenues (tel. 246-8989 or 757-1941), is considered one of the best buys in town. As a member, you subscribe to plays, poetry readings, and musicals. During its Mainstage Season, it premieres plays by well-known contemporary writers performed by such actors as Glenn Close, Bernadette Peters, and Sam Waterston. The best way to see the club's plays is to become a subscriber, or member, by buying a five-play series membership for the September-to-June season. Memberships go for as little as $60 (call 288-2638 for details), and single tickets, which go on sale as each play opens, start at $25.

For musicals, comedy, and drama, the **West Side Theater,** at 407 W. 43rd St., between Ninth and Tenth Avenues (tel. 541-8394), is a good place to go. Ticket prices average $17.50 to $24. Recent productions have included *Orphans* and *Penn & Teller.*

The **Equity Library Theater,** a private theatrical company sponsored in part by the actor's union, gives performances from September to June at the Master's Institute, 103rd Street and Riverside Drive. Performances are Tuesday through Sunday at 8 p.m., with a matinee on Saturday and Sunday. Call 869-9266 for information and reservations. The suggested contribution for tickets is only $7.

One inexpensive theater which gets kudos from the *Village Voice* is the

American Place Theater, 11 W. 46th St., near Radio City (tel. 246-3730). Since its inception in 1964, the theater has won almost 20 *Village Voice* Obies, awards for outstanding theater outside the mainstream. The theater produces plays by living American playwrights. Its talent list includes such recognized writers as Steve Tesich, who wrote the screenplay for *The World According to Garp,* and Sam Shepard. The theater premiered *Do Lord Remember Me,* which moved to Broadway with good reviews, and *Jubilee,* a celebration of Black American culture. Tickets cost $15.

For Spanish speakers and students, **Repertorio Español,** 138 E. 27th St., between Lexington and Third Avenues (tel. 889-2850), performs classic Spanish works and contemporary Latin American drama, comedies, and musicals. Once a year the company, which performs in the Gramercy Arts Theater at the same address, features a performance of flamenco dance. Tickets usually run from $10 to $15, with a $3 discount available to students and seniors.

Off-Off-Broadway

Many of the off-off-Broadway theaters have gained reputations for producing excellent, innovative shows. Indeed, the theaters' departure from the slick Broadway tradition is considered a selling point by the most sophisticated theater fans. Under a special agreement with the actors' union, known as Actors' Equity, the off-off-Broadway, or "showcase," theaters use only Equity members. Though they work on very low budgets out of about 150 tiny theaters scattered about the city, the off-off-Broadway companies are considered a nurturing ground for up-and-coming actors, directors, and writers. Each year a few showcase productions move to Broadway, where they often achieve critical acclaim. If you're willing to experiment, you may be one of the first to see a Broadway hit or a new star, and at a relatively low cost.

One offbeat group which has received *Village Voice* Obies is the **Squat Theater Company,** 256 W. 23rd St., between Seventh and Eighth Avenues (tel. 206-0945). In the Squat Theater building, the company writes, produces, and performs original plays. In between play seasons, when the company members are gearing up, the theater sometimes offers 24-hour movie marathons featuring such films as *Dick Tracy* and *In Cold Blood.* Tickets for the plays are $10, and for the movies, $4.

The **Hudson Guild Theater,** at 441 W. 26th St., between Ninth and Tenth Avenues, and **Playwright Horizons,** at 416 W. 42nd St., also between Ninth and Tenth Avenues, have also received good reviews. The Hudson Guild has produced such award winners as *On Golden Pond* and *Da.* The theater's season runs from September to June. Tickets start at $12 and can be reserved by calling 760-1980. Playwright Horizons features new shows by American writers. Among its most notable is Chris Durang's *Sister Mary Ignatius,* which moved to off-Broadway. Some plays in the process of being written are presented in workshops, free of charge. Tickets, starting at $18, can be reserved at 564-1235.

The **Asia Society,** 725 Park Ave., at 70th Street (tel. 288-6400), a nonprofit organization promoting a better understanding of Asian culture, sponsors both traditional and contemporary performing arts from Asia. Usually performed by visiting Asian artists or by Americans of Asian extraction, the society's performances combine drama, dance, music, and even puppetry. The high quality of its presentations is evidenced by the society's winning of a 1985 Obie for its contribution to off-Broadway theater. Admission to the society's 258-seat auditorium usually costs $8 to $20, although there are a limited number of the best tickets sold at half price to students, and some shows are free. Most performances are from September to June, but call for a current schedule.

For theater fans with a penchant for politics, there are two innovative companies sure to be intriguing. The **Veterans' Ensemble Theater Company** (tel. 664-0086) produces plays year round about everything from Agent Orange to veterans still living in Vietnam. Performances, which have included John Sedlak's *A Few Good Men*, are held at the Raft Theater, 432 W. 42nd St., between Ninth and Tenth Avenues, and in the Public Theater, 425 Lafayette St. Tickets at the Raft are $6, and at the Public, $14. The **New Federal Theater Group**, 466 Grand St. (tel. 598-0400), uses minority issues as themes for plays that run from September to June. *For Colored Girls Who Have Considered Suicide / When the Rainbow is Enuf*, which got rave reviews when it later hit Broadway, premiered here. This company also received a *Village Voice* Obie in 1983. Tickets for general-admission performances Thursday through Sunday cost $6. Since they don't have a continuous schedule, call first.

Note: For a backstage tour of Broadway, see our "More Sights/Unusual Tours" section in this chapter.

POETRY/PROSE: As one of the world's publishing centers, New York always has something literary going on, whether it be a poetry reading, a book signing, or a symposium, and such events don't always take place in formal theaters. Often churches, major bookstores, and universities sponsor such events, and generally at little or no charge. The *New York Times* entertainment section, the *Village Voice*, and *New York* magazine are good sources to check for current happenings.

A forum for some of the most highly regarded poets is the Poetry Center of the **YM-YWHA** (called the 92nd Street Y by New Yorkers), at Lexington Avenue and 92nd Street (tel. 427-6000). Umberto Eco, Mark Strand, Harold Pinter, Gjertrud Schnackenberg, and Eugene Ionesco are among those who have recently read their work there. They follow Dylan Thomas, who made this theater the stage for his fabled readings in the 1950s. There is usually a large and interesting selection of poetry readings and lectures. Tickets, which sell on a first-come, first-served basis (unless you are a member, in which case they are reserved at the beginning of the season) cost $6 and up. Performances are usually on Monday nights from mid-October to late May; for the current schedule, check listings in the *New York Times* entertainment section or write to the Poetry Center at the above address. A $70 membership fee includes admission to all 30 events of the season.

PEN, a writers' organization based at 568 Broadway, near Prince Street (tel. 334-1660), periodically sponsors literary events such as readings, symposia, and conventions at its headquarters as well as at other locations around the city. Call for a current schedule.

Many branches of the **New York Public Library,** 455 Fifth Ave., at 42nd Street (tel. 221-7676), sponsor literary readings. Usually the most famous writers can be seen either at the **Donnell Library Center,** 20 W. 53rd St., off Fifth Avenue (tel. 621-0618), or at the **Jefferson Market branch** in the Village, 425 Avenue of the Americas, between 9th and 10th Streets (tel. 243-4334). Call or stop by any branch for information.

The Writer's Voice, a literary program sponsored by the West Side YMCA, 5 W. 63rd St., between Broadway and Central Park West (tel. 787-6557), offers authors' readings every Friday from September to May at 8 p.m. All genres from mysteries to poetry are featured, and admission runs $5 to $8, depending on the individual event. The admission price also includes a reception and book party afterward, as well as half-price admission to certain nightclubs when the party's over.

CONCERTS: Free classical music performances are plentiful in New York. The

POETRY READINGS / CONCERTS   203

Juilliard School, at Lincoln Center, Broadway at 66th Street (tel. 799-5000), is considered the best music school in the nation, and it offers a wide assortment of free concerts and recitals. Symphony, opera, dance, and chamber music are among the musical performances given most Friday nights at 8:00 p.m. between September and May. On occasion there is also a weekday performance. Phone for information and schedules.

For decades, to play **Carnegie Hall,** Seventh Avenue at 57th Street (tel. 247-7800), has meant "making it" for classical musicians. Fortunately for music lovers with more taste than money, the hall—which presents orchestras, instrumental and vocal recitals, and chamber music—offers student rush tickets (also available to seniors) for $3 on the day of performance. Check that day with the box office to be sure tickets will be available. Carnegie Hall is closed in August.

Avery Fisher Hall, Broadway at 65th Street, in Lincoln Center (tel. 874-2424), is home to the New York Philharmonic, which has its season from September to May. Student rush tickets go on sale half an hour before performance time, generally on Tuesday and Thursday, and cost $5.

The **Alice Tully Hall,** also in Lincoln Center, at 1941 Broadway (tel. 362-1911), presents recitals and chamber music. Because performances there are produced by various parties, check with the box office for specific shows.

Symphony Space, 2537 Broadway, at 95th Street (tel. 864-5400), offers a grab bag of concerts with everything from classical to contemporary music. The theater also presents dance, literary readings, and drama. While the price of tickets varies with the performance, it usually runs between $6 and $10. James Joyce devotees will want to catch the annual Bloomsday celebration in June, which marks the anniversary of the day chronicled in *Ulysses* with readings from Joyce's works by an all-star cast. Travelers with children might want to take the kids there to see the very popular Paper Bag Players, a theater troupe for children, during January and February.

Two quaint brownstones in the center of Greenwich Village are home to the **Greenwich House Music School,** 46 Barrow St., off Seventh Avenue South (tel. 242-4770). On Friday and Saturday evenings, faculty, students, and guests perform all types of classical music—on occasion, with free admission. For information, phone the school or send a self-addressed, stamped envelope to the address above.

Many of the city's major churches, such as **Riverside Church,** 490 Riverside Dr., at 121st Street (tel. 864-2929), The **Cathedral of St. John the Divine,** Amsterdam Avenue at 112th Street (tel. 678-6888), and **St. Peter's Episcopal Church,** 336 W. 20th St., between Eighth and Ninth Avenues (tel. 807-8154), sponsor free or low-priced concerts, as do a number of universities and libraries. Call or stop by for information.

Many of the major midtown skyscrapers, such as the **IBM building,** 590 Madison at 55th Street (tel. 407-3500), and **the Citicorp Center,** 153 E. 53rd St., at Lexington Avenue (tel. 559-4259), offer free concerts in their atria, especially during lunchtime.

In addition, the **New York Philharmonic** sounds off during the summer on Central Park's Great Lawn and also in other parks in all five boroughs. Some people who attend the concerts think the fireworks that accompany many of the performances are even better than the music! Call 580-8700 for details.

The **Brooklyn Museum,** Eastern Parkway and Washington Avenue, Brooklyn (tel. 718/638-5000, ext. 402), holds poetry readings as well as concerts. Performances are on Sunday from October to April. Call for specific schedules. To reach the museum, take the IRT–Seventh Avenue express subway to Eastern Parkway, the Brooklyn Museum station.

Norman Seaman's Theatre Club, 2067 Broadway (tel. 855-9293), is one of the best ways to get inexpensive concert tickets. The $29.95, 12-month membership fee allows you two orchestra tickets to at least 100 concerts at Avery Fisher Hall, Alice Tully Hall, and Carnegie Hall. Members also get half-price tickets—known as twofers—to most Broadway and off-Broadway shows, and substantial discounts at a number of movie theaters and restaurants.

OPERA: Some of the finest opera in New York is also inexpensive. The very popular **New York City Opera** at the New York State Theater, Lincoln Center, 64th Street and Broadway (tel. 870-5570), sells tickets for as little as $6. Check the *New York Times* or *New York* magazine for listings.

Bel Canto, 747 Third Ave. (tel. 752-4210), is one of the city's most notable up-and-coming companies. Their performances include classical productions such as *Lakmé* and *La Duenna*, and on occasion a modern musical play. Call for performance times and ticket schedules.

The **Amato Opera Theater** performs in the Robert F. Wagner Junior High School at 319 Bowery, near East 2nd Street (tel. 228-8200), featuring younger performers in productions such as *Hansel and Gretel*, Verdi's *Falstaff* and *Aïda*. Tickets for the 40 operas in its repertoire begin at $7.

The **Light Opera of Manhattan** specializes in Gilbert and Sullivan operettas. While the singing can be quite good, the productions are accompanied by only piano and tympanni rather than a full orchestra. Tickets cost $12 to $20. As of this writing, the company was in transition between theaters. Call 718/383-5541 for performance information.

The **Opera Shop of the Vineyard Theater,** 309 E. 26th St. (tel. 683-0696), specializes in neglected and rare chamber operas, often featuring works by Donizetti. It produces two operas a year, one in December and one in April, with nine performances each. Tickets cost $10 to $12.

The **Village Light Opera Group** puts on two shows a year at the Fashion Institute of Technology's main auditorium, 227 W. 27th St., at Seventh Avenue (tel. 563-1771). The fall show is typically a Gilbert and Sullivan operetta, while the spring show is either an operetta or a musical, such as *Brigadoon*, that comes close. The group does six performances of each show, with tickets costing $9 and $16.

The **Brooklyn Lyric Opera** produces four operas a year, with most performances at the Holy Name Auditorium at 96th Street and Amsterdam Avenue (tel. 718/837-1176). Admission is $5.

The Metropolitan Opera

The Metropolitan Opera House, Lincoln Center, 64th Street and Broadway (tel. 362-6000), houses one of the finest opera companies in the world. In its modern and quite awesome theater, the company performs classics with an occasional foray into modern pieces. Performers include such internationally acclaimed operatic stars as Luciano Pavarotti, Placido Domingo, Birgit Nilsson, Renata Scotto, and Marilyn Horne. But don't expect to enjoy the theater's musical fare without paying a high price. The company offers free summertime concerts in Central Park, which are noted in local newspapers. But the only regular bargains are the $5 to $8 standing-room tickets, which go on sale the Saturday before the performance. We recommend arriving two hours before the box office opens because lines are long and tickets sell fast. Other tickets range in price from $8 to $75 for orchestra seats. Reservations can be made by phone for a $2 handling charge per ticket. The box office is open Monday to Saturday between 10 a.m. and 8 p.m., on Sunday noon to 8 p.m.

DANCE: From the Rockettes to Nureyev, from Alvin Ailey to Tommy Tune,

New York City is the apex of dance in the nation and the world. The city helped pioneer theatrical dance in the early 20th century, modern dance into the 1950s and today, and is still a beacon for the great names in dance. A typically glittering season includes visits by touring international troupes, from the Royal Danish Ballet to the Stuttgart Ballet. And we have our own New York City Ballet and the American Ballet Theater, as well as many smaller companies, covering everything from classical ballet to the experimental.

The **American Ballet Theater,** under the direction of the renowned Mikhail Baryshnikov, is the resident company at the Metropolitan Opera House (tel. 362-6000 or 799-3100). The ABT presents classics like *Les Sylphides* as well as new ballets by Lynne Taylor-Corbett, John McFall, and Twyla Tharp, among others. Generally, the ballet and opera companies keep the opera house busy year round, with the lights dimming only for August vacation.

Ticket prices for the ABT go as high as $42.50. You can ask for lower-priced balcony seats (about $14), or top-of-the-house Family Circle tickets (bring opera glasses!) for $8. Standing-room tickets ($5) are sold the day of the performance, starting when the box office opens at 10 a.m. (at noon on Saturday); but be forewarned that many fans come at dawn with coffee and blankets in the hope of getting tickets. Family Circle standing-room tickets ($5) go on sale only if the performance sells out.

The **New York City Ballet** performs at the New York State Theater in Lincoln Center (tel. 870-5570). The spring season is all of May and June, and from November to February in winter. The 1985 spring season featured two new works by Peter Martins and one by Jerome Robbins. *The Nutcracker* is performed all December. Ticket prices at the New York City Ballet range from $6 to $36, with standing room going for $3 on the day of performance.

Justly famous as they are, the ABT and the New York City Ballet are far from the only dance performance options. We have listed a variety of other New York City troupes, from the new to the well known. For starters, there's the **Beacon Theater,** 2124 Broadway, at 74th Street (tel. 787-1477), which presents everything from modern dance to the Korean National Dance Company. Ticket prices vary with the performance and group, ranging from $3.50 to $7.50.

The **Brooklyn Academy of Music,** 30 Lafayette Ave., in Brooklyn (tel. 718/636-4100), is well respected for its presentations of ballet and modern dance, from the classical to the avant-garde. The academy is old, and has seen the debuts of a century of greats, from Sarah Bernhardt to Richard Dreyfuss to the American debut of Nureyev. The theater has an express bus from Manhattan to Brooklyn and back for performances. Call for times, prices, and boarding points—also for the latest ticket prices (at this writing, they were in the process of being raised).

The **City Center,** 131 W. 55th St., between Sixth and Seventh Avenues (tel. 246-8989 or 757-1941), is in a landmark building that was once a Masonic Temple. The City Center is the place to see performances by innovative American companies like Alvin Ailey, Merce Cunningham, and comic-ballet troupes from abroad like the all-male Trocadero de Monte Carlo. There is also the space theater where productions like *Digby* are presented. Tickets are generally priced between $5 and $35.

The **Theater at Riverside Church,** 490 Riverside Dr., at 121st Street (tel. 864-2929), is one of the many cultural and other activities sponsored by this busy church. A highlight of the many types of dance performed under its auspices is the dance festival beginning each September. The season, including visiting groups, runs from September to December, and from January to June. General admission is $7; students, $5. Come early enough to look around the church.

The **Joyce Theater,** 175 Eighth Ave., at 19th Street (tel. 242-0800), reopened in 1982 in the venerable former Elgin Theater. Its program is mostly dance, with the Elliot Feld Ballet its resident company. Tickets are $12 to $20. We are looking for a strong future from the Joyce.

The **Cubiculo Playhouse,** 414 W. 51st St., between Ninth and Tenth Avenues (tel. 265-6374), presents experimental theater, with multimedia productions as well as dance, all year long. Ticket prices are only $7.

The **Martha Graham Center of Contemporary Dance,** 316 E. 63rd St. (tel. 832-9166), comprises the country's oldest dance company (founded in 1926 by the great lady herself, who still acts as its director) as well as a school where students are drawn from 30 different countries. The company generally performs a spring season in New York every year or two, with the location varying from year to year. Tickets to regular performances cost $4 to $35, but studio performances—which take place six times a year and feature students and company members—are free or cost only $2 or $3. Call the center to see if there is a performance scheduled during your stay.

Performance Space 122, 150 First Ave., at 9th Street (tel. 477-5288)—formerly P.S. 122—features mostly experimental works in dance, theater, and music. Current offerings are always listed in the *Village Voice,* and tickets cost $6.

The **Ethnic Folk Arts Center,** 179 Varick St. (tel. 620-4083), has performances by various resident companies on Saturday, Sunday, and Monday from September to June. Most performances are of postmodern dance, and tickets generally cost $5 to $7. Call for current schedule.

The **José Limon Dance Foundation** sponsors a fall and a spring performance series at the Limon Dance Center, 38 E. 19th St. (tel. 777-4764). The New Dance Series feature small companies performing modern dance in the Limon aesthetic. Tickets run $5 and $6.

The 20-year-old **Dance Theater Workshop,** at 219 W. 19th St. (tel. 924-0077), is both a performance space for such established artists as Diane Jacobowitz and D. J. MacDonald, and a forum for new choreographers and dancers. The workshop offers regular performances year round, and every Tuesday night it puts on "Fresh Tracks," a program of five or six new works by up-and-coming choreographers. Tickets are $7.

The world-famous **Dance Theater of Harlem,** 466 W. 152nd St. (tel. 977-7751), was founded in 1969 by Arthur Mitchell and Karel Shook as Mitchell's personal commitment to the people of Harlem following the assassination of Martin Luther King, Jr. It comprises both the renowned ballet company, which tours the world and performs at various New York theaters, and a school of allied arts. If you catch the company while it's in town, you're in for an impressive show, generally for prices that run from $10 to $25. If you don't catch them, you might want to attend one of the school's open houses, which take place at 3 p.m. the second Sunday of every month from September to June. Depending on who's in town at the time, students and company and workshop ensemble members perform. Admission is only $3 for adults and $2 for children.

The cultural program at the **Cooper Union,** 41 Cooper Square, at Third Avenue and East 7th Street (tel. 254-6300), includes free dance performances during fall and spring. Call to see what's scheduled for the Union's Great Hall.

Of course you'll find that dance activities change week by week. Check the newspapers and local magazines, especially the *Village Voice* and *New York* magazine, when you arrive. Chances are you'll find something interesting. And before you call the box office, consider these money-saving tips. Some companies have "rush" tickets, sold at discount the day of performance to senior citizens and students with identification. Not all box offices have this, but if you qualify, ask! At the New York State Theater, as of this date, "rush" tickets are sold for the opera (but not, unfortunately, for its sister, the New York City Ballet) for only $5. Both New York City Opera and Ballet give group discounts on tickets sold in blocks of 20 or more to some performances, but this must be established in advance.

Finally, try the "long-hair" version of TKTS, the **Bryant Park Music and Dance Tickets Booth,** at 42nd Street just east of the Avenue of the Americas, at the edge of Bryant Park, for low-priced ballet and concert tickets to events at such places as Lincoln Center, Carnegie Hall, and the 92nd Street Y. Tickets are sold on the day of performance at half price, with a small service charge. The booth is open on Tuesday, Thursday, and Friday from noon to 7 p.m., on Wednesday and Saturday from 11 a.m. to 7 p.m., and on Sunday from noon to 6 p.m. Call 382-2323 after 12:30 p.m. for information on ticket availability.

4. Entertainment

TELEVISION: TV people are always looking for audiences to fill up their studios. Unfortunately for us, Hollywood has lured a lot of the entertainment industry away from New York, so there aren't nearly as many shows to visit now as there were in the early days of television. Participating in a studio audience is always a fun way to see how a show is produced, so it's worth a try to find a show that's open. Unless you're very lucky and see a network employee handing out tickets in Rockefeller Center on a weekday afternoon (which has happened to us), your best bet is to write to the studios way in advance. And there's another attraction to these studio broadcasts—they're absolutely free!

Below are the procedures the networks have set up for obtaining tickets.

National Broadcasting Company (Channel 4)

NBC, located at 30 Rockefeller Plaza with an entrance on West 49th Street under the familiar peacock sign (tel. 664-3055), asks that you write ahead because some shows have long waiting lists. NBC has several popular shows based in Manhattan: the "David Letterman Show," "Saturday Night Live," "Donahue," and "The Cosby Show." To write for tickets, address your request to NBC Tickets (name of show requested), 30 Rockefeller Plaza, New York, NY 10112 (postcards only). There is a limit to two tickets per request, and you must be at least 16 years old to get into the studio. NBC doesn't air many pilots, and tickets for those pilots are usually given out the day before airing.

American Broadcasting Company (Channel 7)

ABC, at 1330 Avenue of the Americas, also asks for a written request at least six months in advance. Requests, with a specific date, should be sent to ABC Guest Relations, 36A W. 66th St., New York, NY 10023 (not the Avenue of the Americas address). At press time, ABC ticketholders were invited to watch "The Morning Show," a talk show airing at 9 a.m. You, the audience, arrive at 8 a.m.

Columbia Broadcasting System (Channel 2)

At the time we went to print, CBS had no audience participation shows in the city. We can only say again that you can't go wrong by calling, as we have seen CBS employees (frequently in snappy blue blazers) in Rockefeller Center handing out tickets for an afternoon run of a pilot series. Call or write the CBS Ticket Bureau, 524 W. 57th St., New York, NY 10019 (tel. 975-2476). By the way, CBS corporate headquarters is housed in a black-glass tower, sometimes called the "Black Rock" by locals, at 51 W. 52nd St., between Fifth Avenue and Avenue of the Americas.

MOVIES—FIRST RUN, CLASSIC, AND OTHERWISE: No city in the world has a selection of films comparable to New York's. As could be expected, there are a number of places where the cinema buff can see first-run films at bargain prices, and several museums where classic, avant-garde, and documentary films are screened for the price of admission. The **St. Mark's Cinema,** on Second Avenue at 8th Street (tel. 533-9292), shows American and foreign movies. While first-run films play uptown for $6, they play here a month or so after their release for only $4, usually as part of a double feature. Another theater with low admission prices is the **Olympia Quad,** at Broadway and 107th Street (tel. 865-8128), where shows are $4 ($3 before 5 p.m.).

The **Museum of Modern Art,** 11 W. 53rd St., just west of Fifth Avenue (tel. 708-9490), screens free film classics from their fine collection every day beginning at 11 a.m. The museum admission ($4.50 for adults, $3 for students) entitles you to admittance to the screening. The museum has two theaters, Titus 1 and Titus 2, and films are shown weekdays (except Wednesday when the museum is closed) at 2, 3, 6 and 6:30 p.m., and on weekends at 2, 2:30, 5, and 5:30 p.m., with special children's programming at 12:30 p.m. on weekends. Also, on Monday nights at 8 p.m. the museum screens films by independent filmmakers.

The New American Filmmaker's Series at the **Whitney Museum,** 945 Madison Ave., at 75th Street (tel. 570-0537), is one of the most important showcases for new, independent American film in the nation. The series features avant-garde, documentary, and feature films that are not apt to be shown in commercial theaters. Films are shown daily (except Monday when the museum is closed) each afternoon and on Tuesday evenings, but not in the summer. The Whitney also screens experimental video film in its second-floor film and video gallery. (Check the museum's daily calendar for titles and showing times.) The $3 admission charge gets you in to both the museum and the film series.

Also at the **Whitney Museum** is the Films and Video on Art Series, sponsored by the education department. This special summer series on artists and art movements is usually held in July or August every day (except Monday when the museum is closed).

The **Donnell Library Media Center,** 20 W. 53rd St., a public library branch between Fifth and Sixth Avenues, has a large collection of movies, and you can check out feature films as well as shorts with a permanent library card. You must, however, reserve most films in advance. Call 621-0609 to find out what's available. There are free screenings in the Donnell Auditorium, with frequent showings of documentaries, comedy classics, and children's movies. You can also request to screen film and video features in the study center. A copy of the bimonthly publication *Events,* available free at the Donnell or any public library, lists current showings.

The **New York Public Library,** at 42nd Street and Fifth Avenue, and many of its 83 branches present free film programs, readings, and musical events throughout the year. Again, consult the publication *Events,* or call the library's public relations office at 221-7676.

The **American Museum of Natural History,** Central Park West between 77th and 81st Streets (tel. 873-4225), presents anthropological and travel films in its auditorium at various times during the week. Your contribution upon entering the museum is the only cost. The museum also shows films in its Naturemax Theater. The screen is four stories high and 66 feet wide, and is one of 12 of its kind in the Western Hemisphere. During the week, screenings are every hour from 10:30 a.m. to 4:30 p.m.; on the weekends, to 7:30 p.m. Admission is $3, $1.50 for children (on Friday and Saturday, free after 5 p.m.).

Exceptional Japanese films, not readily available elsewhere, are regularly shown at the **Japan Society,** 333 E. 47th St. (tel. 752-0824). Screenings are usually on Friday at 7:30 p.m. and occasionally on Saturday and Sunday at 2 p.m. Admission is $5. All films are in Japanese with English subtitles.

The **French Institute,** 22 E. 60th St., just east of Fifth Avenue (tel. 355-6100), and **Goethe House,** 1014 Fifth Ave., between 82nd and 83rd Streets (tel. 744-8310), also present films from abroad that are unlikely to gain commercial release in this country. Call for schedules and prices.

Free documentary films of topical interest are shown weekly at the **Public Theater,** 425 Lafayette St., near Astor Place (tel. 598-7171). Showings are every Friday, Saturday, and Sunday at 2 p.m. Ticket distribution begins at 1 p.m.

The **Millennium Media Center,** 66 E. 4th St., between Second Avenue and the Bowery (tel. 673-0090), includes an avant-garde film series, usually on weekend evenings but not in the summer. Filmmakers are often present to show and discuss their work. A contribution of between $3 and $4 is asked for. Millennium also has a policy of open screenings—anyone can bring in his or her film and show it on most Friday evenings from 8 to 11 p.m.

The **8th Street Playhouse,** 52 W. 8th St., between Fifth and Sixth Avenues (tel. 674-6515), frequently runs festivals, such as an annual 3-D movie festival, and always has midnight showings of cult classics like the *Rocky Horror Picture Show* and *A Clockwork Orange,* as well as first-run features. Call for exact times of shows, prices, and current listings.

The **American Museum of the Moving Image,** 34–31 35th St., Astoria, Queens (tel. 718/784-4742), presents a film series—avant-garde, silent, historical retrospectives, animation, and experimental films—on Saturday nights at 7:30 p.m. from October to December and March to May. At 6:30 p.m., before the screenings, video art is shown in the gallery. The museum will move into its renovated building at 34–12 36th St. (tel. 718/784-4520), the former East Coast facility for Paramount Pictures, in April 1987.

A.I.R. Gallery, 63 Crosby St., (tel. 966-2111) has film, video, and performance series held at various times during the year. Call for schedules and prices.

Other recommended theaters which regularly feature classic, foreign, and avant-garde films and retrospectives, are the **Thalia,** Broadway at 95th Street (tel. 222-3370); the **Bleecker St. Cinema,** 144 Bleecker St., between LaGuardia Place and Thompson Street (tel. 674-2560); the **Film Forum,** 57 Watts St., two blocks north of Canal at Sixth Avenue (tel. 431-1590); the **Metro Cinema,** at 99th Street and Broadway (tel. 222-1200); **Cinema Village,** on 12th Street, east of Fifth Avenue (tel. 924-3363); the **Hollywood Twin,** Eighth Avenue at 47th Street (tel. 246-0717); the **Regency,** Broadway at 67th Street (tel. 724-3700); **Theater 80,** 80 St. Mark's Pl., near First Avenue (tel. 254-7400); and the **Carnegie Hall Cinema,** Seventh Avenue at 57th Street (tel. 757-2131).

Finally, not a week goes by without a special screening or film festival somewhere in the city. Check the weekly listings in the *Village Voice* or the Sunday *New York Times* for information.

5. Zoos and Botanical Gardens

The world-famous **Bronx Zoo** serves both as a fascinating educational and recreational center for animal lovers of all ages, and as one of the world's most successful repository/breeding centers for the earth's diminishing wildlife. With 265 acres, it's the largest urban zoo in the U.S. and is home to nearly 4000 wild animals. Among them are 50 species considered endangered and four species officially extinct in nature (look for them: Père David's deer, Mongolian wild horses, Formosan Sika deer, and the European bison). Each year there are more than 1000 births among the zoo's animal population; other zoos throughout the country—and even the world—look to the Bronx Zoo for new acquisitions.

One of the zoo's most popular features is Wild Asia, an exciting 37 acres in which 15 species of Asian animals roam an open expanse of land cultivated to simulate their natural environment. The area is accessible only by monorail ($1.25 for adults, 75¢ for children), with a half-hour tour narrated by a knowledgeable guide. Wild Asia hosts Siberian tigers, Asian elephants, guar (the world's largest wild cattle), and axis deer, all of which pass before the windows of the monorail. The zoo's newest and most ambitious project is Jungle World, a one-acre wood- and glass-enclosed habitat in which animals wander more or less freely through a re-created volcanic scrub forest, a mangrove swamp, a lowland evergreen rain forest, and a mountain rain forest. It uses an artful combination of real and artificial elements to simulate the natural habitats of the species it contains.

One of the zoo's unique attractions is its participatory Children's Zoo, in which youngsters don giant fox ears and owls' eyes, climb a giant rope spider web, and crawl through a prairie dog tunnel to see what it's like to be an animal. For an overview of the zoo, take the Safari tour train (closed in winter); to get from one end of the zoo to the other quickly, board the Skyfari tramway (also closed in winter). But for real excitement, climb into a llama-drawn cart or atop a camel or an elephant—rides definitely not to be missed!

You can easily spend an entire day at the zoo; and for those who do, there's a cafeteria with reasonably priced meals, snackbars throughout the park that stock traditional zoo fare—hot dogs, hamburgers, and sodas—or you can pack a lunch and eat at picnic tables.

Zoo hours are 10 a.m. to 5 p.m. Monday through Saturday, to 5:30 p.m. on Sunday and holidays (one hour earlier during the winter months). Admission is free Tuesday through Thursday; other days it's $3 for adults, $1.25 for children 2 to 12, and free for children under 2 and senior citizens. Rides and tours charge fees throughout the week. To get to the zoo by subway from Manhattan, take the IRT–Seventh Avenue no. 2 train to Pelham Parkway and proceed west to the Bronxdale entrance. Liberty Lines provides express bus service from stops in Manhattan on Madison Avenue (call 652-8400 for schedule and stops); the fare is $3 and you must have the exact change.

Near the zoo, but a healthy walk away, is the **New York Botanical Garden,** 200th Street and Southern Boulevard, Bronx Park. It is a lovely 250 acres of woods and waterways, lawns and carefully cultivated gardens, and a spectacular glass conservatory. Here, for a good part of a day, you can lose the sights of the city—if not its sounds—and you might even get lost yourself. Stroll through Rhododendron Valley or down Azalea Way, resplendent in late May and early June. Roam a 40-acre hemlock forest—the only uncut woodland in New York City. Follow the path along the Bronx River, past a waterfall to a restored 19th-century mill that now houses a riverside café. Above all, don't miss the famous Enid A. Haupt Conservatory, an acre of gardens in a gorgeous crystal palace, modeled after the 1844 Palm House of the Royal Botanical Gardens at Kew, England. Admission to the conservatory is $2.50 for adults, $1.25 for children; free on Wednesday. Open daily from 10 a.m. to 4 p.m..

The museum building houses a gift shop for plant fanciers, and for the serious student of flora, one of the largest horticultural libraries in the world (open Monday through Thursday from 9:30 a.m. to 6 p.m., on Friday and Saturday to 4 p.m.). The garden grounds are open year round from dawn to dusk. That's typically until 5 p.m. from October through May, 8 p.m. June through September. Call 220-8700 for information. By subway, take the IRT–Lexington Ave. no. 4 train to 200th Street and Jerome Avenue; on the IND–Sixth Avenue D train, ride to Bedford Park Boulevard. By railroad, take the Metro North Harlem local from Grand Central Station to the Botanical Garden Station.

While the old **Central Park Zoo** is being refurbished by the same folks who brought you the wonderful Bronx Zoo (the New York Zoological Society), the **Central Park Children's Zoo** remains open to the public. Located near the eastern rim of the park, at 65th Street and Fifth Avenue, the zoo should not be missed if you come with children to the East Side or Central Park. The zoo features playhouses in the style of a castle (home to the zoo's goats) and a barn (home to a donkey, cow, and barnyard birds that roam at will). There's also an awe-inspiring giant whale, with a helpless Jonah peering from inside the whale's gaping mouth. Admission is an inflation-proof 10¢, and adults must be accompanied by a child. Open daily from 10 a.m. to 4:30 p.m. Outside the Children's Zoo, at the south end of the old Central Park Zoo, there are pony rides for 75¢. They're the pint-sized equivalent of the horse-drawn carriage rides so popular with tourists at Central Park.

Though outsized and outscoped by the Bronx gardens, the **Brooklyn Botanic Garden,** just east of Prospect Park, is nevertheless among the nation's leading botanical gardens. Reclaimed from a waste dump in 1910, the garden's 50 acres are densely planted with more than 12,000 types of vegetation. Most famous are the Japanese gardens. In May and June the spectacle of masses of flowering cherry trees and fragrant magnolias is a sight to behold. The Rose Garden, at its peaks in June and September, is the third-largest collection of roses on display in the U.S., boasting over 900 varieties. There is also a herb garden, a fragrance garden for the blind, a temple garden, a fresh fruit and vegetable garden grown by children, and a Shakespeare garden—carpeted with the violets, rosemary, and chamomile from the Bard's plays and sonnets. The 10,000-square-foot conservatory displays plants grouped by their natural climate: tropical, temperate, and desert. From March to mid-November, guided tours leave every Sunday from the administration building at 1 p.m. Open year round. For information, call 718/622-4433. To get to the garden, take the IRT–Seventh Avenue express no. 2 or no. 3 train to the Eastern Parkway station.

Popular as a pastoral respite for local residents, and worth a visit if you're in the borough, is the **Queens Botanical Gardens,** 43–50 Main St., in Flushing (tel. 718/886-3800). The gardens were built upon land recovered from use as a garbage dump, and the transformation has been complete. The 39 acres are planted with rose gardens (more than 4000 bushes), a "wedding garden" (available by appointment for the big event), a crab apple grove, and an "all-American" display of native North American plants. In spring and summer the gardens present outdoor concerts, and year round there are lectures and workshops open to the public. An indoor shop sells plant-related items, and a plant shop on the grounds offers indoor and outdoor flora at well-below-retail prices. The gardens are open from 9 a.m. to dusk. To get there from Manhattan by subway, take the IRT–Flushing line (no. 7 train) from Times Square or Grand Central, and get off at the last station, Main Street. Then take the Q44 bus south —or walk ten minutes—down Main Street to the Botanical Gardens on the right.

Nearby, and another favorite local retreat, is the **Queens Zoo** (tel. 718/699-4042), where animals roam relatively unconfined and visitors view them from across dry moats. Everything on the small zoo's 18 acres is indigenous to the North American continent. There are pony rides for children and a carousel—this one a turn-of-the-century relic from Coney Island. The zoo is open from 10 a.m. to 4 p.m. daily. Take the IRT–Flushing line (no. 7 train) from Times Square or Grand Central to 111th Street in Queens. Proceed south five blocks to the old New York Hall of Science. The zoo is behind the hall's grounds.

High on the banks of the Hudson River, in the hilly, tranquil Riverdale section of the Bronx, is the **Wave Hill** estate, at West 249th Street and Independence Avenue. Once home to the likes of Mark Twain, Theodore Roosevelt, Jr., and Arturo Toscanini, the 28-acre estate is now a public garden and cultural center with programs in education, garden history, and the visual and performing arts. For aspirants to the country-estate "good life" or just city-weary travelers, a visit to Wave Hill—with its manicured grounds, historic houses, and sweeping view of the Hudson River and the Palisades—is well worth the 45-minute bus and subway ride (20 minutes by car) it takes to get there. Built in 1843, the estate served for more than a century as home to various eminent Americans and foreign dignitaries. It was presented to the City of New York in 1960 by its last proprietors and has been officially designated a historic landmark.

Today visitors can explore its four greenhouses, nature trails, English-style formal and wild gardens, herb and aquatic gardens, and the only public alpine house east of the Rockies. In summer and fall Wave Hill hosts concerts and outdoor theater; year round there are lectures, and garden and bird walks; on Sunday at 2:15 p.m. there are guided greenhouse and garden tours. Wave Hill also boasts an archive of rare commercial recordings of Toscanini, as well as memorabilia from the maestro. Call 549-2055 for information on scheduling of events.

The estate is open daily from 10 a.m. to 4:30 p.m. (from Memorial Day to Labor Day to 5:30 p.m.); on summer Wednesdays, to sunset; on summer Sundays, from 11 a.m. to 7 p.m. Admission is free Monday through Friday; on Saturday and Sunday, $2 for adults, $1 for seniors, and free for children under 14. Concerts, scheduled intermittently, are frequently on Saturday and Sunday afternoons, with admissions running from $4 to $9. To get there: Via the IRT–Seventh Avenue subway, take the Broadway–Van Cortlandt Park train (no. 1) to the 231st Street station. Board the no. 7 or 10 City Line bus at the northwest corner of 231st Street and Broadway. Leave the bus at 246th or 252nd Street. Walk across the parkway bridge and along the parkway, north from 246th or south from 252nd, to 249th Street. Proceed west to Wave Hill gate at 249th Street and Independence Avenue. Express bus service is provided by Liberty Lines from mid-Manhattan via both the East and West Sides. Have the exact fare ready: $3. Call 652-8400 for the Mid-Manhattan Riverdale Express bus schedule.

6. Sports and Recreational Facilities

BASEBALL: The **New York Yankees** play from April to October at Yankee Stadium in the Bronx (tel. 293-6000). With Billy Martin back in the manager's seat, George Steinbrenner still in the owner's box, and Dave Winfield and a crop of new players on the field, the Bronx Bombers offer a consistently exciting and controversial brand of baseball. Grandstand tickets start at $4.50 (on sale two hours before game time); box seats are on sale at the stadium ticket office. To reach Yankee Stadium, take the IND–Sixth Avenue D train or the IRT–Lexington Avenue no. 4 train (marked Woodlawn) to the Yankee Stadium stop.

The **New York Mets** play at Shea Stadium in Queens. Sparked by such young stars as Dwight Gooden and Darryl Strawberry, the Mets are once again "amazin'." The general admission seats at big, beautiful Shea afford a fine view of the action. Tickets start at $4. You can reach Shea Stadium by taking the no. 7 IRT–Flushing train to the Shea Stadium stop.

SPORTS

BASKETBALL: For basketball fans, New York is a great town. Professionally, the **New York Knickerbockers** (the Knicks) play at Madison Square Garden (tel. 564-4400). Tickets are usually easy to get at the door and start at $8. Reach the Garden by taking the IRT–Seventh Avenue no. 1, 2, or 3 train to the 34th Street–Pennsylvania Station stop.

The up-and-coming **New Jersey Nets** play at the Brendan Byrne Arena at the Meadowlands Sports Complex, East Rutherford, New Jersey (tel. 201/935-8888). Ticket prices start at $6. The arena is only a short bus trip from the Port Authority Bus Terminal (at Eighth Avenue and 42nd Street), and special buses run regularly on game nights.

On the college level, Madison Square Garden is also the home of the famous postseason N.I.T. collegiate tournament. The tournament is held in March and attracts top college teams from around the nation. Call the Garden for ticket information.

BICYCLING: During the warm-weather months, Central Park's many bike trails and wide park roads (which are closed to traffic on weekends) are jammed with cyclists. You can rent a bike at the Loeb Boathouse, Park Drive North at 72nd Street (tel. 861-4137), for $4 for the first hour and $1.75 for each subsequent half hour, up to $15 a day. If you go a few blocks away from the park, you can rent a bike for about $3 an hour at **West Side Bicycle Store,** 231 W. 96th St., at Broadway (tel. 663-7531); **Metro Bicycles,** 1311 Lexington Ave., at 88th Street (tel. 427-4450); **Gener's Bicycles,** 242 E. 79th St., at Second Avenue (tel. 249-9218)—where after the first 3½ hours, the rest of the day is free—and **A & B Bicycle World,** 663 Amsterdam Ave. (tel. 866-7600). All the above businesses require identification and/or a substantial deposit. Call for details.

From early spring until well into the fall, **American Youth Hostels,** 132 Spring St. (tel. 431-7100), organizes weekly bicycle tours (from $69 to $125) of the city and outlying areas. The tours are led by an experienced leader and are a great way to see the city. Call AYH for details and a schedule.

BOATING: Rent a rowboat at Central Park's **Loeb Boathouse,** Park Drive North at 72nd Street (tel. 288-7281). From March to December you can drift along the lake and enjoy the beauty of Central Park from the water. It's only $5 an hour, but you must leave a $20 deposit.

If you prefer sailing on a 70-foot schooner, the **Petral,** which is the fastest sailboat in New York Harbor, sails from Gangway A at Battery Park, right next to the Statue of Liberty excursion lines (tel. 825-1977). Prices range from $7 for 45 minutes to $20 for three hours. Closed during the winter.

BOXING: Madison Square Garden stages periodic boxing bouts and occasionally a championship fight. The Felt Forum, a part of the Garden sports complex, also hosts the annual Golden Gloves amateur tournament, held in the spring. Phone 564-4400 for details on upcoming matches.

FOOTBALL: The **New York Jets** are still nominally New York's home team even though they've left (some say deserted) Shea Stadium for the newer Giants Stadium in the Meadowlands Sports Complex across the river in New Jersey (tel. 201/935-8111). The Jets, who play from early September to December, have plenty of company, as both the **New York Giants** and the **New Jersey Generals** also play there. Tickets for the Jets start at $15; those for the Giants at $14, but they're hard to come by in the former case and nearly impossible in the latter, because of all the season ticket holders. That is definitely not the case with the New Jersey Generals, the New York area's entry in the new United States

Football League. The Generals play at Giants Stadium from March to July. Tickets are $6 and $12.

HOCKEY: The competition between the **Islanders** and the **Rangers** makes New York a great place for rabid hockey fans. See the Rangers at Madison Square Garden (tel. 564-4400), tickets starting at $11. The Islanders skate at the Nassau Coliseum, Hempstead Turnpike, Uniondale, N.Y. (tel. 516/794-9100), where tickets start at $16. To reach the Coliseum, take the Long Island Railroad from Penn Station to Hempstead, and then take a bus from there (ask at the Hempstead station for directions to the bus).

HORSERACING: New York's most popular spectator sport is available year round. **Belmont Park,** Hempstead Turnpike and Plainfield Avenue, Elmont, N.Y. (tel. 718/641-4700), races thoroughbreds from May through July and September through October. The Long Island Railroad goes to Belmont from Penn Station. **Aqueduct Racetrack,** Rockaway Boulevard at 108th Street, Jamaica, Queens (tel. 718/641-4700), presents thoroughbred racing January through May and October through December. The **Meadowlands Racetrack,** in East Rutherford, N.J. (tel. 201/935-8500), also races thoroughbreds September through mid-December and presents trotters late December through August. **Roosevelt Raceway,** in Westbury, Long Island (tel. 516/222-2000), presents trotters year round when they are not racing at Yonkers. **Yonkers Raceway,** in Yonkers, N.Y. (tel. 914/968-4200), also races trotters. All the tracks have special bus service from the Port Authority Bus Terminal, 42nd Street and Eighth Avenue in Manhattan.

RIDING: The **Claremont Riding Academy,** 175 W. 89th St., between Columbus and Amsterdam Avenues (tel. 724-5100), will provide you with a horse for cantering on the nearby Central Park bridle path. The cost is $20 an hour and you must be experienced riding in an English saddle. They also give riding lessons. It's open seven days a week from 6:30 a.m. to dark, 6:30 a.m. to 5 p.m. on weekends.

RUNNING: Contact the **New York Road Runners Club,** 9 E. 89th St., between Fifth and Madison Avenues (tel. 860-4455), for information concerning races ranging from short runs through Central Park to full-fledged marathons. (The Road Runners sponsor the annual New York City Marathon in October.)

SKATING: Indoor ice skating is available year round at the **Skyrink**—billed as the world's highest rink—located at 450 W. 33rd St., between Ninth and Tenth Avenues (tel. 695-6556). Admission is $4 to $6.50, plus $2 for skate rental. A winter tradition is a whirl around the ice at the **Rockefeller Center Ice-Skating** Rink (tel. 757-6230). Few things are as enjoyable as skating around the giant Rockefeller Center Christmas tree on a brisk winter's evening. Sessions are $7, plus $3 skate rental.

The roller-skating craze seems to get bigger every year. The acknowledged home of the serious skater is the **Village Skating Rink,** 15 Waverly Pl. (tel. 677-9690). This is where New York's flashiest skaters go to polish their moves. Weekend afternoon sessions are $3, plus $1 for skate rental. The **Roxy Roller Rink,** 505 W. 18th St., between Tenth and Eleventh Avenues (tel. 675-8300), is favored by celebrities and other fashionable types. Weeknight admissions start at $8, $2 for skate rentals. If you've got your own skates—or just want to watch some fancy moves—go to the area of Central Park just east of the Sheep Meadow. You'll always find a crowd on a sunny weekend afternoon.

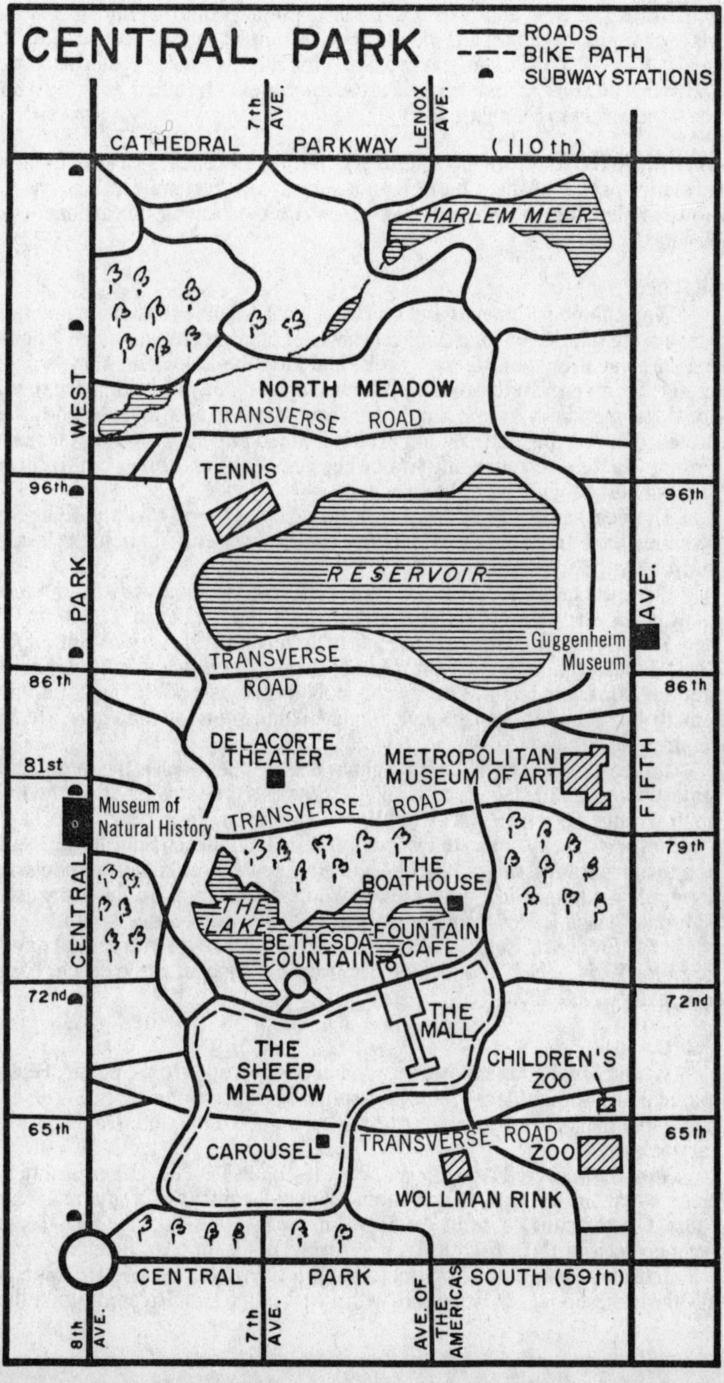
CENTRAL PARK
ROADS
BIKE PATH
SUBWAY STATIONS
7th AVE.
LENOX AVE.
CATHEDRAL PARKWAY (110th)
HARLEM MEER
NORTH MEADOW
TRANSVERSE ROAD
TENNIS
96th
RESERVOIR
WEST
PARK
CENTRAL
TRANSVERSE ROAD
Guggenheim Museum
86th
DELACORTE THEATER
METROPOLITAN MUSEUM OF ART
81st
Museum of Natural History
TRANSVERSE ROAD
FIFTH AVE.
79th
THE BOATHOUSE
THE LAKE
BETHESDA FOUNTAIN
FOUNTAIN CAFE
72nd
THE MALL
THE SHEEP MEADOW
CHILDREN'S ZOO
65th
CAROUSEL
TRANSVERSE ROAD
ZOO
WOLLMAN RINK
CENTRAL PARK SOUTH (59th)
8th AVE.
7th AVE.
AVE. OF THE AMERICAS

SOCCER: The **New York Cosmos** soccer team plays international teams from May to August at the Meadowlands Sports Complex in East Rutherford, N.J. (tel. 201/460-7100). Tickets start at $9 ($4 for children under 16 and seniors 65 and over), and buses run from the Port Authority Bus Terminal, Eighth Avenue and 42nd Street in Manhattan.

SWIMMING: New York has a number of fine ocean beaches for swimming and recreation, none of them more than a subway or short train ride away. The crowds reflect the polyglot mix that is New York—stronger on earthiness than elegance.

Beaches

World-famous **Coney Island** on Brooklyn's Atlantic coast has a fine sandy beach more than seven miles long and a welter of other attractions: roller coasters, carnival attractions, ferris wheels, and loop-the-loops. On a fine summer Sunday the air is overburdened with cries, laughter, and music while the smell of hot dogs and sticky cotton candy pervades the air, and rows of bodies are stretched out on the sand. Yet for all its continued popularity, Coney Island is in a rundown area, certainly safe by day because of the enormous crowds in season, but best avoided by night.

The beaches at Coney Island are free. To get there, take the IND–Sixth Avenue D or F trains, or the BMT West End or Sea Beach lines, to the last stop in Brooklyn, Stilwell Avenue.

If you are taking a day at the beach, be sure to stop in at Astroland Amusement Park, which towers above the boardwalk and the beach. Great fun. The **New York Aquarium** is nearby at West 8th Street and Surf Avenue (tel. 718/266-8711). Housing hundreds of examples of the world's fresh- and saltwater marine life, the Aquarium features three seal pools and a whale pool. The hours are 10 a.m. to 4:45 p.m. Monday through Sunday. Admission is $3 for adults, $1.25 for children.

Just east of Coney Island is **Brighton Beach.** The beach is the same but the atmosphere is a little less frenetic and the crowds a little smaller. Take the IND–Sixth Avenue D or the BMT N or QB train to the Brighton Beach stop.

Beyond the city limits, but worth a visit, is **Jones Beach State Park.** In addition to a beautiful series of beaches, there are tennis courts, heated pools, outdoor roller-skating rinks, and fishing. You can get there on the Long Island Railroad, which leaves from Pennsylvania Station and connects with a shuttle bus at the Freeport, Long Island, station. The railroad offers a special day-trip ticket for $7.50, which also includes showers and a locker at the beach. For details, call 718/739-4200.

Pools

Within Manhattan there are a number of pools open to the public. Fees are minimal and some offer facilities for sports and picnicking as well. The city's pools are open generally from the first week in July until Labor Day; hours may vary seasonally.

West 59th Street Pool, 533 W. 59th St. (tel. 397-3170). Other facilities include a gymnasium with weight room, handball court, and a small basketball court. Open from 11 a.m. to 7 p.m. Admission is free. Take the IRT–Seventh Avenue no. 1 or IND–Eighth Avenue A train to Columbus Circle.

John Jay Pool, East 77th Street and FDR Drive (tel. 397-3159). This is usually the busiest pool in Manhattan, with a view of the East River for sunbathers.

Open from 11 a.m. to 7 p.m. Admission is free. Take the IRT–Lexington Avenue no. 6 train to 77th Street and Lexington Avenue. Transfer to the crosstown bus on 79th Street going east.

East 23rd Street Pool, First Avenue and FDR Drive (tel. 397-3184). Open from 11 a.m. to 7 p.m. Admission is free. Take the IRT–Lexington Avenue no. 6 train to 23rd Street and transfer to a crosstown bus or walk four long blocks.

For more money ($8 on weekdays, $10 on weekends; children, half price), you can swim all day at the pool at the **Sheraton City Squire Motor Inn,** 790 Seventh Ave., at 51st Street (tel. 581-3300). See "Swimming" in Chapter VIII for more details.

TENNIS: The annual **U.S. Open Championship** is played at the National Tennis Center at Flushing Meadow Park every fall during Labor Day week. The center can be reached by taking the IRT–Flushing line (no. 7 train) to the Shea Stadium stop. For ticket information, call 949-9112.

WRESTLING: Nowhere has wrestlemania hit harder than New York. You can catch Hulk Hogan and "Rowdy" Roddy Piper in action at Madison Square Garden (tel. 564-4400). Ticket prices start at $7.

7. More Sights

These are places we like and enjoy—places we urge those with longer visits to see.

BOAT TRIP AROUND MANHATTAN: One of the best ways to view New York's famous skyline, bridges, and other architectural marvels is via a seagoing trip on one of the **Circle Line** boats (Manhattan, you will remember, is an island). The three-hour, 35-mile trip takes you on a cruise down the Hudson River, past the Statue of Liberty, across the lower harbor of Manhattan, under the Brooklyn Bridge, then up the East River past the U.N., across the Harlem River, under the George Washington Bridge, and back down the Hudson again. Along the way, a trained guide comments over a loudspeaker on the sights you pass.

Circle Line boats leave from Pier 83, at the foot of West 43rd Street (on the Hudson River). Boats begin operating in early March and continue through mid-November. From mid-June to the first week of September boats depart every 45 minutes, beginning at 9:30 a.m. up until 5 p.m. The rest of the year there are two trips per day (phone first to check the exact schedule: 563-3200). Fare for adults is $12; children under 12, $5; and seniors, $8.

THE NEW YORK EXPERIENCE: An inspiring introduction to New York is the New York Experience Theater at the bottom of the McGraw-Hill Building on Avenue of the Americas, between 48th and 49th Streets (tel. 869-0345). New York Experience is a multimedia, multisensory production involving 45 projectors, 16 screens, and 68 special effects that lets you see and feel New York's past and present without leaving your seat. You discover the island of Manhattan with its discoverers, participate in the dedication of the Statue of Liberty, see the city's major festivals and parades, and stroll down yesteryear Broadway and see its transformation today. Free with admission to the "Experience" is Little Old New York, an arcade re-creating turn-of-the-century New York.

The show is one hour and is presented every hour on the hour, from 11 a.m. to 7 p.m. Monday through Thursday, to 8 p.m. on Friday and Saturday, and from noon to 8 p.m. on Sunday. Admission is $4.50 for adults, $2.75 for children under 12, and on weekdays there's a discount for seniors.

OCEAN LINERS: There are still ocean-going luxury liners and they still embark with fanfare, amid teary-eyed well-wishers and jubilant confetti throwers. You can see all this, and also explore the ships themselves, because you're in one of the world's greatest ports. For $1 you can visit the remaining huge Atlantic ocean liners—the *Oceanic,* the *Atlantic,* the *Veracruz,* and the *Bermuda Star*—when they tie up at the West Side piers of the Hudson River, between 46th and 55th Streets.

Call 765-7437 for sailing information or pick up a copy of the *New York Times* and find the "shipping notices," usually on the third-to-last page of the paper. These list all the sailings for the next few days, telling where and when each big ship will depart. On sailing days only, the liners receive visitors. For $1 (paid to the Port Authority) you get a pass that allows you on board up until an hour before its departure.

Wander through the lavish dining rooms and elegant ballrooms, all ready and waiting for the ships' lucky passengers. A half hour before departure, a whistle tells visitors to debark. Back on the pier, join friends and relatives of the voyagers to wish them bon voyage. To reach the piers, take any midtown crosstown bus west to Twelfth Avenue, on 42nd, 49th, or 57th Street.

TRAMWAY: Glide along a steel tightrope high above the East River for a breathtaking five minutes on the **Roosevelt Island Tramway.** For 50¢ each way, you can rise high above it all and arrive almost instantly in Manhattan's newest and nearest commuter community (formerly Welfare Island, once a hospital and prison center), where garbage is collected by vacuum tubes and electric buses replace cars. The tramway departs from 60th Street and Third Avenue, and runs every quarter hour on the quarter hour until after midnight, every 7½ minutes during rush hour. Once on the island, have a stroll around and enjoy the green parks and clean streets.

NEW YORK AQUARIUM: Sharks! Big ones, and plenty of them . . . dazzling little butterfly fish . . . a colony of comical penguins . . . white whales from the arctic and fearsome piranhas from the tropics. These and nearly 20,000 marine creatures are on display at the New York Aquarium (tel. 718/266-8711), practically on the ocean at Coney Island in Brooklyn. Included in the price of admission ($3 for adults, $1.25 for children 12 and under; seniors, free after 2 p.m. except weekends) is a whale- and dolphin-training show, an electric eel demonstration, and various special exhibits and demonstrations. For the kids there's a special children's cove, where you are invited to touch and handle sea stars and horseshoe crabs. Feeding times for the penguins, sharks, seals, and walruses vary, so call 718/266-8500 to catch the feedings. The Aquarium's hours are 10 a.m. to 4:45 p.m. daily.

To reach the aquarium, take the IND–Sixth Avenue F train to the West 8th Street Station in Brooklyn and walk down the ramp to Surf Avenue.

ARCHITECTURAL AND NEIGHBORHOOD TOURING: For students of architecture, New York is a wonderland. From the very old to the very latest, it offers more variety of styles, forms, and types than probably any other New World city. From the fancifulness of the New York Yacht Club at 37 W. 44th St. and the

Italian Renaissance Villard Houses on Madison Avenue between 50th and 51st Streets, to the cast-iron warehouses of SoHo, you'll find treasures throughout the city just as you tour on your own. Check on what's happening in architecture in the city by reading Paul Goldberger's frequent columns in the *New York Times,* or consult his *The City Observed,* a guide to the architecture of New York.

The **Municipal Art Society** (tel. 935-3960) offers a "Discover New York" tour series which includes weekend walks through architectural areas of the city. Recent tours included "The City on the River," "City Hall to South Street Seaport," and "New York's First Suburbs." Guided walks are $8 for nonmembers and take place on Saturday and Sunday, every other week. Ask about midweek lectures on the New York area for the month.

Friends of Cast-Iron Architecture is an organization dedicated to the appreciation and preservation of one of New York's most interesting architectural heritages. Nowhere in the country can you find a greater concentration of cast-iron buildings than in SoHo and Tribeca. Friends' occasional guided tours, led by professional architects and architectural historians, cost only $3. They are given sporadically in the spring and fall. Call 427-2488 to see if you can catch one.

Our favorite guided tours of New York are offered by a group of graduate students in urban planning at Hunter College. **Planners' New York Tours** take you to the more unlikely areas for tourists—New York's neighborhoods and boroughs—and give you far more insight into the social reality of the city than you're likely to get from other tours. You will be taken by bus to such places as East Harlem, the South Bronx, Queens, and Brooklyn, as well as the more frequented neighborhoods of Manhattan. The guides—steeped in the nature and problems of urban life—will tell you the histories of various neighborhoods and explain the challenges they are facing in the 1980s and beyond. Tours are given in October and November, and in April and May. They last 3½ to 4 hours and are well worth the cost—$11 for adults and $8 for students at this writing. Call 772-5605 for the most recent prices and scheduling.

Take a "historywalk" with **Joyce Gold,** who teaches Manhattan history at the New School for Social Research, and gives tours of the financial district, Greenwich Village, and Chelsea, three Sundays each spring, summer, and fall for $8. She is also available anytime to give private tours to individuals or groups, and will mail you her book, which is a self-guiding walking tour to lower Manhattan, for $3.75, including postage. Call or write to Joyce Gold, 141 W. 17th St., New York, NY 10011 (tel. 242-5762).

The **Museum of the City of New York** offers walking tours all over Manhattan with an emphasis on the architectural wonders of the city and the personal-interest stories of the people who made the Big Apple what it is today. Tours run from April through October on Sunday and cost $8. For details, call 534-1672.

Experts in their fields, the guides with the **92nd Street Y** tours come from all walks of life and can offer you everything from walking tours of gourmet eating places, artists' studios, or the political history of New York, to a Valentine's Day tour which takes you to the house where Marilyn Monroe lived and the residence where Valentino began his womanizing career. The Y specializes in "theme tours," and they do everything imaginable in this city that offers the most unimaginable things. Celebrate Independence Day the weekend before the Fourth of July by taking an all-night tour, including an escort by a fife-and-drum band and a visit to the mayor's office, or take a tour on roller skates or a bicycle. Tours are given every Sunday and often midweek, and are well worth the $8 to $13 fee. For around $40, the Y also offers tours outside the city to places like the wine vineyards in rural New Jersey, the Boston Harbor, and the apple orchards and antique shops in upstate New York. For more information, write or call Batia Plotch, The 92nd Street Y, 1395 Lexington Ave., New York, NY 10128 (tel. 427-6000, ext. 179).

NATURE TOURS: You may not have come to the city to find nature, but the **Urban Park Rangers** offer interesting tours in all five boroughs of the many parks—over 500—in the area. For instance, in Manhattan's Central Park the rangers will take you on an early-morning wildlife walk with sightings of rabbits, raccoons, and all kinds of native birds. They also have a geology tour of glacial periods and rocks, history tours, and landscape design tours. In Brooklyn, the rangers have fashioned a nature trail at Marine Park, a chance to see the salt marshes and wetlands of an undeveloped area. They also give a "mounted tour" of Prospect Park—on horseback. Call two weeks in advance for this popular tour, which is the only one with a fee—$20. All the rangers' tours are offered all year round, usually on weekends, and best yet, they are *free*. Phone the borough offices for more information: Bronx (tel. 548-7880), Brooklyn (tel. 718/856-4210), Manhattan (tel. 397-3091), Queens (tel. 718/699-4202), and Staten Island (tel. 718/442-1304).

Pick your own wild food with **"Wildman" Steve Brill**, who is an expert on the identification, collection, and use of the hundreds of vegetables, berries, fruits, nuts, herbs, seeds, and mushrooms that you can find—where you least expect them—in the city's parks. Mr. Brill offers leisurely four-hour walks, with a stop for lunch, on Saturday, Sunday, and holidays, March through November, and you can stuff yourself with such delights as black raspberries, cherries, and mulberries, or take home a load of gourmet mushrooms and wild carrots. These charming and educational walks will enchant anyone who has looked at a field of greenery and seen only grass. Call or write to "Wildman" Steve Brill, 143–25 84th Dr., #6C, Jamaica, NY 11435 (tel. 718/291-6825). The fee is $15 in advance, sliding scale for those who can't afford that, or $20 late registration. Mr. Brill is also available for private groups.

MORE TOURS: "Exploring the world within our reach . . . within our means" is the motto of **Adventures on a Shoestring**, a 22-year-old organization that arranges near-daily group visits to the unique places and people that make New York the exciting city it is. The group has some 2000 members—including residents of 25 other states who visit the city regularly—all bound together by their common desire to explore the city's more offbeat and least-explored treasures. In recent years shoestringers have toured a yogurt factory, backstage at the Metropolitan Opera House, and a subway training school for motormen and conductors, and have met with a vampire researcher, a Broadway playwright, a famous New York novelist, and a lie-detection expert.

For a free brochure describing the dozens of novel adventures, write Shoestring at 300 W. 53rd St., New York, NY 10019 (tel. 265-2663). Shoestring events cost members $3; an annual membership is $35. Events open to nonmembers cost them $5 per person. Shoestring also offers "Shoestring Safaris" for groups of five or more visiting the Big Apple. These walking tours are offered in different colorful areas of the city—from the Lower East Side and Chinatown, to the SoHo artists' area and even Brooklyn Heights. Often Shoestring will customize a tour to the interest of the group. Each tour features talks with members of the visited communities. For safaris, the fee varies according to the length of the tour, so call or write to arrange.

A guided tour of New York's largest, and the world's most famous, black community—Harlem—is offered by the **Penny Sightseeing Company,** 305 W. 42nd St. (tel. 246-4220). The three-hour guided bus tour winds its way through East Harlem, Spanish Harlem, and black Harlem, taking in the areas' notable neighborhoods. Among the stops are Harlem's great commercial center, 125th Street, City College of New York, the Morris-Jumel Mansion, the Schomberg Center for Black Research and Culture, and the Abyssinian Baptist Church, one of the oldest and largest churches in the country. The tour is conducted three times a week, on Monday and Thursday at 10 a.m., and on Saturday at 11 a.m. Tickets are $10 on Monday and Thursday, $15 on Saturday, when tourtakers also see a live gospel music concert at a local church. Reservations are required.

Theater lovers can take a unique, one-hour backstage tour of a Broadway theater through the graces of a group called **Backstage on Broadway.** The tours are led by Broadway stage managers, directors, lighting designers, and even leading actors and actresses. You'll see how a show is put together, from the hanging of the scenery to the blocking of the stage. Tours are usually scheduled for Monday through Saturday at 10:30 a.m., and advance reservations by phone only are essential—tours fill fast. For reservations, call 575-8065. Admission is $6 for adults, $5 for students and seniors. For information, write Backstage on Broadway, Suite 344, 228 W. 47th St., New York, NY 10036.

A great way to spend a Sunday afternoon is touring **Shapiro's Winery.** It's the only remaining winery in New York City, and the tour ends with a tasting of some of Shapiro's 31 varieties of wine. The tour takes you through the wine cellar and includes a chat with the winery's fourth-generation owner. Tours are every Sunday on the hour from 11 a.m. to 4 p.m., and they're absolutely free. Shapiro's is on the Lower East Side, at 126 Rivington St. (tel. 674-4404).

8. Churches and Synagogues

Many of New York's religious institutions are among the city's architectural gems. They are fascinating museums of religious art, and their tree-shaded churchyards are pleasant sanctuaries from the city's tumult. The budget-conscious traveler can also look to many of these houses of worship for inexpensive, high-quality entertainment. No longer are the melodic sounds emanating from altars and choirs limited to Gregorian chants, traditional organ tunes, and chorus recitals. New York's churches and synagogues have become increasingly alive with the sound of contemporary music, especially jazz, and they host first-rate concerts, dance recitals, and plays. Many of these events are free, and others can be attended at little cost. Listed below are some of the city's best-known houses of worship, with a few brief facts about each.

LOWER MANHATTAN: Trinity Church: This famous Episcopal church, dedicated in 1846, is the third Trinity to stand at the corner of Broadway and Wall Street (a corner valued at more than $25 million). The first, dating back to 1617, was destroyed in the Great Fire of 1776, and the second was torn down because of structural defects. Trinity may well be the city's première Gothic Revival church; in the mid-19th century its spire was the highest structure on the New York skyline. Alexander Hamilton, Robert Fulton, Capt. James ("Don't give up the ship") Lawrence, and other historic figures are buried in a small adjacent cemetery. The church is open from 7 a.m. to 6 p.m. on weekdays, from 8 a.m. to

4 p.m. on weekends. Its museum, with exhibits relating to Trinity's history, is open from 9:45 to 11:45 a.m. and 1 to 3:45 p.m. For details, phone 602-0800.

St. Paul's Chapel: This Episcopal church, at Broadway and Fulton Street, is the oldest public building in Manhattan, dating from 1764. It is also one of the city's première examples of Georgian Revival–style architecture. Much of the chapel's interior, including a hand-carved altar and a handsome winding stair, was designed by Pierre L'Enfant, the designer of Washington, D.C. George Washington prayed here from 1789 to 1791 (his pew is intact), and the chapel was also the place of worship for the Marquis de Lafayette, Major André, Lord Cornwallis, Benjamin Harrison, and Grover Cleveland. St. Paul's now serves as a parish chapel for Trinity Church. There are free noonday concerts at both churches during the week. For details, phone 602-0800.

St. Mark's in the Bowery: St. Mark's, at East 10th Street and Second Avenue, dates from 1799 and stands on the site of the Peter Stuyvesant family chapel. A blend of disparate styles, it has an Italianate cast-iron portico, a Georgian chapel, and a Greek Revival–style steeple. Stuyvesant is buried in a crypt beneath the church along with 70 of his descendants, and a bust of him (donated by Queen Wilhelmina of the Netherlands in 1915) stands in the tree-shaded courtyard. Heavily damaged by fire in 1978, the building is now almost fully restored. There are services at 6 p.m. on Wednesday and at 10:30 a.m. on Sunday. St. Mark's is extremely active in the cultural and artistic life of the East Village. It hosts bimonthly dance concerts, weekly writing workshops, and weekly poetry readings. The readings are particularly noteworthy; they've been going on for 19 years and often feature such well-known poets as Allen Ginsberg and Ann Waldman. Call 674-6377 for exact times and performer information.

Friends Meeting House: This typical Quaker meeting house is a good place to see in combination with a visit to St. Mark's. It's located at 15 Rutherford Pl., off East 15th Street between Second and Third Avenues. Built in 1860, the red-brick house is understated, especially for structures in the Gothic Revival style. In its southeast corner you can see a granite hitching post from William Penn's Philadelphia home. Meetings are on Sunday at 9:30 and 11 a.m. For details, phone 777-8866.

Marble Collegiate Church: Marble Collegiate, at the corner of West 29th Street and Fifth Avenue, is the city's oldest Dutch Reformed church. Its elegant facade was constructed entirely of marble, hence the church's name. The church boasts a number of firsts: it was the first to be built with hanging balconies, the first to install an electronically operated pipe organ, the first to be air-conditioned, and the first to use closed-circuit television for overflow congregations. For years Marble Collegiate was the site where Dr. Norman Vincent Peale, the world-renowned author and theologian, gave his spirited sermons. The Sunday service is at 11:15 a.m. For information, call 686-2770.

Church of the Transfiguration: This picturesque Episcopal church, at 1 W. 29th St., near Fifth Avenue, is known throughout the world as "the little church around the corner." Built in 1848, it sits in a shrubbery-filled garden that's the closest thing New York has to an old English churchyard. The church is a traditional favorite with stage people—and with lovers too. In fact, legend has it that this church has seen more weddings than any other its size, and there's a "bride's altar" (in the Holy Family Chapel) built with funds donated by the thousands of couples who were married here. Among the church's many famous parishioners were writers Stephen Vincent Benet and William Sydney Porter (O. Henry). The chapel is open from 8 a.m. to 6 p.m. daily. A tour is given every Sunday after the 11 a.m. service. For details, phone 684-6770.

MIDTOWN: St. Patrick's Cathedral: St. Patrick's, at 50th Street and Fifth Avenue, is the city's major Roman Catholic cathedral. Everything about the church (the second largest in Manhattan) is majestic. Its twin spires (modeled after the Cathedral of Cologne) rise to 330 feet above street level, and its great Rose Window measures 26 feet in diameter. Completed in 1879, the cathedral took 21 years to build. Inside, there's an impressive array of altars and shrines, including those of Elizabeth Ann Seton and John Neumann, the first American-born saints. The cathedral is open for worship or visiting from 7 a.m. to 8 p.m. daily. Sunday services are at 7, 8, 9, 10, and 11:45 a.m., and at 12:45, 4, and 5:30 p.m. For information, phone 753-2261.

St. Peter's Lutheran Church: This modernistic church is nestled in a corner of the Citicorp skyscraper at 54th Street and Lexington Avenue. Built in 1977, the church impresses on visitors a sense of simplicity, dignity, and strength. In contrast to the bank's sleek, 900-foot aluminum-clad tower, the granite outer walls of the church reach humbly into the sky like two hands in prayer. The feeling is continued in the main sanctuary, an immense angular tent with butcher-block pews, and a small chapel designed by Louise Nevelson, the world-renowned artist. (The walls of the chapel are lined with three of Nevelson's enigmatic wood assemblages.) St. Peter's is particularly well known for its deep commitment to the performing arts. Its basement theater was the launching pad for the play *The Elephant Man*. And many of the greatest names in jazz have performed at Jazz Vespers—a worship service held every Sunday at St. Peter's at 5 p.m. A more traditional Lutheran service takes place on Sunday at 8:45 and 11 a.m., and during the week. For details, call 935-2200.

This is a good place to see in combination with a trip to the Citicorp complex, right next door, which features a fabulous collection of shops and restaurants.

St. Bartholomew's Church: This 150-year-old Episcopal church, on Park Avenue between 50th and 51st Streets, was originally located downtown on Lafayette Street. In 1918 the church moved to its current home, which is distinguished by an Italian Romanesque portal and dome. Services are held at 9 and 11 a.m. on Sunday, and at various times during the week. Call 751-1616 for details.

Central Synagogue: This reform Jewish synagogue, at East 55th Street and Lexington Avenue, has been called the finest example of Moorish Revival–style architecture in the city. It was erected in 1872 and has been designated an official city landmark. Although the sanctuary is only open to the public during Friday-evening and Saturday-morning worship services, you can arrange for a tour by writing the synagogue office, 123 E. 55th St. For information, phone 838-5122.

Temple Emanu-El: Temple Emanu-El, at Fifth Avenue and East 65th Street, is the world's largest Reform Jewish synagogue. It's also the third-largest house of worship in New York City, after the Cathedral of St. John the Divine and St. Patrick's. Built in 1929, this gray limestone structure is a lofty mix of Romanesque, Byzantine, and Gothic architecture, with occasional flourishes of art deco. Its stately and awe-inspiring main sanctuary is 77 feet wide, 147 feet long, and 103 feet high, with seating for 2500. Daily services are at 5:30 p.m. A guide is available by appointment only. For information, phone 744-1400.

Congregation Shearith Israel (The Spanish and Portuguese Synagogue): Almost directly across the park from Temple Emanu-El, at Central Park West and 70th Street, is the Spanish and Portuguese Synagogue. Founded in 1654, this Orthodox congregation is the oldest Jewish congregation in America. (Its first members were descendants of Jews who fled Spain and Portugal during the Inquisition and made their way to New York via Brazil.) In keeping with the Jewish tradition of not representing human images, the windows of this landmark, neoclassical structure were designed by Louis Comfort Tiffany in simple yet elegant patterns. Services are held daily—mornings and evenings. You can arrange for a tour by writing the synagogue office, 8 W. 70th St. For information, phone 873-0300.

UPPER WEST SIDE: Cathedral Church of St. John the Divine: St. John the Divine, at West 112th Street and Amsterdam Avenue, is the city's major Episcopal church and the largest Gothic cathedral on earth. (In fact, among all the world's churches, only St. Peter's Basilica in Rome is larger.) Its immense nave stretches more than 600 feet, the length of two football fields, and has a seating capacity of 10,000. Though its first ground-breaking ceremony took place in 1892, the building is still only two-thirds completed. Currently, in a building program evocative of the Middle Ages, a dozen young apprentices are putting chisel to stone to raise two 294-foot towers on the cathedral's west front. You'll want to spend lots of time at this church; its nave is bordered by an array of small, beautiful, and intimate chapels. And you can relax in the church's "Biblical Garden," which is planted with a variety of herbs and flowers mentioned in the Bible. Services are held on Sunday at 8, 9:30, and 11 a.m., and at 7 p.m. There are tours Monday through Saturday at 11 a.m., and on Sunday at 12:30 p.m. For information, call 678-6888.

The Riverside Church: The best way to see this famous church is in conjunction with a trip to **Grant's Tomb.** Both are located on Riverside Drive near West 122nd Street. As befits its status as one of the city's most active churches, Riverside's 392-foot tower looms high above the Upper West Side. Built in 1930, the Gothic-style church was funded by John D. Rockefeller, Jr., and modeled on the Cathedral of Chartres. Its main chapel features heroic statues of six Christian preachers, and one of the largest church organs (13,000 pipes) in the world.

Be sure to take an elevator to Riverside's 20th floor, where a fascinating bell exhibit and antique practice clavier can be seen. From there, a narrow staircase winds through a 74-bell carillon (the largest in the world) to an observation platform, 355 feet above ground. For 25¢ you can purchase platform tickets in the lobby and get an unobstructed bird's-eye view of Manhattan and its environs.

Riverside's 10:45 a.m. Sunday services are often flavored with politics. The church's pastor, Dr. William Sloan Coffin, Jr., is a renowned orator and political activist. And the congregation (interdenominational, interracial, and international) is in the forefront of the disarmament movement.

Carillon recitals are given before and after the Sunday service, and on Saturday at noon and on Sunday at 3 p.m. For information, call 222-5900. Also, in September Riverside hosts one of the nation's most diverse and prestigious dance festivals. The festival features more than 60 dance companies, ranging from the American Ballet to a Yugoslavian folk troupe. Dance performances are given till June, at 8 p.m. Wednesday through Sunday. Tickets are $7 for general admission and $5 for senior citizens and students. For information, call 864-2929.

HARLEM: The Abyssinian Baptist Church: New York's oldest and largest black church is at 132 W. 138th St., near Lenox Avenue. Built in 1808, the church is an intriguing mix of Gothic and Tudor architecture. In the 1950s and 1960s it was best known as the parish of Harlem's renowned congressman and preacher, the Rev. Adam Clayton Powell, Jr. Now the church is famous for its 75-member choir, which has sung with the New York Philharmonic and Boston Pops orchestras. You can hear the choir any Sunday at 11 a.m. For information, phone 862-7474.

9. Historic Houses

Beneath that famed Manhattan skyline you can still find the old New York, in buildings and homes preserved by concerned citizens and the city government. Here are a few of our favorites, arranged by geographical location.

LOWER MANHATTAN: Fraunces Tavern: Built in 1719, this landmark building at the corner of Broad and Pearl Streets is a rare vestige of colonial America —an America of old Dutch homes, cobblestone streets, and trading ships. The building takes its name from Samuel Fraunces, the West Indian innkeeper who converted it into a tavern in 1762. It was here, in a long banquet room on the second floor, that George Washington bade an emotional farewell to his officers in 1783. (Later, when Washington became president, Fraunces became his chief steward.) Restored in 1907, the tavern now serves as a restaurant (open weeknights from 7:45 to 9 p.m.) and as a museum of early Americana (see "Museums," above). Its collection of Revolutionary War memorabilia—flags, musketry, colonial maps, and paintings—is particularly noteworthy.

Open weekdays from 10 a.m. to 4 p.m.; closed weekends and holidays (except for Washington's Birthday and July 4th). To get there, take the BMT local subway (RR train) to the Whitehall station and walk to Pearl Street. For information, call 425-1778.

Federal Hall National Memorial: A few blocks north from Fraunces Tavern, at the corner of Wall and Nassau Streets, is the Federal Hall National Memorial—the site of George Washington's inauguration as our country's first president. John Quincy Adams Ward's famous statue of Washington stands in front of the building. Completed in 1842, the building is considered one of the city's finest examples of Greek Revival architecture. A reconstruction of the original Federal Hall—the nation's first capitol building—it served as a U.S. Customs House and as a subtreasury before being converted into a national memorial. Inside, there's a museum with Washington's inaugural suit as well as several exhibitions commemorating the inauguration. There's also a colonial folksinger who recreates, through song, the history of colonial New York.

Open Monday through Friday from 9 a.m. to 5 p.m. Admission is free. For information, call 264-8711.

Old Merchant's House: Now a museum, the Old Merchant's House at 29 E. 4th St., between Lafayette Street and the Bowery, is a perfectly furnished period piece in an area that has been largely taken over by trucking companies. That the house survived is not surprising once you know its story. The five-story Georgian brick house was built in 1832 and bought three years later by Seabury Tredwell, a prosperous hardware merchant. Three of his six daughters lived there all their lives, keeping the house just as it had always been, and refusing to depart when the fashionable area of town moved north. When the youngest of those daughters died in 1933 at the age of 93, hardly anything had changed. The house still lacked plumbing and electricity; its original furnishings, linens, china, and family memorabilia were all intact. Closets and cabinets were filled with old clothes, much of it dating from the 1800s, remarkably preserved and apparently not touched for nearly a century: a playbill from an 1860s theatrical production was found in the pocket of one dress. More than most such museums, the house has the haunting quality of time's having stopped, and the visitor cannot help but wonder at the lives of the reclusive spinster sisters who lived there. It has classic Greek Revival parlors with the original mahogany furniture, fine decorative plaster molding, and handsome hand-carved columns.

Three of the house's five stories are open to the public on Sunday from 1 to 4 p.m. (closed in August). Admission is $2 for adults and $1 for students and senior citizens. The museum can be reached by taking the IRT–Lexington Avenue local (no. 6) subway to the Astor Place–8th Street station and walking south on Lafayette to 4th Street. For special group tours or lectures, phone 777-1089.

Theodore Roosevelt House: This landmark house at 28 E. 20th St., east of Fifth Avenue, is the birthplace of Teddy Roosevelt, the gutsy "Rough Rider" who first led the charge up San Juan Hill and later became the nation's 26th president. Built in 1850, the Gothic brownstone is filled with its original Victorian furnishings and other 19th-century relics. Free chamber music concerts are presented September through June on Saturday from 2 to 3:30 p.m. in the fourth-floor auditorium.

The house is open Wednesday through Sunday from 9 a.m. until 5 p.m. Admission is 50¢ for adults, free for senior citizens and for children under 16. To get there, take the IRT–Lexington Avenue no. 6 (local) subway to 23rd Street and Park Avenue South, or take the BMT RR subway to Park Avenue South and Broadway. For information, call 260-1616.

MIDTOWN EAST: Abigail Adams Smith Museum: Sitting on a raised grassy site at 21 E. 61st St., between York and First Avenues (tel. 838-6878), is one of the few 18th-century buildings left in Manhattan. It was built in 1799 as the carriage house on the estate of Abigail Adams Smith, the daughter of President John Adams. Made of schist, a stone quarried in colonial Manhattan, the house is furnished with several museum-quality antiques from the Federal period. Outside there's a path leading to a quiet garden and sitting area—a mainstay of colonial homes.

Open Monday through Friday from 10 a.m. to 4 p.m.; closed during the month of August. Admission is $2 for adults, $1 for senior citizens. Free admission for children under 12. To get there, take the IRT–Lexington Avenue subway to 59th Street, then either take a crosstown bus or walk four blocks east to First Avenue.

HARLEM: Morris-Jumel Mansion: This white-columned Georgian mansion, at the corner of Edgecombe Avenue and 161st Street, is a remnant of a time when Upper Manhattan was predominantly rural: the summering place of New York's aristocracy. Built by Col. Roger Morris in 1765, it sits atop a grassy hill in the middle of a park filled with lilac and magnolia trees. Outside, there's a colonial herb garden surrounded by a brick wall. This peaceful setting served first as Washington's headquarters and then as British headquarters during the Revolutionary War; later the widow of Stephen Jumel lived there with Aaron Burr, her second husband. The house recently became an accredited museum and there's a special exhibitions gallery on the third floor.

The mansion and museum are open Tuesday through Sunday from 10 a.m. to 4 p.m.; closed Monday. Admission is $1 for adults, 50¢ for students and senior citizens. Children under 6 are admitted for free. For information, call 923-8008. To get there, take the IND–Eighth Avenue AA local train to West 163rd Street. You can also take the Madison Avenue no. 2 or no. 3 bus.

WASHINGTON HEIGHTS: The **Dyckman House:** This 18th-century Dutch Colonial farmhouse was built of brick, wood, and stone to replace one that was destroyed by the British. Occupied by both the Continental and British armies during the Revolutionary War, the house, at 204th Street and Broadway, is now a museum containing Dutch and English period furniture and possessions of the Dyckman family.

Open Tuesday through Sunday from 11 a.m. to 4 p.m. Admission is free. For information, call 304-9422. To get there, take the IND–Eighth Avenue A train to the last stop, 207th Street, and walk three short blocks south on Broadway.

THE BRONX: Poe Cottage: This wooden-frame cottage was the last home of author Edgar Allen Poe, the place where he wrote "Annabel Lee," "The Bells," and "Eureka." Built in 1812 and opened as a museum in 1917, it is a memorial to Poe, his life and times.

Poe Cottage is located on the Grand Concourse at East Kingsbridge Road. To get there, take the IRT–Lexington Avenue no. 4 train to Kingsbridge station. Open on Sunday and Wednesday through Friday from 1 to 5 p.m., on Saturday from 10 a.m. to 4 p.m. Admission is $1. For information, call 881-8900.

STATEN ISLAND: Richmondtown Restoration: This recently completed restoration shows the development of a Staten Island village through the 17th, 18th, and 19th centuries. It includes a Dutch schoolhouse, general store, carriage house, and historical museum. The museum is open Wednesday through Friday from 10 a.m. to 5 p.m., and on Saturday and Sunday from 1 to 5 p.m. Admission is $2 for adults, $1.50 for seniors, $1 for children, and $5 for a family. To get there, take the Staten Island Ferry; when you reach the other side, pick up a no. 113 bus to St. Patrick's Place, then walk to 441 Clarke Ave. For information, phone 718/351-1611.

Chapter IV

A STROLL OR TWO

        1. Greenwich Village
        2. The Lower East Side
        3. The Garment Center
        4. Yorkville
        5. SoHo
        6. The Upper West Side: Columbus Avenue
        7. Chinatown and Little Italy
        8. Chelsea
        9. Tribeca
        10. Central Park
        11. Times Square

    TO US, THE MOST FASCINATING free activity in New York is a simple walk through several of Manhattan's fabled neighborhoods, including Greenwich Village, the Lower East Side, the Garment Center, Yorkville, SoHo, the refurbished Columbus Avenue area on the Upper West Side—and, of course, Chinatown and Little Italy downtown. Put on a pair of comfortable shoes and let's begin.

1. Greenwich Village

    Take any IND subway (AA, A, B, CC, D, E, or F train) to the West 4th Street station. Get out at the uptown exit, which will bring you to 8th Street and Sixth Avenue. Walk east on **8th Street** toward Fifth Avenue. This is one of the Village's main shopping streets, and as people have been saying for the past 40 years about the Village, it's not what it used to be. Fast-food restaurants, discount shoestores, and flashy clothing shops have invaded the street. There are still a few handcrafted jewelry and book stores, but you're more likely to find cheap gift shops or record stores blaring disco music. Yet it's worth visiting. Just ignore the "joint" salesmen and occasional weirdos and concentrate on imagining Bob Dylan or Jack Kerouac walking this street.

    When you reach Fifth Avenue, turn right and you'll see the magnificent Washington Square Arch, which was once treated with an antigraffiti chemical to prevent its being defaced by New York's indigenous art form. The Arch leads directly to **Washington Square,** the finest Village sight of all.

    In its time, Washington Square has been many things—parade ground, cemetery, scene of riots and meetings—but it has always been the Village's major loafing place, and still is. On any day, the people in attendance will be partly made up of chess players, who fill the tables at the southwest corner;

mothers and children; strollers and bench-warmers; skateboarders and disco roller-skaters; street performers and students, just sitting around the edge of the fountain in the center of the park. Summer Sunday afternoons are particularly lively, often filled with rock and jazz musicians. And over it all, the marble Washington Square Arch—gateway to Fifth Avenue—watches serenely. Unfortunately, that's not to say that the park doesn't have a seamier side. Winos and pot smokers (and worse) among others use the park, as do pickpockets and other petty thieves. So use the park with the caution you would any other New York public place.

The north side of the square is lined with lovely, old buildings (dating back to the 1830s), one of which—no. 16—was the scene of Henry James's famous novel *Washington Square*. Some of the houses are still occupied by private individuals, but others have been taken over by various offshoots of New York University, whose headquarters are on the east side of the square.

To the south sprawls the old Italian section of town, a conglomeration of tenements, inexpensive restaurants, grocery stores whose windows are filled with hanging cheeses and cans of olive oil, funeral parlors, and finally, the famous nightclubs and coffeehouses of Greenwich Village.

Walk completely across the square to the south side, and then start exploring the streets to the south of the square: **MacDougal Street, Bleecker Street, Sullivan Street, Thompson Street**—all of which hold the largest cluster of nightspots and coffeehouses in the area, and all of which are as enjoyably seen in the daytime as at night.

MacDougal Street, once the heart of Bohemia, is now a blend of brassy boutiques and sidewalk stands selling shish kebab or pizza. Bleecker Street has many faces, ranging from the artistic to the earthy to the flashy.

East of Sixth Avenue, you're reminded how sleazy commercialism can be. Still, the mood is lively and the street teeming with life. West of Sixth Avenue, Bleecker houses Italian food markets and private homes. Between Seventh and Eighth Avenues, Bleecker Street is an antique hunter's paradise with a greater variety of vintage wares than anywhere else in the city. Over 20 shops are clustered in the seven-block stretch, and the emphasis is on French country furniture.

When you have seen this area, walk back to Sixth Avenue and find West 4th Street—another important shopping street. Walk up West 4th Street to **Sheridan Square,** and then start exploring the streets and areas west of Sheridan Square—which are the most unchanged and most typical residential areas of the Village and currently the heart of New York's gay community. In particular, ask any passerby to point the way to: **Gay Street** (only one block long, but so crooked that you can't see one end from the other); **Christopher Street** (narrow, historic, and housing the famous Theatre de Lys, now the Lucille Lortel Theater, earliest and most successful of the off-Broadway theaters); **Bedford Street** (which contains the Edna St. Vincent Millay House, two stories high, but only eight feet wide).

You might want to spend extra time wandering around **Greenwich Avenue,** that famous angled street that runs into 8th Street; it is on these two streets that you'll see some of the Village's best boutiques and lots of uptowners coming to see what's happening in the Village. Start at upper Greenwich Avenue, working your way down toward 8th Street.

An Architecture Tour

Greenwich Village abounds with interesting 19th-century architecture, but the area at the base of Fifth Avenue is perhaps the most interesting; it contains three streets filled with notable examples of early 19th-century architecture. A visit here is a must for history buffs who want to see some unusual relics of the past.

MacDougal Alley, a tiny street lined with buildings that used to be stables, is one of the most picturesque. The area was created in 1833 and through the years its buildings have been renovated into studios and private homes. The alley is situated on MacDougal Street, between 8th Street and Waverly Place.

Around the corner on the north side of **Washington Square** is a group of buildings regarded by the City Landmarks Commission as "the most important and imposing blockfront of early 19th-century town houses in the city." Built in the early 1830s, these Greek Revival buildings were the homes of prosperous merchants and bankers.

As you walk east on Washington Square North, the next intersection you'll come to is Fifth Avenue. Turn left and a few steps in on your right you'll come to another delightful mews area. **Washington Mews,** a cobblestone street that is longer than MacDougal Alley, was also used in the 19th century to stable the horses of prominent families but is now used as private homes by lucky New Yorkers who can afford these unique vestiges of a bygone era.

2. The Lower East Side

For 50 years the Lower East Side was the home of tens of thousands of immigrant Jews from Eastern Europe, who soon proceeded to provide the city with important leaders in the labor movement, politics, education, industry, science, and the entertainment world. Today most of the old tenement buildings of this area still stand, but mixed among them on the narrow streets are modern housing projects. And side by side in what was once an exclusively Jewish neighborhood live Italians, Puerto Ricans, Ukrainians, blacks, and free-'n'-easy young types, as well as a few of the older Jewish residents who originally gave the area its flavor.

A trip to the Lower East Side will appeal not only to the sociologist, but to the bargain hunters as well. The streets abound in tiny stores of every variety, selling merchandise at prices a good 20% to 30% lower than in any other neighborhood in New York. Wear comfortable shoes, for after a subway ride down to Delancey Street, it's by foot all the way.

If you're planning to take your car, make sure you don't attempt to drive into the neighborhood, especially on a Sunday when it is crowded and impossible to park. Take the IND–Sixth Avenue F subway downtown to Delancey Street. When you leave the Delancey Street Station, walk west to Essex Street, turn left down Essex Street, and on the east side of the street, between Broome and Delancey Streets, you'll come to the first of the four city markets that stretch up to Stanton Street (three blocks across Delancey). It's fun to browse through the Essex Street Markets.

The cavernous indoor markets are crammed with stands and stalls (each rented from the city by private shopkeepers) displaying an enormous variety of food and delicacies, dry goods, hardware, clothing—even home furnishings. The markets cater almost equally to the Jewish and Spanish residents of the neighborhood, and you can buy *cabrito* (goat meat) or *queso blanco* (soft, white milk cheese), as well as the Jewish items more usually associated with the area— kosher pickles to munch on as you walk, or slabs of creamy halvah (ground sesame-seed candy).

As you leave the markets, look to your left toward East Broadway. East Broadway was once the Fleet Street of the Lower East Side, but now the last of the famous Yiddish newspapers, the *Forward,* has moved. At Rivington Street

STROLLS: GREENWICH VILLAGE & LOWER EAST SIDE **231**

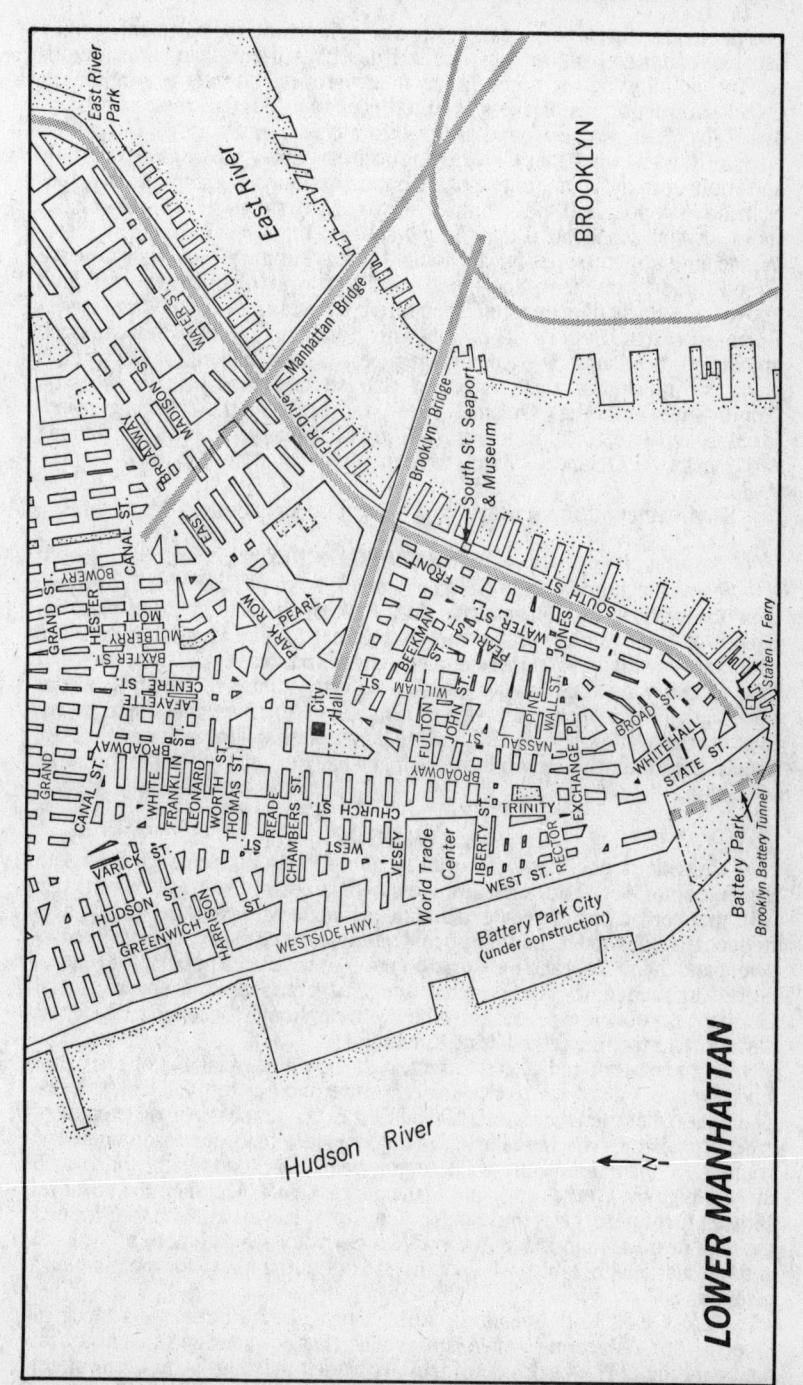

LOWER MANHATTAN

(north of Delancey Street), head west, passing shops housing barrels of smoked fish, bins of unusual candies, jars of dried fruits, bags of lentils, and similar exotica. The clothing and toy stores display their wares right on the sidewalk, each owner carrying on his business from the doorway. Many of these stores are owned by Orthodox Jews, and are therefore closed on Saturday, but all are open on Sunday, when they do a thriving business. Cross Allen Street, turn left, and you'll be in the center of one of the busiest antique sections in the city, specializing in copper and brass items. Narrow, dusty stores sell copper candlesticks, crystal chandeliers, antique gilt frames, brass headboards, and decorative antique accessories for the home—but no furniture. Now walk down to Grand Street, turn right, and you'll soon pass rows of bridal shops selling budget-priced wedding apparel. Then turn back and cross Allen Street again. Remain on Grand Street as it becomes a linen and fabric section. You can stock up here on sheets and towels at bargain prices, or have draperies or bedspreads made for much less than you'd be charged anywhere else in the city. Grand Street intersects Orchard Street, the heart of the shopping scene. From Grand Street, return to Essex. Turn left at Essex and continue walking two blocks to Delancey Street, where you'll come to the IND subway station.

See Chapter VII for specific shopping recommendations in this area.

3. The Garment Center

Save a lunchtime for the Garment Center, heart of New York's, and perhaps the world's, fashion industry. The bulk of the activity takes place on Broadway or Seventh Avenue from 34th Street to around 42nd Street. The streets are crowded with carts of women's clothes pushed recklessly by boys and men of every nationality who look up only to admire the models, whose trademark—the makeup bags—give them away. You'll see salesmen, executives, workers, all gathered in front of buildings, often spilling over into the busy streets, gesturing with their hands, talking, wheeling, dealing—all in the name of fashion.

4. Yorkville

Yorkville is one of our favorite neighborhoods. Its center is East 86th Street, one of New York's liveliest crosstown streets. Bustling during the day with shoppers, it becomes even more alive at night with pleasure seekers who frequent its cafés and restaurants, beer halls, and dance palaces. Places like **Little Finland** (at no. 247) and the **Corso** (at no. 205) have been popular for generations. Although some of the restaurants tend to get expensive, there are several German and Viennese restaurants where you can stop in for coffee and delicate pastries. Our favorite is the **Kleine Konditorei** (no. 234).

At the eastern end of 86th Street, past the commercial section, lies East End Avenue, one of the city's most expensive and quietest residential areas. There, also, between the East River and East End Avenue is a broad expanse of greenery called **Carl Schurz Park,** a place peopled with joggers, skateboarders, youngsters, and older people who sit on the benches in good weather and watch the world go by. At the north end of the park is **Gracie Mansion,** the beautiful 18th-century house that is the home of New York's mayor. You can walk around the park near the mansion, and if you're lucky you'll get a glimpse of the local and international notables who pop in and out of the house for meetings and receptions.

Across East End Avenue between 86th and 87th Streets is a block of Queen Anne 19th-century town houses which has been designated a historical landmark area. The back side of these red-brick buildings is on a tiny street called **Henderson Place,** which you can enter from 86th Street. It has the flavor of a turn-of-the-century village—unless you look to one side, where a massive apartment house looms to dwarf the tiny houses underneath it.

For suggestions about restaurants in the neighborhood, see Chapter II.

5. SoHo

Within the last decade SoHo has become the working center of the city's contemporary art scene. The area begins at its northern end at Houston Street, an east-west thoroughfare that bisects the island of Manhattan. SoHo is centered in the streets between Avenue of the Americas (Sixth Avenue) and the Bowery. Formerly this was a commercial district, with warehouses and factories in the 19th-century cast-iron buildings that line its streets. Now it's home to some 2000 artists, photographers, craftspeople, dancers, filmmakers, and other creative talents who keep the area humming. SoHo is a place to see the latest in art and browse through unusual, often way-out shops.

You'll find an amazing variety of boutiques featuring avant-garde fashion, clothing that is art, pottery, antiques, records, books, and appealing health-food restaurants as well as gourmet dining spots. Within the boundaries of SoHo you can find elegant creations which would be at home anywhere as well as the most experimental and trendy clothes you have ever seen. This is where the blue- and pink-haired New Wave types, walking their dyed-to-match punk-rock puppies, come to buy their leopard skin/vinyl/mini or whatever clothes.

The street life of SoHo is inarguably one of the most exciting in the city. Walk north from Canal Street on West Broadway on any weekend afternoon and you'll see impromptu flea markets set up on the corners or artists hawking their latest creations. We've seen a street performance by a Japanese artist who spent three days screwing common building screws into a platform while his colleague recorded his every move and the crowd's reaction. We've also heard myriad groups of street musicians, and once viewed a movie company filming in the dead of night on Thompson Street. SoHo, it seems, never sleeps.

Walk down West Broadway to Broome Street, turn left, and criss-cross the area west to Mercer Street. Most of the activity centers around these boundaries. To get to SoHo, take the IND–Eighth Avenue E or CC trains to the Spring Street station. See Chapter II for the best places to get a meal.

6. The Upper West Side: Columbus Avenue

The Upper West Side, recently dubbed by *New York* magazine as the "Yupper West Side" in honor of the hordes of "yuppies" who have settled in here, has experienced a tremendous gentrification in the last few years. Heart of the action is Columbus Avenue, which has been transformed from a dirty, grimy thoroughfare into a smaller version of Greenwich Village, a lively strip for nonstop shopping, strolling, dining, drinking, people-watching. Centering around 72nd Street, extending north up into the 80s and south into the 60s, the avenue is lined with bistros and boutiques and crowds frequenting both. Old brownstones on the side streets have been transformed from grubby rooming houses into private homes and luxury apartments. The best time to experience Columbus Avenue is from late afternoon through early evening: some of the shops stay open until 8 p.m. Begin your stroll at 81st Street and walk south toward Lincoln Center. On your way down, you may want to meander off the avenue and stop in at the American Museum of Natural History at 77th Street, or the New-York Historical Society at 77th Street and Central Park West.

Two streets west of and parallel to Columbus, **Broadway** and **Amsterdam Avenue,** have retained some of the flavor of the "melting pot" West Side, but they too are changing fast. On Amsterdam you'll find botanicas and zapaterías

234 NEW YORK ON $45 A DAY

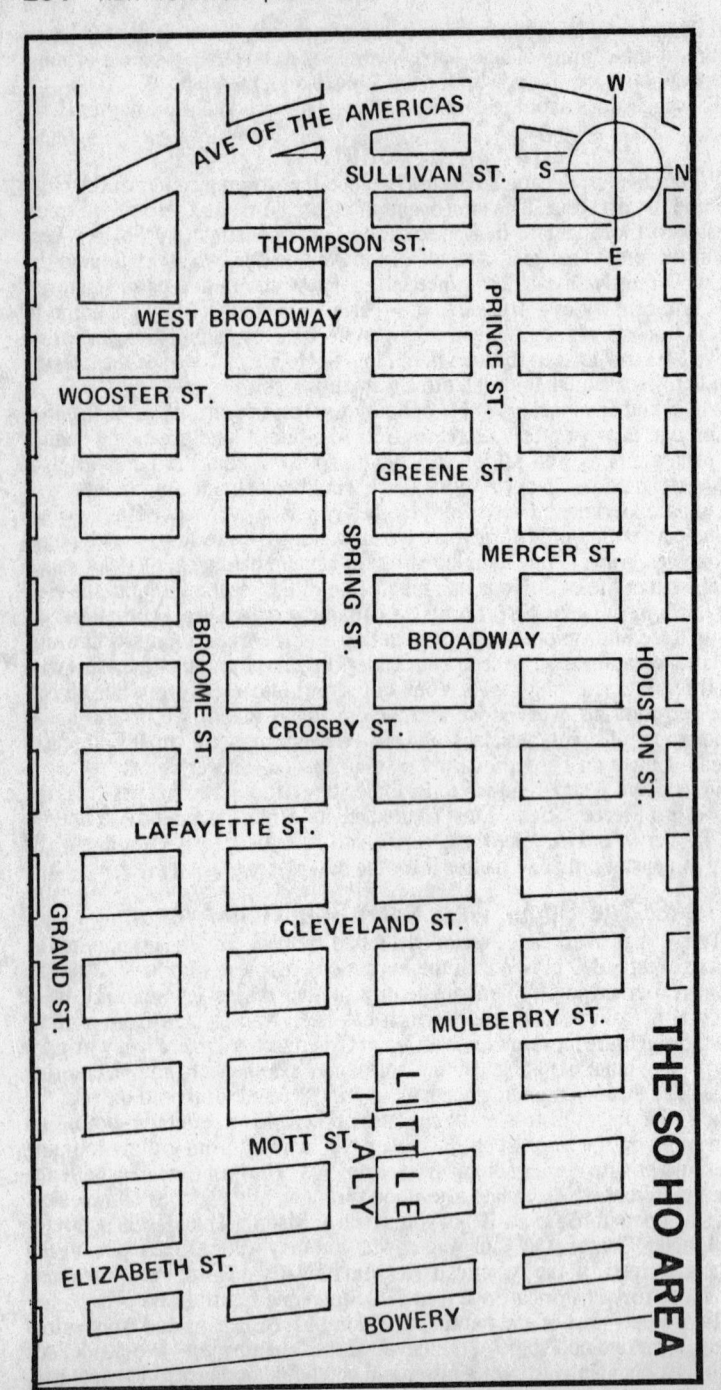

THE SOHO AREA

next door to antique shops and boutiques forced off Columbus Avenue by skyrocketing rents. Stroll downtown on Broadway from about 85th Street to 79th Street and stop into **Zabar's** on 80th Street for gourmet treats par excellance. The **Apthorp** at Broadway and 78th Street and the **Ansonia** at 74th Street are quintessential Broadway apartment buildings and interesting examples of long-gone architectural styles.

7. Chinatown and Little Italy

One of the liveliest sections in the city, day or night, is **Chinatown**, a small area downtown bounded on the south by Worth Street, on the north by Canal Street. Its main commercial area stretches only a few blocks west from the Bowery. Best known for its abundance of low-priced Chinese restaurants, it is full of gift shops catering to the tourist trade and grocery and vegetable stores that are stocked with all kinds of Oriental foods. Its main streets are **Mott Street, Mulberry Street, Pell Street,** and **Doyers Street**—narrow, teeming roads that wind and intersect through the tiny neighborhood. You can enter the area from Canal Street at Mott or Mulberry, or from the Bowery at Pell Street. The Second Avenue bus is a good way to get here; ask the driver to let you off at Chatham Square. See Chapter II for our favorite eateries.

After you've seen Chinatown, walk up Mulberry to Canal Street, and as you keep going on Mulberry you will have entered the home of generations of Italian immigrants who have settled in this European-like community called **Little Italy.** Mulberry Street, above Canal, is the center of a booming activity from afternoon on, in restaurants and cafés that offer the best and lowest priced Italian food in town. Besides the cafés and restaurants, there are lots of tiny shops that sell imported Italian groceries, cheeses, housewares, and a great array of sausage, and meat stores and tiny bakeries. The area, particularly Mulberry Street, has enjoyed a recent *risorgimento*—an effort to enhance and preserve the neighborhood's special character, its intimate scale, and bustling street life.

8. Chelsea

Like so many once-rundown areas of Manhattan, Chelsea is enjoying a renaissance. The area, which is loosely defined as bounded by Fifth Avenue on the east and the Hudson River on the west, runs from 14th Street to 34th Street. Chelsea was the center of the city from the mid-to late-19th century and is rich with historical interest. Before funding for the erection of the Statue of Liberty was completed, her hand (complete with torch) rested in **Madison Square Park** (Madison Avenue at 23rd Street). Madison Square Park, by the way, was the location of the original Madison Square Garden which encompassed the entire city block, Fourth Avenue (now Park Avenue South) to Madison Avenue, 26th to 27th Streets.

Don't miss the **Flatiron Building,** a unique structure at the triangle formed by Broadway and Fifth Avenue at 23rd Street.

Walk west on **23rd Street,** once the heart of New York's theater district, dominated by the long-gone Grand Opera House on the corner of 23rd Street and Eighth Avenue. The **Chelsea Hotel** at 222 W. 23rd St., between Seventh and Eighth Avenues, has been home to noted show business and literary figures, including Sherwood Anderson, O. Henry, Isadora Duncan, and Dylan Thomas. Today many rock stars enjoy the relative privacy of the Chelsea. Continue west on 23rd Street to Ninth Avenue, once the site of the home of Clement Clark Moore who wrote "The Night Before Christmas." Chelsea owes its name to Moore's father-in-law, a sea captain, who named his estate after a home for retired seamen—not the famous London district. When Moore died, he willed the land between 20th and 21st Streets between Ninth and Tenth Avenues to the

General Theological Seminary. The seminary's beautiful gardens are open to the public during daylight hours.

The segment of Sixth Avenue in Chelsea from about 18th to 23rd Streets was known as **Ladies Mile** during the mid-19th century and the street was lined with exclusive shops and stores. Ladies Mile continues to the east, on Broadway, from 20th Street south to 10th Street. The building on the southwest corner of Broadway and 20th Street, for example, was an early location of Lord & Taylor's department store.

Farther uptown, on Sixth Avenue, is the wholesale flower district between 26th and 29th Streets. Buy yourself a bargain posy or stroll along West 28th Street between Fifth Avenue and Broadway and imagine it 100 years ago when it was the world's Tin Pan Alley.

9. Tribeca

Another Manhattan artistic community is named for its location—the *Tri*-angle *be*-low *Ca*-nal Street—and extends (loosely) south of Canal Street to the World Trade Center, and west of Broadway to the Hudson River. It can be reached by the IRT East Side subway, no. 4, 5, or 6 train to the Brooklyn Bridge stop. You'll emerge from the subway near **City Hall Park,** the scene of one of the first public readings of the Declaration of Independence, an event witnessed by George Washington and his troops. Several blocks south of the park on Broadway and Vesey Street, is **St. Paul's Chapel.** Built in 1766, it's the oldest church building in Manhattan. Walk one block north from St. Paul's, along Broadway, and you'll encounter the **Woolworth Building.** This magnificent example of Gothic architecture was built in 1913 and for 18 years held the title of the world's tallest building. This "Cathedral of Commerce" possesses one of the most beautiful lobbies we have ever seen, with marble walls and floors, bronze wall decorations, and mosaic ceiling. If you enter the building from the Broadway entrance, look closely at the first archway to your left, and you'll see representations of Mr. Woolworth and his architect in each corner. In the rear of the lobby, a plaque details the history of the building.

Continue up Broadway to **Warren Street** and turn west toward the Hudson. This street is a bargain hunter's mecca, so do indulge if you'd like to buy a $30 man's shirt for $3.99, or a $27 book for $4.99.

North on Greenwich Street from Warren Street you'll see many factory buildings which have been born again as lofts. Despite fears of high-rent development, the loft-dwellers coexist peacefully with the olive oil/nut/coffee/produce businesses in the neighborhood. Continue up Greenwich Street to **Harrison Street** and you'll see a row of original Federal town houses, saved from the wrecker and sold, by lottery, twenty years ago to lucky bidders.

Hudson Street, which runs parallel to and is one block east of Greenwich Street, is the main street of Tribeca. The shops, galleries, and cafés in Tribeca will give you a feeling of what SoHo was like before commercialization.

10. Central Park

A leafy oasis in the heart of Manhattan runs from Fifth Avenue to Eighth Avenue and from 59th to 110th Streets—a total of 840 acres of boating, tennis, gardens, playgrounds, bridle paths, and statuary smack in the middle of some of the world's most expensive real estate. Plan to spend an afternoon in Central Park; it's perfectly safe during daylight hours as long as you proceed with caution, i.e., don't let your wallet hang out of your back pocket or flash expensive jewelry.

You'll be able to experience a microcosm of city life in the park, from the

English nannies and their charges, the East Side types sunning themselves behind the Metropolitan Museum to the sounds of salsa, reggae, and rap drifting from the northernmost end of the park.

From the **horse-and-buggy rides** (hire a hack on the 59th Street side) to the free Shakespeare in the **Delacorte Theater,** to our personal fond memories of playing softball in the **Sheep Meadow,** we love our park and hope the city continues to resist the real estate moguls who want to develop this prime territory.

One final, and somewhat melancholy sight in Central Park, is **Strawberry Fields,** a park memorial to John Lennon. You can find it opposite the Dakota Hotel where Lennon was shot, on the west side of the park—enter on 72nd Street; it runs from 71st to 74th Streets.

11. Times Square

The Times Square area runs from 49th Street and Broadway to 42nd Street. Within these few blocks are crammed enough porno shows, pinball emporiums, pizza and souvlaki shops, and movie houses to supply the world. The area is nothing if not colorful. Broadway and 42nd Street has been called the crossroads of the world and rumor has it that if you stand on the corner long enough, you're sure to see at least half of all your friends. We can't guarantee that, surely, but you might see one of each type of person you've ever heard of. Clergy and streetwalkers, performers, cops, super-salesmen, pimps, office workers, out-of-towners, photographers, and just plain New Yorkers flock to the area for the movies, the girlie shows, and the theater. There may be more gigantic billboards block for block here than anywhere else in the world.

Chapter V

ONE-DAY EXCURSIONS FROM NEW YORK

1. Up the Hudson Valley
2. Long Island
3. New Jersey

IF YOU'RE PLANNING to be in New York for a few weeks, you might very well want to spend some of your time traveling just outside of New York City—to the surrounding country areas which are noted for scenic beauty and a wide variety of gardens, beaches, old houses, and historical attractions. Most of these are within an hour or two's driving distance of mid-Manhattan. You can either rent a car and be on your own, or take a tour by bus or railroad. One trip offers a particular delight: a cruise up the Hudson River in one of the few remaining side-wheelers, the last of the great ships that once ran from New York City to Albany on the old Hudson River Day Line.

The excursions described in this chapter will take you through the scenic Hudson River Valley to see Bear Mountain and West Point, Sleepy Hollow Restorations, Boscobel, and Hyde Park (the home of Franklin D. Roosevelt), and Waterloo Village; then on to the unspoiled beauties of Long Island and to New York's favorite playground, Jones Beach; and perhaps some trips New Jersey-way.

1. Up the Hudson Valley

WEST POINT AND BEAR MOUNTAIN: Besides giving you a breath of air after you've pounded the city pavements, this boat cruise introduces you to the beauties of the Hudson River Valley. At Bear Mountain there's plenty of room for swimming, hiking, picnicking. **Circle Line,** which now runs the Hudson River Day Line, schedules boat service from the end of May to the middle of September, daily except Monday and Tuesday. No reservations are needed. The round-trip fare Wednesday and Thursday is $12 for adults, $6 for children under 12; on Saturday, Sunday, and holidays, $15 for adults, $7.50 for children; $10 for senior citizens at all times. Boats leave from Pier 81, at the foot of West 41st Street, at 9:30 a.m., and return at 6:30 p.m.

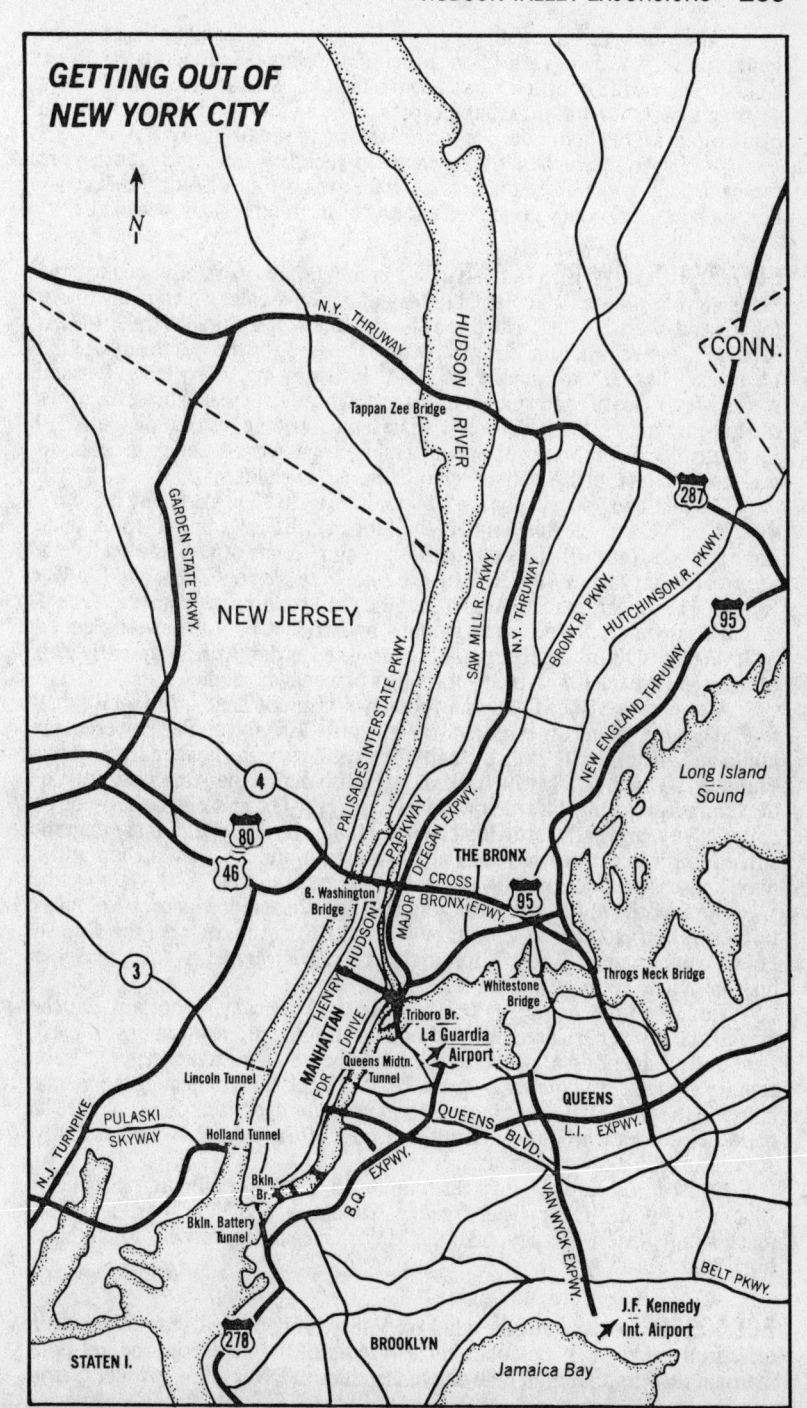

HUDSON VALLEY EXCURSIONS 239

If the youngsters are with you, take the same boat farther along to **West Point,** the very next stop after Bear Mountain. A bus ($3 for adults, $1.50 for children) meets the boat and whisks you to the U.S. Military Academy, where you might observe a full-dress parade, or visit the museum and buildings. Take a picnic along for the boat ride. For further information call 563-3204.

Note: Not only are these trips cheaper on weekdays, but they're much more pleasant. New Yorkers take the trips when they've got time off—on weekends—and the boats are usually jammed then, especially so on holiday weekends.

SLEEPY HOLLOW RESTORATIONS: In addition to its natural beauty, the Hudson Valley has a rich colonial history and is an area in which many of our folk legends were created. The three Sleepy Hollow Restorations (tel. 914/631-8200) in the lower Hudson Valley were made possible by the generosity of John D. Rockefeller, Jr., who made his home in nearby Pocantico Hills. Located within a few miles of each other in the Tarrytown area, they span three centuries of Hudson Valley history. A three-visit ticket to all of the restorations costs $10 for adults, $6.50 for senior citizens and children ages 6 to 14. Separate tickets to each cost $4 for adults, $3.50 for senior citizens and children.

The first one you will come to if you drive from New York City is **Sunnyside,** in Tarrytown, one mile south of the Tappan Zee Bridge on West Sunnyside Lane (just off Route 9). This was the 19th-century home of Washington Irving, the great literary figure who gave us *The Legend of Sleepy Hollow* and *Rip Van Winkle.* The gingerbread house is one of the most picturesque homes in America and is surrounded by orchards, gardens, and wooded paths that were planned by Irving himself. Inside, the rooms are furnished as they were in the early 19th century and are filled with many of Irving's personal mementos.

After you've visited Sunnyside, get in your car and head north on Route 9 to **Philipsburg Manor,** two miles away in North Tarrytown. The stone manor house and gristmill date from the early 1700s and were the headquarters of the Philipses, a Dutch family who backed the British during the American Revolution and subsequently lost their vast land holdings. The gristmill is the scene of daily activity, and early farm implements and agricultural methods are demonstrated in the reconstructed barn nearby. A beautiful colonial kitchen in the main house is presided over by a hostess in period costume.

Our favorite of the three restorations is **Van Cortlandt Manor,** a few miles farther up, off Route 9 in Croton-on-Hudson. To get there, take the Croton Point Avenue exit off Route 9, turn right at South Riverside Avenue, and go a quarter mile to the manor entrance.

This one-time home of an 18th-century politically important Dutch-English family is considered one of our most authentic restorations of early America. It features a Dutch-style manor house, a restored tavern, 18th-century gardens, fruit orchards, and a 750-foot brick wall connecting the manor house to the inn. There are plantings of flowers for every season and guides in period costumes who give horticultural tours of the estate, as well as Early American craft demonstrations.

Each of the Sleepy Hollow Restorations is open daily all year round, from 10 a.m. to 5 p.m.—except Thanksgiving, Christmas, and New Year's Days. To reach Route 9 from the city, take the Major Deegan Expressway to the New York State Thruway.

BOSCOBEL: Deeper into the Hudson Valley, but still less than a two-hour drive from midtown, is Boscobel (tel. 914/265-3638), the splendid Federal-style mansion that graces a bluff high above the Hudson River in the town of Garrison. It boasts one of the finest collections of Federal furnishings anywhere. The Dyckman family, descendants of Dutch colonists, who built the house in 1807, shopped for most of the furniture in New York and many of the pieces you will see came from the workshop of cabinetmaker Duncan Phyfe. Take time to stroll through the rose garden, the wildflower garden, and the herb garden, and visit the gift shop, with tasteful reproductions of Boscobel bowls, pottery, French linens, candles, and other items reminiscent of the 19th century. Boscobel is eight miles north of the Bear Mountain Bridge on Route 9D. It is open throughout the year—except the months of January and February, on Tuesday, and on Thanksgiving, Christmas, and New Year's Days—from 9:30 a.m. to 4:30 p.m. (till 3:30 p.m. in November, December, and March). Admission is $4 for adults, $2 for children 6 to 14.

HYDE PARK: In the same area, you should not miss a visit to **Hyde Park,** home and birthplace of the late Franklin D. Roosevelt. This is our favorite excursion. The house is maintained as it was during the Roosevelts' lifetimes, and both Franklin and Eleanor are buried in the Rose Garden, near the house. Don't miss seeing the library. It houses FDR's personal and presidential papers, as well as displays of priceless gifts he received while in the White House. Open seven days a week from 9 a.m. to 5 p.m. from Memorial Day through Labor Day. Admission is $1.50 for both house and library; children under 16 and senior citizens free. Admission also includes a free pass for a visit to the **Vanderbilt Mansion,** located two miles farther north on Route 9. This is the millionaire's impressive home, built between 1896 and 1898. Phone 914/229-9115 for further information.

The **Hyde Park Town Hall,** located in Hyde Park, 1½ miles north of the FDR Library on the corner of U.S. 9 and Main Street, has a display of FDR material pertaining to Hyde Park. This building is open weekdays from 8:30 a.m. to 4 p.m. Admission free.

Antique collectors and fans should be sure to visit the **Hyde Park Antiques Center,** located between the Roosevelt and Vanderbilt Mansions right on Route 9. Over 35 dealers feature furniture, glassware, china, jewelry, prints, toys, Orientalia, and collectibles. It's open daily from 10 a.m. to 5 p.m. For information, phone 914/229-8200.

To drive to Hyde Park from Manhattan, take the West Side Highway to the Henry Hudson Parkway to the Saw Mill River Parkway to the Taconic Parkway. Then take Route 84 West to Route 9 North at Fishkill, and follow Route 9 to Hyde Park. Or take the Major Deegan Expressway to the New York Thruway and get off at Exit 18 (New Paltz), following signs to the Mid-Hudson Bridge. After the bridge crossing, take the right ramp and follow signs to Route 9 North.

MUSEUM VILLAGE IN ORANGE COUNTY: Here, in Monroe, New York (tel. 914/782-8247), is one of the country's largest outdoor museums of 19th-century American technology. Over 30 buildings contain thousands of objects and tools, portraying the era of homespun crafts and the emerging industry that characterized that time. There are daily demonstrations of broommaking, weaving, pottery, blacksmithing, and printing. A good place to take children. Open daily except Monday from April 15 to October 31, 10 a.m. to 5 p.m. Admission is $4.75 for adults, $2.75 for children ages 6 to 15 (under 6, free). Museum Village is 50 miles from New York City. To get there, take the New York State Thruway to Exit 16 at Harriman. Follow Route 17 West for about four miles and watch for the signs (Exit 129).

OLANA: About an hour's drive north of Hyde Park (and an hour's drive south of Albany) is what looks like an Islamic castle on the banks of the Hudson. This is the Olana Historical Site, and all of it—house, studio, paintings, landscaping, furnishings—reflects the genius of the man who created it, the renowned landscape painter of the Hudson River School, Frederick Edwin Church. Inspired by a visit to Europe and the Near East in 1867, Church and his wife created a palace fit for an Oriental potentate, its lush Oriental trappings curiously mixed with Victorian furnishings. Outdoor views compete with those indoors: Olana is situated on a 500-foot hill overlooking the Hudson at a point where it abruptly becomes two miles wide, affording breathtaking vistas of the river and the Catskill Mountains.

The grounds of Olana are open all year from 8 a.m. to dusk. The castle can be viewed only on a guided tour: these are held Wednesday through Sunday from Memorial Day weekend through the last Sunday in October, and also on Memorial Day, Independence Day, and Labor Day. Tours begin at 10 a.m., and the last tour is at 4 p.m. There is a nominal fee for the tour, and because it is extremely popular, reservations are a must: phone 518/828-0135 or write to Olana State Historic Site, R.D. 2, Hudson, NY 12534. For driving directions to Olana, which is on Route 9G, five miles south of Hudson, phone the above number.

HUDSON VALLEY WINERIES: Attention oenophiles! A delightful way to explore the Hudson Valley is to combine your sightseeing with a visit to a winery in the area—or plan your entire day around such a visit. There are at least 16 wineries in the region, most of them about a two-hour (or less) drive from New York. At most you're not only taken on tours and given free samples, but you'll be able to chat with the winemakers, savor local cheeses and other goodies, wander through the vineyards, stay and enjoy a picnic for as long as you like. There is a small admission charge to most wineries. Two of our favorites are the Brotherhood Winery in Washingtonville (close to Newburgh and West Point), and, farther north, the Hudson Valley Winery in Highland, not far from Poughkeepsie and Hyde Park.

The **Brotherhood Winery,** 35 North St., Washingtonville, NY 10992 (tel. 914/496-3661), is the oldest winery in the United States. Visitors are taken on an extensive tour, invited to visit the underground cellars and the processing-bottling operation, and to taste the wines. Especially enjoyable is a visit to the Hors d'Oeuvrerie, a flower-bedecked outdoor patio, where you can nibble on cheeses, pastas, and pâtés while sipping wine by the glass or carafe. Seasonal events are held frequently: you could run into an authentic Maine clambake or a western-style barbecue. Open weekends mid-February through mid-November from 11 a.m. to 4 p.m.; Monday through Thursday April to mid-November 11 a.m. to 4 p.m. Admission is $2 for adults; children visit free. Phone for reservations and details.

The **Hudson Valley Winery,** Blue Point Road, Highland, NY 12528 (tel. 914/691-7296), boasts an entire "wine village," 315 acres overlooking the Hudson River. Visitors see everything, from vineyards to bottling line. You can have a picnic here, enjoy a hayride through the vineyards, take home souvenir wine glasses. On weekends, wine is served with breadsticks and cheese. Tours are held April through October weekdays from 11 a.m. to 4 or 5 p.m., weekends from 11 a.m. to 4 p.m.; mid-November through December weekends only 11 a.m. to 4 p.m. Admission is $3 for adults, $1 for children during the week; $5 for adults, $1 for children on weekends; and $6 for adults, $3 for children on festival weekends. Phone for reservations and details.

To get a free booklet on winery tours in the Hudson River region, plus information on historic sites and special events, phone 914/265-3066, or write to Hudson River Valley, 72 Main St., Cold Spring, NY 10516.

Note to parents: A visit to a winery makes for a delightful family outing—although the youngsters will not be given free samples!

2. Long Island

The **Long Island Rail Road** offers about 80 excellent, inexpensive escorted tours of Long Island, famed for its beaches and historic homes; they're scheduled during the summer months. The price of a ticket usually includes all admissions, transfers, and one meal. Write for the latest schedule to "Tours," Customer Services, Long Island Rail Road Co., Jamaica, Long Island, New York, NY 11435 (tel. 718/739-4200 or 718/990-7498). Tickets for all tours may be purchased in advance or even 20 minutes before train time at the Long Island ticket office at Pennsylvania Station, 34th Street and Seventh Avenue.

There are two tours we think are most representative of what the area has to offer. First, the **Famous Homes and Garden Tour,** which will take you about 35 miles from the city, through Long Island's beautiful North Shore. You'll visit Sagamore Hill, home and summer White House of President Theodore Roosevelt; and then stop at the John S. Phipps Mansion and Old Westbury Gardens, one of the finest American examples of Georgian architecture, with the beautiful grounds surrounding it. Total cost (including dinner at the Milleridge Inn) is $25 for adults, $15 for children 5 to 11 years.

Some other Long Island Rail Road tours worthy of your attention include a Monday tour to **Falaise,** the home of Harry F. Guggenheim, and to beautiful **Clark Gardens;** a Tuesday visit to the **Sunken Forest** of the famed Fire Island; an all day train-bus-boat tour on Wednesday to the **Cold Spring Harbor Fish Hatchery;** a Saturday or Sunday **ferryboat cruise** from Stony Brook Village to Bridgeport, Connecticut; and an all-day, 300-mile trip to the tip of Long Island, **Montauk Point.**

JONES BEACH: Beach lovers simply must not miss Jones Beach, just a little over 30 miles from midtown. It offers everything from superb ocean swimming and white sandy beaches to paddle tennis and other sports, as well as a famous open-air theater for evening entertainment. Yes, it's crowded, especially on weekends. During the summer, a Long Island Rail Road package takes you there for a round-trip fare of $7.50 for adults, $4 for children. Another Long Island Rail Road package takes you to nearby Long Beach; the charge of $8 for adults includes admission to Ocean Beach Park. For information, phone 718/739-4200 or 718/990-7498.

If you have your own wheels, you can drive to Jones Beach in about 1½ hours from midtown Manhattan. Jones Beach is at the end of the Meadowbrook and Wantagh State Parkways. You might also consider driving another 15 miles farther on to slightly less crowded Robert Moses State Park at the southern end of Sunken Meadow State Parkway. And if you prefer the mild waters of Long Island Sound to the sometimes rough surf of Jones Beach and Robert Moses State Park, try Sunken Meadow State Park, which is at the northern end of that same Southern Meadow State Parkway. For information, phone 516/669-1000.

3. New Jersey

WATERLOO VILLAGE: New Jersey's restored Colonial-period hamlet in Stanhope is only 55 minutes by car from the George Washington Bridge. Set in the Allamuchy Mountain area, it offers a journey through American history. The little canal village contains historical homes and buildings dating from 1740 to 1860. Among them are the Canal House, a Revolutionary-period stone structure; a gristmill built in 1760; a blacksmith shop; the Victorian Wellington House, dating from 1859. In all, 90 rooms have been refurbished in authentic period style. The village is also the scene of busy activity by craftspeople trained in early arts, whose work is sold in the general store that is part of the reconstruction.

On summer weekends, Waterloo is the site of a music festival with everything from orchestral and chamber concerts to jazz and bluegrass, featuring internationally known musicians—anyone from Arlo Guthrie to Alicia DeLarrocha or Pete Seeger. Ticket prices start at $20, but the music festival is included with the village admission on most Sunday afternoons. For details, phone 201/347-4700.

Admission to the village Tuesday through Friday is $6 ($4.50 for senior citizens, $3 for children 6 to 12); Saturday and Sunday, $7.50 ($5 for senior citizens, $3 for children). Open Tuesday through Sunday from 10 a.m. to 6 p.m., from just after Easter through December (to 5 p.m. beginning in October). To get there, take the George Washington Bridge to Route 80 West to Exit 25. Follow Route 206 north to the second traffic light and turn left. Waterloo is on the left about two miles from there. For further information, phone 201/347-0900.

ON SAFARI: Great Adventure, in Jackson, New Jersey—the $100-million family entertainment park with 2000 wild animals—is also worth a visit. See Chapter VIII for details.

Chapter VI

BARGAIN NIGHTSPOTS

1. Bar Hopping
2. The Music Spots
3. Dance, Dance, Dance
4. Theatrical and Nightclub Entertainment

AFTER DUSK FALLS, New York City's frantic daytime scurry reemerges in the nighttime spots—the cafés, clubs, bars, and cabarets. Quiet or closed during the day, they are transformed into glittery, swirling havens for people whose happiest times are at night. They become a night-person's paradise. You can do or find anything. There are piano bars, cabarets, and elegant watering holes for sophisticated fun. There are places for quiet conversation and a drink. And there are disco, jazz, and punk clubs for hot, sensual nights.

A night on the town can be expensive—as much as $100. But for the price of a moderate cover charge, or even just a drink, you can find lively and interesting entertainment. We've highlighted these places below.

Bars, which can be anything from chic celebrity hangouts to rowdy beer joints, make up the first section. They're described briefly with attention to atmosphere and crowd. Live music—from oldtime show tunes to jazz and New Wave—is a New York City trademark and the topic of the second section. The type of music, performers, and prices are noted. Our third major topic is the city's opportunities for you to "boogie," New York's dance spots. Cabarets and nightclubs comprise the final section. Again, prices and performers are noted.

1. Bar Hopping

ROOMS WITH A VIEW: The view from the top of New York's skyscrapers is overwhelming. It spreads across Manhattan to the five boroughs, showing off miles of crowded avenues, massive buildings, and elegant brownstones. Viewing all of this can be done relatively cheaply—provided you limit yourself to one cocktail.

At the top of the World Trade Center, with a 180-degree view, is the **Hors d'Oeuvrerie,** One World Trade Center (107th floor; tel. 938-1111). Here you can have afternoon or evening drinks, along with tasty ethnic-style hors d'oeuvres, while taking in the Statue of Liberty, Staten Island, or the Brooklyn Bridge and Queens. Open to the public from 3 p.m. until midnight nightly, with hors d'oeuvres served after 4 p.m. Men must wear jackets, and no blue jeans are allowed.

The 65th-floor **Rainbow Room**, at 30 Rockefeller Plaza (tel. 757-9090), rests about 850 feet above the city and the view from its three sides spreads at least 50 miles. You can see downtown Manhattan and Central Park directly below, and then as far afield as New Jersey. Meals at the restaurant are very formal and expensive. But for the price of a cocktail—$3.50 and up—you can sit in one of the lounges and still enjoy the view. The north cocktail lounge of the Rainbow Room is open Tuesday to Saturday from 4 p.m. to 1 a.m., on Sunday to midnight, and on Monday to 10 p.m. The south lounge is open from 5 p.m. to 2 a.m. Monday to Saturday.

At **Mitchell's Place** at Top O'Tower, atop the Beekman Tower Hotel, 49th Street and First Avenue (tel. 355-7300), the view spreads from the East River to the Empire State Building and the United Nations. There's also an outdoor terrace from which the scenery is even more pleasant. There's no cover or minimum, but drinks are expensive—between $2.80 and $5.50 apiece. Tuesday through Saturday a pianist entertains between 9 p.m. and 2 a.m.

Another skyscraper café is **Top of the Sixes,** on the 39th and top floor of 666 Fifth Ave. (tel. 757-6662). The scenery through its large windows includes Central Park, downtown Manhattan, and parts of New Jersey. Drinks are moderately priced at about $3.50 for cocktails and $2.50 for beer. There's entertainment Tuesday through Saturday. Open daily from 11:30 a.m. to midnight.

HANGOUTS: On a weekend night in Manhattan, the bars and cafés are as seductive as anything in town. In the Village and on the East and West Sides they dot nearly every block; and when passing by you can't help but be enticed by what's inside—long bars lined with gleaming bottles and glasses, chatter and music that spills into the street, and the glitter of the famous and high-powered that frequent many of them. There is a bar for everyone—for artists, actors, students, musicians, politicos, and business types. They are the "in" places—though not always expensive—and as much a New York trademark as the Stock Exchange and Broadway.

We have listed the popular, famous, and more intriguing bars. Some have already been covered in the restaurant section, and in this case our description is cursory. Any drink prices not covered are moderate.

Upper East Side

Oak wood bars, art nouveau, and Tiffany-style lamps are ubiquitous in Upper East Side bars. These are elegant and lavish watering holes, hoping also to become second homes for the chic or famous.

Elaine's, 1703 Second Ave., between 88th and 89th Streets (tel. 534-8103), takes that image to its zenith. The bartender will tell you that Francis Ford Coppola and producer Robert Evans were in before you, and mention a few others familiar only to those with an insider's knowledge of the celebrity scene. For the price of a drink—about $3.35—you can sit at the bar and watch for celebrities, but don't expect gracious service unless you fit in with the glitterati. Open nightly until 2 a.m.

Maxwell's Plum, at 64th Street and First Avenue (tel. 628-2100), used to be *the* East Side "in-spot" for locals and singles. It's still "in," but mainly with out-of-towners and business types who come to enjoy the plush decor and eclectic mix of art pieces, Tiffany-style lamps, and tuxedoed waiters. The elegant, slightly elevated bar is a perfect roost for people-watching. Open nightly till about 2 a.m.

Housed in a 19th-century red-brick building, **P. J. Clarke's,** 915 Third

Ave., at 55th Street (tel. 759-1650), is a remnant of a time when bars, tenements, and antique shops gave this area a real neighborhood feel. Next to the towering headquarters of Skidmore, Owings and Merrill, Clarke's looks tiny and inconsequential. But inside it's the type of place that garners an avid following of celebrities and noncelebrities alike. It has one of the city's most ornate cut-glass and mahogany bars, and its two back dining rooms have black-and-white tiled floors covered with sawdust. What's more, Clarke's has one of the best jukeboxes in town, with oldies by Sinatra, Peggy Lee, the Ink Spots, and the Mills Brothers. All this and you can get a beer for $1.50. Open nightly until 4 a.m.

A similar ambience, with a preppy twist, fills **Ruppert's,** 1662 Third Ave., at 93rd Street (tel. 831-1900). The split-level bar draws a young professional crowd which sports polo shirts, crew-neck sweaters, and tweed jackets. A pianist performs four nights a week upstairs, and food is served downstairs until 12:30 a.m. Open nightly until 4 a.m.

Drake's Drum, 1629 Second Ave., between 84th and 85th Streets (tel. 988-2826), has the feel of a British tavern. Rumor has it that the English tourists are almost always directed to the bar—which is owned by Englishmen—and that most regular customers have Cockney accents. British flags are stretched across the ceiling and the floor is covered with sawdust in this friendly and low-key bar. Open nightly until 4 a.m.

Whether your taste runs to flirting on the dance floor or to whispering "sweet nothings" over a quiet drink, you can find your niche in the Upper East Side singles bars.

The best spot in the neighborhood for singles on the prowl is **T.G.I. Friday's,** 1152 First Ave., at 63rd Street (tel. 832-8512), where you can try out your best one-liners till 1 a.m. weeknights and till about 3 a.m. on Friday and Saturday. The bartenders are chatty, friendly, and extremely well schooled in the art of moderating a boy-girl repartée.

If you like to single-mingle without being pressured, a good choice is **Martell's,** 1469 Third Ave., at 83rd Street (tel. 861-6110). The crowd is relaxed and easy-going, making this bar/restaurant just as suitable for friends and couples. There's an outdoor café, a jukebox with old jazz recordings, and 28 kinds of imported beer. Drinks are priced at $1.80 for a draft and $2.95 for a cocktail. Open Sunday through Thursday until 2 a.m., on Friday to 4 a.m., on Saturday to 3 a.m.

Upper West Side

McGlade's New Pub, 154 Columbus Ave., at 67th Street (tel. 874-9638), is reputed to be one of the best bars in New York. Its customers include many of the staff from ABC's network headquarters across the street. This is a relaxed bar for young professionals, and has a good mix of neighborhood people, writers, and artists. Open nightly until 4 a.m.

Take a window seat at **Marvin Gardens,** 2274 Broadway, between 81st and 82nd Streets (tel. 799-0578), and watch the crowds along Broadway. This clean, comfortable bar attracts a sophisticated set. Open Sunday through Wednesday until 2 a.m., Thursday through Saturday until 3 a.m.

Pershing's, 323 Columbus Ave., between 70th and 71st Streets (tel. 595-5420), is a classy place to drink. Local celebrities and crew from other neighborhood restaurants and bars show up here. Vintage war posters, wainscot paneling, and a white, pressed-tin ceiling add elegant touches. Friendly bartenders too. Open from noon to 4 a.m.

Artists love **Nanny Rose,** 301 Columbus Ave., at 74th Street (tel. 787-3801). Crayons and papers are provided at the tables, and samples of customers' surprisingly talented art are displayed in the windows and on the walls. This busy restaurant and bar attracts a mixed age group. Open nightly until 12:30 or 1 a.m.

Tap-A-Keg, 330 Columbus Ave., between 75th and 76th Streets (tel. 874-8593), lives up to its motto "hell of a joint." Lots of young drinkers here, and the jukebox tunes, a range of classic oldies and raucous dance numbers, are so good you won't want to leave. Play pinball, or mill around the wood-paneled room. No food. Open from 2 p.m. to 4 a.m. daily.

A step up is **Tap-A-Keg East,** 305 Columbus Ave., between 74th and 75th Streets (tel. 874-9052). This tasteful interior includes a lovely copper bar, plants, and a jukebox with classy selections, such as Billy Holiday tunes. The regulars who frequent Tap-A-Keg East make for a professional, relaxed crowd. There's a pool table in the back. Open from 2 p.m. to 4 a.m.

Dobson's, 341 Columbus Ave., at 76th Street (tel. 362-0100), offers one of the more up-scale bars in an already up-scale neighborhood. Blue-and-white checked tablecloths and pleasant bartenders add charm. A lot of dancers and actors come here. Open until midnight Sunday through Thursday, on Friday and Saturday until 1 a.m.

The outside of **J. G. Melon's,** at 76th Street and Amsterdam Avenue (tel. 874-8291), is painted green like a ripe, juicy watermelon. Inside, the melon motif continues with watermelon paintings, stuffed watermelons, and other melon bric-a-brac. Rich brass railings and etched glass on the front door add up to a pleasant escape. This bar's atmosphere attracts a lot of single women, who feel comfortable relaxing and having a drink. Meals are served also. Open from 11:30 a.m. to 3 a.m.

Fun is the name of the game for young professionals who flock to **Amsterdam's,** 428 Amsterdam Ave., between 80th and 81st Streets (tel. 874-1377), from all over Manhattan. This bar and rotisserie has the flavor of a college football crowd ready to go wild and start cheering at any moment. Open from noon to 3 or 4 a.m. daily.

On the same block is **KCOU Radio,** 430 Amsterdam Ave., between 80th and 81st Streets (tel. 580-0556). This bar rivals Amsterdam's in attracting local young professionals. Highlights of KCOU include a streamlined look with touches of blue neon lighting, and a jukebox that features rock and rhythm and blues. Open nightly until 4 a.m.

Another late night hangout on the Upper West Side is **Shelter,** 2180 Broadway, at 77th Street (tel. 362-4360). The crowd is vintage Upper West Side: lots of young professionals, writers, artists, and neighborhood people. Open nightly until 4 a.m.

Teacher's, 2249 Broadway, between 81st and 82nd Streets (tel. 787-3500), and **Teacher's Too,** 2271 Broadway, between 82nd and 83rd Streets (tel. 362-4900), are both particularly amiable and companionable places. These sister establishments offer warm, dark interiors decorated with work by local artists and photographers. Both are open until midnight or 1 a.m. Sunday through Thursday, on Friday and Saturday until 2 a.m.

At **Saratoga Turf Tavern,** 2550 Broadway, between 95th and 96th Streets (tel. 864-8796), you're likely to find yourself trading stories with the locals. This bar features horseracing prints and photographs. And no wonder: the owner, Joe Gleason, owns a number of horses. As a diversion, a scull and craft hangs above the bar. In the summer, sit outside beneath a red canopy. Open from 11:30 a.m. to 4 a.m.

Hanratty's West, 732 Amsterdam Ave., between 95th and 96th Streets (tel. 864-4224), attracts all varieties of people—young, old, locals, visitors, bikers, yuppies, professionals, and laborers. This mixed and lively crowd all know a good thing when they see it. Open nightly until 3 or 4 a.m.

At **Augies's**, 2751 Broadway, between 105 and 106th Streets (tel. 864-8707), you might find a customer absent-mindedly drinking a beer while absorbed in a book. Others, both locals and older Columbia University students, you'll find playing chess or listening to the low-key music, such as a trio featuring a stand-up bass. During the breaks the musicians pass the hat. This small bar with its high ceiling and glassed-in front is decorated with old art prints and paintings. Open from 5 p.m. to 4 a.m. daily.

On a busy night at the **West End Café**, 2911 Broadway, between 113th and 114th Streets (tel. 666-8750), chaos reigns. Featuring a huge circular bar, beer-sticky floors, videos showing on a TV screen, and couples necking in the corner, this famous hangout—which once drew the likes of Allen Ginsburg and Jack Kerouac—packs in rowdy college students. And with 14 types of beer on tap, and more than 70 varieties in stock, no wonder. Open nightly until 4 a.m.

Midtown West / Times Square

Around Midtown West/Times Square, the bars and pubs attract audiences and performers from the nearby theater district, and if you're lucky you might very well stumble upon a Broadway star.

Try the fabled and very beautiful **Russian Tea Room**, 150 W. 57th St., between Sixth and Seventh Avenues (tel. 265-0947). It has a second-floor bar that's a perfect roost for watching the passing parade of celebrity diners. A favorite with Carnegie Hall concert-goers, the restaurant was refurbished in the red-velvet opulence of a czar's palace. This is not a place to come in jeans and T-shirts, especially if you expect to get good service. While you're here, you might try one of the vodka specials that go by names like Ivan the Terrible, the Ballet Russe, the Moscow Mule, and the Nureyev. Open weekdays till 12:30 a.m., on Saturday till 1:30 a.m.

The line of young professionals waiting to get into the **Hard Rock Café**, 221 W. 57th St. between Sixth and Seventh Avenues (tel. 489-6565), is usually quite long, as befits this New York version of owner Isaac Tigrett's legendary London restaurant/bar. Like its London counterpart, this Hard Rock is a museum of rock-and-roll memorabilia, including 100 gold records, Prince's jacket from the movie *Purple Rain*, Chubby Checker's boots, and the guitars of Eric Clapton and Eddy Van Halen. Even the bar is shaped like a guitar. Open from 11:30 a.m. to 4 a.m.

The preferred watering hole of the Lincoln Center set is the **Ginger Man**, 51 W. 64th St., between Columbus Avenue and Central Park West (tel. 399-2358). Employees warn that this is not a casual bar, but a place for a quiet drink or light meal after the ballet or symphony. The crowd here is heavily sprinkled with celebrities, and the bar's interior is as elegant as its patrons. Brass railings ring the oak bar and old Lincoln Center posters (they've become collectors' items) line the walls. Open nightly until midnight.

Less expensive but also star-studded is **Joe Allen's**, 326 W. 46th St., between Eighth and Ninth Avenues (tel. 581-6464), open daily till 2 a.m.; food served until 1:30 a.m. Another is the very similar **Charlie's**, 236 W. 45th St., between Broadway and Eighth Avenue (tel. 354-2911), open later, till 4 a.m.

For a more romantic, steeped-in-history atmosphere, head west to the **Landmark Tavern**, 625 Eleventh Ave., at 46th Street (tel. 757-8595). But don't wait too late; it closes at midnight during the week and at 1 a.m. on Saturday and Sunday.

Lodged in a historic oak dining room built by Andrew Carnegie, **Lavin's Restaurant and Wine Bar**, 23 W. 39th St., between Fifth and Sixth Avenues (tel. 921-1288), is a relaxing place to educate your wine palate. The bar, with its cool white marble countertop and etched-glass lamps hanging overhead, is a genteel refuge on a hot summer day. The bar emphasizes California wines, though there are European wines available by the glass as well. Pleasant wines cost about $3.50 for each glass, but there is always a superior quality wine on tap as well ($10 to $18.75). Weekdays only, from noon to 10 p.m.

Another cheerful wine bar and restaurant is **Tastings Restaurant** at the **International Wine Center,** 144 W. 55th St., between Sixth and Seventh Avenues (tel. 757-1160), offering a variety of wines at about $3 a glass. The tile bar keeps your elbows cool and the soft green lamps are easy on the eyes. An award-winning wine list is served by an extremely knowledgeable staff, all educated at the wine school on the second floor. Open weekdays from noon to midnight, on Saturday from 5:30 to 11 p.m.; closed Sunday.

Greenwich Village

In Greenwich Village the bars tend to be more casual, less expensive, and livelier. In any one of a number of clubs and nightspots you can join an offbeat crowd of students, artists, musicians, and locals for music, a drink, and a good time.

The **Cottonwood Café,** 415 Bleecker St., between West 11th and Bank Streets (tel. 924-6271), is a lone and rising star in the Village. New to the Village scene, it has broken the mold. It's Texas in Manhattan, serving up great Tex-Mex food, a can't-be-beat friendliness, and live folk and country-western music every night except Sunday. The bar closes at 1 a.m. nightly.

Sazerac House, 533 Hudson St., at the corner of Charles Street (tel. 989-1313), serves New Orleans–style food but its ambience is pure Old Village. It's a local crowd that frequents Sazerac's bar, but you can break in and provide some out-of-towner talk. Open nightly till 2 a.m.

For those with a literary bent, there's the **Lion's Head,** 59 Christopher St., just off Seventh Avenue South (tel. 929-0670). It's one of the most famous writers' bars in the city. Besides that, it's cozy and pubby. Open most nights till 4 a.m.

The legendary **White Horse Tavern,** 560 Hudson St., at the corner of West 11th Street (tel. 243-9260), is where Dylan Thomas once wolfed down 18 shots of whiskey in less than 20 minutes, and died several days later. The White Horse is still host to writers and artists. It serves good hamburgers and omelets, and is open until 1 or 2 a.m. every night.

For romance, there's **Ye Waverly Inn,** 16 Bank St., at Waverly Place (tel. 243-9396). This old and dimly lit tavern is perfect for a romantic date. It's not open very late though: Monday through Thursday until 10 p.m., on Friday and Saturday until 11:15 p.m., and on Sunday until 9:15 p.m.

One bar that's popular without drawing a specific type of crowd is **Montana Eve,** 140 Seventh Ave. South, between 10th and Charles Streets (tel. 242-1200). It has a mix of regulars and occasionals, making for a friendly and even pleasantly rowdy atmosphere. Good food is served until 1 a.m. every day; the bar closes at 3 a.m.

If you want a late-night espresso instead of a drink, the **Peacock Caffè,** 24 Greenwich Ave., off 10th Street (tel. 242-9395), is a popular coffeehouse hangout. Its classical music and baroque columns provide a restful, pensive break from sightseeing or bar hopping. Open till 1 a.m. Tuesday through Thursday and on Sunday, till 2 a.m. on Friday and Saturday. Closed Monday.

For late-night munchies, nothing beats **Sandolino's,** 11 Barrow St., off West 4th Street (tel. 255-6669). Top off your late-night roamings with anything from a hearty sandwich to cheese blintzes. Open, serving food, until 1 a.m.

Chumley's, 86 Bedford St., at Barrow Street (tel. 675-4449), is the quintessence of old Village atmosphere. The entrance is unmarked because it used to be a speakeasy, and this two-room basement establishment seems not to have changed a bit since the old days. The neighborhood regulars and local bohemians make Chumley's a relaxed and convivial place. Open seven nights a week until 1:30 a.m.

East Village

Jack the Ribbers, or "J.R.'s," 25 Third Ave., between St. Mark's Place and East 9th Street (tel. 677-0151), attracts a lot of the fraternity students from nearby New York University. This college crowd appreciates Happy Hour beer for 75¢ and mixed drinks for $1.50. Old railroad prints liven up the walls. Open daily from 3 p.m. to 4 a.m.

You'll feel welcome at **Dojo's**, 24 St. Mark's Pl., between Second and Third Avenues (tel. 674-9821), in the heart of the East Village. There are lots of friendly faces and good conversations here. Drink at the light-wood bar or, in the summer, under a canopied porch. Open Sunday through Thursday from 11 a.m. to midnight, on Friday and Saturday to 1 p.m.

The **Centre Pub,** 29 St. Mark's Pl., between Second and Third Avenues (tel. 254-2462), with its dark-wood interior and comfortable booths, is a place where you'll find students studying with a beer. During the summer, relax in the beer garden in the back, complete with large umbrellas to keep the sun off. If you're hungry, try the burgers or other fare. Open from noon to 4 a.m.

No tour of the East Village bars would be complete without a visit to the **Grassroots Tavern,** on the same block at 20 St. Mark's Pl. (tel. 475-9443), a fun, noisy bar with lots of life, and a solid crowd of regulars. Open from 4 p.m. to 3 a.m.

You'll find **Holiday,** 75 St. Mark's Place (tel. 777-9637), usually crowded with locals, whether they are sitting on the jukebox or gathered around the bar. Lots of hard drinking is done in this smokey, boisterous establishment. Christmas lights, up all year round, add a bit of the holiday spirit. Open from 9 a.m. to 1 a.m. daily.

When uptown professionals venture to **WCOU,** 115 First Ave., at 7th Street (tel. 245-4317), you know it has to be good. WCOU's clean, streamlined look and its antique bar attracts crowds of all ages. Open from 4 p.m. to 4 a.m. daily.

Lots of white-paint graffiti art decorate the black walls of **Downtown Beirut,** 156 First Ave., between 9th and 10th Streets (tel. 777-9011). There are even drawings of rolls of barbed wire, suggesting off-limits areas of Beirut. Downtown Beirut has a clubhouse atmosphere for a younger set of punks and East Village types. Open daily from noon to 4 a.m.

Officially **King Tut's WaWa Hut,** on the southeast corner of 7th Street and Avenue A (tel. 254-7772), has no name. Still, it is one of the more imaginative bars in the area. A huge empty picture frame adorns a back wall. Dressmaker mannequins splattered with paint add a Kafka-esque tone. In the back room, furniture is arranged in little conversational settings. This is definitely a New Wave, punk hangout you won't want to miss. Open from 4 p.m. to 4 a.m. daily.

The gentrified atmosphere at **The Pharmacy,** 141 Avenue A (tel. 260-4798) attracts many of the newer, up-and-coming residents of the East Village. But older, established artists who have been drinking here since this pioneer bar opened keep coming back. Open Sunday through Thursday until 2 a.m., on Friday and Saturday until 4 a.m.

Beulah Land, 162 Avenue A (tel. 473-9310), is a great place to meet people. Everyone, from those wearing business suits to those sporting the latest punk attire, mingles in one large room. Often you'll find people dancing in the middle of the floor to the jukebox. Large New Wave art displays add pizzazz to the white walls. Open till 4 a.m.

Walk into **Caramba!**, 684 Broadway, at Great Jones (East 3rd) Street (tel. 420-9817), and you walk into a fiesta. Students and young professionals gather at the large front bar to party and meet friends. They come especially for the margarita slushes, featured in three sizes: small (3½ ounces), medium (12 ounces), and ridiculous (26 ounces). Open from noon to midnight.

Although only men were allowed into the rustic rooms of **McSorley's Old Ale House**, 15 E. 7th St., near Third Avenue (tel. 473-8800), until 1970, the pub now hosts both men and women. There's a solid college crowd here, but old-timers sit around in front of the pot-bellied stove as well, downing steins of draft ale.

SoHo

Over in SoHo, the **Broome Street Bar**, corner of Broome Street and West Broadway (tel. 925-2086), is popular among artists, writers, and musicians. There's an accent on tropical drinks, and jazz plays from the bar's sound system. Open nightly till about 2:30 a.m.

There's a similar clientele at the **Ear Inn**, 326 Spring St., between Washington and Greenwich Streets (tel. 226-9060). Ear Inn offers a good jukebox, poetry readings, and for the creative customer, butcher-paper tablecloths, and crayons for scribbling. The bar is open until around 4 a.m., with food served until 1 a.m.

For a warming hot toddy in winter or a cooling piña colada in summer, you might make a SoHo stop at the **Prince Street Bar and Restaurant**, 125 Prince St., corner of Wooster Street (tel. 228-8130). It's popular with SoHo locals. Open until 2 a.m. weekdays, to 3 a.m. on Friday and Saturday.

For wine and apéritif connoisseurs, a SoHo must is the **Wine Bar**, 422 West Broadway, between Prince and Spring Streets (tel. 431-4790). The Wine Bar serves 50 varieties of wine, by the glass or the bottle. Open until 2 a.m. nightly.

Tribeca

In Tribeca you can head for a late-night drink to **Smoke Stacks Lightnin'**, 380 Canal St., at West Broadway (tel. 226-0485), open until 2:30 a.m. weekdays, until 4 a.m. on Friday and Saturday. Or there's the lovely, lofty **211 West Broadway**, at Franklin Street (tel. 925-7202), a place typical of Tribeca's warehouse-turned-bar/restaurants, with a pressed-tin ceiling and cast-iron columns. There's always a neighborhood crowd at the **Washington Street Café**, between Vestry and Desbrosses Streets (tel. 925-5110), open for late-night drinks and socializing. And down the street, you can have a drink in one of the prettiest of the Tribeca warehouse-restaurants: **Capsouto Frères**, 451 Washington St., at Watts Street (tel. 966-4900).

Sports fans will love **The Sporting Club**, 99 Hudson St., between Harrison and Franklin Streets (tel. 219-0900), where the main draw is a ten-foot video screen and its companion, a computerized scoreboard, which tower above the oval bar.

One of the best places to hang out in the South Street Seaport area is the **North Star Pub**, 93 South St., at Fulton Street (tel. 509-6757), which serves several varieties of British ale in keeping with its British decor.

PIANO BARS: This is becoming one of New York's most popular scenes, and understandably so! Piano bars are more romantic, more fun, and more relaxed than singles bars. And since few piano bars have either minimums or cover charges, they tend to be less expensive than jazz clubs.

NIGHTLIFE: BARS

Broadway Joe, 315 W. 46th St., between Eighth and Ninth Avenues (tel. 246-6513), is a favorite with stage people, and the waiters say they have served Carol Burnett and Frank Sinatra, among others. Michael Edelstein, a jazz and pop pianist, plays from 10 p.m. until closing Tuesday to Saturday. His Gershwin is top-notch and he also has some very funny Victor Borge–style routines.

Only a stone's throw farther is **Silver Lining,** 349 W. 46th St. (tel. 315-1049). The new management aims to keep the place open 24 hours, with a pianist in the bar from 3 p.m. to 4 a.m. Nightclub acts in the back room range from $7 to $15. A before-theater five-course dinner special costs $11.75, is available Monday to Saturday from 5 to 8 p.m., and includes such choice entrees as roast beef and leg of lamb.

One of the largest and most esteemed piano bars in Manhattan is **Joe's Pier 52,** 163 W. 52nd St., between Sixth and Seventh Avenues (tel. 245-6652), a seafood restaurant and bar founded by a famous Broadway producer. Teddy Robson performs jazz in the "showboat lounge" from 8 p.m. until 1 a.m. Tuesday through Thursday. On weekends the bar taps the circuit of well-known touring jazz musicians. Drinks run $3 and $4, excellent cold appetizers (mostly seafood) run $10 and up and are available in the lounge, with many patrons cracking their lobsters as they sit at the bar.

An extremely dark and cozy piano bar is found at **Le Vert Galant,** 109 W. 46th St., between Sixth and Seventh Avenues (tel. 382-0022). You may find it hard to leave the sumptuous leather bar stools as a pianist performs popular show tunes from 7 p.m. until 1 a.m. Tuesday to Saturday. There's no minimum or cover, but drinks are $3.75 and up, and jackets are required for both bar and restaurant. It's located next to the American Place Theatre, with an elevator that will take you from the plaza level to the bar and restaurant on the second floor.

Piano bars are also popular on the Upper East Side. One of the most frequented is **Mimi's,** 984 Second Ave., at 52nd Street (tel. 688-4692). A pianist is on duty Monday through Saturday between 9 p.m. and 4 a.m., and on Sunday from 6 p.m. to 3 a.m. On three of those nights (Monday, Tuesday, and Saturday), the customers are coaxed along by an amiable, pleasant-voiced pianist named Jackson, who's been performing here for more than 25 years.

Marianas, 986 Second Ave. (tel. 759-4455), is right next door. Its decor is a bit more elegant than Mimi's, and it has a pianist from 7 p.m. till 1 a.m. Monday through Saturday.

The Toy Bar, 401 E. 78th St., between First and York Avenues (tel. 650-0659), is a tiny hole-in-the-wall offering jazz piano music from 9 p.m. to 2 a.m. Tuesday through Sunday. On Monday a fortune teller holds the floor.

Mortimer's, 1057 Lexington Ave., corner of 75th Street (tel. 861-2481), is actually two places rolled into one. The front room is a bar, serving drinks from noon until 1 a.m. Large mirrors on the walls let you see and be seen. In the back room you can have lunch or dinner amid cozy surroundings, with live piano music Tuesday through Saturday from 11:30 p.m. to 2:30 a.m. Lunch is served from noon to 3:30 p.m. weekdays, and 12:15 to 4:30 p.m. weekends. On Sunday and Monday, when there is no live music, dinner is served from 6 p.m. to midnight. Bar service for tables in the back room continues until 2:30 a.m. when live music is offered. Check the prices before sitting down.

Hanratty's, 1754 Second Ave., between 91st and 92nd Streets (tel. 289-3200), is decorated in ice-cream-parlor style, and offers boogie-woogie and other styles of piano music nightly from 8:30 p.m. to 12:30 a.m.

Other piano bars in the Upper East Side include **La Camelia,** 225 E. 58th St., between Second and Third Avenues (tel. 751-5488), with live music from 10 p.m. till 2 a.m. nightly; and **Nickels,** 227 E. 67th St., between Second and Third

Avenues (tel. 794-2331), where piano music can be heard from 8 p.m. to midnight.

Over in Murray Hill, pianist Lenny Metcalfe brings lots of warmth to **David Copperfield,** 322 Lexington Ave., between 38th and 39th Streets (tel. 684-8227). Not surprisingly, the British-born songster is given to tunes like "Maybe It's Because I'm a Londoner" and other old favorites. The audience coaxes him on and often joins in. This is a cozy pub with a distinctly Dickensesque flavor. There's music Monday through Saturday from 9 p.m. to about midnight.

Another highly recommended piano bar is at the **Village Green,** 531 Hudson St., between West 10th and Charles Streets (tel. 255-1650). Pianist Murray Grand seems to know every sing-along tune there is, and the bar has attracted the likes of Mikhail Barishnykov, Debbie Reynolds, and Jessica Lange. Open from 8:30 p.m. to 1 a.m. Sunday through Thursday, until 2 a.m. on Friday and Saturday. The piano is in the upstairs lounge.

Covent Garden, 133 W. 13th St., between Sixth and Seventh Avenues (tel. 675-0020), is an elegant place where you can lounge on a velvet sofa while the pianist plays "easy-listening" music, and where folks occasionally sing along. The baby grand is alive after 7 p.m. weeknights, after 8 p.m. on Friday and Saturday; no music on Sunday.

HOTEL BARS: You may not be able to afford a room in some of New York's posh hotels, but that shouldn't prevent you from enjoying their distinctive ambience or their cocktail hours.

The **Carlyle,** at Madison Avenue and 76th Street (tel. 744-1600), has its share of celebrity guests. You may glimpse a few in **Bemelman's Bar** (named after the illustrator whose delightful murals adorn the walls), a pleasing place with decorated columns, small dark tables, and a grand piano for the singers who perform nightly at 9:30 p.m. The cover charge is $5; during the entertainment, drinks start at $5.50. Adjoining the bar is the Gallery where you can sip your drinks while sitting on velvet couches and comfortable upholstered chairs. (In the afternoon—from 5 until 7 p.m. daily—it's a tea room.) The bar is open nightly till 1 a.m.

Also in the hotel, the elegant **Café Carlyle** is open for drinks and musical entertainment till 1 a.m. Performers do two shows nightly, at 10 p.m. and midnight. The cover charge varies, according to who's at the piano. (Note: The Café Carlyle is closed for the summer.)

The **Barbizon,** Lexington Avenue at 63rd Street (tel. 838-5700), has a pleasant, spacious café/bar on two levels which are connected by a carpeted, winding staircase. Food is available from noon till midnight, and the drinks start at $3.25. Open nightly till 2 a.m.

At the **Regency,** Park Avenue at 61st Street (tel. 759-4100), the wood-paneled bar with its subdued lighting and dramatic red floral murals attracts an international crowd. For the price of a glass of wine ($4.25) or a cocktail ($4.75 and up), you can enjoy the piano music every night from 6 till 9 p.m. and again from 10 p.m. till 1 a.m. Complimentary hors d'oeuvres are served from 5 till 7 p.m. Open nightly till 2 a.m.

For *New Yorker* magazine fans, or anyone interested in things literary, what could be more exciting than a drink at the **Algonquin Hotel,** 59 W. 44th St., at Sixth Avenue (tel. 840-6800). The Algonquin was home to the magazine's celebrated "Round Table"—Franklin Pierce Adams, James Thurber, Dorothy Parker, Alexander Wolcott, and Heywood Broun. You can still see *New Yorker* writers and editors sipping drinks in either the lobby bar or the adjoining blue bar. Both bars serve drinks until 1 a.m. The bartenders make a point of being gracious to everyone.

At the **Waldorf Astoria,** Park Avenue and 50th Street (tel. 355-5000), an international clientele gathers nightly at three distinctive and extravagantly decorated bars. **Sir Harry's Bar** has an African-safari motif with trophy heads and zebra skins on the walls.

Peacock Alley: is next to a two-ton, nine-foot-tall, bronze clock that's capped with a miniature of the Statue of Liberty. The main attraction at this famous bar is songwriter Cole Porter's personal piano. Porter lived at the Waldorf for several years, and his tunes are played on the piano nightly. Open nightly until 2 a.m. There are no cover charges at either bar, but drinks are expensive: about $4.65 for cocktails and $3.35 for beer.

Harry's is an inexplicably popular name for New York hotel bars. **Harry's** at the **Harley Hotel,** 212 E. 42nd St. (tel. 490-8900), has one feature not to be missed—a lavish complimentary buffet served between 5 and 7:30 p.m. which includes shrimp cocktails, fresh vegetables, and quiches. A pianist entertains while you dine. Drinks are expensive, at $4.65 for cocktails and $3.50 for wine, but anyone with a large appetite will make out fine. The bar closes at 2 a.m. on weekdays and at 1 a.m. on weekends.

The **Helmsley Palace,** at 455 Madison Ave. (tel. 888-7000), has yet another **Harry's Bar,** named for Mr. Helmsley himself! For $5.25 you can buy a glass of wine and pretend you're staying at one of the world's most expensive hotels. The bar has a pianist between 6 p.m. and 1 a.m. On the way out, you can stroll around the Villard Houses, a landmark and the hotel's trademark.

But if it's a summery evening, you might want to sit at the outdoor **Café de la Paix,** at the **St. Moritz,** 50 Central Park South (tel. 755-5800). For the price of a glass of wine ($4.50), this Parisian-style café offers the perfect setting for a romantic interlude or a tête-à-tête. Open daily from noon until 3:30 p.m. and from 5:30 to 11:30 p.m.

PLACES TO SEE AND BE SEEN: The watering holes of the glitterati flame and die as unpredictably as the stars they attract. Still popular, though, is the **Odeon,** 145 West Broadway, in Tribeca (tel. 233-0507). Formerly a working-class cafeteria, it was refurbished and redecorated to become a sleek-looking place with lots of chrome and art deco set against a color scheme of black and white. It attracts painters, sculptors, and entertainers. Andy Warhol, Robert DeNiro, and Jack Nicholson are said to be among the regulars. Open weekdays until 2 or 3 a.m. depending on the crowd, on weekends until 4 a.m.

Café des Artistes, 1 W. 67th St., off Central Park West (tel. 877-3500), attracts soap opera stars filming at the nearby WABC studios. The bar is decorated with turn-of-the-century Howard Chandler Christy murals, with some of the artist's original sketches. For some, these wood nymphs may prove as intriguing as the stars. Open Monday to Saturday from noon to 3 p.m. and 5 p.m. to midnight, on Sunday from 10 a.m. to 2 p.m. and 5 to 9 p.m.

The **Empire Diner,** 210 Tenth Ave., at 22nd Street (tel. 243-2736), is the pride of Chelsea. Ensconced in an old roadside diner, it was refurbished in 1976 into a fashionable, art deco restaurant/bar with chrome chairs, stainless-steel walls, and black tabletops. Open 24 hours a day, this is the place to go after the nightclubs close. It has 16 types of imported beer and serves everything from standard diner fare to elaborate meals. The atmosphere is one of candlelight and romance, and a pianist performs from 8:30 to 11 p.m. Sunday through Thursday, and from 11 p.m. to 3 a.m. on Friday and Saturday.

The **River Café,** 1 Water St., Brooklyn (tel. 718/522-5200), is housed in an old barge that floats beneath the Brooklyn Bridge. It has one of New York's best views of the river and lower Manhattan. This restaurant/bar is elegantly simple with wooden floors, fresh flowers, and one wall made entirely of glass. Though it's extremely expensive (dinner costs $42), you may want to drop by for a glimpse and a drink—also expensive at $3.75 a cocktail. Open nightly until 1:30 a.m.

2. The Music Spots

New York is a mecca for musicians; there are more places for them to perform than anywhere else, and the city is home to a plethora of clubs, bars, and music cafés where you can hear them play every night of the week. For the music lover, it's a feast. You can hear some of the best contemporary music in jazz clubs and lofts, as well as oldtime favorites at the many piano bars scattered through town. There are places that feature country music and others where rock is the fare. Some clubs charge no admission or minimum; others tack on a music charge ranging in steepness, depending on who's playing that night. To be certain, phone ahead to ask what the cover or minimum is that evening.

Before we start, here are two indispensable phone numbers which will fill you in on New York's music scene—who is playing where and what is available around town. Call **Jazzline** (tel. 421-3592) for all the jazz doings, and the **Bluegrass Club of New York** (tel. 427-1488) for the latest country music events.

JAZZ: For jazz lovers, New York is a paradise. Nowhere in the world will you find more jazz per square foot than in the Big Apple, and most of it is concentrated in Greenwich Village. We list both major clubs and those that are good bargains—happily, there's often a coincidence of good talent and good prices. For what's playing, check the weekly "Cafes and Clubs" listings in the *Village Voice*.

The most famous jazz club in New York—and perhaps in the world—is the **Village Vanguard,** 178 Seventh Ave. South, at 11th Street (tel. 255-4037). For more than 30 years jazz aficionados have been walking down the long flight of steps into the Vanguard's smokey, dark basement room to hear the likes of John Coltrane, Miles Davis, Charles Mingus, Sonny Rollins, and Pharaoh Sanders. Today the Vanguard is as popular as ever, and still attracts the biggest names in town. Unlike many other jazz clubs, the Vanguard treats both its audience and its musicians with respect. There are no ringing cash registers in the background or hustling for drinks; customers are invited to sit back, relax, and concentrate on the music. Musicians love the place as much as does the audience; dozens of live albums have been recorded in the club over the years, and any night's performance can turn into a rousing, jumping jam session. Be sure to check out the Monday-night shows, with the Mel Lewis Big Band—fast becoming a New York jazz tradition. Admission is $8.50, and there's a one-drink minimum per set. Open daily with sets at 10 p.m., 11:30 p.m., and 1 a.m.

Around almost as long as the Village Vanguard is the famed **Village Gate,** 160 Bleecker St., at Thompson Street (tel. 475-5120). In the past few years the Gate has been presenting more off-Broadway musical revues, such as *One Mo' Time,* and cabaret singers such as Nacha Guevera. But big names still appear at the club. One of the best shows in town is the recently initiated Monday night "Salsa Meets Jazz" series. Each week a top Latin bandleader, such as Tito Puente or Eddie Palmeri, appears with a top jazz soloist such as Woody Shaw or Arthur Blythe, and the interaction is really something to hear. Admission varies with the performer and the evening: for musical revues, tickets are $15 on weeknights, $22 and $27.50 weekends; the Monday-night salsa shows are $12. On weekends there's a $6 drink minimum. The Village Gate is open seven days a week, with jazz sets usually at 10 p.m. and midnight. The Monday-night set begins at 9 p.m. and goes on till 2:30 a.m.

Lush Life, 184 Thompson St., at Bleecker Street (tel. 228-3788), is rapidly becoming another mainstay of the Greenwich Village jazz scene. It's a quiet and intimate room, offering "jazz and cocktails" and the best sound system of any club in the Village. It draws a respectful and knowledgeable audience and strong, imaginative bookings. Recent bookings have included Joe Farrell, Mose Allison, McCoy Tyner, and Gary Burton. Lush Life is a serious jazz lover's paradise. Monday through Thursday the cover is $7; Friday to Sunday, $8—with a $6 minimum at the tables. If you arrive early enough to catch a seat at the bar, however, there is no minimum and the cover includes one free drink. Open nightly, with shows at 9:30 and 11:30 p.m. and another at 1:15 a.m. Reservations are recommended for all nights.

Another relatively new Village club is the **Blue Note**, 131 W. 3rd St., off Sixth Avenue (tel. 475-8592). According to the jazz-knowledgeable bartender, there have been dozens of clubs at this address, going all the way back to speakeasy days. This wood-paneled, blue-carpeted beauty of a club seems to be doing an admirable job of keeping up the tradition. The Blue Note books top jazz stars, many of them from the bebop era. Admission is a little high: there's a $15 to $25 cover and a $5 minimum at a table. If you arrive early and sit at the bar, however, there's a $7.50 cover and a one-drink minimum. Open nightly with sets at 9:30 and 11:30 p.m. and 1:30 a.m. Food is also served.

Seventh Avenue South, 21 Seventh Ave. South, at Leroy Street (tel. 242-4694), is a pleasant, two-story jazz club with a nice view of the street from the window tables. Downstairs is a restaurant and bar; upstairs is the music room, where food and drink are also served. Seventh Avenue South is another favorite with musicians—it's owned by the trumpet-playing Brecker Brothers, who also play there frequently—and there's always a smattering of well-known players in the audience. It's not unusual to see musicians from the audience join the players on stage for a late-night jam session. Bookings range from mainstream to avant-garde. Dave Sanborn and Jaco Pastoras have played the club recently. Weeknights the cover charge is $6, with a $6 minimum. On weekends there's an $8 cover and a $6 minimum. Sets are at 9:30 and 11:30 p.m. nightly. Reservations suggested on weekends.

Sweet Basil, 88 Seventh Ave. South, between Bleecker and Grove Streets (tel. 242-1785), with its dozens of hanging plants and its glass facade, is one of the handsomer jazz clubs in the Village. It also books top jazz groups, and a wide range of them: from mainstream small combos to avant-garde big bands. If you sit at a table there's an $8 to $10 cover with a $6 minimum. At the bar the cover is $10, which includes one free drink. Open nightly, with music beginning at 10 p.m.

One of the best places to hear jazz piano and bass in New York is the **Knickerbocker Saloon**, 33 University Pl., at 9th Street (tel. 228-8490). It's a pleasant corner restaurant and bar that's always crowded with attentive listeners—for good reason. Some of the most accomplished and most famous jazz pianists and bassists in the world play in the plush dining room at Knickerbocker's every night. Billy Taylor, Roland Hanna, Ron Carter, Walter Bishop, Jr., and Cecil McBee are just a few. The best seats are in the main dining room, where there's a $7 minimum on music nights after 10 p.m. In the lounge there's also a $7 minimum, but you can sit at the bar and enjoy the music for the price of a drink. Music from 9:30 p.m. Tuesday through Saturday.

For both good jazz and fine food, **Zinno**, 126 W. 13th St., between Sixth and Seventh Avenues (tel. 924-5182), may be the place to go. Dinners at this comfortable Italian restaurant start at $9.75 and come with a very good small combos seven nights a week. There is no cover charge, but the minimum is $10 per person at the tables. You may also sit at the bar, where the minimum is $6, but the combination of good food and music seems to be the thing here. The first set each evening starts at 8 p.m., the last one at 11:30 p.m.

Good conversationalists and all-star piano/bass duos are the hallmark of **Bradley's,** 70 University Pl., at 9th Street (tel. 228-6440). At times the din of voices in this dark, stained-wood room can be deafening; serious listeners would do well to sit up front, near the bandstand. Musicians like Ron Carter, Tommy Flanagan, Red Mitchell, and Hank Jones play there regularly, with music nightly at around 9:45 p.m. There's no cover, but there is a $5 food and drink minimum at tables and at the bar.

Razzmatazz, a new spot at 110 MacDougal St. (tel. 505-9152), aims to be a "musicians' club," says owner Vinnie Cordusco. It's a small, dark, smokey venue open "legally" until 4 a.m. nightly, but with jazz musicians often jamming much later behind closed doors for those who stay. On weekends it's Brazilian and Latin jazz. Monday nights include poetry readings. A $5 cover charge and two-drink minimum here, with shows starting at 10:30 p.m.

SoHo

5 & 10 No Exaggeration, 77 Greene St. (tel. 925-7414), is an irrepressibly creative "total environment" with live big-band era music in a restaurant whose fine antique furnishings and art deco decorations are for sale. It also has a jewelry and antique shop and an art gallery, so you can dine, shop, and listen to bands playing Glenn Miller, Benny Goodman, and the Andrews Sisters. The cover charge changes depending on the act, but never exceeds $5. Dinner items on the varied menu start at $4.75 for a half-order of fettuccine. There is no minimum. The live music runs Wednesday through Saturday, and reservations are recommended at all times. Closed Monday.

Also in the hot SoHo area is **A Discovery of Soho,** 451 Broome St. (tel. 334-1222). This restaurant and bar features live jazz combos Monday through Wednesday. There is a $5 music charge and no minimum at the tables or the bar, though dinner menu prices with tips will run you at least $12 to $15.

At **Amazonas,** 492 Broome St., near West Broadway (tel. 966-3371), quality Brazilian jazz and an Amazon jungle-like decor create a unique ambience. There is no cover or minimum, but dinner will run at least $25 to $30 per person, including tips. If that's too pricey, try the bar, where there is no minimum. Or check out the restaurant's weekend brunches, when you can take in the same music along with all you can eat of various Brazilian dishes at a fixed price of $14.95, from 12:30 to 4:30 p.m. on Saturday and Sunday. At night music runs from 8 p.m. to midnight Monday through Thursday, from 5:30 p.m. to 1:30 a.m. on Friday and Saturday, and from 7 to 11:30 p.m. on Sunday.

One Hudson, is at 1 Hudson St., naturally enough, on the corner of Hudson and Chambers Streets (tel. 608-5835). It may also be pricey to eat at, but there is no cover and no minimum at the bar. From there you can take in soft, mellow jazz combos playing amid the exquisite 17th-century tapestries that bedeck the high-ceilinged restaurant. Sunday brunches are also available here for $14.95, when you can hear a jazz or classical guitarist playing background music. The music is on Tuesday through Friday from 5 to 11 p.m. and on Saturday from 6 to 11 p.m. Closed Monday.

Chelsea

The **Angry Squire,** at 216 Seventh Ave., between 22nd and 23rd Streets (tel. 242-9066), is a long, nautical-ambience pub and restaurant that has been a Chelsea fixture for many years. The Squire features contemporary vocalists, pianists, and hard-bop bands. There's a $3 to $6 cover and a two-drink minimum at the tables, but no cover at the bar. Good food is served, and the atmosphere is warm and lively. Music on weekends only; sets start at 8 p.m.

A choice spot for a late-night dinner and music is the out-of-the-way **West Boondock,** 114 Tenth Ave., at 17th Street (tel. 929-9645). It's a friendly soul food and jazz joint, featuring a jazz piano soloist Sunday through Thursday from 7:30 p.m. to 12:30 a.m. On Friday and Saturday there's a jazz duo, with music from 8 p.m. to 2 a.m. No cover or minimum, but do partake of the pork chops, ribs, candied yams, and collard greens.

For the most ardent of jazz fans, the **Jazz Cultural Theatre,** 368 Eighth Ave., between 28th and 29th Streets (tel. 244-0997), is a must. Its modest coffeehouse-style room offers the whole spectrum of modern jazz, but the accent is definitely on bebop. Musicians such as Junior Cook, Clifford Jordan, and Slide Hampton are regulars. In the wee hours of Sunday morning, jazz great Art Blakey leads regular jam sessions with other musicians who drop in after their Saturday-night gigs. The jams, which start at 3 a.m. cost $5, with breakfast offered at an additional charge. The other weekend shows are $6 with an advance telephone reservation, $8 at the door, and $5 for senior citizens. Show times are 10 p.m., 11:30 p.m., and 1 a.m. Tuesday and Thursday nights feature open jam sessions with a $5 admission. Monday and Wednesday nights watch spirited music classes conducted by owner Barry Harris, who has himself played with some of the best.

Murray Hill / Gramercy Park

For an evening with big-name jazz musicians in a cozy atmosphere, **Fat Tuesday's,** 190 Third Ave., at 17th Street (tel. 533-7902), is the place to go. This supper club features only headliners such as Dizzy Gillespie, Les McCann, and Stan Getz, and since it only seats 100, the view and sound from anywhere is good. There are two performances nightly, at 9 and 11 p.m. On Friday and Saturday show times are 8 p.m., 10 p.m., and midnight. The cover charge is $10 with a $5 minimum, applicable to food or drink, but there's no minimum at the bar. Reservations are suggested.

Midtown West

Soundscape, 500 W. 52nd St., between Tenth and Eleventh Avenues (tel. 581-7032), is unique among New York's jazz lofts. Owner-manager Verna Gillis is a trained ethnomusicologist and a serious patron of ethnic music. She has made her club home to a number of jazz musicians exiled from Cuba, among them Daniel Ponce, Cuban conga player, and Paquito D'Rivera, Cuban saxophonist. Admission is generally $6 to $8. There is food and drink available, but seating is on folding chairs, arranged in rows (no nightclub ambience here). But the music is first-rate, and deserves the undivided attention its audiences give. Call for a recorded message with the latest information on shows and prices.

Upper West Side

A ramshackle college bar with lots of good traditional jazz is the **West End Café,** 2911 Broadway, between 113th and 114th Streets (tel. 666-8750). The bar/restaurant offers fine music in the swing style from some of the best musicians of that era—Doc Cheatham, Benny Waters, and Eddie Durham, to name a few. On occasion there's also more modern-style jazz by performers such as saxophonist Lee Konitz. Performances are nightly between 9 p.m. and 1 a.m. There's a $3 drink minimum but no cover charge.

Mikell's, 760 Columbus Ave., at 97th Street (tel. 864-8832), offers a potpourri of sounds from jazz fusion to ragtime to pop. Performers include Milt Jackson, Ray Brown, Roy Ayers, and Who It Is—a popular jazz fusion band. Cover charges range from $5 to $10 depending on the group, and there's a two-drink minimum. Open daily from 4 p.m. to 4 a.m., with music every night except Sunday.

Upper East Side

In an area populated by high-profile hangouts like Maxwell's Plum and T.G.I. Friday, **Gregory's**, 1149 First Ave., at 63rd St. (tel. 371–2220), is unique. The focus at this intimate little club is the music: a mix of light jazz, mellow show tunes, and bebop. The music—a trio with vocalist Alicia Sherman—begins nightly at 10 p.m. and goes till 3 a.m. As an added bonus, there's a pianist and vocalist on hand Monday through Friday from 5 till 10 p.m. The crowd is attentive and low-key; the performers are appreciative. There's a $4.50 cover Sunday through Thursday, a $6 cover on Friday and Saturday night, and a two-drink minimum if you sit at either the piano bar or a table.

Eric's, 1700 Second Ave., at 88th Street (tel. 534–8500), features jazz and jazz fusion, with occasional light rock, Tuesday through Saturday. Cover charge is generally $5 with a $5 minimum. There is also a dinner menu.

Harlem

Harlem, the bubbling mother lode of creative jazz culture, offers **Sutton's**, 403 W. 145th St., at the corner of St. Nicholas Avenue (tel. 283–9523). This small, friendly jazz treasure features some of the musicians you would pay much more to see downtown. Gloria Lynne, Arthur Prysock, and Etta Jones are among the artists who have appeared recently. On Thursday night renowned bassist Reggie Workman brings in friends for regular, rollicking jam sessions. Pianists from Moscow and singers from Japan are just as likely to drop in with the eclectic Workman. On Sunday there are art and photography showings, fashion shows, and poetry readings over brunch, when many Harlemites drop in after church. Music nights are Thursday through Saturday, with a $5 cover and a two-drink minimum. Sunday brunches are an all-you-can-eat soul food smörgåsbord, for $5. A moderately priced soul food menu is also offered at night until 10 p.m. Show times are 10 p.m. and midnight on Thursday, at 10 p.m., midnight, and 2 a.m. on Friday and Saturday.

Dixieland

Red Blazer Too, 1571 Second Ave., near 82nd Street (tel. 535–0847), is home to Roaring '20s and Dixieland jazz enthusiasts. Live bands perform Wednesday through Sunday and usually attract a mostly middle-aged crowd to the dance floor. As a bartender noted, the theme of this very New York–looking bar, with Tiffany-style lamps and pictures of celebrities along the walls, is nostalgia. There's no cover and drinks are moderately priced. Open nightly until 4 a.m.

Michael's Pub, 211 E. 55th St., between Second and Third Avenues (tel. 758–2273), is also known as Woody Allen's pub, because the actor/director/writer plays clarinet with a Dixieland band here on Monday. Mr. Allen doesn't always show up on Monday, so don't be disappointed if you hear Dixieland without his clarinet. Closed Sunday. No cover and no minimum.

Jimmy Weston's, 131 E. 54th St., between Lexington and Park Avenues (tel. 838–8384), has traditonal jazz music by artists such as Tommy Furtado and Billy Daniels. The bar is open Monday through Saturday for listening and dancing until 3 a.m. There's a $10 cover charge at tables but not at the bar.

NEW WAVE/ROCK: The Drongoes, the Drab Numbskulls, and Youthinasia are the names of some of New York's New Wave groups. The clubs—as bizarre as the groups' names—might typically have Renaissance-style paintings and old lace hanging next to black lights and strobes. The crowd's style—as cacophonous as the music—might be leopard stockings and Mohawk haircuts. For the past few years New Wave clubs have been thriving in New York. We've listed some of the most popular.

Granddaddy to the New Wave clubs, and still going strong, is **CBGB**, 315 Bowery, at Bleecker Street (tel. 982-4052). The club feels a bit like the inside of a rundown stable, with its exposed beams, splintery wood posts, and general decrepit state. Bookings include the likes of Richard Hell and the Dancin' Hoods. On Saturday and Sunday there are "hardcore matinees" ($5) featuring "severe punk" with groups like Government Issue and The Faction. Cover ranges from $4 to $8, and there's a two-drink minimum.

Some 20 years ago an obscure Manhattan nightspot burst onto the scene with the energy of a dance craze called the Twist. Now reopened in a different spot, the **Peppermint Lounge,** 100 Fifth Ave., at 15th Street (tel. 989-9050), features New Wave groups like Raunch Hands, Sonic Youth, and 3 Teens Kill 4–No Motive. This grandiose three-level club has two stages and three dance floors and bars. Once inside, finding the exit is no easy task. A remarkable video system shows the Peppermint's own videos and old films like *Gone with the Wind*. The famous who used to frequent the club—Joey Dee, Chubby Checker, and the Beatles—have rivals in the new celebrity patrons. On any given night you might hear that Deborah Harry and David Bowie are upstairs in the VIP lounge. The cover ranges from $2 to $10 depending on the band. On Wednesday and Thursday there's no charge for students with college identification. On Friday and Saturday admission is $7 before 11 p.m. and $10 afterward. Closed Sunday through Tuesday.

The Ritz, 119 E. 11th St., between Third and Fourth Avenues (tel. 228-8888), is a 19th-century dance hall turned rock/New Wave club, booking major names such as B. B. King, Eddie Palmieri, the Police, Robin Trower, and the Neville Brothers. The interior is worth a visit in itself. *Raging Bull* was filmed there. The 40- by 50-foot dance floor is surrounded above by an art deco balcony. A revolving mirrored chandelier casts a sparkle on the dancers, just like in the movies. Admission for big names and on the weekends is $12.50 to $15, but lesser bands play on Monday and Tuesday, when you can get in for less. The Ritz also books an occasional reggae band. Call or check the *Village Voice* for performers.

Trax, 100 W. 72nd St., between Columbus Avenue and Broadway (tel. 799-1448), is both a New Wave and rock and roll club. The cover is $5 on weekdays and $7.50 on weekends. There's no minimum and the bar is open until 2 a.m. on weekdays and 4 a.m. on weekends.

If you want to hear some of New York's hottest new bands, the **Pyramid Club,** 101 Avenue A, near East 7th Street (tel. 420-5700), is the place to go. Although you might find bartenders with shaved heads and patrons with green hair here, the crowd is filled with "just folks" types too.

8 B.C., 337 E. 8th St., between Avenues B and C (tel. 254-4698), is still one of the few inhabited buildings on this desolate block. But this doesn't stop the hard-core punk crowd who seem to come out of nowhere to fill the dark, lower-level club to capacity for their latest, favorite bands. In today's world of reverse chic, 8 B.C. is a club of choice. Performances start late; check for cover prices and hours. Open until 4 a.m. Closed Monday and Tuesday.

Neither/Nor, 703 E. 6th St., between Avenues B and C (tel. 474-5758), earned its name because it is neither a club nor a bookstore—it's both, as well as a "performance space" for everything from poetry to experimental music. Friday nights are rhythm and blues. Saturday nights are funk and dance. Other nights vary from Latin music to jazz. Cover charges vary, but are generally about $5. Neither/Nor is on the fringe of the East Village, in a neighborhood to be careful in. The club itself is on the fringe as well, with a loose, makeshift interior. Store hours are 2 to 7 p.m. Performances start at 10 p.m. Open Tuesday through Sunday.

J.P.'s, 1471 First Ave., between 76th and 77th Streets (tel. 288-1022), is a journeyman's rock bar. Local up-and-coming bands frequent its small stage and the clientele is mostly from the neighborhood. Admission to this casual music spot is $3 to $7, depending on the act, with a $5 minimum at the tables. There is no minimum at the bar.

BLUES: Tramps, 125 E. 15th St., between Third Avenue and Irving Place (tel. 777-5077), is New York's top blues club, featuring rhythm and blues singer-pianist Charles Brown playing Wednesday through Saturday. On Sunday through Tuesday Tramps often has surprise guest appearances by luminaries in rock 'n roll, pop, and rhythm and blues. Southside Johnny, Mitchell Rider, David Johannsen, and Wilson Pickett have all appeared in the past. Music begins around 9 p.m., and the club is open until 4 a.m. There's a $5 to $10 cover and a two-drink minimum at tables.

For nothin' but blues, head to **Dan Lynch,** 221 Second Ave., near 14th Street (tel. 473-8807). Though the tunes can be soulful, the atmosphere is lively and friendly. The club is small and intimate, getting you right up with some of the city's best-known blues musicians. No cover; no minimum. Sets start late and the music plays till 2:30 a.m. weeknights and 4 a.m. on weekends.

Classy, yet laid back and casual, **Preacher's,** 145 Bleecker St. (tel. 533-4625), serves up good American fare and polished rhythm and blues acts. New York University students, Broadway people, and others who appreciate good music come for acts such as Vicky Lynn, an excellent songstress who appears every Monday. No cover and only a $5 minimum for food and/or drinks make this friendly spot a bargain. Showtimes are 10 p.m., 11:30 p.m., and 1:15 a.m., seven nights a week.

COUNTRY: The **Lone Star Café,** 61 Fifth Ave., at 13th Street (tel. 242-1664), brings the ambience of Austin, Texas, to New York, and presents country, blues, and rock artists from all around. Try to arrive early—the place opens at 7:30 p.m. on weekends—to grab a seat upstairs at one of the balcony tables. Friday and Saturday are country/rock nights, with admission $8. Monday through Thursday, when the big names often show, the cover is $8 to $14, and there's a two-drink minimum nightly. At the bar, however, you can nurse one drink for as long as you can and take in the music as you do. Lone Star is open Monday through Friday from 11:30 a.m. until 3 a.m., on Saturday and Sunday from 7:30 p.m. to 4 a.m. You can reserve a table for parties of eight or more by prepaying tickets during the week.

If it's pure country music and bluegrass you want, try **O'Lunney's,** 915 Second Ave., at 49th Street (tel. 751-5470). One of the oldest country music spots in the city, O'Lunney's features local and big-name country bands and an occasional bluegrass group. Bands like King Vito and Da Bronx Cowboys, Tommy Joe White and Southern Cooking, and Steel Angel perform here regularly. Performances are Monday through Thursday from 9:30 p.m. to 2 a.m., on Friday and Saturday to 3 a.m., on Sunday from 8:30 p.m. to 1:30 a.m. There's a $3 cover charge and a $3 drink minimum at the tables. But if you sit at the bar you can hoot and holler with the bands for the price of a drink. Open Sunday through Thursday until 3 a.m., on Friday and Saturday until 4 a.m.

REGGAE: The syncopated sounds of reggae can be heard Wednesday through

Sunday nights at the **Reggae Lounge,** 285 West Broadway, corner of Canal Street (tel. 226-4598). Most of the groups are local (but then New York has the largest Jamaican population outside Kingston), with an occasional headliner from the island. Between and before sets, DJs spin the hottest reggae hits over mammoth loudspeakers, and there's always dancing on the floor. Music starts at around 11 p.m. Students with ID are admitted for $6; women are admitted free on Wednesday and for $3 on Thursday. The rest of the week admission varies between $8 and $10.

MIXED BAGS: If there's a folk-rock equivalent of the Village Vanguard, it's **Folk City,** 130 W. 3rd St., between Sixth Avenue and MacDougal Street (tel. 254-8449). Bob Dylan made his first New York appearance here, and Dave Van Ronk, Joan Baez, Simon and Garfunkel, and Arlo Guthrie all made the club their home in the 1960s. Today Folk City still presents the best in folk music, as well as an exotic blend of blues, jazz, country, rock, and comedy. The bigger names, such as Paul Butterfield, Big Joe Turner, and Roger McGuinn, usually appear on Friday and Saturday nights. Sunday is comedy night, and Tuesday is given over to some of the best local singers and songwriters. Wednesday nights feature up-and-coming New Wave rock bands in a highly acclaimed new series. Monday night is hootenanny night; if you've always wanted to perform, here's your chance. Drop by at 7 p.m. and pick up a number, which will entitle you to a 12-minute spot on stage. Anyone can get up and perform—comics, singers, guitar players, even dancers. There's no admission charge on Monday; on Sunday and Tuesday admission is only $1; Wednesday costs $3. The rest of the week admission is $6 to $8, depending on who's playing.

Another famous former folkie haven that now presents a variety of rock, reggae, folk, jazz, comedy, and country acts is the **Other End Cabaret,** 149 Bleecker St., between Thompson Street and LaGuardia Place (tel. 673-7030). The Other End is one of the few top Village clubs that still presents two or three performers a night, usually a couple of lesser-known opening acts and a headliner. This is a good place to catch some rising stars before they graduate to bigger (and more expensive) clubs. The cover is $4 to $10, depending on who's appearing and the night. There's a two-drink minimum at the tables and a one-drink minimum at the bar. The club is open five to seven nights a week, with shows at 10 p.m. and 12:30 a.m. Reservations are accepted for advance tickets. Adjoining is a pleasant and moderately priced café and restaurant where new, local talent is showcased.

The Village's premier showcase for top rock and jazz groups is the **Bottom Line,** 15 W. 4th St., corner of Mercer Street (tel. 228-7880). It's sort of the fancy supper club of the rock crowd, and you're expected to spring for dinner on top of the admission charge. It is, however, perfectly acceptable to stand at the bar, and no one will throw you out for nursing a beer at the tables—if they aren't filled by diners. The best thing about the Bottom Line is its large stage (good views from every corner of the room), excellent sound system, and first-rate bookings, such as Gil-Scott Heron, the Art Ensemble of Chicago, Lou Reed, Arlo Guthrie, and McCoy Tyner. Tickets are usually between $8 and $10. Shows on Sunday through Thursday are at 8:30 and 11:30 p.m., on Friday and Saturday at 9 p.m. and midnight. Advance tickets are on sale at the box office or through the mail, and they are advised for the really popular acts.

Kenny's Castaways, 157 Bleecker St., near Thompson Street (tel. 473-9870), presents rock, blues, jazz, and folk as well as an occasional off-Broadway play. On Monday there's a midnight jazz jam session; Tuesday through Sunday, sets start at 9:30 p.m. and midnight. No cover, but a two-drink minimum per person per set. Closes at 4 a.m.

The nearby **Back Fence,** 155 Bleecker St. (tel. 475-9221), adds country to its repertoire of rock, blues, and folk. Again, no cover, but a two-drink minimum. Sets start at 8:30 p.m. and the club is open till 2 a.m. on weekdays, till 4 a.m. on weekends.

S.N.A.F.U., 676 Sixth Ave., corner of 21st Street (tel. 691-3535), presents three bands in three sets each night—usually rock and New Wave—and features an occasional comedy act as well. There's a cover charge of $5 to $8, depending on the act, and a two-drink minimum at the tables. Open every night but Monday, usually until 1:30 or 2 a.m.

Folk lives and thrives at **Speakeasy,** 107 MacDougal St., near Bleecker Street, in the heart of the Village (tel. 598-9670). Walk right through the unexceptional-looking Greek restaurant in front to the darkened, intimate club in back. Operated by a local folk musicians' co-op in cooperation with the owner, some of the strongest acts in folk music appear here regularly. The Washington Squares, Josh White, Jr., and Jesse Winchester are a few recent ones. Cover charge ranges from $2 to $7, depending on the act, and it all goes to the musicians. There is a two-drink minimum per set, or order a meal of Greek or Middle Eastern cuisine from the kitchen. Shows start at 9 and 11 p.m. Tuesday through Saturday, and at 8:30 p.m. on Sunday.

The Bitter End, 147 Bleecker St., near LaGuardia Place (tel. 673-7030), is a longtime Village fixture whose cellar-like brick walls shake with sounds from some of the hottest and hungriest rock, blues, and pop bands in town. A popular student and singles hangout even on weeknights, the Bitter End's current roster ranges from Kenny Rankin to the Persuasions, though less known local acts are more common. Tuesday nights are for stand-up comedy with acts like Henny Youngman. Cover charge is $5, with a two-drink minimum at the tables and one-drink minimum at the bar. Shows start at 9 p.m. and go on until 4 a.m., seven nights a week.

If you love traditional Irish music, run, don't walk, to the **Eagle Tavern,** 355 W. 14th St., between Eighth and Ninth Avenues (tel. 924-0275). Ignore the dark, somewhat seedy-looking bar in front and walk straight back to the rear room. There you'll find a friendly, welcoming crowd sipping Guinness between dancing and clapping to the jigs and reels. On Friday from 9 p.m. to 1 a.m. there is traditional Irish dancing and music with Greg Rylan and Brian Conway on guitar, fiddle, and all manner of pipes. Admission is $4. On Saturday, American bluegrass takes over, with first-rate banjo, hammer dulcimer, and fiddle players for a $5 admission. Monday night is an open stage for Irish musicians, singers, and poets, and is free. On Wednesday there is a continuing Irish concert series that brings in some of Ireland's most popular musicians. Admission to this is generally $5 with shows at 8 and 10 p.m., and it's wise to reserve your tickets in advance by telephone.

Tucked into the corner of Carnegie Hall, **Carnegie Tavern,** 165 W. 56th St., at Seventh Avenue (tel. 757-9522), is a pre- and post-concert stop for orchestra members as well as concert-goers. Some of the musicians, like the erstwhile members of the Philadelphia Orchestra, are summoned back to the hall by electronic beepers. Tony Tamburello, a pianist praised by the *New York Times* for his "cornucopia of choice tunes and imaginative interpretations," plays daily from 9 p.m. until midnight Drinks average $2.50, and there is a reasonably priced lunch and dinner menu as well. Reservations suggested.

Every Sunday night at 7 p.m., **People's Voice Café** presents a roster of folk performers inside St. Clement's Church, 423 W. 46th St., between Eighth and Ninth Avenues (tel. 245-9394). Much of the folk music has a political bent, and coffee, tea, and juices are served at this laidback, friendly gathering. Call on Sunday after 6 p.m. for further information.

If you're in the mood—and money—for a good splurge, go to **Upstairs at Greene Street,** 101 Greene St., between Prince and Spring Streets (tel. 925-2415). Greene Street, a popular yuppie dinner spot in fashionable SoHo, is a complex of three separate restaurants; "Upstairs" is the least expensive. Its low lights, intimate acoustics, and immaculate white-tablecloth settings set the tone. The entertainment may be comedy, rhythm and blues, country and western, or a musical revue, so call ahead to make sure what's scheduled suits you. On weekends reservations are advised. There is a $10 entertainment charge. With cheaper items on the food and wine menu, the evening will be yours for under $25 with gratuities.

3. Dance, Dance, Dance

The dance scene in New York is more popular than ever. You'll find everything from old-style ballrooms offering swing music to "mixed media" clubs like Area, Limelight, and the Palladium, which feature sultry rock videos, stunning architecture, and exhibitions of the artwork of some of New York's top artists. While New York's clubs are generally open from 10 p.m. until the wee hours of the morning, most people show up after 11 p.m. (If celebrity-watching is on your agenda, we suggest sticking around until at least 2 a.m.) Although some clubs have live bands, most offer only recorded music—the same mix of disco, reggae, New Wave, and hard rock that you'll hear on FM radio. Dance styles range from John Travolta–style disco to punk jumping bean.

Depending on the venue, the cover charge can range anywhere from $5 to $20, with drinks costing more than $4 apiece at the more expensive clubs. And be forewarned: you might have to wait as long as an hour to get into the more popular clubs, and at the more exclusive and expensive ones you'll be subjected to the ever-present "selection committee," which hovers on platforms or doorsteps above the crowd in search of a stylish mix of people.

THE HOT SPOTS: At the **Palladium,** 126 E. 14th, near Broadway (tel. 473-7171), you'll find stockbrokers in three-piece suits dancing within feet of Boy George look-alikes, and maybe even Boy George himself. Designed by one of Japan's most noted and innovative architects, the Palladium is a visual extravaganza—some of the city's best-known artists, such as graffiti artist Keith Haring, were commissioned to decorate the corridors, top-floor bar, and even the bathrooms. Admission is steep: $15 on weeknights and $20 on weekends.

Area, 157 Hudson St., south of Canal Street (tel. 226-8423), draws a beguiling mix of celebrities, Wall Street types, artists, models, you name it. The club changes its theme—and decor—every two weeks. When the theme was carnival, for example, Area was tranformed into a festive games arcade with bizarre side shows. And when faith was the motif, the club became a mesmerizing landscape of Egyptian tombs and Buddhist temples. Admission is $15.

If you're turned off by the crowds and selection committee at either Area or the Palladium, try **Visage,** 610 W. 56th St. (tel. 247-0612), where you can disco the night away against a background of velvet walls, American Realist sculptures, and Lalique crystal masks. Admission is $15 during the week and $20 on weekends.

Limelight, 47 W. 20th St., at Sixth Avenue (tel. 807-7850), also offers a distinctive setting. Housed in a former church, this celebrity-frequented disco features rock videos (in what used to be the church's chapel) and upbeat pop and rock music. Admission is $15.

And then there's **Studio 54,** 254 W. 54th St. (tel. 489-7667). Although this once-vaunted club is no longer a haunt of the rich and famous, it can still be fun—especially on Friday, when Willoughby, one of New York's best dance DJs, is at the turntable. Admission is $15 on weekdays and $18 on weekends.

LESS GLITTER, BUT LOTS OF FUN: The **Surf Club**, 415 E. 91st St. (tel. 410-1360), is a favorite with the preppie crowd. The uniform of choice: white shirts and black skirts or pants. Admission is free on Tuesday, $5 on Wednesday, and $10 on weekends. Closed Monday.

Paradise Garage, 84 King St., near Varick Street (tel. 989-2975), has one of the best sound systems around. The club is only open to the public on Friday nights though, and be prepared to pass through an electronic frisking device when you enter. Admission is $15.

The **Cat Club,** 76 E. 13th St. (tel. 505-0090), features one of the city's largest dance floors, an extravagant light show, and (on weekends) a half-hour rock video show starring the club's own dancers. It costs $10 to get in during the week and $15 on weekends.

Another video haven is **Private Eyes,** 12 W. 21st St., between Fifth and Sixth Avenues (tel. 206-7770), where the cover is $8 on weeknights and $15 on weekends.

LIVE BANDS: **Danceteria,** 30 W. 21st St., between Fifth and Sixth Avenues (tel. 620-0790), is a supermarket of auditory and visual stimuli, with a changing repertoire of video screens, recorded disco, and live music from local bands. The club has three levels, with dance floors and bars on each. The third—at the top of a long and winding staircase—is the most elaborate. Male and female dancers high up on raised platforms gyrate and slide, demonstrating the newest and hottest moves. The music is mostly New Wave and the crowd usually thick. There's a $3 admission on Sunday, Monday, and Tuesday, and a $5 cover charge on Wednesday and Thursday. The cover on Friday and Saturday is $8 before 11 p.m. and $12 thereafter.

The **Pyramid Club,** 101 Avenue A, near East Seventh Street (tel. 420-1590), is one of the most popular of the new clubs now dotting the East Village —and a great place to go on a Sunday night. The cover is $10.

The **Ritz,** 119 E. 11th St., between Third and Fourth Avenues (tel. 254-2800), features live bands (many of them either famous or up-and-coming) and music ranging from punk to jazz. It all takes place in a huge, two-tiered auditorium, with some of the most inventive rock videos around playing above the dance floor. The cover can be anywhere from $5 to $18 depending on the band.

A few blocks away is the **Peppermint Lounge,** 100 Fifth Ave., at 15th Street (tel. 989-9505), another of rock-and-roll's fabled breeding grounds. Admission to the club is generally around $11.

Uptown, the **Kangaroo Club,** 334 E. 73rd St. (tel. 570-1116), boasts the largest dance floor in New York and attracts a mixed crowd of yuppies and East Village types. In addition to disco and live music, the club features regular art shows and movies. Admission is $10 on weeknights, $15 on weekends.

For live progressive music and a raucous good time, you might also try **Trax,** 100 W. 72nd St. (tel. 799-1448), or the **The Fives,** 555 W. 57th St. (tel. 757-4303). Admission at both clubs ranges from $5 (on nights when there is no live band) to $10.

MUSIC OF ANOTHER ERA: Disco is only one facet of New York's burgeoning dance scene. For example, if your tastes run to swing music, there's the 65-year-old **Roseland** ballroom, 239 W. 52nd St. (tel. 247-0200). Admission is $7 on Friday, $10 on Saturday, and $8 on Thursday and Sunday. A Latin band adds to the festivities on Thursday and Sunday till midnight and on Saturday until 11 p.m.

If you're willing to spend more, you can also "swing" at the **Rainbow Room,** 65th Floor, 30 Rockefeller Plaza (tel. 757-9090), on Friday and Saturday; at **Windows on the World,** top floor of One World Trade Center (tel. 938-1111), nightly from 7:30 to 12:30 p.m.; and at the **Café Carlyle** in the Carlyle Hotel, 35 East 76th St. (tel. 744-1660), where the admission is $20 during the week and $25 on weekends.

For '50s and '60s music there's **Heartbreak,** 179 Varick St. (tel. 691-2338), where a live band plays on Monday and admission is $10 on weeknights and $15 on weekends.

Be-boppers will enjoy the **Roxy Roller Rink,** 515 W. 18th St. (tel. 675-8300), which features roller dancing Sunday through Wednesday and hip-hop music on Friday and Saturday. Admission is $10.

And you can dance to the sounds of the '40s and '50s at the **Red Parrot,** 67 W. 57th St. (tel. 247-1530), where there's a 16-piece orchestra on Friday and Saturday nights, with contemporary music played during the band's breaks. The cover here is $15.

REGGAE: At the **Reggae Lounge,** 285 West Broadway (tel. 226-4598), a crowd heavily sprinkled with Rastafarians, Africans, and Europeans dances to pop and Jamaican reggae in a setting of jungle greens and browns. Admission is $8 for women and $10 for men on Friday (women are admitted free on Wednesday and pay $3 on Thursday), $10 for everyone on Saturday, and $6 at all times for students.

LATIN: One of the hottest places to dance in all of New York is **SOB's (Sounds of Brazil),** 204 Varick St. (tel. 243-4940). The club devotes its programming to the music of Brazil and every night turns into a Rio-style Carnivale, often featuring some of the hottest Brazilian, African, and Latin bands in the city. The club also offers some of the city's best Brazilian cuisine, along with a roster of exotic drinks. SOB's is open until the wee hours and attracts an international crowd. Admission is $8 for diners, $12 for others.

Hips and arms sway in time to the rhythms of salsa at the **Corso Latin Ballroom,** 205 E. 86th St., off Third Avenue (tel. 534-4965), which features an 80-foot bar and no fewer than three Latin bands each Saturday night. Admission is $7 on weekends; free for women on Wednesday, Friday, and Sunday until 11 p.m.

Club Senzallee, 59 Murray St., near the World Trade Center (tel. 227-6912), is another lively Latin club, this one drawing a heavily professional crowd. Tuesday through Thursday you can dance to salsa, Latin, and disco music for a $3 admission fee. On Friday there's a live Latin band, with a $5 to $8 cover depending on the band, and on Saturday there's a Brazilian band (cover: $10). Every Sunday the club is the scene of a Brazilian beach party (no cover).

4. Theatrical and Nightclub Entertainment

The nightclub entertainment in New York varies from glossy cabarets to Middle Eastern belly dancing to improvisational comics, whose biggest act is drawing the audience into the show and sometimes up on stage.

Don't Tell Mama, 343 W. 46th Street, between Eighth and Ninth Avenues (tel. 757-0788), is at once a jazz piano bar, cabaret, and video games parlor. The lively crowd sometimes sings with the entertainers, as does the bartender. Depending on the performer, there's a $5 to $11 cover charge for the cabaret at 8:30 and 11 p.m., with occasional shows added at 6 p.m. and 1 a.m. on the weekends. Open until 4 a.m.

A club in the same genre is **Palsson's,** at 158 W. 72nd Street, between

Broadway and Columbus Avenue (tel. 595-7400). The show *Forbidden Broadway* starts at 8:30 p.m., with an additional 11:30 p.m. show on Friday and Saturday. Seats here range from $19 for the 8:30 p.m. Saturday-night show to $12 for the 11:30 p.m. show on Friday nights. The meal is not included. Weeknights an 11:30 p.m. cabaret is offered for $5. Reservations are required. Open until 4 a.m.

J's, 2581 Broadway, between 97th and 98th Streets (tel. 666-3600), is the Upper West Side's new supper club. It features a variety of entertainment ranging from jazz quintets and piano music to comedy acts while you sup on such delicacies as Créole oysters, pasta primavera, and fresh fish and shellfish. Open from 6 p.m. to midnight Sunday through Thursday, to 3 a.m. on Friday and Saturday. The cover ranges from $3 to $10, depending on the act.

Panache, 149 E. 57th St. (tel. 371-3266), is a small, charming cabaret located on the second floor of the Magic Pan restaurant. Seven nights a week the cabaret features fine musical entertainment—singers, jazz performers, or revues. Shows begin nightly at 8 p.m.; on Friday and Saturday there's an additional late show at 11 p.m. The cover charge is $4 to $10, depending on the featured performer. There's a $7.50 minimum for food or beverage. If you're planning on dinner, come an hour before show time. The restaurant is noted for its wide variety of entree and dessert crêpes.

The Ballroom, 253 W. 28th St. (tel. 244-3005), features cabaret acts, singers, comedians, and dancers. There are shows Tuesday through Saturday at 7, 9, and 11 p.m., with a $10 admission and a two-drink minimum.

COMEDY: The Improvisation, 358 W. 44th St., off Ninth Avenue (tel. 765-8268), is the city's première breeding ground for new talent. This highly regarded restaurant/nightclub features a constantly changing lineup of young singers and young comics. The club's famous alums include Rodney Dangerfield, Liz Torres, Robert Klein, and Robin Williams. The action begins nightly at 8 p.m., and there is an additional show at midnight Friday through Sunday. The cover charge is $4 Monday through Thursday and $6 Friday through Sunday, and there's a $5 drink minimum. But if you've just come from a Broadway show, be sure to display your ticket stubs to the bartender or waiter; the stubs will entitle you to a free round of drinks once you've reached the minimum. Reservations are essential on weekends.

One of the best-known New York comedy clubs is **Dangerfield's,** 1118 First Ave., between 61st and 62nd Streets (tel. 593-1650). The club is owned by Rodney ("I can't get no respect") Dangerfield, who performs whenever he's in town. Other performers have included Redd Foxx, Red Buttons, Jackie Mason, and Robin Williams, when he happens to be in the audience. There are shows Monday through Thursday at 9:15 and 11 p.m., with an $8 cover and a $7 minimum; on Friday and Saturday at 9 p.m. and midnight, with a $10 cover and a $7 minimum; and on Sunday there's a showcase for new talent at 9:30 p.m. ($6 cover, two-drink minimum). Reservations are recommended, especially on weekends.

Good comedy can also be found at **Catch a Rising Star,** 1487 First Ave., near 78th Street (tel. 794-1906). The club features some of the same headliners as at Dangerfield's, but it's best known as *the* place to see up-and-coming comics. From Sunday through Thursday there's a show at 9 p.m., $5 cover; on Friday and Saturday shows are at 8:30 p.m. and midnight, with a $6 cover. Monday is audition night. There's a two-drink minimum, and reservations are suggested.

There are more laughs to be had at the following clubs:

Goodtimes, 499 Third Ave., at 31st Street (tel. 686-4250 or 725-8130). This informal club has nightly comic and music acts with up-and-coming performers and on occasion a headliner. Pat Benatar is said to have tried out her talents on the Goodtimes crowd. Shows are Monday through Saturday at 9:30 p.m. The cover is $4 on Friday, $5 on Saturday, and $2 on all other nights. There's a two-drink minimum on weekends. Reservations aren't necessary, but keep in mind that the club is small.

At the **Comic Strip,** 1568 Second Ave., near 82nd Street (tel. 861-9386), aspiring comedians perform Sunday through Thursday at 9 p.m., with a $5 cover; on Friday at 9 p.m. and midnight, and on Saturday at 8:30 p.m., with a $7 cover on both nights. There's a two-drink minimum. Reservations are suggested.

Caroline's, 332 Eighth Ave., between 26th and 27th Streets (tel. 924-3499), is one of the hottest of the new comedy clubs. There are shows Tuesday through Sunday at 9 p.m. ($10 cover charge), and on Friday and Saturday at 9 and 11:30 p.m. ($12 cover). If you get hungry, you can feast on Chinese dim sum and desserts during the shows.

At the **Comedy Cellar,** 117 MacDougal St. (tel. 254-3630), there are shows Sunday through Thursday at 9 p.m. ($3 cover), and on Friday and Saturday at 9 and 11:30 p.m. ($6 cover). There's also a two-drink minimum.

Similarly priced comedy can be found at **Comedy U,** 86 University Pl., between 11th and 12th Streets (tel. 206-1296). There's an audition night on Wednesday and all-female comedy on Thursday; shows start at 8:30 p.m., with a $4 cover. On Friday and Saturday there are shows at 8:30 and 10:45 p.m., with a $6 cover. On all nights there's a two-drink minimum.

You can also find top-notch comedy at **Who's On First,** 1205 First Ave., at 65th St. (tel. 737-2772), on Thursday at 10 p.m., and on Friday and Saturday at 10 p.m. and midnight, for a $4 cover; at **Folk City,** 130 W. 3rd St., off Sixth Avenue (tel. 254-8449), on Wednesday night at 9 and 11 p.m., for a $2 cover; and at the **Duplex Cabaret,** 55 Grove St. (tel. 255-5438), on Friday and Saturday after midnight, for $5. At each place there's a two-drink minimum.

LAS VEGAS IN NEW YORK: Though most nightclubs in Manhattan have Manhattan-style entertainment, some bring to mind Las Vegas rather than New York. One is the **Rainbow Grill,** at 30 Rockefeller Plaza (tel. 757-8970). Twice nightly the club features *Legs,* a production in which glossily costumed showgirls enact through dance the musical history of the United States. The club is on the 65th floor and the view includes the five New York boroughs and parts of New Jersey. The scenery alone may be worth the cover charge ($10 weeknights, $12 on Saturday and Sunday).

Club Ibis, 151 E. 50th St., between Lexington and Third Avenues (tel. 753-3429), is just as elegant but the entertainers' style is more Egyptian than Las Vegas. This classy and attractive club on the floor above the posh Café Versailles has nightly two-hour belly-dancing shows with live Arabian music. There's no minimum, but drinks are expensive, at about $7 a piece. Cover charge is $4 on weekdays and $6 on weekends. Open weekdays until 3:30 a.m., weekends until 4 a.m.

Chippendales, 1110 First Ave., at 61st St. (tel. 935-6060), is a phenomenon of the '80s which gives new meaning to the phrase "girls' night out." Whatever happened to Mahjongg and bridge? The club draws a lively crowd, many of whom are women from out-of-town, who sit on bleacher-style seats in this arena/theater where an all-male burlesque revue ultimately gets down to the bare necessities—their G-strings. The show starts at 8:30 p.m. Wednesday to Saturday. Admission on Wednesday and Thursday is $15; on Friday and Saturday, $20. The seats closest to the stage cost an additional $7 on Wednesday and Thursday, an additional $9 on Friday and Saturday, and can only be purchased at the time of admission. Drinks are priced at $3 to $5. Reservations required.

After the show, at about 10:30 p.m., the club becomes a disco and the stage a dance floor. If you've just seen the show, the disco is free. If you're just coming in to dance there's a $15 cover charge. Open till 4 a.m.

Comedians, Taiwanese acrobats, and female impersonators have all enlivened the stage at the **Latin Quarter,** 200 W. 48th St., between Seventh Avenue and Broadway (tel. 586-3903), a mirrored nightclub with spotlit tables. Shows start at 10 p.m. Thursday to Saturday, with occasional matinees, and are equivalent in price to an off-Broadway show. From 5 to 10 p.m. there's live or deejayed Latin music served with a Latin buffet for $7 to $12, depending on the night. Call for the current schedule.

COLLEGE HANGOUTS: Among the nightspots we have described, there are a number of college hangouts—music clubs with lots of students, and bars where the drinks are reasonably priced and talk is of classes and beer blasts. We have listed some of these by area.

Upper West Side

Amsterdam's, 428 Amsterdam Ave., between 80th and 81st Streets (tel. 874-1377).

Augie's, 2751 Broadway, between 105th and 106th Streets (tel. 864-8707).

Marvin Gardens, 2274 Broadway, between 81st and 82nd Streets (tel. 799-0578).

Shelter, 2180 Broadway, at 77th Street (tel. 362-4360).

Tap-A-Keg, 330 Columbus Ave., between 75th and 76th Streets (tel. 874-8593).

Teacher's, 2249 Broadway, between 80th and 81st Streets (tel. 787-3500).

Trax, 100 W. 72nd St., between Columbus Avenue and Broadway (tel. 799-1448).

West End Café, 2911 Broadway, between 113th and 114th Streets (tel. 666-8750).

Upper East Side

Ruppert's, 1662 Third Ave., at 93rd Street (tel. 831-1900).

East Village

Jack the Ribbers, 25 Third Ave., between St. Mark's Place and 9th Street (tel. 677-0151).

King Tut's WaWa Hut, southeast corner of East 7th Street and Avenue A (tel. 254-7772).

McSorley's Old Ale House, 15 E. 7th St., near Third Avenue (tel. 473-8800).

SINGLES BARS: Here are a few around town.

Upper East Side

Martell's, 1469 Third Ave., at 83rd Street (tel. 861-6110).
Maxwell's Plum, First Avenue at 64th Street (tel. 628-2100).
Ruppert's, 1662 Third Ave., at 93rd Street (tel. 831-1900).
T.G.I. Friday's, 1152 First Ave., at 63rd Street (tel. 832-8512).

Upper West Side

Marvin Gardens, 2274 Broadway, between 81st and 82nd Streets (tel. 799-0578).

Shelter, 2180 Broadway, corner of 77th Street (tel. 362-4360).

Midtown West
Hard Rock Café, 221 W. 57th St. (tel. 489-6565).

East Village
Caramba!, 684 Broadway, at Great Jones (East 3rd) Street (tel. 420-9817).

Greenwich Village
Montana Eve, 140 Seventh Ave. South, between 10th and Charles Streets (tel. 242-1200).

Chapter VII

THE BEST SHOPPING BUYS IN TOWN

1. Men's and Women's Clothing
2. An Alphabetical Miscellany
3. Food

THERE IS ONE POINT that all visitors—and all New Yorkers too—seem to agree on: New York is the shopping capital of the United States. Nowhere else in the world is there such a wealth of goods—made right here or imported from all over the world—to tempt the purchaser. Mexican wedding shirts, chic French jeans (even for pregnant women), African fabrics, Japanese kimonos, Berber capes, the latest imports from Peoples Republic of China, Ukrainian Easter egg decorating kits, Indian saris—you'll find it all here, and much more, in great profusion. Indeed, shopping is one of the city's finest entertainments.

But the thrill of shopping in New York goes even beyond the seemingly infinite variety of merchandise. For whether you're looking for a new camera, a violin, a Parsons table, or a Dior original—you can get it for less in the Big Apple. The purpose of this chapter, then, is to steer both the visitor and the resident to the most exciting bargains in town. We'll begin with men's and women's clothing, then proceed alphabetically, listing everything from antiques to wallpaper. And we'll wind up with a gastronomical tour of the town—where to buy everything from eggroll wrappers to homemade mozzarella cheese.

Note: Many, many stores—especially on the Lower East Side—are open on Sunday, a viable shopping day in this city.

1. Men's and Women's Clothing

Ready-made clothing—well styled, well made, and yet inexpensive—is what New York excels at. The Garment Center of New York—an area that runs along Seventh Avenue from 20th to 40th Streets—produces nearly half the dresses and suits worn in the United States. We'll tell you how to do some shopping there at wholesale. But first, try the following:

WOMEN'S CLOTHING AND ACCESSORIES: For stylish clothing—in fact, for high-fashion gear in general—head for **Ohrbach's**, 34th Street between Fifth and Sixth Avenues (tel. 695-4000). Ohrbach's is a specialty store that prides itself on fashion and value, including clothing, outerwear, shoes, and accessories. Their buyers shop the world to provide low prices on the latest fashions. In addition, Ohrbach's carries many famous makers' merchandise and private labels, all at Ohrbach's affordable prices. (Good buys for men and children too.) Open weekdays from 10 a.m. to 6:45 p.m., on Saturday to 6 p.m., and on Sunday from noon to 6 p.m.

Over on the East Side of Manhattan is another giant of a store for clothing bargains. **Alexander's,** at Lexington Avenue and 58th Street (tel. 593-0880), is known for its high-fashion ready-to-wear at discount prices. It's filled to the brim with merchandise from all parts of the world, selected by crack buying and merchandise teams who travel throughout the United States, Europe, South America, and the Far East in search of their wares. There are usually great buys in cashmere sweaters and knitwear. Alexander's is actually a diversified discount department store selling items that range from perfumes to video cassettes, to toys, books, and appliances. Open 10 a.m. to 9 p.m. Monday through Saturday, on Sunday from noon to 5 p.m. If you're touring downtown New York, stop in at the Alexander's at the World Trade Center.

May's is another large discount department store, with several branches in the boroughs, and one major store at 14th Street and Broadway (tel. 677-4000). Newspaper ads usually appear on Wednesday, Thursday, Friday, and Sunday in the *Daily News* featuring fantastic savings. Appliances, apparel, housewares, and durable goods are great buys. May's Boutique attracts the smart set with high fashion designer clothes, objets d'art, and fine jewelry. Open daily from 10 a.m. to 7 p.m., on Monday till 7:30 p.m., and on Thursday till 8 p.m.

Now for an oddball among the city's inexpensive clothing shops. **Richards Army-Navy,** at 233 W. 42nd St., between Seventh and Eighth Avenues (tel. 947-5018), was once a typical warehouse-type outlet for military surplus, and indeed the store's major stock in trade remains such items as regulation navy pea jackets, of which they sell several thousand a year. But Richards is also well known to designers of high-camp styles, the chicest dames in town, and even Yves St. Laurent, whose visits a few seasons back resulted in a line of military-looking clothes designed specifically for women, as well as sporting wear modeled after military fashions. Richard's has all these (at a much lower price than anywhere else), plus Levi denim jeans, and much more—everything from Nike and Adidas footwear to basketballs, to leather flight jackets to new camouflage fatigues. And it also has one of the largest swim shops, with year-round selections of men's and women's professional and fashion swimsuits, goggles, and accessories. This is also one of the city's largest repositories of skin- and scuba-diving equipment, in case you're interested. Open Monday through Saturday from 9 a.m. to 7 p.m.

Another army-navy store catering to the uptown blue-jean set is **Ar-Bee,** 1598 Second Ave., at the corner of 83rd Street (tel. 737-4661), where shirts, jackets, and raincoats are available at rock-bottom prices. We bought a heavy-weather hooded navy raincoat for $21.85. Another branch across the street at 1601 Second Ave. features camping equipment. Open Monday through Friday from 9 a.m. to 6:45 p.m., on Saturday till 5:45 p.m.

Designer and Other Discount Shops

Two of the shops we've named (Ohrbach's and Alexander's) concentrate on low-priced copies of expensive originals. If you'd prefer to buy the originals themselves (sometimes with the original labels), if you're eager for styles of the well-known European and American fashion designers and fashion houses—designers such as Cacharel or Carol Horn, companies such as Anne Klein—but at reduced-from-list prices, then the following New York outfits will fill the bill.

The leader of the designer discount chains is **Loehmann's**. It has three branches in New York, the main one at Fordham Road and Jerome Avenue in the Bronx (tel. 295-4100); the others at 19 Duryea Pl., at Beverly Road, in Brooklyn, off Flatbush Avenue (tel. 718/469-9800), and in Rego Park, Queens, in Lefrak City (tel. 718/271-4000). Loehmann's offers an enormous selection of women's coats, suits, dresses, and sportswear, often in styles that are simutaneously being sold in Manhattan department stores for twice the price! Since there's an awful lot of dross among the gold, you may have to plow through seemingly dozens of racks, but the end result of your search can be a superb dress at a wonderfully low price. *Caution:* All sales are final; there are no exchanges of refunds.

Phone each store for exact hours. To get to the Bronx store, take the IRT–Lexington Avenue subway (Woodlawn Avenue express, no. 4 train) to the Fordham Road station, or the IND–Sixth Avenue subway (D train) to Fordham Road and the Grand Concourse. An alternative method that beats riding the subway but takes longer is the express bus from Manhattan that stops at various locations along Madison Avenue between 26th Street and 96th Street and costs under $3 each way. Buses run daily at least every 30 minutes until 10 p.m. See our transportation section for further information or call Riverdale Transit (tel. 652-8400) for the exact schedule. To reach the Brooklyn location, take the BMT–Brighton line to Beverly Road; Loehmann's is located 3½ blocks west of the station.

Right in Manhattan, in the downtown financial district (easily reached by taking the IRT–Seventh Avenue subway to Park Place), is another treasuretrove of designer clothing at discount prices: **Syms**, 45 Park Pl., between Church Street and West Broadway, two blocks north of the World Trade Center (tel. 791-1199). The women's departments are on the third and fourth floors. Everything has the nationally advertised price on it. Syms marks down ladies' dresses, ensembles, and suits every ten days: for example, a $100 outfit goes on the racks at $59; after ten days it goes down to $48; ten more days, to $38; after 30 days, when the price becomes final, it's $29. The dates of markdowns are on the ticket, so you might want to trust your luck and wait for the lowest prices. We've also found excellent bargains here in fine leather bags, gloves and scarves, and lingerie. This is pipe-rack shopping and crowded community dressing rooms, but the bargains make it all worthwhile. Syms is open Monday to Wednesday from 9 a.m. to 7 p.m., on Thursday and Friday to 8 p.m., and on Saturday to 6 p.m.

Although the prices are definitely discount—30% to 60% below regular prices on designer labels—the ambience at **Peta Lewis,** 1120 Lexington Ave., corner of 78th Street, second floor (tel. 744-7660), is definitely boutique, with attention to personalized service; the staff here will even help you with personal wardrobing. Peta Lewis carries both career woman and fun clothing, mostly for an over-30 clientele; sizes run 12 to 16. The price range is wide, anything from $19.95 to $200. We've seen labels like Diane B., Daniel Caron, Dino Valiano, and Paula Saker, among others. Open Monday to Saturday from 11 a.m. to 7 p.m., on Thursday to 9 p.m., on Sunday from noon to 6 p.m.; closed summer Sundays.

Juniors can have a field day shopping for name-brand sportswear at **What's New,** at 166 Madison Ave., between 32nd and 33rd Streets (tel. 532-9226), where we spotted the likes of $64 cotton dresses for $35, $30 shawls at $8, $24 sweat pants and shirt set for $14. The store is tiny so it's best avoided during the lunch hour, when nearby office workers are out in full force. There's another What's New store at 122 E. 42nd St., on the subway level (tel. 867-0574). Hours are 10 a.m. to 6 p.m. weekdays, to 5 p.m. on Saturday.

SHOPPING: CLOTHES

Another good bet for juniors are the **Kazootie** stores, which offer brand names at a discount. On our last visit we noticed dress pants for $12.99 that we had seen for $35 elsewhere, and skirts that would normally sell for $25 to $30 were $12.99 here.

There are two Kazootie stores: at 303 Park Ave. South, at 23rd Street (tel. 674-1967), open weekdays from 9:30 a.m. to 7:30 p.m., and on Saturday from 11 a.m. to 6 p.m.; and at 61 Nassau St., between John Street and Maiden Lane (tel. 964-4218), open weekdays from 8 a.m. to 6:30 p.m.

If you're in the Lincoln Center area, you may want to walk a few blocks to check out the neighborhood branch of **Labels for Less**, 186 Amsterdam Ave., between 68th and 69th Streets (tel. 787-0850), which sells designer fashions at good discounts. There are almost a dozen other locations throughout Manhattan.

True scavengers might like to plow through the tables of merchandise at **Gabay's**, 225 First Ave., between 13th and 14th Streets (tel. 245-3180), a secondhand shop that gets damaged merchandise (sometimes damages are hardly noticeable, sometimes they're major) from many of New York's most famous department stores. Diligent shopping occasionally produces great bargains here, but you must check everything carefully, and make sure you concentrate on the front of the store first, where the better merchandise is often put. Bargains in shoes and boots can be especially good. Gabay's also has men's and children's clothing, and occasionally furniture, appliances, and bric-a-brac. Open Monday through Saturday from 9 a.m. to 5:45 p.m., on Sunday from 11 a.m. to 5 p.m.

"No waiting for end-of-season sales" is the slogan at **Ruth Brooks**, 1138 Third Ave., at 66th Street (tel. 744-5412), one of the better discounters around town. Her lines of sports and better clothing, top-designer fashions, and famous-name brands are all discounted by 40% to 80%, and all merchandise is new and perfect. Open Monday to Saturday from 10:30 a.m. to 6 p.m., and from noon to 4:30 p.m. on spring and fall Sundays.

There are hefty discounts on designer sportswear at **Fishkin's**, 314 Grand St., at Allen Street, and at 63 Orchard St., near Grand Street (tel. 226-6538)—sweaters, separates, bathing suits, cruisewear, shoes, handbags, etc. An additional unit at 318 Grand St. concentrates on fun weekend wear. Open weekdays from 10 a.m. to 5 p.m., on Friday to 4 p.m., on Sunday from 9 a.m. to 4:30 p.m.

And while you're perusing Lower East Side shops, don't miss **Sam's Knitwear**, 93 Orchard St., between Delancey and Broome Streets (tel. 966-0390), where discounts of 50% and more are offered on name-brand and designer clothes. Sales are held year round. We bought a dress here for $30 that we had seen (but only coveted) at $80 elsewhere. Open weekdays from 11 a.m. to 6 p.m., on Sunday from 9 a.m.

Wherever you go in Manhattan, it seems, you'll find a **Bolton's**. And no wonder: Bolton's is Manhattan's largest women's discount chain. It offers current contemporary merchandise at 20% to 50% off major department and specialty-store prices. Bolton's prides itself on buying key fashion merchandise made of top-quality fabrics and workmanship; there's no junk to weed through here, just lots of good buys in coats, dresses, suits, sportswear, loungewear, sleepwear, and accessories; we've had good luck here with handbags many times. Most branches of Bolton's are open Monday to Saturday from 10 a.m. to 7 p.m. (on Thursday to 8:30 p.m.), and on Sunday from noon to 5 p.m. You'll find them on the East Side at 1180 Madison Ave., at 86th Street (tel. 722-4454); 1193 Third Ave., at 69th Street (tel. 628-7553); 4 E. 34th St., just off Fifth Avenue (tel. 684-3750); and 225 E. 57th St., near Second Ave. (tel. 755-2527). On the West Side, Bolton's is at 27 W. 57th St., between Fifth and Sixth Avenues (tel. 935-4431), and 2251 Broadway, at 80th Street (tel. 873-8545). In the Village, the address is 43 E. 8th St. (tel. 475-6625); downtown, it's 59 Liberty St. (tel. 349-7464), closed Saturday.

You no longer have to go all the way to Boston to enjoy the legendary shopping buys of **Filene's Basement of Boston.** You just have to go to Queens, specifically to the Fresh Meadows Shopping Center in Flushing, to sample the wares of the world's original "bargain basement." While this new version of Filene's Basement lacks the frantic pace and frenzied atmosphere of the original, the bargains are still the same, if on a much smaller scale, and there is even an improvement: dressing rooms, which somehow they never thought of in Boston. Filene's buys up huge lots of perfect and "nearly perfect" merchandise from leading manufacturers, and also from famous stores which may need to dispose of unsold goods or which are going out of business. Many of the original store labels—Neiman-Marcus, Saks Fifth Avenue, I. Magnin, Sakowitz—are right on the garments. And the prices are always fractions—small fractions—of the originals. We've seen Neiman-Marcus sports coats for $98, Maggie London dresses for $60, handbags from Stone Mountain at $20, Buxton all-leather clutches at $5. Designer names show up frequently among the name-brand merchandise. Buys in lingerie and loungewear are outstanding. There's also a shoe department, a big children's department, and a downstairs store for the men. There's giftware too, and on occasion even Oriental rugs—whatever Filene's gets a great buy on. New merchandise arrives daily, so if you don't find anything you need one day, come back the next, and the next. Yes, they do give refunds.

Filene's is a bit of a trip by subway—IND–Eighth Avenue E train to 169th Street, then the Q17A bus—but it's easy driving: take the Long Island Expressway to Exit 25. There are other Filene's Basements on Long Island: in Manhasset at the Miracle Mile, 1400 Northern Blvd.; in Huntington on Route 110, adjacent to Walt Whitman Mall; in Levittown at Nassau Mall, Hempstead Turnpike. All stores are open seven days a week, Monday through Saturday from 10 a.m. to 9:30 p.m., on Sunday from noon to 6 p.m.

For sheepskin coats and jackets (men's and women's), down coats and jackets, pile-lined suede coats, fun and fake furs—all at 25% to 50% less than department store prices—head over to **Mitchel's Sportwear, Inc.,** 19 Orchard St., between Canal and Hester Streets (tel. 925-6757). Open Sunday through Friday from 9 a.m. to 5 p.m.

Paris Fashions, Inc., 512 Seventh Ave. (6th floor), between 37th and 38th Streets (tel. 382-1895), is filled with coats, raincoats, suits, separates, and sportswear bearing labels like Pauline Trigere, Regina Porter, London Fog, Botany 500, Harvé Benard, Capri, and more. Discounts can go as high as 50%. Open weekdays from 11 a.m. to 4 p.m. and on Saturday from 9 a.m. to 3 p.m. except June through August.

Aaron's, 627 Fifth Ave., between 17th and 18th Streets, in *Brooklyn* (tel. 718/768-5400), is a marvelous store that specializes in high-fashion women's wear at discount prices. Famous-brand, expensive knit dresses that go from $125 to $500 elsewhere cost from $88 to $333 at the most here. Designer clothes of every type, coats, sportswear, top-quality furs, cashmere sweaters, even handbags are sold here. There's a large community dressing room, but the sales staff is courteous and helpful. Open Monday through Saturday from 9:30 a.m. to 6 p.m., on Thursday until 9 p.m. Aaron's own parking field is across the street.

To get there by subway, take the BMT RR local to Prospect Avenue. Walk one block to Fifth Avenue.

And our good friend Sam Wernick of **Better Made Coat and Suit Company** lets people come into his showroom at 270 W. 38th St., off Eighth Avenue (tel. 944-0748), where he sells beautifully made designer coats and suits at big discounts. There's only a small charge for alterations, and Sam has been known to custom-cut coats on request. Coats are in the $159 to $189 range. Open weekdays from 10 a.m. to 4 p.m., on Saturday till 3 p.m.

Across the street from New York's prestigious Fashion Institute of Technology, a small cluster of designer discount stores have opened in the last several years. Weekends are a big shopping time here, and all stay open on Sunday. One of the nicest to shop in—wide aisles, spacious dressing rooms where salespeople will hang up your coat and rush out to bring you selections—is **Harris's**, 275 Seventh Ave., between 25th and 26th Streets (tel. 989-9765). Discounts on designer fashions for women—dresses, coats, sportswear, etc.—range from 30% to 40%. We once lucked in on a sale and spent $50 for a Giorgio Sant'Angelo dress that was $70 at a discount store nearby, and $100 uptown. Open Monday to Saturday from 10 a.m. to 5:45 p.m., on Sunday (except in summer) from 11 a.m. to 5 p.m.

Very "in" with fashion-conscious New York women is **The New Store**, 289 Seventh Ave. between 26th and 27th Streets (tel. 741-1077), which offers beautiful designer clothes at a fraction of the regular prices. European sportswear and after-five clothes are some of the offerings. In addition to their regular discounts, frequent sales offer blazers, sweaters, pants, suits, skirts, and culottes—all from famous makers—at discounts of as much as 50% to 66% and more! Always worth checking. We've had good luck here with silk blouses. Open Monday through Friday from 10 a.m. to 8 p.m., on Saturday and Sunday to 6:30 p.m.

S & W has four stores at the corner of 26th Street and Seventh Avenue (tel. 924-6656), all offering incredible buys in top-designer clothing. The shop at 165 W. 26th St. offers designer misses and junior sportswear, suits, and dresses; 283 Seventh Ave. carries designer handbags, shoes, accessories, and evening wear; 287 Seventh Ave. has designer coats; and 291 Seventh Ave. is where you'll find moderate-priced and budget designer sportswear. In *Brooklyn*, S & W is at 4217 13th Ave. (tel. 718/438-9679).

Everything from cotton basics, 26 styles in 23 colors, to wild American and international designs, is featured at **Unique Clothing Warehouse**, 718-726 Broadway, below 8th Street (tel. 674-1767). They also show work from New York's underground designers. Prices are really low. And they also have fabulous accessories and toys. Open Monday to Saturday from 10 a.m. to 9 p.m., on Sunday from noon to 8 p.m.

Bogies, 201 E. 10th St., near Second Avenue (tel. 260-1199), is a mess, a jumble, a mixture of incredible designer, antique, and recycled clothing. If you know how to pick through the tables you'll find bargains galore. We've seen models and other chic types sitting on the floor going through the piles. We've even seen patchwork quilts here in fairly good condition for low prices. Prices are so low they're unbelievable. Some items are in perfect condition, but many need a little fixing up. If you're clever with a needle, you could put together an entire wardrobe for about $100. Open from 12:30 to 5:30 p.m. Monday to Friday. Open winter Saturdays from 12:30 to 6 p.m.

I. Buss, 738 Broadway, near 8th Street (tel. 242-3338), is another place for recycled military clothing: everything from doormen's hats for a couple of dollars to English police capes to bush jackets. And that's not to mention the shorts, coats, shirts, sweaters, Italian walking shoes, English army shoes, and scores of accessories. Open Monday to Saturday from 10 a.m. to 7 p.m., on Sunday from 1 to 6 p.m.

Trash and Vaudeville, 4 St. Mark's Pl. (which is East 8th Street) east of Third Avenue (tel. 982-3590), has both new clothing (terrific skirts, for example, from Mexico and elsewhere) and a great collection of antique clothes (from about $28 to $50) in its upstairs store. Men's gabardine shirts start at $16. Downstairs is devoted to a wide variety of incredible rock 'n' roll wear, much of it imported from London, plus footwear. Open weekdays from noon to 8 p.m., on Saturday from 11 a.m. to 8 p.m., and on Sunday from 1 to 7 p.m.

One of the best stores of this genre—and a tremendous favorite with young people—is **Canal Jean Co.**, 504 Broadway or 304 Canal St. (tel. 226-1130). A short walk from Chinatown, Little Italy, or the heart of SoHo, this store offers a wide selection of colorful merchandise, from antique clothing and military surplus to better sportswear for men and women to accessories and lingerie—and all at super-low discount prices. Start in front of the store, where bins always offer plenty of good values for inveterate bargain hunters. We once saw antique tweed coats and jackets for 99¢ and antique sweaters at three for $5. Inside, look for such popular basics as 100% cotton dyed T-shirts (five styles, ten colors at any given time at $5 each, or three for $12), or their own 100% cotton Shaker knit sweaters, a real value at $20. Or expect the unexpected! Perhaps a Hawaiian aloha shirt at $9, all-leather military surplus hiking boots from $10 to $20, a 100% cotton Canal Jean beach towel for $4, or '50s and '60s vintage sunglasses from Paris at $4 to $9. Canal Jean Co. is open seven days from 10 a.m. to 8 p.m.

Century 21, 12 Cortlandt St., between Church and Broadway (tel. 227-9092), is a smart shopper's paradise. First-quality, current-season, moderately priced to expensive designer clothes are offered at good and sometimes huge discounts. Also children's clothes, men's clothes, ladies undergarments and sleepwear, beautiful shoes, linens, giftware, appliances, and much, much more. Open Monday through Wednesday from 7:45 a.m. to 6:10 p.m., on Thursday and Friday until 6:25 p.m. They're also in Brooklyn at 421 86th St. No try-ons allowed, but they do offer full refunds on all purchases.

If you have a preppie taste in clothing but don't have any allowance from daddy to go with it, **Deals,** 142 W. 72nd St. (tel. 873-0790) and 81 Worth St. (tel. 966-0214), will outfit you in Ivy League style and leave you enough to take in a polo match. You'll find top name-brand "khakis," rugby shirts, shoes, shirts, sweaters, and dresses at good (20% to 30%) discounts. Even accessories such as leather wallets, address books, and umbrellas by top designer names are discounted. Men's clothing too. Deals is open on Monday, Tuesday, Wednesday, and Friday from 8:30 a.m. to 6 p.m., on Thursday until 8 p.m., on Saturday from 9 a.m. to 6 p.m., and on Sunday from 10 a.m. to 5 p.m.

Down the block and across Broadway from the uptown Deals, **Fashion Aloft,** one flight up at 208 W. 72nd St. (tel. 724-9815), is always worth popping into if you're looking for big discounts on medium-priced women's sportswear. We've bought pants, tops, sweaters, skirts, etc., for anywhere from 20% to 40% off regular prices, and the staff is very helpful. Prices start around $15. Open daily from 10:30 a.m. to 6:30 p.m.; closed Sunday and Monday in July and August.

If you've been an admirer of the Finnish designs of **Marimekko,** there's an entire store for you at 7 W. 56th St., between Fifth and Sixth Avenues (tel. 581-9616). The clothes are beautiful and pricey, but you can buy the fabric by the yard, or inexpensive address and note books covered with the brightly covered cloth. Open Monday through Friday from 10 a.m. to 6:30 p.m., on Saturday to 6 p.m.

Big sellers in Europe and Japan, the clothing creations of **Reminiscence** are a favorite with the under-30 international set. Don't miss a visit to their new anchor store at 74 Fifth Ave., near 13th Street at the top of Greenwich Village (tel. 342-2292). Green and pink walls, neon signs, and spotlights set the scene for Stewart Richer's award-winning designs that are a redefinition of the '50s with a New Wave accent. Richer designs clothes, mostly in natural fabrics, that

SHOPPING: CLOTHES

are fun, comfortable, and exciting, a blend of antique and ultra-contemporary. Flight suits, army surplus pants, coveralls, and jackets are all dyed unusual and brilliant colors—even turquoise and raspberry pink. They also do a thriving business in reproductions of antique and nostalgic clothing such as their own "Hawaiian" shirts, exact duplicates of the patterns and styles sold during the '50s. Also, beautiful interpretations of turn-of-the-century silk men's shirts and ladies' dresses (in lovely pale colors), or "50-ish" suede jackets in very '80s colors of electric blue or lavender, among many other things. In the front of the store is a selection of genuine antique clothes, all reasonably priced. Open Monday through Saturday from 12:15 to 8 p.m. There are also Reminiscence boutiques on the second floor of Macy's and the fourth floor of Bloomingdale's.

Fiorucci, 125 E. 59th St., between Park and Lexington Avenues (tel. 751-5638), is an assault on your eyes (they specialize in *bright*-colored clothing) and ears (and they play *loud* music), and is definitely a must visit in New York if you are interested in what the rest of the nation will be wearing two or three years in the future. Fiorucci stocks the fad of the minute, from miniskirts to paper clothing to blinking electrified earrings. Elio Fiorucci's penchant for combining the classic with the absurd—for example, cowboy boots in gold leather, or a map of the world on a pleated accordion skirt, or industrial textiles used for earrings and belts—is evident everywhere. His far-out collection of T-shirts, along with designer jeans, form the basis of his collection. While prices here are not budget, it's well worth a visit for shopping as theater: live window displays, free cappuccino and espresso, and contemporary music tapes. Accessories at Fiorucci are reasonable, and there is a supply of reduced clothing downstairs. Open Monday and Thursday from 10 a.m. to 8 p.m.; on Tuesday, Wednesday, Friday, and Saturday until 6 p.m.

The Gap, 22 W. 34th St., west of Fifth Avenue (tel. 695-2521), sells jeans, sweat clothes, shirts, blouses, and other casual sportsclothes for men and women at reasonable prices. Their merchandise is all top-quality and current design. Open Monday through Saturday from 9:30 a.m. to 7 p.m., on Thursday until 8:30 p.m., and on Sunday from noon to 5 p.m. There are Gap branches all over the city. Check the New York Telephone Directory for other addresses and phone numbers.

The Forgotten Woman, 888 Lexington Ave. (tel. 535-8848), caters to the larger-size woman who has difficulty finding stylish clothing at a reasonable price and who would like a decent selection. The store stocks many fashionable and comfortable clothes that could be considered bargains since one dress which fits well is worth five that pinch, stretch out of shape, rip at the seams, or are uncomfortable. Store hours are Monday through Saturday from 10 a.m. to 6 p.m.

Downtown, the fashion-conscious larger woman has an ally in Carol Lefkowitz of **The Greater N.Y. Woman,** at 215 E. 23rd St., between Second and Third Avenues (tel. 725-0505), who has a great eye for high style at decent prices. Sportswear, executive dressing, and a special section for dressy, glamorous, "After Five" clothes. A must for the big woman. Open Monday to Saturday from 11 a.m. to 7 p.m., on Thursday to 9 p.m.

Maternity

The immense selection of maternity clothing at **Reborn Maternity Discount,** 1449 Third Ave., between 81st and 82nd Streets (tel. 737-8817), is almost equal to all the other maternity shops in the city (including department stores) combined. First-quality merchandise costs 10% to 50% less than you'd pay at other stores. Expect to pay from $25 and $30 up. They're also featuring sophisticated designer fashions for pregnant women, including designer jeans by Sasson and Jordache. Lingerie and excercise leotards are also discounted. Open Monday to Wednesday and Friday from 10 a.m. to 7 p.m., on Thursday to 8:30 p.m., on Saturday to 6 p.m., and on Sunday from 11 a.m. to 5 p.m.

Bridal Gowns, Wholesale and Retail

Bridal gowns are far from inexpensive these days, so every prospective bride should know about the buildings at 1385 Broadway and 499 Seventh Ave. in the Garment Center; they house some of the leading bridal manufacturers and designers in the country. On Saturday mornings, between 10 a.m. and noon, 1385 Broadway is wide open for brides, bridesmaids, mothers of the bride, and flower girls. To shop efficiently here, shop elsewhere first: know your merchandise and prices before you set foot in the door. Then you'll have a guide for comparison shopping; and in some—but not every case—the savings can be enormous. For the best bargains, check the discontinued and sample racks.

It's sometimes more difficult to gain access to the showrooms at 499 Seventh Ave.; ask the elevator starters what floors will be open. Good bets are Floors 15 and 21. **Barbara Quincy** not only has fabulous bridal gowns, but also graduation and prom dresses at true wholesale prices. The talented young bridal designer **Johanna** is at 134 W. 37th Street, 8th floor. We've seen dresses that retail for over $600 in the $300 range here.

Want to keep within your budget and look as if you've spent a mint? We'll let you in on a special secret. For upward of $250 and $300 you can rent a fabulous creation by **Gene London**, a copy of a couture or antique wedding gown (or even a Victorian original for a higher price). These gowns sell for thousands, and some are made of Battenberg lace and have mile-long cinema satin or candlelit satin trains. Gene's customers are many of the stars from movies and television, and his loft is a great adventure. By appointment only: Gene London, 10 Gramercy Park South (tel. 533-4105).

It will be well worth your while to take a trip to **Brooklyn** to shop for wedding clothes at **Kleinfeld and Son**, Fifth Avenue and 82nd Street, Bay Ridge (tel. 718/833-1100). Kleinfeld is known for one of the largest selections of designer bridal gowns, mother-of-the-bride clothes, designer evening wear, and special-occasion clothes in the country. Discounts range from 20% to 40%. There are many imports from England, France, and Italy in misses and junior sizes. Open Tuesday and Thursday from 11 a.m. to 9 p.m.; on Wednesday, Friday and Saturday till 6 p.m.; closed Sunday, Monday, and Saturday during July and August.

To get to Kleinfeld, take the BMT RR train to 86th Street.

Special-Occasion Dresses

If you're looking for party, prom, mother-of-the-bride, and other special-occasion dresses, make note of the wholesale building at 498 Seventh Ave. Call designer **Anne Marie Gardin** at 736-2895 to make an appointment: she has beautiful dresses, long and short, in lace, linen, and silk, and many mother-of-the-bride outfits. Prices are $100 to $400 wholesale. On the 18th floor of this building you can find beaded and sequined evening wear, from $275 to $800, plus silk dresses and pants for less. Alas, no try-ons, no returns, and cash only. Open weekdays from 10 a.m. to 6 p.m. You can also call **Maria Scotto** at 237 W. 35th St. and make an appointment to come up and see her special-occasion dresses in silk, cotton, crêpes, and chiffon, sizes 6 to 14. Prices range from $80 to $200, and would be double that retail.

Resale Shops

Some of the best-dressed women in New York—glamorous types who look as if they've just stepped off the pages of *Vogue* or *Town and Country*—are actually wearing secondhand clothes which they purchased at chic Madison Avenue resale shops! These are the places where society women, actresses, models, and fashion editors on the best-dressed lists often take dresses, gowns, suits, and coats which they've worn only a few times. (The society columnists would notice, perish the thought, if they showed up in the same clothes too often!) The castoffs are then resold to customers like you, in excellent condition (they've received a thorough cleaning), and at a fraction of their original prices.

The resale shop with the highest fashion styles is **Michael's,** at 1041 Madison Ave., at 79th Street, second floor (tel. 737-7273), which resembles Bergdorf Goodman's more than a secondhand store. The clothing available here comes from some of the wealthiest and best-dressed women in the world; when they empty their closets, they fill Michael's with the very best collection of designer names you're apt to find under one roof anywhere: Valentino, Calvin Klein, Yves St. Laurent, Cardin, Halston, Blass, etc. We've seen $500 coats priced at $95 (and you'd never know they weren't new). Believe it or not, there is even a $10 rack on which you might find a treasure. Open Tuesday through Saturday from 9:30 a.m. to 6 p.m.; closed Saturday during July and August.

After exhausting the possibilities at Michael's, you'll do well to walk five blocks uptown to the **Encore Resale Dress Shop,** at 1132 Madison Ave., at 84th Street (tel. 879-2850), which also stocks an enormous supply of women's outer apparel at prices averaging a third what the original owners paid. In addition to terrific buys on designer clothing, you'll also find incredible values in fine furs. Many of the famous have unloaded wardrobes here. There are two floors to browse through. Open Monday through Saturday from 10:30 a.m. to 6 p.m., (on Thursday to 7 p.m.), and on Sunday from 12:30 to 6 p.m. Closed Sunday from July to mid-August.

Buttons and Buckles

And now, after scouring the resale shops for bargains, you may decide all your new dress needs is some elegant buttons. A charming shop, **Tender Buttons,** at 143 E. 62nd St., between Lexington and Third Avenues (tel. 758-7004), carries every kind of antique and modern button, plus exquisite antique buckles. Some buttons even have fascinating histories, which proprietresses Diana Epstein and Millicent Safro will be happy to tell you about. Note, too, that Tender Buttons has the largest collection of men's blazer buttons (antique and new) in the world, as well as antique men's cufflinks, dress sets, studs, and stickpins. Open Monday through Friday from 11 a.m. to 6 p.m., until 5:30 on Saturday. Closed Saturday in July and August.

Lingerie

Charles Weiss, 38 Orchard St., at Hester Street (tel. 226-1717), claims the city's largest bra and foundation department, and largest brand diversity—all at typical Orchard Street discount prices. Open Sunday through Thursday from 9 a.m. to 5:30 p.m., on Friday until 3 p.m. Closed Saturday.

Another huge selection of the top names in ladies' lingerie can be found at **Goldman & Cohen, Inc.,** 54 Orchard St., between Hester and Grand Streets (tel. 966-0737). Discounts range from about 20% to 70%. Open Sunday to Thursday from 9 a.m. to 5:30 p.m., on Friday till 4 p. m.

Ditto **A. W. Kaufman,** 73 Orchard St., between Grand and Broome Streets (tel. 226-1629), which has vast selections of designer lingerie at greatly discounted prices: loungewear, sleepwear, camisole sets, ensemble sets, hostess gowns, cashmere and wool robes, bedjackets, slippers, even hand-embroidered half slips in pure silks, satins, and cottons. Open Sunday through Thursday from

10 a.m. to 5 p.m., on Friday to 2:30 p.m.

Ultra Smart, 15 E. 30th St., between Fifth and Madison Avenues (tel. 686-1564), buys up stockings from the big mills and puts them out under their own label. These are the exact stockings you'd pay up to five times as much for under a designer label. Open weekdays only from 8 a.m. to 5 p.m.

When Channel 5 did a survey of New York hosiery stores for the "10 O'Clock News," they cited **Wingdale,** 16 W. 30th St., off Fifth Avenue (tel. 684-4291), as the store offering the best prices to the consumer. We've seen Hanes control-top pantyhose discounted here, and Hanes support pantyhose. Men's support hose are also discounted. There's a wide selection of brands and styles, and service is courteous. Open weekdays only from 7:30 a.m. to 4 p.m.

Handbags

The familiar Ohrbach's and Alexander's can be counted on for a vast selection of inexpensive handbags, but for the best values in better handbags, head for the Lower East Side and **Fine and Klein Handbags,** 119 Orchard St., between Delancey and Rivington Streets (tel. 674-6720). Their huge selection of name and designer bags spans three floors and offers such names as Pierre Cardin, Christian Dior, and Halston at discounts of 35%. Open daily except Saturday from 8:45 a.m. to 5:30 p.m.

Another good source of beautiful designer bags is **Aly's Hut,** 85 Hester St., between Orchard and Allen Streets (tel. 226-5475), where names like J.W.M. Derr, Bonsoir, Anne Klein, Sabrina, and the like are sold at 20% to 50% off list price. Open Sunday through Thursday from 9:30 a.m. to 5 p.m.

You should also know about **Ber-Sel,** 79 Orchard St., between Broome and Grand Streets (tel. 966-5517), where Anne Klein, Liz Claiborne, Dior, and many other top-brand and designer bags are sold at discounts of about 30%, along with beautiful wallets and umbrellas. Open Sunday to Friday from 9:30 a.m. to 5:30 p.m.

Shoes

The **Shoe Outlet,** 348 E. 76th St., between First and Second Avenues (tel. 988-0722), has all kinds of women's shoes for $5 to $10. Golo boots, Veneziano, and many other name brands are all available, but not every size in every style. Shoes are from current stock at their retail stores, called **S & T Shoes,** at 1467 Second Ave. (76th Street) and 1043 Lexington Ave. (between 74th and 75th Streets), and are sent to this shop when only a few sizes in each style are left. Open Monday through Saturday from 1 to 5 p.m.

Check the basement-level "budget store" of **Gimbels,** Broadway at 33rd Street (tel. 736-5100), for fabulous bargains in discontinued shoes from its elegant sister store, Saks Fifth Avenue. Prices could start as low as $15, and when you've bought your shoes, you can peruse all the other bargains here. Gimbels is open on Monday, Thursday, and Friday from 9:45 to 8:30 p.m.; on Tuesday, Wednesday, and Saturday till 6:30 p.m.; on Sunday from noon to 5 p.m.

For good prices on high-fashion shoes, women should also check out **Anbar Trading Company,** 93 Reade St., between Church Street and West Broadway (tel. 227-0253). These retailers of women's shoes do not have all sizes, but if you're lucky you'll get a bargain. Many designer names.

Under the same ownership, **Shoe Steal,** around the corner from Anbar at 116 Duane St. (tel. 964-4017), has shoes at even lower prices ($12 to $39 a pair). Both stores are open weekdays from 8 a.m. to 5:30 p.m., on Saturday from 11 a.m. to 5 p.m. Closed Saturdays in July and August.

Several stores on the Lower East Side are well worth checking out, among them:

The **Orchard Bootery,** 75 Orchard St., between Broome and Grand Streets (tel. 966-0688). Many designer shoes here—Jacques Cohen, Bandolino, Evan Picone, Ferragamo, etc.—all discounted 30% or more. Open Monday to Friday from 9:30 a.m. to 5:30 p.m., on Sunday to 6 p.m.

Aly's Hut, 85 Hester St., between Orchard and Allen Streets (tel. 226-5475), carries a wide selection of top-brand footwear: Bass, Mia, Sebago, Hippopotamus, etc. Discounts are in the 20% to 50% range. Aly's Hut is open Sunday through Thursday from 9:30 a.m. to 5 p.m.

Leslie Bootery, 36 Orchard St. (tel. 431-9196), has two floors devoted to women's shoes (their downstairs store is given over to men's shoes; see ahead). On the main level, ladies' shoes such as Caressa, Frye, and Reebok are all sold at 20% discount; on the upstairs level, designer shoes such as Bally, Allure, Beene Bag, Amalfi, Paloma, etc., are also discounted at 20%. Open Sunday to Thursday from 9:30 a.m. to 5:30 p.m., on Friday to 4:30 p.m.

M. M. Shoe Center, 302 Grand St. (tel. 966-2702), is the place to go for low prices on all-leather shoes for men and women. You should be able to find a style to suit your taste from their large selection of top name-brand sandals, shoes, and boots. They stock everything from high-style designer shoes to comfortable everyday styles, and everything is first-quality, current stock. Open Sunday through Thursday from 9:30 a.m. to 5:30 p.m.; closed Friday and Saturday.

Furs

Some of the best bargains in New York on gently used furs can be found at the **Ritz Thrift Shop,** 107 W. 57th St., between Sixth and Seventh Avenues (tel. 265-4559). This is where New York's society women shed their furs, sometimes after only a few months' wear. All the coats, stoles, and jackets are in excellent condition. Mink coats begin at about $600; fitch, beaver, and nutria from $500; raccoon from $600; or lynx from $1000. Open Monday through Saturday from 9 a.m. to 6 p.m. (closed Saturday during July).

A huge selection of used furs—as well as outstanding buys in new furs—can be found at the **New Yorker Fur Thrift Shop,** 822 Third Ave., between 50th and 51st Streets (tel. 355-5090). Although the store specializes in "finer quality coats" (a good used mink would begin at $1500), they also have lots of antique fun coats—remember sheared raccoons and sheared beavers, muskrats, and Persians?—in the $250 to $300 range. Since New Yorker is a manufacturer, they can also offer brand-new fur coats at factory prices; we've seen fox jackets at around $400. All told, there are about 2000 garments on hand. And the men's department is growing. Open Monday through Saturday from 9 a.m. to 5 or 6 p.m. (closed in summer on Saturday).

Also check the aforementioned **Mitchel's,** 19 Orchard St., for fake furs and fun furs.

MEN'S CLOTHING AND ACCESSORIES: Before launching into our listings for menswear, we refer you back to **Richard's Army-Navy, Unique Clothing Warehouse,** and the downtown wholesale shoe district, which carry goods for men also and are described above in our "Women's Clothing and Accessories" section.

Suits, Pants, Jackets, Coats

For traditional executive wear at discount prices, go to **L. S. Men's Clothing,** 23 W. 45th St., between Fifth and Sixth Avenues (tel. 575-0933). Designer suits, jackets, natural shoulder suits, and coats are all American made and sold at 45% to 65% off their typical retail prices of $375 to $650. They also have a large selection of silk and wool ties and slacks. Free cuffs, but alterations are extra. Open on Sunday from 11 a.m. to 4 p.m., on Monday from 9 a.m. to 7 p.m., Tuesday to Thursday to 6 p.m., on Friday to 5 p.m.

Harry Rothman at 111 Fifth Ave., near 18th Street (tel. 777-7400), is patronized by some of the best-dressed men in town, who appreciate the discounts—as high as 50%—on expensive brand-name clothing. As we went to press, the store lost its lease but was planning to reopen somewhere nearby on Fifth Avenue. Call for current information.

Fenwick Clothes, on the fifth floor of 22 W. 19th St., west of Fifth Avenue (tel. 243-1100), is a manufacturer of quality men's clothing which has opened its doors to the public. As a result you get to buy at wholesale prices and can purchase suits, overcoats, topcoats, jackets, slacks, etc., for about 50% off retail price. Suits that would retail for $400 are $200 here; sports jackets that cost $325 to $350 in the stores are $165; and slacks retailing for $95 to $105 are only $49 or $59. Quality is excellent. Alterations extra. Open weekdays from 9 a.m. to 5 p.m., on Saturday until 4 p.m.; closed summer Saturdays.

Syms, 45 Park Pl., between Church Street and West Broadway, two blocks north of the World Trade Center (tel. 791-1199), has three entire floors of men's apparel and accessories, including shoes. Many designer labels in every department, and the savings can be incredible. Men will find everything at Syms, from designer coats and suits, to jeans, to shirts, to warm-up suits, to pajamas. Syms is open from 9 a.m. to 7 p.m. weekdays, except Thursday and Friday when the store stays open to 9 p.m.; 9 a.m. to 6 p.m. on Saturday.

Buyer's Factory Outlet, 149 Fifth Ave., at 21st Street, on the sixth floor (tel. 254-0059), is another big outfit. Suits for $125 to $155, some sports coats for $85 to $105, slacks at $25 to $35; many designer and big-name brands. Open seven days, from 9:30 a.m. to 5:30 p.m.

On the Lower East Side, check out the following shops:

Haar & Knobel, 49 Orchard St., between Grand and Hester Streets (tel. 226-1812), has everything for men. They buy big lots of sportswear, jeans, etc., and pass on the savings. Open Sunday to Thursday from 9 a.m. to 5 p.m., on Friday from 9 a.m. to 3 p.m.

Sam Popper, 85–87 Orchard St., between Grand and Broome Streets (tel. 226-0679), takes only cash for his sportswear, sweaters, and shirts. Nice merchandise, including designer jeans. Open Monday to Friday from 9 a.m. to 5 p.m., on Sunday to 4:30 p.m.

For designer jeans, **Arnie's Place,** 37 Orchard St., at Hester Street (tel. 925-0513), is a good bet. Good discounts on Calvin Klein, Lee, Sasson, Levis, and Landlubber jeans, among others. Open weekdays from 9 a.m. to 5 p.m., on Sunday from 9:30 a.m. to 5:30 p.m.

A tradition of quality and service keep the customers coming back to **Pan Am Men's Wear,** 50 Orchard St., between Grand and Hester Streets (tel. 925-7032). They carry coats, jackets, suits, shirts, and sportswear by such top designers as Perry Ellis, Polo by Ralph Lauren, Alexander Julian, Marzotto of Italy, and a full line of Italian designers. Discounts are sizeable and expert tailoring is free. Garments may be returned within 14 days of purchase. Open Sunday through Wednesday from 9:30 a.m. to 6 p.m., on Thursday till 8 p.m., on Friday to 3 p.m.

Similar wares and bargains are across the street at **G & G Projections,** 53 Orchard St. (tel. 431-4530)—Oleg Cassini and Egon Von Furstenberg sweaters, Virany all-wool pea coats, Van Gill, Adolpho and Geoffrey Beene suits, and much more. Free alterations. Open Sunday to Wednesday from 9 a.m. to 6 p.m., on Thursday till 8 p.m., on Friday till an hour before sundown.

Shirts

On the Lower East Side's Orchard Street, you can pick and choose among many stores selling men's shirts at a discount. Our favorite is the **Victory Shirt Company,** 96 Orchard St., between Delancey and Broome Streets (tel. 677-2020); 10 Maiden Lane, between Broadway and Nassau Street (tel. 349-7111); and 345 Madison Ave., at 44th Street (tel. 687-6375). They make all their own shirts, specializing in 100% cotton, and since you're buying from the manufacturer, savings are great. You can also get handmade silk ties and women's shirts at Victory. The Orchard Street store is open weekdays and Sunday from 9 a.m. to 5 p.m.; the Maiden Lane store is open weekdays only from 9 a.m. to 6 p.m.; and the Madison Avenue store is open weekdays from 9 a.m. to 6 p.m., and on Saturday from 9:30 a.m. to 5 p.m.

The **Penn Garden Grand Shirt Company,** 58 Orchard St., between Grand and Hester Streets (tel. 431-8464), has designer and famous-name men's shirts at incredibly low prices—20% to 30% less than you'd pay elsewhere. Open every day but Saturday, from 9 a.m. to 6 p.m. in summer, until 4 p.m. on Friday in winter, on Thursday to 8 p.m.

Shoes

Leslie Bootery, 36 Orchard St., between Canal and Hester Streets (tel. 431-9196), offers 20% discounts on designer and name-brand men's shoes. This three-level store has its men's shoes—Rockport, Reebok, Clarks of England, Bally, etc.—on the downstairs level. The top floors feature women's shoes from top designers. Open Monday to Thursday from 9:30 a.m. to 5:30 p.m., on Friday to 4:30 p.m., and on Sunday from 9 a.m. to 6 p.m.

For sneakers—Puma, Adidas, Nike, etc.—head to one of these four stores, all under the same ownership, and all open seven days a week from 9:30 a.m. to 5:30 p.m.: **Jules Harvey,** 132 Orchard St.; **H & J Shoes,** 131 Orchard St.; **All Star Shoes,** 135 Orchard St. (these three between Rivington and Delancey Streets); and **Peck & Chase Shoes,** 163 Orchard St., between Rivington and Stanton Streets (tel. 982-0840 for all four stores). They also carry many name-brand and designer shoes, boots, dress shoes, and work shoes, including Timberland.

Sherman Shoes, 121 Division St., at the south end of Orchard Street, one block south of Canal Street (tel. 233-7898), is a find for men looking for discounts of up to 50% on high-quality designer shoes. You'll find top brands from the U.S., France, and Italy, cowboy and dress shoes in both discontinued and up-to-the-minute styles. Open from 8:30 a.m. to 4:30 p.m. Sunday through Thursday; they close early on Friday, and all day Saturday.

See, as well, **Frankel's General Store,** under "Western Wear," ahead.

Ties

New York has a string of low-price tie shops where you can select from among a large assortment of patterns and materials for as low as $2.99 a tie (maximum price is $7.99 for a silk tie). **Tie City** has locations at 205 W. 34th St., between Seventh and Eighth Avenues (tel. 564-4234); 591 Lexington Ave., near 52nd Street (tel. 421-5327); and Grand Central Station (tel. 725-2025). All are open Monday to Saturday from 8 a.m. to 6 p.m.

On the Lower East Side, **Allen Street** is tie street, with about ten stores located between Delancey and Houston Streets. You can simply walk in and out of each shop until you find what you're looking for. All offer the low prices you'd expect in this area.

2. An Alphabetical Miscellany

ANTIQUES: A personal favorite among the city's many antique shops is **Carol Alderman Antiques,** 353 Third Ave., at 26th Street (tel. 532-7242). Shopping here is always an adventure, since you never know what might turn up at this serendipitous spot: it could be anything from an art deco chandelier to an old perfume bottle. Great for gift giving: Carol's large collection of one-of-a-kind earrings, necklaces, bracelets, made of old artifacts, from $12.50 to $85. You'll probably also find mirrors, lamps, stained glass, and much more. Open Monday to Saturday, more or less from 1 to 7 p.m.

You'll need to make an appointment to see the collection of vintage clothing and props at **Early Halloween,** 10 W. 19th St., off Fifth Avenue (tel. 691-2933). You could find a slinky satin nightie, a poplin print housedress, or woolen jodhpurs. Shoes, ties and hats, jackets and coats, accessories in excellent condition—many never-worn items—at reasonable prices. Open weekdays from noon to 6 p.m., by appointment only.

Connoisseurs of brass will want to peruse the merchandise at the **Brass Antique Shoppe,** 32 Allen St., between Canal and Hester Streets (tel. 925-6660), which specializes in small items such as candlesticks and andirons at good prices. This Lower East Side shop also has vases, old Russian samovars, antique drawer pulls, kiddush cups, and much more. Open Sunday to Thursday from 10 a.m. to 4:30 p.m., on Friday to 2:30 p.m.

These are but a fraction of the city's antique shops. For a weekend browsing session, you can explore Hudson Street in Greenwich Village, Amsterdam Avenue from 79th to 86th Streets on the Upper West Side, or the cross streets from 72nd to 86th Street on the upper east side—all are areas with a concentration of antique shops.

APPLIANCES: We'd never buy a stereo, radio, TV, camera, toaster, blow dryer, watch, sewing machine, blender, washing machine—or any other major or minor household appliance—without first comparison-shopping along Canal and Essex Streets on the Lower East Side. The stores listed below all stock a wide variety of brand-new, major-brand household appliances, in perfect condition, with the usual warranties—at prices up to 50% less than those in major department stores! Unless you know exactly what brand and model appliance you want, however, it's a good idea first to stop in at one of the city's better department stores and discuss pros and cons of every make and model with a knowledgeable salesperson. Then simply check out these Lower East Side shops (where gracious service is almost unheard of), and buy where the price is best: they won't give prices on the phone. Ask about refund and exchange policies when you buy, as some of these stores have neither. One last warning—you don't know the meaning of the word "mobbed" if you haven't seen one of these shops on a Sunday; best to go during the week, and preferably in the morning.

Along Essex Street, between Hester and Canal Streets, try:

Dembitzer Bros. Export Company, 5 Essex St. (tel. 254-1310), open Sunday to Thursday from 10 a.m. to 5:45 p.m., on Friday till 2 p.m.

Lewi Supply Company, 15 Essex St. (tel. 777-6910), open Sunday to Thursday from 9 a.m. to 5:30 p.m., on Friday to 2 p.m.

Essex Camera & Electronic Discount Center, 17 Essex St. (tel. 677-6420), open Sunday to Thursday from 10 a.m. to 6 p.m., on Friday to 3 p.m.

Foto Electric Supply Company, 31 Essex St. (tel. 673-5222), open Sunday to Thursday from 9 a.m. to 7 p.m., on Friday till 2 p.m.
Central Electronics, 39 Essex St. (tel. 673-3220), open Sunday to Thursday from 9 a.m. to 6 p.m., on Friday till 2 p.m.
On Canal Street, between Essex and Orchard Streets, try:
ABC Trading Company, 31 Canal St. (tel. 228-5080), open Sunday to Thursday from 10 a.m. to 6 p.m., on Friday to 2 p.m.
Bondy Export Corporation, 40 Canal St. (tel. 925-7785), open Sunday to Thursday from 10 a.m. to 6 p.m., on Friday till 2 p.m.
Kunst Sales Corporation, 45 Canal St. (tel. 966-1909), open Sunday to Thursday from 9 a.m. to 6 p.m., on Friday till 2 p.m. (usually closed Friday during July and August).
Benny's Import & Export, Inc., 51 Canal St. (tel. 925-7535), open Sunday to Thursday from 10 a.m. to 6 p.m., on Friday till 2 p.m.

ARTIST'S SUPPLIES: Worth checking out for art supplies is **Eastern Artists,** 352 Park Ave. South, between 25th and 26th Streets (tel. 725-5555). Housed in a loft on the 11th floor, Eastern offers a full line of artist's supplies at 20% to 50% less than regular prices. Open weekdays from 8:30 a.m. to 6 p.m., on Saturday from 11 a.m. to 5:30 p.m. except during June, July, and August.

Also popular with New York artists for good prices on supplies is **Pearl Paint Company,** 308 Canal St., between Broadway and Church Street (tel. 431-7932). Open Monday to Saturday from 9 a.m. to 5:30 p.m., on Sunday from 11 a.m. to 4:45 p.m. (Closed on Sunday in July and August.)

AUCTIONS: The best place to find major antique pieces at sensible prices is at auction houses. Our favorite is **Sotheby's Arcade Auctions,** 1334 York Ave., at 72nd St. (tel. 606-7410), the "budget" gallery of the wildly expensive Sotheby's. You might be lucky enough to pick up a room-sized Persian carpet for under $1000 at their 10:15 a.m. Tuesday auctions. Items are on exhibit the preceding Thursday, Friday, Saturday, and Monday from 9:30 a.m. to 5 p.m. While you're there, don't hesitate to go up to Sotheby's main galleries on the second floor to ogle, perhaps, the likes of Egyptian carvings or Monet watercolors, or ice-cube-size diamond rings.

The **Lubin Galleries,** 30 W. 26th St., between Fifth and Sixth Avenues (tel. 924-3777), is another place to pick up reasonably priced furniture at auction. Every other Saturday all through the year, beginning at 11 a.m., used and antique furniture is put on auction. Beds, couches, chests of drawers are all available, plus silver, bronzes, Oriental rugs and tapestries, porcelain, china, etc. You can see the items on display the Thursday (10 a.m. to 7 p.m.) and Friday (9 a.m. to 3 p.m.) before the sale. If you can't make the auction, you can leave your bid with a $25 or 25% deposit.

Other auctions of interest:
The **Police Department Auctions of Vehicles and General Property** (tel. 406-1369) for a complete recording of current police auction information—days, times, locations, etc.; for further information, phone 374-5905 and talk to a live person.

The **General Post Office Auction** holds sales every four to six weeks. Phone 971-7761 for information, or check the classified sections of the local papers.

Call the **U.S. Customs Auction** (tel. 466-2924, -2925, or -2926 for information on auction times, dates, locations, etc.). A notice appears in the classified pages of the *New York Times* three Sundays before the day of the auction. At any of the above you might pick up anything and everything, from an unclaimed sofa to a box of hankies, all at extraordinary bargain prices.

BABY CARRIAGES, TOYS, AND FURNITURE: A number of discount-type shops specialize in furniture and accessories for babies.

Albee Baby Carriage, 715 Amsterdam Ave., corner of 95th Street (tel. 662-5740), carries what may be the city's largest selection of carriages: everything from a lightweight aluminum umbrella stroller to custom-made English-style prams. In addition, they carry a full line of juvenile furniture and furnishings, plus a marvelous selection of cribs, beds, toys, infant wear, and dresses—all made by leading manufacturers, yet all selling at a considerable discount. They'll quote prices on the phone. Open from 9 a.m. to 5:30 p.m. Monday to Saturday.

Maclaren strollers, made in England and the biggest-selling strollers in the world, are discounted at **Schneider's,** 20 Avenue A, at the corner of East 2nd Street (tel. 228-3540), in the East Village. Larger strollers and carriages include the Guess line from Germany; these are soft-bodied, have windows, and begin at $175. Schneider's also offers discount-priced baby furniture, as well as a full line of children's toys and nursery accessories. Open Monday to Saturday from 10 a.m. to 6 p.m., on Sunday to 5 p.m.

In business since 1911, emphasizing customer service and very low prices, **Ben's Babyland,** 87 Avenue A, near East 6th Street (tel. 674-1353), is a large store with a wide selection of children's furniture, carriages, layettes, and all related items. A complete line of Silver Cross English prams is priced from $240; the German Teutonia line begins at $200. Open weekdays from 9 a.m. to 6 p.m., on Saturday till 5:30 p.m., and on Sunday till 5 p.m.

Ben's for Kids, 1380 Third Ave., between 78th and 79th Streets (tel. 794-2330), has everything your child will need from the time it is born to the age of about 3—a complete layette department, cribs, crib accessories, high-chairs, toys, clothing, you name it—at way below department store prices. Open Monday to Friday from 10 a.m. to 5 p.m., on Thursday to 8 p.m., on Saturday from 11 a.m. to 5 p.m.

BEAUTY PARLORS AND BARBERSHOPS: Hair care is very expensive in New York, but many women—and men too—have learned to beat the high costs by patronizing beauty schools or training sessions at some of the city's finest beauty salons. You'll be worked on by qualified students who need some live heads to practice on. No need to be alarmed—you can choose the style, the results are usually excellent, and the prices will certainly make you *feel* beautiful.

The biggest school, almost like a private beauty salon, is the **Robert Fiance Hair Design Institute,** 1628 Broadway, at 50th Street (tel. 564-4616), where a complete restyling by an advanced student—haircut, shampoo, and set—begins at $3.50 and can go up; check the price before you start. If you don't want to trust a student to cut your hair, this is still an excellent place to come for a $2 wash and blow dry, a $2 manicure, a $2 eyebrow trim; they also do hair coloring and just about any other service you would receive at a regular salon, but at about half the price. Day hours: Monday through Saturday from 9:30 a.m. to 3 p.m. Evening hours: Monday through Thursday from 6 to 7:30 p.m. There's a senior citizen discount (50%) Monday through Friday from 9:30 a.m. to 2 p.m. No appointment necessary.

Atlas Barber School, 44 Third Ave., between 9th and 10th Streets (tel. 475-1360), cuts men's, women's, and children's hair for $2.75. Hairstyling is $4, a shave is $1, and a facial, $3. Open Monday through Friday from 9 a.m. to 6:30

p.m., on Saturday till 6 p.m. No appointment necessary.

The nicest thing about the training sessions at the fine beauty salons is that you can get your hair done absolutely free! Service is on a first-come, first-served basis (no appointments necessary), at **Daines**, 833 Madison Ave., between 69th and 70th Streets (tel. 535-1563), which has training classes Tuesday and Friday evenings at 6 p.m. And you must arrive at 6 p.m. exactly to get your free shampoo, complete restyling (your choice of hairdo), and blow dry. Daines specializes in a soft, natural look.

A rather different sort of hair shop, performing a rather unique function (and heavily patronized by women seeking absolutely straight hair), is **Jaffry's,** 717 Seventh Ave., at 48th Street (tel. 245-5540), which for over 50 years has been eliminating kinks, curls, and what have you from people's hair. But like all good things, people are finding out about Jaffry's—and when we last visited, there were many clients waiting to be decurled. The reason: a price of only $36 for straightening short hair, which includes a wash and set. (They'll give you an estimate for long hair.) You'd get the same treatment for much more at other salons with results—take it from us—not nearly as good. Phone for an appointment, unless you feel like waiting. Open Tuesday to Friday from 10 a.m. to 7:30 p.m. (last customer at 5:30 p.m.), on Saturday from 8 a.m. to 4 p.m. (last customer at 3 p.m.)

BOOKS, NEW AND SECONDHAND: The most exciting bookstore for bargain-hunters in town has to be the **Barnes & Noble Sale Annex**, occupying a full city block on Fifth Avenue between 17th and 18th Streets (tel. 807-0099). It's the only bookstore we've ever seen that provides supermarket baskets, but that's what you'll need to carry out your finds. Every book in the store (and there are hundreds of thousands) is discounted, from *New York Times* hardcover bestsellers at 33⅓% off, paperbacks from 10% to 25% off, children's books, remainders, reviewers' copies, and scholarly books. It also houses one of the largest classical record departments in New York City. Just across the street is the main Barnes & Noble, which stocks nearly three million hardcovers, paperbacks, and new and used textbooks. Both Barnes & Noble stores are open weekdays from 9:45 a.m. to 6:45 p.m., on Saturday to 6 p.m., and on Sunday from 11 a.m. to 5 p.m.

In the busy midtown area, budget-conscious bookworms head for the **Barnes & Noble** at 600 Fifth Ave., at 48th St. (tel. 765-0590), which offers generous discounts: 15% to 40% off on all hardcover books; 10% to 25% off on all paperback books; and 33⅓% off on all *New York Times* hardcover bestsellers. Open from 9:45 a.m. to 6:45 p.m. weekdays, on Thursday until 8 p.m., until 6 p.m. on Saturday, and from noon to 6 p.m. on Sunday. Both this branch and the downtown store sell discounted records and tapes, mostly classical. You'll also find many smaller Barnes & Nobles in various parts of town: all offer good discount prices.

The once-famous secondhand book area of New York, between Fourth Avenue and Broadway, from 8th to 14th Streets, is declining, but a few stores are still doing business in the old neighborhood. One of the best is the **Abbey Bookshop**, 79 E. 10th St., between Third and Fourth Avenue (tel. 260-5740). Its quarters are jam-packed with secondhand, used, and out-of-print books at discounts of 40% to 50% off, and tables outside offer thousands of books at $1 apiece. Open Monday to Saturday from 11 a.m. to 8 p.m., on Sunday from noon to 6 p.m.

Another vast collection is found at the **Strand**, 828 Broadway, at the corner of 12th Street (tel. 473-1452). At both stores, browsing is not only permitted, but encouraged. It's open weekdays from 9:30 a.m. to 9:30 p.m., on Saturday to

6:30 p.m., on Sunday from 11 a.m. to 5 p.m. The Strand stocks more than two million books on eight miles of bookshelves. It has the largest selection of used books anywhere in the United States, with an emphasis on current reviewers' copies, including bestsellers and new paperbacks at half the publisher's list price.

Forbidden Planet has its original store downtown at 821 Broadway, between 11th and 12th Streets (tel. 473-1576), and a newer store uptown at 227 E. 59th St. (tel. 751-4386). Both locations feature science-fiction books, old and new comic books, original art from comic books, space and science-fiction-oriented toys and games, and sci-fi film memorabilia. They call themselves the largest of their kind, and we believe it. Open from 10 a.m. to 7 p.m. Monday to Saturday, on Sunday from 11 a.m. to 6 p.m.

"Small but mighty" is the way the owners of the **Science Fiction Shop,** 56 Eighth Ave., at Horatio Street in Greenwich Village (tel. 741-0270), characterize their store, in business for over a dozen years and well known to readers worldwide, from Japan to Sweden to Sri Lanka. Visiting science-fiction buffs come from all over the globe to visit the shop when they are in New York. The Science Fiction Shop deals exclusively in the literature of science fiction and fantasy, with a large backstock of titles in print in the United States, supplemented with books brought in from England, both hardcover and paperback. You may find yourself running into an autograph party or special event for such famous writers as Arthur C. Clarke, Isaac Asimov, Anne McCaffrey, and many others. Open weekdays from 11 a.m. to 7:30 p.m., on Saturday to 6 p.m., and on Sunday from noon to 6 p.m.

There's no better bookstore for kids in all New York than **Eeyore's Books for Children,** with locations at 81st Street on both East and West Sides of town: at 1066 Madison Ave. (tel. 988-3404) and at 2252 Broadway (tel. 362-0634). Eeyore's sells only children's books, has a huge selection through which youngsters are invited to browse, and a friendly staff to advise the parents. Look here for hard-to-find classics as well as current children's books, fiction and nonfiction; Eeyore's has them all. As if that weren't enough, they also schedule a number of special events and story hours during the year, all of them free; you might find Isaac Bashevis Singer here signing books, or a magic show, or a slide show on the wonderful world of sharks. If you'd like a schedule of these events, which are held January through May and September through December, or a mail-order catalog, write to either location. The Broadway store is open Monday to Saturday from 10 a.m. to 6 p.m., on Sunday from 10:30 a.m. to 5 p.m.; the Madison Avenue store is open Monday to Saturday from 10 a.m. to 6 p.m., on Sunday from noon to 5 p.m. In the summer the Broadway store's Sunday hours are shortened to noon to 5 p.m., and the Madison Avenue store is closed.

CAMERAS AND COMPUTERS (See also "APPLIANCES"): A dizzying display of photographic paraphernalia meets your eyes when you enter **Willoughby Camera Stores,** at 110 W. 32nd St., near Herald Square (tel. 564-1600). You can get just about anything in the photographic line here, from a Kodak pocket camera for around $20 to a Nikon that goes up into the hundreds. There are projectors, film photo albums, and a complete line of developing and darkroom gear. In addition to all that, Willoughby Peerless has recently expanded to become a leader in the computer, video equipment, audio, and electronic lines as well. They offer one of the largest selections of personal computers and advanced video equipment in the metropolitan area. Bargains are great! They're open weekdays from 9 a.m. to 7 p.m., on Thursday until 8:30 p.m., and on Saturday from 10:30 a.m. to 5:30 p.m. You can also come in from 7:30 a.m. on for early developing and printing services.

When New York's professional photographers need new equipment or film, chances are they'll head for a branch of **Camera Barn,** at 1272 Broadway near 32nd Street, 341 Madison Ave. at 44th Street, downtown at 198 Broadway, and other locations (tel. 947-3510, 867-9280, and 233-3080, respectively). Whether you're interested in a simple Polaroid camera or a sophisticated 35-mm system, you'll find the right prices and a helpful staff. Most branches are open from 8:30 a.m. to 5:45 p.m. on weekdays, on Saturday at 1272 Broadway to 6 p.m., but there is some variation so call to check if you want to make a last-minute purchase.

The buys are often spectacular in cameras, electronics, computers, typewriters, dictation equipment, watches, fine jewelry, and much more at **Forty Seventh Street Photo,** 67 W. 47th St. between Fifth and Sixth Avenues, 115 W. 45th St. between Sixth and Seventh Avenues, 116 Nassau St., and 35 E. 18th St. between Fifth Avenue and Broadway (the latter called the "Professional Photography Store"), (tel. 260-4410 or 608-6934, or toll free 800/221-5858 out of New York state). Huge ads in the *New York Times* list bargains almost daily. The store is often crowded, but the staffs are knowledgeable and the bargains just great. We've seen portable cassette players with earphones selling for almost half the regular department store price, for example. Their prices on film can't be beat either! Open Monday to Thursday from 9 a.m. to 6 p.m., on Friday to 2 p.m., and on Sunday from 10 a.m. to 4 p.m.; closed Saturday. Their catalog is available free for the asking.

Brothers is another big name in New York for good buys in cameras, electronics, and video. Their East Side location at 466 Lexington Ave., corner of 45th Street (tel. 986-3323), is open Monday to Saturday from 8:30 a.m. to 5 p.m., on Sunday from 10 a.m. to 6 p.m. The West Side location, 130 W. 34th St., opposite Macy's (tel. 695-4158), stays open on Monday, Thursday, and Friday from 9 a.m. to 8:30 p.m.; on Tuesday, Wednesday, and Saturday from 9 a.m. to 7:30 p.m.; on Sunday from 10 a.m. to 6 p.m.

CARPETS: **ABC Carpet Company,** two huge stores at 881 and 888 Broadway, at East 19th Street (tel. 677-6970), is perhaps New York's best-known name for rug and carpet values, with thousands of rolls of rugs at very good prices: a recent trip turned up all-wool imported Berber broadlooms, valued at $40 per square yard, selling for $9.90 here. The carpet collection is huge, encompassing everything from fine Orientals for thousands to handmade Indian rugs that might go for as little as $100 for a 9′ by 12′. There are beautiful area rugs, tiles, shades, and Levolor vertical and mini blinds, the latter discounted at 50%. Of course, they deliver and install. People come from all over the area to shop here, so ABC has thoughtfully provided free parking at two nearby garages for its customers: at 17th Street between Broadway and Fifth Avenue, and at the 20th Street Garage, between Fifth and Sixth Avenues. Open 9 a.m. to 6 p.m. Monday through Saturday, on Thursday until 8 p.m., on Sunday from 11 a.m. to 5 p.m. Closed Sunday June through August.

Uptown, on the busy Upper West Side, the **Rug Warehouse,** Broadway at 79th Street (tel. 787-6665), draws those with a keen eye for values. Owner Larry Feldman carries almost 3000 new and used Oriental carpets of the finest quality and at some of the lowest prices you'll find anywhere in this country. Prices begin at less than $200 for a 9- by 12-foot Oriental-style carpet. Open seven days a week from 11 a.m. to 5 p.m.

CHILDREN'S CLOTHING: For fabulous discounts on children's clothing, we suggest you venture across the river and into **Brooklyn.** If you're willing to brave the largest shopping crowds you've ever encountered (leave the children at home when you visit this store), you'll discover superb discounts on better children's clothing (brand names every mother will recognize) at **Natan Borlam,** 157 Havemeyer St., near South 2nd Street, *Brooklyn* (tel. 718/387-2983). You'll find underwear, dresses, suits, snowsuits, coats, tights, polo shirts, etc.—many with top-name labels still in them and most at discounts ranging from 25% to 50%. They also carry teenage and ladies' clothing. Take the IRT–Lexington Avenue subway to Brooklyn Bridge, then change to the BMT (Jamaica line) QB train. Take the BMT to Marcy Avenue, get off, and walk four blocks to 157 Havemeyer St. Borlam's is open Sunday to Thursday from 10 a.m. to 5 p.m., on Friday from 10 a.m. until 2:30 p.m. If Borlam's doesn't have what you want (which is highly unlikely), then browse around Havemeyer Street; it's dotted with discount shops offering children's furniture and clothing.

The discount houses offer the best value in new children's clothing; the **resale shops** offer the biggest bargains in hand-me-downs, some of them quite elegant and bearing name tags from high-fashion stores like Saks Fifth Avenue and Bergdorf Goodman. One of the oldest and best of these in town is **Second Act,** 1046 Madison Ave. (upstairs), between 79th and 80th Streets (tel. 988-2440), where you can purchase outgrown clothing in excellent condition, often items that have been worn only a few times, at prices 50% less than the original. Many French and English imports, as well as American-made coats, toddlers' snowsuits, girls' skirts, boys' slacks, Levis, jackets, etc. We've even seen ski and riding gear. Every item is freshly cleaned and only the latest styles are sold. In addition, Second Act has a large selection of children's books (from 15¢ to $3), a smattering of handcrafted items at less than boutique prices, and used ice skates. Open Tuesday to Saturday from 10 a.m. to 5 p.m.; closed Saturday in July and August.

As for New York department stores, **Ohrbach's** and **Alexander's** (see "Women's Clothing and Accessories," above, for addresses) are known for inexpensive children's clothing, with Ohrbach's often selling imported children's clothes at considerably less than those of the Fifth Avenue emporiums. But nothing can beat the twice-yearly sales (usually around January and July) at **Saks Fifth Avenue,** 611 Fifth Ave., between 49th and 50th Streets (tel. 753-4000), when crowds of hungry mothers from everywhere swoop down on the children's department to realize savings of anywhere from 30% to 50% on beautiful merchandise. (Savings are huge all over the store during these sales.) Saks is open Monday to Saturday from 10 a.m. to 6 p.m., and on Thursday nights to 8 p.m.

A favorite of budget-wise East Side mamas is **Melnikoff's,** at 1594 York Ave., corner of 84th Street (tel. 288-2419), where name-brand children's merchandise is all discounted 10%. They specialize in clothing and equipment for sending children to camp. Open Monday through Saturday from 9 a.m. to 6 p.m.

West Side mothers watch for the twice-yearly sales (July–August and January–February) at **Morris Brothers Department Store,** 2322 Broadway, at 84th Street (tel. 724-9000), when the pickings are good in name-brand children's clothing. The store has a large and varied selection and specializes in jeans—many of them for mothers and fathers as well as kids. Open from 9:30 a.m. to 6:30 p.m. Monday through Saturday.

On New York's Lower East Side you should check out the following:

A & G Infants & Children's Wear, 261 Broome St., between Orchard and Allen Streets (tel. 966-3775), sells name-brand (Healthtex, Ruth Scharf, Youngland, Carter, etc.) children's clothes at discounts of about 25%. You can get clothes here for infants to preteens. Open Sunday to Thursday from 10 a.m. to 5 p.m., on Friday to sundown.

Similar wares and hours at **Rice & Breskin,** 323 Grand St., corner of Orchard Street (tel. 925-5515); **Nathan Kurtz Textiles,** 27 Canal St., between Essex and Ludlow Streets (475-6550), which also has good buys on linens and hosiery for men and women; **Kleins of Monticello,** 105 Orchard St., between Delancey and Broome Streets (tel. 966-1453); and **M. Kreinen & Co., Inc.,** 301 Grand St., between Allen and Eldridge Streets (tel. 925-0239).

CHINA, POTTERY, CRYSTAL, AND GLASSWARE:

We have no problem making our choice here: the most exciting, low-cost shop in the country for modern design in home accessories, tableware, and cookware is the **Pottery Barn,** which has eight New York City branches: a huge warehouse store at 231 Tenth Ave., between 23rd and 24th Streets (tel. 206-8118), consisting of three floors and a basement; a store at 117 E. 59th St., between Park and Lexington Avenues (tel. 753-5424); at 250 W. 57th St., at Eighth Avenue (tel. 315-1855); one at 51 Greenwich Ave., between Sixth and Seventh Avenues in the Village (tel. 807-6321); at 2109 Broadway at 74th Street (tel. 595-5573); at 700 Broadway, at 4th Street (tel. 505-6377); at 1451 Second Ave., at 76th Street (tel. 988-4228); and at 87th Street and Lexington Avenue, just behind Gimbels East (tel. 289-2477). All are under the imaginative management of Hoyt Chapin, who—through mass purchasing and low overhead—manages to sell stunning imported modernistic designs, most of which are manufactured according to his own specifications, at low, low prices. You'll find kitchenware, dishes, glassware, mugs, vases, baskets, picture frames, rugs, storage systems, and casual furniture. Many items are now manufactured in China. Pottery Barn will ship anywhere in the United States. All stores are open on Sunday from noon to 5 p.m., and from 10:30 a.m. to 6:30 p.m. weekdays; most stores have some evening hours. A recent visit turned up excellent buys in frames, white porcelain dinnerware, and 11-ounce wineglasses.

A high-rent, prime midtown location does not deter **Robin Importers,** 510 Madison Ave., between 52nd and 53rd Streets (tel. 753-6475 or 752-5605), from offering generous discounts—30% to 60% on most items—on china, stainless flatware, stoneware, giftware, and table linens by major manufacturers. They show over 150 patterns in stainless and china. Open Monday to Friday from 9 a.m. to 6 p.m., on Saturday from 10 a.m. to 5 p.m. They ship anywhere in the United States via UPS: for ordering out of New York state, call toll free 800/223-3373.

For gifts or china and crystal for your own home, **J. Finkelstein** at 95 Delancey St., between Orchard and Ludlow Streets on the Lower East Side (tel. 674-9582), has a superb selection of name-brand items and art objects at 20% to 50% lower than uptown prices. They also have a fine collection of cabinets, screens, chests, and other Oriental furniture, much of it from mainland China. Open Sunday to Friday from 9 a.m. to 5 p.m.

Similar wares and discounts are found at these other Lower East Side shops, most of which also carry sterling silver:

Crystal Clear, 55 Delancey St., between Allen and Eldridge Streets (tel. 925-8783), open Sunday to Thursday from 10 a.m. to 5 p.m.

Rogers and Rosenthal, Inc., 105 Canal St., corner of Forsyth Street (tel. 925-7557), open weekdays only from 10 a.m. to 5 p.m.

Greater New York Trading Company, 81 Canal St., between Allen and Eldridge Streets (tel. 226-2808), open Monday to Thursday from 10 a.m. to 6 p.m., on Friday till 3 p.m., and on Sunday from 9:30 a.m. to 5:30 p.m.

Lanac Sales Company, 73 Canal St., corner of Allen Street (tel. 925-6422), open Monday to Thursday from 10 a.m. to 6 p.m., on Friday till 2 p.m., and on Sunday from 9 a.m. to 5 p.m.

Over on Grand Street, between Ludlow and Essex Streets, check out **Grand Sterling Company, Inc.**, 345 Grand St. (tel. 674-6450), open Sunday to Thursday from 10:30 a.m. to 5:30 p.m.; closed Friday. They have another store at 4921 Thirteenth Ave. in *Brooklyn* (tel. 718/854-0263).

East Side Gifts and Chinaware, 351 Grand St. (tel. 982-7200), open Sunday to Thursday from 9 a.m. to 5:30 p.m., on Friday to 3:30 p.m.

CIGARS: Cigar lovers should run over to **J-R Tobacco**, 11 E. 45th St., just off Fifth Avenue (tel. 869-8777), where cigars are 30% to 40% off retail. A free newsletter (ask to be put on the mailing list) tells which cigars will be specially discounted; one brand is featured daily. Open weekdays from 8 a.m. to 6 p.m., on Saturday from 9 a.m. to 4 p.m. Other locations are: 1410 Broadway, at 39th Street; 505 Park Ave., at 59th Street; and 219 Broadway, between Vesey and Barclay Streets, downtown.

COSMETICS: For fantastic buys in top-quality cosmetics, head for the **Make-Up Center,** 150 W. 55th St., between Sixth and Seventh Avenues (tel. 977-9494), where models and actresses have been shopping for years. The center sells its own line of products, called "Allure," for half of what regular name brands cost. Available treatments are eyebrow shaping and tweezing, makeup consultations, facials, manicures, and pedicures. Because so many models have their makeup applied here, you must make an appointment for the consultation. Best of all, there's no pressure to buy the products. Open Monday through Friday from 4 a.m. to 6 p.m., until 8 p.m. on Thursday, until 5 p.m. on Saturday.

Clairol Consumer Research Center, 345 Park Ave. (tel. 546-2707), is always seeking consumer responses to their new and existing hair- and skin-care products. Women and men are invited to make an appointment to come in to test products—using them as they would at home. You might be asked to test a hair color, cream rinse, or skin-care product. Each consumer is given a complimentary package of samples. Call the above number to arrange an appointment. To be absolutely sure of getting a convenient appointment, it might be wise to write or phone several weeks before your visit.

If you'd like to relax with a facial while you're in New York, call the **Christine Valmy International School,** 260 Fifth Ave., at 28th Street (tel. 581-1520). The beauty school from this famous Fifth Avenue salon will cream, massage, and pamper you for the bargain rate of $12.50. All the operators have completed the school course and are putting in hours of hands-on training. Your facial will be completely supervised by an instructor. All products and techniques are exactly the same as at the salon, and are for men as well as women. In addition, waxing is offered at less-than-salon rates. Appointments, which should be scheduled two to three days in advance, are available Monday to Friday only, at 10 and 11:30 a.m. and at 2 and 4 p.m.; on Monday and Wednesday, also at 6:30 p.m.

"i" Natural Cosmetics, 737 Madison Ave. (tel. 734-0664), sells cosmetics that sound, look, and smell so good you might be tempted to eat them instead of using them on your skin, but don't! They'll do better things for the outside of your body than for the inside. Try some Real Grapefruit Freshener or Chamomile Lemon Shampoo. Open Monday through Saturday from 10 a.m. to 6 p.m.

Caswell-Massey Co., Ltd., 518 Lexington Ave. (tel. 755-2254), is still formulating and selling the same cologne that George Washington used. Try some if you're feeling presidential, or if you're in a lighter mood, buy a cake of any of their aromatic hard-milled soaps. Caswell-Massey is the oldest chemists and perfumers in America, founded in 1752, with a superb line of toiletries and personal-care items, many from Great Britain and Europe. The main store on

Lexington Avenue is open weekdays from 9 a.m. to 6 p.m., on Saturday from 10 a.m. to 6 p.m. There are branches at 21 Fulton St., at the South Street Seaport (tel. 608-5401), open Monday to Saturday from 10 a.m. to 10 p.m. and on Sunday from noon to 8 p.m. in season (Monday to Saturday from 10 a.m. to 9 p.m. and on Sunday from noon to 6 p.m. out of season); and at One Herald Square (tel. 244-0411), open on Monday, Thursday, and Friday from 9:45 a.m. to 8:30 p.m., on Tuesday and Wednesday to 6:45 p.m., on Saturday to 6 p.m., and on Sunday from noon to 6 p.m.

Boyd Chemist, 655 Madison Ave. (tel. 838-5524), is the place to go for unusual and imported cosmetics and beauty supplies. The cosmeticians will gladly give you a demonstration of any product you buy, such as eye shadow, for a glamorous professional look. They also carry designer fashion jewelry. Open Monday through Friday from 8:30 a.m. to 7 p.m., on Saturday from 9:30 a.m. to 6 p.m. Closed Saturday in July and August.

DISCOUNT HOUSES: The city's cheapest discount shop is the **99¢ Shop,** with branches at 591 Lexington Ave., corner of 52nd Street (tel. 753-6969); 1457 Broadway, between 41st and 42nd Streets (tel. 354-0111); 89 Chambers St., between Church Street and Broadway (tel. 267-6722); 33 W. 8th St., between Fifth and Sixth Avenues (tel. 475-6951); 144 Fulton St., between Broadway and Nassau Street (tel. 964-2142); and 250 W. 57th St., between Broadway and Eighth Avenue (tel. 581-1040). Every single item in these stores—including such drugstore goods as toothpaste, shaving creams, and makeup—is sold for only 99¢. At the 57th Street branch there are also $1.99, $3.99, and $9.99 departments. The regular manufacturers' prices are left on the merchandise display signs to remind you of your savings. There's a complete hardware and auto accessory department, a gadget and novelty section, food and candy department, toys and a book department, and a gigantic housewares department. The 591 Lexington Ave. store is open Monday to Wednesday from 7:30 a.m. to 7 p.m., on Thursday to 9 p.m., and on Friday to 6 p.m.; the 1457 Broadway store, Monday to Wednesday from 8 a.m. to 7 p.m., on Thursday to 9 p.m., on Friday to 6 p.m., and on Sunday from noon to 6 p.m.; 89 Chambers St. is open weekdays only from 8 a.m. to 6 p.m.; 33 W. 8th St. is open Sunday to Thursday from 11 a.m. to 10 p.m., on Friday and Saturday to midnight; hours for the Fulton Street store are 7:30 a.m. to 6 p.m. weekdays. The 57th Street branch is open weekdays from 8 a.m. to 7 p.m., on Saturday from 11 a.m. to 6 p.m., and on Sunday from noon to 6 p.m.

DRUGS AND VITAMINS: Prescriptions Limited has three locations: at 1151 Madison Ave., at 85th Street (tel. 628-3210); at 880 Madison Ave., at 71st Street (tel. 737-1800); and at 1147 Third Ave., at 67th Street (tel. 879-5115). This is the place to head to if you need a prescription filled. All drugs are at least 30% less (and often 50%) than at regular commercial pharmacies. The bargains are equally good in vitamins, as **Vitamin Factory Outlets,** located in Prescriptions Limited, offers a huge selection and very low prices (even lower than mail order) on all natural and organic vitamins: no sugar, starch, artificial colors, flavoring, salt, or preservatives. You can get a free vitamin consultation and a free catalog, which enables you to order from home via a toll-free number. Other health products, such as surgical supplies and appliances, are also discounted. Show them this listing and receive an additional 10% discount. All branches are open Monday through Friday from 9 a.m. to 6 p.m., on Saturday from 10 a.m. to 2 p.m.

For a complete line of drugstore items, as well as prescriptions, try the **Drug Loft** at 1103 Lexington Ave., at 77th Street (tel. 879-0910). Ordinary drugstore products are sold at a discount of at least 20%. Prescriptions are 20% to 50% lower than at regular drugstores. Vaporizers, hair dryers, surgical stockings, Thermoses, electric heating pads, hot-water bottles, and everything else are all at low, low prices. And since the Fair Trade laws have now been repealed, cosmetics too are also discounted. Open Monday through Friday from 8:30 a.m. to 7:30 p.m., on Saturday from 9 a.m. to 5 p.m.

DRY GOODS: For towels, linens, curtains, bedspreads, comforters with matching sheets, decorative pillows, and draperies, **Ezra Cohen,** 305 Grand St., at Allen Street, on the Lower East Side (tel. 925-7800), is a bargain shop that offers name brands at prices at least 20% lower than comparable uptown shops. Send for their free catalog. Open Sunday to Friday from 9 a.m. to 5 p.m.

Continuing along Grand Street, between Allen and Forsyth Streets, you'll find over ten more dry goods stores stocking similar wares. It's a good idea to comparison-shop for the best styles and prices.

The Wholesale House, 2960 Avenue U, off Nostrand Avenue, *Brooklyn* (tel. 718/891-5800), is worth a trip on the BMT to buy designer bedroom and bathroom linens and accessories at tremendous discounts. All the major brands are sold at below "White Sale" prices. They can custom-design your bedroom using sheet fabrics of your choice. Open Monday through Saturday from 10 a.m. to 5:30 p.m. Take the IRT–Lexington Avenue subway to Brooklyn Bridge, and charge there for the BMT (Brighton Beach line, QB train). Get off at Avenue U and take the Avenue U bus to Nostrand Avenue.

ELECTROLYSIS: Electrolysis need not be expensive. At the **Kree Institute of Electrolysis,** 1500 Broadway at 43rd Street, fifth floor (tel. 730-9700), you can have a student, under professional supervision, work on you for just $10 an hour. (Electrolysis is the only A.M.A.-approved method of permanent hair removal.) Come in Monday to Friday from 10:30 a.m. to noon or 3 to 5 p.m.; no appointment necessary.

"Experience is what counts in electrolysis," says **Margaret Railton-Jones,** who claims she can get as much done in a quarter hour—for which she charges $15—than others can in a much longer period of time. Margaret, who is at 850 Seventh Ave. (tel. 582-5338), gives personalized, very professional service, and also offers very good rates on waxing, facials, and eyebrow styling, a particular specialty. Please mention this book for special rates.

EYEGLASSES: The very best choice for huge discounts is **Cohen's Optical,** 117 Orchard St., corner of Delancey Street (tel. 674-1986), where the choice, including all top-designer frames—Givenchy, Dior, Pierre Cardin, Yves St. Laurent, etc.—numbers into the thousands! You get a free examination when you buy glasses here, and prices for a complete pair begin at $14.95. They also have contact lenses. Another advantage at Cohen's is two hours of free parking (they reimburse you) at the Municipal Garage on Essex Street between Rivington and Delancey Streets. Open Monday to Saturday from 9 a.m. to 6 p.m., on Sunday to 5:45 p.m.

You can choose from hundreds of first-quality frames—many of them by top designers—at **Empire Optical,** 19 W. 34th St., between Fifth and Sixth Avenues, Room 1107, 11th floor (tel. 244-8588). Discounts on frames and lenses are in the 30% to 50% range. Bring your prescription or a correct pair of glasses. Open Monday to Thursday from 10 a.m. to 6 p.m., on Friday to 2 p.m.

Another good bet for leading designer frames is the half-century-old **Manhattan Optical,** 235 Canal St., corner of Centre Street (tel. 226-8050). They also carry contact lenses and do examinations on the premises. Discounts are about

30%, with glasses beginning at $18.95. Open weekdays from 9 a.m. to 6 p.m., on Saturday to 5 p.m., on Sunday from 10 a.m. to 4 p.m.

FABRICS, LOW COST: The Lower East Side of New York is the place to find fabrics at the cheapest prices in America. The streets here are jammed with little stores that are themselves jammed with bolts of cloth, scraps of cloth, bits of fur, and suit materials.

Also, be sure to shop West 40th Street between Seventh and Eighth Avenues for an exciting array of high-fashion fabrics at reasonable prices.

Your first stop could be at one of **Sam Beckenstein's** two establishments. The shop at 125 Orchard St. features men's suiting fabrics, many from England and Italy, in pure worsteds and blends, for a fraction of the price charged in midtown textile marts. The ladies' shop, at 130 Orchard St., carries laces, embroideries, imported wools, and silk couturier fabrics, as well as patterns and notions, and also slipcovers, upholstery goods, and custom draperies made to order. The phone number for both is 475-4525; they are located between Rivington and Delancey Streets, and both are open Sunday through Friday from 9 a.m. to 5:30 p.m.

Pay a visit, too, to **Harry Snyder,** 70 Hester St., between Allen and Orchard Streets (tel. 925-0855), which has lovely imports and designer fabrics—woolens, silks, cottons, novelty fabrics, etc., at about one-third the original cost. Open Sunday to Thursday from 9 a.m. to 5:30 p.m., till 5 p.m. on Friday.

An uptown store specializing in low-priced fabrics is **Ashil Fabrics,** at 101 W. 34th St., at Broadway, underground, near the subway entrance (tel. 560-9049). It carries every conceivable type of cloth, from cotton remnants to elegant brocades and upholstery fabrics, all sold at discount prices. Open Monday to Saturday from 9:30 a.m. to 6 p.m.

Another good place to buy fabrics at near-wholesale prices is **Art Max,** 250 W. 40th St., between Seventh and Eighth Avenues (tel. 398-0755). The store is jammed with bolts of imported and domestic fabrics of all types and patterns. Bridal fabrics—imported French laces, Swiss embroidered organza, and the like—are specialties here, as are "mother of the bride fabrics"—imported beaded silk chiffons, chantilly and metallic laces. Salespeople are highly knowledgeable and are fluent in most languages. Be sure to go downstairs where lots of bargains are to be found. Open from 8:30 a.m. to 6 p.m. Monday through Friday, on Saturday from 9 a.m. to 5 p.m.

If you're handy with a needle or know somebody who is, check out the terrific values at **Frontier Fabrics,** 144 Chambers St. (right at the IRT subway stop), a warehouse-outlet store for a huge line of fabrics for dresses, sportswear, and upholstery as well. Biggest sellers here are the printed materials (percale, poly-cotton blends, all cotton, etc.) for $1.75 a yard, which would sell for $4 to $6 elsewhere, and their solid-color materials at $1.50 and $1.75 a yard. Artists come here for their canvases, $1.50 and $2.50 a yard. And upholstery fabrics start at a low $3 a yard. Open Monday to Saturday from 9:30 a.m. to 6 p.m., on Wednesday to 7 p.m.

The **Fabric Warehouse,** 406 Broadway (tel. 431-9510), is three floors of fabrics, trimmings, patterns, and anything else you might ever need for home sewing at amazing discount prices—they have a great selection of fabrics for under $2 a yard. Open Monday, Tuesday, Wednesday, and Friday from 9 a.m. to 6 p.m., on Thursday to 7:30 p.m., and on Saturday and Sunday from 10 a.m. to 5 p.m.

FLEA MARKETS: New Yorkers are far from immune to the nationwide flea market fever. And at the risk of bragging, or markets feature great selections of unusual and interesting collectibles, antiques, and junk. Also, many feature cut-rate factory overruns, seconds, and just plain bargains from metropolitan area factories and businesses, including designer jeans, tools, cosmetics, and shoes. Some of the best are:

Annex Antiques and Flea Market, Avenue of the Americas and 26th Street (tel. 243-5343), is open on Sunday from April through October. There's an admission charge for adults; children are let in for free. Primarily antique dealers, but you can find beautiful Victorian petticoats side-by-side with antique cameras or magazines. It's one of Manhattan's largest outdoor fleas.

Walter's World Famous Le Flea Market, 252 Bleecker St. in Greenwich Village (tel. 255-0175), is housed in a former supermarket, but the goodies are much more exciting now: collectibles, antiques, art deco furnishings, old and new jewelry, rare phonograph records, collectors' toys, movie memorabilia, lots more. It's great fun. Walter's is open year round, on Thursday and Sunday from noon to 8 p.m., on Friday until 9 p.m., on Saturday until 10 p.m.

Canal Street Flea Market, Canal and Greene Streets (tel. 226-7541), is where you'll find New Wave women trying on pointy-toed shoes and uptown dealers buying pocket watches for their shops—it's very eclectic. Open Saturday and Sunday from 9 a.m. to 6 p.m. year round (weather permitting).

You'll have to leave Manhattan to find one of the *nation's* largest fleas. **Barterama,** at Aqueduct Racetrack, South Ozone Park, Queens (tel. 516/775-8774), sells mainly new merchandise. Here's where you'll find the jeans you've seen in department stores at $35 plus for less than $20. The same is true for shoes, sneakers, lunch boxes, cowboy hats, tools, cosmetics, ad infinitum. Barterama operates at Aqueduct on Tuesday, Saturday, and Sunday from mid-April to mid-December; a similar flea market is at Belmont from early May through October and again from late October through late December. For exact dates, consult the local papers or phone the number above (on Wednesday only). Admission is $1 per carload on Tuesday, $1.50 per carload on the weekend.

FLOWERS AND PLANTS: The wholesale flower district of New York is located on Sixth Avenue around 28th Street—it's a tourist attraction in itself—and many of the wholesale distributors will sell to individuals at prices quite a bit lower than your corner florist would charge. If you're looking for something in particular—window box plants, cacti, etc.—check out all the stores and comparison-shop.

One of the best stores in the area is **Bill's Flower Market,** 816 Sixth Ave., at 28th Street (tel. 889-8154), where top-quality fresh flowers can be had for very reasonable prices. Bill's also has dried flowers, seeds, and lovely silk flowers. They offer all florist services too—FTD, Interflora, etc. Open Monday to Friday from 8 a.m. to 5:30 p.m.

FOAM: The **Economy Foam Center,** 173 E. Houston St., at First Avenue (tel. 473-4462), cuts foam to size, custom covers cushions in vinyl or fabric, sells materials, quilts, pillows, mattresses, and highriser covers, all at discounted prices. Herculon upholstery fabric costs $7.50 here; it's normally $12.50 a yard or more elsewhere. You can also buy bedding, sheets, and pillow cases. Open Sunday through Friday from 9:30 a.m. to 6 p.m.

FRAMES: **Make a Frame,** 406 Third Ave., near 28th Street (tel. 684-1215), is the place to go for do-it-yourself framing in a friendly, informal atmosphere. Low prices and plenty of help in this neighborhood shop where everyone from youngsters to local matrons to artists works together framing their own creations or someone else's. Savings are considerable. Open Monday to Thursday from 11 a.m. to 8:30 p.m., on Friday and Saturday to 7 p.m.

FURNITURE: The **Salvation Army Stores,** the larger of which is at 536 W. 46th St., between Tenth and Eleventh Avenues (tel. 757-2311), are two large warehouses full of furniture, books, toys, clothing, and bedding. The furniture is old, some of it antique, some even stylish, but it costs peanuts, and can often be used for those staple furniture items (beds, for instance) whose appearance you may not care about. Speaking of beds, the Salvation Army Store has nearly an entire floor of them, assembled or disassembled into mattresses, frames, and bedsteads. A double bed with box spring, headboard, mattress, and frame recently went for $95. Open from 9 a.m. to 5 p.m. Monday through Saturday. Delivery service is available. There are six other Salvation Army Stores in Manhattan; check your phonebook for listings.

Perhaps the most imaginative budget-priced furniture stores in town are the **Bon Marché** shops, in the Bon Marché building at 55 W. 13th St., between Fifth and Sixth Avenues (furniture on the sixth floor, lamps and accessories on the seventh floor) (tel. 620-5550), and also at 1060 Third Ave., at 63rd Street (tel. 620-5592). They have literally cornered the market of young couples who want to decorate their apartments inexpensively in Scandinavian-modern style. They are best known for their price and range on all kinds of drawer units and bookcases (we've seen big teakwood bookcases selling for $60 each), Danish teak extension tables, and quality Italian chrome goods. Prices on their exclusive glove-soft leather sofas, made for them in Italy, are so extraordinary—about $859 for an 84-inch sofa, $1150 for a convertible double bed—that shipments regularly sell out. A recent trip turned up marble tops from Italy and Portugal selling at one-third to one-quarter off the going price. Prices are considerably lower than comparable merchandise elsewhere. And, rare for New York, everything that's on the floor is in stock—which means instant delivery. Customers can pick up or pay for delivery. Just browsing here is a pleasure. All three stores are open Monday to Saturday from 10:30 a.m. to 6:30 p.m.; the Third Avenue store stays open till 9 p.m. on Thursday nights.

The **Castro Convertible Clearance Center,** 43 W. 23rd St., between Fifth and Sixth Avenues (tel. 255-7000), has many floors (plus a mezzanine) jam-packed with convertible sofas, modular groups, recliners, tables, bedroom furniture, wall units, box springs, mattresses, lamps, and much more. Convertibles can be custom-covered to your order; dozens of floor samples are ready for immediate delivery. Open Monday to Friday from 10 a.m. to 9 p.m., on Saturday to 7 p.m., and on Sunday from 11 a.m. to 6 p.m. They ship anywhere. There's free parking on the premises at all times.

Plexi-Craft Quality Products Corporation, 514 W. 24th St., between Tenth and Eleventh Avenues (tel. 924-3244), is a factory that sells to the public at net prices—about 50% less than retail! They have Plexiglas and Lucite tables, chairs, magazine racks, telephone stands, cubes, shelving, you name it. Shipping is available. Open weekdays from 9:30 a.m. to 5 p.m., on Saturday from 11 a.m. to 4 p.m.; closed Sunday.

Along the **Bowery,** between Hester and Delancey Streets, are many restaurant supply stores that also sell to the public at far below list prices. The range of goods is wide—everything from bar stools, to tables, to commercial dishes and cooking equipment, cabinets, tables, chairs, etc.

GIFTS AND MISCELLANEOUS ITEMS (See also "CHINA, POTTERY, CRYSTAL, AND GLASSWARE"): **Noto,** 245 W. 72nd St., between Broadway and West End Avenue (tel. 877-7562), is the place for tasteful gift items, at

prices considerably less than those on the East Side or in the department stores. Note the the beautiful hand-printed bedspreads in Indian cotton fabric, from $15; the jewelry (especially earrings) from Bali, China, India, and Mexico, some of it costly, but a good deal in the $15 range; the imported lamps from Italy and the Orient; the tastefully matted and framed prints, beginning at $30; and the hand-finished reproductions of fanciful decorative mirrors, copies of French, Florentine, and English antiques, very popular, from $12 to $35. A large back gallery features occasional pieces, some from the Far East, some American country pieces. There are tasteful cards and free gift wrapping too. Noto is open Monday to Saturday from 10 a.m. to 7 p.m., on Sunday from noon to 6 p.m.

Collector's Cabinet, 153 E. 57th St., between Lexington and Third Avenues (tel. 355-2033), is one of several stores sharing the same address. It's like visiting a museum, with price tags. There are semiprecious minerals and gems, fossils, seashells, and an impressive collection of ancient art and artifacts. You can buy, for instance, an ancient Roman bronze statue, life-size, for $250,000. In other words, bring your children only if you're comfortable around such pricey tags. Open Monday through Saturday from 10 a.m. to 6 p.m.

Depending on what they have in stock on the day you visit, a stop at **Job Lot Trading Company, Inc.** (also known as "The Puschcart"), at 140 Church St., between Chambers and Warren Streets, and at 80 Nassau St., near Fulton Street, downtown (tel. 962-4142), and 412 Fifth Ave., at 37th Street (tel. 398-9210), could be one of the memorable shopping experiences of New York. You'll find everything and anything from famous-name children's toys to fishing rods, from toothpaste to knapsacks, to boxes of candy, all of them discounted at least 50%. The crowds are thick. The uptown store is open Monday to Saturday from 8:30 a.m. to 6:30 p.m.; the downtown Job Lots are open from 7:45 a.m. to 6:15 p.m. Monday to Saturday.

New York's Japanese shops are good places for inexpensive gifts. The most exciting selection of wares is at **Azuma**—wicker furnishings, basketry, bedspreads, clothing, paper lampshades, toys, stationery, mugs, saki sets, tea services, posters, paper flowers, papier-mâché boxes, you name it! You'll feel as if you're at an exotic fair. One of the fine Azuma stores is at 666 Lexington Ave., near 56th Street (tel. 752-0599); see the phone book for other addresses.

Odd Job Trading, 7 E. 40th St., just off Fifth Avenue (tel. 686-6825), 149 W. 32nd St., between Sixth and Seventh Avenues, at the Penta Hotel (tel. 564-7370), and 66 W. 48th St., between Fifth and Sixth Avenues (tel. 575-0422), sells brand-name close-out toiletries, linens, stationery, glassware and china, tools, toys, and just about anything else you could think of at low, low prices. Open Monday through Friday from 8 a.m. to 6 p.m. All stores close early on Friday nights during the winter and are closed all day Saturday. Open on Sunday from 10 a.m. to 5 p.m. (except July and August).

Welcome to New York City, 26 Carmine St., near Bleecker Street and Avenue of the Americas (tel. 242-6714), is a good source for unusual New York souvenirs. They carry antique and modern maps, photos, posters, prints and memorabilia, plus unusual T-shirts and souvenirs. Stop in and treat yourself to a one-of-a-kind remembrance of your trip. Open Monday through Saturday from 11 a.m. to 8 p.m., on Sunday from 1 to 5 p.m.

Hoffritz For Cutlery has several locations around Manhattan, at Grand Central Station (tel. 682-7808), Penn Station (tel. 736-2443), 331 Madison Ave. (tel. 697-7344), and 203 W. 57th St., between Seventh and Eighth Avenues (tel. 757-3431). Try one of the shops for pocket knives, scissors, kitchen gadgets, and unique shaving equipment. They hold 50%-off sales on their high-quality cutlery periodically, and you can really get an excellent buy at that time. The stores are usually open from 9 a.m. to 5 p.m. Monday through Saturday; check with each individual store for exact hours.

If you like crystals or geodes, amber or semiprecious jewelry, check out **Astro Mineral Gallery,** 155 E. 34th St. (tel. 889-9000). They have an extensive, well-priced collection of rocks, petrified wood, sculpture, and jewelry, all sold in a relaxed and beautiful gallery setting (with fountains and ponds). Their selection of crystals is outstanding. Admire precious rocks selling for thousands of dollars or purchase a string of beggar beads for under $10. There's a large selection of jewelry including tiger eye, garnet, carnelian, malachite, and rose quartz in the $10- to $20-per-strand price range. You may luck into a 50%-off sale. Open Monday through Friday from 10 a.m. to 6 p.m., on Saturday and Sunday from noon to 6 p.m.

The **South Street Seaport** and its new **Marketplace** have a bevy of exciting shops already, and more are in the offing. Shops are entertaining, but not of the bargain variety. Of special interest is **Bowne & Co. Stationers,** a re-creation of a print shop typical of those found in mid-19th century New York, and named for a real firm established in 1775. It's located at 211 Water St., on the first floor of a Greek Revival building dating back to the 1830s. Here you will find demonstrations of letterpress printing, workshops, and classes, plus stationery items, antique and contemporary, for sale.

Have a look, too, in Schermerhorn Row, at **Brookstone,** which looks like a giant mail-order catalog of unusual hardware and gadgets come to life; and at **Captain Hook's,** laden port to stern with marine antiques, brass fittings, seashells, and seashell jewelry. Around the corner from Schermerhorn Row are the Front Street Shops, where you should have a look at **Mickey & Co.,** which boasts an unbelievable array of Mickey Mouse–themed clothing; and at **Maja,** with heaps of stunning costume jewelry at reasonable prices. Stop to browse through the $1 outside bins and the vast array of books indoors at the **Strand Book Store,** a branch of the famed bookstore on 12th Street and Broadway (see above).

Cannon's Walk, just across from the Fulton Market, is another charming little shopping area. **Ambassador Cove Pottery** has many nice handmade things at reasonable prices. And there's a branch here of **Caswell-Massey,** America's oldest apothecary shop, whose goods arrived from Europe 200 years ago on these very docks. Try something traditional: perhaps the Williamsburg Potpourri for $7, whose fragrance fills the store.

Over 100 new shops, restaurants, and cafés were set to open at the Seaport's newest addition, **Pier 17 Pavilion,** after this book went to press. Shopping here promises to be the most scenic in New York: public promenades of the steel-and-glass pavilion, set on a pier that extends out into the East River, open to vistas of the Brooklyn Bridge to the north and New York harbor to the south.

HARDWARE: Come to Canal Street and rummage for bargains (job lot and close-out merchandise, for the most part) in the bins that line both street and stores in this area. **Quality Hardware,** 322 Canal St., between Broadway and Church Street (tel. 226-0128), is open daily from 8 a.m. to 6:30 p.m. and carries everything from twine to power tools. Other stores worth checking out: **Canal Hardware,** 311 Canal St., corner of Mercer Street (tel. 226-0825), open Monday to Saturday from 8 a.m. to 6 p.m., on Sunday from 10 a.m. to 5 p.m.; and **Canal Street General Store,** 312 Canal St., between Broadway and Church Street (tel. 925-4705), open seven days a week from 10 a.m. to 6 p.m.

KITCHENWARE (See also "CHINA, POTTERY, CRYSTAL, AND GLASSWARE"): For pepping up your kitchen, the very French-looking but budget-priced **The Bridge,** at 212 E. 52nd St., between Second and Third Avenues (tel. 688-4220), carries the most extensive and interesting housewares selection in town, and at substantially reduced prices—we've comparison-shopped. Prices start at 95¢ for wooden-handled spatulas (hard to find elsewhere), and go way up for gigantic copper pans which would cost much more anywhere else. This is where Julia Child buys the tiny French paring knife she used constantly on her television show "The French Chef." They also carry French white porcelainware, a full line of stainless-steel items, and the Zester, to make vegetable strips, twists, etc. Open weekdays from 9 a.m. to 5:30 p.m., on Saturday from 10 a.m. to 5 p.m.

Believe it or not, **Zabar's,** 2245 Broadway, at 80th Street (tel. 787-2000), world-famous home of appetizers, delicacies, fresh coffee, everything, has among the best prices in town on all kitchen equipment including the well-known Cuisinart. We bought a model here for $130, and saw it selling elsewhere for $180. A marvelous shopping adventure. Open Monday to Friday from 8 a.m. to 7:30 p.m., on Saturday to midnight, on Sunday from 9 a.m. to 6 p.m. The mezzanine is open from 9 a.m. to 6 p.m. daily.

And **Conran's,** the American branch of the well-known London-based Habitat chain, has some fabulous buys in pottery, kitchenware, china, glass, and lots of other things (including furniture). Marvelous browsing here, even if you don't buy. One store is in the Citicorp Building, entrance at Third Avenue and 54th Street (tel. 371-2225); another is at 2-8 Astor Pl., near Broadway and 8th Street (tel. 505-1515). Open weekdays from 10 a.m. to 9 p.m., on Saturday to 7 p.m., and on Sunday from noon to 6 p.m. A $2 quarterly catalog is available at the stores, or via mail from 145 Huguenot St., New Rochelle, NY 10801.

LAMPS AND LIGHTING FIXTURES: On the Bowery, two stores offering vast selections of lamps, ceiling fans, and lighting fixtures at substantial discounts are: **New York Gas Lighting Co., Inc.** 145–149 Bowery, between Broome and Grand Streets (tel. 226-2840), open from 10 a.m. to 4 p.m. daily, closed Saturday in July and August; and on the same block, **Bowery Lighting Corporation,** 132 Bowery (tel. 966-4034), open daily from 9:30 a.m. to 5:30 p.m.

LUGGAGE: You simply can't beat the prices at **Bettinger's Luggage Shop,** 80 Rivington St., off Allen Street (tel. 674-9411). They offer discounts of 25% to 40% on first-quality brand-name luggage—Hartman, American Tourister, Samsonite, etc.—plus exact replicas of the extremely popular nylon Sportsacs for 25% less, a full line of business and attaché cases, wallets, and much more. They also stock some seconds and irregulars. Open Sunday to Friday from 9:30 a.m. to 6 p.m.

MILLINERY AND NOTIONS: West 38th Street between Fifth Avenue and Avenue of the Americas is where New Yorkers go for ribbons, veils, zippers, buttons, feathers, hats, stones, and jewelry-making items. Wander in and out of the various shops, making sure to stop at **Manny's Millinery Supply Company,** 63 W. 38th St. (tel. 840-2235), where combs are only $2.50 a dozen and flowers to decorate them start at 39¢ a bunch. Open weekdays from 9 a.m. to 5:45 p.m., on Saturday from 9 a.m. to 3:30 p.m. (closed Saturday during the summer).

Sheru Bead, Curtain, & Jewelry Designers, 49 W. 38th St. (tel. 730-0766), is the spot for hobby supplies, buttons, flowers, millinery, ribbons, cloisonné, appliqués, beads, etc. Open weekdays from 9 a.m. to 6 p.m., on Saturday from 9 a.m. to 5 p.m.

Cinderella Flower and Feather Company, 57 W. 38th St. (tel. 840-0644), has everything you need to decorate your hat yourself—flowers, feathers, combs, etc. Open weekdays from 8:30 a.m. to 4:30 p.m., on Saturday from 10:30 a.m. to 3 p.m.

And slightly off the beaten path, **Arden Bridal**, 1014 Avenue of the Americas, between 37th and 38th Streets (tel. 391-6968), sells both retail and wholesale, with excellent prices for headpieces, veils, and accessories, as well as millinery supplies, flowers, feathers, combs, ribbons, etc. Open weekdays from 9:30 a.m. to 6 p.m., on Saturday from 10 a.m. to 5 p.m.

MUSICAL INSTRUMENTS: For great buys (40% or more off) in new and secondhand musical instruments, particularly violins, call the **Ardsley Musical Instrument Service** in Westchester: 914/693-6639. We also found new and used band instruments of every type, and tiny violins for tiny musicians. Open Monday to Saturday, by appointment only.

All kinds of band instruments can be bought at **Terminal Music,** 166 W. 48th St., between Sixth and Seventh Avenues (tel. 869-5270). Discounts of 20% to 66⅔% on guitars, electric pianos, amplifiers, and drums and other percussion instruments. Guitars run from $25 to $1800—the majority, of course, in the lower price range. Terminal has the city's largest collection of recorders, that ancient instrument that is currently enjoying such popularity. Prices for those begin at $2. They also carry historic instrument music. Open Monday through Saturday from 9 a.m. to 6 p.m.

PERFUME: Why spend a small fortune for expensive French perfumes when you can buy quality reproductions of the famous fragrances at a fraction of the price? Here's where to do it:

Essential Products Company, Inc., 90 Water St., New York, NY 10005, between Wall Street and Hanover Square (tel. 344-4288), sells all its perfumes for a mere $18 an ounce. They offer 43 scents, including a highly popular new version of Giorgio, as well as Ombre Rose, Opium, Bal à Versailles, Joy, Shalimar, and Halston. Also available are 14 men's colognes, the newest a version of Yves St. Laurent's Kouros. Mail orders are shipped promptly. Essential will send you free five fragrance cards, a fragrance list, and an order form if you call or write for information.

Tuli-Latus Perfumes, Ltd., does a marvelous job of replicating such scents as Joy, L'Air du Temps, Lauren, Madame Rochas, Giorgio, Calandre, Opium, etc., as well as Gucci's Pour Homme and other men's colognes. Their version of Chanel No. 5 (Tuli-Latus No. 6) has long been a personal favorite. Prices range between $15 and $25 an ounce. They also have an excellent line of skin-care products. Phone 718/746-9337 for a catalog, or write them at 146-36 Thirteenth Ave., P.O. Box 422, Whitestone, NY 11357. You can also visit their retail boutique at 136-56 39th Ave., Suite 450, Flushing, Queens, weekdays from 9:30 a.m. to 4:30 p.m.

PETS AND PET SUPPLIES: Want to adopt a poor deserving little dog—an orphan, no less? Then go to the **ASPCA,** 441 E. 92nd St., corner of York Avenue (tel. 876-7711), and your only costs will be $8.50 for a license, which you can purchase right there, plus a $40 adoption fee. In addition to dogs, you can pick up cats, of course, as well as more unusual animals (which occasionally include parakeets, hamsters, etc.); the ASPCA will examine the animal, inoculate it, and give it an optional free medical examination for up to two weeks after adoption, free spay/neuter, and free feline leukemia testing. You can come in to adopt a pet from 10 a.m. to 7 p.m. on Monday, Tuesday, Wednesday, Saturday; to 8 p.m. on Thursday and Friday; and from noon to 6 p.m. on Sunday. You must be at least 18 or have ID with your present name and address. The ASPCA also proudly presents the "Purina Pets for People" program for senior citizens aged 60 years and over who can adopt free of charge. For further information on this program, call the above number Monday through Friday from 10 a.m. to 6 p.m.

Another worthy animal-adoption agency is the smaller **Bide-A-Wee Home,** 410 E. 38th St., between First Avenue and the East River (tel. 532-4455 or 532-4457). They place dogs and cats, and ask a $15 to $40 donation depending on the animal you select. All animals here have been inoculated, already neutered if they are six months or older, and in perfect health. You must be at least 21 to adopt and have two forms of certifiable ID. Open Monday through Saturday from 9 a.m. to 7 p.m., on Sunday to 5 p.m.

Everything you'll need to keep your new pet comfy and contented can be found—often at a discount—at **Pet Bowl,** 421 Amsterdam Ave., at 80th Street (tel. 595-4200). In addition to dog and cat food (including prescription diets), they carry a large stock of accessories and furniture, including beds, toys, collars, leashes, etc. Stop in to put your name on their mailing list; you'll receive their catalog and be notified of special sales. Open Monday to Friday from 10 a.m. to 7 p.m., on Saturday from 9:30 a.m. to 6 p.m.

PRINTS AND POSTERS: **Associated American Artists,** 20 W. 57th St., off Fifth Avenue (tel. 399-5510), has original graphics, etchings, lithographs, serigraphs, and woodcuts bearing the artists' signatures beginning at $40. Open Tuesday to Saturday from 10 a.m. to 6 p.m.; closed Saturday June through August.

The **Argosy Book Store,** 116 E. 59th St., between Park and Lexington Avenues (tel. 753-4455), places enormous bins of old maps, prints, and books out in front of the store (prints begin here at $2; inside, they begin at $1 and go way up). They also have catalogs of Americana, medicine, rare books, autographs, etc. Open weekdays from 9 a.m. to 6 p.m., on Saturday from 10 a.m. to 5 p.m. (closed Saturday from mid-May through Labor Day).

The **Gallery of Graphic Arts,** 1601 York Ave., between 84th and 85th Streets (tel. 988-4731), presents top-notch graphic art in an intimate, neighborhood setting. Owner Ellie Seibold is an avid collector (and seller) of contemporary American, European, and Japanese lithographs, etchings, woodcuts, original posters, and authentic Mexican and New England tombstone rubbings. She's always on the lookout for works by young artists, and delights in selling quality work at prices people can afford. Prints begin at around $30, and would sell for much more in a fancier gallery. She also does some very special framing work (some of the leading museums are her clients) and takes pride in framing the hard-to-frame—full-size quilts, tapestries, antique textiles, Indian beadwork, or whatever. If you need such work done, drop in to see Ellie or call and discuss it with her: send her the object, and she'll frame it superbly and mail it back to you. Her motto: "If there's any way to get it on the wall, we do it." Gallery of Graphic Arts is open Monday to Saturday from 11 a.m. to 6:30 p.m.

Poster Originals has two locations, one at 924 Madison Ave., near 73rd Street (tel. 861-0422), in the uptown art district, and another downtown at 158 Spring St. (tel. 226-7720), in SoHo, New York's dynamic downtown art neighborhood. Both galleries carry an exciting array of posters by contemporary painters, both European and American. You might find Polish circus posters, as well as some from opera, theaters, and museums. Prices are reasonable, beginning at $10 for unframed posters. The Madison Avenue gallery is open Monday through Saturday from 10 a.m. to 6 p.m.; the SoHo gallery, Tuesday through Sunday from 10 a.m. to 6 p.m.

Untitled, 159 Prince St. (tel. 982-2088), is a postcard store the likes of which you've never seen. Subjects run the gamut from cave paintings to the very latest in New Wave art cards. This is the place to finally start a postcard collection for yourself, or invest in a starter set for a friend as a remembrance of New York. Hours are noon to 7 p.m. seven days a week.

RECORDS: Big record selections at great prices? You'll find them at **Sam Goody's** two Manhattan locations: 51 W. 51st St., at Sixth Avenue (tel. 246-8730), and 666 Third Ave., at 43rd Street (tel. 986-8480). Goody's is one of the world's largest record and tape dealers in both classical and popular music; they also handle a full line of compact discs, radio equipment, and all associated accessories. Each branch carries a complete line of these products, all selling at substantial discounts. Watch the newspapers for special sales. Both stores are open weekdays from 9:30 a.m. to 6:45 p.m., on Saturday to 6:15 p.m., and on Sunday from noon to 5 p.m.

 Tower Records, 692 Broadway, at 4th Street (tel. 505-1500), is as much a Village "happening" as a record store, with its three floors of records and tapes throbbing with excitement 365 days a year. The *New York Post* once called it "the hottest place to meet a member of the opposite sex," and that it is, as the crowds watch videos, attend special events, listen to music, and get to know one another. Well, even if you're just looking to buy records or tapes at good prices, Tower Records is good to know about. The largest eastern outpost of the well-known western chain, Tower has one of the world's largest collections, in all categories, from classical to rock to rhythm and blues. Records are often sold for as little as $5.95. There's another Tower Records uptown in the Lincoln Center area at 1967 Broadway, at 66th Street (tel. 799-2500), and a block north of that, at 1977 Broadway (tel. 496-2500), Tower Video. All three stores are open every day of the year, from 9 a.m. to midnight.

SCIENCE AND SPIRIT: Something like 2000 products which show that "science and spirit are not incompatible" can be found at **Star Magic,** 834 Broadway, near 8th Street (tel. 228-7770). Star Magic is a unique and magical store that should be experienced by anyone tuned in to either inner or outer space. Celestial music, flashing lights, unusual objects set the scene for a futuristic space in which you can find anything from telescopes, globes, robots, prisms, holograms, and model space shuttles, to healing crystals, gemstone pendants, pyramids, books on higher consciousness, and statues of the Buddha. Tapes and records run the gamut from synthesized electronic space music to Tibetan gongs. The price range is wide, from $8 sterling silver earcuffs among the Space Age jewelry, to $240 rose quartz spheres to telescopes that run up to $675. There's another Star Magic in San Francisco, and their newest shop is at 275 Amsterdam Ave. (tel. 769-2020). For a free catalog, you can call them toll free (outside of California) at 800/222-1070.

SPORTING GOODS: The three outstanding sporting goods stores in New York are **Herman's, Paragon,** and **Hudson's.** Each of them has complete selections of name-brand equipment.

 Herman's World of Sporting Goods, at 135 W. 42nd St., between Broadway and Avenue of the Americas (tel. 730-7400), has an enormous supply of tennis and ski equipment as well as all kinds of other sports items. Their end-of-the-season markdowns offer terrific values: late September and early October for tennis equipment, February and March for skis, as well as parkas, hunting jackets, and sleeping bags. Open weekdays from 9:30 a.m. to 7 p.m., on Saturday to 6 p.m. Other branches of Herman's are at 39 West 34th St., off Fifth Avenue (tel. 279-8900), open the same hours, plus Sunday from noon to 5 p.m.;

845 Third Ave., at 51st Street (tel. 688-4603), open Monday to Saturday from 9:30 a.m. to 7 p.m.; and downtown in the financial district, at 110 Nassau St., between Ann and Beekman Streets (tel. 233-0733), open weekdays from 9 a.m. to 6 p.m., on Saturday to 5 p.m.

Paragon, 867 Broadway, between 17th and 18th Streets (tel. 255-8036), has comparable items and specializes in camping equipment. Their prices are rock bottom for all kinds of backpacking and climbing gear, tents, and camping clothing, not to mention a wide variety of sporting goods and sports clothing. Open Monday through Saturday from 9:30 a.m. to 6:30 p.m., on Thursday to 7:30 p.m., and on Sunday from 11 a.m. to 6 p.m.

Hudson's, 97 Third Ave., from 12th to 13th Streets (tel. 473-7320), is a whole city block of a store specializing in outdoor clothing and equipment. They have a big selection of leather jackets, jeanswear (501 jeans), footwear, and sports apparel at discount prices. Open Monday to Saturday from 9:30 a.m. to 6:30 p.m., on Sunday from noon to 5 p.m.

STEREO AND ELECTRONIC EQUIPMENT (See also "APPLIANCES"):
One of the best places to buy stereo components—speakers, amplifiers, and turntables—is **Lafayette,** 49 W. 45th St., near Sixth Avenue (tel. 819-0213), where you'll find not only stereo equipment, but radios, tape recorders, etc.—all at rock-bottom prices. Open Monday to Friday from 10 a.m. to 7 p.m., on Saturday to 6 p.m., and on Sunday from noon to 5 p.m.

THRIFT SHOPS:
Along Second and Third Avenues in the 70s is a string of thrift shops which feature used merchandise—of every sort—sold in "as is" condition. The shops are staffed by public-spirited ladies in colorful smocks who donate their time and proceeds from sales to hospitals, nursing homes, and other charitable institutions. Some of the merchandise, admittedly, is hand-me-down, but very often you turn up excellent buys here. Many smart shoppers regularly canvas these shops for real finds.

Top choice of these shops is the **Girls' Club of New York Thrift Shop,** 202 E. 77th St., between Second and Third Avenues (tel. 535-8570), which is almost elegant in appearance compared to many others of the genre. They feature men's, women's, and children's clothing in "mint condition": 60% of their clothing is new. Prices go from $5 up. They sell designer clothing and fine furs at reasonable prices. Also, furniture, bric-a-brac in excellent condition, many antiques in all categories, and books from 25¢ up. Store hours: Monday through Saturday from 10 a.m. to 5 p.m.

Among the others, you might try:

Irvington House Thrift Shop, 1534 Second Ave., at 80th Street (tel. 879-4555), which sells women's and men's clothing, from dollar items to designer numbers. They also have furs, linen, furniture, rugs, decorative accessories, paintings, porcelains, books, silver, and glassware. Proceeds go to Irvington House Institute for Medical Research, affiliated with the Albert Einstein College of Medicine and Rockefeller University.

The **Trishop Quality Thrift Boutique,** 1689 First Ave., between 87th and 88th Streets (tel. 362-2411), is a well-kept secret among many of the city's better-dressed women: this place handles mostly top-quality, brand-new merchandise contributed by manufacturers and famous Fifth Avenue department stores (proceeds from sales benefit the Mental Health Association of New York and Bronx Counties). You might find designer clothes anywhere from $14 to $40. While 90% of the clothing is new, most of the furniture, lamps, bric-a-brac, etc., is used. The shop is open Tuesday to Saturday from 9:30 a.m. to 4:30 p.m.

Downtown, the thrift-shop fans swear by:

St. George's Thrift Shop, 175 Third Ave., between 16th and 17th Streets (tel. 260-0350), sells gently used clothing for men, women, and children, as well as bric-a-brac, books, records, linens, and lots more. Open Monday to Saturday from 10 a.m. to 4 p.m., on Thursday till 7 p.m.

TOYS: For new and antique dollhouses, miniatures, and dolls, a good bet is **The Doll House,** 176 Ninth Ave., at 21st Street (tel. 989-5220). There is at least a 20% discount on everything and the selection is overwhelming for such a little place. Open Sunday to Friday from 10 a.m. to 4:30 p.m.

Mythology, 370 Columbus Ave., at 78th Street (tel. 874-0774), sells wind-up toys, pretty erasers, pins, unusual rubber stamps, posters, and books, both new and collectible. They have a great selection of toy robots. It's one of our favorite stores in New York, stuffed to the ceiling with items that make you want to look, touch, try, and buy. If you can leave this interesting little store without buying something, you have more sales resistance than we do! Unusual flip books, all kinds of tiny toys at tiny prices, and much, much more. Open Monday to Friday from 11 a.m. to 9 p.m., on Saturday to 7 p.m., and on Sunday to 6 p.m.

B. Shackman & Co., 85 Fifth Ave., near 14th Street (tel. 989-5162), sells wonderful reproductions of antique toys and dolls, and has an extensive selection of dollhouse furniture as well. Here you'll find the kind of whirligigs, china dolls, and teddy bears that are sold in museum gift shops. Cat lovers will enjoy their Kitty Cucumber T items. Open Monday through Friday from 9 a.m. to 5 p.m., on Saturday from 10:30 a.m. to 4 p.m.

If you'd like to buy a toy souvenir for a child back home, why not visit **Childcraft,** 150 E. 58th St., between Third and Lexington Avenues (tel. 753-3196), and 155 E. 23rd St. (tel. 674-4754), and buy one that will teach a skill or a craft? Childcraft stocks a beautiful line of wooden toys too. Open Monday through Friday from 10 a.m. to 6 p.m., on Saturday to 5 p.m.

Dollsandreams, 1421 Lexington Ave., at 93rd Street (tel. 876-2434), is a dream of a toy store. They stock a lovely selection of dolls, toys, and art supplies, as well as a full line of Swiss Caran D'Ache art supplies (crayons, paints, markers, etc.). The dolls and toys here are of the highest quality, and prices are always fair. Open Monday through Friday from 9 a.m. to 5 p.m., on Saturday from 10 a.m. to 6 p.m.

UMBRELLAS: If you've never been able to find the perfect umbrella in your local stores, **Gloria Umbrellas,** 39 Essex St. (tel. 475-7388), should have one in stock to suit your fancy—and at a 30% discount! Whether you're looking for an oversize, folding, or windproof umbrella, we're sure you won't be disappointed here. They are also expert at repairing all types of umbrellas. Open Sunday through Thursday from 9 a.m. to 5 p.m., on Friday until 2:30 p.m.

WALLPAPER AND PAINT: Expect to find very good bargains in wallpaper, paints, decorative plumbing, and more at **Wallpaper Mart,** 187 Lexington Ave., between 31st and 32nd Streets (tel. 889-4900). The price you see on the tag is already discounted 10% to 25% off list prices. Regular wallpapers and vinyls are represented among the very large stock of wallpapers. You can also order from sample books at discount. Open Monday through Friday from 10 a.m. until 6:30 p.m., on Thursday until 7 p.m., on Saturday to 5 p.m.

Pearl Paint Company at 308 Canal St., between Broadway and Church Street (tel. 431-7932), is a bargain-hunter's store, and everyone from famous-name artists to household painters comes to Pearl's to stock up. Items are available by mail. They also have a showroom and gallery at 42 Lispenard St., around the corner from the store. Open Monday through Saturday from 9 a.m.

to 5:30 p.m., on Sunday from 11 a.m. to 4:45 p.m. Closed Sunday in July and August.

WESTERN WEAR: Frankel's Discount Store, 3925 Third Ave., at 40th Street, *Brooklyn* (tel. 718/788-9402), is an excellent source for discount-priced western wear. They've been selling cowboy boots here for ages (the store is almost half a century old) long before the recent fad. The store specializes in discontinued styles and odd lots, and you, the customer, benefit from discounts that can go as high as 50% and more, on boots, sneakers, clogs, jeans, as well as down vests, hats, baseball gloves, and lots more. A great find! Open Tuesday to Saturday from 10 a.m. to 7 p.m.; closed Sunday and Monday.

3. Food

Food, food, beautiful food. In New York, everyone's a gourmet. For the best prices on the essentials—plus the frills from Spanish saffron to Hungarian prune whip—consult the following:

CHEESE: New York abounds with cheese stores, but it's hard to beat the prices at **Cheese of all Nations,** 153 Chambers St., between Hudson and Greenwich Streets (tel. 732-0752). Almost a thousand varieties are in stock, all modestly priced. A trip down here is well worthwhile since the neighborhood abounds in bargain stores. And Chambers Street is right at the IRT-Seventh Avenue subway stop (take the no. 1, 2, or 3 train). Open Monday to Saturday from 8 a.m. to 5:30 p.m.

Fairway, 2127 Broadway, at 74th Street (tel. 595-1888), has a marvelous cheese section, at some of the best prices anywhere. Up front are acres of super-fresh fruits and vegetables, which, along with the cheeses and pastas and other goodies, bring the customers from far and wide. A few blocks farther uptown, at Broadway and 80th Street, **Zabar's** (tel. 787-2000), New York's great gourmet grocery, has another superb selection of cheeses (more highly priced, however, than Fairway). Both stores are open every day.

Ideal Cheese, 1205 Second Ave., at 63rd Street (tel. 688-7579), just might be the best cheese store in New York—the best of everything, including the largest selection of goat and sheep cheese in the country; many are American made. They also sell gift baskets, gourmet coffees, and pâtés. A free catalog goes with all cheese and gift items. Open weekdays from 9 a.m. to 7 p.m., on Saturday to 6 p.m.

Dean & De Luca, 121 Prince St., between Greene and Wooster Streets (tel. 254-7774), has every type of cheese, great loaves of black bread, sweet ham, savory pies, pastries, pastas, condiments, coffees, and croissants to name a few categories. Worth a trip to the SoHo area just to bring a goodie home. Open Monday to Saturday from 10 a.m. to 7 p.m., on Sunday to 6 p.m.

Ben's, 181 E. Houston St., between Allen and Orchard Streets (tel. 254-8290), features homemade baked flavored farmer and cream cheese—strawberry, pepper, walnut, raisin—irresistible and relatively inexpensive. Not to mention fresh tub butter, and hundreds of varieties of domestic and imported cheeses. Open Sunday to Friday from 8 a.m. to 6 p.m. (closing at 3 p.m. on Friday in winter).

Murray's Cheese Store, 42 Cornelia St., between Sixth Avenue and Bleecker Street (tel. 243-3289), has hundreds of varieties of imported cheeses at unbeatable prices. Frequent specials and excellent quality. Open Monday to Saturday from 8 a.m. to 6 p.m.

COFFEES AND TEAS: McNulty's has been serving coffee- and tea-loving New

Yorkers for around 90 years at 109 Christopher St., between Hudson and Bleecker Streets (tel. 242-5351). They sell over 20 varieties of choice coffees and many rare, hard-to-obtain teas. Open Monday through Saturday from 11 a.m. to 11 p.m., on Sunday from 1 to 7:30 p.m.

FRESH AND FANCY: Gourmets who would like to buy their fish and truffles, game and produce, and other imported specialty items from the same source that celebrated restaurants like Lutèce shop, have two days a week to be in gourmet's heaven. That's when **Flying Foods International** in Long Island City (tel. 718/706-0820), wholesale distributors of fancy fresh foods from all over the world (they never carry anything frozen), open their doors to the public and do not raise their prices above wholesale. The best way to come is with an open mind and mingle with the other adventurous shoppers to see what's on hand in the always-changing selection: you might find, for example, rouget barbet (red mullet) from the Mediterranean, crayfish from Louisiana, haricots verts from France, exotic wild mushrooms and buffalo mozzarella from Italy, baby vegetables, quail and duck breasts among the game, exotic olive oils, vinegars, and mustards. The staff is at the ready to give you cooking ideas and recipes in which to use the exotic ingredients. Out-of-season fruits are another specialty—like tender raspberries in the cold of a New York winter. Flying Foods International is open to the public on Friday and Saturday only, from 10 a.m. to 3 p.m. The warehouse is at 43-43 9th St., in Long Island City, which is just about ten minutes from midtown Manhattan, across the East River from the 59th Street bridge. By public transportation, take the IRT–Flushing no. 7 train from Times Square or Grand Central to Vernon-Jackson Boulevard; or the IND E or F train to 23rd and Ely Avenues, and ask directions for the short walk to Flying Foods.

GOURMET GROCERIES: Uptowners who crave Middle European specialties, but don't want to break the budget to get them, like **Lekvar by the Barrel,** 1577 First Ave., corner of 82nd Street (tel. 734-1110), which specializes in such things as Hungarian salami, and fresh Hungarian prune whip doled out of a huge barrel. They also have wide arrays of jams and honeys, egg noodles, Hungarian cookbooks; imported Brazilian, Dutch, Chinese, and Indonesian specialties; plus dried and candied fruits, teas, everything for baking and cake decoration, gourmet candy, kitchenware, Hungarian peasant pottery, fresh herbs and spices. A free catalog is available on request. Open Monday to Saturday from 9 a.m. to 6:30 p.m.

Also in the Yorkville section, **Paprikas Weiss Importers,** at 1546 Second Ave., between 80th and 81st Streets (tel. 288-6117), specializes in Middle European foods, as well as unusual kitchen utensils from all over the world. Hard-to-find spices are available here in bulk (it's cheaper to buy it this way, rather than in the fancy bottles you get at the supermarket). Coffees and teas, ready-to-use strudel dough sheets, Hungarian salamis, nuts, cheeses, homemade jams and syrups, every kind of canned good imaginable, a huge selection of French pâtés, foie gras, and fresh goose livers, plus continental candies, make this place an international food bazaar par excellence. They also sell gift items from Hungary: hand-embroidered peasant blouses, kerchiefs, and shawls, for example. Send $1 to subscribe to their mail-order catalog. Open Monday through Saturday from 9 a.m. to 6 p.m.

Still shopping Yorkville: **Bremen House,** 220 E. 86th St., between Second and Third Avenues (tel. 288-5500), is a great place for cold cuts and sausages in every size, shape, and texture, cooked and raw. Cheeses, candies, German herrings, mustards, jams, herb teas, kitschy gift items like Black Forest cuckoo clocks, spices, European records, European cosmetics, and all sorts of imported canned and packaged goods, as well as German newspapers and magazines are also sold. A free catalog is available. Open Monday to Saturday from 9 a.m. to 8 p.m., on Sunday from 11 a.m. to 7 p.m. Well worth a visit to the Yorkville area just to see this store.

While you're in the neighborhood, stop in at **Schaller and Weber** for "gold medal award-winning" cold cuts and gourmet products. They're on Second Avenue, corner of 86th Street (tel. 879-3047); and the **Elk Candy Co.**, at 240 E. 86th St., between Second and Third Avenues (tel. 650-1177), for every kind of sweet imaginable.

Basior-Schwartz, 421 W. 14th St. (tel. 929-5368), is an enormous cooler which is also a large wholesale supplier to stores and restaurants. It services the retail customer as well, selling cheeses, pâtés, smoked fish, crackers, and biscuits at very big discounts, and much, much more. Olive oil, dried fruits and nuts, and tuna fish at great savings too. Open from 5 a.m. to noon, weekdays only. It's in the bustling wholesale meat market district.

HEALTH AND NATURAL FOODS:
It sometimes seems that half the people in New York are on a health and fitness kick. As a result, there are health-food stores every few blocks, plus huge natural-food emporiums here and there. Some of the best:

Commodities, 117 Hudson St., at the corner of North Moore Street, in Tribeca (tel. 334-8330), is a macrobiotic superstore, with what they call perhaps the largest selection in the world of macrobiotic products. But there's also plenty for those who are not into macrobiotics in this huge store where almost 95% of the goods are organically grown—and that includes fresh fruits and vegetables, grains, beans, seaweeds, unusual flours (chestnut, chickpea, etc.), even the very pleasant Altura coffee from Mexico, which has half the usual amount of caffeine. Rows of bins house staple items; there are fresh herbs in bulk; homeopathic and herbal remedies (including Dragon Eggs, a line of Chinese herbal medicines) comprise a natural pharmacy. Sections of cookwares and natural cosmetics too. And prices on these hard-to-find items are all discounted: from 7% to 20%. Many people from out of the neighborhood come here on weekends to stack their cars with the good buys. Commodities is open from 10 a.m. to 9 p.m. seven days a week, and closes only on Christmas Day.

Almost everything at **Pete's Spice and Everything Nice**, 174 First Ave., between 10th and 11th Streets (tel. 254-8773), is sold in bulk (from one ounce to 100 pounds), and that everything includes 500 herbs and spices; 20 blends of coffee; 100 grains, flours, and dried beans; 60 kinds of dried fruit; 65 varieties of shelled and unshelled nuts; plus varied imported and gourmet items—all at budget prices. Try the coffee beans—mocha java goes for $4.49 a pound. Open Monday to Saturday from 10 a.m. to 7 p.m.

Popular on the West Side is **World Health**, 2320 Broadway, at 84th Street (tel. 874-0988), with excellent selections of all natural foods. Their organic fruits and vegetables are carefully certified; they also carry a complete line of vitamins, grains, beans, nuts, dried fruits, honeys, meat, fish, and dairy products. Open Monday to Friday from 11 a.m. to 7:30 p.m., on Saturday to 7 p.m.

The Good Earth, 1334 First Ave., between 71st and 72nd Streets (tel. 472-9055), carries a wide array of organic and natural foods—fruits, vegetables, meats, dairy products, breads, cakes—natural cosmetics, natural vitamins, etc. Their other store at 182 Amsterdam Ave., at 68th Street (tel. 496-1616), is just two minutes from Lincoln Center. Open Monday, Wednesday, and Thursday from 10 a.m. to 7 p.m., on Tuesday and Friday to 8 p.m., on Saturday to 6 p.m.

Nutrition may be the "in" thing now, but at **Brownies**, 91 Fifth Ave., between 16th and 17th Streets (tel. 242-2199), healthful eating has been the vogue for 47 years. Famed for its natural-foods restaurant around the corner on 16th Street, Brownies purveys vitamins, grains, beans, seeds, etc. Their home-baked cakes—carrot, maple walnut, carob, to give you an idea—are both healthful and scrumptious, using only whole-grain flours, honey, and other natural ingredients. The retail store is open Monday through Friday from 9 a.m. to 7 p.m., until 6 p.m. on Saturday.

HERBS AND SPICES: In Greenwich Village, **Aphrodisia,** 282 Bleecker St., between Sixth and Seventh Avenues (tel. 989-6440), is the place to go for exotic herbs and spices. You can also purchase flower oils to make your own perfume or potpourri, *fo ti teng* (an Oriental herb reputed to have great health-giving and aphrodisiac qualities), and dandelion root (a healthful coffee substitute); they even carry crystallized roses, a perfect cake decoration, which are hard to find. Lots of books for sale here on nature's own medicines, health foods, recipes, aphrodisiacs, and magical herbs. Open Monday to Saturday from 11 a.m. to 7 p.m., and on Sunday (except in July and August) from noon to 5 p.m.

And don't forget the aforementioned **Pete's Spice,** 174 First Ave.

PRODUCE: The cheapest produce—as well as groceries, meat, and other items—in town is sold in the **City Markets,** which are warehouse-type buildings in which pushcart peddlers and other small food entrepreneurs place their carts, stalls, and bins. The food is more exotic than you'd find in the commercial groceries, very little of it is canned, and the prices are rock bottom. Several such markets exist, our favorite being the one located on **Essex Street,** between Stanton and Broome Streets, on the Lower East Side (tel. 254-6655). For the most exotic fare, there's still another on **Park Avenue** (La Marqueta), between 111th and 116th Streets (tel. 722-6716), selling all varieties of Spanish fruits and vegetables. Both are open Monday to Saturday from 8 a.m. to 6:30 p.m.

J.J. Starace, 7 Little West 12th St., at Ninth Avenue (tel. 589-9404), is the place to go to buy the best of the crop—that is, if you get up at 5 a.m. This wholesale operation, which sells mainly to restaurants, will sell leftovers and extras to consumers who wend their way downtown in the wee hours. Usually nothing is left after 11 a.m., and they close up completely by noon, so come early. Weekdays only.

SWEETS AND DRIED FRUITS: Best buys here are on the Lower East Side. **Wolsk,** 81 Ludlow St., between Broome and Delancey Streets (tel. 475-7946), has been here since 1939, both wholesaling and retailing dried fruits, nuts, candies, chocolates, halvah, and more. They have 50 varieties of nuts for eating or baking, 30 varieties of domestic and imported dried fruits. Nuts are roasted fresh daily on the premises. Hand-dipped chocolates, made of only the finest and purest ingredients, are made weekly. In lots of 100 or more, one can buy imported and domestic hard candies, licorice, gummies, boxed chocolates, etc., at 20% to 50% below regular retail prices. Open Sunday to Thursday from 8 a.m. to 5 p.m., on Friday until 2 p.m. Mail order is available; they ship UPS.

Good buys are also available nearby at **Mutual Dried Fruit,** 127 Ludlow St., between Rivington and Delancey Streets (tel. 673-3489), open Sunday to Thursday from 9 a.m. to 5:30 p.m., on Friday to about 4:45 p.m.

WINES AND SPIRITS: Offering one of the city's most comprehensive and inexpensive selections of domestic and imported wines is **Astor Wines and Spirits,**

12 Astor Pl., between Broadway and Lafayette Street, just below 8th Street (tel. 674-7500). You can get a very nice imported French table wine for under $3, and prices on all their stock—especially their own Astor label—are most reasonable. In addition, a wide choice of liquors and liqueurs is sold at the lowest prices permitted by the New York State Liquor Authority. Open Monday through Saturday from 9 a.m. to 9 p.m.

THE BRONX'S ARTHUR AVENUE: One of the city's most unusual shopping areas is not in Manhattan but in the Bronx. The Arthur Avenue section is predominantly Italian, with lots of food shops and bakeries as well as a smattering of retail shops selling clothing and household items. But food is first on Arthur Avenue, and a walk along the avenue is a must for every gourmet who enjoys eating and cooking Italian food. Shoppers will be glad to learn that prices are considerably lower here than in most parts of Manhattan.

Our favorite stretch of the avenue is between 184th and 187th Streets, where a number of the best shops are located. For fish go to **Randazzo's** at 2340 Arthur Ave. (tel. 367-4139). On the sidewalk in front of the store a raised bench full of ice shavings holds an interesting array of mussels, clams, and unusual small fish. Inside you can buy anything from porgies to lobster, and the fish is always fresh and well priced. Occasionally the owners themselves have caught the fish they sell. Open Monday to Saturday from 7 a.m. to 6 p.m.

Before you go elsewhere on the avenue, let us lead you to a bakery around the corner, where the bread is absolutely the best we've ever eaten. The **Arena Bakery,** 651 E. 183rd St., between Hughes and Belmont Avenues (tel. 733-6221), turns out bread, rolls, and pizza dough for restaurants and groceries, but they also sell retail in the little store connected to the bakery. The family in charge here has been baking for four generations. Open around the clock, Monday to Saturday.

Back on Arthur Avenue (no. 2344) is the **Arthur Avenue Retail Market** (tel. 364-9321), a big city public market chock full of privately operated stalls, each offering vegetables and fruit at competing prices. You can walk through and buy what you want after checking the price and quality of the various vendors. Meats and poultry, cheeses and sausages, espressos, coffees, pastries, all Italian specialties, housewares and candies, spices, too, are all sold here under one roof and the atmosphere is very European. A good place to do your budget shopping. Open Monday to Saturday from 8 a.m. to 6 p.m.

187th Street, which intersects Arthur Avenue, is a continuation of the Italian food shopping in this area. On the first block off Arthur Avenue, **Ceglie's Italian Delicatessen,** 604 E. 187th St. (tel. 364-3867), is worth a visit for sausages, cheeses, cold cuts, homemade mozzarella, etc. Open Monday to Saturday from 7 a.m. to 6 p.m., on Sunday to 1 p.m.

Next door, at 606 E. 187th St., **De Lillo Pastry** (tel. 367-8198) offers all types of Italian goodies baked right on the premises. Open Tuesday to Saturday from 8:30 a.m. to 7:30 p.m., on Sunday to 6:30 p.m., and on Monday to 5 p.m.

Danny's Pork Store, 626 E. 187th St. (tel. 933-1690), sells every cut of pork imaginable, as well as homemade pork sausage that is made fresh daily. Open Monday to Saturday from 9 a.m. to 5:30 p.m.

To reach the Arthur Avenue section by subway, take the IND–Sixth Avenue D train uptown to Fordham Road in the Bronx. Then take the no. 12 bus from Fordham Road to Hoffman Street, and walk one block to Arthur Avenue. The shopping area is three blocks away.

CHINATOWN: A market shopping tour of Chinatown is educational as well as fun. Not to be missed is the fascinating **Kam Man Food Products, Inc.,** 200

Canal St., between Mott and Mulberry Streets (tel. 571-0330), a vast emporium offering everything from fish, meat, housewares, and vegetables, to furniture and exotic Chinese remedies for whatever ails you. Not only is the food and produce of excellent quality and relatively inexpensive, but the drug products come in intriguing little metal boxes and wonderful wrappings, all worth saving. The line in the front is generally for the barbecued duck hanging in the window. Wonderful for gift shopping or just browsing. Open every day from 9 a.m. to 9:15 p.m.

Kam Kuo, 7 Mott St., near Park Row (tel. 349-3097), is a spanking-clean supermarket-like store selling everything from utensils to the actual ingredients —everything you need for Chinese cookery. Open the same hours as Kam Man.

The **United Super Market,** 84 Mulberry St., between Bayard and Canal Streets (tel. 962-6440), specializes in Chinese meats—pork and liver sausages, dried duck, etc. Open daily from 9 a.m. to 7:30 p.m.

A little out of the immediate Chinatown area, **Yat Gow Min Co., Inc.,** 100 Reade St., between Church Street and West Broadway (tel. 233-7200), offers Oriental food products, noodles, eggroll skins, almond and fortune cookies in large amounts at wholesale prices. Open weekdays from 9 a.m. to 4 p.m., on Saturday to 3 p.m.

A LITTLE ITALY GASTRONOMIC ADVENTURE: The neighborhood people who live in Little Italy, a section that runs the length of Mulberry Street from East Houston Street to Canal Street, swear by the quality and low prices at the many food shops in the area. We have several favorites of our own (see also Chapter II).

For Italian-style sausages, we go to **D. De Santis and Sons** at 158 Mott St., between Broome and Grand Streets (tel. 925-4540), who offer four varieties made fresh daily on the premises, without preservatives or coloring, from family recipes. Sweet or hot sausages, pepper and onion sausages, and cheese sausages sell for around $3 to $3.50 a pound. Open Monday through Saturday from 8:30 a.m. to 6 p.m.

Another good bet for sausages—they've been making them at the same location since 1890—is **Fretta Brothers Italian Pork Products,** 116 Mott St., at Hester Street (tel. 226-0232). They call their products "the Cadillac of sausages." Open Tuesday to Saturday from 8 a.m. to 6 p.m., on Sunday from 8:30 a.m. to 1:30 p.m.

For excellent homemade pasta, try either of the following:

Piemonte Ravioli Company, 190 Grand St., between Mott and Mulberry Streets (tel. 226-0475), where owner Mario Bertorelli turns out ravioli, manicotti, cannelloni, gnocchi, cavatelle, spinach noodles, spinach lasagne, egg lasagne, and a host of other pastas. Open Tuesday through Saturday from 8 a.m. to 6 p.m., and from 8 a.m. to 3 p.m. on Sunday.

Raffetto's, 144 W. Houston St., between MacDougal and Sullivan Streets (tel. 777-1261), is open Tuesday to Saturday from 8 a.m. to 6 p.m.

For cheese, we like a store that has been doing business at the same address for over 50 years. **Di Palo's,** 206 Grand St., between Mott and Elizabeth Streets (tel. 226-1033), features cheese that is made on the premises—fresh mozzarella and ricotta made with whole milk—plus a good selection of imported cheeses. Provolone is available in weights from 2½ to 100 pounds. Store hours are 8 a.m. to 6 p.m. Monday through Saturday, till 2 p.m. on Sunday.

In business even longer than Di Palo's, **Alleva Dairy,** 188 Grand St., at Mulberry Street (tel. 226-7990), has been offering fresh ricotta and mozzarella (try the smoked mozzarella) since 1892. They are the oldest makers of these products in America. Open from 8:30 a.m. to 6 p.m. Monday to Saturday, till 1:30 p.m. on Sunday.

For bread, sausage, cheese, and fresh salads, visit the **Italian Food Center,** just next door at 186 Grand St. (tel. 925-2954), open daily from 8 a.m. to 7 p.m.

The biggest supplier of bread in the area is the little **Parisi Bakery,** at 198 Mott St., between Kenmare and Spring Streets (tel. 226-6378). Large crusty loaves of bread sell for 80¢ each. You can also buy "lard and pepper" cookies and butter biscuits for $2.50 a pound. Open Monday to Saturday from 7:30 a.m. to 6:30 p.m.

We get our Italian vegetables at **Caruso's Fruit Market,** 152 Mott St., between Broome and Grand Streets (tel. 226-2978), which supplies some of the finest restaurants in Little Italy. All the hot and sweet peppers you may desire, as well as a good selection of the freshest fruits and a wide variety of other vegetables. Open 7 a.m. to 6 p.m. Monday through Saturday.

A NINTH AVENUE GASTRONOMIC ADVENTURE: The city's most colorful market area, where prices are exceptionally low, is Ninth Avenue from 37th to 43rd Streets. Everywhere you look here, the eye is attracted by vivid color, the nose by tantalizing smells. Up and down the street, bins are overflowing with fresh seafood (crabs, shrimp, squid, mussels), fruits, and vegetables; bakery windows are crowded with still-warm French and Italian loaves and flaky pastries; huge cheeses, ripe enough to burst, beckon invitingly from inside dark groceries; butchers proudly advertise their rock-bottom prices, and announce via window posters fresh game, baby lamb, and other delicacies.

Take an hour or more to see this one day. Start at **De Leonardi's Fish Company,** 672 Ninth Ave., between 46th and 47th Streets (tel. 245-9117). It's what a fish store was meant to be: ultra-clean, with a supply of fresh fish, all with bright eyes and red gills. A chart on the wall shows all the fish that live in North American waters, many of which you'll be able to buy here. De Leonardi's is a wholesaler to many of the big-name, fancy restaurants in the city, but will sell to the public. Some of what we saw included fresh brook trout, striped bass, shrimp, and Little Neck clams. Open Monday through Friday from 7 a.m. to 3 p.m.

Especially hospitable, and a personal favorite, is the family-owned **Poseidon Oriental Pastry Shop,** 629 Ninth Ave., between 44th and 45th Streets (tel. 757-6173), a guaranteed hit if you're a fan of honey-rich delicacies made with the purest ingredients in a spotless environment. Look toward the back of the store and you'll see one of the good-looking sons of the owner in front of a large wooden table, busily spreading out the 16-square-foot sheets of paper-thin phyllo dough, used to make exotic pastries and strudels. Buy it and freeze it. Pistachio-filled honey rolls, rich baklava, and innumerable other exotic delights are for sale. Delicious cheese, spinach, and meat pies are available in both cocktail and regular sizes. Everything, incidentally, can be frozen. Open Tuesday to Saturday from 9 a.m. to 7 p.m., on Sunday from 10 a.m. to 4 p.m.

Stop in at the **Washington Beef Company,** 573 Ninth Ave., between 41st and 42nd Streets (tel. 563-0200), whose very reasonably priced beef, pork, poultry, lamb, and other meats draw New York's most knowledgeable shoppers. Open Monday to Wednesday and Saturday from 6 a.m. to 5:30 p.m., until 6:30 p.m. on Thursday and Friday.

The block between 39th and 40th Streets is where you'll find fresh fruit and spices. At **International Groceries and Meat Market,** 529 Ninth Ave. (tel. 279-5514), boxes of imported spices line the sidewalk, and inside are row upon row of burlap sacks filled with more spices (over 50 kinds in all), beans, and grains. You'll also find Middle Eastern and European delicacies here—everything from stuffed grape leaves to Spanish saffron. They also have a wide selection of olive oils and cheeses, plus fresh pita bread daily. Open from 8 a.m. to 6 p.m. Monday to Saturday.

Across the street, at 494 Ninth Ave., between 37th and 38th Streets (tel. 564-4944), you'll be attracted to the **D'Aiuto Pastry Shop,** where Italian pastries, luscious cheesecakes, rum cakes, and home-baked cookies are on appetite-whetting display. Open Monday to Friday from 6 a.m. to 7 p.m., on Saturday from 8 a.m. to 7 p.m.

Hungry by now? Stop in at **Manganaro's Hero Boy Restaurant,** 492 Ninth Ave., between 37th and 38th Streets (tel. 947-7325), and order a "mile-high special," heaping big portions of meat and cheese: prosciutto, salami, mortadella (Italian baloney), capicola (cold shoulder loin of pork), cooked salami, provolone, fried peppers, tomato, lettuce, and spices. If you simply want to rest your feet, this is a good place to get a delicious cappuccino (Italian espresso coffee served with steamed milk and cinnamon). Next door at 488 Ninth Ave. (tel. 563-5331) is its retail store, where you can buy the ingredients for the sandwich just described. Great cheeses and salamis are suspended from the ceiling, along with giant bags of Italian candy and pasta. The restaurant is open Monday to Saturday from 6:30 a.m. to 7:30 p.m.; store hours are 8 a.m. to 7 p.m. on Monday and Saturday, to 8 p.m. Tuesday through Friday. More about Manganaro's in Chapter II.

GOURMET'S WALK AT THE SOUTH STREET SEAPORT: New York's exciting South Street Seaport is not only a living museum that brings back the days of the tall ships (see Chapter II), but it's also one of the city's newest, most engaging and entertaining marketplaces. The center of the food excitement here is the Fulton Market at 11 Fulton St., whose entire main floor is given over to fresh foods from the city's finest purveyors. Here you'll find, for example, **Evan & Lewis Limited,** whose specialty is English farmhouse cheese—cheddar, Cheshire, Double Gloucester, Leicester, Wensleydale, and Caerphilly, for a start. They also have quite a few goat cheeses from France and Italy, all the well-known cheeses, and all at good, competitive prices. Other tempting gourmet items here include pâtés from Au Petit Cochon, smoked meats and fresh sausages from Schaller and Webber, pastas and salads from Pasta and Cheese, plus caviar, smoked fish, sun-dried tomatoes, and more. A must stop.

Huge sacks of fragrant coffee beans perfume the air at **Merchant's Coffee, Tea and Spices,** which may well have the largest selection of coffees and pure-water-process decaffeinated coffees in the country. Consider, for example, decaffeinated Amaretto, Irish cream, Swiss mocha almond, espresso roast, etc., for about $7 a pound. Luscious flavored coffees like Dutch mocha mint, cinnamon mocha royale, and chocolate cherry are about $6. Coffees from Africa, South and Central America, the Caribbean, and the Pacific are featured, and all are sold fresh and ground on the premises. They also offer coffee makers and mugs, cappuccino machines, loose and packaged teas, and more.

Another favorite of ours is **Provisions,** whose gourmet delicacies, mostly French, would make lovely small hostess presents. It's hard to resist the likes of Lime Tree honey from the Alps of Haute-Provence, pistachio spread from Provence, pure maple syrup from Canada, or Sweet Heat chutney. At least have a giant chocolate truffle; they're flown in fresh every week from San Francisco and go for $1.75 each.

Zaro's Bread Basket gives you the chance to sample traditional New York Jewish-style baking (everything here is kosher, by the way). Wonderful strawberry and blueberry cheesecakes, hearty breads like raisin pumpernickel, luscious pastries, goodies galore are here. Warning: This one is hard to resist.

Guss Pickles, the legend of the Lower East Side, is here at the Marketplace with all those wonderful sours, half-sours, and sour tomatoes, that have nourished generations of hungry New Yorkers. A dollar buys two pickles from the barrel; $2, a quart jar to take home.

The **Seaport Fruiton Market** has a mind-boggling array of fresh fruits and vegetables; the **Fulton Market Retail Store** has quality fish and seafood; and **Nutcracker Treats** has both imported and domestic nuts and seeds, dried fruit, and freshly made peanut butter each day.

For food-related gifts, **A & D Mercantile** is great fun, with scads of goodies like cookie crocks, pâté pots, all sorts of gadgets, kitchen magnets, spoon rests, plus charming "character mugs" at small prices.

If candy is your thing, cross the street from Fulton Market to the Front Street Shops, where you'll find the **Rocky Mountain Chocolate Factory,** the first of the popular Colorado-based chain to open east of the Mississippi. Several times a day chocolates are hand-dipped in the main selling area. A pound of hand-dipped chocolates runs about $11; fudges, about $7. You can get a huge strawberry dipped in white chocolate for 75¢, an apple dipped in caramel and candy toppings for $2.50.

If all this food shopping has made you hungry, go back to the Fulton Market and head up to the restaurants and snack shops on the upper floors. Some of our favorite take-out food establishments here (people who work in the nearby Wall Street area swear by them) are **Ming's Bau House** for Chinese dim sum cooked in clay pottery, and **Jimbay,** who prepare classic sushi presentations in a lunch box with rice, fresh ginger, and a leaf of seaweed. Eat here, or take your picnic out to the benches by the sea and enjoy!

Chapter VIII

NEW YORK WITH CHILDREN: BUDGET TIPS

1. Cultural and Educational Attractions
2. Recreation
3. Entertainment
4. Shops for Children
5. Services for Children
6. Eating Out With Children
7. Mapping Out Your Days

WITH ITS SKYSCRAPERS and busy streets, New York is a nonstop carnival for children. There's an endless list of activities for young people here, and chances are that small feet will grow tired long before you exhaust the full range of things to do.

We have listed activities that can be enjoyed with little or no expense. There are seven sections in this chapter: cultural and educational attractions; recreation; entertainment; shops; services; restaurants; and touring. Although the programs we've listed are for kids, adults may enjoy them too.

1. Cultural and Educational Attractions

MUSEUMS FOR CHILDREN: Although New York is home to some of the most sophisticated museums in the adult world (as described in Chapter III), the city has been generous in its efforts to provide museum activities that are of interest to young people. Exhibits and special programs for children cover a wide range of interests, and most are either free of charge or require a nominal contribution.

From Tyrannosaurus Rex to Star Wars

Most native New Yorkers have fond childhood memories of the **American Museum of Natural History,** Central Park West at 79th Street (tel. 873-1300). This huge museum is a budding scientist's gold mine, featuring exhibits on animals, plants, humans, and the evolution of life as we know it. The dinosaur room, filled with huge skeletons of our prehistoric predecessors, is one of the museum's most popular exhibits. Visit the People Center, which offers lectures, poetry readings, and educational activities for children of all ages in the fall and spring. Other highlights are the Natural Science Center and the Discovery Room, which give kids a chance to learn about plants, animals, and geology of New York City. And don't miss the popular science films that are shown in the Naturemax Theater—it has a screen that's four stories tall.

There's enough in this museum to fill several afternoons, so plan your hours carefully. It's worth a call to find out the schedule of activities. Open daily from 10 a.m. to 5:45 p.m., and until 9 p.m. on Wednesday, Friday, and Saturday evenings. Admission is pay-what-you-wish, with suggested fees of $3 for adults, $1.50 for children. On Friday and Saturday evenings admission is free.

For a dramatic journey in time and space, travel right next door to the **Hayden Planetarium,** Central Park West and 81st Street (tel. 873-8828). For more than 50 years the planetarium has been taking viewers of all ages out of this world with glittering sky shows on its huge domed ceiling. There's also a 14-ton meteorite, an exhibit exclusively devoted to the sun, and a laser show accompanied by classical and rock music (for show times, call 873-5714). Open from 12:30 to 4:45 p.m. Monday through Friday; from October through June, also open from 10 a.m. to 5:45 p.m. on Saturday and from noon to 5:45 p.m. on Sunday (from June through September, open Saturday and Sunday from noon to 4:45 p.m.) Special laser shows are often shown in the evening. Admission is $3.75 for adults, $2.75 for students and senior citizens with ID cards, and $2 for children.

One block to the south, children over 10 may find much that's interesting at the **New-York Historical Society,** 170 Central Park West, at 77th Street (tel. 873-3400). Its presentations are somewhat staid, but the fine collections here include Early American tin and cast-iron toys and carriages, Tiffany lamps, and watercolor paintings of birds by John Jay Audubon. Open from 11 a.m. to 5 p.m. Tuesday through Friday, from 10 a.m. to 5 p.m. on Saturday, and from 1 to 5 p.m. on Sunday. Admission is $2 for adults, 75¢ for children.

Museum Mile

Just across Central Park is the queen of Fifth Avenue's "Museum Mile" and one of the world's greatest museums—the **Metropolitan Museum of Art,** Fifth Avenue at 82nd Street (tel. 553-7710). To the eye-opening delight of children, there are displays of mummies, knights in armor, a real Egyptian temple, and some of the world's most famous paintings—all complemented by the beauty of the building itself and the Central Park backdrop. What's more, some of New York's finest street performers use the sidewalk in front of the museum as their stage.

Throughout the year the museum offers a busy schedule of workshops, films, and gallery talks for young people. To join a workshop, parents should show up on the day of the activity. We suggest you arrive early, since places are given on a first-come, first-served basis. Weekend family programs run on Saturday and Sunday from 11:30 a.m. to 4:30 p.m., September through June. Studio workshops charge $1.50 for materials. Films and gallery talks are free. Call in advance for the schedule of events. Open Wednesday through Sunday from 9:30 a.m. to 5:15 p.m., on Tuesday evening till 8:45 p.m. Suggested admission fees are $4 for adults, $2 for students and senior citizens.

To give your children a glimpse of New York City before the invasion of skyscrapers and high-rise apartments, visit the **Museum of the City of New York,** Fifth Avenue at 104th Street (tel. 534-1672), where slide shows, dioramas, and other exhibits trace the city's history from its founding as a Dutch colony in 1625. While older children may find the historical information here interesting, younger children can take a look at the museum's doll and dollhouse collection, which is the largest of its kind in the city. Displays of old fire engines, maps, and toys will also appeal to youngsters. Open Tuesday through Saturday from 10 a.m. to 5 p.m., on Sunday and holidays from 1 to 5 p.m. Admission is free.

Although the **Guggenheim Museum,** Fifth Avenue at 89th Street (tel. 860-1300), doesn't have special children's programs, it is housed in a spectacular spiral building designed by the architect Frank Lloyd Wright. Visitors generally take the elevator to the top floor, then walk downhill in wide circles, viewing artworks along the curved walls. While parents view the museum's collection of avant-garde art dating back to the late 19th century, kids can get a kick out of the building's playful design. Open Wednesday to Sunday from 11 a.m. to 5 p.m., on Tuesday till 8 p.m.; closed Monday. Admission is free on Tuesday evening from 5 to 8 p.m. Other times, $3 for adults, $1.75 for students and seniors with ID cards, and free for children under 7. No strollers.

The **Cooper-Hewitt Museum,** 91st Street at Fifth Avenue (tel. 860-6898), recently discontinued its education department, but it plans on soon resuming its extensive children's programming. When it does, this museum—located in the former Carnegie Mansion—is a must visit for aspiring designers and artists. As the Smithsonian Institution's National Museum of Design, it has an immense collection of historical and modern objects and designs from all over the world. While the permanent collection is not on view, the changing exhibits focus on various aspects of design, from canes to skyscrapers. Open on Tuesday from 10 a.m. to 9 p.m., Wednesday through Saturday to 5 p.m., and on Sunday from noon to 5 p.m. Admission is free on Tuesday night from 5 to 9 p.m.; otherwise it's $2 for adults, $1.50 for senior citizens and students over 12, and free for children under 12.

The **Museum of Modern Art,** 11 W. 53rd St. between Fifth and Sixth Avenues (tel. 708-9400), concentrates its educational efforts on classroom and school group activities, but this beautiful, recently expanded museum has plenty of powerfully communicative art children can appreciate. Monet's *Water Lilies,* Chagall's *I in the Village,* Calder's *Mobile,* Jackson Pollack's *No. 1,* and Picasso's *Goat* (in the sculpture garden) are just a few of the works popular with children. Open Friday to Tuesday from 11 a.m. to 6 p.m., and until 9 p.m. on Thursday; closed Wednesday. Admission is $4.50 for adults, free for children under 16 accompanied by an adult, and free on Thursday from 5 to 9 p.m.

El Museo del Barrio, 1230 Fifth Ave., at 104th Street (tel. 831-7272), records the vivid culture of Puerto Rico and Latin American through sculpture, paintings, graphics, and photography. On permanent view are pre-Columbian artifacts, supplemented by changing exhibits that focus on Puerto Rican culture on the island, in New York City, and in the Americas. For children interested in learning more about a vibrant but little-known culture shared by more than five million U.S. citizens, this museum is a must. Open Tuesday through Friday from 10:30 a.m. to 4:30 p.m., on Saturday and Sunday from 11 a.m. to 4 p.m. Voluntary contributions.

The **Jewish Museum,** Fifth Avenue at 92nd Street (tel. 860-1888), houses the world's largest collection of Jewish ceremonial art and historical objects. The museum offers some special family programs, usually for children 5 to 12, which focus on current exhibitions or upcoming Jewish holidays. Advance reservations are required, so call ahead to the education department (tel. 860-1863) for schedules and reservations. Open on Monday, Wednesday, and Thursday from noon to 5 p.m., on Sunday from 11 a.m. to 6 p.m., on Tuesday from noon to 8 p.m., and on Friday from noon to 3 p.m. Admission is $2.50 for adults, and $1.50 for senior citizens, students, and children ages 6 to 16.

Especially for Kids

The **Children's Museum of Manhattan,** at 314 W. 54th St., near Eighth Avenue (tel. 765-5904), is the borough's only participatory museum for children. This is a strictly hands-on place, where children have fun and learn by doing. In a recent exhibit on comic strips, for instance, museum employees dressed as comic-strip characters, and visitors drew their own comic strips. Designed for children ages 2 to 12, the museum's changing exhibits bring the world down to a manageable, explorable dimension. Open Wednesday through Sunday from 1 to 5 p.m. Admission on weekdays is $1 for adults, $2 for children; on weekends, $2 for adults, $3 for children.

Kids and parents alike will have a ball at the **Brooklyn Children's Museum,** 145 Brooklyn Ave. and St. Mark's Avenue, in the Crown Heights section of Brooklyn (tel. 718/735-4400). The museum—the first and oldest of its kind in the world—is housed in a remarkable $5-million multitiered structure and is a playground of participatory fun. Children enter by crossing a steel-mesh bridge and popping through the museum's entrance, an old-fashioned trolley-car kiosk. Inside they find themselves skittering down the People's tube—a huge, simulated river with locks, dams, waterwheels, and a turbine that can be worked to make the water level rise or fall. The museum has a greenhouse, where children mix soil and gather seeds to grind into flour in a gristmill. On the more traditional side, the museum houses a collection of more than 20,000 artifacts from ancient China, Egypt, Europe, and Colonial America, along with a collection of more than 2500 rare dolls. A number of daily workshops, classes, and films for children are offered, and there's a lending collection from which children can take home objects for a period of two weeks.

Open Monday, Wednesday, and Thursday from 1 to 5 p.m., on Saturday and Sunday from 10 a.m. to 5 p.m.; closed Tuesday. Admission is free. To get there by subway, take the IRT–Seventh Avenue line (the no. 3 "New Lots" train) to Kingston station. Walk one block west to Brooklyn Avenue and then six short blocks up to Kingston Avenue and St. Mark's Avenue (you'll see Brower Park on the corner).

The **Staten Island Children's Museum** is snug in its new home—in Snug Harbor, near the famous Richmondtown Restoration. The museum occupies a four-story building and offer exhibitions on architecture, music, and the fine arts. It's famous for Meadowfair, its annual spring arts fair that attracts more than 5000 people. After-school programs are open to out-of-town youngsters (reservations required). The museum was just reopening as we were getting ready to go to press. They will be open from Tuesday through Sunday but call 718/273-2060 for exact hours. Suggested donation is $2 per visitor.

Ahoy Matey!

New York's still-thriving harbors are celebrated at the **South Street Seaport,** located along Fulton and Water Streets at Piers 15 and 16 (tel. 732-7678). Recently restored and expanded, the Seaport is filled with exhibits, galleries, antique ships, and seafood markets. To give children a feel for waterfront life 100 years ago, take them to **South Street Venture,** 210 Front St. (tel. 608-6696), a multimedia presentation complete with sea spray and fog. (Admission is $3.75 for adults, $3 for seniors, $2.50 for children.) Maritime exhibits and films can also be found at the **South Street Seaport Museum,** 171 John St. (tel. 669-9400), which coordinates walking tours of the area and visits aboard the Seaport's antique ships. (Admission is either $3 or $5 for adults and $1.50 or $3.50 for children, depending on the activities and tours selected.) There are numerous restaurants and food concessions here, all drawing on the world-renowned Fulton Fish Market.

Exhibits are open seven days a week, but hours vary. To get to the Seaport, take the IRT–Seventh Avenue express (no. 2 or 3 train) to Fulton Street; walk east toward the water.

The **Intrepid Sea–Air–Space Museum,** on the Hudson River at the foot of West 46th Street, at Pier 86 (tel. 245-2533), is a fascinating museum of technology housed on an old aircraft carrier. There are four theme halls—each devoted to a particular aspect of our country's recent achievements on the seas, in the air, and beyond. Each hall offers a related film. Admission is $4.75 for adults, $2.50 for children under 12. Open Wednesday through Sunday from 10 a.m. to 5 p.m.

Howdy Doody

The more than 20,000 videotapes and radio shows at the **Museum of Broadcasting,** 1 E. 53rd St., just off Fifth Avenue (tel. 752-7684), show younger generations that, yes, there was life before rock videos. Visitors can select tapes from the museum's holdings, and view them at individual consoles on a first-come, first-served basis. Why not pick out a few of your own favorite kids' shows—"Howdy Doody" and "Kukla, Fran, and Ollie" are all here—or let your kids choose reruns of their own favorites? Open Wednesday through Saturday from noon to 5 p.m., on Tuesday to 8 p.m. Suggested donations are $3 for adults, $2 for students, and $1.50 for children under 13.

3-D

Children and adults will enjoy being confounded at the **Museum of Holography,** 11 Mercer St., in SoHo, half a block north of Canal Street and one block west of Broadway (tel. 925-0526), where 3-D images seem to be alive and kicking in their own complete worlds. This museum features extensive educational displays, including a selection of the earliest and state-of-the-art holograms. Admission is $3 for adults and $1.75 for children. Open Wednesday through Sunday from noon until 6 p.m.

First Aid for Dolls

The **New York Doll Hospital,** 787 Lexington Ave., between 61st and 62nd Streets (tel. 838-7527), is the place to bring grandmother's wax doll for a facelift, or your injured Cabbage Patch kid for a specialist's care. The Doll Hospital began over 60 years ago as a concession to a hairdressing salon—children could get their doll's hair done just like their mother's. Although there aren't any ambulances here, you're welcome to observe any of the "operations" and view the collections of bisque, foreign, and celebrity dolls. To get there, ring the bell at the sidewalk door and then go up one flight of crooked old stairs after you're buzzed in. Open Monday through Friday and Saturday (except in summer) from 10 a.m. to 6 p.m. Admission is free.

The Birth of America

A visit two centuries into the nation's past is the subject of the **Federal Hall National Memorial,** at the corner of Wall and Nassau Streets (tel. 264-8711). The memorial, administered by the National Park Service, is housed in an 1842 building on the site where the Declaration of Independence was read in July of 1776, where the first Congress met to count the electoral votes of the first presidential election, and where George Washington was inaugurated in 1789 as the nation's first president. Exhibits include films for children of different ages. Open Monday through Friday from 9 a.m. to 5 p.m. Admission is free.

America's Greatest Tinkerer

Most children will enjoy an entire museum devoted to one of America's best-known homespun geniuses, inventor Thomas Edison. The **Con Edison Energy Museum,** 145 E. 14th St., just west of Third Avenue (tel. 460-6244), focuses on the development of electricity, from Edison's invention of the electric lightbulb to the present, and includes some hands-on exhibits. Open Tuesday through Saturday from 10 a.m. to 4 p.m. Admission is free.

Fire Engines

Nearly two centuries of fire-fighting history are stored away at the **Fire Department Museum,** 104 Duane St., between Church Street and Broadway (tel. 570-4230). The oldest engine here dates back to 1820 and was hand-pulled by a team of volunteer firemen to the scene of a New York fire. Also on display are leather fire hoses, steam engines, Brooklyn's first fire bell, and pictures and drawings (including a Currier and Ives) of famous fires. There's even a stuffed dog named Chief, who earned his stripes by saving cats from burning buildings. Open from 9 a.m. to 4 p.m. Monday through Friday; closed holidays. Admission is free.

(*Note:* Other, more descriptive displays of vehicles and fire-fighting paraphernalia can be seen at the Museum of the City of New York and the New-York Historical Society.)

New York's Finest

If anyone in your family is interested in the men in blue, try a visit to the **Police Academy Museum,** 235 E. 20th St., between Second and Third Avenues (tel. 477-9753). This museum boasts one of the world's largest collections of police memorabilia—from weapons to handcuffs—plus exhibits on current police procedures and uniforms. Open Monday through Friday from 9 a.m. to 3 p.m. Admission is free.

Aspiring policemen also may want to take a look behind the scenes at the **Police Headquarters Building,** 1 Police Plaza, behind the Municipal Building (tel. 374-3804). The communications system for police in all five boroughs is a lot bigger than the home computer game your child may be used to, and makes an interesting 45-minute tour. These are given September through May at 10 a.m. and 1 p.m. on Tuesday and Wednesday. Arrangements should be made at least two weeks in advance by phone. Admission is free. To get there, take the IRT–Lexington Avenue subway to the Brooklyn Bridge station, and walk through the Municipal Building.

The Hidden Wonders of Harlem and Washington Heights

Many guidebooks—and even natives—give the impression that sightseeing in northern Manhattan stops with the Upper West Side. This is an unfortunate misapprehension, and we would like to set the record straight! Manhattan continues to fascinate . . . even beyond 200th Street.

But before proceeding, it is wise to note that while this area is not dangerous if explored wisely, Harlem, more than anywhere else in Manhattan, demands street-smarts. Unless you are traveling with someone who lives in or is familiar with the neighborhood, visit during the day. You can map out the stops you want to make and take the most direct routes via several public transportation lines. MTA buses go uptown on Broadway and on Riverside Drive; the IRT and IND subway lines also serve the area. Consult subway and bus maps or call MTA route information (tel. 718/330-1234), for specifics. There are many organized tours that go through Harlem; for information, call the Uptown Chamber of Commerce (tel. 427-7200).

Budding designers can view the country's largest collection of black fashion design and memorabilia at the **Black Fashion Museum,** 126th Street between Lenox Avenue and Adam Clayton Powell, Jr., Boulevard (tel. 666-1320). The oldest pieces date from the late 1600s and the most recent from such Broadway plays as *The Wiz* and *Timbuktu.* Open by appointment only. Admission is free.

The **Studio Museum in Harlem,** 144 W. 125th St., between Lenox and Seventh Avenues (tel. 864-4500), is an elegant museum dedicated to black American culture and Harlem's vibrant local art. Programs for children—for example, weekend classes in batik, collage, silkscreening, and African masks—are offered throughout the year. They cost $3 to $5 and require reservations. Other frequently scheduled events include films and puppet shows about events in black American history (e.g., Rosa Parks and the bus boycott), and concerts, lectures, and readings by nationally known artists and scholars. Museum hours are 10 a.m. to 5 p.m. on Wednesday, Thursday, and Friday, and 1 to 6 p.m. on Saturday and Sunday. Admission is $1.50 for adults and 50¢ for children.

Once upon a time there lived a woman who saved so many toys and dolls in her lovely Harlem brownstone that she could hardly find room for them. Her name was—and is—Aunt Len, and you can meet her at **Aunt Len's Doll and Toy Museum,** located on one of Harlem's most historic blocks between 141st and 142nd Streets and Hamilton Terrace (look for the wooden sign near the corner; tel. 281-4143). This is a very personal collection of more than 5000 dolls and 100,000 assorted toys and trinkets; it includes antique black dolls from all over the world, an American revival choir, Shirley Temple dolls, life-size English dolls sitting down to a tea party, and a Michael Jackson doll. Aunt Len (her real name is Mrs. Holder Hoyt) gives classes in dollcraft to local children and is the inspiration behind a yearly doll pageant in Harlem. Open by appointment only; donation suggested.

Unfortunately, **Audubon Terrace,** Broadway between 155th and 156th Streets, does not attract the visitor's attention the way it once did. The area has grown lackluster, is given little promotion, and there is talk of moving one of the museums either downtown or to another state. But this is still an impressive cultural enclave—a constellation of five museums and research institutions and on the estate of John Jay Audubon, the naturalist and painter.

For a glimpse of America's indigenous past, visit the **Museum of the American Indian–Heye Foundation** (tel. 283-2420). The museum is filled with artifacts from tribes as far north as the Arctic and as far south as Tierra del Fuego. There are masks, games, tomahawks, and the personal possessions of such famous chiefs as Red Cloud, Sitting Bull, Crazy Horse, and Arapoosh. Admission is $2 for adults, $1 for students and senior citizens. Hours are Tuesday through Saturday from 10 a.m. to 5 p.m., on Sunday from 1 to 5 p.m. This is the museum that's generated all the talk about moving elsewhere, so call first before making a special visit up to Harlem to see it.

Two other museums in the complex may be of special interest to older children:

The **Hispanic Society of America** (tel. 926-2234) has a small yet lively collection of paintings by El Greco, Velázquez, Goya, and other Hispanic artists. With its terracotta floors and high ceilings, the building replicates a small Spanish villa. Walk through the Sorrolla Room, where there is a vivid series of murals painted by Joaquin Sorrolla y Bastida in 1911; the walls burst with scenes of fiesta life in regional Spain. Admission is free but a donation is appreciated. Open Tuesday through Saturday from 10 a.m. to 4:30 p.m., on Sunday 1 to 4 p.m.

Coin collectors will appreciate the **American Numismatic Society** (tel. 234-3130). The society recently completed installation of "The World of Coins," a comprehensive exhibit surveying the history of the world's coinage and paper money. Kids will delight in seeing coins made of salt, shells, and beads—and in learning how and why money has made "the world go round" for millennia. There's a computer on hand to provide detailed information on any coin or object in the show. Open Tuesday through Saturday from 9 a.m. to 4:30 p.m., on Sunday from 1 to 3 p.m. Admission is free.

OTHER EDUCATIONAL ATTRACTIONS: In addition to the better-known museums, there are smaller, offbeat sights that will appeal to children as well.

Read All About It

The **New York Times**, 229 W. 43rd St., between Seventh and Eighth Avenues (tel. 556-1310), gives public tours of its editorial and composing rooms each Friday at noon. The tour, which lasts about an hour, meets in the lobby. Small children can visit, but keep in mind that people will be at work. Admission is free. Reservations are not needed except for large groups.

Banking

For a glimpse of the world of finance, young entrepreneurs should visit the **Federal Reserve Bank**, 33 Liberty St., between Nassau and William Streets (tel. 791-6130). The tour here includes a visit to the gold vault, the currency-processing department, and an exhibit hall that explains the Federal Reserve's role in the economy. Tours are given by reservation only—Monday through Friday at 10 a.m., 11 a.m., 1 p.m., 2 p.m.—and must be made at least one week in advance by phone or by mail.

The World's Largest Post Office

Kids 14 and older can see the U.S. mail at work in the huge **James A. Farley Post Office** at Eighth Avenue and 33rd Street (across from Penn Station), but you must make arrangements at least two weeks in advance. Write to the Postmaster, Room 3215, James A. Farley Building, New York, NY 10001 (tel. 971-5331). Children must be at least 14, and you must have ten or more people in your group. The post office will send you a letter confirming your reservation—be sure to bring it on the day of the tour. Tours take about 45 minutes. The Farley Building is one of the nicer public buildings in the city—the block-long lobby has a magnificent ceiling and there aren't any loiterers. Admission is free.

Manhattan by Movie

The **New York Experience** is a 12-year-old multimedia presentation that still captures the verve of New York City, past and present. Sixteen screens full of music and excitement will give you a sense of what it's like to live here. The movie shows downstairs at the McGraw-Hill Building, 1221 Avenue of the Americas, between 48th and 49th Streets (tel. 869-0345). Show times are Monday to Thursday from 11 a.m. to 7 p.m., on Friday and Saturday to 8 p.m., and on Sunday from noon to 8 p.m. Admission is $4.25 for adults, $2.50 for children under 12. Come early to let your kids enjoy the exhibit "Little Old New York" (free), which re-creates turn-of-the-century Manhattan. The Antique Amusement Arcade features old working pinball machines and games for 25¢. There's also an inexpensive café for snacks.

Around the World

From Australia to Zambia, governments from all over the world have consulates, tourist bureaus, and information offices scattered around the city. You will come away from any of them with an armload of posters, brochures, and newspapers. Budding linguists can try using a few phrases of elementary French or Spanish, and others can try to decipher a newspaper written in Arabic. To get phone numbers or information, look up the country of your choice in the Manhattan White Pages. Most offices are open during regular business hours.

A Super Supermarket

La Marqueta, Park Avenue between 111th and 116th Streets, may very well be the world's largest supermarket. Food from Jamaica, Puerto Rico, Cuba, Italy, Haiti, Spain, and other far-away places can be purchased here. Located under the Park Avenue railroad tracks, La Marqueta is mouthwatering proof of New York's melting pot and the variety of foods that go into it.

Great Graffiti

You don't have to go to Harlem to see graffiti in New York, but some of the best—and best intentioned—can be found at the **Graffiti Hall of Fame,** a neighborhood-improvement project on the playground walls behind Junior High School No. 13 at 106th Street and Park Avenue. Kids will appreciate the energy, vivid colors, and messages embedded in the designs. Other graffiti art can be seen on 125th Street between Fifth and Seventh Avenues. The merchants here hire graffiti and spray-paint artists to decorate the roll-down shutters of their shopfronts.

ZOOS FOR CHILDREN: If there's anyplace you can take your children and have just as much fun as they do, it's the zoo. New York's **Bronx Zoo,** at Fordham Road and Southern Boulevard, is among the world's finest. It is home and breeding ground for nearly 4000 wild animals, many of which are endangered species, some even considered extinct in nature. The zoo is lovely as well as interesting, and the perfect place to take yourself and your children for a day away from the city proper.

Aside from the myriad animals in imaginative settings, the Bronx Zoo offers a special children's zoo. Conceived as a "participatory" zoo, it's a place where children can assume the behavior, live in the environments, and even don the sensory apparatus (fox's "ears," owl's "eyes") of wild animals, to find out just what it's like to be an animal. There's a prairie dog tunnel that is child-size and a giant rope spiderweb for climbing.

Also not to be missed are rides on elephants and camels, and in llama-drawn carts (closed during winter), and a monorail ride ($1.25 for adults, 75¢ for children) through Wild Asia, where tigers, rhinos, and wild Asian deer roam relatively unconfined in a 38-acre area designed to simulate their natural environment. The zoo's newest and most ambitious project is Jungle World, a one-acre wood- and glass-enclosed habitat in which animals wander more or less freely through a re-created volcanic scrub forest, a mangrove swamp, a lowland evergreen rain forest, and a mountain rain forest.

The zoo is open daily from 10 a.m. to 5 p.m. in the winter, and until 5:30 p.m. in the summer. Admission is free on Tuesday, Wednesday, and Thursday (rides and special exhibits have separate charges); Friday through Monday, admission is $3 for adults and $1.25 for children. To reach the zoo by subway, take the IRT–Seventh Avenue no. 2 express train to Pelham Parkway, or the IRT–Lexington Avenue no. 5 train to East 180th Street and transfer to the IRT–Seventh Avenue no. 2. From Pelham Parkway, walk west to the Bronxdale entrance to the zoo. Express bus service is available from mid-Manhattan; the fare is $3 (exact fare required). Call 652-8400 for schedule and stops.

Central Park has its own adorable **Lehman's Children's Zoo,** with its entrance at East 64th Street and Fifth Avenue (tel. 360-8287). A 10¢ admission brings children and adults into a fantasyland of miniature bridges, a red barn,

Noah's Ark, and a sculpted blue whale. The zoo's inhabitants are winsome ducks, rabbits, cows, and goats, plus more exotic critters like ferrets and African pony goats. Open daily from 10 a.m. to 4:30 p.m. Call the above number or park information (tel. 390-3100) for story-telling and special events. Outside the Children's Zoo, at the south end of the old Central Park Zoo, there are pony rides, for 75¢. Also in Central Park, there's the **Carousel Ride,** a nice stroll in from either side of 65th Street. A ride on one of the gaily painted horses is 50¢. And if your children still have the heebie-jeebies, rustle them over to the **Alice in Wonderland statue** next to the model boat pond near the East 77th Street entrance to the park, and let them climb to their heart's content.

Brooklyn's **Prospect Park Zoo,** Empire Boulevard and Flatbush Avenue (tel. 718/965-6587), offers everything most people expect in a zoo, including the **Children's Farm,** where kids can pet domestic animals and enjoy pony-cart rides. Admission is free. Open daily from 11 a.m. to 4:45 p.m., until 4 p.m. from mid-April through September. To get there, take the D, N, or QB subways to Prospect Park.

In Queens, the place to talk to the animals is the **Queens Zoo and Children's Zoo,** 111th Street and 54th Avenue at Flushing Meadows/Corona Park (tel. 718/699-7239). Here the children's zoo is modeled after a farmer's barnyard, and features a carousel, pony rides, and wagon rides in addition to your standard barnyard residents. Admission is free. Open daily from 10 a.m. to 4 p.m. To get there, take the IRT–Flushing (no. 7) subway to 111th Street.

An internationally renowned collection of reptiles—including every species of U.S. rattlesnake—can be found at the **Staten Island Zoological Park and Children's Zoo,** 614 Broadway, Staten Island (tel. 718/442-3100). The zoo also features a waterwheel, pond, and feedable animals such as goats and sheep. Open daily from 10 a.m. to 4:45 p.m. Admission is $1 for adults, 75¢ for children, free for senior citizens and kids under 3; on Wednesday, free to all. To get there by car, take the Verrazano Narrows Bridge to the Staten Island Expressway, to the Slosson Avenue exit. Follow Slosson to the zoo parking lot at Clove Road. By bus from the Staten Island Ferry depot at St. George, take bus 107 to Forest Avenue at Broadway, then walk three blocks up Broadway.

2. Recreation

Children who get cabin fever after a long hotel stay can run off steam in the city's wide range of recreational facilities. Below we've listed some inexpensive ways to take advantage of Manhattan's "great outdoors," which means Central Park—one of the best running, jumping, walking, ball-playing, ice-skating, roller-skating, theater-going, bicycling, kite-flying, picnicking, horseback-riding, concert-listening, napping, folk-dancing, sail-boating, and people-watching spots anywhere.

BICYCLING: Central Park's roadways are closed to cars on weekends throughout the year so that peddlers can make their way through the park unhindered. Biking hours are 7 p.m. Friday to 6 a.m. Monday. From early May to early November the park is closed to cars from 10 a.m. to 3 p.m., and from 7 to 10 p.m.

Among the shops where bicycles can be rented is **West Side Bicycles,** 231 W. 96th St., (tel. 663-7531). Open daily from 9:30 a.m. to 6:30 p.m., it rents three-speed bikes for $3 per hour or $15 per day; ten-speeds for $5 per hour or $25 per day (deposit required: $50 or credit card or $20 plus driver's license). **R & B Bicycle,** 663 Amsterdam Ave., near 92nd Street (tel. 866-7600), is open from 9 a.m. to 6 p.m. Monday through Saturday, and from 10 a.m. to 7 p.m. on Sunday. Rates for three-speeds are $3.50 per hour or $12 per day, and for ten-speeds, $4.50 per hour or $17.50 per day (deposit: leave ID card). **Midtown Bi-**

NEW YORK WITH CHILDREN

cycles, 360 W. 47th St., between Eighth and Ninth Avenues (tel. 581-4500), is open daily from 9:30 a.m. to 6:30 p.m. Three-speeds are $3 per hour or $15 per day; ten-speeds are $5 per hour or $25 per day (deposit: leave credit card, or driver's license and $20).

BOATING: There's nothing like a boat ride in Central Park on a sunny afternoon. You can rent rowboats at the **Loeb Boathouse,** on the east side of the 72nd Street lake (tel. 288-7281). Open seven days a week beginning in April (and until the weather becomes prohibitive) from 11 a.m. to 6 p.m. Monday through Friday, 9 a.m. to 7 p.m. Saturday and Sunday. A $20 deposit and $5 per hour gets you afloat.

CHESS: Have a grandmaster in your family? The **Manhattan Chess Club,** on the tenth floor of Carnegie Hall at 154 W. 57th St. (tel. 333-5888), was established in 1870 and is one of the oldest chess clubs in the world. Bobby Fischer, among other chess stars, has played here. Your child can play chess all day for $3. Open noon to 10 p.m. daily.

You can also bring your child to the **Chess and Backgammon Club,** 212 W. 72nd St. (tel. 874-8299). Open daily from 10:30 a.m. till late evening. The playing fee is $1.50 per hour.

HORSEBACK RIDING: Eager equestrians can rent horses at the **Claremont Riding Academy,** 175 W. 89th St., from 6:30 a.m. to 4 p.m. on weekends and until an hour before dusk on weekdays for $20 an hour (no deposit required). Riding lessons and classes at different skill levels are also offered. Private lessons are $22 a half hour; group lessons, $22 an hour. For reservations and information, call 724-5101.

ICE SKATING: The **Lasker Memorial Skating Rink,** at 107th Street in Central Park, at the 110th Street entrance opposite Lenox Avenue (tel. 397-3142), is an outdoor rink that doubles as a swimming pool in the summer. The winter season is from November through mid-March. Admission is $1 for children, $2 for adults on weekdays; $2.50 for adults on weekends and holidays. Open Monday through Friday from noon to 9 p.m., on Saturday and Sunday from 11 a.m. to 10 p.m. Closed Monday.

For indoor skating year round, visit the **Sky Rink,** 450 W. 33rd St., between Ninth and Tenth Avenues (tel. 695-6555). The rink has afternoon and evening sessions for children and adults; call for the exact schedule. Admission is $6 for evening sessions, $5.50 for afternoon sessions. Skates can be rented for $2 a pair.

KITE FLYING: The best place in Central Park to fly kites is in the Sheep Meadow, opposite the West 67th Street entrance to the park (also a good place to spread a blanket and relax).

For an unusual kite, try **Go Fly A Kite,** which has two stores—the main store at 1201 Lexington Ave., between 81st and 82nd Streets (tel. 472-2623), and one in the Citicorp Center, at 53rd Street and Lexington Avenue (tel. 308-1666). The main store is open Monday to Saturday from 10:30 a.m. to 5:45 p.m. The Citicorp store is open Monday to Friday from 10:30 a.m. to 7:45 p.m. At both stores prices start at $2.50 and fly all the way up to $500.

MODEL BOAT SAILING: **Conservatory Lake,** in Central Park at 72nd Street and Fifth Avenue (tel. 249-3772), is the place to launch your model boat. You'll see as many adults as children here, and some serious sailors and intricate sloops. Races are held every Saturday from 9 a.m. till 5 p.m.

ROLLER SKATING: Roller skating has become a popular activity in New York in recent years. You can rent skates at the **Mineral Springs Pavilion,** in Central Park at the West 72nd Street entrance (tel. 861-1818). Rates are $4 for the first hour and $1.50 for each additional half hour. A $5 deposit with two major pieces of identification is required for rentals. Open daily from 10 a.m. to 5:30 p.m., to 6:30 p.m. on weekends.

SWIMMING: The city also operates several swimming pools, open generally from Memorial Day to Labor Day, depending on the city budget. One favorite is the **John Jay Pool** on East 77th Street, one block east of York Avenue at Cherokee Place (tel. 397-3159). It's open daily from 11 a.m. to 7 p.m. Admission is free, but bring a lock for lockers.

Central Park has its own pool, the **Lasker Memorial Rink** at 107th Street (tel. 593-8253), which hangs up its skates for towels during the summer. Enter from East 110th Street opposite Lenox Avenue. Lasker has an Olympic-size pool (but only about three feet deep) and two wading pools. Admission is free. Open weekdays from 11 a.m. to 7 p.m., weekends from 10 a.m. to 7 p.m.

If you're willing to pay to leave the crowds behind, swim at the **Sheraton City Squire Inn,** 790 Seventh Ave., between 51st and 52nd Streets (tel. 581-3300). The pool, located on the fifth floor, is open to nonguests daily from 7:30 a.m. to 8 p.m. Fees are $8 on weekdays, $10 on weekends; children under 12 are half price. Towels and comfortable locker facilities are included, and you can stay all day if you wish. The pool is moderate-sized, with glass walls on three sides.

PICNICS: On a warm, sunny day, a picnic is a special delight in the city, and it's as easy as picking up sandwiches and spreading a blanket. Central Park, of course, is just about the best place to go to stretch out, sunbathe, and let your kids run. In addition to the hot-dog vendors and orange-juice squeezers on most streetcorners, there are summertime kiosks at the **Bethesda Fountain** in Central Park at 72nd Street, where you can buy franks, sausages, drinks, and other snacks. More expensive (around $10 a person and up) are the special picnics-to-go that you can pick up at the **Tavern on the Green** restaurant and other elegant eateries on the Upper East and West Sides. One that doesn't require advance orders is **TBLS Cuisine,** Lexington Avenue at 78th Street.

On the West Side, you'll find a nice little park for lunch or a rest stop on West 50th Street between the Avenue of the Americas and Seventh Avenue, not far from Radio City Music Hall. The park has white patio chairs and tables, a fountain, and bronze life-like sculpture of a teenage boy reading a book on fishing. It's so realistic that you can read about angling over his right shoulder, but don't ask him to share the hamburger he also holds!

Another serene haven in the heart of the city is **Paley Park,** a few steps east of Fifth Avenue on 53rd Street, a tiny oasis about the size of a tennis court. High brick walls on three sides, vaulting honey locust trees, ivy, and pots of begonias shield you from the city's bustle. You can dine alfresco at patio tables, and there's a refreshment stand for light snacks. Open from 8 a.m. to 7 p.m.

There are numerous **city-sponsored playgrounds,** but one of the roomiest and most pleasant is on First Avenue between 67th and 68th Streets. It has safety swings, mini-theaters, and a log mountain with a giant slide. There's also a toddler area with a smaller slide and sand to play in. There are lots of tall trees and shaded benches. The park closes at dusk.

3. Entertainment

THEATER AND PERFORMANCES: Stage lights and grease paint hold a special thrill for children, and New York theaters put on a wide variety of shows throughout the year that are appropriate for young people of all ages. Many productions are participatory, so your children may get a chance to step into the limelight.

For the most current and complete listings, check the *New York Times,* the *New Yorker, New York* magazine, and the *Village Voice.* Below are a few playhouses and other entertainment establishments that regularly feature children's shows.

One of the most popular kids' attractions in the city is a magic show at the **Magic Towne House,** 1026 Third Ave., between 60th and 61st Streets (tel. 752-1165). Open only in the summer, the playhouse features an hour-long show for children ages 4 to 12. The magician often asks for help from the audience. Tickets are $4 for adults and children, and reservations are recommended.

Audience participation is part of the charm at the **13th Street Repertory Company,** 50 W. 13th St., between Fifth and Sixth Avenues (tel. 675-6677). The company performs two hour-long plays, *Snow White* and *Rumpelstiltskin,* and is planning to add a third show that dramatizes folk tales. Show times are Saturday and Sunday at 1 and 3 p.m. Admission is $3 for adults and children. Reservations are recommended. If you'd like to hold your child's birthday party here, call ahead and the company will set up a special table with birthday decorations (cost: $10; you provide the food). Admission to the show is $2.50 for birthday guests.

The **Little People's Theater,** at the Courtyard Playhouse at 39 Grove St., near Seventh Avenue South (tel. 765-9540), is one of the city's longest-running children's theater groups. From Labor Day till the end of June, it offers *Alice in Wonderland* and other traditional children's shows geared for kids between the ages of 3 and 8. Show times are 1:30 and 3 p.m. on Saturday and Sunday. Admission is $4 for adults and children; reservations are a must.

Other popular attractions include:

The **Market at Citicorp Center,** East 53rd Street at Lexington Avenue (tel. 559-2330), which presents a wide range of entertainment for children on Saturday from 11 a.m. to noon. Free admission. Call for schedule.

Fourth Wall Theater, 79 E. 4th St., between the Bowery and Second Avenue (tel. 254-5060), which presents a rock 'n' roll musical for kids called *Toto and the Wizard of Wall Street* at 3:30 p.m. on Saturday and Sunday. Admission is $4 for children, $7 for adults. Closed from mid-June through August.

The **Big Apple Circus** is a delightful one-ring circus that performs at Lincoln Center, on Broadway between 62nd and 63rd Streets, from November through January, then travels from borough to borough during the spring and summer. Call 369-5110 to check its schedule. Admission prices vary, from $8 to $24.

The **Paper Bag Players,** 50 Riverside Dr., at 77th Street (tel. 362-0431), a much-praised theater group that uses costumes made out of commonplace household items in an hour-long show of musical skits and sketches. Call for schedule.

And the **Library for the Performing Arts at Lincoln Center,** 111 Amsterdam Ave., at 65th Street (tel. 870-1633), sponsors puppet shows, films, and other performances.

Department stores also schedule various programs for children. In particular, watch for events at **F.A.O. Schwarz,** 745 Fifth Ave., at the corner of 58th Street (tel. 644-9400), **Gimbels,** at 33rd Street and Broadway (tel. 564-3300);

and **Barnes & Noble Bookstore,** Fifth Avenue at 18th Street (tel. 675-5500).

OTHER ATTRACTIONS: Fun for children is not limited to the stage. Below are other events and entertainment that kids will enjoy.

Record Breakers

Located in the concourse of the Empire State Building, which gets honorable mention here as the third-tallest building in the world, the **Guinness World Records Exhibit Hall** (tel. 947-2335) may seem tacky to adults, but holds great appeal for children. Most of the displays are replicas of record holders, including a statue of the world's tallest man (8 feet 11 inches) and a model of the hand with the longest fingernails (uncut from 1952 to 1981). Admission is $3 for adults, $2 for children 12 and under. Open daily from 9:30 a.m. to 6 p.m., to 8 p.m. in summer.

Boat Excursions

The **Staten Island Ferry** is still the best deal in town, at 25¢ a ride. On a clear day you'll get a full view of the bay, including the Statue of Liberty, Brooklyn, Manhattan, New Jersey, Staten Island, Governor's Island, and the Verrazano Narrows Bridge. To get to the ferry, take the IRT–Seventh Avenue no. 1 subway all the way to the South Ferry station. The Staten Island Ferry is used by commuters, so it's best to avoid rush hours when you go.

The **Statue of Liberty Ferry** to Liberty Island leaves from Battery Park (tel. 269-5755). It runs every hour from 10 a.m. to 4 p.m. Wednesday through Sunday. Adult fares are $2; children under 12 pay $1.

The **Circle Line** tour boats sail completely around Manhattan from Pier 83 at West 43rd Street (tel. 563-3200). The schedule changes, so call ahead for information on these three-hour tours. The pier is located in an area of town that should be approached with caution in the evening. Fares are $12 for adults, $5 for children under 12.

Wild Animals and Amusement Park

If you feel like getting out of the city for a short day trip, you can go on a safari to the wilds of New Jersey at **Great Adventure,** Jackson, N.J. (tel. 201/982-2000). The 500-acre park has lions, bears, and giraffes which run freely in a natural setting. You can drive your own car through the safari route (windows and doors must be locked) or take a guided bus tour. There's also a big amusement park here, with all the expected rides and attractions.

The safari park is open from 9 a.m. to 5 p.m. A combined ticket for the safari and amusement park is $14.95. Admission to the park alone is $13.95, to the safari is $4.95. Children under 3 are admitted free.

Great Adventure is about an hour's drive out of the city. By car, take the Jersey Turnpike to Exit 7A and follow signs to I-95 East. Exit at Mount Holly and turn south onto Route 537, which takes you to the park.

THIS AND THAT ABOUT TOWN: Even traveling around New York can be an exciting adventure. The subways are filled with graffiti that can appear straight out of an MTV video or a science fiction thriller. Many buildings, especially in SoHo and Greenwich Village, have been decorated with huge murals and designs.

If you're on East 42nd Street, the art deco home of the city's largest-circulation newspaper, the **Daily News Building,** at 220 E. 42nd St., at Second Avenue, is worth a peek. The main lobby, open 24 hours a day, contains a huge globe that turns, and sometimes there's a show of newspaper photographs.

One block east, the **Ford Foundation** building, at 320 E. 42nd St., looks like a huge terrarium. A small, fern-lined pool of water keeps the air moist for a jungle of plants. Sometimes, when enough moisture condenses on the glass roof above, there's a "rainstorm" inside the building. The garden is open to the public weekdays from 9 a.m. to 5 p.m.

The **Flatiron Building** is a fine example of how architects have used every available space in the city to create unusual structures. Wedge-shaped to fit into a triangular piece of property at the intersection of Broadway and Fifth Avenue, at 23rd Street, the building got its nickname for its obvious resemblance to the old-fashioned iron.

Parades, Street Fairs, Festivals, Etc.

Each year New York hosts parades and festivals on a grand scale. The color and hoopla make them great events for kids, so we've sketched out a few time-tested favorites to watch for.

Topping the parade list is the **Macy's Thanksgiving Day Parade,** a must-see pageant of Disney creatures, decked-out high school bands, mounted horsemen and women, wonderous flower-bedecked mechanical floats, gigantic helium balloons, and marching celebrities. The parade usually begins around 9 a.m. at Central Park West and 72nd Street, and travels down Broadway to Macy's at Herald Square (West 34th Street).

St. Patrick's Day (March 17) is the occasion for the grandaddy of all New York's parades. You'll be surprised by how many Irish accents you hear, but then, everyone's a little bit Irish on St. Paddy's Day. Be prepared for the revelry to get pretty wild. The parade travels up Fifth Avenue from 38th to 86th Streets.

Chinatown and Little Italy both have raucous celebrations of their own. The **Chinese New Year,** on the first day of the full moon between January 21 and February 19, is ushered in with a dragon parade and fireworks. Make a night of it with a meal at one of Chinatown's many restaurants (see our Chinatown section in Chapter II). And right next door to Chinatown is Little Italy, scene of the **Feast of San Gennaro,** in mid-September on Mulberry Street between Spring and Park Streets. The feast is like a half-mile-long church fair, with game booths and stalls selling all kinds of Italian food.

Keep in mind that both Chinatown and Little Italy are among the oldest sections of New York, with narrow streets that are usually mobbed by nightfall of the respective celebration days. Those with small children in tow or claustrophobia should come early (in the afternoon, if possible) to beat the thickest crowds. Hang onto your wallets and have fun!

Come Easter, the Parks Department holds its annual **Easter Egg Rolling Contest** in Central Park. Check the newspaper for the time and location (other groups hold egg hunts as well, some free) or call the Parks Department at 472-1003.

A good number to call for information on just about anything happening in the city is the **Office of Special Events;** 566-4074.

Christmas is a special time in New York. The stores and streets are as pretty —and busy—as the songs say. The following stores usually have special windows for the holidays, with mechanized puppets and trains that tell a story or theme. Dress warmly, because chances are you'll have to stand in line. And call first to make sure the windows are up.

Lord and Taylor, 425 Fifth Ave., at 38th Street (tel. 391-3344).
B. Altman and Co., Fifth Avenue at 34th Street (tel. 689-7000).
Saks, 611 Fifth Ave., at 50th Street (tel. 753-4000).
Gimbels, Broadway at 33rd Street (tel. 564-3300).

4. Shops for Children

Toys are part of what being a kid is all about, and venerable **F.A.O. Schwarz,** 745 Fifth Ave., at the corner of 58th Street (tel. 644-9400), is a three-story toyland packed with the world's best toys. Although you'll find Louis XVI dollhouses and Italian racing cars priced in the thousands, there are lots of cute toys (wind-up ducks, etc.) priced for much less. Open Monday through Saturday from 10 a.m. to 6 p.m., till 8 p.m. on Thursday.

If you really want to do some buying, **Woolworth's** has discounts on Fisher-Price toys and other brands. Two of the chain's largest local branches are at 34th Street and Avenue of the Americas, across from Macy's (tel. 563-3523); and at Third Avenue and 59th Street (tel. 755-8634). They generally open around 10 a.m. and stay open till various times throughout the week.

Alexander's, Lexington Avenue at 58th Street (tel. 593-0880), also has good buys in toys and other children's things. Open Monday through Saturday from 10 a.m. to 9 p.m., on Sunday from noon to 5 p.m.

Macy's, Broadway at 34th Street (tel. 695-4400), has a great, if higher-priced, children's section on the fifth floor. There's also a full pet store with fish, birds, and puppies and kittens who live in mini-brownstones. Macy's is open from 9:45 a.m. (noon on Sunday) till 6:45 p.m., till 6 p.m. on weekends. Open till 8:45 p.m. on Monday, Thursday, and Friday.

Polk's Model Craft Hobbies, in the basement at 314 Fifth Ave., near 32nd Street (tel. 279-9034), has a good selection of kits and models—airplanes, boats, trains, rockets, scientific displays, etc. Don't miss the case of beautiful wooden ships, priced into the thousands. The handcrafted paddleboats, sidewheeler steamers, and clipper ships are lovely to behold. Open from 9:30 a.m. to 5:45 p.m. Monday through Saturday.

Gateway Hobbies, 62 W. 38th St., between Fifth and Sixth Avenues (tel. 221-0855), is the place to go for military and car models from around the world. In the back is a case of painstakingly completed models with magnificent detailing, and a jumbled work area where staffers work on models in their free time. It's a fascinating shop. Open Monday through Friday from 10 a.m. to 5:45 p.m., on Saturday to 5 p.m.

Mary Arnold Toys, 962 Lexington Ave., between 70th and 71st Streets (tel. 744-8510), has a nice selection of toys and classic family games that could be just what a desperate parent needs. Harried hotel-bound parents might also consider story tapes and cassettes, from $7.50 to $12. Open Monday through Friday from 9 a.m. to 6 p.m., on Saturday from 10 a.m. to 5 p.m.

Named after the woeful character in *Winnie the Pooh,* the two **Eeyore's,** 2252 Broadway, at 81st Street (tel. 362-0634), and 1066 Madison Ave., at 81st Street (tel. 988-3404), are bustling centers of activity. In addition to selling children's books for all ages, in at least three foreign languages, year round, the stores sponsor story readings, art contests, and author appearances. The West Side branch is a cozy little place; the newer store on the East Side is attractively laid out, and has a huge stuffed Eeyore in the back for kids who want to cuddle between book browsing. Call or drop by to get a list of the store's activities.

After a day of gallery hopping with adults in SoHo, take the children to **Wendy's,** 456 West Broadway, between Prince and West Houston Streets (tel. 533-2305). This quaint little shop carries imported toys and handmade clothes for infants to 10-year-olds. In the front cases of the store are displays of antique toys, games, and paper theaters. Prices vary widely, but there's a good deal that's affordable. Open Tuesday through Saturday from 11 a.m. to 7 p.m., on Sunday to 6 p.m.

While the **Enchanted Forest,** 85 Mercer St., in SoHo (tel. 925-6677), celebrates "the spirit of the animals, the old stories, and the child within," it is not exclusively a children's store. Many of the stuffed, carved, and painted animal figures are unique collector's items with price tags in the hundreds of dollars. See the *Wolf in Dapper Clothing* on the landing, for instance, and the exquisite *Puss 'n' Boots*. But the shop does stock plenty of less costly animal items for children, and it's worth a trip to see the shop's rainbow-colored rooms, waterfall, and tree-house-like second floor. A rabbit hutch will open here soon. Unusual, one-of-a-kind stuffed animals range in price from $10 to $20, and animal trinkets, notecards, coloring books, and wind-up toys are available from $2 to $10.

Although it carries standard pet-store items, the main attraction at the **Crystal Aquarium,** 1659 Third Ave., at 93rd Street, is row after row of glass aquariums and their seemingly endless varieties of fish. In fact, local biology teachers often visit the store with their classes because it carries such a large stock of exotic sea creatures.

If you're after real bargains in kids' clothing, try some of the discount shops closely congregated on the Lower East Side. Many shoppers move from one store to the next. Orchard Street features a number of stores, including **Little Rascals,** at 101 Orchard St. (tel. 226-1680), which sells elegant imported kids' wear at up to 50% discounts. Another street to try is Grant Street, where, among others, you can find **Rice & Breskin,** 323 Grand St. (tel. 925-5515). This store has three floors of just about everything for kids, with all the better-known American brands.

5. Services for Children

BABYSITTERS: The sitters at **Gilbert Child Care Agency,** 206 E. 81st St. (tel. 744-6770), come highly recommended. They charge $4.25 an hour for children nine months or older (infant care is more expensive) and 50¢ per hour for each additional sibling. The agency requires a minimum of four hours' work and asks you to pay $2 a day for the sitter's transportation before 8 p.m., and $4 after 8 p.m.

Barnard College women run a small babysitting service (tel. 280-2035) and the charge is $3.50 an hour, plus the sitter's cabfare home after 9 p.m.

BARBERS: Michael's is a barbershop specializing in haircuts for children. Located at 91st Street and Madison Avenue (tel. 289-9612), they charge $12.50 per haircut. Hours are 9 a.m. to 5 p.m. Appointments are necessary.

F.A.O. Schwarz, at 58th Street and Fifth Avenue, still has **Mr. Rudy's Barber Shop** (tel. 644-9461), for many years one of kids' favorite barbershops in the city. Now in semi-retirement, Mr. Rudy cuts hair on Friday and Saturday from 10 a.m. to 6 p.m. Haircuts are $8.50, and appointments are suggested.

Older children may prefer going to the hippest haircutters in the Village, **Astor Place Barbers,** at the corner of Astor Place and Broadway near 8th Street. The barbers here can cut your hair in any odd shape and color you can imagine —or stick to more conventional looks. Go early to avoid the crowds. Opens about 9:30 a.m., but by noon, particularly in summer, customers are lined up outside, creating a festive atmosphere as they wait their turns under the scissors. Haircuts are $7, $2 extra if you want your hair washed.

6. Eating Out With Children

Eating out is one of New York's great pleasures—and it's one that older kids may enjoy almost as much as their parents. But for diners with young children, a little bit of planning helps ensure a more pleasant meal. For one thing, most Manhattan restaurants just aren't accustomed to serving children—

particularly the more fashionable or exotic spots. Often, waiters and waitresses haven't learned that serving families first helps them as well as you. For another thing, many restaurants don't have the kind of space a hungry, fidgety family needs—tables tend to be small and close together.

One easy way of settling on a restaurant that welcomes kids is to call ahead (even if it doesn't require recommendations) and ask if it has highchairs. Many restaurants don't. The ones that do usually are used to serving families. Some New York parents recommend lugging along a "Sassy Seat" for your young child, if that's not too much trouble; this is an inexpensive, easily portable highchair that fits onto the end of just about any table.

Before you ever get to a restaurant, though, you and your kids will be tempted by savory smells on nearly every streetcorner. You'll find pushcarts and peddlars hawking a tremendous variety of foods—hot dogs, soft pretzels, roasted chestnuts, knishes, empañadas, little shish kebabs. For $1 or so apiece, you can literally eat your way down the street.

But save some room for pizza! Pizza joints abound everywhere, especially in areas like Greenwich Village, and nearly all sell pizza for $1 a slice.

And don't forget dessert! All over town, sweet tooths will find all kinds of ice-cream and cookie stands, Italian ices, and Tofutti.

Below we've listed a few, well-known, child-pleasing places.

The **Horn and Hardart Automat,** 200 E. 42nd St., at Third Avenue (tel. 599-1665), is a longtime children's favorite. The treat here is putting the tokens into the sandwich machines, and there's a David's Cookies stand in the restaurant for dessert.

Nathan's Famous, Broadway at 43rd Street (tel. 382-0620), is one of the best places in town for a hot dog and fries. Originally a Coney Island institution, Nathan's has an amusement park atmosphere, with murals of Coney Island, video games, brightly colored chairs and tables. The wide selection includes corn on the cob, knishes, even frog legs!

For reasonably priced barbecued chicken and ribs (always a kids' favorite), try the **Dallas Jones Bar-B-Q** chain at 21 University Pl. (tel. 674-4450), 316 Sixth Ave. (tel. 741-7390), 27 W. 72nd St. (tel. 873-2004), and 336 E. 86th St. (tel. 772-1616). The decors range from dining-hall nondescript uptown to chrome-and-black slick downtown. Small orders of chicken and ribs can be had for $2.50 to $5. Other tasty down-home standards are chicken pot pie for $5.95, and gargantuan orders of onion rings for $1.95 or $2.95. There's also an early-bird special, between 4 and 6:30 p.m. Monday through Saturday, that's a real bargain at $6.95 for two.

One of New York's best ice-cream parlors is **Peppermint Park,** 1231 First Ave., at 66th Street (tel. 879-9484). Everything is fresh, and there are more than enough flavors to satisfy the pickiest palates. Take-out ice-cream cones are $1 for a single scoop, plus an assortment of floats, sundaes, egg creams, frozen yogurts, and pastries. The café is cozy and bright, with white tables and green booths, and prices are moderate by New York standards.

Rumpelmayer's, in the St. Moritz Hotel, mid-block on glittering Central Park South (tel. 755-5800), is a New York institution that's worth a peek if you're in the area. Venerable Rumpelmayer's is wildly expensive for an ice-cream parlor, even a famous one. There are stuffed animals for sale, and an elegant marble soda fountain with pink padded stools. Beyond is the café, with mirrored arches, pink tables, and hanging ferns.

7. Mapping Out Your Days

As any New Yorker will tell you, one of the keys to getting all you can of what the city offers is careful planning. That's particularly true when you're seeing the city with kids who want frequent pit-stops to eat, rest, or just be kids. Despite the city's simple street layout and its comprehensive transit system, getting around this crowded metropolis takes time. In other words, if you try to sightsee in more than a couple of areas of the city in one day, be prepared to spend a lot of time in subways, buses, or taxis.

Here we've listed suggestions for what to do with kids in different areas of Manhattan. For more information, check the detailed entries in other parts of this chapter and the rest of the guide. Keep in mind that streets are often crowded, even on Saturday, so a stroller for a small child is a good idea. And it's also a good idea to map out beforehand where you're going and how to get there.

LOWER MANHATTAN: Lower Manhattan begins at the southern tip of the island, at **Battery Park** and the **Staten Island Ferry,** north to around **City Hall** and the **Brooklyn Bridge.** In between, the many sights and attractions include **Wall Street,** where you'll find the **stock exchanges, Federal Hall,** and **Trinity Church** and its cemetery, where such early American luminaries as Alexander Hamilton and Robert Fulton are buried. There's also the **South Street Seaport,** the **World Trade Center** (the observation deck on top is a must), the **Woolworth Building** at 233 Broadway, and **City Hall Park,** the site at which, on July 9, 1776, the Declaration of Independence was read to George Washington and his troops.

SOHO: SoHo and Tribeca are actually names that describe each area. SoHo stands for "South of Houston Street"; Tribeca is the "Triangle Below Canal Street." Architecturally, SoHo is noted for its cast-iron loft buildings that house influential art galleries, and an ever-increasing number of fashionable restaurants and shops. Sights include the **Museum of Holography** (11 Mercer St.), but the real attractions are the galleries and shops, among them kids' clothing stores such as **Wendy's** (456 West Broadway) and the **Enchanted Forest** (85 Mercer St.). The best sightseeing streets are West Broadway, Greene Street, Prince Street, and Spring Street. It's an easy walk east of Broadway to Little Italy and Chinatown.

GREENWICH VILLAGE: Greenwich Village generally covers the area north of Houston Street up to West 12th Street, between Broadway and the Hudson River. Here, the place to begin is **Washington Square Park,** at the foot of Fifth Avenue. Kids may like a stroll down Eighth Street, one block north, a bustling street crowded with stores, record shops, and a wide variety of eateries, including **Dallas Jones Bar-B-Q** at the corner of University Place. Head west a few blocks, past Sixth Avenue, to find the narrow, winding streets that the Village is known for. Here also you'll find two children's theaters, the **13th St. Repertory Company** at 50 W. 13th St., and the **Little People's Theater,** at 39 Grove St. For the best in records, try **Tower Records** at 692 Broadway.

EAST VILLAGE / LOWER EAST SIDE: In just the last few years the East Village and the Lower East Side have become a magnet for artists, musicians, and punk style in general. It's also the center of the city's Ukrainian community. Here, attractions include the **Public Theater,** at Astor Place; the rapidly increasing number of ultra-hip shops and restaurants; and the Indian restaurants on East 6th Street.

MIDTOWN EAST: Midtown East takes in the area east of Fifth Avenue, and north of 42nd Street to Central Park. A walk east on 42nd Street from **Grand**

Central Terminal will take you past the **Chrysler Building**, the **Daily News Building**, the **Ford Foundation**, over to the **United Nations** at the East River's edge. A stroll up Fifth Avenue will take you to a host of world-famous places and stores: **Rockefeller Center, Radio City Music Hall, St. Patrick's Cathedral, Brooks Brothers, Tiffany's, Steuben Glass, F.A.O. Schwarz, Saks Fifth Avenue, Elizabeth Arden,** and more. A great place to stop for meals is the **Citicorp Center,** at Lexington Avenue and 53rd Street, which offers at least a half dozen different restaurant options, from a coffeeshop up to **Alfredo the Original of Rome,** which is a tad pricey but does offer great pasta and highchairs.

MIDTOWN WEST: Midtown West includes the area west of Fifth Avenue, north of 42nd Street to Central Park. Attractions for kids are spread out, but one place to stop, rest, and get some fresh maps is the **Visitor Information Center** at 42nd Street and Broadway, at the base of **Times Square.** You'll probably want to avoid walking farther west on 42nd Street, which has become fairly seedy and for the unwary can be a dangerous place at night. Elsewhere in the area, special places for kids include: the **Intrepid Sea-Air-Space Museum** at the foot of 46th Street and the Hudson River; the **New York Experience,** a multimedia presentation at the McGraw-Hill Building at 1221 Avenue of the Americas; and the **Children's Museum of Manhattan,** at 314 W. 54th St.

PENN STATION/CHELSEA: The focal point of another focal point of Manhattan activity is **Penn Station** (downstairs) and **Madison Square Garden** (upstairs), located at West 32nd Street between Sixth and Seventh Avenues. A couple of blocks away is **Herald Square,** at the intersection of Sixth Avenue, Broadway, and 34th Street. There you'll find the mammoth main stores of **Macy's** and **Gimbels.** And one block farther east at Fifth Avenue lies everyone's favorite tall building, the **Empire State Building** with the **Guinness World Records Exhibit Hall** down in the concourse.

UPPER EAST SIDE: The Upper East Side, east of Central Park over to the East River, is generally considered the most elegant part of Manhattan. A sure kid-pleaser is the **Lehman's Children's Zoo** in Central Park, at 65th Street and Fifth Avenue. "Museum Mile" along Fifth Avenue includes the **Metropolitan Museum of Art** at 82nd Street, the **Guggenheim Museum** at 89th Street, the **Cooper-Hewitt Museum** at 91st Street, the **Jewish Museum** at 92nd Street, and the **Museum of the City of New York** at 104th Street. For shopping, head one block east to Madison Avenue to **Eeyore's,** at 81st Street; or for hamburgers, try **Jackson Hole Restaurant** at 91st Street.

UPPER WEST SIDE: Most kids' attractions on the Upper West Side, the area west of Central Park, will be found around the **American Museum of Natural History** at Central Park West and 79th Street. Nearby are the **Hayden Planetarium,** behind the museum at 81st Street, and the **New-York Historical Society** at 77th Street. Pricey shops and restaurants line Columbus Avenue south to **Lincoln Center,** located between 65th and 62nd Streets. **Dobson's** restaurant at 341 Columbus Ave., has fairly reasonable prices, large tables, and yes, highchairs.

Chapter IX

HELPFUL NEW YORK CITY LISTINGS AND GENERAL INFORMATION

HERE WE GIVE YOU a whole range of tips, tricks, and hints to help you make your way through New York as though you've lived here all your life. Few things are more frustrating than being in a strange city, having a tooth flare up and not knowing where to find a dentist, or getting front-row tickets to the show the critics are raving about and not having the faintest idea where to find a reliable babysitter. Check the alphabetical entries here and you can be well on your way to solving those problems. From the mundane to the serious, we offer the ABCs of life in New York, and hope they will help you feel right at home with the intricacies of the Big Apple.

AIRPORT TRANSPORTATION: Carey Transportation (tel. 718/632-0500) offers frequent bus service between New York City and both LaGuardia and John F. Kennedy International Airports with a connecting service to Newark International Airport. You can catch the buses at one of two locations: 125 Park Ave., near Grand Central Station between 41st and 42nd Streets; or at the Airport Transportation Center at the Port Authority Bus Terminal, 42nd Street between Eighth and Ninth Avenues. For John F. Kennedy, buses leave every 30 minutes from the Park Avenue terminal and about every 30 minutes from Port Authority ($8 one way, $13 round trip). For LaGuardia, buses leave every 15 minutes from the Park Avenue terminal, and every 30 minutes from Port Authority ($6 one way, $10 round trip). Plan on arriving about two hours early at Kennedy and an hour and a half before your flight time at LaGuardia. Buses to Newark Airport leave from the Port Authority Bus Terminal. The half-hour ride costs $4, and the schedules vary, so call ahead for bus times.

There's also the **Train to the Plane,** the express to JFK Airport. Catch it downstairs at the IND Subway Station at 50th Street and Rockefeller Center, or call 858-7272 for other stops (IND–Sixth Avenue stations at 57th Street, 50th Street, 42nd Street, 34th Street, West 4th Street, Chambers Street, Broadway-Nassau Street, and Borough Hall, Brooklyn). The train runs regularly from 5 a.m. to midnight; the connecting shuttle bus to the airport from 5:30 a.m. to 11:55 p.m. Trains leave every 20 minutes. It costs $6, including subway fare. Allow at least one hour for the trip.

Cab fares are high, but you can cut costs by sharing. Fare from midtown to LaGuardia is approximately $15, about $25 to JFK, and $25 to Newark. Meter fares double when you cross state lines (i.e., going to Newark Airport). Cab drivers are supposed to give you an official airport fee schedule on request—beware of excessive fares.

For reliable information on the best and least expensive way to get to any of New York City's airports (including Newark) from wherever you are, call toll free 1-800/A-I-R-R-I-D-E, a service of the Port Authority. You'll find out where in the city you'll get your ride, how often it runs, and how much it costs.

ALCOHOLISM: To get help with problems of alcoholism, call **Alcoholics Anonymous** at 473-6200.

AMBULANCE: If an emergency arises, call the police at 911-1234, or simply dial the Operator, say there is an emergency, give him or her your telephone number, and describe the problem.

ANIMAL HOSPITAL: If your pet gets injured or becomes sick, call the **Humane Society of New York**, 306 E. 59th St., near Second Avenue (tel. 752-4840). The society is open by appointment only on weekdays from 9 a.m. to 4 p.m., until 6 p.m. on Wednesday and Thursday, on Saturday to 3 p.m., and on Sunday from noon to 2 p.m. There are also numerous 24-hour veterinary services in the city.

APARTMENTS: The market is so tight in New York that finding an apartment can take weeks or months of tracking down leads and combing real estate ads. But if you want to stay for a while, try the Sunday real estate section of the *New York Times*, which comes out late Saturday night. Check the ads in the *Village Voice* (at the newsstands on Wednesday), and in the *Chelsea Clinton News* and other neighborhood papers. More important, though, ask all your friends and acquaintances—the best apartments are usually let before they even reach the real estate ads.

BABYSITTERS: The sitters at **Gilbert Child Care Agency,** 206 E. 81st St. (tel. 302-3200), come highly recommended. They charge $4.75 an hour for children nine months or older (infant care is more expensive) and 50¢ per hour for each additional sibling. The agency requires a minimum of four hours' work and asks you to pay $2.50 a day for the sitter's transportation before 8 p.m., and $5 after 8 p.m.

Barnard College women also run a small babysitting service (tel. 280-2035), and the charge is $3.50 an hour, plus the sitter's cabfare home after 9 p.m.

BUILDING AND HEAT COMPLAINTS: Call 960-4800.

BUSES: The price of a bus ride in the city is currently $1, and they require exact change or a subway token. Bus drivers do not give change. If you need a transfer slip, ask for it as you board. The New York Convention and Visitors

NEW YORK CITY GENERAL INFORMATION 339

Bureau at Columbus Circle gives out excellent bus route maps, or call 718/330-1234 for bus information.

CALENDAR OF SPECIAL EVENTS: These New York celebrations can be one of the highlights of a visit. The dates vary, so call or write ahead for details to the **New York Convention and Visitors Bureau,** 2 Columbus Circle at West 59th Street (tel. 397-8222); Madison Square Garden, 4 Pennsylvania Plaza (tel. 564-4400); the New York Coliseum, Columbus Circle at West 59th Street (tel. 757-5500); or to the **Jacob K. Javits Convention Center,** 33rd Street and Seventh Avenue New York, N.Y. 10121 (tel. 563-4848). Be sure to call 755-4100 every few days to get a recorded message from the city's Parks and Recreation Department listing exciting things to do and see day by day.

Note: The Coliseum will close on March 31, 1986. When an event is followed by an asterick (*), it will take place in 1987 at the Javits Convention Center, which was in the final stages of construction at this writing.

January: Chinese New Year celebrations in Chinatown, on the first full moon after January 21; Ice Capades at Madison Square Garden; National Boat Show at the New York Coliseum*; Winter Antiques Show at the Seventh Regimental Armory, Park Avenue at 67th Street (tel. 288-0200); New York Automobile Show at the New York Coliseum*; Martin Luther King, Jr. Concert, on the third Sunday in January, at the Brooklyn Botanic Garden (tel. 718/622-4433).

February: USA National Track and Field Championships at Madison Square Garden; Westminster Kennel Club Dog Show at Madison Square Garden; International Antiques Show at Madison Square Garden; Black History Month, programs in all five boroughs; Washington's Birthday Parade on Fifth Avenue.

March: St. Patrick's Day Parade on Fifth Avenue; Golden Gloves boxing finals at Madison Square Garden; Greek Independence Day Parade on Fifth Avenue; New York Flower Show of the Horticultural Society of New York (tel. 757-0915), at the Hudson Exhibition Pier near 50th Street.

April: Baseball season opens at Yankee and Shea Stadiums (call 397-8222 for exact dates); Ringling Brothers and Barnum & Bailey Circus at Madison Square Garden; Macy's Spring Flower Show (tel. 560-4495); Easter Parade in front of St. Patrick's Cathedral, Fifth Avenue at 50th Street on Easter Sunday, late morning. Wear your finest spring outfit and join in.

May: Japanese Cherry Blossom Festival (with Japanese arts and entertainment) at the Brooklyn Botanic Garden (tel. 718/622-4433); Big Apple Circus at various locations (tel. 369-5110); Armed Forces Day Parade on Fifth Avenue; Ninth Avenue International Festival (food and crafts), 37th to 57th Streets on Ninth Avenue; Washington Square Spring Art Festival on Memorial Day weekend; New York City beaches open on Memorial Day weekend.

June: Museum Mile Celebration on Fifth Avenue between 82nd and 105th Streets; Hispanic Expo Fair at the Seventh Regimental Armory, Park Avenue at 67th Street (tel. 288-0200); Kool Jazz Festival at various locations (tel. 787-2020 or 873-0733); Puerto Rican Day Parade on Fifth Avenue; Dr. Pepper Popular Music Festival begins (tel. 249-8870); Salute to Israel Parade on Fifth Avenue; Gay Pride Day Parade and street fair (tel. 777-1800); 52nd Street Festival on Father's Day, 52nd Street from Third to Ninth Avenues.

July: Shakespeare in the Park begins at Delacorte Theater in Central Park (tel. 535-5360); Mostly Mozart Concerts at Lincoln Center (tel. 874-2424); Fireworks on the Fourth of July (call Macy's at 695-4400 for time and place); New York Philharmonic concerts in Central Park (tel. 397-3100).

August: U.S. Open Tennis Championships at the USTA National Tennis

Center in Queens (tel. 718/592-8000); Washington Square Autumn Art Festival on Labor Day weekend; Harlem Week in various locations around Harlem—check newspaper listings for specifics.

September: Labor Day Parade on Fifth Avenue; Fifth Avenue Mile Footrace between 62nd and 82nd Streets; Flatbush Frolic, Footrace and Fair on Cortelyou Road in Brooklyn (tel. 718/282-9200); Feast of San Gennaro in Little Italy on Mulberry Street (tel. 226-9546); Columbus Avenue Festival (food and crafts) from 66th to 79th Streets—check newspaper listings for more information; New York Book Fair on Fifth Avenue (tel. 593-3983); TAMA County Fair on Third Avenue from 14th to 34th Streets (tel. 674-5094); One World Festival on 35th Street and Second Avenue (tel. 686-0710); East Side Festival on Third Avenue between 69th and 96th Streets (tel. 734-9800).

October: New York City Marathon (to run in the race or volunteer, call 860-4455 well in advance); Columbus Day Parade on Fifth Avenue; Pulaski Day Parade on Fifth Avenue; National Arts and Antiques Festival at the Seventh Regimental Armory on 67th Street and Park Avenue (tel. 288-0200); Halloween Parade in Greenwich Village; Rockefeller Center ice-skating pond opens (tel. 489-4300).

November: Big Apple Circus at Lincoln Center (tel. 369-5110); Macy's Thanksgiving Day Parade on Fifth Avenue; Veteran's Day Parade on Fifth Avenue; National Horse Show at Madison Square Garden.

December: Big Apple Circus at Lincoln Center (tel. 369-5110); Chanukah candle lighting at City Hall; Midnight Run and Fireworks in Central Park; Christmas windows in department stores; lighting of Rockefeller Center Christmas tree; New Year's Eve at Times Square; Christmas Star Show at the Hayden Planetarium.

CAR STORAGE: The cheapest in town on a weekly basis is the famous **Auto Baby Sitters** in Brooklyn. Call 718/493-9800 or write to them at 827 Sterling Pl., Brooklyn, NY 11216. They will pick up your car from the city (time permitting) and store it for $35 a week, $67 a month, and less for longer periods. Vans cost more. They offer a $1 discount to readers who mention this book. Their hours are 9 a.m. to 5 p.m. Monday through Friday, to midnight on Saturday. Closed Sunday and holidays.

CHESS: If you want to while away an afternoon over a chess game, you can play for 90¢ an hour at the **Chess Shop,** 230 Thompson St., at West 3rd Street (tel. 475-9580). They're open from noon until midnight every day of the year.

CLEANERS: New York City seems to have a dry cleaner on every block, and most of them can provide express service on the same day. Such speedy service, however, does cost more. If your clothes are just rumpled from a suitcase, try this old trick: hang the offending item in your hotel bathroom, shut the door, and run a hot shower (preferably with you in it to conserve water). In a few minutes the wrinkles should be steamed out and the garment ready to wear.

CONSUMER-RELATED PROBLEMS: To report any problems with merchants or ask consumer-related questions, call either the **Better Business Bureau** (tel. 533-6200) or the **Department of Consumer Affairs** (tel. 577-0111).

CRISES: If you need counseling and expert advice for any kind of real problem —loneliness, wife or child abuse, depression, extreme bewilderment—call **Help Line** (tel. 532-2300) or **Victim Services** (tel. 577-7777). Or call 664-0505 and ask for **The Samaritans,** who are there to lend an ear when you need a friend.

NEW YORK CITY GENERAL INFORMATION

DEAF CRISES: Deaf people can call toll free 800/342-5347 and leave a message with a TTY machine if an emergency arises.

DENTISTS: If a tooth acts up in the middle of your visit, call the **New York University College of Dentistry,** 421 First Ave., near 24th Street (tel. 481-5924), weekdays only from 10 a.m. to noon and 1:30 to 4 p.m. August hours are 9 a.m. to 2 p.m. The **Dental Emergency Service** (tel. 679-3966) is a 24-hour answering service that will try to refer you to a dentist.

DEPARTMENT OF HEALTH: To report food poisoning or other health problems related to a restaurant or take-out eatery, call 334-7753. For problems with food bought in a grocery store or market, call 488-4820.

DIAPER SERVICE: A reliable, inexpensive diaper laundry is **Riteway Diaper Service,** 3329 Atlantic Ave., Brooklyn (tel. 718/647-9000).

DOCTOR: Call the **Doctor's Emergency Service** of the New York Medical Society (tel. 718/745-5900 or 718/238-2100) or the emergency services number, 911. Emergency wards are always open at **St. Vincent's Hospital,** Seventh Avenue and 11th Street (tel. 790-7000); **New York Hospital,** Cornell School of Medicine, East 70th Street at York Avenue (tel. 472-5454); and **Mt. Sinai Hospital,** at Madison Avenue and 100th Street (tel. 650-7171).

DRUGSTORES: A good drugstore that is open 24 hours a day is **Kaufman's,** 50th Street and Lexington Avenue (tel. 755-2266). **Windsor Pharmacy,** at Sixth Avenue at 58th Street (tel. 247-1538), is open daily from 8 a.m. to midnight.

ELECTRICAL APPLIANCES: You can rent or buy anything and everything with a cord at **Electrical Appliances Rental and Sales Company,** 40 W. 29th St., near Broadway (tel. 686-8884).

EYE CARE: An inexpensive place to get a general eye examination or referral is the Optometric Center, the clinic of the **State College of Optometry,** State University of New York. The offices are located at 100 E. 24th St., between Park Avenue South and Lexington Avenue. Call 420-4900 for information, 420-4950 for appointments. Exams cost $28. Hours: Monday to Thursday from 8:45 a.m. to 6:30 p.m., on Friday from 9 a.m. to 4 p.m. Closed weekends and holidays.

FBI: Its main number in Manhattan is 553-2700.

FIRE: Dial 911 to report a fire.

FISHING: Probably the best sport fishing in New York City is in the Hudson River. There are free fishing locations on the river at 92nd Street and 83rd Street at Riverside Park. Unfortunately, pollution of the Hudson has caused New York state to issue a health notice advising people to eat only one meal a month of fish from the river. The state also advises that pregnant women, nursing mothers, women of childbearing age, and young children should not eat any fish from the Hudson.

If it's ocean fish you're after, Long Island Sound offers some of the East Coast's best angling. Numerous charter companies and "party boats" line the sound on Long Island and in Connecticut. Similar services are located on Long Island and in New Jersey for fishing in the Atlantic Ocean.

FOOD STAMPS: For information about the food stamp program in New York, call 718/237-7372; for information in Spanish, 718/237-7371.

FOREIGN CURRENCY: If you're going abroad, you may want to take a small amount of the currency of the first country on your itinerary. Numerous New York agencies sell foreign currency. You can go to the excellent **Deak-Perera Fifth Avenue, Inc.** (tel. 757-6915), in Rockefeller Center at 630 Fifth Ave., or **Deak-Perera International, Inc.**, at 41 E. 42nd St., off Madison Avenue (tel. 883-0400).

Exchanging foreign currency for dollars is also quite easy. **New York Foreign Exchange, Inc.**, at Olympic Towers, 645 Fifth Ave. at 51st Street (tel. 888-5891), will give dollar equivalents for any foreign currency. Their hours are 9 a.m. to 5 p.m. weekdays and on Saturday from 10 a.m. to 4 p.m. And **Citibank** has three foreign currency exchanges: at 54th Street and Lexington Avenue, at 51st Street and Fifth Avenue, and at JFK Airport. Many midtown hotels will exchange foreign currency if you are a registered guest.

GAY AND LESBIAN CONCERNS: Call **Gay Switchboard** (tel. 777-1800), with hours from 6 p.m. to midnight, seven days a week. The volunteers staffing this telephone information and referral service have listings of more than 100 organizations and agencies ready to deal with the gay-related concerns of resident and visitor alike, regarding health, legal questions, religious issues, or whatever. When the volunteers aren't available, the same number will get you a recorded message listing gay social and entertainment possibilities.

HANDBAG REPAIR: **Artbag Creations,** 735 Madison Ave., at 64th Street (tel. 744-2720), will change the shape of last year's bag to keep up with the current fashions, mount needlepoint, or provide new handles when they get worn. Chain handles cost $12.50 and up; relustering starts at $30. There is no charge for estimates.

HELP FOR THE HANDICAPPED: The city has many events and programs designed for those who are deaf, blind, or confined to a wheelchair. For information, call the **Mayor's Office of the Handicapped,** 52 Chambers St., Room 206 (tel. 566-0972); **New York Association for the Blind,** the Lighthouse, 111 E. 59th St. (tel. 355-2200); or the **New York Society for the Deaf,** 344 E. 14th St. (tel. 673-6500).

INFORMATION: Questions about New York will be answered by the **New York Convention and Visitors Bureau** (tel. 397-8222—and be patient). Open 9 a.m. to 6 p.m. weekdays, 10 a.m. to 6 p.m. weekends and holidays, the Visitors Bureau also has two walk-in centers, open the same hours: 2 Columbus Circle at West 59th Street, and 1465 Broadway at 42nd Street. The bureau is a gold mine of information about the city. It provides a guide and map to New York in six languages, lots of different brochures, guides to restaurants and stores in all boroughs, a list of free New York activities, bus maps, subway maps, tickets for TV shows, and twofers (two-for-the-price-of-one theater tickets), plus a complete listing of seasonal attractions. For a recorded message giving a rundown on all free events in New York, call 755-4100.

NEWSPAPERS AND MAGAZINES (LOCAL): New York City has three daily newspapers, including one, the *New York Times,* that is arguably the nation's finest. The city is also home to several weekly newspapers and two weekly magazines that you may find helpful. All are available on almost any newsstand in the city, or you might want to pick up an issue several weeks before you visit, since most events, cultural and otherwise, are announced in the press a few weeks ahead of time, and you'll be able to make reservations or buy tickets in advance.

Daily Newspapers: the *New York Times* (especially Friday and Sunday), *Daily News* (especially Friday), *New York Post* (especially Saturday).

Weekly Publications: *The New Yorker* (good for cultural events), *New York* magazine (now incorporates *Cue,* with excellent general listings), and the *Village Voice* (particularly for music, cheap events, freebies, and off- and off-off-Broadway performances).

NEWSPAPERS (OUT OF TOWN): Hotaling's, 142 W. 42nd St., between Broadway and Seventh Avenue (tel. 840-1868), carries over 200 newspapers—everything from the *San Diego Union* to *Le Monde.*

OPTICIAN: You can get one-hour service at **Cohen's Optical Company,** 117 Orchard St., corner of Delancey Street (tel. 674-1986). Cohen's has undoubtedly the lowest prices for eyeglass service in New York: about $8 to replace a broken lens, $19.95 for complete eye examinations and new glasses. Even better, Cohen's is open on Sunday from 9 a.m. to 6 p.m., Monday through Saturday until 5:30 p.m.

PARKS DEPARTMENT EVENTS: New York's many beautiful parks are great not only for general recreation but also as the sites for an extraordinary array of musical and operatic performances, plays, festivals, poetry readings, and much more. Of course, almost all of these outdoor events are in the summer. Call 755-4100 to get the Parks Department's recorded message, changed daily, giving all free events in the parks and in the rest of the city.

PHOTOGRAPHY: New York is a photographer's dream, not only because of its numerous visual treats but also because of its camera stores, which boast the lowest prices for camera equipment to be found in the United States. Dozens of cut-rate photo-supply stores dot the West Side. One of the best-known is **47th Street Photo,** 67 W. 47th St., between Fifth and Sixth Avenues, plus its other branches—see listing in Shopping chapter (tel. 260-4410). Some tips on buying: Comparison-shop before you let a smooth-talking salesman con you into something you don't want, and try to bargain with the cut-rate places.

If you have your own equipment already, try to bring more than one lens—a 35-mm, 50-mm, and 135-mm lens should cover any photographic opportunity. Also, don't attract attention to your camera equipment by carrying it in a flashy, expensive camera bag. Bring a nondescript, surplus-type bag if you can. Don't bring your camera along to any area you don't feel comfortable in yourself, such as a lonesome, dark street late at night.

For a week's stay, you might want to bring 14 rolls of film, about two per day. Ten rolls (black and white or color) should be slow speed (ASA 64 or 100) and the remainder fast speed (ASA 400 or 1000) for taking either indoor photos without flash or night photos.

POISON CONTROL CENTER: For immediate 24-hour first-aid—or hospital referral if necessary—call 340-4494 or P-O-I-S-O-N-S (764-7667).

POLICE: Call **911** for life-threatening emergencies only; 374-5000 for normal matters.

POLLUTION COMPLAINTS: To report on air-, water-, sewer-, or noise-pollution violations, call the **New York Department of Environmental Protection** at 966-7500.

POST OFFICE: The **General Post Office**, 33rd Street and Eighth Avenue (tel. 971-7176), is open from 8 a.m. to 6 p.m. and operates an emergency window until midnight.

RADIO AND TELEVISION STATIONS: It would take a chapter to list them all. Here are some major ones:
    AM Radio: 660 (WNBC, pop music); 710 (WOR, talk, easy-listening music); 880 (WCBS, all news); 1010 (WINS, all news); 1050 (WHN, country music); 1560 (WQXR, classical music).
    FM Radio: 88.3 (WBGO, jazz music); 92.3 (WKTU, disco music); 93.1 (WPAT, easy-listening music); 93.9 (WNYC, Public Radio, classical music); 99.5 (WBAI, listener-sponsored radio); 101.1 (WCBS, "golden oldies" rock); 102.7 (WNEW, progressive rock); 104.3 (WNCN, classical music); 107.5 (WBLS, soul and Latin rock).
    Television Stations: Channel 2 (WCBS, network); Channel 4 (WNBC, network); Channel 5 (WNEW, local); Channel 7 (WABC, network); Channel 9 (WOR, local); Channel 11 (WPIX, local); Channel 13 (WNET, public television); Channel 47 (WNJU, mostly Spanish).

RAILROAD INFORMATION: New York has excellent rail connections to its suburbs and other major cities in the Northeast. For **Metro North** information (for Westchester County and other northern suburbs), phone 532-4900; phone 718/739-4200 for **Long Island Rail Road** information (for all of Long Island); call 1-800/USA-RAIL for **Amtrak** information.

REDUCED BUS AND SUBWAY FARE: Residents of the five boroughs who are 65 years old and over, and not working full time, can ride on city transportation at half fare during special hours. Call 577-0819 for details.

SUBWAYS: For information on how to get from one place to another on the subway, call 718/330-1234.

SUICIDE: If you feel depressed, call **Save-A-Life League** at 718/492-4067 for help and counseling. There are also walk-in mental-health clinics in most city hospitals—ask for an emergency appointment.

TELEGRAMS: Phone 962-7111 for **Western Union**, which will also send a mailgram, singing telegram, cablegram, candygram, flowergram or opiniongram (to elected officials only).

TELEPHONE CALLS IN THE NEW YORK CITY AREA: The area code for Manhattan and the Bronx is 212. To call any other area code location (Brooklyn, Queens, and Staten Island, 718; Long Island, 516; Westchester and Rockland Counties, 914; Connecticut, 203; New Jersey, 201) dial 1, then the area code and number.

TELEPHONE DIRECTORIES (OUT OF TOWN): The **New York Public Library**, 42nd Street and Fifth Avenue, maintains telephone directories of virtually every city in the world.

TELEPHONE INFORMATION: Dial 411 to get the number of any establishment or person in Manhattan and the Bronx; 718/555-1212 for the other boroughs. Long-distance information can be obtained by dialing 1, the area code of the city you want, then 555-1212.

TELEPHONE RECORDINGS: New York boasts a large collection of informational, interesting, and unique telephone services, all of which cost extra to reach. You can call the **Children's Story**, 976-3636; **Dial-A-Joke**, 976-3838; **Dow Jones Report**, 976-4141; **New York Lottery Results**, 976-2020; **Off-Track Betting**, 976-2121; **Sportsphone**, 976-1313.

For Jean Dixon's Daily Horoscope, dial **Aries**, 976-5050; **Taurus**, 976-5151; **Gemini**, 976-5252; **Cancer**, 976-5353; **Leo**, 976-5454; **Virgo**, 976-5656; **Libra**, 976-5757; **Scorpio**, 976-5858; **Sagittarius**, 976-5959; **Capricorn**, 976-6060; **Aquarius**, 976-6161; **Pisces**, 976-6262.

TIME: Phone 976-1616.

TIPPING: The following should generally prove satisfactory: bellhops, 50¢ per bag; taxis, 15%, 50¢ minimum; waiters, 15%; chambermaid, $1 to $1.50 per night (for double or single room); barbers and hairdressers, 15%; manicurists, $1. Naturally, if any of the above provide extra services, your tip should be increased accordingly. Do not tip hotel desk clerks, theater ushers, employees of cafés where a "no tipping" sign is displayed, subway or bus operators.

TRAVELERS AID: If you're a stranger in the city, lost or destitute or in need of help of any kind, these folks can help. They have three offices: 2 Lafayette St., near City Hall (tel. 577-7700); 1465 Broadway, corner of 42nd Street (tel. 944-0013); and at the International Arrivals Building at JFK Airport (tel. 718/656-4870).

V.D. INFORMATION: Call 226-5353 for helpful information, including the names and addresses of clinics where V.D. can be treated.

WEATHER—WHAT TO WEAR: The saying for New England's weather holds true for New York as well: if you don't like the weather, just wait a few minutes and it'll change. To be prepared for any contingency, always check the forecast in the morning. Phone 976-1212 for up-to-the-hour forecasts.

New York's temperature swings from the low average of 32 degrees Fahrenheit in January to a high of 86 degrees Fahrenheit in July. However, those are just averages; any New Yorker will tell you that it gets much warmer and colder than that. To help you decide what to pack for winter or summer in New York, here are some tips:

In **winter,** try to dress in layers. Not only will you be warmer, but you'll be able to take off layers when you go inside the frequently overheated restaurant or museum. A comfortable pair of warm, winter boots are essential if you want to take any winter walks, as are a hat, scarf, and gloves. An ideal coat for New York winter is a lightweight down-filled one. So if you own a parka, bring it along. It's considered perfectly acceptable in all but the poshest places.

Summer in New York can be downright blistering. Be sure to take along a lightweight hat to shade your head from the sun, thick-soled sandals or summer shoes to protect your feet from burning-hot pavement, and plenty of lightweight clothing. You might also want to tote a light sweater or jacket, since many restaurants and theaters keep a heavy hand on the air-conditioning switch.

If you dress for moderate weather in the **spring** and **fall,** you can't go wrong. And bring an umbrella in all seasons!

NOW, SAVE MONEY ON ALL YOUR TRAVELS!
Join Arthur Frommer's $25-A-Day Travel Club

Saving money while traveling is never a simple matter, which is why, over 23 years ago, the **$25-A-Day Travel Club** was formed. Actually, the idea came from readers of the Arthur Frommer Publications who felt that such an organization could bring financial benefits, continuing travel information, and a sense of community to economy-minded travelers all over the world.

In keeping with the money-saving concept, the annual membership fee is low—$18 (U.S. residents) or $20 (Canadian, Mexican, and foreign residents)—and is immediately exceeded by the value of your benefits which include:

(1) The latest edition of any TWO of the books listed on the following page.

(2) An annual subscription to an 8-page quarterly newspaper *The Wonderful World of Budget Travel* which keeps you up-to-date on fastbreaking developments in low-cost travel in all parts of the world—bringing you the kind of information you'd have to pay over $25 a year to obtain elsewhere. This consumer-conscious publication also includes the following columns:

Hospitality Exchange—members all over the world who are willing to provide hospitality to other members as they pass through their home cities.

Share-a-Trip—requests from members for travel companions who can share costs and help avoid the burdensome single supplement.

Readers Ask . . . Readers Reply—travel questions from members to which other members reply with authentic firsthand information.

(3) A copy of *Arthur Frommer's Guide to New York*.

(4) Your personal membership card which entitles you to purchase through the Club all Arthur Frommer Publications for a third to a half off their regular retail prices during the term of your membership.

So why not join this hardy band of international budgeteers NOW and participate in its exchange of information and hospitality? Simply send $18 (U.S. residents) or $20 U.S. (Canadian, Mexican, and other foreign residents) along with your name and address to: $25-A-Day Travel Club, Inc., 1230 Avenue of the Americas, New York, NY 10020. Remember to specify which *two* of the books in section (1) above you wish to receive in your initial package of members' benefits. Or tear out this page, check off any two books on the opposite side and send it to us with your membership fee.

FROMMER/PASMANTIER PUBLISHERS   Date_____
1230 AVE. OF THE AMERICAS, NEW YORK, NY 10020

Friends, please send me the books checked below:

$-A-DAY GUIDES
(In-depth guides to low-cost tourist accommodations and facilities.)

☐ Europe on $25 a Day	$11.95	☐ New Zealand on $25 a Day	$10.95
☐ Australia on $25 a Day	$10.95	☐ New York on $45 a Day	$9.95
☐ England on $35 a Day	$10.95	☐ Scandinavia on $35 a Day	$9.95
☐ Greece on $25 a Day	$10.95	☐ Scotland and Wales on $35 a Day	$10.95
☐ Hawaii on $35 a Day	$10.95	☐ South America on $25 a Day	$9.95
☐ India on $15 & $25 a Day	$9.95	☐ Spain and Morocco (plus the Canary Is.) on $35 a Day	$9.95
☐ Ireland on $25 a Day	$9.95	☐ Washington, D.C. on $40 a Day	$10.95
☐ Israel on $30 & $35 a Day	$10.95		
☐ Mexico on $20 a Day	$9.95		

DOLLARWISE GUIDES
(Guides to accommodations and facilities from budget to deluxe, with emphasis on the medium-priced.)

☐ Austria & Hungary	$10.95	☐ Caribbean	$12.95
☐ Egypt	$11.95	☐ Cruises (incl. Alaska, Carib, Mex, Hawaii, Panama, Canada, & US)	$10.95
☐ England & Scotland	$10.95	☐ California & Las Vegas	$9.95
☐ France	$10.95	☐ Florida	$10.95
☐ Germany	$11.95	☐ New England	$11.95
☐ Italy	$10.95	☐ Northwest	$10.95
☐ Japan & Hong Kong (avail. Apr. '86)	$11.95	☐ Skiing USA—East	$10.95
☐ Portugal (incl. Madeira & the Azores)	$11.95	☐ Skiing USA—West	$10.95
☐ Switzerland & Liechtenstein	$11.95	☐ Southeast & New Orleans	$11.95
☐ Bermuda & The Bahamas	$10.95	☐ Southwest	$10.95
☐ Canada	$12.95		

THE ARTHUR FROMMER GUIDES
(Pocket-size guides to tourist accommodations and facilities in all price ranges.)

☐ Amsterdam/Holland	$4.95	☐ Mexico City/Acapulco	$4.95
☐ Athens	$4.95	☐ Montreal/Quebec City	$4.95
☐ Atlantic City/Cape May	$4.95	☐ New Orleans	$4.95
☐ Boston	$4.95	☐ New York	$4.95
☐ Dublin/Ireland	$4.95	☐ Orlando/Disney World/EPCOT	$4.95
☐ Hawaii	$4.95	☐ Paris	$4.95
☐ Las Vegas	$4.95	☐ Philadelphia	$4.95
☐ Lisbon/Madrid/Costa del Sol	$4.95	☐ Rome	$4.95
☐ London	$4.95	☐ San Francisco	$4.95
☐ Los Angeles	$4.95	☐ Washington, D.C.	$4.95

SPECIAL EDITIONS

☐ Bed & Breakfast—N. America	$7.95	☐ Museums in New York	$8.95
☐ Fast 'n' Easy Phrase Book (Fr/Ger/Ital/Sp in *one* vol.)	$6.95	☐ Shopper's Guide to England, Scotland & Wales	$10.95
☐ Guide for the Disabled Traveler	$10.95	☐ Swap and Go (Home Exchanging)	$10.95
☐ How to Beat the High Cost of Travel	$4.95	☐ Travel Diary and Record Book	$5.95
☐ Marilyn Wood's Wonderful Weekends (NY, Conn, Mass, RI, Vt, NJ, Pa)	$9.95	☐ Urban Athlete (NYC sports guide)	$9.95
		☐ Where to Stay USA (Lodging from $3 to $30 a night)	$9.95

In U.S. include $1 post. & hdlg. for 1st book; 25¢ ea. add'l. book. Outside U.S. $2 and 50¢ respectively.

Enclosed is my check or money order for $_____

NAME_____

ADDRESS_____

CITY_____ STATE_____ ZIP_____